American Evangelicalism
An Annotated Bibliography

American Evangelicalism
An Annotated Bibliography

Norris A. Magnuson

William G. Travis

LOCUST HILL PRESS
West Cornwall, CT
1990

Library of Congress Cataloging-in-Publication Data

Magnuson, Norris A., 1932-
   American evangelicalism : an annotated bibliography / Norris A.
Magnuson, William G. Travis.
   495p.   cm.
   Includes bibliographical references.
   ISBN 0-933951-27-2 (lib. bdg. : alk. paper) : $45.00
   1. Evangelicalism--United States--Bibliography.
   2. Fundamentalism--Bibliography. 3. Pentecostalism--United States-
-Bibliography. 4. Revivals--United States--Bibliography. 5. United
States--Church history--Bibliography. I. Travis, William G.
II. Title
Z7778.U6M34 1990
[BR1644.U6]   90-33989
0.16.2773'082--dc20   CIP

Printed on acid-free, 250-year-life paper
Manufactured in the United States of America

Contents

Acknowledgments • *vii*

Preface • *ix*

Introduction • *xiii*

The Bibliography • *1*

    I. General, Reference and Bibliographical Works • *1*

    II. History of Evangelicalism
        A. General Studies • *15*
        B. Colonial Era • *33*
        C. Nineteenth Century • *40*
        D. Twentieth Century • *49*
        E. Post-World War II • *57*
        F. New Evangelicalism • *75*
        G. Young/Radical Evangelicalism • *86*
        H. The American South • *92*
        I. Great Britain • *95*
        J. Outside the United States and Britain • *103*
        K. Missions • *116*

    III. Specialized Studies of Evangelicalism
        A. Black Evangelicalism • *123*
        B. Jews and Evangelicals • *129*
        C. Women in Evangelicalism • *136*
        D. Individuals • *143*
        E. Politics • *159*
        F. Society and Religion • *171*
        G. Science • *193*
        H. Education • *198*
        I. Communications • *207*
        J. Literature and the Arts • *211*
        K. Theology • *215*
        L. The Bible • *244*
        M. Wesleyanism • *259*

N. The Holiness Movement • *262*
O. Millennialism • *265*
P. Pietism • *268*
Q. Spiritual Life • *270*
R. Denominations • *275*
S. Parachurch Organizations • *290*
T. Social Science Studies • *292*

IV. Fundamentalism
A. General Studies • *307*
B. History • *315*
C. Post-World War II • *332*
D. Fundamentalism and Politics • *339*
E. Social Science Studies • *349*

V. Pentecostalism
A. Origins • *359*
B. History • *364*
C. Biblical and Theological Studies • *379*
D. Pentecostalism Outside the U.S. • *392*
E. Social Science Studies • *397*

VI. The Charismatic Movement
A. History • *403*
B. Biblical and Theological Studies • *415*
C. Personal Accounts • *429*
D. Social Science Studies • *431*

VII. Revivalism
A. General Studies • *435*
B. Eighteenth Century • *441*
C. Nineteenth Century • *445*
D. Twentieth Century • *451*
E. Social Effects of Revivalism • *453*

VIII. Ecumenism • *457*

Selected Periodicals • *473*

Index of Authors/Editors • *475*

Acknowledgments

Special thanks are due to:

Beth Langstaff, capable research assistant, without whose thoroughness in searching out relevant books and articles and skills in resolving bibliographical problems this project would have been much less complete and much longer in the making.

Nannette Ward and Lorraine Swanson for their word-processing labors in the early stages of the project.

Gloria Metz, whose very significant contributions included much of the data entry and all of the more difficult data manipulation, along with much expert editing.

Tom Bechtle of Locust Hill Press, for patience in granting repeated extensions of deadlines and for ongoing encouragement and helpfulness in what was for us a large and demanding task.

Preface

Our purpose in this work has been to provide extensive coverage of articles, books, and dissertations relating to the evangelical movement in North America. Although we have intended it to be as nearly complete as possible, the number of relevant items, in combination with lack of indexing for many periodical titles, especially in earlier decades, makes complete coverage a very elusive goal.

For books and dissertations the core list was compiled from the holdings of the libraries of the Consortium of Minnesota Theological Seminaries in subject areas related to evangelicalism, including fundamentalism, pentecostalism, and the charismatic movement. We then sought additional references in bibliographies and bibliographical notes in books and periodicals as well as in separately published bibliographies. For more recently produced material we have depended upon book reviews, publisher's advertisements, and bibliographies such as *Book Publishing Record*, as well as close perusal of our own seminary's recent acquisitions and orders.

For periodical articles, the core list was compiled from items located in the standard periodical indexes. However, because of the large number of unindexed periodicals, and the unindexed years in titles that are currently being indexed, it was necessary to search scores of unindexed or partially indexed periodical titles, concentrating in particular, but not exclusively, upon the post-World War II era.

The problem of the time-lag between the publication of articles and their appearance in printed indexes was resolved partly through the use of automated data bases, and partly through the authors' access to the hundreds of periodicals regularly received by area theological libraries. Our coverage includes, therefore, most of the major theological and religious periodicals received as late as December 1989.

Partly because of the number of entries and partly because of our intent to place our major emphasis upon twentieth century evangelicalism, we have included relatively few titles out of the large volume of literature by and about puritanism and pietism, two of the major streams within the larger evangelical movement.

We have generally limited inclusion to items appearing under appropriate subject headings in indexes or catalogs, as noted above, and to items whose title or subtitle indicates similar areas of coverage. Without that limitation, virtually every book or article originating within evangelicalism (e.g., periodicals such as *Christianity Today, Eternity*, and the *Journal of the Evangelical Theological Society*) could have been included. We will no doubt have missed some significant items by this approach, but it seemed the least fraught with problems, and the surest method of selecting materials that were explicitly dealing with evangelicalism and its related movements.

Among the periodical indexes consulted were *Religion Index One: Periodicals* (American Theological Library Association, 1949-), *Religion Index Two: Multi-Author Works* (ATLA, 1960-), *Christian Periodical Index* (1956-), *Guide to Social Science and Religion in Periodical Literature* (1964-), *Mosher Index* (from 1969 to 1979 the *Subject Guide to Select Periodical Literature*), *Humanities Index* (1974-), and *Social Science Index* (1974-). The latter two indexes superseded the *International Index* (1907-1974). Indexes covering denominational literature include *Catholic Periodical and Literature Index* (1930-), *United Methodist Periodical Index* (1961-1980), and *Southern Baptist Periodical Index* (1965-1984, 1987-). For older materials we used the *International Index, Nineteenth Century Readers' Guide to Periodical Literature 1890-1899, With Supplementary Indexing 1900-1922*, and Richardson's *Periodical Articles on Religion 1890-1899*. For articles in multi-author works, we used *Religion Index Two* and *Essay and General Literature Index*. Perusal of abstracting tools included *Religion Index One* (section: "Author Index With Abstracts," 1975-1985), and *Religious and Theological Abstracts* (1958-).

For dissertations as well as for articles, BRS (Bibliographical Retrieval Services) automated data bases, including Religion Index One and Two, provided coverage of recently published literature. For earlier years we used *Comprehensive Dissertation Index 1861-1972* (Volume 32, Philosophy and Religion). TREN (Theological Research Exchange Network) includes theses and dissertations from a number of evangelical seminaries, some of which are not available elsewhere.

Books and articles representative of the variety of positions on the movements under consideration have been included. The points of view of mainline Protestants, Roman Catholics, fundamentalists, pentecostals, and "new," "young," and "establishment" evangelicals, as well as secular scholars, are represented by journals and popular magazines and by individual books and articles.

Periodicals and books searched also include the spectrum from popular to scholarly, so that the life and thought of the larger church, as well as that of scholars, is represented.

Although the focus is upon North America, we have included articles and books that describe these movements in other lands, in part because of the light they shed on, and their connections with, North American evangelicalism.

We have generally reported rather than evaluated the content of books and articles, although we have occasionally indicated content of special worth. And, although we have in some cases indicated the stance of the author, that may also often be ascertained by the content reported, and, in the case of articles, by the periodicals in which they appear.

Although for earlier years we have searched available indexes, including the indexes produced by the periodicals themselves, most of the items listed and annotated are from the post-World War II era. This reflects in part, of course, the fact that the general indexing of religious periodicals dates largely from this period. The major index produced by the American Theological Library Association, for example, began with a small number of titles in 1949, and only gradually attained its present extensive coverage.

Of great significance for the increasing volume of material is the fact of the resurgence of evangelicalism during the latter part of the 20th century, the entrance of the pentecostal movement much more fully into the larger family of churches during the same period, and the emergence and rapid growth of the charismatic movement during the 1960s and 1970s.

An indication both of the resurgence of evangelicalism in these movements, and of the explosion of material indexed, may be seen in the fact that the number of entries on evangelicalism (not including the cross-reference entries) in *Religion Index One* increased from 37 in the decade 1949-1959, to 18 and then to 87 in the two-year periods 1969-1970 and 1979-1980, and to 69 in the single year 1988. During the same years the totals on fundamentalism were, respectively, 14, 7, 18, and 36, and on pentecostalism and the charismatic movement 8, 9, 29, and 75. Taken together as reflecting the larger movement, the totals are 57 (1949-1959), 39 (1969-1970), 134 (1979-1980), and 180 (1988). To this point, at least, the volume of material shows no sign of abating.

We have annotated many, but not all, of the books, dissertations, and articles cited here. Some were not available to us; a few were located too late to allow for anything beyond the citation.

The references have been arranged by subject areas, numbered consecutively, and used to create a name index as well as cross references, using only the number for each item listed.

Introduction

The English word evangelical is a form of the Greek euangelion, a word meaning "good news." In this general and most basic sense, an evangelical is anyone who espouses the good news in Christ. Although the word has been used from New Testament times it came into frequent use only with the sixteenth century Protestant Reformation. Thus, in its more restricted usage, evangelical describes the inheritors of the Reformation tradition.

In its more specific meaning, as a term describing both a theology and the people who hold the theology, "evangelical" has three components. First, belief in the good news announced through the death and resurrection of Christ: salvation for all who believe. Second, belief in the Bible as the only rule for faith and practice, a belief that issues in several central doctrines. Third, the missionary desire to share the gospel, producing the evangelism and missions emphases so characteristic of the last several centuries.

Evangelicals have not been confined to a single Protestant denomination, either at the time of the Reformation or since. While some denominations are exclusively evangelical in outlook—the Christian and Missionary Alliance, the Wesleyan Church, and the Baptist General Conference, for example—evangelicalism is found throughout American Protestantism, including the "mainline" denominations (middle class groups who are the keepers of a more or less liberal outlook).

Since the movement it describes is loosely structured, the word "evangelical" is always in danger of becoming so stretched as to lose its meaning. During the years since the mid-1970s when evangelicals have been in the public eye in the United States an elasticizing of the term has occurred, as it has been appropriated by persons who do not hold the doctrine of biblical inerrancy, by inerrantists, and by some who have slipped into universalism (the belief that all eventually will be saved). Some persons might call themselves evangelicals because it is popular at the moment or because of pressures in their denomination. Further differences emerge among "young" and "new" and "radical" evangelicals.

The course of evangelicalism in American church and national life is a many-faceted one. Evangelicalism was the prevailing Protestant theology down to the Civil War. Numerous studies demonstrate its cultural hegemony in the colonial and early national periods. After that time, forces both internal and external to the churches came into play, changing the way in which evangelicals saw themselves and lessening their role in the life of church and nation. For the first half of the twentieth century, an apparently diminished evangelical community was caught up in debates about the social gospel and fundamentalism. A public resurgence occurred, beginning in the 1960s, and evangelicalism, though certainly not culturally hegemonous, has again become a significant part of the culture in ways not foreseen by anyone. Signs of internal friction and faction, however, may presage a problematic role for evangelicals from now to the end of the century.

The term "pietism" is frequently connected with evangelicalism. Originally applied to a movement among German Lutherans in the late seventeenth century, pietism advocated a warm-hearted personal faith, holy living, and lay Bible study, expressed in missionary work and social philanthropy.

Pietism was the effective force in the founding of the Moravians, and through the Moravians influenced John Wesley and Wesleyanism. It also nourished a number of European renewal movements in the nineteenth century, and was characteristic of a large segment of American evangelicalism into the twentieth century and to the present.

The term came to apply to any who emphasized the experience side of Christianity, and was often used by critics with the implication that pietists had an unreasoned or legalistic faith. Some later pietists did lose the social thrust of the earlier years and turned to a passive, inward faith. While not all evangelicals were pietists, virtually all pietists were evangelicals.

The rise of theological liberalism, the higher criticism of the Bible, and the social and intellectual changes that led to the beginnings of American pluralism helped create fundamentalism. The name came from two sources: a series of slim volumes published between 1910 and 1915 entitled *The Fundamentals*, that summarized older biblical and theological beliefs contrasted with newer ideas gaining currency; and the founding in 1919 of the World's Christian Fundamentals Association, the major organizational vehicle for fundamentalism in the 1920s.

Views about fundamentalism have changed in recent years. Most historians agree that fundamentalist militancy led to the formation of new schools, denominations, and other organizations. But the stereotype of fundamentalists as bigoted, anti-intellectual, and anti-science gives a false picture, and ignores the variety of persons and ideas in the movement. The Scopes Trial of 1925 was often seen as the apogee of the movement, but recent studies show a vitality in fundamentalism that continued through the 1930s and 1940s, in missions, education, and other endeavors.

In the 1920s fundamentalism and evangelicalism seemed almost synonymous, but fundamentalism had internal rifts in the period between the world wars. When the National Association of Evangelicals (NAE) was founded in 1942 not all fundamentalists joined, an indication of more tensions to come. After World War II a number of conservative evangelical scholars did doctoral studies at major universities, accepted some of the ideas encountered there, gained an appreciation for certain elements of literature and the arts, and came to adopt some aspects of biblical criticism.

At issue in the growing division was the question of "separation"; the fundamentalists condemned Billy Graham's "inclusive" evangelism, the worldliness creeping into church life, and the scholars who had imbibed too many modern ideas. The latter were branded "neo-evangelicals" for their alleged readiness to compromise with the world. By the 1960s this "new" evangelicalism had become the postwar evangelical movement, with the adjective dropped by the 1970s. No longer synonymous, fundamentalism and evangelicalism were related, and at times quarrelsome, movements, evangelicalism in the conservative theological center and fundamentalism on the right.

Recently, some fundamentalists have moved closer to mainstream evangelicalism, though there is still a militant fundamentalism that refuses such realignment. The issue of separation, however, remains a factor.

Evangelicalism, which experienced inner dissension on its right with fundamentalists in the 1950s and 1960s, went through inner dissension on its left in the 1970s with a movement known as "young" or "radical" evangelicalism. Whereas the fundamentalists' critique centered upon compromise with the world, the young evangelicals emphasized failure to engage the world, especially in social and political action. The latter group turned against what it saw as "establishment" evangelicalism's close identification with the status quo in American life, and sought to stimulate social and political activism like that found among some nineteenth century evangelicals. The Sojourners community in Washington, D.C., and its magazine of the same name embody this approach.

As the young evangelicals moved to the political left, some of them moved to the theological left also, creating a left-wing evangelicalism to offset the fundamentalist right-wing. Thus, current evangelicalism has a mainstream center, an "open" evangelicalism on the left and a fundamentalist right wing.

An important element in evangelicalism derives from the nineteenth-century holiness movement, which emphasized personal spiritual development as a two-stage crisis: justification, when one is freed from sins committed; and sanctification, when one is freed from the control of sin.

Initially, the movement was Wesleyan in orientation and therefore emphasized achieving what Wesley called perfect love or entire sanctification, the ability to live without conscious sin. A variation of the emphasis on perfectionism was that which originated with Charles Finney and Asa Mahan, known as Oberlin Perfectionism. The holiness movement organized into the National Holiness Association (formed in 1867 as the National Camp Meeting for the Promotion of Holiness, renamed in 1893) and this in turn became the vehicle for holiness teachings and influence. By century's end, holiness teaching had parted company with Methodism and even led to the founding of new denominations.

A holiness emphasis closer to the Reformed tradition emerged through the Keswick movement, begun in England in 1875 under both English and American auspices. Keswick spoke of victorious Christian living or the overcoming life, but did not use phrases like entire sanctification; sin could be counteracted, but not eradicated. Keswick rapidly permeated evangelical church life, influencing Bible conferences and Bible institutes, and merging with a rising theology: dispensationalism. The Scofield Reference Bible, published in 1909, and a pervasive presence among evangelicals for the next two generations, meant further spread of the Keswick teachings through the Scofield notes.

The holiness movement was to extend its influence through a new and powerful movement that began in the U.S. just after the turn of the century. Pentecostalism, which added the baptism in the Holy Spirit, evidenced by glossolalia, as the sign that the sanctification crisis had taken place, began in part at Charles Parham's Bethel College, Topeka, Kansas, in 1901. In that year students experienced the baptism in the Spirit accompanied by tongues-speaking. Among Parham's students was William Seymour, a black minister from Texas, who had the tongues experience and took the teaching with him when he went to Los Angeles in 1906. There, the famous Azusa Street revival broke out and that, coupled with the events in Topeka, constitutes the beginning of the contemporary pentecostal movement.

In the decade following Azusa Street, pentecostalism quickly spread to other parts of North America and to Europe. Missionary from the start, pentecostalism was soon established in other parts of the world. In 1914 at Hot Springs, Arkansas, a number of the pentecostal groups and leaders met to discuss issues and strategy. Both theological and racial divisions were hardened and denominations like the Assemblies of God, the Church of God, the Church of God in Christ (a black denomination), and "oneness" pentecostals (nontrinitarians) emerged.

In spite of its generally fundamentalist beliefs, pentecostalism's insistence on glossolalia and healing as standard components of Christian experience kept it from acceptance by many evangelicals in the 1920s and 1930s. A breakthrough occurred when pentecostals participated in the founding of the NAE, thus aligning with the moderate evangelicalism that would dominate after World War II. A famous article in *Life* magazine in 1950 described pentecostalism as a "third force" in Protestantism and this further boosted it into the mainstream. At the same time, several prominent pentecostals began to foster rapprochement with mainstream evangelicals and with ecumenists. Together, these events led to a more general acceptance of pentecostalism.

Closely related to pentecostalism was the charismatic movement, beginning in mainline Protestant denominations in 1960, in Roman Catholicism in 1967, and in the Orthodox Church a few years later. These "neo-pentecostals," as they were originally called (the term lost currency in the 1970s), while emphasizing tongues-speaking and healing, remained in their denominations, preferring to bring the teachings to bear on their own religious structures. Further, many of the charismatics did not share the separation views that marked pentecostalism.

The charismatic movement, especially strong among Lutherans, Catholics, and Episcopalians, spawned organizations, magazines, and mass rallies to carry out its message. The charismatic movement peaked in the 1970s and, while it is still a major force, it no longer has the media exposure or the organizational strength it once had.

Recent events show a blending of charismatics with some pentecostals. The Society for Pentecostal Studies (founded 1970) has since

1982 allowed a voice in the organization to anyone interested in charismatic religion. In July 1987 a conference in New Orleans brought pentecostals and charismatics together from many different ecclesiastical communions.

Revivalism was one of the chief characteristics of American Protestantism in the eighteenth and nineteenth centuries, and still retains a powerful influence in many quarters. Revivalism promotes periodic spiritual intensity in church life, during which the unconverted are won to Christ and the converted are shaken out of spiritual lethargy. Revivalism has often led to social reform activities. Unevenly distributed among the denominations, revivalism has been strongest among Baptists, Methodist, holiness, and pentecostal groups and weakest among Lutherans and Episcopalians. Theologically it has been closer to conservative evangelicalism and fundamentalism than to liberalism.

The meaning of terms like revival, awakening, and renewal has prompted much dialogue, but defining revivalism as something happening only in frontier conditions and with emotional appeals is clearly incorrect. Revivalism is both urban and rural, rational and emotional, cutting across all class lines.

The great and general awakening of the 1730s and 1740s marked the major entry of revivalism into American church life. The effects of this Great Awakening were clear enough. Belief in awakenings became the commonly-held legacy of the movement. Detractors came forward, indicative of the divisive effects that revivalism was always to have among American Protestants. Education was also affected, several schools being founded by revival advocates. And in many congregations, experiential piety replaced the religious formalism that threatened post-Reformation Protestantism.

The Second Awakening, usually dated from 1800 with the appearance of the camp meeting and the revival that began in New England, marked the maturing of revivalism, particularly in the career of Charles Finney. By the time the most active phase of his career was completed, in 1835, the marks of modern revivalism were clearly fixed: protracted meetings; preaching for decision; professional itinerating revivalists; techniques for the preparation and conduct of meetings; and even a special musical form, the gospel song.

The career of D. L. Moody, the 1905 revival, and the flamboyant tactics of Billy Sunday were the high points in the century after Finney. Hundreds of lesser-known revivalists crisscrossed the country, lacing the nation with evangelistic meetings. Black churches were as actively revivalistic as white ones. Both the nineteenth century holiness movement and the pentecostal churches that were formed at the beginning of the new century were revivalistic in nature.

Revivalism continued between the two world wars, though with less influence in the general culture and with the stereotypical evangelist, seen in Sinclair Lewis's Elmer Gantry, a staple of the media. With the revival of religion after World War II came a resurgence in revivalism. Both Oral Roberts and Billy Graham came on the national scene in the late 1940s, Roberts representing the continuation of pentecostal healing revivals and Graham initially representing fundamentalism and then the rising neo-evangelicalism. Both Roberts and Graham and their contemporaries used the latest technologies to present the gospel message, but the technologies helped bring disrepute to the revival tradition when the televangelist scandals erupted in the 1980s.

Revivalism remains a strong feature of important segments of contemporary Protestantism and seems unlikely to disappear from the American church scene for the foreseeable future.

Missionary activity has been a constant in evangelicalism, stronger since the end of the eighteenth century than in the colonial era. The great century of missions, the nineteenth, has been followed by an even more extensive missionary enterprise. While the evangelical churches promoted missions all through the twentieth century, there was a special surge following World War II, and that activity has not diminished. With the approach of the millennial point in the year 2000, missionary concern and activity is probably stronger among evangelicals than at any time in the past.

For all its vitality and popularity, evangelicalism enters the 1990s with serious questions about its future. Criticisms have been raised about members of the coming generation with their paucity of Bible knowledge and their ease with the culture. The political surge of right-wing evangelicalism in the 1970s and 1980s has apparently run its course. Complaints are heard about the lack of a strong intellectual tradition among evangelicals. The future course of the movement is no more possible to predict than was its sudden rejuvenation in the 1970s. The books and articles in this bibliography attest well, however, to evangelicalism's variegated past, and document its recent and present vitality.

I

GENERAL, REFERENCE AND BIBLIOGRAPHICAL WORKS

1. Ahlstrom, Sydney E. "Theology in America: A Historical Survey, I. The Shaping of American Religion." In Religion in American Life, eds. James W. Smith, and A. Leland Jamison, 251-71. Princeton: Princeton University Press, 1961.

    Very fine survey of theology from the Puritans to neo-orthodoxy, built around American theology's diversity and derivativeness (more British before 1815, more German thereafter).

2. Barkley, Gary. "The Electric Church: Bibliographic Resources." Review and Expositor 81 (Winter 1984): 97-105.

    Helpful listing of books, articles and dissertations published from the 1930s on.

3. Bass, Clarence B. "Backgrounds to Contemporary Theological Trends." Bethel Seminary Quarterly 10 (February 1962): 38-48. "Contemporary Theological Trends." Bethel Seminary Quarterly 10 (May 1962): 59-71.

    Part one focuses on the historical context with special attention to liberalism, including its decline during the second quarter of the 20th century. Part two "attempts to delineate the significant doctrines and moods of liberalism, fundamentalism, orthodoxy, neo-orthodoxy, Bultmannism, and neo-evangelicalism."

4. Bergquist, James A. "Evangelism in Current Ferment and Discussion: A Bibliographical Survey." Word and World 1 (Winter 1981): 59-70.

    Good survey placed in three categories: mission of the church; movements and counter-movements; current issues and developments.

5.   Billington, Louis. Popular Evangelicalism in Britain and North
        America, 1730-1850. London: Methuen, 1950.

6.   Branson, Mark Lau. The Reader's Guide to the Best Evangelical
        Books. San Francisco: Harper & Row, 1982. 207 p.

        A valuable volume, the selections are "limited to the 1950-1980
        era, with a focus on more recent materials." Part one assesses
        books about the Christian life, "many of which are generally
        more popular," while the much larger part two on the Bible, the
        church, and the world "is for the more serious readers." Each
        topic has an introductory essay, followed by an annotated list.
        Index.

7.   Brunkow, Robert de V., ed. Religion and Society in North America:
        An Annotated Bibliography. Santa Barbara, CA/Oxford, England:
        American Bibliographical Center/Clio Press, 1983. 515 p.

8.   Bundy, David D. Keswick: A Bibliographic Introduction to the
        Higher Life Movements. Wilmore, KY: Asbury Theological Seminary,
        1975. 89 p.

        Short history of the Keswick movement followed by bibliograph-
        ical items divided into theological, biblical and devotional
        studies, hymnody, and periodicals.

9.   Burgess, Stanley M., and Gary B. McGee, eds. Patrick H.
        Alexander, assoc. ed. Dictionary of Pentecostal and Charismatic
        Movements. Grand Rapids: Zondervan, 1988. 914 p.

        More than eight-hundred articles, written by sixty-five
        contributors, cover a wide range of topics, historical and
        theological. Longer articles have attached bibliographies.
        Very helpful general resource.

10.   Buss, Dietrich G. "Meeting of Heaven and Earth: A Survey and
        Analysis of Literature on Millennialism in America, 1865-1985."
        Fides et Historia 20 (January 1988): 5-28.

        Survey of twenty years of literature on Christian
        millennialism, treated chronologically from Puritan times to
        the 20th century.

11.   Calvin Theological Journal, published semi-annually by Calvin
        Theological Seminary, Grand Rapids, MI.

The November issue each year has an extensive bibliography on Calvin studies, some of them on issues pertinent to American evangelicalism.

12. Carden, Allen. "God's Church and a Godly Government: A Historiography of Church-State Relations in Puritan New England." Fides et Historia 19 (February 1987): 51-66.

A summary of Puritan thought on church and state, followed by various and conflicting views about that thought in the writings of historians from George Bancroft to Edmund S. Morgan and David Hall, and suggestions for further research.

13. Carpenter, Joel A., ed. Fundamentalism in American Religion, 1880-1950. New York: Garland, 1988-. Forty-five volumes.

A forty-five volume facsimile series of significant and often rare works documenting the development of a major religious movement.

14. Carpenter, Joel A., and Edith L. Blumhofer. Evangelicalism in Twentieth Century America: A Guide to the Sources. New York: Garland. Forthcoming. c. 250 p.

Lists "important archives, libraries, artifact collections, and locations of periodicals and electronic media materials"; covers "all variety of evangelicals," but focuses on "the post-1945 coalition of evangelicals . . . dominated by ex-fundamentalists."

15. Carter, Paul A. Decline and Revival of the Social Gospel: Social and Political Liberalism In American Protestant Churches, 1920-1940. Ithaca: Cornell University Press, 1956. 265 p.

Best study of the social gospel for the period between the two World Wars. Carter combines fine critical scholarship with appreciation for the movement. Ten-page bibliography. Index.

16. Cauthen, Kenneth. The Impact of American Religious Liberalism. New York: Harper & Row, 1962. 283 p.

The standard work in its field, first published in the early 1950s, reprinted in 1983. Presents the work of eight representative liberal theologians of the late nineteenth and early twentieth centuries. Bibliographical references. Index.

17.   Chase, Elise, comp. Healing Faith: An Annotated Bibliography of
       Christian Self-Help Books. Westport, CT: Greenwood, 1985. 199 p.

       723 titles (from 4,000 "possible candidates") published in
       America since 1970, divided into three chapters (with
       subdivisions in each): spiritual psychodynamics, family and
       developmental issues, and the wider community; selections from
       a variety of theologies: "fundamentalist, conservative evangel-
       ical, neo-evangelical, charismatic, or liberal." Good annota-
       tions. Well-indexed.

18.   Dawsey, James. A Scholar's Guide to Academic Journals in Reli-
       gion. ATLA Bibliography Series, no. 23. Metuchen, NJ: Scarecrow,
       1989. 313 p.

       Aimed at the academic writier, this listing of over 500
       journals is divided into thirty-three categories; each journal
       is well annotated, with cross references among categories.
       Index of journals.

19.   Dollar, George W. "A Bibliography of American Fundamentalism."
       Bibliotheca Sacra 119 (January-March 1962): 20-27.

       Non-annotated list of 175 books by fundamentalists, non-funda-
       mentalists and anti-fundamentalists; special strength for the
       1920s and 1930s.

20.   Elwell, Walter A., ed. Evangelical Dictionary of Theology. Grand
       Rapids: Baker, 1984. 1,204 p.

       Considerably enlarged successor to Baker's Dictionary of
       Theology (1960), with 1200 articles by more than 200 evangel-
       ical scholars. Distinguishing characteristics include articles
       done from a theological perspective, sympathetic but not
       uncritical, popular language, cross references between
       articles, selective bibliographies.

21.   _____, ed. Evangelical Commentary on the Bible. Grand Rapids:
       Baker, 1989. 1,229 p.

       The most recent one volume evangelical commentary: thirty-eight
       evangelical scholars, using the NIV as the basis for their
       comments, provide commentary, outline, and introduction for
       each of the books of the Bible.

22.   Evangelical Archives Conference. Wheaton, July 1988. "Documen-
       tation of the Evangelical Movement." Christian Librarian 33
       (November 1989): 4-11.

Report of the "Documentation Group," one of four groups
established by the Conference, and into which the Conference
divided for working sessions; the Documentation Group explored
"ways for documenting the entire Evangelical movement"; the
four reports were together published in A Heritage at Risk
(1988).

23.   Evans, James H., Jr., comp. Black Theology: A Critical Assessment
        and Annotated Bibliography. Westport, CT: Greenwood Press, 1987.
        205 p.

        Annotations on 461 items--books and articles--cast into three
        categories: the origin and development of black theology;
        liberation, feminism, and Marxism; cultural and global
        discourse. Helpful introduction. Indexes.

24.   Faupel, David W. The American Pentecostal Movement: A Biblio-
        graphical Essay. Wilmore, KY: B. B. Fisher Library, Asbury
        Theological Seminary, 1972. 56 p.

25.   Gaustad, Edwin Scott. Faith of Our Fathers: Religion and the New
        Nation. San Francisco: Harper & Row, 1987. 196 p.

        Study of the half-century from 1776 to 1826, years of option
        and decision as complex for the churches then as for the
        churches now. Constrast between the elite leaders and the
        operations of the churches. Bibliography.

26.   Gifford, Carolyn De Swarte, ed. Women in American Protestant
        Religion 1800-1930. New York: Garland, 1986-.

        Thirty-six volume reprint collection, mostly from mainstream
        Protestantism; seven of the volumes are never-before-published
        anthologies on various aspects of the women's movement; avoids
        material reprinted elsewhere.

27.   Griffin, Leslie. "Catholics, Blacks, Evangelicals: Three Versions
        of the Public Church." New Theology Review 1 (August 1988): 20-41.

        Finds that Catholic bishops "identify moral principles" to
        apply to politics, black churches operate from "a fundamental
        principle of human equality," and evangelicals apply "biblical
        principles in the public realm," creating a struggle for those
        committed to Marty's "public church" idea.

28.   Hall, David D. "On Common Ground: The Coherence of American Pur-
        itan Studies." William and Mary Quarterly (April 1987): 193-229.

Extremely helpful bibliographical essay covering the writings
since 1970 of literary, seminary (the relationship between
Puritanism and Calvinism), and social historians.

29.   Hedstrom, James A. "A Bibliography for Evangelical Reform."
        Journal of the Evangelical Theological Society 19 (Summer 1976):
        225-38.

        Books from the 1960s and 1970s, many with annotations, on a
        variety of topics, couched in a plea for change in evangelical
        life and thought.

30.   Hempton, David. "Evangelical Revival and Society: A Historio-
        graphical Review of Methodism and British Society c. 1750-1850."
        Themelios 8 (April 1983): 19-25.

        The work of historians who assess the role of Methodism in
        England is looked at by way of three questions: Why did
        Methodism grow so rapidly? Why did it decline after 1840?
        What was its impact on British society?

31.   Hughes, Richard T. "The Churches of Christ in the United States
        and the Restoration Ideal: Recent Bibliography." Evangelical
        Studies Bulletin 6 (Spring 1989): 7-9.

        Recent literature--articles, books, dissertations--and archival
        depositories of help to the researcher.

32.   Hunt, Thomas C., and James C. Carper. Religious Colleges and
        Universities in America: A Selected Bibliography. New York:
        Garland, 1988. 386 p.

33.   Hutchison, William R. American Protestant Thought in the Liberal
        Era. Washington, DC: University Press of America, 1983. 243 p.

        Reprint of a valuable anthology (1968) of statements of
        pioneers in American liberal Protestantism. Bibliographical
        references.

34.   _____. The Modernist Impulse in American Protestantism.
        Cambridge: Harvard University Press, 1976. 347 p.

        Best of the monographs on turn-of-the-century liberalism. by a
        writer sympathetic to the liberal cause. on the rise. course.
        and questioning (though not the demise) of the liberal faith.
        Appendixes. Sixteen-page bibliography. Index.

35. Institute for the Study of American Evangelicals. Wheaton College, Wheaton, Illinois.

   A center for the study of the historical significance and contemporary role of evangelicalism. Twice a year publishes the Evangelical Studies Bulletin, a newsletter of bibliographical data and conference announcements. Sponsors conferences.

36. International Directory: Catholic Charismatic Prayer Groups. Ann Arbor: Servant Publications.

37. Jones, Charles Edwin. Black Holiness: A Guide to the Study of Black Participation in Wesleyan Perfectionist and Glossolalic Pentecostal Movements. Metuchen, NJ: Scarecrow Press, 1987. 388 p.

   Nearly 2,400 items, mostly grouped around organizations (with descriptions thereof), not annotated, arranged in six parts: general aspects of the movements; then (the bulk of the volume) three "orientations": Wesleyan-Arminian, finished work of Calvary, and leader-centered; and sections on schools and biography. Very helpful. 55-page index.

38. _____. A Guide to the Study of the Holiness Movement. Metuchen, NJ: Scarecrow Press, 1974. 918 p.

   There are 7,338 items in this six-part guide, most of which are grouped around organizations; the longest section on the holiness movement proper, an extensive section on biography, and sections on the Keswick movement, the holiness-pentecostal movement (of those groups which preceded the 1906 Azusa Street revival), schools, and general works. Brief description of organizations, no other annotations. Essential for holiness studies. 120-page index.

39. _____. A Guide to the Study of the Pentecostal Movement. Metuchen, NJ: Scarecrow Press, 1983. 2 volumes (1,199 p.).

   An exhaustive listing of more than 9,800 entries (most without annotations), in four parts: "literature of the movement without reference to doctrinal tradition"; works classified by doctrinal emphasis (the longest section in the volumes), with brief histories of the denominations listed; schools, with location, sponsorship, and related bibliography; biography on individuals "who are participants or creators of the movement." Essential for pentecostal studies. 140-page index.

40.   Kuklick, Bruce, ed. American Religious Thought of the 18th and
       19th Centuries. New York: Garland, 1988-. 32 volumes.

41.   Leadership '88 Networking Directory: A Guide to Young Leaders in
       the United States. Designed and edited by Olgy Gary. Wheaton:
       Lausanne Committee for World Evangelization 1988. 170 p.

       Prepared for the use of persons attending Leadership '88, "a
       national conference initiated by the Lausanne Committee for
       World Evangelization," with the intent of facilitating
       cooperative ministry among "the new generation of Christian
       leaders . . . emerging across North America." Listings by
       vocational, regional, and organizational groupings, among
       others. Includes, for example, a very helpful listing of
       organizations represented by the participants.

42.   Lesser, M. X. Jonathan Edwards: A Reference Guide. Boston: G. K.
       Hall, 1981. 421 p.

       A significant work on Edwards' scholarship; nearly 1,800
       entries on a wide variety of materials, chronologically
       arranged, covering the period 1729-1978. Introductory essay;
       fifty-four-page index.

43.   Lippy, Charles H., ed. Religious Periodicals of the United
       States: Academic and Scholarly Journals. Westport, CT: Greenwood
       Press, 1987. 626 p.

       Surveying more than one hundred publications, this book
       "concentrates on a sampling of those [periodicals] that focus
       on academic and scholarly concerns," from a range of religious
       groups and institutions, most of them currently in print, a few
       of which are evangelical in orientation. An essay accompanied
       by information sources and publication history describes each
       periodical. Appendixes. Thirty-seven-page index.

44.   Lippy, Charles H., and Peter W. Williams, eds. Encyclopedia of
       the American Religious Experience: Studies of Traditions and
       Movements. New York: Scribner, 1987. Three volumes (1.872 p.).

       Over one hundred especially commissioned topical and thematic
       essays, organized into nine categories, covering "the total
       scope of religious activity and the impact of that activity on
       [North] American life." All religious traditions are included.
       and many of the essays are pertinent to the history and theo-
       logy of evangelicalism. A very valuable resource. Biblio-
       graphies with each essay. 114-page index.

45.   Manspeaker, Nancy. Jonathan Edwards: Bibliographical Synopses.
        New York: Edwin Mellen, 1981. 259 p.

        Built on the bibliographies of John J. Coss (1917) and Stephen
        S. Webb (1962), this annotated work includes "books, chapters
        in books, articles, and monographs" and "works in which
        Edwards' thought or influence is given more than incidental
        consideration." An extremely valuable work.

46.   Martin, Ira Jay, III. Glossolalia: The Gift of Tongues--A Biblio-
        graphy. Cleveland, TN: Pathway, 1970. 72 p.

        Unannotated list of books, articles, tracts, theses and
        dissertations, commentaries, encyclopedias, and dictionaries
        that touch on the subject.

47.   McDonnell, Kilian, ed. Presence, Power, Praise: Documents on the
        Charismatic Renewal. Collegeville, MN: Liturgical Press, 1980.
        3 volumes.

        Volumes 1 and 2 include "Continental, National, and Regional
        Documents"; Volume 3 includes "International Documents."
        Bibliographical references. Index.

48.   McGavran, Donald, ed. The Conciliar-Evangelical Debate: The
        Crucial Documents, 1964-1976. 2d ed., enl. South Pasadena:
        William Carey, 1977. 396 p.

49.   McGiffert, Michael. "American Puritan Studies in the 1960s."
        William and Mary Quarterly 27 (January 1970): 36-67.

        Extremely helpful bibliography of studies of 17th century New
        England Puritanism, "paying particular regard to the work that
        has been done since the death of Perry Miller in 1963."

50.   McKim, Donald L. "The Authority and Role of Scripture (1981-
        1986): A Selected Bibliography." TSF Bulletin 10 (March-April
        1987): 19-22.

        Annotated list of more than forty books, placed in categories
        of historical dimension, theological developments, and biblical
        interpretation.

51.   Melton, J. Gordon. The Catholic Pentecostal Movement: A Biblio-
        graphy. Evanston, IL: Garrett Theological Seminary Library, 1971.
        20 p.

This early bibliography of more than 200 items (about half with brief annotations) exhaustively covers magazine articles and books, and also references some newspaper articles, and mimeographed materials. Index.

52.   Mills, Watson E. Charismatic Religion in Modern Research: A Bibliography. Macon, GA: Mercer University Press, 1985. 178 p.

More than 2,000 items related to classical pentecostalism, the charismatic movement, and the Jesus people movement. Excellent subject index.

53.   _____. Glossolalia: A Bibliography. New York: Edwin Mellen, 1985. 129 p.

Listing of 1,158 books and articles, without annotations, "of the more significant works in this area of glossalalia studies," touching historical, biblical, theological, psychological, and phenomenological areas, preceded by an informative biblographical essay. Indexes.

54.   _____, ed. Speaking in Tongues: A Guide to Research. Grand Rapids: Eerdmans, 1986. 537 p.

Twenty-five articles, published from the 1960s to the 1980s, are here gathered into five categories of study: exegetical, historical, theological, psychological, and socio-cultural; an excellent resource on the subject. Helpful survey of the literature. Thirty-six-page bibliography. Index.

55.   Montgomery, Michael S., comp. American Puritan Studies: An Annotated Bibliography of Dissertations, 1882-1981. Westport, CT: Greenwood Press, 1984. 419 p.

This bibliography brings together 940 doctoral dissertations from American, British, Canadian, and German sources. Montgomery selects dissertations central or important to the study of the world of American Puritans from 1620 to 1730. Most attention is on the New England Puritans, but studies on the influence of Puritanism on American history and culture as well as historiographical studies on the interpretation of Puritanism after 1730 are included. A valuable resource.

56.   Moyles, R. G. A Bibliography of Salvation Army Literature in English--1865-1987. Lewiston, NY: Edwin Mellen, 1988. 250 p.

57. Noll, Mark A. "'American Religious Thought of the 18th and 19th Centuries.'" Church History 58 (June 1989): 211-17.

A review article on the thirty-two volume Garland reprint edition (1988) of works from the 18th and 19th centuries, heavy with New Englanders. "Minor questions of selection aside, this is an absolutely first-rate reprint collection."

58. Peterson, Paul D., ed. Evangelicalism and Fundamentalism: A Bibliography Selected From the ATLA Religion Database. First rev. ed., November 1983. Chicago: American Theological Library Association, 1983. 389 p.

Items are taken from Religion Index One [RIO] (1975-), Religion Index Two [RIT] (various sets of years), and Research in Ministry: An Index, 1981- (doctor of ministry projects); arranged as in RIO: subject index, author/editor index (many with abstracts), book review index; a valuable guide to thousands of items.

59. Pierard, Richard V. "The New Religious Right in American Politics." In Evangelicalism and Modern America, ed. by George Marsden, 161-74. Grand Rapids: Eerdmans, 1984.

A very helpful bibliographic essay covering the historical background as well as the recent resurgence of the religious right into politics.

60. _____. "The Quest for Historical Evangelicalism: A Bibliographical Excursus." Fides et Historia 11 (Spring 1979): 60-72.

Stating that "Evangelical Protestantism has become the focal point of an enormous literary output," he discusses a part of that output, giving special attention to Richard Quebedeaux and his work.

61. Proctor, William. The Born-Again Christian Catalog: A Complete Sourcebook for Evangelicals. New York: M. Evans, 1979. 282 p.

A combination dictionary-encyclopedia-catalog-handbook, with reviews, mini-catalogs, definitions, and with a special focus on "born-again living." Bibliography.

62. Raskopf, Roger W. "Recent Literature on the Pentecostal Movement." Anglican Theological Review [Supplement] 2 (September 1973): 113-18.

63.   Ricard, Laura B. "New England Puritan Studies in the 1970s."
        Fides et Historia 15 (Spring-Summer 1983): 6-27.

        Extremely helpful bibliographical essay concentrating on the
        intellectual and social historians, who in the 1970s softened
        their disputes with each other.

64.   Rienstra, M. Howard. "Christianity and History: A Bibliographic
        Essay." In A Christian View of History?, eds. Marsden, and
        Roberts, 181-96. Grand Rapids: Eerdmans, 1975.

        Articles and books published after 1945 "that self-consciously
        reflect on the many relationships between Christianity and
        history," for historians, philosophers and theologians.

65.   Robeck, Cecil M., Jr. "The Decade (1973-1982) in Pentecostal-
        Charismatic Literature: A Bibliographic Essay." Theology, News
        and Notes 30 (March 1983): 24-29, 34.

        Books only in this very helpful survey.

66.   Roberts, Richard Owen. Revival Literature: An Annotated Biblio-
        graphy with Biographical and Historical Notices. Wheaton: Richard
        Owen Roberts, 1987. 575 p.

        5,983 items listed, with indication of holdings location(s) for
        each. By an insider, a participant, and an authority in the
        literature of revival. The result of four decades of study of
        revivalism, this is the first work to which to turn for the
        researcher in revivalism. While the single alphabet listing is
        formidable, the extensive index aids in finding persons, places
        and movements more readily. Both American and British
        publications, many of them rare.

67.   Sandeen, Ernest R., and Frederick Hale. American Religion and
        Philosophy: A Guide to Information Sources. Detroit: Gale
        Research Company, 1978. 377 p.

        Volume five in The American Studies Information Guide Series;
        excellent annotated bibliography of 1,639 books and articles,
        arranged by subjects, some of which relate to evangelicalism
        (e.g., sections on pentecostalism, fundamentalism, and neo-
        evangelicalism), and accessed by extensive author, title, and
        subject indexes.

68.   Smith-Rosenberg, Carroll. "Women and Religious Revivals: Anti-
        Ritualism, Liminality, and the Emergence of the American Bour-

geoisie." In The Evangelical Tradition in America, ed. Leonard I. Sweet, 199-232. Macon, GA: Mercer University Press, 1984.

An age of Jackson bibliographical study of women whose "enthusiastic response to religious antiritualism and to antistructuralism . . . reflects the greater complexity of women's class relocation," while social differences among women influenced their differing responses to ritual and structure.

69.   Spittler, Russell P. "Suggested Areas for Further Research in Pentecostal Studies." Pneuma 5 (Fall 1983): 39-56.

Thorough analysis of the need for pentecostal studies (with references to work already done) in theology, historical inquiry, exegesis, and socio-psychological topics, together with some of the how and why for doing the studies.

70.   Stuart, Bruce Wayne. "American Religious Historiography: William Warren Sweet, Perry Miller and Sidney E. Mead." Ph.D. diss., University of Minnesota, 1984. 409 p.

71.   Sweet, Leonard I. "The Evangelical Tradition in America." In The Evangelical Tradition in America, ed. Leonard I. Sweet, 1-86. Macon, GA: Mercer University Press, 1984.

Indispensable guide to scores of books and articles on the whole range of evangelicalism; Sweet has done a masterful job of making this material available for the researcher.

72.   _____, ed. The Evangelical Tradition in America. Macon, GA: Mercer University Press, 1984. 318 p.

Ten scholars present as many essays, ranging across the history of evangelicalism in America on such topics as slavery, millennialism, Charles Finney, Native Americans, Blacks, and Women. The editor contributes an extensive (pp. 1-86) and excellent bibliographical essay. Bibliographical notes in each chapter.

73.   Tinder, Donald. "Book Survey: The Holy Spirit From Pentecost to the Present." Christianity Today 19 (9 May 1975): 11-20.

Extremely helpful annotated survey of books on the subject, almost all of them published in the 1970s, placed in ten categories.

74.   Wacker, Grant. "Searching for Norman Rockwell: Popular Evangelicalism in Contemporary America." In The Evangelical Tradition in

America, ed. Leonard I. Sweet, 289-315. Macon. GA: Mercer University Press, 1984.

A bibliographic study showing "that what is growing is not Evangelicalism . . . but rather a segment within Evangelicalism defined by its allegiance to a cluster of values derived from Victorian middle-class society," the "Evangelical Right" seeking a "Christian Civilization."

75.   Weimer, Ferne Lauraine. "The Billy Graham Center Collection." Christian Librarian 33 (November 1989): 12-14.

A division of Wheaton College, the Center "is dedicated to the study and promotion of world evangelization." Its three divisions--Archives, Museum, and Library--"preserve the American heritage of Protestant non-denominational evangelistic and missionary endeavors, and provide resources for research."

76.   Williams, Ethel L., and Clifton L. Brown, comps. Afro-American Religious Studies: A Complete Bibliography with Locations in American Libraries. Metuchen, NJ: Scarecrow, 1972. 454 p.

Articles and books, unannotated, are arranged in five sections in this helpful resource: the African heritage; Christianity and slavery in the new world; the American Negro and the American religious life; the civil rights movement; the contemporary religious scene. Appendixes list periodicals, manuscript collections, and bibliographical sources. Author index.

77.   Wilson, John F., ed. Church and State in America: A Bibliographical Guide. Vol. 1, The Colonial and Early National Periods. Vol. 2, The Civil War to the Present Day. Westport: Greenwood, 1986, 1987.

Part of the Project on Church and State at Princeton, funded by the Lilly Endowment. Indispensable source guide for study of church-state relations. Bibliography. Indexes.

See also items 105, 379, 454, 822, 958, 1079, 1341, 1456, 1657, 1749, 2021, 2275, 2300, 2321, 2344, 2505.

II

HISTORY OF EVANGELICALISM

A. General Studies

78. Ahlstrom, Sydney E. "From Puritanism to Evangelicalism: A Critical Perspective." In The Evangelicals: What They Believe, Who They Are, Where They Are Changing. eds. David F. Wells and John D. Woodbridge, 269-89. Nashville: Abingdon, 1975.

Argues that the term "evangelicalism" refers to "a fairly unified tradition."

79. Allan, J. D. The Evangelicals: An Illustrated History. Commentary by J. D. Allan, with contributions by John Stott, et al. Exeter, U.K.: Paternoster Press; Grand Rapids: Baker, 1989. 154 p.

Briefly tells the story of evangelicalism across the church's 2000 year history, in a number of countries and across a wide range of topics, using scores of photographs and other illustrations.

80. Alley, Cletus E. "Is There Anything Lutherans Can Do in Evangelism that Is Lutheran? An Evaluation of Evangelical Practices in Terms of the Lutheran Confession." D.Min. diss., Luther Northwestern Theological Seminary, St. Paul, MN, 1982. 202 p.

81. Anderson, Marvin W. Evangelical Foundations: Religion in England, 1378-1683. New York: Peter Lang. 1987. 488 p.

Surveys renewal in the English Church. showing the Biblical roots and the centrality of preaching from Wyclif on. including British colonial North America to the time of Roger Williams. Bibliographical references. Bibliography. Index.

82. "Apostolic, Catholic, and Evangelical." International Bulletin of Missionary Research 12 (April 1988): 1.

15

"This given" of elements which "must come together--apostolic
faithfulness, catholic vision, and evangelical commitment--if
we are to realize our calling and destiny in Jesus Christ,"
"runs through our current issue like a bright thread."

83.   Askew, Thomas A. "A Response to David F. Wells." In A Time to
        Speak: The Evangelical-Jewish Encounter, eds. A. James Rudin, and
        Marvin R. Wilson, 41-44. Grand Rapids: Eerdmans; Austin, TX:
        Center for Judaic-Christian Studies, 1984.

        A response to Wells' paper, "'No Offense: I Am An Evangeli-
        cal,'" in the same volume. Askew offers a four-part definition
        of evangelicalism.

84.   Averill, Lloyd J. "Can Evangelicalism Survive in the Context of
        Free Inquiry?" Christian Century 92 (22 October 1975): 924-28.

        Because of a university's commitments to intellectual freedom,
        the complex character of truth, inclusiveness, and moral
        learning, "there is an inherent incompatibility between
        Christian evangelicalism and the idea of a university."

85.   Baxter, James Sidlow. Rethinking Our Priorities; the Church: Its
        Pastor and People. Heart-to-Heart Talks With Ministers, Music
        Directors, Leaders, and Workers in Our Evangelical Churches.
        Grand Rapids: Zondervan, 1974. 255 p.

        Taking his cue from Richard Baxter, The Reformed Pastor (1656),
        Britisher Baxter has some strong words about the role of the
        Bible, Pentecost, and public worship in evangelical churches.

86.   Bebbington, David W. Patterns in History: A Christian View.
        Downers Grove: InterVarsity, 1979. 211 p.

        A "Study in historical thought"; Bebbington looks at various
        views of history--cyclical, progressive, historicist, Marxist
        --from an evangelical point of view, and develops the evangel-
        ical perspective in some detail. Fourteen page annotated
        bibliography. Index.

87.   Bockmühl, Klaus. "Karl Barth 1886-1986: An Evangelical Apprai-
        sal." Crux 22 (September 1986): 28-32.

        Discusses two elements as "particularly noteworthy and of
        continuing relevance: 1) his passion for the primacy of God,
        and 2) his struggle in recovering the reality of God."

88.   Bowden, Henry Warner. A Century of Church History: The Legacy of
        Philip Schaff. Carbondale: Southern Illinois University Press,
        1988. 375 p.

        Ten bibliographical essays on a variety of subjects in church
        history, three of them pertinent to American topics: Jay P.
        Dolan, "Immigration and American Christianity: A History of
        Their Histories"; John F. Wilson, "Civil Authority and
        Religious Freedom in America: Philip Schaff on the United
        States as a Christian Nation"; Gerald H. Anderson, "To the Ends
        of the Earth: American Protestants in Pursuit of Mission."

89.   Branson, Mark Lau. "Fundamentalism--Left and Right." TSF
        Bulletin 5 (May-June 1982): 2-3.

        An appeal to walk a centrist line, avoiding the closed-minded
        approaches of both the theological left and the theological
        right.

90.   Brown, Harold O. J. "Evangelicalism in America." Dialog 24
        (Summer 1985): 188-92.

        Discusses evangelicalism in terms of its sources (Lutheran,
        Pietist, and Revivalist) and characteristics (Brown cites six),
        distinctions within, and its future.

91.   Brown, John Bossert, Jr. "Wholistic Health Care: An Evangelical
        Perspective." Journal of Pastoral Practice 6, no. 2 (1983):
        45-53.

        Briefly surveys the assumptions of the movement, which
        developed in the late 1960s, and offers words of appreciation
        as well as of criticism.

92.   Cailliet, Emile. "The Mind's Gravitation Back to the Familiar."
        Theology Today 15 (April 1958): 1-8.

        Comments about the positive and negative in fundamentalism,
        evangelicalism, and eclecticism.

93.   Carnell, Edward John. "Orthodoxy: Cultic vs. Classical."
        Christian Century 77 (30 March 1960): 377-79.

        The doctrine of the church divides cultic (fundamentalism) from
        classical orthodoxy, the former's separatism dividing it from
        the historical denominations and thereby losing touch with the

church universal, in contrast to the latter's willingness to
maintain contact with the church universal.

94.   Castlen, James Eudelle. "Jubilate! Church Music in the Evangelical Tradition: A Programmed Adaptation for the Philippines."
D.M.A. diss., Southern Baptist Theological Seminary, 1986. 319 p.

95.   Citron, Bernhard. New Birth: A Study of the Evangelical Doctrine
of Conversion in the Protestant Fathers. With a preface by Hugh
Watt. Edinburgh: The University Press, 1951. 215 p.

Written from the Reformed perspective, but with "loving
admiration" for all the saints of the church, by one who was
pastor and scholar. Views the life of the Christian from its
first awakening, and how that progress is reflected in the
church's doctrine. Bibliography. Indexes.

96.   Craig, William Lane. Apologetics, an Introduction. Chicago:
Moody Press, 1984. 214 p.

Good example of a recent evangelical approach to the subject.
Bibliographical references. Index.

97.   Curry, Lerond. "Will the Real Evangelical Please Stand Up?"
Christian Century 93 (26 May 1976): 512-16.

Asserting that he is both evangelical and liberal, Curry
castigates those evangelicals who take over the word and its
meaning for themselves, to the exclusion of others with equally
valid claims on the term.

98.   Davis, John Jefferson. Evangelical Ethics: Issues Facing the
Church Today. Phillipsburg: Presbyterian and Reformed, 1985.
299 p.

An evangelical seminary professor examines nine issues that
include "Reproductive Technologies," "Homosexuality,"
"Abortion," and "Infanticide and Euthanasia." Bibliographical
references.

99.   _____. "Future Directions for American Evangelicals." Journal
of the Evangelical Theological Society 29 (December 1986): 461-67.

With the passing of the founding generation of evangelicals,
new emphases should include the Word of God as power vis a vis
the world religions, the Spirit of God in pentecostal power,
and world mission.

100.   DeHoney, Wayne. An Evangelical's Guidebook to the Holy Land.
         Nashville: Broadman, 1974. 159 p.

101.   Dobson, Edward, and Edward E. Hindson. "Who are the 'Real'
         Pseudo-Fundamentalists?" Fundamentalist Journal 2 (June 1983):
         10-11.

         Biblical and historical perspectives on those who subtract from
         or add to the essential doctrines of Christianity.

102.   Dudley-Smith, Timothy. "Yesterday and Tomorrow: Evangelical
         Points From the Past." Churchman 93, no. 3 (1979): 199-210.

         Discussion of evangelical enthusiasm, evangelical attributes,
         and the evangelical essentials: the search for holiness, the
         spread of the gospel, and the cross of Christ.

103.   Earle, Ralph M., Jr. "Liberalism on the Defensive." Asbury
         Seminarian 3 (Summer 1948): 59-61.

         Notes the programs at the meetings of the National Association
         of Biblical Instructors, as well as articles in The Journal of
         Bible and Religion, and the book, Religious Liberals Reply
         (1947).

104.   Ellingsen, Mark. "Common Sense Realism: The Cutting Edge of
         Evangelical Identity." Dialog 24 (Summer 1985): 197-205.

         Evangelicalism has a philosophical heritage derived from common
         sense realism while Protestant mainliners are in a Kantian
         philosophical mold, thus explaining many of the differences
         between the two groups; suggestions for rapprochement in the
         conclusion. Further explication in Ellingsen's The Evangelical
         Movement (1988).

105.   Evangelical Archives Conference. Wheaton, July 1988. A Heritage
         at Risk: The Proceedings of the Evangelical Archives Conference,
         July 13-15, 1988. Wheaton: Billy Graham Center, Wheaton College,
         1988. 47 p.

         An urgent call to gather, preserve, and use the documents of
         the evangelical movement: creators, users, and curators met to
         discuss what materials to preserve, how to preserve them, and
         how to make them useful.

106.   Fison, Joseph Edward. The Blessing of the Holy Spirit. London/
         New York: Longmans/Green, 1950. 226 p.

"In a religious situation in which liberal protestantism has
lost touch with the supernatural and evangelical pietism and
catholic mysticism have lost touch with the natural, the
supreme need of the Christian church is a rediscovery of the
blessing of the Holy Spirit . . . . Only the Holy Spirit can
point the way forward to a revival of genuine religion." Set
in the context of liberal and conservative developments during
the post-World War I decades.

107.   Frey, Harald Christian Andreas. "Critiques of Conciliar Ecumenism
        by Conservative Evangelicals in the United States." Th.D. diss.,
        Boston University, 1961. 303 p.

108.   Fuller, David Otis, ed. Valiant for the Truth: A Treasury of
        Evangelical Writings. Introductions by Henry W. Coray. New York:
        McGraw Hill, 1961. 460 p.

        Nearly forty selections, from the early church to J. G. Machen,
        most of them on biblical and theological subjects.

109.   Gerstner, John H. "The Theological Boundaries of Evangelical
        Faith." In The Evangelicals: What They Believe, Who They Are,
        Where They Are Changing, ed. David F. Wells and John D.
        Woodbridge, 21-37. Nashville: Abingdon, 1975.

        Traces the history of evangelicalism from the Reformation to
        recent decades.

110.   Helm, Paul. "Is Evangelicalism Just a Cult?" Banner of Truth no.
        52 (January 1968): 13-15.

        Not when it is "meaningfully set in the midst of human life."
        "Not when it is true to itself and to the logic of its belief.
        Unhappily this is not the case at present."

111.   Hickman, James T. "The Polarity in American Evangelicalism."
        Religion in Life 44 (Spring 1975): 47-58.

        Defines evangelicalism as the merging of Protestant orthodoxy
        and pietism that originated in the Great Awakening; the
        polarity comes between communication of the gospel and the
        presentation of orthodoxy; three motifs, particularly on social
        issues, in the 20th century: fundamentalism (the preservation
        pole), evangelicalism, and neo-evangelicalism (the communi-
        cation pole).

112.   Inch, Morris A. The Evangelical Challenge. Philadelphia:
         Westminster, 1978. 165 p.

         A professor at Wheaton College presents evangelicalism in its
         history, theology, emphasis on evangelism and missions.
         Helpful "Reader's Summary" at the end of each chapter.
         Bibliography. Index.

113.   Ippel, Henry P. "Evangelicals Attempt the Impossible: A Handbook
         to the History of Christianity." Fides et Historia 10 (Spring
         1978): 61-69.

         An essay reviewing Eerdmans' Handbook to the History of
         Christianity (1977).

114.   Jacobs, Anton K. "Evangelicalism and Capitalism: A Critical Study
         of the Doctrine of Atonement in the History of American Religion."
         Ph.D. diss., University of Notre Dame, 1985. 250 p.

115.   Kantzer, Kenneth S., ed. Evangelical Roots: A Tribute to Wilbur
         Smith. Nashville: Thomas Nelson, 1978. 250 p.

         Seventeen essays by evangelicals on various questions of
         history, theology, and the Bible. Bibliographical references.

116.   _____. "The Future of the Church and Evangelicalism." In
         Evangelicals Face the Future. Scenarios, Addresses, and Responses
         from the 'Consultation on Future Evangelical Concerns' held in
         Atlanta, Georgia, December 14-17, 1977, ed. Donald E. Hoke,
         127-46. Pasadena: William Carey Library, 1978.

         Reviews evangelicalism's historic meaning, presents multiple
         meanings, and projects a positive future, although with several
         warnings.

117.   _____. "Love of God Demands Love for His Church." Christian-
         ity Today 25 (17 July 1981): 14-16.

         In spite of the problems and sin in the church, it is still the
         institution founded by Christ and therefore needs our
         commitment and love.

118.   _____. "Of Prophetic Robes and Weather Vanes." Interview by
         Harvey G. Cox. et al. Christianity Today 22 (7 April 1978):
         21-26.

Sixteen persons pose questions to Kantzer as he assumes the
editorship of Christianity Today.

119.   Katsh, Abraham I. The Biblical Heritage of American Democracy.
        New York: KTAV, 1977. 246 p.

        The impact of the language and message of the Hebrew Bible on
        Western civilization, the Puritans, legislation, concepts of
        justice, and English and American literature. Appendixes.
        Bibliography. Indexes.

120.   Kay, Thomas O. "Evangelicalism's Debt to the Mediaeval Church."
        New Oxford Review 50 (October 1983): 10-16.

        Theology based on Scripture, emphasis on the transcendence and
        immanence of God, mysticism, missions, the integration of faith
        and learning, and social service are all part of the debt.

121.   Kevan, E. F., and D. M. Lloyd-Jones. "The Evangelical Library."
        Evangelical Quarterly 17 (July 1945): 221-25.

        Description of a new library in London stressing evangelical
        history and doctrine, and an address given by Lloyd-Jones at
        its opening.

122.   Kinder, Ernst. Evangelical: What Does it Really Mean? Translated
        by Edward and Marie Schroeder. St. Louis: Concordia Pub. House,
        1968. 105 p.

        Professor of Systematic Theology at the University of Munster,
        Germany, and author of numerous books and articles, examines
        the word's meaning in the New Testament, its reclaiming in the
        Reformation, and the ecumenical posture that ought to mark
        evangelicals today.

123.   King, John Owen, III. The Iron of Melancholy: Structures of
        Spiritual Conversion in America from the Puritan Conscience to
        Victorian Neurosis. Middletown, CT: Wesleyan University Press,
        1983. 457 p.

        Heavy with Freud and Weber, a psychohistory analysis of the
        progress from Puritan "cases of conscience" to the Victorian
        neurological "case." Among evangelicals, only Jonathan Edwards
        is treated. Bibliography. Index.

124.   Kraus, C. Norman. "Anabaptism and Evangelicalism." In Evangeli-
        calism and Anabaptism, ed. C. Norman Kraus, 169-82. Scottsdale,
        PA: Herald Press, 1979.

Analyzes both movements, finding more contrast than similarity,
with the exception of the radical "Young Evangelicals."

125.   , ed. Evangelicalism and Anabaptism. Scottdale, PA:
Herald Press, 1979. 187 p.

Resurgent evangelicalism analyzed from an Anabaptist-Mennonite
perspective. Topics include Biblical inerrancy, eschatology,
and the pentecostal/charismatic movement. First given as
lectures (1977-1978) at Goshen College. Bibliographical
references.

126.   . "Introduction: What is Evangelicalism?" In Evangelicalism and Anabaptism, ed. C. Norman Kraus, 9-22. Scottdale, PA:
Herald Press, 1979.

He presents evangelicalism as a highly diverse coalition that
stands in the tradition of 17th and 18th century Protestant
Orthodoxy, held together by emphases that include biblical
authority, evangelism, "born-again" experience, and
Americanism.

127.   Kuhn, Annie W. "The Influence of Paul Gerhardt Upon Evangelical
Hymnody." Asbury Seminarian 3 (Spring 1948): 21-28.

Reprinted in Asbury Seminarian 35 (October 1980): 10-25. The
17th century German hymn writer, "the greatest hymn writer
Germany has produced," whose work was very influential upon the
Wesleyan movement.

128.   Leonard, Bill J. "A Theological Evaluation of Evaluations: The
Evangelicals." Theological Education 22 (Autumn 1985); 7-25.

A Southern Baptist defines evangelicalism, shows its diversity,
and describes the tensions the evangelical seminaries face--
confessionalism and soul liberty; the relation to culture;
relation to constituents--and the effects on evaluation the
tensions bring.

129.   Lindsell, Harold. The New Paganism. San Francisco: Harper & Row,
1987. 279 p.

Here the historian rather than the theological controversialist, Lindsell chooses "paganism" rather than "secular humanism"
to describe the displacement in the West of the Judeo-Christian
tradition, a displacement he traces to the Enlightenment;
includes a description of contemporary American society, an

analysis of Karl Barth's thought. and a program for the church
in the pagan society. Appendixes. Bibliography. Index.

130. _____. "Who Are the Evangelicals?" Christianity Today 9
(18 June 1965): 3-6.

Some history of the term evangelical, especially as consonant
with the Reformation and rooted in the Bible; the variety of
uses of the term in the 1960s and the threat of dilution.

131. _____. "Who or What is an Evangelical? (Why a Leading Evangelical Recommends the Term 'Fundamentalist')." Fundamentalist
Journal 3 (February 1984): 28-30, 37.

Because of recent changes in how people define it, the term
evangelical "seems to be a confusing label and probably [is] a
lost cause."

132. Lovelace, Richard F. The American Pietism of Cotton Mather:
Origins of American Evangelicalism. Grand Rapids: Christian
University Press, Eerdmans, 1979. 350 p.

Placing Mather (1663-1729) "in the center of the genetic line
from the colonial Puritans to the later evangelicals," this
monograph (originally Lovelace's Princeton Ph.D. dissertation)
in "spiritual theology" ("the rise and progress of religion in
the soul") pictures Mather not as an aberrant Puritan (other
than his egocentricity and florid writing style) but as a
bridge to the Great Awakening and later manifestations of
evangelicalism. Bibliographical essay. Index.

133. _____. "A Call to Historic Roots and Continuity." In The
Orthodox Evangelicals: Who They Are and What They Are Saying, ed.
Robert E. Webber and Donald Bloesch, 43-67. Nashville: Thomas
Nelson, 1978.

Surveys the sweep of Christian history, in an appeal for a
"recovery of our full Christian heritage," of "evangelical
catholicity."

134. Mabie, Henry Clay. Under the Redeeming Aegis: An Exposition of
the Evangelical Principle. London: Hodder & Stoughton. 1913.
157 p.

135. MacKay. Donald M. "The Health of the Evangelical Body: What Can
We Learn From Recent History?" Journal of the American Scientific
Affiliation 38 (December 1986): 258-65.

Centers on "things that can go wrong organically with the
corporate life of an evangelical body" and asks for a loving
relationship among evangelicals to avoid the spiritual ill-
health to which groups are prone.

136.   Mariner, Kirk. "Historical Origins of Contemporary American
Evangelicalism." Ph.D. diss., Wesley Theological Seminary, 1979.

137.   Marsden, George M. "Evangelicals, History, and Modernity." In
Evangelicalism and Modern America, ed. George Marsden, 94-102.
Grand Rapids: Eerdmans, 1984.

Though "evangelicals' views of history, like their intellectual
assumptions, are early modern as opposed to contemporary
modern," the principle by which to judge the good and the bad
in either view of history (and thereby save some of the
evangelical heritage) is the Incarnation.

138.   ____. "The Plight of Liberal Protestantism." Fides et
Historia 20 (January 1988): 45-50.

A review article of Liberal Protestantism: Realities and
Possibilities, ed. Robert S. Michaelson and Wade Clark Roof
(New York: Pilgrim Press, 1986). Reviews contributions which
run the range from defense to critiquing of liberal
Protestantism, by such scholars as Peter Berger, William
Hutchison, and Leonard Sweet.

139.   Martin, Roger H. "An Evangelical Chair at Harvard?" Christianity
Today 27 (4 February 1983): 14-16.

An associate dean at Harvard Divinity School describes the
evangelical presence at Harvard and advocates the appointment
of an evangelical to the faculty. Responses by Kenneth
Kantzer, Richard Lovelace, and Norman Geisler in the same issue
(pp. 17-20).

140.   Marty, Martin E. The Public Church: Mainline-Evangelical-
Catholic. New York: Crossroad, 1981. 170 p.

Hoping to create a "communion of communions" among the
churches, Marty "draws on biblical, theological, and political
motifs to offer a mode for self-understanding and mission in
the years ahead."

141.   ____. "The Shape of Religious Thought and Assumptions." In
Evangelicals Face the Future. Scenarios, Addresses, and Responses

from the 'Consultation on Future Evangelical Concerns' held in
Atlanta, Georgia, December 14-17, 1977, ed. Donald E. Hoke,
110-21. Pasadena: William Carey Library, 1978.

Provides the larger religious context: we will remain a
religious people; we are in the third stage of an extended
religious revival, which has not, however, substantially
altered American life; cautions the church in its interaction
with modern society.

142.   _____. "The Years of the Evangelicals." Christian Century 106
(15 February 1989): 170-74.

"Comment[s] on the current shape of evangelicalism from the
vantage of a friendly critic or a critical friend." Concludes
that "the next 12 years cannot be the Years of the Evangelicals
in the same way the previous ones were. A period has ended."

143.   McDonnell, Kilian. "A Catholic Looks at Evangelical Protestantism." Commonweal 92 (21 August 1970): 408-13.

Assessment of the variety, weaknesses, strengths and success of
the evangelicals, who "have something to teach their Catholic
brethren, especially in the matter of evangelism."

144.   McGoldrick, James E. "Three Principles of Protestantism." Banner
of Truth no. 52 (January 1968): 7-18.

Protestantism as a "revival of the biblical faith, a revival of
New Testament Christianity, with a positive emphasis upon the
doctrines of Scripture, grace and faith."

145.   McIntire, Carl, and Ronald A. Wells, eds. History and Historical
Understanding. Grand Rapids: Eerdmans, 1983. 296 p.

Eight essays, five by evangelicals, that began as papers or
lectures, aiming "to get at what insights Christian faith may
bring to our understanding of historical process and historical
knowledge and study, and then the exploration of what we may
gain from such insights." Bibliographical references. Index.

146.   McLoughlin, William G. "Is There a Third Force in Christendom?"
Daedalus 96 (Winter 1967): 43-68.

Argues that religion goes through reorientation as it finds a
new consensus in culture, and when it does it produces groups
at the fringes. The so-called third force is basically these

fringe groups, who will likely not be included in the completed
reorientation and therefore are not a third force.

147.   Mead, Sidney E. "American Protestantism since the Civil War. II.
         From Americanism to Christianity." Journal of Religion 36 (April
         1956): 67-89.

         Changes in American life such as the rise of industrialism and
         its consequences, and changes in thinking like the rise of
         "scientific modernism," led to divisions in Protestant theology
         ranging from conservative orthodoxy to liberalism, and promoted
         the social gospel and the rise of fundamentalism.

148.   Montgomery, John Warwick. "'Born Againism': An Evangelical
         Innovation?" Christianity Today 26 (22 October 1982): 80.

         Modern evangelicalism is not a deviant phenomenon of church
         history but mainstream Christianity.

149.   Mouw, Richard J. "New Alignments: Hartford and the Future of
         Evangelicalism." In Against the World for the World, ed. Peter L.
         Berger and Richard John Neuhaus, 99-125. New York: Seabury, 1976.

         An evangelical signer of the Hartford Appeal (1975) explains
         who the evangelicals are, describes new alignments (theological
         polarization and politicization) among them, offers a critique
         of evangelicalism, notes its suspicion of ecumenism, and shows
         the similarities between right and left-wing evangelicals.

150.   Nichols, John Broadhurst. Evangelical Belief: Its Conflict With
         Rome. 2d ed. London: Religious Tract Society, 1903. 367 p.

         Classic statement of the anti-Roman Catholic stance common
         among some evangelicals, in this case by a British churchman.
         Bibliography. Index.

151.   Noll, Mark A. "The Conference on Faith and History and the Study
         of Early American History." Fides et Historia 11 (Fall 1978):
         8-18.

         Proposes an ideal for this organization of evangelical
         historians, then uses the newsletter and journal (Fides et
         Historia) as sources to look at what members have been doing in
         their writing.

152.   _____. "Evangelicals and Reformed: Two Streams, One Source."
         Reformed Journal 31 (April 1981): 8-14.

The single source is the gospel by way of the Reformation. The
evangelical stream differs from the Reformed (here, the
Christian Reformed Church), in having gone through two experiences that affected it profoundly: the American Revolution and
the fundamentalist-modernist controversy.

153.   Padilla, C. Rene, ed. The New Face of Evangelicalism: An Inter-
         national Symposium on the Lausanne Covenant. London: Hodder and
         Stoughton, 1976. 282 p.

         Fifteen authors (ten of them either citizens or residents of
         Third World countries) discuss the fifteen sections of the
         Lausanne Covenant (1974), a document aimed at eliminating the
         dichotomies between evangelism and social concern, evangelism
         and discipleship, and evangelism and church renewal. Biblio-
         graphical references.

154.   Quebedeaux, Richard. By What Authority: The Rise of Personality
         Cults in American Christianity. San Francisco: Harper & Row,
         1982. 204 p.

         Includes "an overview of evangelical resurgence in popular
         culture." Examines the nature and impact of popular religion
         in America, its celebrity leadership and the social impact of
         the mass media and technological advance on modern American
         religion. Bibliography.

155.   Ramm, Bernard. The Evangelical Heritage. Waco: Word, 1973.
         180 p.

         In a "study of theological geography," Ramm puts evangelicalism
         in its historical contexts, notes the conflicts it has faced
         since the Enlightenment, and suggests its possible future.
         Bibliographical references. Index.

156.   Rausch, David A., and Carl Hermann Voss. Protestantism--Its
         Modern Meaning. Philadelphia: Fortress, 1987. 211 p.

         An historical and contemporary treatment of Protestantism, that
         gives much attention to evangelicalism, "Puritanism and
         Pietism," fundamentalism, and the pentecostal and charismatic
         movements. Bibliographical references.

157.   Rifkin, Jeremy, with Ted Howard. The Emerging Order: God in an
         Age of Scarcity. New York: Putnam's, 1979. 303 p.

Argues that the five-century long economic expansion era is coming to a close as a new age of scarcity appears, at the same time that a second Protestant Reformation spearheaded by charismatics and evangelicals is creating a new covenant vision for America to serve as steward and protector of God's creation. Bibliography. Index.

158.   _____. "Hope for a Second Reformation." Sojourners 8 (September 1979): 10-15.

This excerpt from Rifkin and Howard, The Emerging Order (1979), suggests that with the coming age of scarcity "the charismatic and evangelical movements are beginning to establish a radically new theological prescription for an ecologically balanced steady-state future."

159.   Roth, Wolfgang. "Euaggelion: The History of a Word: 'Evangelical Counsels' in the Middle Ages." Explor 2 (Fall 1976): 9-10.

Also known as the "Counsels of Perfection," the "Evangelical Counsels" "describe Christian behavior which goes beyond the requirements of the Decalog."

160.   Schaff, Philip. The Creeds of the Evangelical Protestant Churches. With translations. London: Hodder and Stoughton, 1877. 880 p.

Beginning with the Augsburg Confession (1530) and Luther's Catechism (1529), an eminent 19th century church historian examines creedal statements through the late 19th century. In three sections: the evangelical Lutheran Churches' creeds of the 16th century; the evangelical Reformed Churches' creeds of the 16th and 17th centuries; and "Modern Protestant Creeds" of the 17th through the 19th centuries.

161.   Schwarz, Fred. "Evangelical Misinformation Concerning Communism." Christian Anti-Communism Crusade 29 (15 May 1989): 1-2.

Schwarz misuses the word evangelical in this opposition to an article that equates communism with practical Christianity.

162.   Sell, Alan P. F. Theology in Turmoil: The Roots, Course and Significance of the Conservative-Liberal Debate in Modern Theology. Grand Rapids: Baker, 1986. 199 p.

Centers on the period 1880-1930, in both Britain and the U.S., with chapters on immanentism, biblical criticism, evolution,

the reception of Ritschl's thought. and conservatives and
liberals; ending with a plea for theological balance.
Bibliographical references. Index.

163.   Sernett, Milton C. "Welcoming the 'Evangelicals' -- A Call to End
One-Upmanship." Currents in Theology and Mission 6 (June 1979):
154-58.

Look past the institutional and party labels in their confusing
array to find and appreciate the essence of evangelical, says
Lutheran Sernett.

164.   Shaw, Mark R. "Drama in the Meeting House: The Concept of Conversion in the Theology of William Perkins." Westminster Theological
Journal 45 (Spring 1983): 41-72.

Asserts that contrary to the opinions derived from Perry
Miller, Perkins did not whittle down 16th century Calvinism by
means of covenant theology and his morphology of conversion.

165.   Smith, Timothy L. "Evangelical Christianity and American
Culture." In The Believable Futures of American Protestantism,
ed. Richard John Neuhaus, 1-17. Grand Rapids: Eerdmans, 1988.

Also published as "Evangelical Christianity and American
Culture," in A Time to Speak: The Evangelical-Jewish Encounter,
eds. A. James Rudin and Marvin R. Johnson, 58-75 (1987).
Evangelical Christianity was from the first religiously plural,
created a biblical culture, tied religious experience to moral
commitment, and had its millennialism become the concept of a
transformed society.

166.   _____. "A Shared Evangelical Heritage." In The Evangelical
Round Table. Eastern College and Eastern Baptist Theological
Seminary (St. Davids, PA, 1986). Evangelicalism: Surviving Its
Success, moderator Kenneth Kantzer, editor David A. Fraser, 12-28.
Princeton: Princeton University Press, 1987.

Stresses the non-sectarian. ecumenical nature of historic
evangelicalism, placing special emphasis (pp. 16-28) on its
social concern and practice.

167.   Stafford, Thomas Albert. Christian Symbolism in the Evangelical
Churches, with Definitions of Church Terms and Usages. New York:
Abingdon/Cokesbury, 1942. 176 p.

Defines evangelicalism broadly as the "type of Christianity which emphasizes the authority of the Holy Scripture rather than the authority of the Church"; discussion centers more on the symbols than on the theological position. Bibliography. Index.

168.   Stein, K. James. "Euaggelion: The History of a Word, From the Reformation to Today." Explor 2 (Fall 1976): 4-8.

Notes that "since the Reformation the word 'evangelical' has been appropriated by theological parties who claim that their doctrines in a unique way constitute the gospel"; describes its usage by British evangelicals, American evangelicals, various denominations, and in the name of Explor's publisher, Garrett-Evangelical Theological Seminary.

169.   Szasz, Ference Morton. The Divided Mind of Protestant America, 1880-1930. University: University of Alabama Press, 1982. 196 p.

Narrative of how the mainline Protestant denominations (excepting the Lutherans), who in 1880 exercised hegemony in America, gradually split into liberal and conservative factions, culminating in the fundamentalist-modernist controversy, opening the way for pluralism and pushing Protestantism to the periphery of national life. Seventeen-page bibliography. Index.

170.   Underwood, Brian. Faith at the Frontiers: Anglican Evangelicals and Their Countrymen Overseas. London, England: Commonwealth and Continental Church Society, 1974. 134 p.

A "much simpler and an abbreviated version" of a dissertation submitted to the University of Durham. Relates the 150 year history of the Commonwealth and Continental Church Society, one of a number of societies begun by Anglican evangelicals of the early 19th century. "References" section. Index.

171.   Wauzzinski, Robert Alan. "God and Mammon: The Interrelationship of Protestant Evangelicalism and the Industrial Revolution in America, 1820-1914." Ph.D. diss., University of Pittsburgh. 1985. 369 p.

172.   Wells, David F., and John D. Woodbridge. eds. The Evangelicals: What They Believe, Who They Are, Where They Are Changing. Rev. ed. Grand Rapids: Baker. 1977. 325 p.

First published in 1975 (Nashville: Abingdon. 1975. 304 p.); twelve essays and a "Guide to Further Reading" by a number of

leading evangelicals written at the time when evangelicalism
was regaining national attention and when others were assessing
its stance. The revised edition has expanded bibliographical
references and indexes.

173.   , eds. Reformed Theology in America: A History of Its
        Modern Development. Grand Rapids: Eerdmans, 1985. 317 p.

        Fifteen essays (and two general statements) on ten Reformed
        theologians and the five schools in which they are placed:
        Princeton, Westminster, the Dutch schools, the southern
        tradition, and neo-orthodoxy. Bibliographical references.
        Index.

174.   Wells, Ronald A., and Thomas A. Askew. Liberty and Law: Reflec-
        tions on the Constitution in American Life and Thought. Grand
        Rapids: Eerdmans, 1987. 208 p.

175.   Wells, William W. Welcome to the Family: An Introduction to Evan-
        gelical Christianity. Downers Grove: InterVarsity, 1979. 184 p.

        An introductory treatment by an evangelical historian and
        theologian. The volume's three parts relate to evangelical-
        ism's view of the Bible, its heritage, and its lifestyle.
        Bibliographies. Index.

176.   "What Does It Mean to Be Evangelical?" Christianity Today 33 (16
        June 1989): 60, 63.

        Describes the proceedings and results when more than 350
        evangelical leaders met at Trinity Evangelical Divinity School
        for four days in May 1989 to produce a concise definition of
        evangelical belief and practice.

177.   Wood, A. Skevington. "Evangelicalism: A Historical Perspective."
        TSF Bulletin 60 (Summer 1971): 11-20.

        Use of the term evangelical in the church's history, and its
        collateral terms: orthodox, apostolic, primitive, catholic,
        reformed, protestant.

178.   Woodbridge, John D., Mark A. Noll, and Nathan O. Hatch. The
        Gospel in America: Themes in the Story of America's Evangelicals.
        Grand Rapids: Zondervan, 1979. 237 p.

        In the wake of evangelical resurgence in the 1970s, a fine
        introduction to evangelical beliefs about the church, the

world, and the life of the mind, from three young evangelical
scholars. Bibliography. Index.

See also items 20, 21, 27, 29, 58, 64, 72, 190, 285, 288, 337, 346, 532,
533, 544, 553, 569, 576, 789, 1104, 1105, 1121, 1122, 1191, 1192,
1224, 1234, 1248, 1272, 1413, 1427, 1472, 1476, 1480, 1485, 1498,
1583, 1599, 1702, 1706, 1707, 1733, 2494.

B. Colonial Era

179.   Alline, Henry. Henry Alline: Selected writings. Ed. George A.
        Rawlyk. New York: Paulist Press, 1987. 343 p.

        An important eighteenth century evangelical in Nova Scotia.
        Bibliography. Indexes.

180.   Balmer, Randall H. A Perfect Babel of Confusion: Dutch Religion
        and English Culture in the Middle Colonies. New York: Oxford
        University Press, 1989. 224 p.

        Attempts to set right a neglected part of history, the Dutch in
        New York and New Jersey prior to the Revolution, and the ortho-
        dox camp (as opposed to the pietists, supporters of revivalism)
        in the Dutch Reformed Church; both the Dutch culture and the
        church experienced "a long, steady decline" after the defeat by
        England in 1664. Nineteen-page bibliography. Index.

181.   Bloch, Ruth H. Visionary Republic: Millennial Themes in American
        Thought, 1756-1800. Cambridge: Cambridge University Press, 1985.
        291 p.

        Contends not that millennialism caused the American Revolution
        nor that millennial religious ideas provided the ideological
        basis for it, but that millennialism illuminates how many
        Americans understood the ultimate meaning of the revolutionary
        crisis and the birth of the American nation. Bibliographical
        references.

182.   Bonomi, Patricia U. Under the Cope of Heaven: Religion, Society,
        and Politics in Colonial America. New York: Oxford University
        Press, 1986. 291 p.

        Survey of colonial religion; major contention is that the
        eighteenth century was a time of religious vitality, not
        decline, and that religion was, therefore, an important element

of the fabric of American life. Fifty-seven pages of
bibliographical notes. Index.

183.   Bozeman, Theodore Dwight. To Live Ancient Lives: The Primitivist
         Dimension in Puritanism. Chapel Hill: University of North
         Carolina Press, 1988. 460 p.

         Rather than seeing in Puritanism a precursor of a number of
         modern ideas, Bozeman finds in it the desire to return to the
         church and society of biblical times; a provocative study that
         could begin a new direction in Puritan studies. Appendixes.
         Thirty-three page bibliography. Index.

184.   Brown, C. G. "Itinerancy and Loyalty. A Study in Eighteenth
         Century Evangelicalism." Journal of Religious History 6 (June
         1971): 232-45.

         The suggestion that Methodists and evangelicals differed on
         itinerancy, the latter abhorring the practice, and on loyalty
         to the Church of England, cannot be sustained.

185.   Buckley, T. E. "Evangelicals Triumphant: The Baptists' Assault on
         the Virginia Glebes 1786-1801." William and Mary Quarterly 45
         (January 1988): 33-69.

         The fight over the glebe-lands in Virginia, ending in success
         for the Baptists, forced "the legislature to undo a major
         social-political compromise of the Revolution," and, more
         significantly, "helped lay the foundations for an evangelical
         bloc ready to impose, by legislation if necessary, its values
         and culture on the American body politic"; and points "to the
         interaction of religion and politics present throughout
         American history."

186.   Butler, Jonathan M. "Enlarging the Bonds of Christ: Slavery,
         Evangelism, and the Christianization of the White South,
         1690-1790." In The Evangelical Tradition in America, ed. Leonard
         I. Sweet, 87-112. Macon, GA: Mercer University Press, 1984.

         Seeks to advance understanding of American evangelicalism by
         describing Southern religion after 1750, including the
         symbiotic relationship between slavery and Southern white
         Christianity.

187.   Carden, Allen. "The Communal Ideal in Puritan New England. 1630-
         1700." Fides et Historia 17 (Fall-Winter 1984): 25-38.

Based on the idea of covenant. and never fully realized, the
ideal in the Massachusetts Bay Colony included obedience to
God, a self-sacrificing public spirit, and mutual subjection
and edification for the good of the whole; but not social
equality.

188.   Coalter, Milton J., Jr. Gilbert Tennent, Son of Thunder: A Case
Study of Continental Pietism's Impact on the First Great Awakening
in the Middle Colonies. New York: Greenwood, 1986. 227 p.

Sheds light on Tennent's story, and on pietism, the Great
Awakening, Presbyterians, and other facets of life in the
Middle Colonies. Twenty-page bibliography. Index.

189.   Cohen, Charles L. God's Caress: The Psychology of Puritan
Religious Experience. New York: Oxford University Press, 1986.
310 p.

Cohen says conversion was the axis in Puritan life, hanging on
the helplessness of the sinner and the power of God. Cohen and
Hambrick-Stowe (q.v.) reach the high-water mark in the study of
Puritan feelings, both clergy and lay. Fifteen page bibliographical essay. Index.

190.   _____. "Two Biblical Models of Conversion: An Example of
Puritan Hermeneutics." Church History 58 (June 1989): 182-96.

Using the frequent sermons on Lydia and David as examples,
Cohen argues that the Puritan divines used "a flexible
hermeneutic which allowed pastoral expertise and the dictates
of Reformed theology to eclipse the underlying Scriptures."

191.   Corrigan, John E. The Hidden Balance: Religion and the Social
Theories of Charles Chauncy and Jonathan Mayhew. Cambridge:
Cambridge University Press, 1987. 161 p.

Study of the mid-18th Century Boston Congregationalists who
marked the transition from Puritanism to religious rationalism
and who provide the concept of balance as "fundamental to
cosmic order itself" in the "broad search for order and for
meaning" that propelled many thinkers of the time. Appendix.
Bibliography, Index.

192.   Currey, Cecil B. "Eighteenth-Century Evangelical Opposition to
the American Revolution: The Case of the Quakers." Fides et
Historia 4 (Fall 1971): 17-35.

Argues that until the mid-eighteenth century, the Quakers combined orthodoxy in doctrine with being "severely evangelical in zeal"; contends that, to maintain their pacifism under the pressures of the Revolutionary War, they renounced their evangelicalism and with it their power.

193.   Geissler, Suzanne B. Jonathan Edwards to Aaron Burr, Jr.: From the Great Awakening to Democratic Politics. New York: Edwin Mellen, 1981. 276 p.

Another interpretation of the enigmatic Burr, grandson of Edwards, this one placing Burr in the context of the secularization of the evangelical message between 1750 and 1800; argues that though Burr did not demonstrate his grandfather's faith, his "political ideas--social reform and western expansion--are easily in the Edwardsean tradition." Originally a Syracuse Ph.D. dissertation. Twenty-seven-page bibliography. Index.

194.   Guelzo, Allen C. Edwards on the Will: A Century of American Theological Debate. Middletown, CT: Wesleyan University Press, 1989. 34 p.

Discussion of Edwards's famous treatise on the will, from his involvement in it and Guelzo's analysis of it through the debate among New Divinity, Old Calvinist, and Middle Atlantic Presbyterians, culminating in the work of Nathaniel Taylor as "the end of its importance as a theological question." Bibliography. Index.

195.   Hall, David D. Worlds of Wonder, Days of Judgment: Popular Religious Belief in Early New England. New York: Alfred A. Knopf, 1989. 316 p.

Lay people and clergy shared more common ground in New England than in Europe; at the same time, lay people both agreed with their clergy (consensus) and disagreed with them (resistance). The points of agreement centered around a world of wonder and of judgment, which lay people interpreted in ways not always the same as the clergy. A book stressing the cultural role of religion and culture's effect on religion. Bibliographical references. Index.

196.   Hall, David D., and David Grayson Allen, eds. Seventeenth-Century New England. Boston: Colonial Society of Massachusetts, 1984. 340 p.

Nine essays given at a conference held in 1982, three of which
are on religious subjects: Puritan portraits, Puritan establishment and the supernatural. Bibliographical references.

197.   Heimert, Alan. Religion and the American Mind: From the Great
        Awakening to the American Revolution. Cambridge: Harvard
        University Press, 1966. 668 p.

        Connects the Revolution with the Great Awakening and especially
        with Jonathan Edwards' theology. In the Perry Miller tradi-
        tion, contends that the theological "Calvinists" (evangelicals)
        rather than the theological liberals talked most about liberty
        and freedom and therefore trained the Revolution generation to
        think in those terms. Massive research. Seventy-six pages of
        bibliographic references. Index.

198.   Holifield, E. Brooks. Era of Persuasion: American Thought and
        Culture, 1521-1680. Boston: Twayne, 1989. 200 p.

        Defining persuasion as "in contrast to thought that was
        dispassionate, disinterested or speculative," Holifield finds
        the motif in the writings of the 200 or so explorers and
        colonists covered here; moves through all parts of the
        continent, with a heavy concentration on New England.
        Bibliographical essay.

199.   Isaac, Rhys. "Evangelical Revolt: The Nature of the Baptists'
        Challenge to the Traditional Order in Virginia, 1765-1775."
        William and Mary Quarterly 31 (July 1974): 345-68.

        The gentry style of the Virginia elite was challenged by the
        more somber Baptists and the Baptist incorporation of converted
        slaves as brothers and sisters, resulting in major disagreement
        over the question of "order"--the Virginia elite and the
        Baptists each saw order in their own style.

200.   Jackson, Harvey H. "Hugh Bryan and the Evangelical Movement in
        Colonial South Carolina." William and Mary Quarterly 43 (October
        1986): 594-614.

        Bryan (1699-1753), converted under Whitefield in 1740, had a
        short-lived career in "enthusiastick Prophecies," including
        preaching to slaves; his career offers "insights into the
        building of regenerate communities in early America and into
        the origins of evangelical efforts to christianize slaves."

201.   Mattson-Boze. M. Howard. "Evangelical Participation in the
        American Revolution: An Essay Review of Alan Heimert's Religion
        and the American Mind." Fides et Historia 4 (Fall 1971): 4-16.

        After arguing that evangelicals turn out to be "the Revolu-
        tionaries," "the radical democrats," drawing as they did on
        their experience in the awakening and from Scripture, Mattson-
        Boze asks why their influence did not continue to be evident,
        and suggests it may have been due to the fact of communicating
        largely through sermons, and partly due to the general blurring
        of disagreements in the enthusiasm of the Revolutionary era. A
        briefer version appears in Eternity 22 (July 1971): 16, 53.

202.   Miller, Glenn T. "The Rise of Evangelical Calvinism: A Study in
        Jonathan Edwards and the Puritan Tradition." Th.D. diss., Union
        Theological Seminary in the City of New York, 1971. 552 p.

203.   Noll, Mark A. "The Bible in Revolutionary America." In The Bible
        in American Law, Politics, and Political Rhetoric, ed. James
        Turner Johnson, 39-60. Philadelphia: Fortress, 1985.

        Treats the Bible and the founding fathers, the Bible in
        revolutionary political theory, and the Bible and social values
        in the early national period; "In Revolutionary America the
        Bible was being read doctrinally, morally, and devotionally,
        but almost never culturally."

204.   _____. "Christian and Humanistic Values in Eighteenth Century
        America: A Bicentennial Review." Christian Scholar's Review 6
        (1976): 114-26.

        The seventeenth century Christian humanism of the Puritan
        synthesis dissolved in the 18th century, was not revived by the
        Great Awakening, and was replaced (though with some noteworthy
        exceptions) by Whig humanism, so that "both humanistic and
        Christian values were compromised."

205.   _____. "Moses Mather (Old Calvinist) and the Evolution of
        Edwardseanism." Church History 49 (September 1980): 273-85.

        Tracing the lineage of thought from Jonathan Edwards to the
        Edwardseans like Timothy Dwight. Noll discovers that Mather
        (1719-1806). a moderate opponent of Edwards and the Great
        Awakening. "appears to have thought along lines followed later
        by the proponents of the Second Great Awakening."

206.   Pointer, Richard W. "American Ideas on the Relation of Freedom
         and Truth." Fides et Historia 19 (June-July 1987): 20-31.

         American Protestants accepted the notion of "truth triumphant"
         via Locke, Milton, and revolutionary generation Americans, that
         allowed public opinion to replace the state as the "resolving
         force" of all truth questions; but it placed too much emphasis
         on freedom as a concomitant of truth, and displayed a naive
         trust in human rationality.

207.   _____. Protestant Pluralism and the New York Experience: A
         Study of Eighteenth-Century Religious Diversity. Bloomington:
         Indiana University Press, 1988. 205 p.

         Questions the standard interpretation that pluralism was only
         reluctantly and with little thought entered into by the
         Protestant denominations, by suggesting that there was a
         thoughtful grappling with the issues of freedom, tolerance, and
         equality; New York Protestants presaged the pluralism of
         nineteenth and twentieth century Protestants. Eighteen-page
         bibliography. Index.

208.   Schneider, Lenore. "Colonial Evangelicals: Repressed?" Fides et
         Historia 13 (Fall 1980): 72-76.

         A review article about Philip Greven's The Protestant Tempera-
         ment: Patterns of Childrearing, Religious Experience and the
         Self in Early America (1977); "categorizes colonial Americans
         according to temperaments shaped by religious experience as
         well as childrearing styles," with evangelicals, moderates, and
         the genteel being the three groups.

209.   Speck, W. A., and Louis Billington. "Calvinism in Colonial North
         America, 1630-1715." In International Calvinism, 1541-1715, ed.
         Menna Prestwich, 257-83. Oxford: Clarendon Press, 1985.

         "[A] synthesis of current scholarship on the doctrine, disci-
         pline, and social history of Congregationalism in New England",
         and "an account of the contributions of Dutch, French and
         Presbyterian Calvinists to the development of colonial
         society."

See also items 12, 28, 30, 42, 45, 49, 55, 57, 63, 132, 164, 513, 514,
    529, 545, 546, 547, 561, 568, 714, 804, 815, 816, 821, 822, 832, 866,
    902, 905, 906, 946, 948, 1002, 1303, 1316, 1334, 1432, 1439, 1447,
    1486, 1487, 1488, 1489, 1562, 1676, 1681, 1773, 2482, 2484, 2504,
    2507, 2513, 2514.

C.   Nineteenth Century

210.   Abell, Aaron Ignatius. The Urban Impact on American Protestant-
        ism, 1865-1900. Cambridge: Harvard University Press, 1943. 275 p.

        Classic study of the religious and social effects of urban
        development on American Protestantism, and the consequent rise
        of social Christianity, both evangelical and liberal.
        Bibliographical essay.

211.   Adams, Charles. Evangelism in the Middle of the Nineteenth
        Century: Or, an Exhibit Descriptive and Statistical of the Present
        Condition of Evangelical Religion in All Countries of the World.
        Boston: C. H. Pierce, 1850. 316 p.

212.   Banner, Lois W. "Religion and Reform in the Early Republic: The
        Role of Youth." American Quarterly 23 (December 1971): 677-95.

        Includes the role of young evangelicals in social and political
        reform.

213.   Barker, William S. "The Social Views of Charles Hodge: A Study in
        19th-Century Calvinism and Conservatism." Presbyterion: Covenant
        Seminary Review 1 (Spring 1975): 1-22.

        Examines "Hodge's social thought to determine to what extent"
        the interpretation is accurate that holds orthodox Presbyter-
        ianism, and Hodge in particular, to have been exclusively
        conservative by that era. Concludes that Hodge's social
        thought "contained potential for social progress," but that the
        potential was not actualized.

214.   Barnard, John. From Evangelicalism to Progressivism at Oberlin
        College, 1866-1917. Columbus: Ohio State University Press, 1969.
        171 p.

        Centering on "the changing ways in which students at Oberlin
        thought about social issues between 1866 and 1917," Barnard
        shows how the energy "that had once gone into the advancement
        of evangelism was redirected to the pursuit of learning,"
        explaining thereby the affinity between evangelicalism and
        progressivism. Ten-page bibliography.

215.   Berk, Stephen E. Calvinism Versus Democracy: Timothy Dwight and
        the Origins of American Evangelical Orthodoxy. Hamden, CT: Archon
        Books, 1974. 252 p.

The role of Dwight, grandson of Jonathan Edwards and president of Yale, in the emergence of a conservative evangelical consensus in the early nineteenth century. Seventeen-page bibliography. Index.

216.   Bowden, Henry Warner. "Robert Baird: Historical Narrative and the Image of a Protestant America--1855." Journal of Presbyterian History 47 (June 1969): 149-72.

American Robert Baird (1798-1863) traveled extensively in Europe and the United States on behalf of evangelical causes, and published in the 1840s and 1850s the widely acclaimed Religion in America, which defined the true churches along two lines: (1) orthodox theological confessions, and (2) actively doing God's work on earth (the latter carried out through collective programs--voluntarism).

217.   Briggs, J. H. Y. "Image and Appearance: Some Sources for Nineteenth Century Nonconformity." Baptist Quarterly 23 (January 1969): 15-31; 23 (April 1969): 59-72.

The sources include fiction, biographies, sermons, hymns, records of charitable works, and froth and gossip; has implications for similar American studies.

218.   Brown, Ford K. Fathers of the Victorians: The Age of Wilberforce. Cambridge, England: University Press, 1961. 568 p.

Evangelicals in the Church of England, with special focus upon William Wilberforce (1759-1833). Bibliography.

219.   Brumberg, Joan Jacobs. Mission for Life: The Story of the Family of Adoniram Judson, the Dramatic Events of the First American Foreign Mission, and the Course of Evangelical Religion in the Nineteenth Century. New York: Free Press, 1980. 302 p.

Also published in 1984 by New York University Press, with shortened sub-title, "The Judson Family and American Evangelical Culture." A description of 19th century evangelical culture, the "complex of values, behaviors, and institutions that were deliberately promoted by antebellum evangelicals," seen through the family of Baptist missionary Judson (1788-1850), down to 1900. Bibliography. Index.

220.   Butler, Francis Joseph. "John Henry Newman's 'Parochial and Plain Sermons' Viewed as a Critique of Religious Evangelicalism." S.T.D. diss., The Catholic University of America, 1972. 304 p.

221.   Carwardine, Richard. "The Know-Nothing Party, The Protestant
        Evangelical Community and American National Identity." In
        Religion and National Identity, ed. Stuart Mews, 449-63. Oxford:
        Basil Blackwell, 1982.

            Though evangelicals were unanimous in their anti-Catholicism,
            they disagreed over methods of expressing it, and some
            paticularly felt the Know-Nothing party "vitiate[d] their
            highest national ideals and values," by favoring "a flawed,
            exclusive democracy."

222.   Collier, William, ed. Evangelicana or Gospel Treasury, Containing
        a Great Variety of Interesting Anecdotes, Remarkable Providences,
        and Precious Fragments. Selected chiefly from the London Evangel-
        ical Magazine, by William Collier. Boston: Hastings, Etheridge
        and Bliss, 1809. 312 p.

            Many short pieces illustrate the interests, style of writing,
            and humor of early 19th century evangelicals.

223.   Conforti, Joseph. "Antebellum Evangelicals and the Cultural
        Revival of Jonathan Edwards." American Presbyterians: Journal of
        Presbyterian History 64 (Winter 1986): 227-41.

            By the time of the 1808 edition of his works, aided by New
            Divinity advocates and the start of the Second Awakening,
            Edwards was emerging as a man of remarkable piety, a brilliant
            thinker, and authority on revivalism.

224.   _____. "Jonathan Edwards's Most Popular Work: 'The Life of
        David Brainerd' and 19th Century Evangelical Culture." Church
        History 54 (June 1985): 188-201.

            The Life of Brainerd created for 19th century evangelicals a
            genuine hero to emulate, a means of transmitting Edwardsian
            thought (especially his ethics), a rationale for religious
            reform, an inspiration for missionary activity, and particu-
            larly a model of holiness as disinterested benevolence.

225.   Conser, Walter Hurley, Jr. "Church and Confession: Conservative
        Theologians in Germany, England, and America, 1815-1866." Ph.D.
        diss., Brown University, 1981. 676 p.

226.   Craufurd, A. H. "The Strength and Weakness of Evangelicalism."
        The Thinker 3 (1893): 201-09.

227.   Crunden, Robert M. Ministers of Reform: The Progressives'
       Achievement in American Civilization, 1889-1920. New York: Basic
       Books, 1982. 307 p.

       Answering the question, "What was Progressivism?" Crunden
       examines the lives of one hundred Progressive Era reformers
       (centering on twenty-one with national roles, a number of them
       in the arts), to demonstrate his thesis that the reformers
       "absorbed the severe, Protestant moral values of their parents"
       and applied them to careers other than the ministry, so they
       became "preachers turning moral reform on institutions as well
       as individuals." Bibliography. Index.

228.   Dabney, Robert L. Discussions: Evangelical and Theological.
       London: Banner of Truth Trust, 1967. Two volumes (728, 684 p.)

       A reprint of volumes first published in 1890, the work of a
       professor at Union Theological Seminary in Virginia, widely
       recognized as among the most prominent of American theologians
       of his day.

229.   Davis, Christian R. "The Rhetoric of Nineteenth-Century American
       Evangelical Autobiography." Ph.D. diss., Pennsylvania State
       University, 1985. 265 p.

230.   DeJong, Mary A. "I Want to be Like Jesus: The Self-Defining Power
       of Evangelical Hymnody." Journal of the American Academy of
       Religion 54 (Fall 1986): 461-93.

       Studies the Christ-hymns in thirty-two 19th century hymnals to
       show that they reflected "current gender-role prescriptions,"
       leading men and women to "respond differently to certain
       Christian ideals" which "in turn had social consequences,"
       i.e., confirming of social roles.

231.   Dole, C. F. "The Evangelical Movement in America." New England
       Magazine 12 (July 1895): 533-44.

232.   Eens-Rempel, Kevin. "The Fellowship of Evangelical Bible Churches
       and the Quest for Religious Identity." Mennonite Quarterly Review
       63 (July 1989): 247-64.

       Details the origins and development of a Mennonite group that
       adopted late nineteenth century American evangelicalism. The
       EBC dropped the word "Mennonite" from its title (Evangelical
       Mennonite Brethren Conference) because of perceived negative
       connotations.

233.   Ellis, George M. "The Evangelical and the Sunday Question, 1830-
         1860: Organized Sabbatarianism as an Aspect of the Evangelical
         Movement." Ph.D. diss., Harvard University, 1952. 175 p.

234.   Frank, Douglas W. Less Than Conquerors: How Evangelicals Entered
         the Twentieth Century. Grand Rapids: Eerdmans, 1986. 310 p.

         An analysis of the loss of influence and power that evangel-
         icals experienced between 1850 and 1920; due, Frank suggests,
         to dispensationalism, the Keswick movement, and Billy Sunday
         revivalism. Bibliography. Index.

235.   Gabriel, Ralph H. "Evangelical Religion and Popular Romanticism
         in Early 19th Century America." Church History 19 (March 1950):
         34-47.

         As a romantic faith, 19th century Protestantism focused on the
         individual and emphasized the importance of the emotions. As
         such, it had both ties with and influences on the ecstasy of
         the frontier revival and the mysticism of Transcendentalism.

236.   Gallichan, W. M. "The Rearguard of the Christian Army." West-
         minster Review 135 (April 1891): 353-63.

237.   Glover, Willis B. "English Baptists at the Time of the Downgrade
         Controversy." Foundations 1 (July 1958): 41-51.

         Blames much of the weakness of Baptists (and evangelicals) of
         the time on "an almost incredible weakness in theology" (that
         had not kept pace with the currents of biblical criticism).

238.   _____. Evangelical Nonconformists and Higher Criticism in the
         Nineteenth Century. London: Independent Press, 1954. 296 p.

         This study of non-Anglican evangelicals, especially in the
         period 1880-1900, notes the background, the decline of
         inerrancy, and the phases by which historical criticism was
         accepted; although initially enervating, historical criticism
         has "deepened" Christian thought and made it "more honest and
         realistic." Index.

239.   Graham, Stephen R. "Philip Schaff and the Protestant Mind in the
         Nineteenth Century: A Critique of Religion and Society." Fides et
         Historia 21 (January 1989): 32-49.

         Listening to neither secularist nor sectarian appeals, Schaff
         was a "liberal, tolerant, ecumenically-minded 'Christian

Consensus' person," as shown in his ideas on ecumenism,
cosmopolitanism, and the role of Christianity in American
nationality.

240.   Heath, Richard. "The Waning of Evangelicalism." Contemporary
         Review 73 (May 1898): 649-65.

241.   Hoeveler, J. David, Jr. "Evangelical Ecumenism: James McCosh and
         the Intellectual Origins of the World Alliance of Reformed
         Churches." Journal of Presbyterian History 55 (Spring 1977):
         36-56.

         President of Princeton from 1868, McCosh brought a philosophi-
         cal mind and a dedicated evangelicalism to his belief that
         ecumenical organizations offered the best hope for stemming the
         tide of German and British liberalism.

242.   Humphreys, Fisher, ed. Nineteenth Century Evangelical Theology.
         Nashville: Broadman, 1983. 416 p.

         Using a rather broad definition of evangelicalism, Humphreys
         gathers fifty-six readings from thirty-two British and American
         authors, arranged in theological categories, aimed at enriching
         the theology and ministry of 20th century Christians.

243.   Jordan, Philip D. The Evangelical Alliance for the United States
         of America, 1846-1900: Ecumenism, Identity and the Religion of the
         Republic. New York: Edwin Mellen, 1982. 277 p.

         Traces the course of the Evangelical Alliance in the U.S. from
         its context in the early republic to organization in the 1840s,
         gradual expansion through the middle decades, and gradual slow-
         ing by 1900, seeing the Alliance "as the vehicle of nineteenth
         century attempts to articulate an evangelical and American
         identity conducive to religious unity. Originally his 1971
         Iowa Ph.D. dissertation. Seventeen-page bibliography. Index.

244.   Kraus, C. Norman. "Evangelicalism: The Great Coalition." In
         Evangelicalism and Anabaptism. ed. C. Norman Kraus. 39-61.
         Scottdale, PA: Herald Press, 1979.

         Describes, with helpful charts, the historical and theological
         roots of the fundamentalist-pentecostal coalition that he holds
         to be one of the most hopeful signs within the evangelical
         movement.

245.   Marsden, George M. The Evangelical Mind and the New School
         Presbyterian Experience: A Case Study of Thought and Theology in
         Nineteenth-Century America. New Haven: Yale University Press,
         1970. 278 p.

         Based on Marsden's Yale dissertation (1966). Focuses on the
         Reformed and Calvinist elements in evangelicalism, emphasizing
         vigorous intellectual life. Bibliography. Index.

246.   _____. "Unity and Diversity in the Evangelical Resurgence."
         In Altered Landscapes: Christianity in America, 1935-1985, ed.
         David Lotz, 61-76. Grand Rapids: Eerdmans, 1989.

         The distinctives in fundamentalism inherited by evangelicalism,
         and the negative and positive forces that make it "impossible
         to regard American evangelicalism as a single coalition with a
         more or less unified and recognized leadership."

247.   Martin, Roger H. "Evangelical Dissenters and Wesleyan-style
         Itinerant Ministries at the End of the Eighteenth Century."
         Methodist History 16 (April 1978): 169-84.

         The Village Itinerancy Society (founded 1796) represents a
         number of dissenting societies "which not only resembled, but
         could easily have rivalled many of Wesley's itinerant
         circuits," and whose existence show the contributions of
         dissent to the 18th century evangelical revival.

248.   Marty, Martin E. Modern American Religion. Vol. 1: The Irony of
         It All, 1893-1919. Chicago: University of Chicago Press, 1986.
         374 p.

         While the irony theme is difficult to sustain in this first of
         a projected four-volume series, Marty's short narratives on a
         large variety of American religions, including evangelicalism,
         are done with insight into the bewildering array of religious
         expressions. Forty-seven-page bibliographical essay.

249.   McLoughlin, William G., ed. The American Evangelicals, 1800-1900:
         An Anthology. New York: Harper & Row, 1968. 213 p.

         Includes one of the best brief introductions to evangelicalism.
         Bibliographical references.

250.   _____. "Cherokee Slaveholders and Baptist Missionaries, 1845-
         1860." Historian 45 (February 1983): 147-66.

251.   "Meeting of Evangelicals in St. Louis." Baptist and Reflector 108
        (7 May 1942): 3.

        Report on the meeting at which the formation of the NAE was
        proposed.

252.   Miller, Perry. The Life of the Mind in America: From the Revol-
        ution to the Civil War. New York: Harcourt, Brace, and World,
        1965. 338 p.

        Miller's proposed but not fully completed work on the subject;
        part one, "the evangelical basis," is included and is built
        around the principle that American Protestantism, "amid a
        multitude of forms," thought "revivalism was the primary force
        in maintaining 'the grand unity of national strength.' This
        was the evangelical heritage." Index.

253.   Muir, Andrew Forest. "Franklin Samuel Rising, Radical Evangeli-
        cal." Historical Magazine of the Protestant Episcopal Church 24
        (December 1955): 366-99.

        An account of the life and career of one who was the spokesman
        of the "radical evangelical party" in his denomination, and one
        whose career "graphically illustrates what was happening to
        evangelicalism in the mid-Victorian period."

254.   Mullin, Robert Bruce. Episcopal Vision/American Reality: High
        Church Theology and Social Thought in Evangelical America. New
        Haven: Yale University Press, 1986. 247 p.

        Describes the alternative social and intellectual vision of a
        high church Episcopalianism surrounded by evangelical
        Protestants in antebellum America; focuses on John Henry Hobart
        (1775-1830) and his successors as they developed theological,
        devotional, and social principles for the movement; and the
        decline of the Hobartian synthesis after 1845. Twenty-six page
        bibliography. Index.

255.   Murdoch, Norman H. "Evangelical Sources of Salvation Army
        Doctrine." Evangelical Quarterly 59 (July 1987): 235-44.

        The eleven articles in the Salvation Army creed began (1865) as
        similar in doctrine to the Evangelical Alliance's ecumenical
        creed (adopted 1846). but by 1876. advocating Wesleyan views on
        holiness and eternal security. had turned the Army into a
        narrower, sectarian organization.

256.   Nichols, James Hastings. "Philip Schaff: Evangelical Catholic."
        Ecumenical Trends 11 (January 1982): 11-13.

        The United States' "most eminent Protestant ecumenist of the
        nineteenth century," the "guiding spirit" of the Evangelical
        Alliance for more than two decades, and a scholar whose
        contributions to historical and biblical studies were "massive
        and significant."

257.   Pocock, Emil. "Evangelical Frontier: Dayton, Ohio, 1796-1830."
        Ph.D. diss., Indiana University, 1984. 189 p.

258.   Pritchard, Linda K. "Religious Change in a Developing Region: The
        Social Contexts of Evangelicalism in Western New York and the
        Upper Ohio Valley During the Mid-Nineteenth Century." Ph.D.
        diss., University of Pittsburgh, 1980. 351 p.

259.   _____. "Religious Change in Nineteenth-Century America." In
        The New Religious Consciousness, ed. Charles Y. Glock and Robert
        N. Bellah, 297-330. Berkeley: University of California Press,
        1976.

260.   Rausch, David A., and Carl Hermann Voss. "The Century of Evan-
        gelicalism." Ashland Theological Journal 19 (Fall 1987): 71-82.

        A chapter from their book, Protestantism: Its Modern Meaning
        (1987). Discusses the 19th century, covering such subjects as
        evangelism, revivals, the benevolent empire, and trends in
        theology.

261.   Rogers, J. Guinness. "Is Evangelicalism Declining?" Contemporary
        Review 73 (1898): 814-28.

262.   Scott, Donald Moore. "Watchmen on the Walls of Zion: Evangelicals
        and American Society, 1800-1860." Ph.D. diss., The University of
        Wisconsin, 1968. 502 p.

263.   Swanson, Michael Richard Hans. "Robert Baird and the Evangelical
        Crusade in America, 1820-1860." Ph.D. diss., Case Western Reserve
        University, 1971. 340 p.

264.   Wilson, Major L. "Paradox Lost: Order and Progress in Evangelical
        Thought of Mid-Nineteenth Century America." Church History 44
        (September 1975): 352-66.

        Seen in four mid-century periodicals, the paradox--belief in
        order (supernatural origins of the Republic) and in progress

(natural changes over time)--was "lost" when the future seemed
to overwhelm the past, and the hope failed that revivalism
could recapture the order.

265.   Winter, Rebecca J. The Night Cometh: Two Wealthy Evangelicals
Face the Nation. South Pasadena: William Carey, 1977. 84 p.

An account of Lewis and Arthur Tappan in 19th century
evangelicalism. Bibliography. Index.

266.   Wood, Gordon S. "Evangelical America and Early Mormonism." New
York History 61 (1980): 383.

Lengthy social description of evangelicalism from the
Revolution to 1830; out of that milieu came Mormonism, which
"blended the folk inclinations and religiosity of common people
with the hardened churchly traditions and enlightened gentility
of modern times."

See also items 25, 30, 40, 57, 162, 169, 171, 194, 218, 289, 513, 514, 515,
516, 520, 521, 522, 523, 524, 525, 526, 528, 530, 535, 536, 537, 538,
539, 540, 542, 552, 553, 555, 556, 557, 563, 564, 566, 571, 572, 573,
574, 577, 640, 656, 659, 677, 708, 709, 713, 717, 752, 757, 759, 761,
762, 766, 767, 769, 770, 773, 781, 786, 787, 788, 798, 811, 818, 822,
824, 829, 835, 835, 837, 843, 844, 848, 850, 852, 868, 881, 883, 884,
903, 954, 967, 968, 971, 973, 977, 978, 982, 989, 997, 1002, 1003,
1004, 1005, 1008, 1010, 1012, 1013, 1014, 1016, 1018, 1020, 1021, 1022,
1024, 1027, 1029, 1036, 1040, 1049, 1051, 1053, 1056, 1065, 1078, 1081,
1097, 1098, 1099, 1102, 1104, 1128, 1129, 1133, 1135, 1167, 1168, 1171,
1173, 1176, 1177, 1178, 1179, 1224, 1252, 1262, 1277, 1302, 1302, 1303,
1329, 1355, 1371, 1398, 1399, 1425, 1436, 1437, 1446, 1450, 1454, 1465,
1466, 1467, 1468, 1469, 1470, 1471, 1473, 1474, 1475, 1477, 1499, 1536,
1537, 1544, 1547, 1550, 1555, 1557, 1567, 1580, 1598, 1627, 1660, 1664,
1667, 1793, 2038, 2482, 2495, 2521, 2529, 2541, 2548, 2637.

D. Twentieth Century

267.   Ahlstrom, Sydney E. "The Traumatic Years: American Religion and
Culture in the '60s and '70s." Theology Today 36 (January 1980):
504-22.

In a slightly revised form of an article in Daedalus 107
(1978): 13-29, Ahlstrom contends that seen against the
background of the 1950s, a well-balanced religious era, the
years 1960-1975 produced enough turmoil to create a "new
America" for the 1980s.

268.   Beckwith, Burnham P. "The Decline in American Religious Faith
        Since 1913." Humanist 41 (March/April 1981): 10-14, 54.

        Summarizes "the most relevant results" of fifteen different
        studies (beginning with that of Leuba in 1913), "nearly all" of
        which "support the general conclusion that the amount of
        religious belief among U.S. adults has been declining,"
        particularly among educated persons; concludes that the trend
        will likely continue.

269.   Boyd, Nancy. Emissaries: The Overseas Work of the American YWCA
        1895-1970. New York: The Woman's Press, 1989. 416 p.

270.   Butler, Farley P., Jr. "Billy Graham and the End of Evangelical
        Unity." Ph.D. diss., University of Florida, 1976. 308 p.

        An "examination of the process through which the unity of . . .
        conservative evangelicalism ended, producing two movements:
        evangelicalism and fundamentalism." Bibliography.

271.   Carpenter, Joel A. "From Fundamentalism to the New Evangelical
        Coalition." In Evangelicalism and Modern America, ed. George
        Marsden, 3-16. Grand Rapids: Eerdmans, 1984.

        Fundamentalism of the 1930s and 1940s, "a hidden part of its
        history," was an important ingredient in welding together the
        new evangelical coalition, symbolized by the founding of the
        NAE in 1942 and youth groups like Youth for Christ (1944).

272.   _____. "The Fundamentalist Leaven and the Rise of an Evangeli-
        cal United Front." In The Evangelical Tradition in America, ed.
        Leonard I. Sweet, 257-88. Macon, GA: Mercer University Press,
        1984.

        The story of a resurgent fundamentalist-evangelicalism seen
        through the organizational history of the National Association
        of Evangelicals during the 1930s and 1940s.

273.   Catherwood, Christopher. Five Evangelical Leaders. Wheaton, IL:
        H. Shaw, 1985. 239 p.

        Popular studies of five British and American evangelicals in
        the 20th century: John Stott, Martyn Lloyd-Jones, Francis
        Schaeffer, James I. Packer, and Billy Graham.

274.   Chafer, Lewis Sperry. "United Action of Evangelicals." Biblio-
        theca Sacra 99 (October 1942): 385-86.

A leading dispensationalist finds "genuine ground for encouragement in the nationwide movement which has been styled the
National Association of Evangelicals for United Action."

275.   Gillie, Robert Calder. Evangelicalism: Has It a Future? London:
        Cassell, 1912. 118 p.

        This short study by Britisher Gillie walks the line between
        "the wonderful glow of Evangelicalism" and "certain possible
        readjustments of thought." Bibliography.

276.   Hammond, Phillip E. "In Search of a Protestant Twentieth Century:
        American Religion and Power Since 1900." Review of Religious
        Research 24 (June 1983): 281-94.

        Between 1880 and 1920 mainline Protestantism experienced a loss
        of nerve in world missions and saw the breaking of the link
        between itself and the exercise of power in America. Thus,
        resurgent contemporary Protestantism is not so much warring
        against modernism as against the diminished political role
        played by religion.

277.   Handy, Robert T. "The American Religious Depression, 1925-1935."
        Church History 29 (March 1960): 3-16.

        "During the period of religious and economic depression, then,
        the 'Protestant era' in America was brought to a close"; these
        were years of significant transition for the American churches.

278.   Hedstrom, James A. "Evangelical Program in the United States,
        1945-1980: The Morphology of Establishment, Progressive, and
        Radical Platforms." Ph.D. diss., Vanderbilt University, 1982.
        516 p.

279.   Henry, Carl F. H. "Dare We Renew the Modernist-Fundamentalist
        Controversy?" Christianity Today, in four parts: "The Modernist
        Revision" 1 (10 June 1957): 3-6; "The Fundamentalist Reduction" 1
        (24 June 1957): 23-26; "The Contemporary Restoration" 1 (8 July
        1957): 15-18; "The Evangelical Responsibility" 1 (22 July 1957):
        23-26, 38.

        Abridgement of lectures on Evangelical Responsibility in
        Contemporary Theology (1957); finds Fosdick's modernist
        revision wanting; finds the fundamentalist temperament "a
        perversion of the biblical spirit"; sees neo-orthodoxy as the
        contemporary restoration; beyond all these is needed a renewed
        evangelicalism.

280.   _____. Evangelical Responsibility in Contemporary Theology.
Grand Rapids: Eerdmans, 1957. 89 p.

Four lectures survey the larger 20th century theological scene
--modernism, fundamentalism, neo-orthodoxy--and then the
responsibility of evangelicalism, the latter in such areas as
biblical theology, preaching, the Christian life, and the life
of the mind. Index.

281.   _____. Fifty Years of Protestant Theology. Boston: W. A.
Wilde, 1950. 113 p.

Occasioned by Henry's addressing the founding meeting of the
Evangelical Theological Society in Cincinnati (1950); he
describes Protestant theology at the beginning of the century,
during the fifty years thereafter, and the mid-century "divide"
between evangelicalism and neo-orthodoxy. Bibliographical
references. Index.

282.   _____. Frontiers in Modern Theology. Chicago: Moody Press,
1965. 160 p.

Appearing originally in Christianity Today, this series of
essays reflects on Barth, Bultmann, issues in revelation, the
end of modern theology, and the European and American
theological scenes. Index.

283.   Hine, Leland D. "Is Evangelicalism Dying of Old Age?" Eternity
23 (March 1972): 21-23.

An evangelical church historian reviews its history, describing
the symptoms ("dogmatism, ritualism, legalism and conformity")
and the true evangelical ("exuberant faith . . . always
searching the Scriptures").

284.   Howden, J. Russell, ed. Evangelicalism. By members of the
Fellowship of Evangelical Churchmen, ed. by J. Russell Howden.
London: Chas. J. Thynne & Jarvis, 1925. 325 p.

Essays on pivotal items in the theology and practice of the
churches (e.g., incarnation, resurrection, atonement, inspiration and authority of the Bible), by members of the FEC, at a
time, in their judgment, of great unrest and changes in the
churches and within evangelicalism. Bibliographical references
in some of the essays.

285.   Hutchison, William R. Between the Times: The Travail of the
        Protestant Establishment in America, 1900-1960. New York:
        Cambridge University Press, 1989. 320 p.

286.   Jacobsen, Douglas. "From Truth to Authority to Responsibility:
        The Shifting Focus of Evangelical Hermeneutics, 1915-1986." TSF
        Bulletin. Part 1 in vol. 10 (March-April 1987): 8-15. Part 2 in
        vol. 10 (May-June 1987): 10-14.

        Fundamentalist evangelicals (1915-1945) such as Torrey and
        Machen, emphasized the truth of orthodoxy; "Classical"
        evangelicals (1945-1975) such as Carnell and Henry shifted the
        defense to the authority of the Bible; post-classical
        evangelicalism (since 1975) places at the hermeneutical center
        responsibility to tradition and culture as well as to the
        Bible.

287.   Keck, Herbert A. "Liberal Evangelicalism." Religion in Life 21
        (Summer 1952): 453-59.

        Liberalism, "a willingness to correlate one's faith with the
        fresh knowledge of the modern day," has three weaknesses:
        negativity, a weak sense of sin, and a readiness to compromise
        with a false naturalism.

288.   Lotz, Davis M., Donald W. Shriver, Jr., and John F. Wilson, eds.
        Altered Landscapes: Christianity in America 1935-1985. Grand
        Rapids: Eerdmans, 1989. 387 p.

        The twenty essays in this festschrift to Robert T. Handy cover
        changes in the churches and in the theological disciplines;
        some are related to evangellcalism. Bibliographical refer-
        ences. Index.

289.   Marsden, George M. "From Fundamentalism to Evangelicalism: A
        Historical Analysis." In The Evangelicals: What They Believe, Who
        They Are, Where They Are Changing, ed. David F. Wells and John D.
        Woodbridge, 122-42. Nashville: Abingdon. 1975.

        Treats a "Century of Change" in terms of four stages: 1870s to
        ca. 1919 (evangelicalism appeared to remain intact); 1919-1926
        (defeats on "all fronts"); 1926 to the 1940s (withdrawal and
        regrouping); and the 1940s to the present (emergence of a new
        evangelicalism with a clear division into evangelicalism and
        separatist fundamentalism).

290.   McCutcheon, William. "The Methodist League for Faith and Life
         (1920s and '30s)." Explor 2 (Fall 1976): 59-67.

         The League was a rallying point for conservative evangelicals
         during the period of the fundamentalist-modernist controversy,
         with several issues of concern: "Doctrinal Issues and the Local
         Church," "Revisions of Church Ritual," and "Conference Courses
         of Study."

291.   Moberg, David O. "A Sociologist's Interpretation of the Recent
         Rapid Growth of the Baptist General Conference." Bethel Seminary
         Quarterly 7 (August 1959): 19-24.

         Focuses on "Swedish neutrality and mediation" on various con-
         troversial issues, including areas of theology, as enhancing
         the former Swedish Baptist Conference's position as "a posi-
         tive, sound, evangelical body." Although accurate prediction
         is not possible, that kind of position may continue to be a
         factor.

292.   Murch, James D. Cooperation Without Compromise: A History of the
         National Association of Evangelicals. Grand Rapids: Eerdmans,
         1956. 220 p.

         The now-classic account of the early history and functions of
         the NAE, illustrating "the only kind of ecumenicity in which
         evangelicals can cooperate." Bibliographical references.
         Index.

293.   Murray, Iain. "The Church and Evangelical Policy." Banner of
         Truth no. 30 (May 1963): 1-7.

         Strongly negative on prevailing policy. Calls for application
         "to the denominations, as such, New Testament standards of
         orthodoxy, discipline and unity."

294.   _____. "Evangelical Reaction to the Ecumenical Movement in
         England." Banner of Truth no. 52 (January 1968): 1-9.

         A conservative evangelical review of developments within
         British evangelicalism, including its literature, during the
         1960s.

295.   National Association of Evangelicals. Evangelical Action! A
         Report of the Organization of the National Association of
         Evangelicals for United Action. Boston: United Action Press,
         1942. 160 p.

296.	Neill, Stephen. "An Historical Understanding." Foundations 25
	(January-March 1982): 9-21.

	Missions historian Neill describes the evangelical basis in the
	19th and 20th centuries for the World Council of Churches; from
	the standpoint of one who has "a profound concern for that
	which is truly evangelical and that which is truly ecumenical."

297.	Ockenga, Harold John. "Christ for America." United We Stand, A
	Report of the Constitutional Convention of the National
	Association of Evangelicals, Chicago, IL (May 3-6, 1943): 11.

298.	Packard, William. Evangelism in America: From Tents to TV. New
	York: Paragon House, 1988. 275 p.

	Poet/novelist/playwright Packard seeks the roots of evangelism,
	with special focus on America: a chapter on American funda-
	mentalism, profiles on Moody, Sunday, and others; broadens the
	definition; hostile to the sweeping claims of traditional
	evangelism. Bibliography. Index.

299.	Paulson, Eric Edwin. Thunder in the Wilderness: Evangelical
	Essays in an Age of Doubt. Minneapolis: Privately printed by
	Augsburg, 1965. 283 p.

	Paulson studied under the prominent fundamentalist, Reuben A.
	Torrey, at the Bible Institute of Los Angeles; analyzes
	conditions in church and world and the evangelical's response.

300.	Proctor, W. C. G. Evangelical Thought and Practice. London: J.
	Clarke, 1946. 95 p.

	Anglican Proctor distinguishes evangelicalism from Catholicism
	and modernism, describing evangelicalism's understanding of the
	Bible and apostolic experience, its doctrines and practices,
	relation to the social order, and to ecumenism. Index.

301.	Renwick, A. M. "The Position and Prospects of Protestantism in
	the Post-War World." Evangelical Quarterly 17 (April 1945):
	133-46.

	Draws a global picture from the numerical, political and
	spiritual points of view, with a positive outlook for the
	future.

302.	Riley, William Bell. "National Association of Evangelicals for
	United Action." Pilot 23 (November 1942): 53-54.

Commends the admirable aim of the NAE, warns that creating a
new organization poses threats of division in fundamentalist
ranks, and hopes the intention of unity will be realized.

303.   Rowdon, Harold H. "Edinburgh 1910, Evangelicals and the Ecumenical Movement." Vox Evangelica 5 (1967): 49-71.

The 1910 meeting did not play the crucial role in ecumenism
usually ascribed to it, for many of its ideas derived from 19th
century sources; however, it was crucial in another way:
"evangelicals began to find themselves edged out of the very
movement they had commenced," and began to part company with
ecumenists.

304.   Schrotenboer, Paul G. "The Continuing Reformation." International Reformed Bulletin no. 31 (October 1967): 1-3.

In the context of what appears to be stagnation in evangelical
Protestantism, he editorializes that "the message of the
Reformation is truly existential in the 20th century," but that
there must be continuing reformation for today's world.

305.   Shelley, Bruce L. Evangelicalism in America. Grand Rapids:
Eerdmans, 1967. 134 p.

A brief history of the National Association of Evangelicals,
written for the occasion of its 25th anniversary, but not an
"official" history. A few bibliographical references included
in the "Notes."

306.   Stackhouse, John G., Jr. "Proclaiming the Word: Canadian Evangelicalism Since World War I." Ph.D. diss., The University of
Chicago, 1987. 264 p.

307.   Stewardson, Jerry L., and Edmund F. Perry. "Expounding Evangelical Faith: From Karl Barth to Carl Henry." Explor 2 (Fall 1976):
35-44.

Stewardson reviews books by Barth, Helmut Thielicke, Donald
Bloesch, and Bernard Ramm, under the topic "the doctrine of the
Spirit: a contemporary weakness"; Perry reviews three books by
Carl F. H. Henry under the topic "strategic preparation for
evangelical witness."

308.   Tenney, Merrill C., ed. The Word for this Century. New York:
Oxford University Press, 1960. 184 p.

Eight evangelicals, administrators or faculty or alumni of
Wheaton Graduate School, mark Wheaton College's centenary with
essays based on its statement of faith. Bibliography.

309.   Walker, Robert. "Robert Walker Reflects Upon 50 Years of
        Christian Life." Interview by Steven Lawson. Charisma 14 (July
        1989): 62-64, 66-67, 69.

        A pioneer in Christian journalism and long-time publisher of
        Christian Life magazine, "talks about the interviews, the
        articles and the people that made journalism history."

310.   Watt, David Harrington. "A Transforming Faith: Essays on the
        History of American Evangelicalism in the Middle Decades of the
        Twentieth Century." Ph.D. diss., Harvard University, 1987.
        226 p.

311.   Weddell, John Weaver. "The Savor of Evangelicalism." Review and
        Expositor 13 (January 1916): 53-64.

        Lilting description of the evangelical minister and evangelical
        preaching.

312.   Williams, George H., and Rodney L. Petersen. "Evangelicals: Soci-
        ety, the State, and Nation (1925-75)." In The Evangelicals: What
        They Believe, Who They Are, Where They Are Changing, eds. David F.
        Wells and John D. Woodbridge, 211-48. Nashville: Abingdon, 1975.

        After introductory comments on the fifty years prior to 1925,
        the authors look at the changing attitudes through the eras of
        Bryan, Sunday, and Graham, noting that too often evangelicals
        tied Christianity to the nation.

See also items 14, 40, 44, 60, 154, 162, 169, 227, 234, 517, 548, 564, 565,
    567, 570, 624, 672, 751, 765, 776, 788, 803, 805, 806, 819, 825, 826,
    827, 829, 841, 847, 874, 915, 934, 937, 954, 982, 1012, 1017, 1018,
    1025, 1049, 1050, 1052, 1063, 1068, 1074, 1077, 1084, 1089, 1119, 1141,
    1152, 1164, 1277, 1290, 1302, 1323, 1371, 1385, 1398, 1425, 1477, 1522,
    1524, 1527, 1540, 1541, 1542, 1549, 1556, 1563, 1566, 1569, 1577, 1585,
    1594, 1660, 1667, 1748, 1818, 2521, 2557, 2559, 2614, 2633.

E.   Post-World War II

313.   Anderson, Clifford V. "The Practice of Evangelical Christian
        Education Since World War II." In Changing Patterns of Religious
        Education, ed. Marvin J. Taylor, 129-43. Nashville: Abingdon,
        1984.

Who the evangelicals are, the kind of education offered in
their churches, organizations auxiliary to the educational
enterprise, and wider evangelical influences.

314.   Askew, Thomas A. "Christian Higher Education: Where Has it Been?
Where is it Going?" Action 47 (March-April 1988): 4-7.

Evangelical higher education since mid-century. A positive
portrayal within a context of large challenges.

315.   "Back to that Oldtime Religion: Gaudy and Vital, U.S. Evangelicalism is Booming." Time 110 (26 December 1977): 52-58.

Featured on the front cover, and given extensive coverage,
presenting some of the key individuals and churches, prospects
and problems, of a "New Empire of Faith."

316.   Baker, Thomas Eugene. Christ and the Even Balance: A Manual of
Fundamentalism. Millersburg, PA: Bible Truth Mission, 1968.
168 p.

317.   Balmer, Randall H. Mine Eyes Have Seen the Glory: A Journey Into
the Evangelical Subculture in America. New York: Oxford University Press, 1989. 240 p.

"This is a book about popular evangelicalism, a kind of travel-
ogue into the evangelical subculture in America, a subculture
that encompasses fundamentalists, charismatics, and pentecostals," persons "who insist on some sort of spiritual rebirth
as a criterion for entering the kingdom of heaven, who often
impose exacting behavioral standards on the faithful, and whose
beliefs, institutions, and folkways comprise the evangelical
subculture in America." Bibliographies. Index.

318.   Banner, Ray. "Evangelicalism in the United States." Evangelical
Quarterly 39 (1967): 154-64.

Treats definitions, organization, doctrine, evangelism and
missions, education, literature, leadership, and problems and
possibilities, in a "reporter's view," rather than a philosophical approach.

319.   Barnhouse, Donald Grey. "'Return to Biblical Theology': Comments
by the Editor-in-Chief on William F. Albright's Remarkable
Manifesto in the Christian Century." Eternity 10 (February 1959):
7-10, 38.

Judges Albright's article in a recent issue of CC to be the
most important of the previous year and perhaps of a generation. Barnhouse reports and interacts with Albright's article
as a significant confirmation of conservative biblical
interpretation.

320.   Baumann, J. Daniel. "Contemporary Themes in Evangelical Preach-
        ing." In "Proclaim the Good News": Essays in Honor of Gordon G.
        Johnson, ed. Norris Magnuson, 173-84. Arlington Heights, IL:
        Harvest, 1986.

        Examines three models of contemporary evangelical preaching--
        evangelistic, life situation, and expository--by analyzing the
        preaching of a prominent example of each.

321.   Bayly, Joseph. "A Salute to 'Mr. Evangelical.'" Eternity 26 (May
        1975): 20-21.

        Tribute to Russell Hitt upon his retirement after more than two
        decades as editor of Eternity magazine. His stamp, and that of
        the magazine: "complete trust in the Bible's authority, and
        belief in a Christian world-and-life view for the present time
        in harmony with the Bible."

322.   Benjamin, Paul. "Some Projections of Evangelical Church Growth."
        In Evangelicals Face the Future: Scenarios, Addresses, and
        Responses from the 'Consultation on Future Evangelical Concerns'
        held in Atlanta, Georgia, December 14-17, 1977, ed. Donald E.
        Hoke, 155-59. Pasadena: William Carey Library, 1978.

        Projected growth for thirteen denominations that responded to
        his letter of inquiry. Concludes that the American church is
        "alive and growing."

323.   Berger, Peter L. "Religion in Post-Protestant America." Commen-
        tary 81 (May 1986): 41-46.

        Since "the Protestant social and cultural establishment has
        ended," differing interpretations of the First Amendment, and
        partisan religous advocacy have created confusion and moral
        pluralism, which the churches as "mediating institutions" can
        help overcome.

324.   Blackwood, Andrew W. "The Evangelical Pulpit Today." Christi-
        anity Today 6 (22 December 1961): 8-10.

Summary of the monthly sermons for 1961 in Christianity Today,
with some suggestions to pastors on sermon preparation.

325.   ____, ed. Evangelical Sermons of Our Day. New York: Harper,
            1959. 383 p.

            Thirty-seven sermons by leading evangelicals of the mid-twen-
            tieth century, selected and with annotations by one who was
            himself one of those leading evangelicals. Brief biographical
            sketches of the contributors.

326.   Campbell, Will D., and J. Y. Holloway. "An Open Letter to Dr.
            Billy Graham, Or, About This Issue." Katallagete 3 (Winter 1971):
            1-3.

            Points out that "the chief function of institutions now is to
            perpetuate themselves by perpetuating myths"; addressed to
            Graham because of his influence in high places.

327.   Cattell, Everett L. "National Association of Evangelicals and
            World Evangelical Fellowship." Christianity Today 9 (29 January
            1965): 12-14.

            The National Association of Evangelicals and the World
            Evangelical Fellowship, their founding and their purposes.

328.   "Christianity Today at Thirty: Looking Back at the Forces and
            Faces of American Evangelicalism." Christianity Today 30 (17
            October 1986): 19-28.

            Nine brief essays describe two dozen influential evangelicals
            and the forces that both shaped and represented their views.

329.   Clancy, Thomas. "Fundamental Facts About Evangelicals." America
            142 (31 May 1980): 454-57.

            Sketch of the evangelical presence in American church life;
            reasons for Catholics to avoid contact with evangelicals;
            reasons for Catholics to know evangelicals better.

330.   Clark, Gordon H. "The Evangelical Theological Society Tomorrow."
            Bulletin of the Evangelical Theological Society 9 (Winter 1966):
            3-11.

            Presents the reason for ETS existence and the essentials of the
            mid-twentieth century situation: "The doctrine of verbal
            inspiration is not only the platform on which the Evangelical

Theological Society stands, it is also the crucial issue in
theological debate today."

331.   Collins, Gary. "The Pit and the Pendulum." Eternity 28 (October
        1977): 40-41.

        Five ways in which "new-breed evangelicals sound like old-breed
        fundamentalists."

332.   Consultation on Future Evangelical Concerns, Atlanta, December
        1977. Evangelicals Face the Future: Scenarios, Addresses, and
        Responses from the "Consultations on Future Evangelical Concerns"
        held in Atlanta, Georgia, December 14-17, 1977, ed. Donald E.
        Hoke. Pasadena: William Carey Library, 1978. 166 p.

        The product of a meeting of seventy-five evangelical leaders,
        who examine prospects, needs, and challenges facing evan-
        gelicals, and possible responses. Bibliographical references.

333.   Continuing Consultation on Future Evangelical Concerns. An
        Evangelical Agenda: 1984 and Beyond. Sponsored by the Billy
        Graham Center, Wheaton College. Pasadena: William Carey Library,
        1979. 202 p.

        Prominent evangelicals review such major issues as the church,
        the Christian family, lifestyle in a secular society, and world
        evangelization. Bibliographical references.

334.   Dayton, Donald W. "Whither Evangelicalism?" In Sanctification
        and Liberation: Liberation Theologies in Light of the Wesleyan
        Tradition, ed. Theodore Runyon, 142-63. Nashville: Abingdon,
        1981.

        The meaning of evangelical; the 19th century holiness movement
        as influential in evangelicalism; the impoverishment that has
        occurred because evangelicals have lost contact with that
        Arminian heritage.

335.   Deck, Allan Figueroa. "Fundamentalism and the Hispanic Catholic."
        America 152 (26 January 1985): 64-66.

        Analysis of fundamentalist Protestant inroads among California
        Hispanics and the relatively ineffective Catholic means to
        counter the move.

336.   Douglass, R. Bruce. "The Waning Credibility of the Mainline
        Protestant Churches' Social Pronouncements." New Oxford Review 56
        (May 1989): 10-15.

Concludes that whereas Catholics and evangelicals are growing
and "moving much more forcefully into the mainstream of
American life," the mainline Protestant influence that has been
very significant, "is clearly on the wane. But how far?" That
issue needs to be faced.

337.   Ellingsen, Mark. The Evangelical Movement: Growth, Impact,
Controversy, Dialog. Minneapolis: Augsburg, 1988. 496 p.

Prepared for the Institute for Ecumenical Research (Strasbourg), this is the best work on the evangelicals from the
mainline perspective; Ellingsen demonstrates prodigious
research, writes sympathetically, is aware of the subtle
differences among evangelicals, and urges dialogue between
evangelicals and conciliarists. Ninety pages of bibliographical references. Indexes.

338.   "Evangelicals Converge on Columbus for 47th Annual Convention."
United Evangelical Action 48 (May-June 1989): 10-12.

Briefly reviews the National Association of Evangelicals'
convention participants and emphases.

339.   "The Evangelicals." Union Seminary Quarterly Review 32 (Winter
1977).

340.   Evans, William Joseph. "The Pocket Testament League: An
Evangelical Response to Social, Political, and Military Crises."
Ph.D. diss., New York University, 1972. 216 p.

341.   Ezell, Macel D. "The Evangelical Protestant Defense of Americanism, 1945-1960." Ph.D. diss., Texas Christian University, 1969.
212 p.

342.   Ford, Leighton. "Images of the Future: An Evangelical Perspective." In Evangelicals Face the Future. Scenarios, Addresses,
and Responses from the 'Consultation on Future Evangelical
Concerns' held in Atlanta, Georgia, December 14-17, 1977, ed.
Donald E. Hoke, 29-41. Pasadena: William Carey Library, 1978.

Keynote address for the conference by a leading American
evangelist, who calls for preparation for several future
scenarios, and for cleansing and unity in evangelical ranks.

343.   "Fuller Theological Seminary and the Evangelical Movement: Four
Addresses from The 1987 President's Lectureship." Theology, News
and Notes 17 (December 1987).

344.   Goodall, Norman. "Evangelicals and Evangelicals." <u>Frontier</u> 1
         (November 1958): 249-53.

         Discusses the movement to separatism and exclusivism within
         evangelicalism, and pleads against further hardening of the
         issues.

345.   Gouldstone, Tim. "Evangelicals and Contemporary Anglican Liberal
         Theology." <u>Churchman</u> 95, no. 2 (1981): 110-22.

         Recent trends in evangelical Anglican theology, current liberal
         Anglican theology, and six "areas which need to be studied and
         lessons that need to be learned by evangelical Anglicans."

346.   Graham, Billy. "An Agenda for the 1980's." <u>Christianity Today</u> 24
         (4 January 1980): 23-27.

         The external world that evangelicals face; their internal
         problems; witness in the 1980s should be marked by integrity,
         compassion, and vision.

347.   _____. "The Evangelist and a Torn World." In <u>The Work of an</u>
         <u>Evangelist: International Congress for Itinerant Evangelists,</u>
         <u>Amsterdam, The Netherlands</u>, ed. J. D. Douglas, 3-9. Minneapolis:
         World Wide Publications, 1984.

         The first message of the Congress, stressing the motive, mes-
         sage, and methods of Biblical evangelism, in one of the most
         significant evangelical gatherings of recent decades.

348.   _____. "The House That Evangelicals Built." <u>Eternity</u> 32 (May
         1981): 19-21.

         Analysis of the reasons for growth in evangelicalism, and five
         dangers faced: pride, worldly methods, traditionalism, per-
         petuating an organization, and complacency.

349.   _____. "A New Theology, A New Morality, and A New Evangelism."
         <u>Eternity</u> 16 (November 1965): 9-10, 45-46.

         Sees a denial of the authority of the Bible, a new example of
         the old immorality, and a substitution of social emphasis for
         personal evangelism.

350.   _____. "What Ten Years Have Taught Me." <u>Christian Century</u> 77
         (17 February 1960): 186-89.

The narrow limits assigned to evangelists, realistic assessment
of the results of mass evangelism, deepened faith in basic
doctrines, wider view of the church, social implications of the
gospel, triumph of the kingdom of God.

351.   _____. "Why Decision?" Decision 1 (November 1960): 2.

Basic purpose: "To provide spiritual food for Christians, and
to publish evangelistic messages and articles aimed at reaching
the secular mind and winning the non-believer to Christ."
Also, to link the Graham Team with its supporters, and to
"encourage the hearts of pastors and missionaries everywhere."

352.   Grounds, Vernon C. "American Evangelicalism: Today and Tomorrow."
In A Time to Speak: The Evangelical-Jewish Encounter, ed. A. James
Rudin and Marvin R. Wilson, 138-51. Grand Rapids: Eerdmans; and
Austin, TX: Center for Judaic-Christian Studies, 1987.

Calls evangelicalism a "divided but dominant and dynamic form
of Protestantism" with a hopeful future.

353.   _____. "American Evangelicalism: Quo Vadis?" TSF Bulletin 10
(May-June 1987): 7-10.

Discusses books by James Davison Hunter and Mark Noll that
focus on the future of American evangelicalism, the first
reviewing possible changes in young evangelicals, and the
latter noting shifts in evangelical biblical scholarship since
1880, warning of perils and suggesting an agenda.

354.   Grubb, Luther L. "The State of the Church Today." Grace
Theological Journal 12 (Fall 1971): 23-33.

One of a series of four articles that discusses the state of
the church, including obstacles ahead, and consideration of how
the church should respond; coverage includes Sunday School
literature, the attitudes of young people, and the "Social
Gospel."

355.   Guinness, Os. "The American Hour, The Evangelical Moment." In
Evangelicalism: Surviving Its Success, moderator Kenneth Kantzer.
ed. David A. Fraser, 192-97. Princeton: Princeton University
Press, 1987.

Originally presented at The Evangelical Round Table in 1986
(Eastern College and Eastern Baptist Theological Seminary. St.
Davids, PA). Describing a crucial period of great national

change at a time of evangelical resurgence. he explores some of
the potential outcomes, asking whether evangelicalism will rise
to the occasion.

356.   Harding, D. N. "Evangelical Fellowship of Canada." Evangelical
Christian (June 1966): 11-12.

The officers and Constitution of EFC as adopted at their annual
conference.

357.   Hatch, Nathan O. "Evangelicalism as a Democratic Movement."
Reformed Journal 34 (October 1984): 10-16.

A chapter in George Marsden, ed., Evangelicalism and Modern
America (1984): 71-82. The driving force behind American
Christianity is not the quality of its organization, the status
of its clergy or the power of its intellectual life, but its
emphasis on the people. The downside to this emphasis has been
a failure to sustain serious intellectual life.

358.   Henry, Carl F. H. "American Evangelicals in a Turning Time."
Christian Century 97 (5 November 1980): 1058-62.

Evangelicalism is strong, not as strong as its proponents
think, but stronger than ecumenical or Catholic Christianity
and therefore needs to push ahead to make its mark on American
life.

359.   _____, ed. Christian Faith and Modern Theology: Contemporary
Evangelical Thought. New York: Channel Press, 1964. 426 p.

360.   _____. Evangelicals at the Brink of Crisis: Significance of
the World Congress of Evangelism. Waco: Word, 1967. 120 p.

Presented also as a lecture series in several seminaries, this
small volume contends that the Congress, "an event of major
importance," brought the growing evangelical movement to the
brink of crisis/decision about major areas (theology. evangelism, social-political. and ecumenical). calling for new
commitment and new unity.

361.   _____. Evangelicals in Search of Identity: Significance of the
World Congress on Evangelism. Waco: Word. 1976. 96 p.

Following the WCE (which he chaired) in Berlin late in 1966.
Henry, then editor of Christianity Today. addressed the
theological, evangelistic, social, and ecumenical crises faced

by evangelicals, with special emphasis on the need for unity
and for deepened commitment to the risen Lord of the Church.

362.   . "Evangelicals: Out of the Closet But Going Nowhere?"
Christianity Today 24 (4 January 1980): 16-22.

Evangelicals have advanced to some extent since the 1950s, are
troubled by both weaknesses and strengths, and need to get
beyond the troubles through a nine-point approach.

363.   Hestenes, Roberta. "Sowing the Seeds of Reconciliation." In
Evangelicalism: Surviving Its Success, moderator Kenneth Kantzer,
editor David A. Fraser, 182-91. Princeton: Princeton University
Press, 1987.

Originally in The Evangelical Round Table printed in 1986 by
Eastern College and Eastern Baptist Theological Seminary, St.
Davids, PA. Focusing on the near future, she provides a
biblical perspective on ministry in relationship to reconciliation, discusses four dangers, makes several suggestions for
the maturation of evangelicalism.

364.   Hewitt, Thomas. "Evangelicals in an Ecumenical Atmosphere."
Christianity Today 9 (29 January 1965): 37-38.

Evangelicals need to overcome their tendency to form sects and
need to heal their divisions, but not at the expense of doctrinal basics.

365.   Hoke, Donald E., ed. Evangelicals Face the Future. See "Consultation on Future Evangelical Concerns."

366.   Hutcheson, Richard G., Jr. Mainline Churches and the Evangelicals: A Challenging Crisis? Atlanta: John Knox Press, 1981.
194 p.

An analysis, by a Presbyterian leader, of the challenge resurgent evangelicalism poses for the mainline churches. Includes
such crisis points as youth, para-church organizations,
overseas missions, the charismatic movement. and church growth.
as well as a "Manual For Mainline Ministers" on coping with the
crisis. Bibliographical references.

367.   "Into the Next Century: Trends Facing the Church." Christianity
Today 30 (17 January 1986): 11-131.

A CT Institute report by 13 authors viewing the trends, challenges and strategies for the years ahead.

368.   Johnston, Jon. Will Evangelicalism Survive Its Own Popularity? Grand Rapids: Zondervan, 1980. 224 p.

Believing that evangelicalism's compromise with American culture "has reached epidemic proportions." Johnston describes eight components in the culture (such as materialism, faddism, youthism) that threaten the vitality of the movement, and urges a return to biblical Christianity. Bibliographical references. Indexes.

369.   Jorstad, Erling. "Pressers On and Holders Fast: Evangelicalism and Popular Culture." Dialog 24 (Summer 1985): 181-87.

How evangelicals relate to popular culture: politics, television, fiction, religious merchandise. The two groups divide on these issues.

370.   Kantzer, Kenneth S. "Evangelicalism: Midcourse Self-Appraisal." Christianity Today 27 (7 January 1983): 10-11.

Ten weaknesses, seven assets of the evangelical movement.

371.   _____. "Reflections: Five Years of Change." Christianity Today 26 (26 November 1982): 14-20.

Kantzer reflects on changes in evangelicalism 1977-1982.

372.   _____. "Which Magnet Draws Evangelicals Together?" Christianity Today 26 (16 July 1982): 12-14.

The magnet is neither liberalism nor secular humanism but commitment to Christ and the Scriptures.

373.   Kantzer, Kenneth S., Richard F. Lovelace, and Norman Geisler. "Why Does Harvard Want an Evangelical Connection?" Christianity Today (4 February 1983): 17-20.

Mixed responses to Roger H. Martin's article in the same issue entitled "An Evangelical Chair at Harvard?" (pp. 14-16).

374.   Kucharsky, David. "Year of the Evangelical '76." Christianity Today 21 (22 October 1976): 12-13.

Broad-stroke survey of the reasons for the rise of evangelicalism in the consciousness of American culture.

375.   Lane, A. N. S. "The Fundamentalism Debate: A Survey of Reviews of
James Barr's Fundamentalism." Evangelical Review of Theology 3
(April 1979): 11-26.

Covers twenty-seven reviews, giving numerous brief quotes,
along with his own evaluative comments, and of "cautions" that
evangelicals need to take to heart. The large conclusion is
that Fundamentalism "makes some important points that need to
be headed [sic] but it is marred by serious inaccuracies."

376.   Lane, Tony. "The Fundamentalism Polemic." Christian Graduate
(September 1977): 77-80.

A critique of James Barr's book, Fundamentalism (1977), dealing
with British conservative evangelicalism; "a significant
milestone in the history of evangelical-liberal polemic,"
which, although marred by serious defects, needs to be taken
seriously.

377.   Lindsell, Harold. "The Shape of Religious Thought and Assump-
tions: Response." In Evangelicals Face the Future. Scenarios,
Addresses, and Responses from the 'Consultation on Future
Evangelical Concerns' held in Atlanta, Georgia, December 14-17,
1977, ed. Donald E. Hoke, 122-26. Pasadena: William Carey
Library, 1978.

A sobering view, including many areas that have not been
affected by the mid-century revival, among them the leadership,
seminaries and the media. Nor has there been much social
impact.

378.   Lundquist, Carl H. "Issues Confronting North American Evangel-
icals." In Serving Our Generation: Evangelical Strategies for the
Eighties, ed. with an introduction by Waldron Scott, 97-106.
Colorado Springs: World Evangelical Fellowship, 1980.

A leading evangelical educator and past president of the NAE
discusses issues facing evangelicalism: fragmentation, biblical
inerrancy, financial accountability, politicizing for evangelical action, and the scholarly integration of faith and
knowledge.

379.   Marsden, George M., ed. Evangelicalism and Modern America. Grand
Rapids: Eerdmans, 1984. 220 p.

Thirteen essays on the rise of evangelicalism in American
culture since World War II, including a bibliographical essay
by Richard Pierard: "The New Religious Right in American
Politics." Bibliographical references in the other essays.

380.   Marty, Martin E. "Religion in America Since Mid-Century."
Daedalus 3 (Winter 1982): 149-63.

Places evangelicalism within the context of "resurgent anti-
modern religion."

381.   _____. "Tensions Within Contemporary Evangelicalism: A
Critical Appraisal." In The Evangelicals: What They Believe, Who
They Are, Where They Are Changing, eds. David F. Wells and John D.
Woodbridge, 170-88. Nashville: Abingdon, 1975.

Historical and contemporary analysis of tensions within
evangelicalism, including theology, social concern and action,
intellectuality, and life patterns.

382.   McKenna, David. "Our Evangelical Agenda." United Evangelical
Action 37 (Spring 1978): 8-11.

Warning about the disciplines needed, based on Micah 6, if
evangelicals are to overcome the hype of "the year of the
evangelical."

383.   Menendez, Albert J. "Who are the Evangelicals?" Christianity
Today 22 (27 January 1978): 42.

Summary of the results of the Gallup survey of 3000 persons,
Religion in America, 1977-78 (1978).

384.   Moberg, David O. "Fundamentalists and Evangelicals in Society."
In The Evangelicals: What They Believe, Who They Are, Where They
Are Changing, eds. David F. Wells and John D. Woodbridge, 143-69.
Nashville: Abingdon, 1975.

A leading evangelical sociologist attempts a definition of
evangelicalism, identifies its adherents, and examines its
growing strength and the consequences of that strength.

385.   Mouw, Richard J. "Evangelicals In Search of Maturity." Theology
Today 35 (April 1978): 42-51.

Aware that evangelicals have several problems--the politicized
way they handle theological debate. differences on the relation

between social and personal dimensions of life. cultural
imperialism--Mouw believes "the evangelical coalition is
deteriorating and will virtually dissolve in the near future."

386.   Murphy, Cullen. "Protestantism and the Evangelicals." Wilson
Quarterly 5 (Autumn 1981): 105-16.

Describes twelve "rings" (groupings) of evangelicalism, showing
their diversity and resiliency; uses Wesleyans as an example of
persistence and diversity; graphs.

387.   "The NAE: Building on Evangelical Consensus." An interview with
Billy Melvin. Christianity Today 26 (8 October 1982): 50-53.

The executive director of the NAE describes its constituency,
programs and relation to other organizations.

388.   Nash, Ronald H., ed. Evangelical Renewal in the Mainline
Churches. Westchester: Good News, 1987. 174 p.

An examination of the evangelical renewal within eight of the
most prominent mainline denominations. Includes a chapter on
the Roman Catholic Church in the United States. Helpful
"Directory of Renewal Groups" in each chapter. Bibliography.

389.   _____. Evangelicals in America: Who They Are, What They
Believe. Nashville: Abingdon, 1987. 125 p.

Written for the general reader, the book is a "short non-
technical introduction to Evangelicalism in America," covering
basic topics. Bibliography. Index.

390.   "1976: 'The Year of the Evangelical.'" Christian Century 93 (29
December 1976): 1165-66.

"In terms of public attention and news coverage, 1976 was
unmistakably the Year of the Evangelical, and much of that
attention . . . came as a result of a 'born-again' Southern
Baptist's campaign for the presidency."

391.   Noll, Mark A. "Evangelicals on the Canterbury Trail: Why is the
Appeal of Sacramentalism Growing?" Eternity 29 (March 1978):
15-19, 40-41.

The answer lies in part in the influence of persons like C. S.
Lewis, of low church Anglicans like John Stott and J. I.
Packer, of new vitality within American Episcopalianism, and of

its position and practice in such areas as worship. sacraments.
and art and culture, areas in which many American evangelicals
are dissatisfied.

392.   ____. "What Has Wheaton To Do With Jerusalem? Lessons From
Evangelicals for the Reformed." Reformed Journal 32 (May 1982):
8-15.

With a number of qualifications connected to each lesson Noll
suggests that "(1) the virtues of practicality, (2) the
individualism of grace, and (3) the intricacies of
Americanization" are needs among the Reformed that evangelicals
can supply.

393.   The Nottingham Statement: The Official Statement of the Second
National Evangelical-Anglican Congress 1977. London: Falcon,
1977.

394.   "One in Five Adults is an Evangelical." Emerging Trends 5 (March
1983): 3.

"The same proportion recorded in surveys conducted in 1981,
1980 and 1976."

395.   Ostling, Richard N. "Those Mainline Blues." Time 133 (22 May
1989): 94-96.

Describes and explains the "unprecedented decline" in membership in the mainline congregations, and substantial growth in
other bodies, including the conservative evangelical churches.
"Critical shortcomings" mark the mainline churches in "virtually every activity concerned with the teaching and spreading
of the faith," including Sunday School, higher education,
foreign missions, and radio and television ministries.

396.   Packer, James I. "Fundamentalism: The British Scene." Christianity Today 2 (29 September 1958): 3-6.

Sees a reinvigorated British "fundamentalism" (evangelicalism),
handles the doctrinal complaints--views of the Bible and the
atonement--and encourages evangelicals to support local
churches and to pursue social involvement.

397.   Paine. Stephen W. "Separation" - Is Separating Evangelicals.
Boston: Fellowship Press. 1951. 43 p.

Deals with the issue of why the two interdenominational
organizations into which "Bible-believing" Christians were
gathered--The National Association of Evangelicals and the
American Council of Christian Churches--had not united. Paine
a former president of the NAE.

398.   Peterson, William J. "25 Years of Eternity." Eternity 26 (April
1975): 10-13, 61-63. "The Magazine That Lived." Eternity 26 (May
1975): 22-24, 64-65.

Part I relates the story of the magazine's origins and early
years under the leadership of the prominent preacher Donald G.
Barnhouse, including stands taken on controversial issues.
Part II in May gives the account of the survival and prosperity
of the magazine under the leadership of Russell T. Hitt.

399.   Pierard, Richard V. "Laussane II: Reshaping World Evangelicalism." Christian Century 106 (16-23 August 1989): 740-42.

Report of the Second International Congress on World Evangelization, held in Manila in July, with attendance of some 4,300:
gave "serious attention to Third World concerns"; adopted
"Manila Manifesto" of evangelical intentions for world
evangelism; softening toward WCC.

400.   Schaeffer, Francis A. The Great Evangelical Disaster. Westchester: Good News, 1984. 192 p.

In Schaeffer's judgment the evangelical church has accommodated
itself to secular society, with a resultant loss of truth and
beauty, compassion and humanness. He calls for a radical stand
against the dominant world spirit of this day. Bibliographical
references.

401.   Scott, Waldron, ed. Serving Our Generation: Evangelical Strategies for the Eighties. Colorado Springs: World Evangelical
Fellowship, 1980. 281 p.

Papers presented in preparation for the 7th General Assembly of
the World Evangelical Fellowship, London, 1980. survey the
world situation, the WEF commissions, and challenges ahead.
Bibliographical references.

402.   Scroggs, Robin. "The Bible as a Weapon in Evangelical-Liberal
Warfare." Chicago Theological Seminary Register 66 (Spring 1976):
61-72.

Discusses the background, including the modernist-fundamentalist controversy and the rise of historical criticism, and
the present situation following the reemergence of conservative
Christianity in strength, concluding with "Prospects and
Questions from a Liberal Bias."

403.   Shelley, Bruce L. "Sampling the Spirit of the Smaller Denominations." Christianity Today 25 (11 December 1981): 24-26.

Six smaller evangelical denominations exemplify the evangelical
renaissance.

404.   _____. "Will American Evangelicalism Survive?" Christianity
Today 28 (15 June 1984): 30.

Evangelicals are making only limited impact on American life.

405.   Smith, Timothy L. "A Fortress Mentality: Shackling the Spirit's
Power." Interview by David Kucharsky. Christianity Today 21 (19
November 1976): 22-26.

A wide-ranging interview on the status, prospects and agenda of
evangelicalism.

406.   Stackhouse, John G., Jr. "A Tour Among the Evangelicals."
Christian Century 106 (17 May 1989): 529-35.

A review article on Randall Balmer, Mine Eyes Have Seen the
Glory: A Journey Into the Evangelical Subculture of America
(1989). Balmer defines evangelicalism, distinguishes various
groups within, and explores "some social manifestations of
American evangelicalism, encompassing as much . . . variety and
balance as he could manage." Criticizes evangelicalism "while
defending it against unjustified attacks by others."

407.   Stott, John R. W., ed. Obeying Christ in a Changing World.
Cleveland: Collins World, 1977. 3 volumes.

The three volumes contain nearly twenty papers from the
Nottingham conference (1977), illustrating the breadth of
evangelical Anglican thought, but always from the starting
point of Scripture, "God's unique and trustworthy revelation."
Bibliographical references.

408.   Stransky, Thomas F. "A Look at Evangelical Protestantism."
Theology, News and Notes 35 (March 88): 21-26.

Detailed mutual views and misunderstandings that can now be
replaced as possible new alignments appear.

409.   Sweet, Leonard I. "The 1960s: The Crises of Liberal Christianity
          and the Public Emergence of Evangelicalism." In Evangelicalism
          and Modern America, ed. George Marsden, 29-45. Grand Rapids:
          Eerdmans, 1984.

          Uses the "complementaries of authority and identity" to suggest
      .   that liberalism lost authority in the "first 1960s" (1960-1967)
          and evangelicalism gained identity in the "second 1960s"
          (1967-1971); warning that 1970s and 1980s evangelicalism may be
          following liberalism in a loss of authority.

410.   _____. "Wise as Serpents, Innocent as Doves: The New
          Evangelical Historiography." Journal of the American Academy of
          Religion 56 (Fall 1988): 397-415.

          Insightful discussion of the works and approaches of contem-
          porary evangelical historians, concentrating on Mark Noll and
          George Marsden, with passing reference to Joel Carpenter,
          Nathan Hatch, Harry Stout and Grant Wacker.

411.   Tarr, Leslie K. "Canadian Evangelicals at the Crossroads."
          Evangelical Christian (August 1966): 17, 20.

          In the context of division and ineffectiveness, the adminis-
          trator of Central Baptist Seminary in Toronto appeals for an
          emphasis that combines truth (doctrinal purity), love (avoid
          excesses and negativism), and proclamation (Gospel witness).

412.   _____. "Master Plan to Sabotage Evangelicals." Eternity 22
          (April 1971): 20-21.

          In the form of communication from Satan's forces, a ten-point
          plan to undermine evangelicals.

413.   Wacker, Grant. "Uneasy in Zion: Evangelicals in Postmodern
          Society." In Evangelicalism and Modern America. ed. George
          Marsden, 17-28. Grand Rapids: Eerdmans. 1984.

          While seeing some value in William McLoughlin's "rigorously
          reductionist scheme" and more value in Martin Marty's "flexible
          functionalist scheme." Wacker suggests two distinguishing
          forces to explain the strength of post-WWII evangelicalism:
          "the peculiar structure of church-state relations" and "the
          religious legacy of the American South."

414.   Warner, R. Stephen. New Wine in Old Wineskins: Evangelicals and Liberals in a Small-Town Church. Berkeley: University of California Press, 1988. 355 p.

An account of a Presbyterian Church in Mendocino, California, which changed, between 1959 and 1982, from a staid mainline church through social emphasis (1960s) and conservativism (1970s) into charismatic evangelicalism. Warner, a sociologist, contends that the congregation reflected the changes in American Protestantism during the past quarter century, and that a pivotal factor in its growth was the evangelistic preaching of a Fuller Seminary graduate, Eric Underwood. Thirteen-page bibliography. Index.

415.   "Why Christianity Today?" Christianity Today 1 (15 October 1956): 20-21.

"Christianity Today has its origin in a deep-felt desire to express historical [evangelical] Christianity to the present generation."

416.   Woodward, Kenneth L. "Born Again! The Year of the Evangelicals." Newsweek 88 (25 October 1976): 68-78.

One of the news article that helped put evangelicals in the media limelight.

See also items 6, 29, 61, 74, 99, 104, 110, 116, 130, 136, 142, 149, 172, 176, 178, 270, 278, 435, 438, 462, 473, 480, 492, 549, 550, 554, 622, 662, 669, 678, 687, 791, 813, 820, 834, 846, 853, 901, 919, 966, 972, 984, 990, 998, 1000, 1023, 1043, 1073, 1140, 1190, 1218, 1230, 1231, 1232, 1237, 1245, 1249, 1253, 1255, 1264, 1265, 1270, 1275, 1276, 1280, 1282, 1283, 1286, 1337, 1338, 1341, 1347, 1362, 1363, 1364, 1366, 1367, 1372, 1374, 1402, 1405, 1417, 1500, 1514, 1529, 1538, 1584, 1609, 1610, 1622, 1623, 1624, 1633, 1645, 1646, 1652, 1670, 1683, 1684, 1701, 1703, 1704, 1705, 1710, 1711, 1713, 1757, 1862, 1863, 2079, 2560, 2588, 2589, 2592, 2599, 2606, 2610, 2616, 2617, 2620, 2636, 2641, 2658.

F. New Evangelicalism

417.   Ashbrook, William A. "Evangelicalism: The New Neutralism." The Voice (October 1956): 6-7, 13. Appears again in a condensed version in Central C. B. Quarterly 2 (Summer 1959): 31-32.

Warning Bible-believing Christians about the new evangelicalism, refers to the movement as the "New Neutralism," charges

it with hostility toward fundamentalism and cordiality towards
even extreme liberals.

418.   . Evangelicalism: The New Neutralism. Columbus: Calvary
Bible Church, 1970. 86 p.

A series of vignettes illustrating militant fundamentalism
opposed to the new evangelicalism.

419.   Benware, Paul. "The Social Responsibility of the Church." Grace
Journal 12 (Winter 1971): 3-17.

Presents and critiques the "Neo-Evangelical View of Social
Responsibility," concentrating on the Scriptural support.

420.   "Bibliography on New Evangelicalism," assembled by Dennis Walton
as of September 1, 1960. Central C. B. Quarterly 3 (Fall 1960):
35-38.

Divided into two sections: materials "favorable to" and
"against" new evangelicalism, including some unpublished
materials.

421.   Bloesch, Donald G. The Evangelical Renaissance. Grand Rapids:
Eerdmans, 1973. 165 p.

Written about the new evangelicalism, Barth, and pietism, at a
time when evangelicalism was re-entering American cultural
consciousness, by one who sees himself as both evangelical and
ecumenical. Bibliographical references.

422.   . "The New Evangelicalism." Religion in Life 41 (Autumn
1972): 327-39.

Seeing it as "wider and deeper than the original surge of 'neo-
evangelicalism,'" Bloesch lays out the central themes and the
weaknesses in new evangelicalism, differentiates it from
neo-orthodoxy, and offers a prognosis for its future.

423.   Brien, Robert C. "New Evangelicalism Rests on Philosophy."
Central C. B. Quarterly 3 (Fall 1960): 29-34.

Brien first describes background causes of the rise of the new
evangelicalism, and then lists seven "philosophic influences"
(e.g., rationalism, empiricism, pragmatism).

424. Clearwaters, Richard V. "The Bible: The Unchanging Evangelical Volume." Sword of the Lord 22 (4 May 1956): 1-2, 5-7.

Also published in the author's Central C. B. Quarterly 3 (Summer 1960): 33-40, this article, written in response to an article ("Is Evangelical Theology Changing?") in the Christian Herald 17 (March 1956): 16-19, warns against emphasis on experience and predicts controversy, before treating eight marks of the new evangelicalism (emphasis, e.g., on science and on scholarship).

425. _____. "The Double Divisiveness of the New Evangelicalism." Central C. B. Quarterly 1 (Summer 1958): 1-6.

Also published in Sword of the Lord; the new evangelicalism is marked by compromise, "pride of intellect," "appeasement of evil." Its advocates are "false prophets."

426. _____. "Forty Years of History Looks Down Upon Conservative Baptists." Central C. B. Quarterly 5 (Spring 1962): 17-22.

"A brief sketch" of CB history, climaxing in the "Manifesto" of June 1953, and presenting the apparent erosion of doctrine in the years since.

427. _____. The Great Conservative Baptist Compromise. Minneapolis: Central Seminary Press, n.d. 224 p.

A potpourri of articles with no apparent schematic arrangement, each on some issue in the fundamentalist versus new evangelical controversy, one phase of which was played out among Conservative Baptists in the 1950s and 1960s. Indexes.

428. _____. "New Evangelicalism's Sectarianism or New Testament Local Church Christianity." Central C. B. Quarterly 2 (Fall 1959): 35-42.

An address delivered at the annual CB meetings in 1959, which presented first the negative "Judgment of History" upon the new evangelicalism, and then the "New Testament Test" of Christian fellowship and of Christian character.

429. Dollar, George W. "Dangers in New Evangelicalism." Central C. B. Quarterly 5 (Summer 1962): 21-32.

A leading fundamentalist historian examines three large issues --the view of Scripture, overemphasis on scholastics, and de-emphasis on separatism--"where New Evangelicals threaten to depart from the moorings."

430.   Erickson, Millard J. The New Evangelical Theology. Westwood, NJ: Fleming Revell, 1968. 254 p.

Fine analysis of new evangelicalism as it had emerged by the late 1960s. More a theological study than a historical one. Fourteen-page bibliography. Index.

431.   Ferm, Robert O. Cooperative Evangelism. Grand Rapids: Zondervan, 1958. 99 p.

A new evangelical defense of Billy Graham's approach to evangelism in light of the Bible and history. Bibliography.

432.   Glover, Willis B. "The Old Evangelicalism and the New." Religion in Life 23 (Spring 1954): 286-96.

The "new" evangelicalism is neo-orthodoxy, which, says the author, should be amalgamated with the "old" (pre-20th century) evangelicalism.

433.   Grounds, Vernon C. "Fundamentalism and Evangelicalism: Legitimate Labels or Illicit Labels?" Denver: Conservative Baptist Seminary, mimeographed and distributed privately, n.d.

434.   _____. "Is LOVE in the Fundamentalist Creed?" Eternity 5 (June 1954): 13-14, 41-42.

435.   _____. "Theological Progress and Evangelical Commitment." Bulletin of the Evangelical Theological Society 4 (November 1961): 69-79.

Exploring the question whether theology still has a "frontier," he concludes that although "between Christianity and contemporary culture there stretches a challenging frontier," within Biblically oriented theology "the frontier has largely been closed though there are still exciting areas to explore and annex."

436.   Helgerson, Carlton. "The Challenge of a New Religion: Neo-Evangelicalism." Central Bible Quarterly. Part 1 in vol. 21 (Spring 1978): 3-17. Part 2 in vol. 21 (Summer 1978): 9-19.

A highly critical two part article by one who earlier was an adherent of the new evangelicalism; focuses on such aspects as its philosophy, witness, theology, message, methods, attitudes, ecclesiology, schools, and challenges.

437. Henry, Carl F. H. "Evangelical Retrospect and Prospect." Standard 46 (23 December 1956): 12-13, 16.

A retrospective look at 1956 included signs of spirituality, ecumenicism, evangelism, and publishing gains; prospects included the Billy Graham New York crusade, evangelical textbooks, and stronger evangelical influence.

438. Holmes, Arthur F. "The 'Death of God' in the Evangelical Church." Gordon Review 10 (Fall 1966): 4-12.

The commencement address at Gordon Divinity School, 1966, published in Eternity 17 (December 1966); Evangelicalism needs "a personalized ministry, . . . a decompartmentalized faith, . . . a living theology"; it needs scholarship as well as piety, social concern as well as evangelism, complex moral decision as well as traditional mores.

439. Houghton, Myron J. "A Look at the Baptist General Conference." Central C. B. Quarterly 7 (Spring 1964): 15-28.

An examination from a fundamentalist viewpoint of one denomination's stance. Deals with organizational structure, the general posture of the Conference, and its college and seminary.

440. "Is Evangelical Theology Changing?" Christian Life 17 (March 1956): 16-19.

Eight currents of thought that indicate the shift from fundamentalism to evangelicalism.

441. "Is Liberal Theology Changing?" Christian Life 17 (April 1956): 20-22.

Five indicators of change reveal that "man-centered, science worshipping liberalism no longer rules the roost," but "the new liberalism is dangerously confusing and misleading."

442. Kantzer, Kenneth S. "The Wheaton College Position on Inspiration: An Interview With Kenneth S. Kantzer." By C. Stacey Woods. Eternity 7 (December 1956): 8-9, 34-35.

The chair of the Department of Bible and Theology is
interviewed by an editor of Eternity and general secretary of
the InterVarsity Christian Fellowship. Accompanied by the
extensive official statement (pp. 9, 36-38).

443.   Killen, R. Allen. "The Inadequacy of the New Evangelicalism and
the Need for a New and Better Method." Journal of the Evangelical
Theological Society 19 (Spring 1976): 113-20.

The historical development of modern apologetics, suggestions
for a new method (based especially on careful analysis of an
opponent's system), and a Christianity vs. Communism case study
of the method.

444.   Kirkwood, Wilson D. "The New Evangelicals and the Biblical
Doctrine of Separation--Book Review." Reformation Review 26
(April 1981): 105-14.

The origins of new evangelicalism, its failure on the doctrine
of separation, and the consequent threat of a slide into
liberalism.

445.   Lightner, Robert P. Neoevangelicalism Today. Schaumburg, IL:
Regular Baptist Press, 1979. 208 p.

First published in 1959 (as Neo-evangelicalism). the first four
sections recount the developments, doctrines, difficulties, and
dangers of neo-evangelicalism, and a fifth section updates the
book; from the pen of a right-of-center evangelical. Annotated
bibliography.

446.   _____. "The New Evangelicals - Bystanders of the Faith."
Discerner. Part 1 in vol. 6 (July-Sept. 1969): 4-10.   Part 2 in
vol. 6 (October-December 1969): 7-10.

So called because "the movement is characterized by a rejection
of the biblical doctrine of separation and a desire to make the
Gospel respectable to the non-evangelicals," as well as a "weak
view of Scripture among so many of their number." Originally
published in The Reformation Review 14 (July 1967): 203-17.

447.   Linton, Thomas H. "Evangelical Compromise." Reformation Review
14 (July 1967): 218-24.

Sees the World Congress on Evangelism. held in Berlin. 1966. as
an example of compromise because of who was invited to attend.
who was excluded, and the continued promotion of "ecumenical
evangelism."

448.   Luchies, John E. "The Contemporary Opportunity for the Evangel-
         ical: An Editorial." Bulletin of the Evangelical Theological
         Society 4 (April 1961): 1.

         To seize the opportunity will require "scholarship of the
         highest order of excellence," using "modes of expression" that
         reflect the "forms of the thought-patterns of our day."

449.   MacEwen, H. F. "New Evangelicalism." Reformation Review 21
         (April 1974): 129-41.

         Using a Babylon motif to explain church history, MacEwen
         contends that new evangelicals have failed to separate
         themselves from apostate groups like the NCC.

450.   Marsden, George M. Reforming Fundamentalism: Fuller Seminary and
         the New Evangelicalism. Grand Rapids: Eerdmans, 1987. 319 p.

         Fuller Seminary as the paradigm of the movement of evangeli-
         calism from mid-twentieth century fundamentalism to the open
         evangelicalism of the 1980s, appreciatively told: good
         portraits of the major participants. Bibliographical
         references. Index.

451.   Marty, Martin E. "Fundamentalism and the Church." Christian
         Century 74 (27 November 1957): 1411-13.

         Review of Gabriel Hebert, Fundamentalism and the Church (1957)
         which Marty applauds as warning that "deviations to the right
         [sc. "new evangelicalism"] are ultimately as dangerous to the
         Christian truth as are those of the left."

452.   _____. "Intruders in the Crowded Center." Christian Century
         74 (3 July 1957): 820-21.

         Review of Carl Henry, ed., Contemporary Evangelical Thought
         (1957), faulted by Marty for its "belligerent and doctrinaire
         attitude and the narrowly confined framework" which could lead
         to a repetition of the controversies of the 1920s.

453.   McClain, Alva J. "Is Theology Changing in the Conservative Camp?"
         Brethren Missionary Herald 19 (23 February 1957): 123-24.

         Defense of the term and the general attitudes of fundamentalism
         over against the "new evangelicalism." Response to an article
         in Christian Life (March 1956), "Is Evangelical Theology
         Changing?"

454.   McCune, Rolland D. "An Analysis of the New Evangelicalism:
        History." Central Bible Quarterly 19 (Spring 1976): 2-26.

        Reviews, from a fundamentalist perspective, the fundamentalist
        conflict with modernism and the early years of the new
        evangelicalism. Helpful documentation and review of relevant
        literature.

455.   _____. "Post-Tribulationism - 'Historic' Premillennialism."
        Central Bible Quarterly 18 (Summer 1975): 2-19.

        The first of a series of articles examines the claims of
        posttribulationism (the position of many new evangelicals) from
        a dispensational perspective, concluding that those claims are
        in error.

456.   McDonald, Morris. "Contemporary Trends in New Evangelicalism."
        Reformation Review 25 (January 1980): 17-43.

        Recap of the history of the new evangelicalism, turmoil in the
        seventies among that group, especially on the question of
        inerrancy, and a warning about the redefined separatism and
        relaxed militancy among fundamentalists like Jerry Falwell and
        John R. Rice.

457.   Nash, Ronald H., ed. The New Evangelicalism. Grand Rapids:
        Zondervan, 1963. 188 p.

        Carefully crafted insider presentation of neo-evangelicalism:
        its distinction from fundamentalism; its beliefs about the
        Bible, the church, and defense of the faith; and its critics.
        Bibliography. Index.   .

458.   "The New Evangelicals." Newsweek 84 (6 May 1974): 86.

459.   Oatley-Willis, B. R. "Neo-Evangelicalism in Missions." Reforma-
        tion Review 24 (January 1979): 21-35.

        Scattered comments indicting a number of faith mission agencies
        "in the New Evangelical orbit" for their willingness to
        compromise and thereby add confusion to the gospel.

460.   Ockenga, Harold John. "From Fundamentalism, Through New Evangel-
        icalism, To Evangelicalism." In Evangelical Roots: A Tribute to
        Wilbur Smith, ed. Kenneth S. Kantzer, 35-48. Nashville: Thomas
        Nelson, 1978.

The sequence of change from fundamentalism to evangelicalism by
one of the prime movers in the change.

461.   ____. "Resurgent Evangelical Leadership." Christianity Today
5 (10 October 1960): 11-15.

Cites persons, publications and organizations as indicators of
the resurgence, which must now continue through the principle
of infiltration (of society and the churches).

462.   Packer, James I., ed. "Fundamentalism" and the Word of God: Some
Evangelical Principles. Grand Rapids: Eerdmans, 1958. 191 p.

In a book influential in neo-evangelicalism, Packer says that
fundamentalism (better called evangelicalism) "is in principle
nothing but Christianity itself"; "authentic Christianity is a
religion of biblical authority" (which leads him into
discussions of the Bible, including inerrancy). Appendixes.
Bibliographical references. Index.

463.   "The Perils of Independency." Christianity Today 1 (12 November
1956): 20-23.

Though desiring to defend the orthodox faith by exalting Christ
and the Bible, independency tends to be divisive, has an
incorrect theology, and promotes unrestrained individualism.

464.   Pickering, Ernest. "New Evangelicalism Reviewed (A Book Review)."
Central Bible Quarterly 7 (Spring 1964): 1-10.

A very negative review by the Dean of Central Conservative
Baptist Seminary of an early presentation of the new evangelicalism, Ronald Nash's book, The New Evangelicalism (1963).

465.   ____. "The Present Status of the New Evangelicalism."
Central C. B. Quarterly 2 (Spring 1959): 1-4.

Discribes new evangelicalism's principles: lists many of the
leading persons, institutions and publications; urges
Christians everywhere to "resist it steadfastly" as lacking
"moral courage . . . doctrinal clarity," and as making
"unwarranted concessions." Reprinted in Reformation Review 7
(April 1960): 150-56.

466.   ____. "Should Fundamentalists & Evangelicals Seek Closer
Ties? An Evaluation of Edward Dobson's Book. 'In Search of
Unity.'" Discerner 12 (Summer 1986): 5-11.

Responds in the negative (but in what appears to be an irenic
spirit), because of a changing and more complex religious
scene, because of questions relating to separatism, because
evangelicals represent "a theological hodge-podge," and because
the road to unity necessitates cooperation with
pentecostal/charismatic Christians.

467.   Pratt, Raymond. "The Social Emphasis of New Evangelicalism."
         Central Bible Quarterly 21 (Winter 1978): 18-47.

Sees "the social application of the Gospel" as "a major tenet"
of the movement. Considers various areas such as racism and
ecology, examining both theory and practice.

468.   Price, Robert M. "Neo-Evangelicals and Scripture: A Forgotten
         Period of Ferment." Christian Scholars Review 15 (1986): 315-30.

Price's thesis, explored especially via E. J. Carnell, is that
"it was the neo-evangelical opening of the question of
inspiration and inerrancy that made possible the subsequent
young evangelical revolution."

469.   Pyles, Volie E. "'Bruised, Bloodied, and Broken': Fundamental-
         ism's Internecine Controversy in the 1960s." Fides et Historia 18
         (October 1986): 45-55.

Carl Henry (1947) and Harold John Ockenga (1957) issued calls
for social responsibility by the new evangelicals, creating an
uproar in the 1960s as fundamentalists dealt with how much
social involvement was proper for them, at the same time
sharpening the distinction between evangelicals and
fundamentalists.

470.   Russell, Alfred U. "A Polemic for Fundamentalism." Central C. B.
         Quarterly 3 (Winter 1960): 33-38.

After noting fundamentalism's "glorious heritage, rich in . . .
scholarship," he calls for separation, castigating the new
evangelicals for their attacks and their compromising.

471.   Sanasac, Rupert L. "The Basis of the New Evangelicalism."
         Central C. B. Quarterly 3 (Summer 1960): 27-32.

Discusses the purpose, precepts and program of the new
evangelicals.

472.   Shaw, James T. "Neo-Evangelicalism." Reformation Review 24
        (April 1979): 96-104.

        The failure of neo-evangelicalism is its unwillingness to
        follow the biblical doctrine of separation.

473.   Smith, Timothy L. "The Postfundamentalist Party." Christian
        Century 93 (4-11 February 1976): 125-27.

        Review of David F. Wells and John Woodbridge, eds., The
        Evangelicals (1975); the twelve essays in the book reveal the
        evangelical mosaic in its many parts, but do not answer the
        subtitle's questions.

474.   Stott, John R. W. "Are Evangelicals Fundamentalists?" Christi-
        anity Today 22 (8 September 1978): 44-46.

        Comments on James Barr, Fundamentalism (1977), pointing out
        Barr's polemical and poorly researched conclusions, and
        suggesting that evangelicals make more use of the Bible's
        double authorship (divine and human) than do fundamentalists.

475.   Tow, Siang Hwa. "Recent Trends in Evangelicalism." Reformation
        Review 28 (January 1983): 22-38.

        Evangelicals are moving toward neo-liberalism and neo-
        liberation as they get affected by ecumenism, the social
        gospel, charismatic renewal, and biblical errancy.

476.   Vanhetloo, Warren. "A Study of Modernism as a Method." Central
        C. B. Quarterly 2 (Spring 1959): 27-34.

        Presenting five "tendencies" (e.g., a de-emphasis on doctrine
        and an emphasis on experience), he applies them also to two
        "closely interrelated" groups, namely new evangelicalism and
        "Ecumenical-Interdenominationalism." Charts.

477.   Walhout, E. "Liberal-Fundamentalist Debate." Christianity Today
        7 (1 March 1963): 3-4.

        Liberalism's strength is its obedience to the Cultural Mandate,
        fundamentalism's its obedience to the Great Commission: both
        obediences are necessary in carrying out Christian missions.

478.   Williams, J. B. "The Dangers of New Evangelicalism." Faith for
        the Family 9 (January 1981): 4-6, 14.

Good example of the militant fundamentalist approach to
evangelicalism, including an eight-point list of where the
compromise between evangelicalism and liberalism is leading.

479.   Woodbridge, Charles J. The New Evangelicalism. Greenville: Bob
         Jones University, 1969. 62 p.

From the most erudite of the fundamentalist opponents, a survey
of the background of the new evangelicalism, and its mood,
method, theology, and ethics; to demonstrate that it "is a
theological and moral compromise of the deadliest sort."

480.   Young, Warren C. "Whither Evangelicalism?" Bulletin of the
         Evangelical Theological Society 2 (Winter 1959): 5-15.

In his ETS presidential address in 1958, Young describes
"tendencies" in evangelicalism: "toward an understanding of
theology as an experiential as well as a rational discipline";
"to listen to what science has to say about man"; "to restudy
the problem of communications in the light of modern
semantics"; and, "to reconsider and restate our understanding
of the doctrine of revelation."

See also items 271, 360, 771, 856, 867, 872, 1047, 1062, 1087, 1210, 1249,
    1253, 1255, 1330, 1331, 1333, 1356, 1372, 1374, 1418, 1509, 1604, 1639,
    1784, 1800, 1811, 1837, 1870, 1880.

G.   Young/Radical Evangelicalism

481.   Bedell, Kenneth B. "Young Evangelicals in the 19th and 20th
         Centuries." Review of Religious Research 30 (March 1989): 255-61.

Challenges James Hunter's view that young evangelicals in their
left-liberal political activism derive from an appearance of
New Class. Analysis of articles in the 1890s journal For the
Right reveals the presence of a group of young evangelicals
without the benefit of New Class.

482.   "A Conversation with Young Evangelicals." Post American 4
         (January 1975): 6-13.

Nineteen representatives of the young evangelicals give a
variety of opinions on social conscience, political involvement
and their understanding of the faith.

483.   Dayton, Donald W. "Updating the 'Young Evangelicals.'" Other
        Side 15 (January 1979): 28-33.

        Review of Richard Quebedeaux's The Worldly Evangelicals (1978);
        Dayton finds the book "frustrating and puzzling, not only in
        itself, but even more for the responses it is evoking from
        various quarters."

484.   _____. "Where Now Young Evangelicals?" Other Side 11 (March-
        April 1975): 30-37, 54-56.

        In contrast to "older" evangelicals, young evangelicals seem
        agreed on a more extensive belief in the cultural conditioning
        of the Bible, on the need for more social witness and
        involvement, on an interest in ecumenism and in the
        indigenization of theology.

485.   De Gruchy, John W. "The Great Evangelical Reversal: South African
        Reflections." Journal of Theology for Southern Africa 24
        (September 1978): 45-57.

        Distinguishes five types of evangelicals on the American scene,
        one of which, radical evangelicals (those interested in social
        involvement), has implications for the way Southern African
        evangelicals operate amidst black-white tensions.

486.   Dobson, Edward, and Edward E. Hindson. "Drifting Evangelicalism."
        Fundamentalist Journal 2 (February 1983): 12-13.

        The left wing of evangelicalism ("young" and "worldly" in
        Quebedeaux's terms) has moved so far "from orthodox roots that
        it is naive even to retain the term 'evangelical'" to describe
        them.

487.   Dockery, David S. "Does Your Evangelical Heritage and Theology
        Create Radical Christian Commitment?" Sojourners 5 (April 1976):
        15-18.

        Five respondents say their evangelical heritage sustains only
        in part their radical commitment.

488.   Gallagher, Sharon. "Radical Evangelicalism: A Conference Report."
        Radical Religion 1 (Summer/Fall 1974): 61-65.

489.   Knapp. Stephen C. "Radical Evangelicals: Who are They? And Where
        in the World are They Headed?" Other Side 15 (January 1979):
        34-39.

Uses Peter Berger's concepts of modernization and demodern-
ization to debate some of Quebedeaux's understanding of worldliness in his The Worldly Evangelicals (1978), and to explain
some of the cultural attitudes of fundamentalists, new
evangelicals and radical evangelicals.

490.   Lane, Bill. "New Directions For the Church. " Post American 2
        (January-February 1973): 4-5.

        Keep the correct doctrinal beliefs, but do not abandon the
        helpless, nor be content with the status quo in government and
        business, nor forsake the role of servant for power and
        influence.

491.   Lyra, Synesio, Jr. "The Rise and Development of the Jesus
        Movement." Calvin Theological Journal 8 (April 1973): 40-61.

        The constituent elements of the Jesus movement (hippie
        lifestyle, fundamentalistic mentality, and charismatic zeal),
        descriptions of its leaders and organizations, and a critical
        analysis of its theology and practices.

492.   MacKay, John A. "Toward an Evangelical Renaissance." Christi-
        anity Today 16 (4 February 1972): 6-8.

        Sees hopeful signs that the renaissance has begun.

493.   Marty, Martin E. "A Taxonomy of the Born-Again." Christian
        Century 95 (4 October 1978): 924-30.

        Marty characterizes Quebedeaux's The Worldly Evangelicals
        (1978) as a "very useful and informative analysis," flawed,
        however, by his "confusion of two categories of worldliness
        throughout the book," and by the quagmire of categories.

494.   McCune, Rolland D. "Second Generation New Evangelicals." Central
        Bible Quarterly 17 (Winter 1974): 2-15.

        A review of Richard Quebedeaux's The Young Evangelicals (1974):
        highly negative, from a fundamentalist perspective, reviewing
        its history, view of the Bible, evangelism, and a number of
        social issues.

495.   Moellering, Ralph L. "New Evangelicals." Currents in Theology
        and Mission 5 (April 1978): 110-15.

Positive appraisal of the "young evangelicals" of the 1970s,
who have overcome the dichotomy between social and spiritual
ministry, moved out of the isolation that pervades mainline
evangelicals, and applied modern scholarship to the Bible
without suffering doctrinal loss.

496.   Mounce, Robert. "Why Criticize Evangelicals?" Eternity 22
         (September 1971): 43, 51.

         Answers a reader's question: "Why are so many of the articles
         in Eternity critical of evangelical Christianity?" Answer
         includes: The nature of social movements/institutions is to
         grow, adding extraneous matter and complexity; it is healthy to
         evaluate in order to "redirect ourselves to the essentials of
         biblical faith."

497.   Pinnock, Clark H. "Charismatic Renewal for the Radical Church."
         Post American 4 (February 1975): 16-21.

         Both charismatics and radical Christians need to take seriously
         the full list of gifts in the New Testament to create a healing
         and reconciling community "such as we have never seen before."

498.   Price, Robert M. "A Fundamentalist Social Gospel?" Christian
         Century 96 (28 November 1979): 1183-86.

         Applauds the evangelical social awakening, but accuses some
         young evangelicals of "hermeneutical ventriloquism" (getting
         Bible-text support for one's thinking; e.g., biblical feminism)
         or "political snake-handling" (following the Bible radically
         without reference to political realities; e.g., the Sojourners
         community).

499.   Quebedeaux, Richard. "The Evangelicals: New Trends and New
         Tensions." Christianity and Crisis 36 (20 September 1976):
         197-202.

         The young evangelicals (many of them named here) are
         symptomatic of the new views of the Bible, social concerns,
         cultural attitudes, and ecumenical interests that characterize
         the trends and create the tensions.

500.   _____. The Worldly Evangelicals. San Francisco: Harper & Row,
         1978. 189 p.

         Argues that both the evangelical establishment (right and
         center evangelicalism) and radical/young evangelicalism (the

left) run the risk of too much influence from American culture,
but the evangelical left offers the greater hope for "pointing
the church as a whole in the right direction." Bibliography.
Index.

501.   . The Young Evangelicals: Revolution in Orthodoxy. New
York: Harper & Row, 1974. 157 p.

Written from within a movement for renewal that rejects both
separatist fundamentalism and mainstream ecumenical liberalism.
Biblically based, and with evangelism and social Christianity
as central concerns. Written just before the full re-emergence
of evangelicalism. Bibliographical references. "Suggestions
for Further Reading."

502.   Rogers, Jack B. "Confessions of a Post-Conservative Evangelical."
Reformed Journal 23 (February 1973): 10-13.

Comments on and illustrations of his hypothesis: "Evangelicals
are not consistently biblical when they approach social
problems."

503.   Sider, Ronald J. "A Plea for More Radical Conservatives and More
Conserving Radicals." In The Evangelical Round Table. Eastern
College and Eastern Baptist Theological Seminary (St. Davids, PA,
1986). Evangelicalism: Surviving Its Success, moderator Kenneth
Kantzer, editor David A. Fraser, 168-78. Princeton: Princeton
University Press, 1987.

At a time of unequalled possibilities, evangelicalism is
characterized, in Sider's view, by conflicts that threaten to
destroy its "historic opportunity." He suggests three
countermeasures: "acknowledging each other's strengths";
attending to precise areas of political disagreement; and, "a
new covenant of integrity."

504.   . "What's in Store for '74? Evangelical Churches."
Christian Century 91 (2 January 1974): 12-13.

Social involvement, evangelism, and social action are in store.

505.   Stephens, W. Richard. "The Evangelical Christian and the
Military-Industrial-Educational Complex." Fides et Historia 3
(Fall 1970): 4-21.

Reviewing the relation of the military to industry, and the
role of the schools in militarism, he concludes that, moved by

our faith and by "the peril of our times," evangelical
Christians must be made "deeply aware of the problem of
militarism" and must be urged to "active commitment to its
eradication from our schools and our way of life."

506. Tholin, Richard, and Lane T. Dennis. "Radical Evangelicals:
Challenge to Liberals and Conservatives." Explor 2 (Fall 1976):
3-54.

"Doctrinally conservative Christians who uphold radical views
of the social-political scene"; defines "radical evangelicalism," presents a typology of the movement, examines its
practice, and discusses its relationship to the larger church
including the evangelical and the mainline churches.

507. Van Elderen, Marlin J. "Evangelicals and Liberals: Is There a
Common Ground?" Christianity and Crisis 34 (8 July 1974): 151-55.

Interweaves comments on Quebedeaux's The Young Evangelicals
(1974) with the social concerns that might be common ground for
liberals and evangelicals, but concert between the two is a
long way off.

508. Wallis, Jim. Agenda for Biblical People. New edition. San
Francisco: Harper & Row, 1984. 109 p.

Revision of Wallis' 1976 book, the most widely-known statement
of the social outlook of the "young" or "radical" evangelicals;
by the editor of Sojourners magazine. Bibliography. Indexes.

509. _____. "The New Evangelicalism." Chicago Theological Seminary
Register 68 (Winter 1978): 7-15.

Discusses the reemergence of evangelical Christianity into the
mainstream of American culture; the impact of acceptance upon
the movement (it is "coming apart, just when it has been
discovered"); its social stance; its emphasis upon conversion,
but of an often diluted sort; and the possibility of major
prophetic social impact.

510. _____. "'New Evangelicals' and the Demands of Discipleship."
Christian Century 91 (29 May 1974): 581-82.

The "characteristically comfortable relationship between the
evangelical churches, and the political and economic status
quo, is being seriously challenged by the growing evangelical
insurgency."

511. _____. "Post-American Christianity." Post American 1 (Fall
1971): 2-3.

An appeal for radical Christians to move away from "the
church's accommodation to non-Christian ways" by speaking out
against corrupt values and injustice in society.

See also items 60, 124, 468, 644, 671, 952, 970, 1031, 1047, 1283, 1625,
1637, 1992.

H. The American South

512.   Boles, John B. The Great Revival, 1787-1805: The Origins of the
         Southern Evangelical Mind. Lexington: University of Kentucky
         Press, 1972. 236 p.

         Rejecting the popular impression of the revival as combining an
         "emotionally charged populace with a frightening theology,"
         this revisionist work sees the origins of the revival in the
         complex intellectual world of the evangelicals, especially the
         "central belief structure" of "Providence, repentance, and
         prayer," creating "a watershed in the religious history of the
         South." Seventeen-page bibliography. Index.

513.   _____, ed. Masters and Slaves in the House of the Lord: Race
         and Religion in the American South, 1740-1840. Lexington:
         University of Kentucky Press, 1988. 257 p.

514.   Calhoon, Robert M. Evangelicals and Conservatives in the Early
         South, 1740-1861. Columbia: University of South Carolina Press,
         1988. 242 p.

         Sees "the manifest progression of evangelicals and conser-
         vatives from conflict to independent action to collaboration
         . . . . Around the edge of that movement of events and beliefs
         --and sometimes in the center of action--will appear the church
         people and politicians who were not so sure they had a fix on
         each other." Thirty-one pages of notes. Index.

515.   Crowther, Edward Riley. "Southern Protestants, Slavery and
         Secession: A Study in Religious Ideology, 1830-1861." Ph.D.
         diss., Auburn University, 1986. 403 p.

516.   Faust, Drew Gilpin. "Evangelicalism and the Meaning of the Pro-
         slavery Argument: The Reverend Thornton Stringfellow of Virginia."
         Virginia Magazine of History and Biography 85 (January 1977):
         3-17.

Baptist Stringfellow (1788-1869). a slaveholder. saw slavery as God-given, and the salvation of slaves a necessity--items that Faust relates not to social control but to the southern evangelicals' belief system.

517.   Harrell, David Edwin, Jr., ed. Varieties of Southern Evangelicalism. Macon, GA: Mercer University Press, 1981. 114 p.

"Essays . . . written by the participants in the Fourth Annual Hugo Black Symposium held at the University of Alabama in Birmingham in 1979," on historical roots and general beliefs, Billy Graham, and the national context of Southern evangelicalism. Bibliographical references.

518.   Hill, Samuel S., Jr. "Fundamentalism and the South." Perspectives on Religious Studies 13 (Winter 1986): 47-65.

More evangelical than fundamentalist, religion in the South has four parties in it, each emphasizing a different characteristic: truth (correct belief; here is where the fundamentalists are); conversion (evangelism), spirituality (personal walk), and service.

519.   _____, et al. Religion and the Solid South. Nashville: Abingdon, 1972. 208 p.

Five university professors look at the South's religion from historical, sociological, and anthropological points of view, arguing the "distinctiveness of religious life in the South," the domination of the region by evangelical Protestantism, and "religion as conservator and reinforcer of, . . . popular (white) southern culture." Bibliographical references.

520.   _____. The South and the North in American Religion. Athens: University of Georgia Press, 1980. 152 p.

Analysis of the two regions at three different points in their history: 1795-1810, 1835-1850 and 1885-1900; shows the divergences present and the lack of interaction between the two. An essay in regionalism rather than a full-blown historical study. Notes.

521.   Holifield. E. Brooks. The Gentleman Theologians: American Theology in Southern Culture. 1795-1860. Durham. NC: Duke University Press, 1978. 262 p.

The admitted minority of Southern clergy, mostly urban, who
were educated and who tried to establish orthodox Christianity
on a reasoned foundation; contrast to stereotypical Southern
preacher as a person only of feeling and biblicism. Forty-five
pages of bibliographical references. Indexes.

522.   Kuykendall, John W. Southern Enterprise: The Work of National
        Evangelical Societies in the Antebellum South. Westport, CT:
        Greenwood Press, 1982. 188 p.

523.   Loveland, Anne C. Southern Evangelicals and the Social Order,
        1800-1860. Baton Rouge: Louisiana State University Press, 1980.
        293 p.

        Explores the southern evangelicals' justification of, and
        implied critiques of, slavery. Bibliography. Index.

524.   Mathews, Donald G. "Religion and Slavery: The Case of the
        American South." In Anti-Slavery, Religion, and Reform: Essays in
        Honor of Roger Anstey, eds. Bolt and Drescher, 207-32. Hamden,
        CT: Archon Books, 1980.

        Suggests that "religion and slavery can be understood equally
        well by looking at slaveholders as well as abolitionists, by
        looking at slaves as well as masters"; the looks reveal that
        "Southern evangelicalism . . . sustained slaves as well as
        slaveholders."

525.   _____. Religion in the Old South. Chicago: University of
        Chicago Press, 1977. 274 p.

        Positive on evangelicals. A volume in the Chicago History of
        American Religion series that characterizes evangelicalism in
        the antebellum South from the Revolution to the Civil War in
        the context of black appropriation of and measurement of that
        evangelicalism. Note on sources; bibliographical references.

526.   Parker, Harold M., Jr. The United Synod of the South: The
        Southern New School Presbyterian Church. Westport, CT: Greenwood,
        1988. 347 p.

        History of the New School experience in the South, embodied in
        the United Synod (1858-1863) and its antecedents, described
        chronologically and thematically. Appendixes. Twenty-page
        bibliography. Index.

527.   Thompson, James J., Jr. "New South, Old Religion." New Oxford
        Review 55 (June 1988): 5-14.

        Lengthy description of southern fundamentalism and its
        incongruous juxtaposition with the forward-looking sunbelt
        South.

528.   Wilson, Charles Reagan. Baptized in Blood: The Religion of the
        Lost Cause, 1865-1920. Athens: University of Georgia Press, 1980.
        256 p.

        Aided and abetted by evangelical denominations, the Lost Cause
        idea--that the (white) South, though defeated in the Civil War,
        still had a transcendent identity separate from the rest of the
        nation--became a civil religion in the former Confederacy.
        Twenty-one-page bibliography. Index.

See also items 173, 185, 186, 413, 708, 715, 717, 878, 1051, 1053, 1060,
        1168, 1178, 1182, 1300, 1359, 1360, 1470, 1517, 1533, 1534, 1535, 1536,
        1538, 1540, 1545, 1546, 1547, 1549, 1553, 1554, 1582, 1585, 1587, 1660,
        1665, 1669, 1715, 1753, 1769, 1775, 1786, 1866, 1878, 1879, 1948, 1956,
        1958, 1970, 1983, 1997, 2059, 2104, 2264, 2290, 2525, 2536, 2546, 2558.

                            I.   Great Britain

529.   Balda, Wesley D. "Ecclesiastics and Enthusiasts: The Evangelical
        Emergence in England, 1760-1800." Historical Magazine of the
        Protestant Episcopal Church 49 (September 1980): 221-31.

        Distinguishes evangelicals (revivalists loyal to the Church of
        England) from Methodists--"Wesley's more unruly and
        enthusiastic preachers" who disregarded the parochial system.
        Helpful to American evangelicalism as one kind of reaction to
        Methodist evangelicals.

530.   _____. "Simeon's 'Protestant Baptists': A Sampling of Moderate
        Evangelicalism Within the Church of England, 1839-1865." Fides et
        Historia 16 (Fall/Winter 1983): 55-67.

        Amends the common picture of the combative, doctrinally rigid
        Victorian evangelical by showing the moderate stance of the
        heirs of Charles Simeon (d. 1836), which means "that some of
        the most cherished Victorian stereotypes of evangelicalism
        cannot be sustained."

531.   Balleine, George Reginald. A History of the Evangelical Party in
        the Church of England. London, New York: Longmans, Green, 1911.
        230 p.

        One of the first surveys of the evangelical party in the Church
        of England; Balleine tells the story from the early 18th to the
        later 19th centuries. Bibliographies. Index.

532.   Barabas, Steven. So Great Salvation: The History and Message of
        the Keswick Convention. With a foreword by Fred Mitchell.
        London: Marshall, Morgan & Scott, 1952. 207 p.

        The standard text, from an insider, on the history and methods
        of Keswick, a detailed analysis of the sequence of teaching at
        a typical Keswick week, and brief sketches of nine of the early
        leaders. Bibliography.

533.   Baring-Gould, Sabine. The Evangelical Revival. London: Methuen,
        1920. 360 p.

        A non-evangelical Anglican takes a detailed and sardonic look
        at Anglican and dissenting evangelicals from the time of Wesley
        and Whitefield to WWI. Scattered references. Index.

534.   Bebbington, David W. Evangelicalism in Modern Britain: A History
        from the 1730s to the 1980s. Winchester, MA: Unwin Hyman, 1989.
        320 p.

        A "newly researched historical study of Evangelical religion"
        from its beginnings in the time of Wesley to the present
        charismatic renewal; it shows the great impact of the
        Evangelical movement on nineteenth-century Britain, accounts
        for its resurgence since the Second World War and argues that
        developments in the ideas and attitudes of the movement were
        shaped most by changes in British culture."

535.   _____. "The Gospel in the Nineteenth Century." Vox Evangelica
        13 (1983): 19-28.

        Description of evangelicals in the British Isles, with passing
        reference to the United States; influence on the United States
        because of the transatlantic nature of much of the nineteenth
        century evangelicalism.

536.   Bennett, Arthur. "Charles Simeon: Prince of Evangelicals."
        Churchman 102, no. 2 (1988): 122-42.

Seeks to make a new approach. "delineating the spiritual
forces" that motivated and made for the greatness of one who
was at once among the most influential of evangelicals and of
Church of England clergymen across the history of those
movements.

537.   _____. "The Spiritual Life and Ministry of Charles Simeon."
Banner of Truth no. 223 (June 1986): 6-11.

The first of a series about an influential evangelical
churchman who has been largely forgotten, particularly as
regards his spirituality.

538.   Best, G. F. A. "The Evangelicals and the Established Church in
the Early 19th Century." Journal of Theological Studies 10 (April
1959): 63-78.

Anglican evangelicals were viewed by other Anglicans with
suspicion because they faced two matters with ambiguity--how
far they should go in cooperating with Dissenters (they saw
both right and wrong in cooperation) and whether or not they
were Calvinists (they were widely accused of so being, and
thereby adversely affecting the parish system).

539.   Bradley, Ian C. The Call to Seriousness: The Evangelical Impact
on the Victorians. New York: Macmillan, 1976. 224 p.

Treats Anglican evangelicalism, 1800-1860, "when the influence
of Evangelicalism was at its height," dominated first by
Wilberforce (d. 1833), then by Shaftesbury (d. 1885), and when
it was "essentially a dynamic movement and the influence it
exerted on society was, on the whole, a positive one."
Bibliographical references. Index.

540.   Brown, C. G. "Divided Loyalties? The Evangelicals, The Prayer
Book and the Articles." Historical Magazine of the Protestant
Episcopal Church 44 (June 1975): 189-209.

Argues that the Anglican evangelicals of the late 18th and
early 19th centuries made good use of the prayer book. and
their moderate Calvinism fit well with the Thirty-Nine
Articles.

541.   The Christian Treasury: Containing Contributions from Ministers
and Members of Various Evangelical Denominations. Edinburgh:
Johnstone, Hunter, 1863. 614 p.

542.   Clegg, Herbert. "Evangelicals and Tractarians." Historical
            Magazine of the Protestant Episcopal Church. Part 1 in vol. 35
            (June 1966): 111-53. Part 2 in vol. 35 (September 1966): 237-94.
            Part 3 in vol. 36 (June 1967): 127-78.

            Investigates the links between the two movements in the early
            19th century and the breaking of those links; argues that the
            two movements were much closer to each other than has been
            generally supposed, diverging in the early 1830s; Clegg
            attempts to set forth the points of agreement and reasons for
            the subsequent divergence.

543.   Clifford, Alan. "The Christian Mind of Philip Doddridge (1702-
            1751): The Gospel According to an English Congregationalist."
            Evangelical Quarterly 56 (October 1984): 227-42.

            Famed hymnwriter Doddridge, noted for his charity with others,
            was a man of strong doctrinal convictions who tempered his
            ecumenism (seen in his opposition to Roman Catholicism) with a
            thoroughly evangelical orthodoxy.

544.   _____. "The Reasons for Past Failure of Evangelical Unity."
            Churchman 101, no. 3 (1987): 227-50.

            Review of the historical developments from the Reformation
            which have produced disunity among evangelicals, centering on
            the issue of separation, and a call for English evangelicals to
            work at a visible unity of their denominations.

545.   Cragg, George G. Grimshaw of Haworth: A Study in Eighteenth
            Century Evangelicalism. Foreword by Thomas Bloomer. London:
            Canterbury Press, 1947. 128 p.

            A study of an 18th century evangelical in the Church of
            England. Grimshaw (d. 1763), parish minister at Haworth,
            England, had ties to Wesley and Whitefield, and was himself
            part of the evangelical revival. Bibliography. Index.

546.   Crooks, George R. "The Evangelical Revival in its Relation to
            Theology." Methodist Review 79 (1897): 177-94.

547.   Davies, George Colliss Boardman. The Early Cornish Evangelicals,
            1735-60: A Study of Walker of Truro and Others. London: S.P.C.K.,
            1951. 229 p.

            Concentrates on Samuel Walker (1714-1761), Calvinist, and
            committed to the local parish (contra the Wesleys), and his
            work of evangelical revival in Cornwall. Bibliography. Index.

548.   Derham, A. Morgan. "England: Evangelical Rain Amid Drought."
         Eternity 27 (December 1976): 22-25, 36, 39, 43.

         An interview with Derham, "one of the keenest observers of the
         evangelical scene in England." Discusses the role of indi-
         viduals (e.g., C. S. Lewis, Billy Graham), denominations, and
         various other questions including American influence in
         general.

549.   Duffield, Gervase. "Amber to Green." Frontier 9 (Summer 1966):
         119-22.

         Doubts whether evangelicals in Britain will form a "United
         Evangelical Church."

550.   _____. "New Evangelical Impetus in England." International
         Reformed Bulletin (October 1964): 12-16.

         The new impetus derives from two recently founded evangelical
         publishing houses, the significance of which he describes in
         the historical and contemporary religious context in Britain.

551.   Elliott-Binns, L. E. The Early Evangelicals: A Religious and
         Social Study. Greenwich, CT: Seabury Press, 1953. 464 p.

         Thorough study of eighteenth-century Anglican evangelicals
         including Methodists. Bibliographical references. Index.

552.   Farley, Ian David. "J. C. Ryle--Episcopal Evangelist: A Study in
         Late Victorian Evangelicalism." Ph.D. diss., University of Durham
         (United Kingdom), 1988. 444 p.

553.   Finlayson, R. A. "How Liberal Theology Infected Scotland."
         Banner of Truth no. 156 (September 1976): 24-28.

         Impact of German theology during the second half of the 19th
         century, first in the Free Church colleges and then rapidly
         through the ministry of the Free Church.

554.   Forster, Roger, ed. Ten New Churches. London: MARC Europe;
         Middlesex: British Church Growth Association. 1986. 176 p.

         Evangelical churches from several denominations in Britain that
         began in the 1970s and 1980s. Forster notes common threads in
         their development. Index.

555.   Hennell, Michael. "The Churchman in the Context of Victorian
        Evangelicalism." Churchman 93, no. 1 (1979): 19-28.

        Begun in 1879, the Churchman was the voice of Anglican
        evangelicalism, emphasizing church work in the towns, overseas
        missionary work and theological issues.

556.   _____. Sons of the Prophets: Evangelical Leaders of the
        Victorian Church. London: S.P.C.K., 1979. 147 p.

        The theological "sons" of Charles Simeon and William
        Wilberforce, these six Anglican evangelicals of the mid-19th
        century demonstrate the vitality of the movement and its
        interest in social reform and overseas missions. Bibliography.
        Index.

557.   Holladay, J. Douglas. "English Evangelicalism, 1820-1850:
        Diversity and Unity in 'Vital Religion.'" Historical Magazine of
        the Protestant Episcopal Church 51 (June 1982): 147-57.

        The evangelical role in humanitarian reform, 1823-1847; the
        values underlying the reform camgaigns; the arguments used to
        promote the objectives of the campaigns.

558.   Hopkinson, Bill. "Changes in the Emphases of Evangelical Belief
        1970-80: Evidence From New Hymnody." Churchman 95, no. 2 (1981):
        123-18.

        Sees "significant changes" in this study of nine British song
        and hymn books (with theme tables appended), which show "strong
        new emphases suggesting a fresh expression of God's saving
        activity."

559.   Hylson-Smith, Kenneth. Evangelicals in the Church of England,
        1734-1984. Edinburgh: T. & T. Clark, 1988. 411 p.

        The first extensive study since Balleine's in 1908; discusses
        origins, growth, influence, scholarship, literature, preaching,
        social action and missions, among numerous subjects.
        Fourteen-page bibliography. Indexes.

560.   Jay, Elizabeth, ed. The Evangelical and Oxford Movements.
        Cambridge: University Press, 1983. 219 p.

        Selections from four evangelicals (including Simeon) and four
        tractarians (including Newman). Helpful introductory essay.
        Bibliographies.

561.   Jeffrey, David Lyle. ed. A Burning and A Shining Light: English
        Spirituality in the Age of Wesley. Grand Rapids: Eerdmans, 1987.
        517 p.

            Selections from 18th century spiritual writing, focusing upon
            evangelicals. Bibliographical references.

562.   Lawrence, Albert Sumner. "Evangelical Anglicanism and the
        Ministry of Preaching." D.Min. diss., Luther Northwestern
        Theological Seminary, MN, 1979. 199 p.

563.   Loane, Marcus Lawrence. Cambridge and the Evangelical Succession.
        London: Lutterworth, 1952. 276 p.

            Demonstrates through biographical studies the succession of
            five 18th and 19th century Cambridge evangelicals: William
            Grimshaw, John Berridge, Henry Venn, Charles Simeon, and Henry
            Martyn. Bibliography. Index.

564.   _____. Makers of Our Heritage: A Study of Four Evangelical
        Leaders. London: Hodder & Stoughton, 1967. 191 p.

            Four evangelical leaders in the Church of England: John Charles
            Ryle; Handley Carr Glyn Moule; Edmund Arbuthnott Knox; Howard
            West Kilvinton Mowil; covering the years 1816 to 1958.
            Bibliography. Index.

565.   MacLeod, A. Donald. "The Way Ahead for Anglican Evangelicals."
        Churchman 102, no. 4 (1988): 325-35.

            Though secession is not an immediate duty, Anglican evangeli-
            cals should so order their lives on behalf of the Gospel that
            they are willing to face separation from the Church of England
            for the sake of the church in England.

566.   MacLeod, John. "Religious Movements of the Past Century in
        England, 1830-1930." Bibliotheca Sacra 87 (October 1930): 405-22.

            Survey of the various groups in the churches in England. with
            special emphasis on the evangelicals. both establishment and
            dissenters.

567.   Manwaring, Randle. From Controversy to Co-Existence: Evangelicals
        in the Church of England. Cambridge. England: Cambridge
        University Press. 1985. 227 p.

Retrenched between the two world wars, Anglican evangelicalism
in recent decades has emphasized scholarship, social involvement, and ecumenism; but it still has an identity problem, and
right, center, and left wings. Bibliography. Index.

568.   McConnell, Francis John. Evangelicals, Revolutionists and Ideal-
ists: Six English Contributors to American Thought and Action.
New York, Nashville: Abingdon-Cokesbury, 1942. 184 p.

The six: William Wilberforce (1759-1833), James Edward
Oglethorpe (1696-1785), Charles Wesley (1707-1788), George
Whitefield (1714-1770), Thomas Paine (1737-1809), and George
Berkeley (1685-1753).

569.   Poole-Conner, E. J. Evangelicalism in England. Rev. ed. London:
Henry E. Walter, 1966. 297 p.

A long look, covering the 15th through the 20th centuries, at
both establishment and dissenting evangelicalism in England.
First published in 1951. Bibliographical references.

570.   Rennie, Ian Scott. "Evangelicalism and English Public Life 1923-
1950." Ph.D. diss., University of Toronto (Canada), 1963. 417 p.

571.   Reynolds, John Stewart. The Evangelicals at Oxford, 1735-1871: A
Record of an Unchronicled Movement, With the Record Extended to
1905. Appleford, England: Marcham Manor Press, 1975. 212, 136 p.

Originally published, Oxford: Blackwell, 1953 (212 p.).
Account of "the consecutive history of evangelicalism at
Oxford," creating a small but strong school of thought,
influential both at Oxford and in the wider religious world.
Biographical appendix of over one hundred Oxford evangelicals.
Bibliography. Index. The section on the years after 1871 has
an additional biographical appendix, bibliography, and index.

572.   Sachs, William Lewis. "Improving the Time: The Worldview of
Activist Evangelicalism in England, 1785-1833." Ph.D. diss., The
University of Chicago, 1981. 229 p.

573.   Sheehan, R. J. "The Decline of Evangelicalism in Nineteenth-
Century England." Banner of Truth no. 278 (November 1986): 15-22.

A consideration of six factors contributing to the decline,
with a brief listing of conclusions.

574.   Toon, Peter. The Anglican Way: Evangelical and Catholic. Wilton,
        CT: Morehouse-Barlow, 1983. 94 p.

575.   _____. "Evangelicals and Tractarians: Then and Now."
        Churchman 93, no. 1 (1979): 29-38.

        Tractarians (Anglo-Catholics) and evangelical Anglicans have
        had a number of common interests and common enemies, but they
        do not agree on a number of important doctrinal and liturgical
        matters; in recent years, evangelicals have grown stronger and
        Anglo-Catholics weaker.

576.   _____. "The Nature of Evangelicalism: An Anglican Perspec-
        tive." Reformed Journal 24 (December 1974): 24-27.

        Recounting of three times in the last century when Anglican
        evangelicals attempted to define or re-define their name, out
        of which efforts Toon draws a list of common principles.

577.   Voll, Dieter. Catholic Evangelicalism: The Acceptance of
        Evangelical Traditions by the Oxford Movement During the Second
        Half of the Nineteenth Century; A Contribution Towards the
        Understanding of Recent Anglicanism. Translated by Veronica
        Ruffer. London: Faith Press, 1963. 150 p.

578.   Webster, Douglas. "Evangelicalism and the Ecumenical Movement."
        Ecumenical Review 6 (July 1954); 385-89.

        Centering on the English context, notes the close ties, both
        theologically and historically, because of the roots of the
        Ecumenical Movement in the missionary movement of the 19th
        century and thus in the Evangelical Revival.

See also items 5, 30, 85, 121, 134, 150, 164, 170, 184, 217, 220, 237, 238,
    242, 273, 293, 294, 345, 375, 376, 396, 407, 640, 677, 756, 822, 827,
    833, 840, 844, 849, 866, 868, 870, 957, 989, 990, 997, 999, 1002,
    1004, 1005, 1057, 1064, 1078, 1081, 1099, 1124, 1143, 1166, 1167, 1171,
    1176, 1177, 1187, 1190, 1229, 1251, 1281, 1296, 1303, 1329, 1334, 1352,
    1355, 1432, 1433, 1441, 1447, 1460, 1469, 1548, 1771, 1792, 1854, 2017,
    2499, 2509, 2510, 2511, 2513, 2514, 2517, 2529, 2530, 2531, 2539, 2540,
    2543, 2581, 2600, 2637, 2653.

                J.   Outside the United States and Britain

579.   Adeyemo, Tokunboh. "African Evangelicals in the '80s." In
        Serving Our Generation: Evangelical Strategies for the Eighties,

ed. Waldron Scott, 31-45. Colorado Springs: World Evangelical
Fellowship, 1980.

Numerical growth along with serious problems; priorities
include contextualizing Christianity, developing a theology of
self-reliance, disciplemaking, and evangelizing, among others.

580.   Alvarez, Carmelo E. "Latin American Pentecostals: Ecumenicals and
Evangelicals." One in Christ 23, nos. 1-2 (1987): 93-97.

Most pentecostal churches (whether missionary, immigration, or
national) have been a divisive force, but five pentecostal
church organizations are trying to be ecumenical.

581.   Aren, Gustav. Evangelical Pioneers in Ethiopia: Origins of the
Evangelical Church Mekane Yesus. Stockholm, Sweden: EFS Forlaget;
Addis Ababa, Ethiopia: Evangelical Church Mekane Yesus, 1978.
486 p.

582.   "Bala 1969: A Correspondent Reports." Banner of Truth nos. 70-71
(July-August 1969): 35-36.

Report of the sessions of the annual Ministers' Conference of
the Evangelical Movement of Wales.

583.   Blocker, Jacques. "All-Africa Conference Put Under Evangelical
Scrutiny." Evangelical Missions Quarterly 6 (Spring 1970):
175-80.

The General Assembly of the All Africa Conference of Churches
(AACC), held in Abidjan, Ivory Coast, in September 1969;
praises the Conference but also criticizes it on several
counts.

584.   Bong, Rin Ro. "Basic Issues in the Asian Church." In Serving Our
Generation: Evangelical Strategies for the Eighties, ed. Waldron
Scott, 47-56. Colorado Springs: World Evangelical Fellowship,
1980.

Emphasizes the need for personal evangelism, leadership
development, lay training, contextualizing, and emphasis on
human rights.

585.   _____. "A Goal of ATA: Strengthen ETS: Eight Developing
Evangelical Theological Societies (ETS) in Asia." Asia
Theological News 15 (January-March 1989): 2-3.

Lists the three objectives adopted by the Asia Theological
Association for promoting evangelical theological education in
Asia. Listing of the various associations, their journals,
memberships, and presidents.

586.   ____. "Theological Trends in Asia: Asian Theology." Asia
Theological News 13 (October-December 1987): 2-3, 15-16.

An editorial by the Executive Secretary of Asia Theological
Association and Dean of Asia Graduate School of Theology.

587.   Bowers, Paul. "Evangelical Theology in Africa: Byang Kato's
Legacy." Evangelical Review of Theology 5 (April 1981): 35-39.

Reprinted from Trinity Journal 1 (1980), a brief analysis of
Kato's sole work, Theological Pitfalls in Africa (1975), in
which he warned that segments of African Christianity had moved
too far toward syncretism with traditional African religion.

588.   Boyd, Forrest J. "Evangelicals 'Up Front, Suddenly,' in Uruguay."
Christianity Today 22 (5 May 1978): 42-43.

Describes the impact of the Luis Palau evangelistic meetings
(spring 1978), not only in the large attendance and
conversions, but also as successfully penetrating politics,
education, business, and the media.

589.   Branson, Mark Lau, and C. Rene Padilla, eds. Conflict and
Context: Hermeneutics in the Americas. Grand Rapids: Eerdmans,
1986. 323 p.

Reports of a conference of North American and Latin American
scholars held in Mexico City, November 1983, sponsored by the
Latin American Theological Fraternity and the Theological
Students Fellowship; no consensus document produced, but good
initiating of discussion on hermeneutic issues. Bibliography.
References.

590.   Brusco, Elizabeth Ellen. "The Household Basis of Evangelical
Religion and the Reformation of Machismo in Colombia." Ph.D.
diss., City University of New York, 1986. 305 p.

591.   Carroll, R., M. Daniel, and Guillermo W. Mendez. "Another Voice
from Latin America: Concerned Evangelicals and the Challenge of a
Continent in Crisis." Modern Churchman New Series. 30. no. 4
(1980): 42-46.

Focuses on the contributions of one evangelical group, the
Latin American Theological Fellowship (LATF) (representative of
"the voice of millions of evangelicals"), which, since its
beginning in 1969, has sponsored various meetings and published
materials "at several levels."

592.   Cattell, Everett L. "Evangelical Cooperation in India." Asbury
         Seminarian 9 (Winter 1955): 42-46.

         A description of the work of the Evangelical Fellowship of
         India (EFI), begun four years earlier, and uniting evangelicals
         across denominational lines, with activities that include
         missions, literature and a theological seminary.

593.   Chao, Jonathan T'ien-en. "Evangelical Cooperation for Future
         Evangelization of China: [Phase One of a China Mission Strategy,
         1975-1995]." International Reformed Bulletin no. 61 (1975):
         73-80.

         The "dean designate" of the China Graduate School of Theology
         in Hong Kong, building on the assumption that there will be
         only gradual change in China during the following two decades
         and that those years ought to be spent in planning and
         preparation, suggests goals and basic strategies.

594.   Chow, Wilson W. "Biblical Foundations: An East Asian Study."
         Evangelical Review of Theology 7 (April 1983): 102-12.

         One of a series of four articles on "Biblical Foundations for
         Evangelical Theology in the Third World" (Latin America,
         Africa, South Asia, East Asia). Without breaking new ground,
     ·   "presents an evangelical position for the foundation of the
         evangelical theological task."

595.   Corwin, Charles. "Evangelicals and Human Action Systems."
         Evangelical Review of Theology 13 (July 1989): 264-73.

         The author, with extensive experience in Asian studies,
         addresses and answers the question: "'How should the
         evangelical church in non-Christian societies relate to those
         human action systems?'"

596.   Costas, Orlando E. "Evangelical Theology in the Two Thirds
         World." TSF Bulletin 8 (September-October 1985): 7-12.

         Based on documents from meetings in Thailand (March 1982),
         Korea (August 1982) and Mexico (June 1984), Costas argues that

two-thirds world evangelicals are divided from their one-third world colleagues in that the latter are still struggling with the theological implications of the Enlightenment while the former are coping with "the explosive social, economic, political, cultural and religious reality of most people in the world."

597.   d'Epinay, Christian LaLive. "Toward a Typology of Latin American Protestantism." Review of Religious Research 10 (Fall 1968): 4-11.

The traditional sociological concepts do not apply well in Latin America, where the processes of nationalization and acculturation are important determinants.

598.   De Chalandeau, Alexander. The Theology of the Evangelical Christians: Baptists in the USSR: As Reflected in the Bratskii Vestnik. Strasbourg, France: S.N., 1978. 311 p.

A Strasbourg Ph.D. dissertation (1978), on the history and theology of evangelicals in the Soviet Union as seen in their periodical, Brotherly Herald; by a descendant of Russian evangelicals. Bibliography.

599.   DePetrella, Lidia Susana Vaccaro. "The Tension Between Evangelism and Social Action in the Pentecostal Movement." International Review of Mission 75 (January 1986): 34-38,

A Church of God leader in Brazil, de Petrella gives seven reasons why "the tension . . . is gradually being overcome in our communities."

600.   Derham, A. Morgan. "Evangelical Perspectives in Western Europe." In Serving Our Generation: Evangelical Strategies for the Eighties, ed. Waldron Scott, 87-96. Colorado Springs: World Evangelical Fellowship, 1980.

An optimistic statement by the president of the European Evangelical Alliance. Stresses the need for unity and cooperation visibly expressed.

601.   Doyle, Barry, and Alan Swift. "Evangelicals in Quebec." Faith Today (November 1977): 6-25.

A three-part article: "The Quiet Revival." "Separatism is not a sin," and "The Forgotten Church," in a preliminary issue of a magazine "for the entire Christian Constituency of Canada."

602.   Emery, George N. "The Origins of Canadian Methodist Involvement
         in the Social Gospel Movement 1890-1914." Bulletin (1977),
         Journal of the Canadian Church Historical Society 19 (March-June
         1977): 104-19.

         Partly a manifestation of "the waning popularity of the
         Methodist evangelical tradition."

603.   Evangelical Witness in South Africa: A Critique of Evangelical
         Theology and Practice, by South African evangelicals. Grand
         Rapids: Eerdmans, 1986. 48 p.

         A document originally published in Transformation; here
         reprinted with a foreword by J. Deotis Roberts.

604.   "Evangelical Witness in South Africa: Evangelicals Critique Their
         Own Theology and Practice." Transformation 4 (January-March
         1987): 17-29.

         132 black evangelicals in South Africa issue a document
         addressed to the crisis in that nation, explaining the
         theological problems in evangelicalism, and relating
         evangelicalism to structural conformity, ecumenism, evangelism
         and missions, and radicalism.

605.   Faught, J. Harry. "The Evangelical Fellowship of Canada."
         Evangelical Christian (January 1966): 19.

         The chairman of the EFC briefly relates the history and
         activities of the group since its beginning in 1963, its
         spiritual purpose, and its hope for cooperative evangelical
         efforts.

606.   "The First Evangelical Conference of Latin America." Ecumenical
         Review 2 (Winter 1950): 179-83.

         Evangelicals from sixteen Latin American countries, along with
         visitors from France, Spain, and the United States, gathered
         (Buenos Aires July 1949), "for the purpose of strengthening the
         links of brotherhood, and of studying our common problem."
         Includes a "Message to Protestant Christians," and a "Declar-
         ation of the First Evangelical Conference of Latin America."

607.   Gehman, Richard J. "The Crisis in the Evangelical Church in
         Africa." Inland Africa (January-March 1977): 10-11.

The crisis is presented as the need for evangelicals of
scholarly stature, able to refute liberal teachings, including
an adequate number of trained pastors for the churches.

608. Genet, Harry. "Latin Evangelicals Chart Their Own Course."
Christianity Today 23 (7 December 1979): 44-46.

News report on the Second Latin American Congress on
Evangelization, Lima, Peru, November 1979, illustrating the
diversity of opinion among Latin evangelicals.

609. Grubb, Kenneth. "Evangelical Religion in Brazil." Frontier 3
(Autumn 1960): 220-23.

Upbeat picture of the evangelical presence in Brazil.

610. Harrison, Patricia J. "Theological Education by Extension--A
Lively Experiment in Latin America." Journal of Christian
Education 13 (October 1970): 113-24.

Arguing that this experiment may afford useful ideas "for an
equally bold advance elsewhere," she discusses the problems of
rapid growth and inadequate training facilities, the answer
that is in process of development, "The Question of Texts," and
some implications.

611. International Conference for Itinerant Evangelists. Amsterdam,
1983. The Work of an Evangelist: International Congress for
Itinerant Evangelists, Amsterdam, The Netherlands. J. D. Douglas,
ed. Minneapolis: World Wide Publications, 1984. 888 p.

Sponsored by the Billy Graham Association. Includes
representative addresses and workshop and seminar reports by
prominent evangelicals on subjects of significance to late
twentieth century evangelicalism. Bibliographical references.

612. Kato, Byang. "Creating Facilities for Evangelical Theological
Training in Africa." International Reformed Bulletin no. 64
(1976): 42-45.

The meaning of "evangelical," the current situation for
theological education in Africa, and suggestions for meeting
the need.

613. Kuzmic, Peter. "Evangelical Witness in Eastern Europe." In
Serving Our Generation: Evangelical Strategies for the Eighties.

ed. with an introduction by Waldron Scott, 77-85. Colorado
Springs: World Evangelical Fellowship, 1980.

Lacking both external power and contact with other evangelicals, their authentically Christian lives, informed by a
"theology of the cross," give them a unique opportunity to
function as a Christian alternative.

614.   Lernoux, Penny. "The Fundamentalist Surge in Latin America."
Christian Century 105 (20 January 1988): 51-54.

Describes the striking growth of conservative Protestant
groups, including the involvement of American fundamentalists.

615.   Mann, James. "A Global Surge of Old-Time Religion." U.S. News &
World Report 90 (27 April 1981): 38-40.

News report of the world-wide evangelical presence.

616.   Miguez-Bonino, Jose. "Our Debt as Evangelicals to the Roman
Catholic Community." Ecumenical Review 21 (October 1969): 310-19.

Describes the crisis of Catholicism in Latin America, and the
traditional relationship of evangelicals to Catholicism;
suggests the debt owed: love, admonition, and the proclamation
of the gospel.

617.   Nelson, Wilton M. "Evangelical Surge in Latin America."
Christianity Today 7 (19 July 1963): 5-8.

Using three early-1960s books Nelson charts the dramatic
increase of evangelical forces in the previous thirty-five
years.

618.   Nesdoly, Samuel J. "Among the Soviet Evangelicals." Banner of
Truth no. 270 (March 1986): 5-9, 15.

Report of late 20th century conditions and suggestions as to
how to be of help to Soviet evangelicals.

619.   Nunez, Emilio Antonio. "Evangelical Theology and Praxis for Latin
America." Evangelical Review of Theology 11 (April 1987): 107-19.

This final chapter of Nunez's book, Liberation Theology (1986),
calls for a clear commitment to evangelical theology (in
contrast to the non-evangelical nature of some liberation
theologies), coupled with an acted-out sense of social
responsibility.

620.   Nunez, Emilio Antonio, and William Taylor. Crisis in Latin
        America. Chicago: Moody Press, 1989. 439 p.

        Includes a brief historical sketch, an overview of Liberation
        Theology, and a summary of theological developments in the
        Roman Catholic and evangelical churches. Brief annotated
        bibliography. Index.

621.   Odunaike, Samuel. "Pentecostals, Evangelicals, Charismatics and
        the Evangelical Movement." In Serving Our Generation: Evangelical
        Strategies for the Eighties, ed. Waldron Scott, 267-81. Colorado
        Springs: World Evangelical Fellowship, 1980.

        A Nigerian layman discusses the relationship of pentecostal and
        charismatic Christians with each other and with the global
        evangelical movement.

622.   Parker, David D. "Deprogramming a Cult: James Barr and Funda-
        mentalism in Australia." Colloquium 17 (October 1984): 18-26.

        Mostly about the varied reception to Barr in Britain and
        America; the neglect in Australia of Barr's work results from
        his failure to assess fundamentalism in Australia as well as
        from the nature of fundamentalism there (described in Parker's
        1982 Ph.D. dissertation, "Fundamentalism and Conservative
        Protestantism in Australia, 1920-1980").

623.   _____. "The Evangelical Heritage of Australian Protestantism:
        Towards an Historical Perspective." Evangelical Quarterly 57
        (January 1985): 43-62.

        A two-hundred-year-old presence in Australia, evangelicalism
        flourishes currently in Protestant denominations and in
        para-church and other interdenominational agencies with the
        same kind of vitality and theological diversity seen in its
        American counterpart. Reprinted in Evangelical Review of
        Theology 11 (April 1987): 135-51.

624.   _____. "The Future of Australia's Evangelical Heritage."
        Evangelical Review of Theology 13 (January 1989): 49-60.

        Noting its effectiveness in the mid-19th century and at
        present, and defining Australian evangelicalism to include
        historical links, and to be marked by evangelism, foreign
        missions, pietism, the Puritan ethic, and doctrine. Parker
        discusses developments in the 1980s, and the future; the latter

will demand both "sophisticated skilful theology" and the
practical living out of the Gospel.

625. _____. "Theological and Bible College Education in Australia:
An Evangelical Perspective." 1. Historical Development. Journal
of Christian Education, no. 86 (July 1986): 5-18. 2. Contemporary
Trends. Journal of Christian Education, no. 87 (December 1986):
29-40.

A thorough report of the history and current practices of
theological and Bible education in Australia.

626. Perez, Pablo E. "Latin America: Hope and Reality." In Serving
Our Generation: Evangelical Strategies for the Eighties, ed.
Waldron Scott, 57-76. Colorado Springs: World Evangelical
Fellowship, 1980.

An analysis that centers on three major recent gatherings in
Latin America, and their implications for evangelicals during
the 1980s.

627. Phillips, Walter. "The Defence of Christian Belief in Australia
1875-1914: The Responses to Evolution and Higher Criticism."
Journal of Religious History 9 (December 1977): 402-23.

Though done in the Australian context, the solutions of
Australian churchmen were similar to those proposed in Britain,
showing "that Christianity and modern knowledge were not
necessarily incompatible."

628. Piggin, Stuart. "Towards a Bicentennial History of Australian
Evangelicalism." Journal of Religious History 15 (June 1988):
20-37.

"Offers reflexions and a preliminary sythesis for a projected
bicentennial history of Australian evangelicalism." Includes a
projected outline for the full history.

629. Pike, Richard. "Evangelicalism in Bermuda: A Report from Richard
Pike." Banner of Truth no. 72 (September 1969): 27-28.

A rather negative evaluation from a Reformed clergyman's
perspective.

630. Richard, John. "Evangelical Fellowship of Asia and Theological
Education." Asia Theological News 15 (April-June 1989): 2-3.

The General Secretary of the Evangelical Fellowship of Asia briefly surveys the EFA and its work. Followed (4-10, 17-19) by questions answered by the leaders from ten nations about the background, main activities and other facets of the work of EFA in their lands.

631. Rubinstein, Murray A. "American Evangelicalism in the Chinese Environment: Southern Baptist Convention Missionaries in Taiwan, 1949-1981." American Baptist Quarterly 2 (September 1983): 269-89.

The years of success (1948-1961), the years of stagnation (1962-1971), and the time for reflection on the dynamics of cultural change and the need for new mission strategies (1970s).

632. Sawatsky, Walter. "Russian Evangelicals Hold a Congress." Religion in Communist Lands 3 (January-June 1975): 12-15.

"The over-riding impression for foreign observers attending the 41st All Union Congress of the Evangelical Christians and Baptists" in Moscow in December 1974 "was one of spiritual triumph." Reported the growth of evangelicalism, emphasis on unity, messages, business matters.

633. _____. Soviet Evangelicals Since World War II. Kitchener, Ontario, and Scottdale, PA: Herald Press, 1981. 527 p.

Attempts to present a "reflective, deliberate, and nuanced response" to the story of evangelicals in the Soviet Union; much attention given to the issue of church and state; both a history and a "descriptive analysis"; writes from an Anabaptist-Mennonite stance. Thirteen-page bibliography. Index.

634. Scarf, Alan. "The Evangelical Wing of the Orthodox Church in Romania." Religion in Communist Lands 3 (November-December 1975): 15-20.

Evangelicalism in Romania originated in contacts of soldiers with evangelical Protestants during World War I. Relates the story of two priests--Tudor Popescu and Josif Trifa--and the movements they originated in the 1920s and 1930s.

635. Scott, Waldron. "Introduction: Evangelical Ambiguity." In Serving Our Generation: Evangelical Strategies for the Eighties. ed. Waldron Scott, 9-27. Colorado Springs: World Evangelical Fellowship, 1980.

A summary by the then President of WEF of the world state of evangelicalism and an overview of the WEF.

636.   Skoglund, Herbert. "The Shape of Evangelical Churches in Japan." Evangelical Missions Quarterly 9 (Spring 1973): 176-79.

Examines the evangelical churches in terms of growth, leadership, theology, and ethics.

637.   Smeeton, Donald Dean. "Evangelical Trends in Europe, 1970-1980." Evangelical Missions Quarterly 16 (October 1980): 211-16.

Discusses several trends: "a growing desire for evangelical cooperation"; "greater exploitation of printed materials"; "a growing concern for evangelism and missions"; "a growing concern for theological education"; in short, a report that is "not overwhelmingly good, but . . . does hold a powerful promise."

638.   Smith, Anthony Christopher. "The Essentials of Missiology From The Evangelical Perspective of the 'Fraternidad Teologica Latinoamericana.'" Ph.D. diss., The Southern Baptist Theological Seminary, 1983. 435 p.

639.   Steeves, Paul D. "Alexander Karev: Evangelical in a Communist Land." Fides et Historia 8 (Spring 1976): 63-81.

Depicts the relationship of evangelicals to the government, using the life of a Russian Baptist leader, reflecting the way in which most Russian believers have responded; provides perspective on the recent history of Russian Baptists and on the problems faced by Christian believers in a communist land.

640.   Stunt, Timothy C. "Geneva and British Evangelicals in the Early Nineteenth Century." Journal of Ecclesiastical History 32 (January 1981): 35-46.

A whole series of British evangelicals, especially the more radical wing, were influenced by the Geneva reveil.

641.   "Theological Issues in Asia." Asia Theological News 13 (October-December 1987): 2-19.

Articles by leading Asian evangelicals that focus in part upon American contributions to developments in Asian theology.

642.   Troutman. Charles H. "Evangelicals and the Middle Classes in
         Latin America." Evangelical Missions Quarterly. Part I, 7
         (Winter 1971): 79-91. Part II, 7 (Spring 1971): 154-63.

         Part I describes the substantial advances by Pentecostals among
         the lower classes and the lack of growth of the "mission
         society oriented churches," churches of the middle class. Part
         II discusses the missionary society oriented churches, placing
         responsibility for the lower growth rates upon the mission-
         aries; suggests reasons for lack of growth and makes several
         recommendations.

643.   Wagner, C. Peter. "Latin American Congress on Evangelism."
         Evangelical Missions Quarterly 6 (Spring 1970): 167-73.

         Reports on the First Latin American Congress on Evangelism
         (CLADE), which met at Bogota, November 21-29, 1969, one of a
         number of continent- wide congresses (North America, Africa,
         Asia had preceded Bogota); discusses significance, mechanics,
         content, "side effects," and benefits; followed by the document
         produced by the Congress, "The Evangelical Declaration of
         Bogota" (pp. 172-73).

644.   _____. Latin American Theology: Radical or Evangelical? The
         Struggle for the Faith in a Young Church. Grand Rapids: Eerdmans,
         1970. 118 p.

         Describes the debate over "the mission of the church in the
         world." analyzing the position of the "new radical left of
         Latin American Protestantism"; critiques that position from the
         standpoint of the church growth position; presents the views of
         several Latin American evangelicals, and his own position, of
         traditional evangelism and the necessity of serving society.
         Bibliography.

645.   Wilson, Everett A. "The Central American Evangelicals: From
         Protest to Pragmatism." International Review of Mission 77
         (January 1988): 94-106.

         Places them "in the context of twentieth century socio-
         political developments, examines the institutional
         characteristics . . . and attempts to identify their
         integrating values."

646.   Yoder. Bill. "Western Evangelicals and Eastern Europe." Reformed
         Journal 32 (April 1982): 10-15.

Develops five reasons why Western Christians respond to Marxism as they do, and suggests how to improve the situation.

647.   Yoder, Derek S. "Doing African Christian Theology: An Evangelical Perspective." AIM International 72 (Summer 1988): 4.

A review of Richard J. Gehman's book, Doing African Christian Theology: An Evangelical Perspective (1986).

See also items 306, 356, 411, 485, 653, 657, 660, 670, 672, 779, 875, 1039, 1118, 1138, 1139, 1282, 1305, 1446, 1555, 1606, 1607, 1653, 1750, 1764, 1817, 1818, 1833, 1994, 2487, 2554, 2567, 2568.

K.   Missions

648.   Ahonen, Lauri. Missions Growth: A Case Study on Finnish Free Foreign Mission. Pasadena: William Carey, 1984. 72 p.

A study of pentecostalism in Finland. Thirteen-page bibliography.

649.   Alexander, John W., ed. Confessing Christ as Lord: The Urbana 81 Compendium. Downers Grove: InterVarsity, 1982. 269 p.

Twenty-one messages given at the Thirteenth Inter-Varsity Student Missions Convention (1981).

650.   Barnhardt, Joy A., and Luther (Lee) E. Barnhardt, III. "The Baptist General Conference Foreign Mission Advance: An Investigation into the Causes of its Emergence." American Baptist Quarterly 6 (September 1987): 172-200.

Concludes that "the precipitating factor seems to have been the theological issue with the ABFMS and the NBC." The fear of modernism in the Northern Baptist Convention was part of a "multiplicity of factors" that led to the break of the Swedish Baptists with the Convention.

651.   Bergman, Marvin L. "North American Evangelical Missions: The Last 100 Years." TSF Bulletin 10 (November-December 1986): 24-26.

Brief summaries of the papers given at "A Century of World Evangelization: North American Evangelical Missions. 1886-1986," a conference held at Wheaton College in June 1986.

652.   Beyerhaus, Peter, Arthur Johnston, and Myung Yuk Kim. "Evangel-
         icals, Evangelism and Theology: A Missiological Assessment of the
         Lausanne Movement." Evangelical Review of Theology 11 (April
         1987): 169-85.

         A paper given in Leuven, Belgium, in June 1986, traces the
         evolution of the Lausanne Movement and discusses "New Tasks and
         Theological Challenges Facing the Evangelical Movement,"
         calling for united effort.

653.   Clymer, Kenton J. Protestant Missionaries in the Philippines,
         1898-1916: An Inquiry into the American Colonial Mentality.
         Urbana: University of Illinois Press, 1986. 267 p.

         Excellent study of the encounter between American culture and a
         target culture; missionaries were both agents and critics of
         American views; probably helped in the long run to democratize
         the Filipino people both socially and politically. An
         appreciative view of the missionaries. Bibliography.

654.   Conn, Harvie M. "Looking to the Future: Evangelical Missions From
         North America in the Years Ahead." Urban Mission 5 (January
         1988): 18-31.

         Writing as an "optimistic newscaster" rather than as a prophet,
         he discusses numbers of missionaries now on the field, and a
         series of anticipated issues.

655.   Coote, Robert T. "The Uneven Growth of Conservative Evangelical
         Missions." International Bulletin of Missionary Research 6 (July
         1982): 118-23.

         Statistical analysis of North American missionary personnel,
         1952-1980, shows that NCC decline was not as dramatic as often
         suggested and that IFMA-EFMA growth was fairly modest.

656.   Donahoo, William D. "The Missionary Expression of American
         Evangelical Social Beliefs." Ph.D. diss., Johns Hopkins
         University, 1977. 279 p.

         The (Congregational) American Board of Commissioners for
         Foreign Missions had its largest pre-Civil War mission field,
         more than 300 missionaries, in the Near East: this study
         elicits social thought from the missionaries' reports as they
         contrast the American system with the other nations: America
         was emerging as the fulfillment of the good society, because it

was a picture of "God's plan for earthly existence for all."
Seventeen-page bibliography.

657.   Escobar, Samuel. "Beyond Liberation Theology: Evangelical
Missiology in Latin America." International Bulletin of
Missionary Research 6 (July 1982): 108-14.

Descriptions of contrasting approaches to witness in Latin
America by liberation theology and evangelicalism; emphasis on
the challenges facing the evangelicals.

658.   "Evangelicals and The Bible Society." Evangelical Missions
Quarterly 6 (Summer 1970): 227-35.

Questions raised by evangelical leaders resulted "in a series
of frank consultations, as well as a Committee for continuing
consultations. Reports the first meeting of that Committee
with the Bible Society (August 1969), including a list of
seventeen questions and answers prepared by the Bible Society
at the Committee's request.

659.   Forbes, Bruce David. "An Assessment of Native American Missions."
Evangelical Studies Bulletin 6 (Spring 1989): 1-4.

Review essay of the historical study of Indian missions in the
United States, with particular emphasis on William McLoughlin,
Cherokee Renascence in the New Republic (1986), and Donald B.
Smith, Sacred Feathers (1987).

660.   Glasser, Arthur F. "China Today - An Evangelical Perspective."
Evangelical Review of Theology 6 (April 1982): 70-84.

Three evangelical concerns: spiritual hunger and the gospel,
radical theology and the truth, and who speaks for the church
in China. Reprinted from Missiology 9 (July 1981).

661.   _____. "A Critical Look at the Wheaton Congress From Five
Perspectives: North American." Evangelical Missions Quarterly 3
(Fall 1966): 1-5.

The Congress (April 9-16. 1966) represented the evangelical
response to the "tension generated throughout the world chiefly
by theologians and ecclesiastics within the Ecumenical
Movement." Lists four questions that were raised in the effort
to develop an evangelical perspective.

662.   . "The Evolution of Evangelical Mission Theology Since
World War II." Evangelical Review of Theology 11 (January 1987):
53-64.

> Reprinted from International Bulletin for Missionary Research
> (January 1985). Six elements in the evolution: affirming the
> Great Commission, discovering church growth, being challenged
> by ecumenists, struggling for a holistic gospel, listening to
> the "third force," and reaffirming the Kingdom of God.

663.   . "Fellowships and Mergers as Demonstrations of
Evangelical Unity." Evangelical Missions Quarterly 4 (Winter
1968): 94-101.

> Presents a number of "prerequisites" for the "relative success"
> achieved in the younger churches and nations; lists several
> "relevant factors" concerning mission mergers, and concludes
> with strong condemnation of the competitive spirit that too
> often rules the churches.

664.   . "Mission in the 1990s." International Bulletin of
Missionary Research 13 (January 1989): 2-8.

> Gives an evangelical perspective, describing that movement's
> "missionary involvement" and suggesting "where they will be at
> the end of the century." Cautious but positive, expecting
> "growth in numbers and maturity."

665.   Hesselgrave, David J. Today's Choices for Tomorrow's Mission: An
Evangelical Perspective on Trends and Issues in Missions. Grand
Rapids: Academie Books, Zondervan, 1988. 272 p.

> A practitioner-professor of missions writes about ten trends
> and issues (including "multiple options," the role of
> Pentecostalism, and the "mounting opposition, for example).
> Appendixes. Bibliographical references. Indexes.

666.   Hogg, W. Richie. "Pages From An African Journal. Part II: On
Faith Missions." Hartford Quarterly 3 (Spring 1963): 25-48.

> Part two of a four part article in this issue: reviews their
> background, including their history and theology, their current
> organization, constituency and methods, focusing at some length
> on the Sudan Interior Mission, and concluding with several
> generalizations, among them that "one can only confess that
> this is work blest of God."

667.   Hollenweger, Walter J. "Charismatic Renewal in the Third World:
        Implications for Missions." Occasional Bulletin of Missionary
        Research 4 (April 1980): 68-75.

        The roots of the renewal are American neo-pentecostalism and
        "oral theology" in the Third World; the fruits are prayer for
        the sick, exorcism and glossolalia; the implications of the
        creation of an intercultural theological approach to the
        gospel.

668.   Hutchison, William R. Errand to the World: American Protestant
        Thought and Foreign Missions. Chicago: University of Chicago
        Press, 1987. 227 p.

        Survey of missions thought from colonial times to the present,
        concentrating on the mainline denominations. Excellent
        introduction to a new field of study. Bibliography. Index.

669.   Kane, J. Herbert. "Inter-Mission Cooperation Among Evangelicals."
        Evangelical Missions Quarterly 1 (Spring 1965): 3-9.

        Declares that "the amount and extent of cooperation among
        evangelical missions is enormous" and began early; the
        many-faceted nature of the cooperation antedated the rise of
        liberalism; and the efforts of the IFMA and EFMA together
        constitute an "encouraging picture of the rapidly expanding
        inter-mission cooperation."

670.   _____. "A Survey of Cooperation Among National Churches
        Overseas." Evangelical Missions Quarterly 1 (Summer 1965): 36-41.

        Based on response to a questionnaire sent to all members of the
        EFMA and IFMA; responses revealed considerable caution by
        mission leaders, particularly regarding doctrinal issues.

671.   Knapp, Stephen C. "Mission and Modernization: A Preliminary
        Critical Analysis of Contemporary Understandings of Mission from a
        'Radical Evangelical' Perspective." In American Missions in Bicen-
        tennial Perspective, 146-209. South Pasadena: William Carey, 1977.

        A heavily-researched article (forty pages of notes and
        bibliography); Knapp contends that Western missions have been
        "uncritically absorbed" in the process of modernization (an
        "integrationist" approach) and offers a "dualist" variation,
        influenced by both Reformed and Anabaptist concepts, and
        outside of mainstream evangelicalism.

672.   Koop, Allen V. American Evangelical Missionaries in France,
         1945-1975. Lanham, MD: University Press of America, 1986. 207 p.

         A balanced account that documents the problems, struggles, and
         failures of the Protestant missionary enterprise on a difficult
         field. Twenty-two-page bibliography. Index.

673.   Lindsell, Harold, ed. The Church's Worldwide Mission: An Analysis
         of the Current State of Evangelical Missions, and a Strategy for
         Future Activity. Waco: Word Books, 1966. 289 p.

         Proceedings of a significant evangelical conference--the
         Congress on the Church's World-Wide Mission--that met at
         Wheaton College in 1966. Sheds light on the larger evangelical
         movement, through its focus on one of the most important
         emphases of that movement. Bibliographies.

674.   Newbigin, Lesslie. "Cross Currents in Ecumenical and Evangelical
         Understandings of Missions." International Bulletin of Missionary
         Research 6 (October 1982): 146-51.

         Three issues are dealt with: 1) evangelism and social action;
         2) mission, missions, and churches; 3) universalism and
         pluralism. Responses by Paul Schrotenboer and C. Peter Wagner,
         illustrating the differences between evangelicals and
         ecumenists. Final rejoinder by Newbigin.

675.   Norton, Wilbert. "Mission in the United States: An Evangelical
         Perspective." International Review of Mission 63 (April 1974):
         192-200.

         Some historical perspective on evangelical missions, and a
         cataloguing of organizations engaged in both home and foreign
         missionary activity.

676.   Peck, George. "The Dialogue, the Mandate, and Our Hermenutical
         Perspective." Foundations 25 (January-March 1982): 31-44.

         Discussion of differing approaches to missions, and strengths
         of each, made by evangelicals and conciliarists.

677.   Piggin, Stuart. Making Evangelical Missionaries 1789-1858: The
         Social Background, Motives and Training of British Protestant
         Missionaries to India. . . .   Abingdon, Oxfordshire: Sutton
         Courtenay Press, 1984. 378 p.

Contains texts of David Bogue's "Missionary Appeal" (1794);
Charles Buck on "Philanthropic Movements" (1800); Sydney Smith
on "Evangelical Missionaries" (1808). Includes list of
missionaries to India recruited in Britain 1789-1858.
Bibliography. Index.

678.   Utuk, Efiong S. "From Wheaton to Lausanne: The Road to Modification of Contemporary Evangelical Mission Theology." Africa
Theological Journal 15, no. 3 (1986): 151-65.

Modifications in evangelical missions, seen in the Wheaton
(1966), Berlin (1966) and Lausanne (1974) meetings, show it to
have a number of ideas in common with ecumenical missions,
making rapprochement between the two a possibility.

679.   Winter, Harry E. "Catholic, Evangelical, and Reformed: An
Ecumenical Strategy for Total Evangelization." In Mission in
Dialogue: The Sedos Research Seminar on the Future of Mission
March 8-19, 1981, Rome, Italy, eds. Mary Motte and Joseph R. Lang,
216-228. Maryknoll: Orbis, 1982.

Definition of the three terms, evangelization techniques of
each, a methodology that could combine the three, and
suggestions for the further exploration of issues.

680.   Winter, Ralph D., ed. The Evangelical Response to Bangkok. South
Pasadena: William Carey, 1973. 153 p.

Reports on the "Salvation Today" conference sponsored by the
commission on World Mission and Evangelism of the World Council
of Churches and held in Bangkok December 29, 1972-January 12,
1973. Bibliographical references.

681.   _____. "The Kingdom Strikes Back: The Ten Epochs of Redemptive
History." Evangelical Review of Theology 6 (October 1982):
237-59.

Reprinted from Winter. ed., Perspectives on the World Christian
Movement (1981), ten 400-year epochs from Abraham to A.D. 2000.
stressing the five epochs since the time of Christ.

See also items 48, 219, 269, 303, 631, 638, 643, 689, 708, 983, 1019, 1022,
     1202, 1232, 1761, 2013, 2015, 2077, 2078, 2080, 2084, 2094, 2219, 2526,
     2609, 2611, 2613, 2631.

III

SPECIALIZED STUDIES OF EVANGELICALISM

A. Black Evangelicalism

682.   Banks, William L. A History of Black Baptists in the United States. Philadelphia: Continental Press, 1987. 160 p.

    A brief survey of the black Baptists from colonial times to the present, with particular stress on black denominational organization. Bibliography.

683.   Brown, Joseph. "The Negro Evangelical and the Race Crisis." Eternity 15 (September 1964): 17, 30.

    Attempts to respond to two typical questions: "Who are these persons called Negro evangelicals? Why have we not heard of them before?" Devotes much attention to the question of evangelicals and the race issue.

684.   Bruce, Calvin E. "Black Evangelical Christianity and Black Theology." In Black Theology II: Essays on the Formation and Outreach of Contemporary Black Theology, eds. Calvin E. Bruce and William R. Jones, 163-87. Lewisburg: Bucknell University Press, 1978.

    Encourages black liberationist theologians to take cognizance of black evangelicals, because dialogue with them enhances theology, because evangelicals have an intensely personal (rather than "theopolitical") understanding of Christianity, and because emphases on the Bible and worship are important evangelical strengths.

685.   Butchart, Ronald E. "Evangelical Christianity and Freedmen's Education." In Northern Schools, Southern Blacks and Reconstruction: Freedmen's Education, 1862-1875. 33-52. Westport. CT: Greenwood Press, 1980.

686.   Faulkner, Barbara L., et al. "Response to Pannell: A Call for
         Evangelical Concern." Fides et Historia 2 (Spring 1970): 15-25.

         Response to Pannell's address (this issue) at the Conference on
         Faith and History (December 1969); Faulkner, Irving Luscombe,
         N. S. Tjernagel, and Richard L. Troutman, call for "renewed
         evangelical Christian concern for black history and black
         people."

687.   Haynes, Michael E. "Three Minutes to Midnight: The Evangelical
         and Racism." Evangelical Missions Quarterly 5 (Fall 1968): 1-6.

         In an address given at the Park Street Church Missionary
         Conference in Boston in April 1968, a black Baptist clergyman
         and representative to the Massachusetts legislature relates his
         own pilgrimage, and issues several challenges to white
         evangelicals in the midst of what he sees as a crisis
         situation.

688.   Hopkins, Jerry Berl. "Billy Graham and the Race Problem,
         1949-1969." Ph.D. diss., University of Kentucky, 1986. 233 p.

689.   Jacobs, Sylvia M. Black Americans and the Missionary Movement in
         Africa. Westport, CT: Greenwood Press, 1982. 255 p.

         Twelve essays describe the important role played by black
         Americans in the Protestant mission movement in Africa down to
         1960; deals with mission ideology, carrying out the mission,
         and the work of the missionary. Bibliographical essay. Index.

690.   LeBlanc, Douglas. "Black Evangelical Leaders to Watch." Eternity
         39 (May 1988): 27.

         Ten important black leaders: Melvin Banks, Bill and Ruth
         Bently, Reuben S. Connor, Elward Ellis, Anthony Evans, Ben
         Johnson, Howard Jones, Crawford Loritts, Bill Pannell, and
         Willie Richardson. Compiled by Aaron Hamlin and Eddie Lane of
         the National Black Evangelistic Association.

691.   Lincoln, C. Eric, ed. The Black Experience in Religion. Garden
         City: Doubleday, 1974. 369 p.

         Twenty-six essays on five subjects: the black church: spiritual
         leadership; religion and protest: cults and sects: African and
         Caribbean religion. Bibliographical references. Index.

692.   Lovett, Leonard. "Black Holiness-Pentecostalism: Implications for
         Ethics and Social Transformation." Ph.D. diss., Emory University,
         Atlanta, 1978. 183 p.

693.   _____. "Black Origins of the Pentecostal Movement." In
         Aspects of Pentecostal-Charismatic Origins, ed. Vinson Synan,
         123-41. Plainfield, NJ: Logos, 1975.

         Reviews several interpretations of the origins of pentecostal-
         ism and concludes that "the modern Pentecostal Movement began
         in the black community." Based on his "Perspectives on the
         Black Origins of the Contemporary Pentecostal Movement."
         Journal of the Interdenominational Theological Center 1 (Fall
         1973): 36-49.

694.   _____. "The Spiritual Legacy and Role of Black Holiness-
         Pentecostalism in the Development of American Culture." One in
         Christ 23, no. 1-2 (1987): 144-56.

         Traces the origins of Black holiness-pentecostalism to three
         roots: Africa (a disputed root), the nineteenth century
         holiness movement, and socioeconomic deprivation; notes the
         role of Blacks in the founding of the twentieth century
         pentecostal movement.

695.   MacRobert, Iain. The Black Roots and White Racism of Early
         Pentecostalism in the USA. New York: St. Martin's, 1988. 142 p.

         Because black Pentecostals had some elements of an African
         pneumatology (with its freer expression of Spirit-possession)
         and had a more participatory view of the church than did white
         pentecostals, the latter re-drew the color line after the
         early, interracial years of the movement. Bibliography.

696.   Massey, James Earl. "The Black Contribution to Evangelicalism."
         The Evangelical Round Table. Eastern College and Eastern Baptist
         Theological Seminary (St. Davids, PA: 1986). Evangelicalism:
         Surviving Its Success, moderator Kenneth Kantzer, editor David A.
         Fraser, 50-58. Princeton: Princeton University Press, 1987.

         A prominent black evangelical discusses three of many black
         contributions to evangelicalism: "the development of black
         evangelical churches"; "a musical tradition that encourages
         self-expression in worship"; "an active witness against racism
         in the church."

697.   Niebuhr, Gustav. "Black Evangelicals Meet." Christian Century
        105 (31 August-7 September 1988): 761.

        Brief report on black evangelical leaders meeting in Atlanta,
        GA, August 1988.

698.   Norton, Will. "A Day in the Life of a Black Fundamentalist."
        Eternity 9 (September 1971): 22-24, 42.

        A day spent with Rev. John Perkins, black fundamentalist
        preacher who had by that date "been instrumental in the
        initiation and organization of 25 to 30 black cooperatives in
        Mississippi," as well as in the Voice of Calvary Bible
        Institute. Describes Perkins, his ministry, his relationship
        with the law and with police, and the "overwhelming" problems
        blacks face.

699.   Oliver, John W., Jr. "Evangelical Campus and Press Meet Black
        America's Quest for Civil Rights, 1956-1959: Malone College and
        Christianity Today." Fides et Historia 8 (Fall 1975): 54-70.

        Presents the evangelical response to the Civil Rights movement
        in the pages of Christianity Today and on the campus of Malone
        College, concluding with the suggestion that it was on its
        campuses rather than in its pulpit or press that evangelicalism
        made "its most enlightened response to civil rights."

700.   Pannell, William E. "The Evangelical Christian and Black
        History." Fides et Historia 2 (Spring 1970): 4-14.

        A slightly revised version of an address given at the
        Conference on Faith and History (December 1969), suggests
        several lessons blacks have learned from history: that blacks
        did build the United States; that violence is thoroughly
        American; that Christianity is inextricably bound up with this
        society; that "rugged individualism" is either dead or
        irrelevant today; concluding that we need to develop a
        Christian interpretation of history.

701.   _____. "Growing Up Evangelical and Black." Theology, News and
        Notes 21 (March 1975): 6-7, 16.

        The pilgrimage of a black evangelical who spent a number of
        years in white evangelicalism and now, like others, sees the
        black church as home; believes evangelical seminaries can serve
        the black church well.

702.   Payne, Eric. "What is Faith Community in the Black Evangelical
         Tradition." In The Recovery of Spirit in Higher Education:
         Christian and Jewish Ministries in Campus Life, ed. Robert Rankin,
         263-84. New York: Seabury, 1980.

         Who the evangelicals are; the black community and evangeli-
         calism; forces inhibiting the formation of faith communities in
         the black evangelical tradition; the growth of faith
         communities in that tradition.

703.   Pike, Garnet Elmer. "The Rise of a Black Pentecostal Church in a
         Changing City: A Historical Case Study." D.Div. diss., Vanderbilt
         University Divinity School, 1972. 110 p.

704.   Proctor, Samuel D. "The Black Community and the New Religious
         Right." Foundations 25 (April-June 1982): 180-87.

         Blurring the line between state and church, and upholding the
         interests of the state as they do, the religious right has
         little to do with the black community.

705.   Raboteau, Albert J. "The Black Experience in American Evangel-
         icalism: The Meaning of Slavery." In The Evangelical Tradition in
         America, ed. Leonard I. Sweet, 181-97. Macon, GA: Mercer
         University Press, 1984.

         While emphasizing revival, conversion, and the Bible, like
         their White counterparts, Black evangelicals have also made
         unique contributions to American evangelicalism.

706.   Roberts, Ronald E. "Leadership Styles in Black Evangelicalism."
         D.Min. diss., Dallas Theological Seminary, 1985. 320 p.

707.   Rooks, Charles Shelby. "Toward the Promised Land: An Analysis of
         the Religious Experience of Black Americans." Black Church 2
         (1972): 1-48.

         Description of the patterns of ministry in the black church,
         how a black theology developed, and what ought to be the
         mission of the black church; written from a non-evangelical
         standpoint.

708.   Sernett, Milton C. Black Religion and American Evangelicalism:
         White Protestants, Plantation Missions, and the Flowering of Negro
         Christianity, 1787-1865. Metuchen, NJ: Scarecrow Press, 1975.
         320 p.

Based on his 1972 University of Delaware Ph.D. dissertation
titled "Black Religion and American Evangelicalism: White
Protestants, Plantation Missions, and the Independent Negro
Church, 1787-1865"; arguing that black religion "was not a
fourth American faith," Sernett carefully lays out the
influence of evangelicalism on black Christianity, the element
of folk religion in the black church, the gospel preached in
the plantation chapel and in the "hush-arbor," and the
emergence of independent black churches. Appendixes.
Fifty-page bibliography. Indexes.

709.   Swift, David E. Black Prophets of Justice: Activist Clergy Before
          the Civil War. Baton Rouge: Louisiana State University Press,
          1989. 376 p.

          Study of six ministers of antebellum independent black
          Presbyterian and Congregational churches, who made major
          contributions to black aspirations and the creation of black
          institutions. Twenty-page bibliography. Index.

710.   Tinney, James S. "Exclusivist Tendencies in Pentecostal Self-
          Definition: A Critique From Black Theology." Journal of Religious
          Thought 36 (Spring-Summer 1979): 32-49.

          White pentecostals use history, theology (fundamentalist and
          evangelical), and praxis (haves vs. have-nots) to arrive at
          their exclusivism; Tinney proposes a simple, inclusive
          definition of pentecostalism: "the tongues-speaking movement."

711.   Turner, William C., Jr. "Black Evangelicalism: Theology,
          Politics, and Race." Journal of Religious Thought 45 (Winter-
          Spring 1989): 40-56.

          Responds "to the evident need to differentiate between evan-
          gelical Christian faith and a socio-political conservatism";
          Black evangelicalism is unique, "rooted in the historic Black
          Church," and marked by ecumenism, "passionate concern for . . .
          souls," concern for "the poor and oppressed," and a high
          ethical standard.

712.   _____. "The United Holy Church of America: A Study in Black
          Holiness-Pentecostalism." Ph.D. diss., Duke University. 1984.
          233 p.

713.   Washington, James Melvin. Frustrated Fellowship: The Black
          Baptist Quest for Social Power. Macon, GA: Mercer University
          Press, 1986. 226 p.

The definitive critical history to date of the Black Baptists
from the beginnings in the late 18th century to the founding of
the first denominational body in the 1890s. Bibliographical
references and essay.

714.   . "The Origins of Black Evangelicalism and the Ethical
Function of Evangelical Cosmology." Union Seminary Quarterly
Review 32 (Winter 1977): 104-16.

There is some confusion on the meaning of black evangelicalism
in the 1970s, but clearly in the later 18th century black
Christians accepted the evangelical doctrines of a literal
heaven and hell, then adapted them to the life situation of
black slaves.

715.   Washington, Joseph R., Jr. Race and Religion in Early Nineteenth
Century America 1800-1850. Lewiston, NY: Edwin Mellen, 1988. 2
volumes (996 p.).

Massive study marred by an opaque prose. Bibliography. Index.

716.   Williams, Melvin Donald. "A Pentecostal Congregation in
Pittsburgh: A Religious Community in a Black Ghetto." Ph.D.
diss., University of Pittsburgh, 1973. 328 p.

717.   Williams, Michael Patrick. "The Black Evangelical Ministry in the
Antebellum Border States: Profiles of Elders John Berry Meachum
and Noah Davis." Foundations 21 (July-September 1978): 225-41.

The careers of Baptist ministers Meachum (1789-1854) in St.
Louis and Davis (1804-1866) in Baltimore, who "were living
symbols that a quiet approach [to emancipation] did not denote
accommodation"; on the contrary, they exhibited "an immense
dedication to freedom and the evangelical mandate."

See also items 23, 27, 37, 76, 513, 525, 876, 979, 1051, 1114, 2048, 2064,
2074, 2150, 2261.

B. Jews and Evangelicals

718.   Armerding, Carl Edwin. "The Meaning of Israel in Evangelical
Perspective." In Evangelicals and Jews in Conversation on
Scripture, Theology, and History. eds. Marc H. Tanenbaum. Marvin
R. Wilson, and A. James Rudin. 119-40. Grand Rapids: Baker. 1978.

What is an evangelical? Israel in the New Testament; Israel in
evangelical history.

719.   Banki, Judith H. "What and How Jews Teach About Evangelicals and
         Christianity." In A Time to Speak: The Evangelical-Jewish
         Encounter, eds. A. James Rudin and Marvin R. Wilson, 91-103.
         Grand Rapids: Eerdmans; Austin: Center for Judaic-Christian
         Studies, 1984.

         "[F]ormal Jewish education teaches relatively little about
         contemporary evangelicals as a group," a bit more about the
         claims of evangelicalism, which claims are rejected "without
         malice or invective."

720.   Bloesch, Donald G. "Sin, Atonement, and Redemption." In
         Evangelicals and Jews in an Age of Pluralism, eds. Marc H.
         Tanenbaum, Marvin R. Wilson, and A. James Rudin, 163-82. Grand
         Rapids: Baker, 1984.

         Interreligious dialogue (which Bloesch approves); the meaning
         of sin; the substitutionary atonement; the drama of redemption;
         salvation by grace.

721.   Grounds, Vernon C. "The Problem of Proselytization: An
         Evangelical Perspective." In Evangelicals and Jews in an Age of
         Pluralism. ed. Marc H. Tanenbaum, Marvin R. Wilson and A. James
         Rudin, 199-225. Grand Rapids: Baker, 1984.

         Affirms that both Judaism and Christianity are missionary;
         describes the faulty ways Christianity has been evangelistic;
         reports on the battle to abandon proselytizing on three
         fronts--civility, history, theology--admitting that theology
         can not be abandoned.

722.   Kantzer, Kenneth S. "Six Hard Questions for Evangelicals and
         Jews." In Evangelicalism and Jews in an Age of Pluralism, eds.
         Marc H. Tanenbaum, Marvin R. Wilson, and A. James Rudin, 257-67.
         Grand Rapids: Baker, 1984.

         The questions deal with anti-semitism (evangelicals dare not be
         anti-semitic) and evangelism--evangelicals must do it.

723.   LaSor, William Sanford. "The Messiah: An Evangelical Christian
         View." In Evangelicals and Jews in Conversation on Scripture,
         Theology, and History, eds. Marc H. Tanenbaum. Marvin R. Wilson.
         and A. James Rudin, 76-95. Grand Rapids: Baker. 1978.

         Approaches the Old Testament accounts from the perspective of
         the New Testament and of history to examine three concepts:
         messianic king, apocalyptic Son of Man, and the Suffering
         Servant.

724.   Levine, Hillel. "Evangelicals and Jews: Shared Nightmares and
        Common Cause." In A Time to Speak: The Evangelical-Jewish
        Encounter, ed. A. James Rudin and Marvin R. Wilson, 152-64. Grand
        Rapids: Eerdmans; and Austin, TX: Center for Judaic-Christian
        Studies, 1987.

        Seeks to dispel the myths held by some evangelicals about Jews,
        in particular that they are anti-tradition and secularist;
        cites S. Zelman and A. J. Gordon as examples of Jew and
        evangelical in a common cause.

725.   Mouly, Ruth W. "Israel: Darling of the Religious Right."
        Humanist 42 (May/June 1982): 5-11.

        "An unlikely alliance has the potential to greatly influence
        U.S. foreign policy in a critical region," a "frightening"
        reality to those "who hope to secure a just solution to the
        Israeli-Palestinian conflict." Aspects discussed include
        reasons for evangelical support, evangelical Christian origins
        of Zionism, and how Israel courts the religious right.

726.   Mouly, Ruth W., and Roland Robertson. "Zionism in American
        Premillenarian Fundamentalism." American Journal of Theology &
        Philosophy 4 (September 1983): 97-109.

        Noting recent examples of support for Israel, the authors treat
        the founding of "premillenarian Zionism" in the late 19th and
        early 20th centuries, and its expression in recent years.

727.   National Conference of Evangelicals and Jews. See Tanenbaum, Marc
        H., ed. (First, 1975, and Second, 1980); and Rudin, A. James, ed.
        (Third, 1984).

728.   Newman, Elias. Fundamentalists' Resuscitation of the Anti-Semitic
        Protocol Forgery, the Tragedy of Tragedies and the Story of a Lie.
        Minneapolis: Augsburg, 1934. 19 p.

729.   Oswalt, John N. "An Evangelical View of the Modern State of
        Israel." In A Time to Speak: The Evangelical-Jewish Encounter,
        eds. A. James Rudin and Marvin R. Wilson. 165-69. Grand Rapids:
        Eerdmans, and Austin, TX: Center for Judaic-Christian Studies,
        1987.

        Israel has a right to exist and to secure that existence, but
        Oswalt does "not feel constrained to endorse all those policies
        and strategies as being necessarily God's will" to maintain
        existence.

730.   Rausch, David A. "Fundamentalism and the Jew: An Interpretive
        Essay." Journal of the Evangelical Theological Society 23 (June
        1980): 105-12.

        Concentrates on Arno C. Gaebelein to demonstrate that the
        common opinion that fundamentalists are anti-semites is without
        significant substantiation.

731.   _____. "Our Hope: An American Fundamentalist Journal and the
        Holocaust, 1937-1945." Fides et Historia 12 (Spring 1980):
        89-103.

        The journal was unique in chronicling "with unbelieveable
        accuracy the plight of the Jews during the Nazi regime," a
        plight which appalled the journal; the thoroughness of coverage
        "must be commended and reevaluated."

732.   _____. A Legacy of Hatred: Why Christians Must Not Forget the
        Holocaust. Chicago: Moody Press, 1984. 222 p.

        Good survey by an evangelical who specializes in Jewish
        studies. Bibliographical references.

733.   _____. "Prospectus for the Future." In Evangelicals and Jews
        in an Age of Pluralism, eds. Marc H. Tanenbaum, Marvin R. Wilson,
        and A. James Rudin, 275-85. Grand Rapids: Baker, 1984.

        Important results of the conference of evangelicals and Jews
        held at Trinity Divinity School, December 1980; further needs:
        for evangelicals to learn more about the Holocaust, and to
        address the issue of "Christian Zionism."

734.   _____. "What and How Evangelicals Teach About Jews and
        Judaism." In A Time to Speak: The Evangelical-Jewish Encounter,
        eds. A. James Rudin and Marvin R. Wilson, 76-90. Grand Rapids:
        Eerdmans, and Austin, TX: Center for Judaic-Christian Studies,
        1987.

        Analysis of some of the literature (Sunday School and
        otherwise) and a few of the fringe groups among evangelicals,
        giving positive and negative impressions of Jews.

735.   _____. Zionism Within Early American Fundamentalism, 1878-
        1918: A Convergence of Two Traditions. New York: Edwin Mellen,
        1979. 378 p.

Based on Rausch's Ph.D. dissertation (Kent State, 1978), this study disputes the alleged anti-Semitism of fundamentalists by an early-period study which clearly shows that proto-fundamentalist (pre-1918) prophecy conferences, Bible institutes, and publications reflect a pro-Jewish, pro-Zionist stance. Twenty-three-page bibliography. Index.

736.   Riggans, Walter. "Towards an Evangelical Doctrine of the Church: The Church and Israel." Churchman 103, no. 2 (1989): 129-35.

Premise is that "the church has no identity or purpose apart from that of Israel; the New Testament . . . [none] apart from the Hebrew Bible; Jesus . . . [none] apart from the God of Abraham." "My proposition is that all Evangelicals should be involved with the Jewish-Christian Dialogue circles, almost entirely devoid at present of evangelical scholarship and witness."

737.   Rudin, A. James. "Current Evangelical-Jewish Relations: A Jewish View." In Evangelicals and Jews in an Age of Pluralism, eds. Marc H. Tanenbaum, Marvin R. Wilson, and A. James Rudin, 29-43. Grand Rapids: Baker, 1984.

Five areas of mutual interest and agreement, and the central problem area: mission/witness.

738.   Rudin, A. James, and Marvin R. Wilson, eds. A Time to Speak: The Evangelical-Jewish Encounter. Grand Rapids: Eerdmans, 1987. 202 p.

The proceedings of the third national Conference of Evangelical Christians and Jews, held at Gordon College (Wenham, MA) in 1984. Bibliography.

739.   Saperstein, Marc. "Points of Dialogue Between Evangelicals and Jews." TSF Bulletin 9 (November-December 1985): 13-15.

The Bible, acceptance of Jesus as Messiah, proselytizing and the view of the state of Israel, are the points of dialogue, to which the author adds a plea for mutual understanding.

740.   Smith, Timothy L. "Biblical Social Ethics: An Agenda for the Eighties." In Evangelicals and Jews in an Age of Pluralism, eds. Marc H. Tanenbaum, Marvin R. Wilson, and A. James Rudin, 64-82. Grand Rapids: Baker, 1984.

Speaking for the "moral minority." Smith outlines some of the
historic links between the social ethics of Judaism and of
Christianity, and lays out an agenda for social ethics in an
era that needs help.

741.   Tanenbaum, Marc H., Marvin R. Wilson, and A. James Rudin, eds.
         Evangelicals and Jews in Conversation on Scripture, Theology, and
         History. Grand Rapids: Baker, 1978. 326 p.

         Eighteen papers from the first National Conference of
         Evangelicals and Jews (New York City, December 1975); seven
         general areas, with an evangelical and a Jewish scholar
         treating each subject, among them: "The Messiah"; "The Meaning
         of Israel"; "Interpretation of Scripture" (four papers); "Moral
         Crises and Social Ferment" (four papers); "Religious
         Pluralism"; and "The Future." Bibliography. Indexes.

742.   _____, eds. Evangelicals and Jews in an Age of Pluralism.
         Grand Rapids: Baker, 1984. 285 p.

         Fifteen papers presented by evangelical and Jewish scholars at
         the second National Conference of Evangelicals and Jews
         (Deerfield, IL, December 1980), with a format similar to that
         of the first Conference. Evangelical scholars included Timothy
         Smith, Bruce Waltke, Donald Bloesch, Vernon Grounds, Kenneth
         Kantzer, and David Rausch. Bibliographical notes.

743.   Voss, Carl Hermann, and David A Rausch. "American Christians and
         Israel, 1948-1988." American Jewish Archives 40 (April 1988):
         41-81.

744.   Wilson, Marvin R. "Current Evangelical-Jewish Relations: An
         Evangelical View." In Evangelicals and Jews in an Age of
         Pluralism, eds. Marc H. Tanenbaum, Marvin R. Wilson, and A. James
         Rudin, 13-28. Grand Rapids: Baker, 1984.

         Background on the recent evangelical-Jewish conversations, and
         an unfinished agenda to be addressed.

745.   _____. "An Evangelical Christian View of Israel." In A Time
         to Speak: The Evangelical-Jewish Encounter, eds. A. James Rudin
         and Marvin R. Wilson, 170-76. Grand Rapids: Eerdmans; and Austin:
         Center for Judaic-Christian Studies, 1987.

         Ten matters in the evangelical understanding of Israel "that
         need further clarification, thought and action."

746.   . "An Evangelical Perspective on Judaism." Journal of
the Evangelical Theological Society 19 (Summer 1976): 169-90.

> The definition of evangelical; the dilemma of dialogue; the
> common heritage; facing the differences between evangelicals
> and Jews. Taken from Tanenbaum, et al., Evangelicals and Jews
> in Conversation (1978).

747.   . Our Father Abraham: Jewish Roots of the Christian
Faith. Grand Rapids: Eerdmans; and Dayton: Center for
Judaic-Christian Studies, 1989. 374 p.

> "Although this work is a biblical, historical, and cultural
> study," it is also "a call for Christians to reexamine their
> Jewish roots so as to effect a more authentically biblical
> lifestyle." From the leading evangelical in the Christian-
> Jewish dialogue. Bibliography.

748.   . "Zionism as Theology: An Evangelical Approach."
Journal of the Evangelical Theological Society 22 (March 1979):
27-44.

> Traces the biblical and historical roots, and makes a four-
> point assessment of Zionism as theology, arguing for a
> "God-ordained future for ethnic Israel" without categorically
> saying the modern state of Israel is that future.

749. Wyschogrod, Michael. "Judaism and Evangelical Christianlty." In
Evangelicals and Jews in Conversation on Scripture, Theology, and
History, eds. Marc H. Tanenbaum, Marvin R. Wilson, and A. James
Rudin, 35-52. Grand Rapids: Baker, 1978.

> The Bible (Old Testament) as an obvious point of contact; the
> Law passages in the New Testament, and the question of the
> place of Jesus in the two faiths.

750. Yamauchi, Edwin M. "Concord, Conflict, and Community: Jewish and
Evangelical Views of Scripture." In Evangelicals and Jews in
Conversation on Scripture, Theology, and History, eds. Marc H.
Tanenbaum, Marvin R. Wilson, and A. James Rudin, 154-96. Grand
Rapids: Baker, 1978.

> Concord is in "their mutual regard for the Old Testament":
> conflict occurs over interpretation of the New Testament
> (anti-semitism in the New Testament, views of the trial, death,
> and resurrection of Jesus); community is in the mutual effort
> against anti-semitism.

See also items 1278, 1729, 2057.

C. Women in Evangelicalism

751.   Bendroth, Margaret L. "The Search for 'Women's Role' in American
        Evangelicalism, 1930-1980." In Evangelicalism and Modern America,
        ed. George Marsden, 122-34. Grand Rapids: Eerdmans, 1984.

        The women's role question "is still waiting for an answer,"
        primarily because "traditionalism and feminism have become the
        poles which, to a large degree, have set the limits of creative
        discussion."

752.   Boylan, Anne M. "Evangelical Womanhood in the Nineteenth Century:
        The Role of Women in Sunday Schools." Feminist Studies 4 (October
        1978): 62-80.

        Rather than seeing womanhood as solely a response to a
        repressive male ideology, Boylan contends that in the case of
        the evangelical Sunday School "women themselves devised both
        the organization and the ideology to express their view of
        female nature."

753.   Cartwright, Desmond W. "'Your Daughters Shall Prophesy': The
        Constitution of Women in Early Pentecostalism." In The
        Distinctiveness of Pentecostal-Charismatic Theology. C1-C13.
        Fifteenth Annual Meeting, Society for Pentecostal Studies, Mother
        of God Community, Gaithersburg, MD: 1985.

754.   Conn, Harvie M. "Evangelical Feminism: Reflections on the State
        of the Union." TSF Bulletin 8 (November-December 1984): 20-23,
        and 8 (January-February 1985): 18-20.

        Conn lays out the egalitarian and hierarchical views, suggests
        a third, centrist, option that bridges between the first two,
        and proposes a five-point study agenda for the future.
        Reprinted from Westminster Theological Journal (Spring 1984):
        104-24. with the title, "Evangelical Feminism: Some Reflections
        on the Contemporary State of the Union."

755.   Corley, Kathleen E.. and Karen J. Torjesen. "Sexuality. Hierarchy
        and Evangelicalism." TSF Bulletin 10 (March-April 1987): 23-27.

        Beginning with the divided meeting of the Evangelical Women's
        Caucus in Fresno. CA. July 1986, the authors discuss sexuality

and hierarchy, concluding that evangelicals need to re-think the relationship of the two concepts.

756. Davis, Robin Reed. "Anglican Evangelicalism and the Feminine Literary Tradition: From Hannah More to Charlotte Bronte." Ph.D. diss., Duke University, 1982. 305 p.

757. Dayton, Donald W. "Evangelical Roots of Feminism." Covenant Quarterly 34 (November 1976): 41-56.

Using "evangelical" in its sense of conversion and new life experience (rather than the sense of doctrinal orthodoxy), Dayton traces feminism from the Evangelical Revival and Awakenings, through the antebellum social reform movement and into late-19th century evangelicalism.

758. Dayton, Donald W., and Lucille Sider Dayton. "Evangelical Feminism: Some Aspects of its Biblical Interpretation." Explor 2 (Fall 1976): 17-22.

Argues the case for the origins of evangelical feminism in the revival movements of the 18th and 19th centuries, antebellum abolitionism and segments of the holiness and pentecostalism movements, all of which offered biblical reasons for the equality of women.

759. Epstein, Barbara Leslie. The Politics of Domesticity: Women, Evangelicalism, and Temperance in Nineteenth-Century America. Middletown, CT: Wesleyan University Press, 1981. 188 p.

Through four phases--Great Awakening, Second Awakening, Woman's Crusade of 1873-1875, woman's temperance movement from 1874-- Epstein traces a developing self-consciousness of women as they discovered "a particularly 'female' set of values and concerns" a self-consciousness parallelled and promoted by "the reorganization of relations between men and women . . . that emerged with the nineteenth-century growth of the market and the beginnings of industrialization." Bibliography. Index.

760. Fraser, Elouise Renich. "Evangelical Feminism: The Threat of Its Survival." The Evangelical Round Table. Eastern College and Eastern Baptist Theological Seminary (St. Davids, PA. 1986). In Evangelicalism: Surviving Its Success. moderator Kenneth Kantzer. editor David A. Fraser, 45-49. Princeton: Princeton University Press, 1987.

A critique of the evangelical establishment from the standpoint
of evangelical feminism, whose survival, the author holds,
promises struggle for evangelicalism.

761.   Ginzberg, Lori D. "Women and the Work of Benevolence: Morality
         and Politics in the Northeastern United States, 1820-1885." Ph.D.
         diss., Yale University, 1985. 381 p.

762.   _____. "Women in an Evangelical Community: Oberlin 1835-1850."
         Ohio History 89 (Winter 1980): 78-88.

         Oberlin's "ideal of the morally superior woman" (following
         Catharine Beecher) was seen as a more effective approach to
         reform than the human rights position of people like the Grimke
         sisters; by 1850 Oberlin was changing.

763.   Hansell, Joy. "An International Forum of Evangelical Women." In
         Serving Our Generation: Evangelical Strategies for the Eighties,
         ed. with an introduction by Waldron Scott, 149-60. Colorado
         Springs: World Evangelical Fellowship, 1980.

         The IFEW functions as the most recent of the WEF commissions.
         Hansell presents the need for IFEW, changes in strategy that
         are taking place, and new possibilities.

764.   Hardesty, Nancy A. Women Called to Witness: Evangelical Feminism
         in the 19th Century. Nashville: Abingdon, 1984. 176 p.

         Portrays the women's movement and the support given it within
         evangelicalism from the early 1800s into the early 20th
         century. Bibliographical references. Index.

765.   Hassey, Janette. No Time for Silence: Evangelical Women in Public
         Ministry Around the Turn of the Century. Grand Rapids: Zondervan,
         1986. 254 p.

         Discovers the extensive role played by women (including in
         Bible Institute circles) 1880-1930, based on theology, social
         activism, and a charismatic leadership style, and notes the
         restrictive elements in fundamentalism after WWI that account
         for "the gradual decline of public ministry opportunities for
         Evangelical women." Thirteen appendixes. Bibliography.
         Indexes.

766.   Hewitt, Nancy A. "The Perimeters of Women's Power in American
         Religion." In The Evangelical Tradition in America, ed. Leonard
         I. Sweet, 233-56. Macon, GA: Mercer University Press, 1984.

Tests the theories of Victor Turner and Mary Douglas through a close analysis of women in Rochester, NY, in the 1830s and 1840s; finds the theories "insufficient to capture the complex and manifold transitions experienced by women in the first half of the nineteenth century."

767. _____. "Yankee Evangelicals and Agrarian Quakers: Gender, Religion, and Class in the Formation of a Feminist Consciousness." Radical History Review 28 (1984).

Contends that, in 19th century Rochester, "women's rights advocates came almost exclusively from the most anti-evangelical ranks of the Hicksite Quakers."

768. Hoch, Carl B., Jr. "The Role of Women in the Church: A Survey of Current Approaches." Grace Theological Journal 8 (Fall 1987): 241-51.

Discusses three approaches: the non-evangelical egalitarian (which does not treat the Bible as authoritative), the evangelical egalitarian (which contends that certain traditional texts have been misinterpreted), and the hierarchical (which holds that male and female are essentially equal while filling different roles); presents Scriptural support in each case, and concludes with eleven questions that "need to be addressed."

769. Hudson, Winthrop S. "Early Nineteenth-Century Evangelical Religion and Women's Liberation." Foundations 23 (April-June 1980): 181-85.

In half a dozen ways, from conversion to participation in women's societies, evangelical religion "contributed much of the psychological and social space that was indispensable in the process of women's liberation."

770. Juster, Susan. "'In a Different Voice': Male and Female Narratives of Religious Conversion in Post-Revolutionary America." American Quarterly 41 (March 1989): 34-62.

Arguing that "the conversion narrative is as much a cultural mirror as a personal statement," this study of over 200 accounts in six evangelical magazines, 1800-1830, shows "the sexual leveling [of men and women] achieved in the regenerate state" and the "androgynous model of regeneration" in contrast to the "separate spheres" argument about men and women in this era (as contended, e.g., by Barbara Epstein, The Politics of Domesticity [1981]).

771.   Knippers, Diane. "The Evangelical Women's Caucus; A Special
         Report." Good News 9 (January-February 1976): 58-60.

         Proceedings of the November 1975 national gathering in Washing-
         ton, DC, with representatives from thirty-five states and a
         "broad spectrum" of denominations, rooted in the "New
         Evangelical" movement.

772.   Mason, Frances. "Evangelical Women's Caucus." Daughters of Sarah
         1 (January 1975): 7, 10.

         About twenty-five women met in connection with the second
         Thanksgiving Workshop of Evangelicals for Social Concern,
         December 1966, resulting in the establishment of the
         Evangelical Women's Caucus (EWC).

773.   McCants, David A. "Evangelicalism and Nineteenth Century Woman's
         Rights: A Case Study of Angelina E. Grimke." Perspectives in
         Religious Studies 14 (Spring 1987): 39-57.

         Using the 19th century evangelical model--spiritual rebirth,
         search for holiness, response to spiritual calling--McCants
         sees a parallel in Grimke's religious experience, with the
         third part of the model leading her into an appeal for woman's
         rights.

774.   Mickelsen, Alvera, ed. Women, Authority and the Bible. Downers
         Grove: InterVarsity Press, 1986. 304 p.

         Fourteen papers, with responses, given at the Evangelical
         Colloquium on Women and the Bible, held in Oak Brook, Illinois,
         October 1984, on biblical authority, biblical views of
         authority and leadership, difficult passages, and changing the
         church. Bibliographical references.

775.   Mollenkott, Virginia Ramey. "An Evangelical Feminist Confronts
         the Goddess." Daughters of Sarah 9 (September/October 1983):
         8-12.

         While rejecting the term "Goddess" as sex-specific, she finds
         much for Jewish and Christian believers to learn from Goddess
         worshipers. Reprinted from Christian Century 99 (20 October
         1982): 1043-46.

776.   _____. "Evangelicalism: A Feminist Perspective." Union
         Seminary Quarterly Review 32 (Winter 1977): 95-103.

Beginnings of the evangelical feminist movement by an early
member, centered on the biblical teaching about male/female
relationships. Mollenkott's position is that "the vast
preponderance of biblical evidence points toward an ideal of
human unity and egalitarian harmony in the body of Christ."

777.   Newman, Amy L. "Evangelicals and Feminism." Asbury Seminarian 31
        (July 1976): 6-10.

        Examines "the theological implications of feminism," focusing
        on three areas: "feminism and the Bible," "language about God,"
        and "male-female roles and 'God's natural order.'" Friendly to
        feminist position.

778.   Radl, Shirley. The Invisible Woman: Target of the New Religious
        Right. New York: Dell, 1983. 199 p.

779.   Reasoner, Esther. "Asian Conference for Evangelical Women."
        Japan Harvest 39, no. 1 (1989): 8-9.

        Eighty-two Christian women from twelve countries met April 3 to
        7, 1989, in Singapore, convened by the Evangelical Fellowship
        of Asia; objectives included unity/cooperation, evangelism/
        missions, and personal relationship and deepened walk with
        Christ; reports on sessions and results.

780.   Roebuck, David G. "Pentecostal Women in Ministry: A Review of
        Selected Documents." Perspectives in Religious Studies 16 (Spring
        1989): 29-44.

        Purpose: to provide bibliographical data for an area in which
        little has been published. Concludes that, "while most
        Pentecostals accept women in some areas of ministry," and many,
        especially independents, encourage full participation, "others,
        especially denominations, tend to exclude women from roles of
        authority and power."

781.   Ryan, Mary P. "A Women's Awakening: Evangelical Religion and the
        Families of Utica, New York, 1800-1840." In Women in American
        Religion, ed. Janet Wilson James, 89-110.   Philadelphia:
        University of Pennsylvania Press, 1978.

        This demographic study discloses that women were "the majority
        of revival converts" and "were also instrumental in a host of
        other conversions among their kin of both sexes", thereby
        contradicting "the interpretation of the Second Great Awakening
        as a rite of youthful independence."

782.   Scanzoni, Letha Dawson. and Susan Setta. "Women in Evangelical,
         Holiness, and Pentecostal Traditions." In Women and Religion in
         America: A Documentary History, 1900-1968, vol. 3., eds. Rosemary
         Radford Ruether and Rosemary Skinner Keller, 223-35. San
         Francisco: Harper & Row, 1986.

         The openness toward women's roles in the church that appeared
         in the late 19th century underwent restriction in the 20th
         century due to evangelicals' limited equality approach,
         reluctance to accept social change, and desire for order.
         Fourteen documents accompany the essay.

783.   Scholer, David M. "Feminist Hermeneutics and Evangelical Biblical
         Interpretation." Journal of the Evangelical Theological Society
         30 (December 1987): 407-20.

         Uses seven typologies to categorize current feminist
         hermeneutics, and then attempts to dialogue between their
         positions and traditional evangelical biblical interpretation.
         Cf. condensed version, "How Can Divine Revelation Be So Human,"
         in Daughters of Sarah 15 (May/June 1989): 11-15.

784.   Spencer, Ralph Wakefield. "Dr. Anna Howard Shaw: The Evangelical
         Feminist." Ph.D. diss., Boston University, 1972. 700 p.

785.   Strachey, Barbara. Remarkable Relations: The Story of the
         Pearsall Smith Women. New York: Universe Books, 1982. 359 p.

         The family of Hannah Pearsall Smith, noted holiness teacher of
         the late 19th century, written by her granddaughter, describing
         the turning away from Hannah's religion that prevailed in her
         family, beginning with her husband. Bibliography.

786.   Sweet, Leonard I. "The Female Seminary Movement and Woman's
         Mission in Antebellum America." Church History 54 (March 1985):
         41-55.

         Between 1820 and 1850 "a decisive shift" occurred toward
         educating women equally with men, resulting from the triumph of
         evangelicalism's doctrines of "usefulness, individualism, and
         millennialism, the emergence of a capitalist economic system,
         and the division of the sexes in a symbolic order by spherical
         idealogy."

787.   _____. The Minister's Wife: Her Role in Nineteenth-Century
         American Evangelicalism. Philadelphia: Temple University Press,
         1983. 327 p.

Shows the contributions of evangelicalism to the liberation of women, with focus on the particular impact on and through the wives of the clergy. Bibliographical references. Index.

788.   Thomas, Hilah F., and Rosemary Skinner Keller. Women in New Worlds. Nashville: Abingdon, 1981. 445 p.

A volume in the Historical Perspective on the Wesleyan Tradition series, these twenty papers on the 19th and 20th centuries were originally given at the Women in Two Worlds conference, Cincinnati 1979, sponsored by the United Methodist Church.

789.   Tucker, Ruth A., and Walter L. Liefeld. Daughters of the Church: Women and Ministry from New Testament Times to the Present. Grand Rapids: Zondervan, 1987. 552 p.

Wide-ranging survey of the importance of women and their ministry in a variety of endeavors in the church, written primarily in a biographical mode. Thirty-page bibliography. Appendixes. Indexes.

790.   Warner, Wayne E. The Woman Evangelist: The Life and Times of Charismatic Evangelist Maria B. Woodworth-Etter. Metuchen, NJ: Scarecrow, 1986. 340 p.

A well-researched, solid biography of Woodworth-Etter (1844-1924), important in pentecostal history and a controversial figure through the forty-five years of her evangelistic work. Appendixes. Bibliography. Index.

See also items 26, 68, 269, 848, 881, 882, 1024, 2033, 2039, 2056, 2088, 2378, 2501.

D.   Individuals

791.   Ehrenstein, Herbert Henry. "Barnhouse at His Best: A Listening/ Reading Guide for the Uninitiated." Eternity 26 (April 1975): 37, 56.

Suggestions of tapes and books by a prominent American evangelical--founder of Eternity magazine. and pastor for thirty years of the influential Tenth Presbyterian Church of Philadelphia, until his death in 1960.

792.   Findlay, James F., Jr. Dwight L. Moody: American Evangelist
        1837-1899. Chicago: University of Chicago Press, 1969. 440 p.

        Still the best account of the life and times of Moody, told
        judiciously and with empathy. Bibliographical references.
        Index.

793.   Frame, Randy. "Modern Evangelicalism Mourns the Loss of One of
        Its Founding Fathers." Christianity Today 29 (15 March 1985):
        34-36.

        Eulogy for Harold John Ockenga (1905-1985), instrumental in the
        founding of the NAE and in the new evangelicalism.

794.   Graham, Billy. "Billy Graham on Separation." Eternity 9
        (November 1958): 17-19, 47.

        "In a personal letter, released for use in Eternity, Billy
        Graham reveals his biblical views on Christian separation,"
        declaring that "the entire weight of scripture lies in the
        direction of fellowship rather than separation."

795.   _____. "Door Interview: Billy Graham." Wittenburg Door no. 19
        (June/July 1974): 4-11.

        At age fifty-five, and as part of an issue of WD that focuses
        on Graham and his Evangelistic Association, he is interviewed
        on topics that include his relationship to American Presidents
        and more broadly his ministry. Reprinted in Eternity 25
        (November 1974): 28-32.

796.   Grier, W. J. "Benjamin Breckinridge Warfield." Banner of Truth
        no. 89 (February 1971): 3-9.

        Part of an issue devoted to a leading conservative Reformed
        theologian of the late 19th century and early 20th century.

797.   Hamilton, James E. "Finney: An Appreciation." Christianity Today
        19 (8 August 1975): 13-16.

        Survey of Finney's thought and his impact on 19th century
        American culture.

798.   Hardman, Keith J. Charles Grandison Finney, 1792-1875: Revivalist
        and Reformer. Syracuse, NY: Syracuse University Press, 1987.
        521 p.

The first critical biography of Finney thus far published; a
sympathetic yet well drawn work; a must for any beginning in
Finney studies. Eleven-page bibliography. Index.

799.   Harkness, Robert A. Reuben Archer Torrey: The Man and His
Message. Chicago: Bible Institute Colportage Association, 1929.
127 p.

The story of a central figure in the fundamentalist movement
through the 1920s: prominent evangelist, associate of D. L.
Moody, and leader in the Bible Institute movement in the late
19th and early 20th centuries.

800.   Harrell, David Edwin, Jr. Oral Roberts: An American Life.
Bloomington: Indiana University Press, 1985. 622 p.

An excellent life and times biography, fundamental to
understanding Roberts and his milieu. 106 pages of notes;
bibliographical essay. Index.

801.   _____. "Oral Roberts: Quintessential Pentecostal." In The
Distinctiveness of Pentecostal-Charismatic Theology, 11-112.
Fifteenth Annual Meeting, Society for Pentecostal Studies, Mother
of God Community, Gaithersburg, MD: 1985.

Sketch of the healing experience, healing evangelism, and
theological outlook of Roberts.

802.   Harris, Eleanor K. "The Thought of Aiden Wilson Tozer: An
Analysis and Appraisal with Special Emphasis on His Mysticism and
Conceptual Approach to the World." Ph.D. diss., New York
University, 1980. 240 p.

803.   Hart, Darryl Glenn. "'Doctor Fundamentalis': An Intellectual
Biography of J. Gresham Machen, 1881-1937." Ph.D. diss., The
Johns Hopkins University, 1988. 427 p.

804.   Hatch, Nathan O., and Harry S. Stout. eds. Jonathan Edwards and
the American Experience. New York: Oxford University Press. 1988.
298 p.

Fifteen essays on Edwards' thought and influence on his own and
subsequent eras; current Edwards scholarship. integrated into a
portrayal of his role in the development of American
consciousness. Bibliographical references.

805.   Heidebrecht, Paul H. "Pragmatic Evangelical: Herbert Taylor,
          1893-1978." Methodist History 26 (January 1988): 98-112.

          A self-made man of wealth who used his resources for Christian
          ends. His life and principles constitute a case study of the
          relationship of evangelicalism to the use of money and to
          American individualism.

806.   Henry, Carl F. H. Confessions of a Theologian: An Autobiography.
          Waco: Word, 1986. 416 p.

          By one who was perhaps the leading architect of the resurgent
          evangelicalism of the past half century. Reflections on a
          lifetime by the dean of American evangelical theologians in the
          twentieth century. Index.

807.   _____. "A Conversation with Carl F. H. Henry." Eternity 39
          (January 1988): 20-21.

          On the eve of his 75th birthday, topics include, among others,
          evangelical education, the political scene, and literature and
          the arts.

808.   _____. Conversations with Carl Henry: Christianity for Today.
          Lewiston, NY: Edwin Mellen, 1986. 191 p.

          More than a dozen interviews in the 1980s shed light on both
          the person and the theology of Henry.

809.   _____. "An Interview With Carl F. H. Henry." By Diana
          Hochstedt Butler. TSF Bulletin 10 (March-April 1987): 16-19.

          Henry advocates an intellectual, cognitive explication of the
          Christian faith, in contrast to the emphasis on decision that
          pervades evangelicalism.

810.   Hitt, Russell T. "Barnhouse of Philadelphia." Eternity 26 (April
          1975): 14-18.

          A leading evangelical (editor of Eternity) on the person,
          education, and ministry of a leading evangelical of the
          previous generation.

811.   Hoeveler, J. David, Jr. James McCosh and the Scottish Intellec-
          tual Tradition: From Glasgow to Princeton. Princeton: Princeton
          University Press, 1981. 374 p.

Excellent biography of McCosh (1811-1894). a Scottish Common
Sense philosopher, president of Princeton College (1868-1888)
and reconciler of evolution and evangelicalism; instructive for
understanding an important thread of 19th century evangelicalism. McCosh bibliography. Bibliographical references. Index.

812.   Hoffelt, Robert David. "Pragmatics of Persuasion and Disciplines
of Duty: The Influence of Timothy Dwight in American Preaching."
Ph.D. diss., Princeton Theological Seminary, 1983. 411 p.

813.   Hurley, James B. "Schaeffer on Evangelicalism." In Reflections
on Francis Schaeffer. ed. Ronald W. Ruegsegger, 269-301. Grand
Rapids: Zondervan, 1986.

"Schaeffer's background and method of communication"; "three
messages he sent to the evangelical churches": be light, be
salt, practice church discipline; his view of the "great
evangelical disaster"; and his legacy; told sympathetically.

814.   Hywel-Davies, Jack. The Life of Smith Wigglesworth: One Man, One
Holy Passion. Ann Arbor: Servant Publications, 1987. 171 p.

A popular history of Englishman Wigglesworth (1859-1947), a
pioneer of the pentecostal movement, much noted for his healing
ministry.

815.   Jenson, Robert W. America's Theologian: A Recommendation of
Jonathan Edwards. New York: Oxford University Press, 1988.
224 p.

Provocative study of Edwards based on his (unpublished)
"Miscellanies"; contends that Edwards resolved the "doubleness"
of American life--a reasoned civil order and a revealed
religious order--through a combination of science and piety.
Bibliographical references. Index.

816.   _____. "Mr. Edwards' Affections." Dialog 24 (Summer 1985):
169-75.

Careful analysis of Jonathan Edwards on the religious
affections. from a sympathetic point of view; anticipates
Jenson's book. America's Theologian: A Recommendation of
Jonathan Edwards (1988).

817.   Johnson, James E. "Charles G. Finney and a Theology of Revivalism." Church History 38 (September 1969): 338-58.

Traces Finney's career as revivalist and professor at Oberlin, his roots in the New Haven Theology, how Finney "repudiated the main tenets of Calvinism"; shows the tenets of the moral government of God and of human ability that led to other components in his theology.

818.   Kilby, Clyde S. Minority of One: The Biography of Jonathan Blanchard. Grand Rapids: Eerdmans, 1959. 252 p.

Solid account of the life of Blanchard (1811-1892), founder of Wheaton College (Illinois) and noteworthy evangelical social activist. Bibliography. Index.

819.   Land, Gary, ed. The World of Ellen G. White. Washington: Review and Herald Publishing Association, 1987. 253 p.

Fourteen essays by Adventist scholars giving background accounts of the 19th century in which Ellen G. White (1827-1915), founder of the Seventh Day Adventists, lived and moved. Topics such as travel, temperance and amusements are briefly outlined and related to specific comments in White's writings. Bibliographical references. Index.

820.   Lee, Earl. "Francis Schaeffer: Prophet of the Religious Right." Humanist 48 (September/October 1988): 27-29.

The "fundamental error" of Schaeffer's philosophy "is that it ascribes the failures of modern society to an anti-Christian influence when, in fact, these failures are the result of a powerful anti-human influence, an explosion of anxiety that Schaeffer has aided."

821.   Lesser, M. X. Jonathan Edwards. Boston: Twayne, 1988. 153 p.

The compiler of Jonathan Edwards: A Reference Guide (1981), here offers an introductory study of Edwards' thought "as a connected series of comments on the doctrine of divine sovereignty," from his early speculative papers to the formal treatises on free will and original sin. Bibliography.

822.   Lewis, Donald M., ed. Dictionary of Evangelical Biography, 1730-1860. Oxford and New York: Blackwell. Forthcoming.

Projected to include upwards of 3,200 entries by more than 300 historians, internationally selected; it will focus on persons associated with the evangelical movement in the English speaking world.

823.   Liefeld, David R. "Lutheran Orthodoxy and Evangelical Ecumenicity
        in the Writings of John Warwick Montgomery." Westminster Theo-
        logical Journal 50 (Spring 1988): 103-26.

        Can confessional Lutheran orthodoxy and evangelicalism be
        synthesized? They can, says the author, on biblical inerrancy,
        but not on confessional teaching about the sacraments. Thus,
        Montgomery's attempt to synthesize does not hold up. Argues
        that the Lutheran belief in inerrancy is not of recent origin,
        derived from fundamentalism, but is long-standing in the
        Lutheran tradition, indeed in the whole of church history.

824.   Loetscher, Lefferts A. Facing the Enlightenment and Pietism:
        Archibald Alexander and the Founding of Princeton Theological
        Seminary. Westport, CT: Greenwood Press, 1983. 303 p.

        Solid study of the founder of Princeton Seminary by a long-time
        faculty member (now deceased). Thirty-four pages of
        bibliographical references. Bibliographical essay. Index.

825.   Marsden, George M. "J. Gresham Machen: Defender of Orthodoxy."
        Eternity 38 (January 1987): 25-27.

        Fifty years after his death, an appreciation of Machen as
        scholar and as defender of orthodox Christianity (less so for
        his separatism), which make him so influential in contemporary
        evangelicalism.

826.   _____. "J. Gresham Machen, History, and Truth." Westminster
        Theological Journal 42 (Fall 1979): 157-75.

        Nicely drawn comments about the strengths and weaknesses in
        Machen's views of history and truth, based on Common Sense
        philosophy and "Baconianism," in the context of the historical
        relativism of Machen's time.

827.   Marshall, I. Howard. "F. F. Bruce as a Biblical Scholar."
        Journal of the Christian Brethren Research Fellowship no. 22
        (1971): 5-12.

        Part of an issue, the topic of which is "The Contribution of F.
        F. Bruce"; Marshall states that "it is principally through
        Bruce's work that conservative evangelical scholarship has won
        a place for itself in the world of modern biblical
        scholarship."

828.   Mattson, John Stanley. "Charles Grandison Finney and the Emerging
        Tradition of 'New Measure' Revivalism." Ph.D. diss., University
        of North Carolina at Chapel Hill, 1970. 331 p.

829.   McClanahan, James Samuel, Jr. "Benjamin B. Warfield: Historian of
        Doctrine in Defense of Orthodoxy, 1881-1921." Ph.D. diss., Union
        Theological Seminary in Virginia, 1988. 671 p.

830.   Muck, Terry. "Home to Lynchburg: Assessing Jerry Falwell after
        Moral Majority and the PTL." Christianity Today 32 (15 January
        1988): 16-17.

        An Executive Editor of CT gives a positive assessment of
        Falwell after the latter's withdrawal from the Moral Majority
        and the PTL.

831.   Mulholland, Robert Joseph. "Carl McIntire: The Early Radio Years
        (1932 to 1955)." Ph.D. diss., Bowling Green State University,
        1984. 280 p.

832.   Murray, Iain. Jonathan Edwards: A New Biography. Edinburgh:
        Banner of Truth, 1987. 503 p.

        First comprehensive biography of Edwards since the 1940s, told
        from a sympathetic view, seeing Edwards not primarily as a
        philosopher of religion but as a revivalist and pastor.
        Bibliography. Index.

833.   _____. "Thirty Years at Westminster." Banner of Truth no. 57
        (June 1968): 1-5.

        A tribute to Martin Lloyd-Jones, eminent British evangelical,
        on the occasion of his retirement from the pastorate of
        Westminster Chapel. Includes his parting letter to his
        congregation.

834.   Nelson, Rudolph L. The Making and Unmaking of an Evangelical
        Mind: The Case of Edward Carnell. Cambridge: Cambridge University
        Press, 1987. 272 p.

        First full-length biography of one of the important creators of
        new evangelicalism in the 1950s and 1960s. Somewhat biased
        against evangelicalism. Bibliography. Index.

835.   Noll, Mark A., ed. Charles Hodge: The Way of Life. New York:
        Paulist Press, 1987. 291 p.

Hodge's The Way of Life and other writings on religious
experience; helpful introduction by Noll. Bibliographical
references.

836.   . "The Surprising Optimism of Donald Bloesch." Center
Journal 3 (Summer 1984): 95-104.

837.   Numbers, Ronald L. Prophetess of Health: A Study of Ellen G.
White. New York: Harper & Row, 1976. 271 p.

An objective history of the most influential person in the
founding of the Seventh Day Adventists; placed here in the
context of the health movement of the mid-nineteenth century.
Fifty-one-page bibliography. Index.

838.   Opie, John. "Finney's Failure of Nerve: The Untimely Demise of
Evangelical Theology." Journal of Presbyterian History 51 (Summer
1973): 155-73.

By D. L. Moody's time, revivalism had become non-theological, a
shift from earlier revivalism that Opie charges came both from
Charles Finney's inability to "preserve the historic paradox
which had given revivalism a distinctive doctrinal and
psychological focus," and from his lapse into Pelagian and
Gnostic ideas.

839.   . "James McGready: Theologian of Frontier Revivalism."
Church History 34 (December 1965): 445-56.

Contending that McGready was "neither the model nor the
advocate" of unrestrained camp meeting revivalism, Opie places
him in the Edwardsean and Puritan theological traditions,
fighting against both the Arminian revivalists and the
anti-revivalists.

840.   Packard, A. Appleton. "An Evangelical Ecclesiastic." Evangelical
Quarterly 33 (October-December 1961): 207-19.

Evaluation of the person and work of Bishop William Warburton,
"one of the foremost English prelates of the eighteenth
century."

841.   Patterson, Bob E. Carl F. H. Henry. Waco: Word Books. 1983.
179 p.

One of the "Makers of the Modern Theological Mind" series from
Word Books; Patterson briefly describes Henry's career. then

details his apologetics. writings on revelation, view of the
Bible, and doctrine of God. Bibliographical references. List
of Henry's books. Index.

842.   Pierard, Richard V. "From Evangelical Exclusivism to Ecumenical
         Openness: Billy Graham and Sociopolitical Issues." Journal of
         Ecumenical Studies 20 (Summer 1983): 425-46.

         Examines Graham's views on race, communism, and America's
         standing before God, to see his altered stances on these
         matters; further, "one may expect to see a continuing
         flexibility in the remaining years of his public ministry."

843.   Politzer, Jerome. "Theological Ideas in the Preaching of Phillips
         Brooks." Historical Magazine of the Protestant Episcopal Church
         33 (June 1964): 157-70.

         Contends that Brooks' preaching was a "truly evangelical and
         orthodox proclamation of the Christian gospel," carrying on
         "the great tradition of evangelical conviction and Christian
         humanism"; reviews the doctrines and practices of the Church in
         the preaching and practice of Brooks.

844.   Pollard, Arthur, and Michael Hennell, eds. Charles Simeon (1759-
         1836): Essays Written in Commemoration of His Bi-Centenary by
         Members of the Evangelical Fellowship for Theological Literature.
         London: S.P.C.K., 1959. 190 p.

         One of the most prominent of early 19th century evangelicals,
         and pivotal for the movement's place within Anglicanism, hon-
         ored on the bi-centenary of his birth by essays focusing on
         various aspects of his life and emphasis, as, for example, the
         Bible, the doctrine of God, the church, pastoral theology, and
         the context and significance of Simeon's work. Bibliography.

845.   Porter, Thomas Henry. "Homer Alvan Rodeheaver (1880-1955):
         Evangelistic Musician and Publisher." Ed.D. diss., New Orleans
         Baptist Theological Seminary, 1981. 324 p.

846.   Price, Robert M. "Clark H. Pinnock: Conservative and Contem-
         porary." Evangelical Quarterly 60 (April 1988): 157-83.

         Helpful overview of Pinnock's thinking: defending biblical
         authority (to 1970); obeying biblical authority (1970s):
         rethinking biblical authority (1980s). Latterly. Pinnock
         rejects verbal inspiration and classical theism. and moves from
         political radicalism to neo-conservatism.

847.   Ramm. Bernard. "An Interview with Bernard Ramm and Alta Ramm."
        By Walter R. Hearn. Journal of the American Scientific Affilia-
        tion 31 (December 1979): 178-86.

        Part of "A Bernard Ramm Festschrift" issue with a special focus
        on his book, The Christian View of Science and Scripture
        (1954); one of the leading evangelical theologians of the last
        half of the 20th century.

848.   Raser, Harold E. Phoebe Palmer: Her Life and Thought. Lewiston:
        Edwin Mellen, 1987. 389 p.

        This book, along with the one done by Charles White (q.v.),
        brings Palmer to the attention of historians and gives her her
        proper place of influence both in the holiness movement of the
        19th century and in later evangelical history. Fourteen-page
        bibliography. Seventy pages of bibliographical notes.

849.   Rawlinson, Leslie. "Some Church Views of J. C. Ryle." Banner of
        Truth no. 76 (January 1970): 15-23.

        The views of the first Anglican Bishop of Liverpool, "an
        outspoken evangelical." Treats Ryle's view of his own church,
        "his attitude to Nonconformists," "his approach to Church
        reunion," and "some suggested lessons for today."

850.   Robert, Dana Lee. "Arthur Tappan Pierson and Forward Movements of
        Late-Nineteenth-Century Evangelicalism." Ph.D. diss., Yale
        University, 1984. 457 p.

851.   Rogers, Jack B. "Francis Schaeffer: The Promise and the Problem."
        Reformed Journal. Part 1 in vol. 27 (May 1977): 12-15; Part 2 in
        vol. 27 (June 1977): 15-19.

        The promise is Schaeffer as evangelist, which he does quite
        well; the problem is Schaeffer as thinker, which he does poorly
        (Rogers illustrates).

852.   Rosell. Garth M. "Charles G. Finney: His Place in the Stream."
        In The Evangelical Tradition in America. ed. Leonard I. Sweet.
        131-47. Macon, GA: Mercer University Press. 1984.

        A pivotal figure in evangelical history in America. Finney is
        shown to have made social reform central to evangelical life
        and faith.

853.   Ruegsegger. Ronald W., ed. Reflections on Francis Schaeffer.
        Grand Rapids: Zondervan, 1986. 320 p.

        Ten thoughtful chapters by nine authors about Schaeffer's
        system of thought, conceptual framework, analysis of the
        disciplines (philosophy, art and music, theology), and his
        critique of culture (history, America, ethics, evangelicalism).
        Bibliography. Index.

854.   Russell, Charles Allyn. "Adoniram Judson Gordon: Nineteenth-
        Century Fundamentalist." American Baptist Quarterly 4 (March
        1985): 61-89.

        Study of the influence and teaching of Gordon, emphasizing his
        thought on the Holy Spirit, healing and prophecy; becomes a
        chapter in Russell's Voices of American Fundamentalism (1976).

855.   _____. "Clarence E. Macartney: Fundamentalist Prince of the
        Pulpit." Journal of Presbyterian History 52 (Spring 1974): 33-58.

        The life and beliefs of Presbyterian Macartney (1879-1957), the
        pulpit his throne, who defended "the Reformed tradition as
        shaped by Princeton theology," showed little interest in social
        problems, and in several ways does not fit the image of a
        "typical" fundamentalist.

856.   _____. "Donald Grey Barnhouse: Fundamentalist Who Changed."
        Journal of Presbyterian History 59 (Spring 1981): 33-57.

        Minister of Tenth Presbyterian, Philadelphia, for over 30
        years, the indefatigable and controversial Barnhouse (1895-
        1960) had radio, publishing and conference ministries, was
        Reformed and dispensational in theology, had very pronounced
        views on social and political matters, and was the
        "fundamentalist who changed, somewhat."

857.   _____. "J. C. Massee: Unique Fundamentalist." Foundations 12
        (October-December 1969): 330-56.

        Georgian Massee (1871-1965) enjoyed a long career as pastor and
        speaker, emphasized evangelism (to the neglect of a social
        gospel), was involved in the "Thirty Years War" in the Northern
        (American) Baptist Convention, and generally conducted himself
        from the standpoint of "a constructive rather than destructive
        fundamentalism."

858. _____. "John Roach Straton, Accusative Case." Foundations 13 (January-March 1970): 44-72.

The colorful and aggressive fundamentalist Straton (1875-1929), pastor of Calvary Baptist Church in New York City, 1918-1929, described in terms of his ministerial characteristics, his social outlook (he was not a social prophet), and his debates with Unitarian Charles Francis Potter.

859. _____. "Mark Allison Matthews: Seattle Fundamentalist and Civic Reformer." Journal of Presbyterian History 57 (Winter 1979): 446-66.

Matthews (1867-1940) for thirty-eight years pastored First Presbyterian, Seattle, largest in the denomination, was noted for his passion on a broad range of social topics, untypical of fundamentalists.

860. _____. "W. A. Criswell: A Case Study in Fundamentalism." Review and Expositor 81 (Winter 1984): 107-31.

Criswell's church (largest in the SBC), his denominational leadership, conservative theology, and conservative social and political views; "Criswell's greatest strength is his preaching ability as a pastor-evangelist."

861. _____. "William Bell Riley: Architect of Fundamentalism." Foundations 18 (January-March 1975): 26-52.

Published originally in Minnesota History (Spring 1972), this award-winning essay recounts Riley's (1861-1947) multiple-role career--pastor, evangelist, educator, organizer, polemicist-- that made him "the most important fundamentalist minister of his generation."

862. _____. "William Jennings Bryan: Statesman-Fundamentalist." Journal of Presbyterian History 53 (Summer 1975): 93-119.

Marred as was Bryan (1860-1925) by the stereotype of the Scopes Trial, this article sets to right his life and thought: his progressive social and political outlook, and his indigenous fundamentalism.

863. Schaeffer, Francis A. "Are Christians Headed for Disaster?" Interview by Melinda Delahoyde. Moody Monthly 84 (July-August 1984): 19-20.

In this last interview before his death. Schaeffer urges
confrontation with the world, and fears the harm accommodation
will bring.

864.   Scorgie, Glen. A Call for Continuity: The Theological Contribution of James Orr. Macon, GA: Mercer University Press, 1988.
189 p.

Flourishing at the turn into the 20th century, Scotsman Orr,
who penned some of the work in The Fundamentals, contributed
overall "a call for continuity with the older orthodoxy,"
though some of his ideas would be repudiated by 1920s fundamentalists; a fine study, emphasizing Orr's comprehensive reading
and large literary output. Twenty-page bibliography. Index.

865.   _____. "James Orr, Defender of the Church's Faith." Crux 22
(September 1986): 22-27.

Orr's legacy to late 20th century evangelicals is "not only a
body of orthodox belief," but his "example of deep responsibility and great respect for the general Christian public."

866.   Secrett, A. G. "Philip Doddridge and the Evangelical Revival of
the Eighteenth Century." Evangelical Quarterly 23 (October 1951):
242-59.

Story of nonconformist Doddridge (1702-1751), contemporary of
the Wesleys and Whitefield (and influential on Whitefield),
pastor, head of an academy, hymn writer, pamphleteer--all in
the cause of evangelicalism.

867.   Sharp, Larry Dean. "Carl Henry: Neo-Evangelical Theologian."
D.Min. diss., Vanderbilt University Divinity School, 1972. 164 p.

868.   Simeon, Charles. Evangelical Preaching. Introduction by John R.
W. Stott. Portland: Multnomah Press, 1986. 296 p.

Includes an introduction to the preaching of Simeon, prominent
early 19th century evangelical, by James Houston. Stott's
introduction to Simeon as a person, and Simeon's sermon
abstracts (the outlines from which he preached).

869.   Smith, Willard H. "William Jennings Bryan and the Social Gospel."
Journal of American History 53 (June 1966): 41-60.

Evidence of Bryan's interest in reform, social justice, and
applied Christianity alongside of, and not contrary to, his
orthodox beliefs.

870.   Snyder. Howard A. "The Making of a Radical Protestant." Asbury
        Seminarian 33 (January 1978): 5-33.

        The 1977-1978 Ryan Lectures at Asbury Theological Seminary. A
        historical review of Wesley's life and ministry to 1740, with
        special attention to his relationship to the Moravians.

871.   Sroka, Barbara. "Some Personalities From the Evangelical Past."
        His 36 (January 1976): 22-26.

        Describes D. L. Moody, Jonathan Edwards, Harriet Tubman,
        Richard Allen, Charles Finney, Elizabeth Blackwell, Charles
        Hodge, and B. B. Warfield.

872.   Stackhouse, John G., Jr. "'Who Follows in His Train?' Edward John
        Carnell as a Model for Evangelical Theology." Crux 21 (June
        1985): 19-27.

        Presents Carnell's achievements, and urges present day evan-
        gelicals "to a similarly uncompromising but humble engagement
        with the world."

873.   Staggers. Kermit L. "Reuben A. Torrey: American Fundamentalist,
        1856-1928." Ph.D. diss., Claremont Graduate School, 1986. 338 p.

874.   Stonehouse, Ned B. J. Gresham Machen: A Biographical Memoir.
        Grand Rapids: Eerdmans, 1955. 520 p.

        The only biography to provide a complete picture of the life
        and work of Machen, given by one of his students in what is at
        times an overly laudatory fashion. Bibliographical references.
        Index.

875.   Tarr, Leslie K. Shields of Canada. Grand Rapids: Baker, 1967.
        218 p.

        Life story of T. T. Shields (1873-1955), long-time Toronto
        Baptist pastor and the most influential man in the Canadian
        wing of militant fundamentalism; not a critical biography.
        Appendixes.

876.   Tinney, James S. "William J. Seymour: Father of Modern-Day
        Pentecostalism." Journal of the Interdenominational Theological
        Center 4 (Fall 1976): 34-44.

        The first article about black minister Seymour. key person in
        the 1906 Azusa Street revival, placing him in his rightful
        position as one of the founders of pentecostalism.

877.   Trueblood, D. Elton. "The Basis of Recovery." In The Evangelical
         Round Table. Eastern College and Eastern Baptist Theological
         Seminary (St. Davids, PA, 1986). Evangelicalism: Surviving Its
         Success, moderator Kenneth Kantzer, ed. David A. Fraser, 179-82.
         Princeton: Princeton University Press, 1987.

         One of the key persons in the renewal of the church since mid-
         century stresses the life of the mind, the need for intel-
         lectual vitality, giving a number of historic and contemporary
         models.

878.   Walker, Charles Lynn. "The Ethical Vision of Fundamentalism: An
         Inquiry into the Ethic of John Franklyn Norris." Ph.D. diss.,
         Southwestern Baptist Theological Seminary, 1985. 224 p.

879.   Weaver, C. Douglas. The Healer-Prophet, William Marrion Branham:
         A Study of the Prophetic in American Pentecostalism. Macon, GA:
         Mercer University Press, 1987. 386 p.

         An excellent study of a relatively unknown person who was a
         major force in pentecostalism in the mid-twentieth century, who
         had significant influence on Oral Roberts and later faith
         healers. Revision of Ph.D. dissertation (Southern Baptist
         Theological Seminary, 1985). Bibliography. Indexes.

880.   Weborg, John. "Philip Jacob Spener: Heartfelt Desires for Reform
         of the True Evangelical Church." Covenant Quarterly 25 (February
         1967): 19-26.

         Considers one of the significant persons within the history of
         evangelicalism, with a particular view to clarifying the role
         of Spener's conventicles in bringing the church "into closer
         subjection to the Word of God and Christian discipline," making
         "reformers out of Christians."

881.   White, Charles Edward. "The Beauty of Holiness: The Career of
         Phoebe Palmer." Fides et Historia 19 (February 1987): 22-34.

         White is among those who have given a more rightful place to
         Phoebe Palmer (ignored until recently) in American religious
         history, due to her influence as a theologian of the holiness
         movement, revivalist, humanitarian and feminist. Fuller
         details in White's book of the same title (1986).

882.   Wozniak, Kenneth William Mulholland. "Ethics in the Thought of
         Edward John Carnell." Ph.D. diss., University of Southern
         California, 1981. 258 p.

883.   Wyatt-Brown, Bertram. Lewis Tappan and the Evangelical War
        Against Slavery. Cleveland: Case Western Reserve University
        Press, 1969. 376 p.

        Fine biography of New England abolitionist Tappan (1788-1873);
        reveals both his shortcomings as a person and his moral fervor
        against slavery, in the context of antebellum evangelicalism.
        Eleven-page bibliographical essay. Index.

884.   _____. "Partners in Piety: Lewis and Arthur Tappan, Evangel-
        ical Abolitionists, 1828-1841." Ph.D. diss., The Johns Hopkins
        University, 1963.

See also items 42, 45, 132, 179, 188, 194, 197, 200, 202, 205, 218, 219,
    223, 224, 228, 239, 241, 253, 256, 263, 270, 326, 347, 350, 351, 517,
    536, 537, 543, 552, 556, 560, 568, 688, 713, 724, 730, 773, 784, 902,
    938, 944, 971, 1023, 1027, 1063, 1077, 1083, 1152, 1206, 1224, 1252,
    1253, 1316, 1330, 1438, 1441, 1442, 1461, 1499, 1503, 1534, 1676, 1677,
    1726, 1798, 1802, 1807, 1819, 1828, 1840, 1842, 1854, 1903, 1932, 1984,
    2039, 2124, 2270, 2288, 2482, 2509, 2512, 2516, 2517, 2535, 2537, 2538,
    2541, 2542, 2552, 2553, 2557, 2558, 2579, 2580.

                              E.   Politics

885.   Bandow, Doug. Beyond Good Intentions: A Biblical View of
        Politics. Westchester: Crossway, 1988. 271 p.

        Works out a Christian political perspective by discussing God's
        purpose for government, the transcendence of the spiritual, the
        problems facing the American nation, a review of principles by
        which to judge proposed policies, and application of those
        principles to specific issues. Bibliographical references.
        Indexes.

886.   Bates, Vernon Lee. "Christian Fundamentalism and the Theory of
        Evolution in Public School Education: A Study of the Creation
        Science Movement." Ph.D. diss., University of California, Davis,
        1976. 232 p.

887.   Baumann, Fred E., and Kenneth M Jensen, eds. Religion and
        Politics. Charlottesville: University Press of Virginia, 1989.
        175 p.

888.   Berg, John Leland. "An Ethical Analysis of Selected Leaders and
        Issues of the New Religious Right." Ph.D. diss., Baylor
        University, 1985. 292 p.

889.   Breisch, Francis. "Why I am a Political Liberal." Eternity 16
        (October 1965): 24, 26-28.

        An Orthodox Presbyterian clergyman, a theological conservative,
        explains why he has moved into the camp of political liberals.
        The same issue carries a companion piece by a political
        conservative.

890.   Bromley, David G., and Anson Shupe, eds. New Christian Politics.
        Macon, GA: Mercer University Press, 1984. 288 p.

        Sixteen papers, some published previously, most from the hands
        of social scientists, looking at the historical background and
        the political impact of the NCR, social support for the NCR,
        and the role of the media in the NCR. Bibliography. Index.

891.   Bruce, Steve. The Rise and Fall of the New Christian Right:
        Conservative Protestant Politics in America 1978-1988. Oxford:
        Clarendon, 1988. 210 p.

        Part of a series on comparative Protestant political movements,
        Bruce has a chapter on social movements theory, then discusses
        why there was a market for the NCR, the mobilization carried
        out by its leadership, "the social and political structure
        within which this mobilization took place," and the apparent
        failure of the movement. Thirteen-page bibliography. Index.

892.   Cerillo, Augustus, Jr., and Murray W. Dempster, eds. Salt and
        Light: Evangelical Political Thought in Modern America. Grand
        Rapids: Baker, 1989. 175 p.

        A collection of essays and commentary demonstrating political
        thought in the evangelical radical left, the fundamentalist new
        right, the evangelical conservatives, and evangelical liberals
        since World War II. The editors present both historical
        context and debate about the important theological and
        political issues. Bibliography.

893.   Cizik, Richard. "Representing Evangelicals in Washington, D.C."
        United Evangelical Action 48 (March-April 1989): 27.

        Represents "church denominations," "biblical and theological
        values," and "a world constituency": provides "constituency
        service (workman), governmental oversight (watchman) and policy
        input (witness)."

894.   Cooper, John C. Religious Pied Pipers: A Critique of Radical
         Right-Wing Religion. Valley Forge: Judson, 1981. 124 p.

         Depicts the born-again movement as the search for certainty in
         the present age, offers a biblical critique of the Moral
         Majority, and prescribes a healthy faith to supplant the
         "corruption of faith, hope, and love" that marks the right-wing
         vision. Brief notes.

895.   Cotham, Perry C. Politics, Americanism, and Christianity. Grand
         Rapids: Baker, 1976. 335 p.

         A four-part approach to the subject in this carefully-drawn
         book: biblical foundations and introductory concepts; styles of
         Christian political life in America; civil religion in America;
         the question of whether America is a Christian nation.
         Bibliographical references. Indexes.

896.   Cromartie, Michael, ed. Evangelicals and Foreign Policy. Essays
         by Richard John Neuhaus, et al. Washington, DC: Ethics and Public
         Policy Center, 1989. 100 p.

         Examines evangelical involvement "in order to stimulate
         thinking on what the role of evangelicals should be"; points
         out past mistakes and offers insights for the future.

897.   Dayton, Donald W. "Some Perspectives on 'The New Christian
         Right.'" Fides et Historia 15 (Fall-Winter 1982): 54-60.

         Comparison between Jerry Falwell and the Moral Majority of the
         1970s and 1980s and the Charles Finney/Tappan Brothers wing of
         1830s and 1840s evangelicalism. Dayton finds a number of
         similarities, but argues that the 19th century group was more
         open to change than the recent New Right.

898.   Dejong, Gerben. "Indochina and Evangelical Consciousness."
         Reformed Journal 24 (January 1974): 17-22.

         Evangelical consciousness--social and political views, not
         religious orthodoxy--on sin, history, authority, and
         eschatology, "sanctioned both the ethos and the policies"
         regarding American intervention in Vietnam.

899.   Flowers, Ronald B. "President Jimmy Carter, Evangelicalism,
         Church-State Relations, and Civil Religion." Journal of Church
         and State 25 (Winter 1983): 113-32.

On specific political issues, President Carter "did not try to
impose his theological viewpoints on others through the
political process," while in matters of civil religion,
particularly human rights, he advocated strong positions
without abrogating religious liberty.

900.   Foley, Michael W. "Evangelical Politics." Commonwealth 107 (29
          February 1980): 104-07.

          Sketches the rise of media-conscious evangelicals in politics,
          traces evangelical political interest back to the 19th century,
          notes the move of contemporary evangelicals toward a centrist
          position, and suggests that "the world of conservative
          Christianity will be in ferment for some time."

901.   Fowler, Robert Booth. A New Engagement: Evangelical Political
          Thought, 1966-1976. Grand Rapids: Eerdmans, 1982. 298 p.

          A thoughtfully done two-part study: first, "different clusters
          of evangelicals" from Christianity Today, Billy Graham, and the
          Schaeffers to Carl Henry to the radicals; second, a look at
          selected issues like race, hunger, the family and Vietnam.
          "Taken together these two approaches expose the richness, the
          diversity, and the complexity of evangelical political and
          social thought." Bibliography. Index.

902.   Grenz, Stanley J. "Isaac Backus: Eighteenth Century Light on the
          Contemporary School Prayer Issue." Fides et Historia 18 (October
          1986): 5-14.

          Baptist Backus, 18th century advocate of religious liberty,
          contended for a view of church and state that might be
          interpreted as support for those who advocate prayer in public
          schools, but Grenz feels that the lessons of the intervening
          years might well teach us (and Backus) that prayer is a
          religious expression, not a civil duty.

903.   Gribbin, William. The Churches Militant: The War of 1812 and
          American Religion. New Haven: Yale University Press, 1973.
          210 p.

          Sets the second war with Britain in "the current of evangelical
          fervor and moral reform." and uses denominational leaders as
          spokesmen for the role played by religion in American life.
          thus providing a case study of attitudes in the early republic
          era. Twenty-three-page bibliography. Index.

904.   Hammond, Phillip E. "Evangelical Politics: Generalizations and
        Implications." Review of Religious Research 27 (December 1985):
        89-92.

            Summary of findings of the articles in this issue of RRR;
            Hammond traces evangelical political involvement to the
            centrist nature of American politics and its response to the
            1960s counter culture.

905.   Hart, Benjamin. Faith and Freedom: The Christian Roots of
        American Liberty. San Bernadino, CA: Here's Life, 1988. 384 p.

            Aiming "to correct the many popular misconceptions about
            America's past," Hart traces the idea of liberty through the
            colonial and revolutionary eras, with interpretations of
            persons and events that not all evangelical historians would
            espouse. Bibliography. Index.

906.   Hatch, Nathan O. The Sacred Cause of Liberty: Republican Thought
        and the Millennium in Revolutionary New England. New Haven: Yale
        University Press, 1977. 197 p.

            Based on an analysis of Congregational clergy sermons over a
            sixty-year period, Hatch contends that millennial thought and
            republican thought converge as a central theme in the rela-
            tionship between religion and politics in Revolutionary New
            England. Bibliography of sermons; bibliographical references.
            Index.

907.   Henry, Carl F. H. "Evangelicals Jump on the Political Bandwagon."
        Christianity Today 24 (24 October 1980): 20-25.

            Warns that the many voices only promote confusion, that
            single-issue politics is dangerous, and that while evangelicals
            ought to be biblical, the Bible gives principles, not detailed
            blueprints.

908.   Henry, Paul B. Politics for Evangelicals. Valley Forge: Judson,
        1974. 127 p.

            Later a U.S. Representative from Michigan, Henry encourages
            entering the political arena and suggests strategies for action
            in politics. Bibliographical references.

909.   Hogan, William. "Why I am a Political Conservative." Eternity 16
        (October 1965): 25-28.

A United Presbyterian clergyman "explains why he thinks the
Bible supports a conservative position." The same issue
carries a companion piece on political liberalism.

910.   Hutcheson, Richard G., Jr. God in the White House: How Religion
         Has Changed the Modern Presidency. New York: Macmillan, 1988.
         267 p.

         Focuses on the post-Watergate presidencies, which responded to
         the "multidimensional moral crisis of the late twentieth
         century," reflected a long-held American belief "that public
         morality is rooted in religion" and that presidents "exemplify
         the common underlying faith in God," and fit well with the
         notion that separated church from state but not religion from
         society. Bibliographical references. Index.

911.   Johannesen, Stanley. "American Republicanism and Christian
         Piety." In The Terrible Meek: Religion and Revolution in
         Cross-Cultural Perspective, ed. Lonnie D. Kliever, 1-23. New
         York: Paragon Press, 1987.

         Sees American civil religion as "a phase of popular religious
         practices and collective perceptions in the West extending
         backward to antiquity," whose narrative context is "the long
         history of remissions [liberty]."

912.   Johnson, Stephen D., and Joseph B. Tamney. "The Christian Right
         and the 1984 Presidential Election." Review of Religious Research
         27 (December 1985): 124-33.

         Sample of 351 Muncie, Indiana, residents discloses that
         "moderate Christian Rightism seems to have played a role in the
         election of Ronald Reagan, but political party identity and
         economic well-being had by far the greatest role in his
         re-election."

913.   Jorstad, Erling. Evangelicals in the White House: The Cultural
         Maturation of Born Again Christianity. New York: Edwin Mellen,
         1981. 171 p.

914.   Kantzer, Kenneth S. "Summing Up: An Evangelical View of Church
         and State." Christianity Today 29 (19 April 1985): 28-31.

         Summary of the Christianity Today Institute forum on the
         Christian as citizen, published in this issue of CT.

915.   Karmarkovic, Alex. "American Evangelical Responses to the Russian
        Revolution and the Rise of Communism in the Twentieth Century."
        Fides et Historia 4 (Spring 1972): 11-27.

        The first of three papers on the general topic, presented at
        the fall 1970 Conference on Faith and History; looks at the
        Russian Revolution, the threat its expansion posed, and the
        American evangelical response, which regards Communism as a
        serious threat, but which believes the answer is in the Gospel
        message.

916.   Linder, Robert D., and Richard V. Pierard. Twilight of the
        Saints: Biblical Christianity and Civil Religion in America.
        Downers Grove: InterVarsity, 1978. 213 p.

        Two evangelical historians examine American civic faith in
        order to determine how Christians should relate to it; the
        civil religion idea, its role in American life, and its claim
        to transcendence, about which evangelicals are warned.
        Bibliography. Index.

917.   Lipset, Seymour Martin, and Earl Raab. "The Election and the
        Evangelicals." Commentary 71 (March 1981): 25-31.

        The swing toward conservatism in the 1980 election "and the
        emergence of a political evangelical movement were parallel
        developments which may have been mutually reinforcing rather
        than related to one another as cause and effect."

918.   Marsden, George M. "Politics and Religion in American History."
        Reformed Journal 38 (October 1988): 11-16.

        Nuanced survey of the topic with reference to Puritanism, the
        revolution, 19th century evangelical-oriented Republicanism,
        the reorientation of 1896 (with the "ideal of secularized
        consensus" in its wake), and the emergence of evangelicals in
        politics since 1968.

919.   McAllister, Ronald J. "Religion in the Public Arena: A Parodox of
        Secularization." Journal of Church and State 30 (Winter 1988):
        15-31.

        Seeing the flaw in the secularization paradigm--"faith and
        daily life are increasingly divorced for modern people"--
        McAllister offers a dynamic model that includes both tradi-
        tional secularization ("disbarring religion and enervating
        religious values") and "reverse" secularization (religion

affecting politics) to explain the complex relations of
religion and politics in American life.

920.   McLoughlin, William G. "The Illusions and Dangers of the New
Christian Right." Foundations 25 (April-June 1982): 128-43.

In its renewed fight against political and religious
liberalism, the NCR mistakenly identifies itself with
Puritanism, 19th century evangelical social action, and an
objective view of science, and incorrectly sees America as a
Christian nation.

921.   Monsma, Stephen V. "Evangelicals on Politics." Christianity
Today 21 (20 May 1977): 34-38.

Review of five books published in 1976 that address the two
issues of involvement in political life and attitudes toward
the nation; the authors vary widely in their approaches.

922.   Mouw, Richard J. "Evangelicals and Political Activism."
Christian Century 89 (27 December 1972): 1316-19.

A dissenter from the evangelical establishment, Mouw believes
the emphasis on political individualism and political passivity
must be replaced by "active political evangelism."

923.   Nemeth, Roger J., and Donald A. Luidens. "The New Christian Right
and Mainline Protestantism: The Case of the Reformed Church in
America." Sociological Analysis 49 (Winter 1989): 343-52.

"[E]xamines the penetration of the NCR social and political
agenda into one mainline Protestant denomination," concluding
that the influence of the NCR in the RCA "is relatively small."

924.   Nesmith, Bruce Forrester. "Presidential Campaigns, White Evangelicals, and the New Republican Coalition." Ph.D. diss.,
University of Illinois at Urbana-Champaign, 1987. 266 p.

925.   Neuhaus, Richard John, and Michael Cromartie, eds. Piety and
Politics: Evangelicals and Fundamentalists Confront the World.
Washington, DC: Ethics and Public Policy Center, 1987. 424 p.

Reprint of twenty-six essays written in the 1980s by and about
evangelicals and fundamentalists in public life. Written from
stances that cover the spectrum of political positions.
Bibliographical references. Index.

926.   Noll, Mark A. One Nation Under God? Christian Faith and Political
        Action in America. San Francisco: Harper & Row, 1988. 213 p.

        Contending that "the demands of faith should always provide the
        framework for political action, rather than the reverse," Noll
        studies the "Christian heritage" (not "Christian nation") of
        America, analyzes several points of Christian influence on
        national political life, from the Revolution to Prohibition,
        and suggests "a framework for Christian political involvement
        today." Appendixes. Bibliographical references. Index.

927.   _____. Princeton and the Republic 1768-1822. Princeton:
        Princeton University Press, 1989. 340 p.

928.   _____, ed. Religion and American Politics: From the Colonial
        Period to the 1980s. New York: Oxford University Press, 1989.
        384 p.

        A collection of seventeen essays on the subject, several by
        evangelicals. Bibliographical references.

929.   _____. "A Tale of Two Revolutions." Reformed Journal 39 (July
        1989): 16-21.

        Compares and contrasts the American and French revolutions,
        evangelical support for both (at least at the beginning), and
        addresses why Christianity was so closely tied to the American
        Revolution but not to the French.

930.   Noll, Mark A., Nathan O. Hatch, and George M. Marsden. The Search
        for Christian America. Westchester: Crossway, 1983. 188 p.
        Expanded edition, Colorado Springs: Helmers and Howard, 1989.
        199 p.

        Three prominent evangelical historians set out to prove a
        twofold thesis: "that early America does not deserve to be
        considered uniquely, distinctly or even predominantly
        Christian"; "the idea of a 'Christian nation' is a very
        ambiguous concept," even "harmful to effective Christian action
        in society." Twenty-eight-page appended bibliographical essay
        by Randall Balmer.

931.   Patterson, James Alan. "Evangelicals and the Presidential
        Elections of 1972, 1976, and 1980." Fides et Historia 18 (June
        1986): 44-62.

Study of Evangelicals for McGovern, support for born-again candidate Jimmy Carter, and the emergence of the New Christian Right in the first Reagan campaign. Demonstrates the variety of political opinion among evangelicals and the temptation they face to wrap political ideology in religious garb.

932.   Peterson, Walfred H. Thy Liberty in Law. Nashville: Broadman, 1978. 185 p.

A theory of religious liberty based on the Bible; "the relationship between theories of religious liberty and the law of liberty"; and, based mostly on Supreme Court decisions, description and assessment of "the American law of religious liberty." Bibliographical references. Index.

933.   Pierard, Richard V. "Evangelicals and the Bicentennial." Reformed Journal 26 (October 1976): 19-23.

Instead of concentrating on conferences, publications, music, trinkets and a distorted picture of a Christian past, American evangelicals "should realistically assess the national goals and the progress being made toward their achievement."

934.   _____. "The Great Eclipse." Eternity 35 (February 1984): 14-19.

Decline from the mid-1920s to 1940s of evangelical political activism, then an increase after WWII, especially strong from 1960 on; in spite of a "regained political activism," evangelicals "still do not speak with one voice."

935.   _____. "Mending the Fence: Reagan and the Evangelicals." Reformed Journal 33 (June 1983): 18-21.

Three Reagan speeches to evangelical audiences characterize his fence-mending; misplaced, says Pierard, because not all evangelicals espouse the same political agenda.

936.   _____. "Religion and the 1984 Election Campaign." Review of Religious Research 27 (December 1985): 98-114.

Religious involvement in presidential politics is not new. nor is it out of keeping with the First Amendment. but religious supporters of Reagan may well have exceeded the bounds of propriety and they were "hardly the decisive element in the Reagan victory."

937.   . The Unequal Yoke: Evangelical Christianity and Political Conservatism. Philadelphia: J.B. Lippincott, 1970. 191 p.

Viewing the yoke as "crippling orthodox Christianity" and
emphasizing the need to reverse "the trend toward political,
economic, and social conservatism," Pierard describes the
nature of the yoke and offers a center to left-of-center
position as a political option for evangelicals. Annotated
bibliography. Index.

938.   Pinnock, Clark H. "A Pilgrimage in Political Theology--A Personal
Witness." In Liberation Theology, ed. Ronald Nash, 105-120.
Milford, MI: Mott Media, 1984.

Pinnock's three-phase pilgrimage (with most attention to the
third): in the mainstream, 1953-1969; on the radical edge,
1970-1978; return to the political center ("neo-Puritan
politics"), 1978-1984.

939.   Pitzer, Donald E. "Revolution and the Evangelicals." Fides et
Historia 4 (Fall 1971): 45-49.

Originally a response to three papers given at the 1970
Conference on Faith and History, on the broad subject of
evangelicals and the American Revolution, attempting to tie
those papers together.

940.   Pratt, Andrew Leroy. "Religious Faith and Civil Religion:
Evangelical Responses to the Vietnam War, 1964-1973." Ph.D.
diss., The Southern Baptist Theological Seminary, 1988. 518 p.

941.   Rochelle, Larry. "Born-Again Politics: Now the Republicans."
Humanist 40 (November-December 1980): 18-25.

Deals with the question whether Reagan can "take the born-again
vote away from Carter in 1980?" discussing their contrasting
positions, and the born-again rhetoric and crusade, noting its
results in Illinois.

942.   Rothenberg, Stuart, and Frank Newport. The Evangelical Voter:
Religion and Politics in America. Washington, DC: The Institute
for Government and Politics of The Free Congress Research and
Education Foundation, 1984. 176 p.

Based on a national survey (1983), a study of evangelicals and
fundamentalists that focuses on a variety of questions related
to political attitudes and behavior, concluding that "there is

no easy way to summarize or categorize the political impact of
the evangelical voter . . . Evangelicals are almost as varied
as the American public at large." Bibliography.

943.   Shupe, Anson. "The Reconstructionist Movement on the New
        Christian Right." Christian Century 106 (4 October 1989): 880-82.

        About "a relatively new creature on the right wing of Christi-
        anity," the "antipluralistic Christian Reconstructionist
        movement and the drastic changes it seeks in American Society."

944.   Streiker, Lowell D., and Gerald S. Stober. Religion and the New
        Majority: Billy Graham, Middle America, and the Politics of the
        70s. New York: Association Press, 1972. 202 p.

        Describes the religion of middle America, epitomized by Billy
        Graham and his fundamentalism, "and the ways in which this
        religion will influence the political decisions made by
        Americans in the perilous days ahead." Notes at end of each
        chapter. Index.

945.   Thomas, Cal. "How Much Politics Can Evangelicals Withstand?" In
        The Evangelical Round Table. Eastern College and Eastern Baptist
        Theological Seminary (St. Davids, PA, 1986). In Evangelicalism:
        Surviving Its Success, moderator Kenneth Kantzer, ed. David A.
        Fraser, 148-55. Princeton: Princeton University Press, 1987.

        A former spokesman for the Moral Majority considers "how far
        the church ought to go in entangling itself in the political
        life of America"; he uses Abraham Kuyper's career as a model
        for what ought to be.

946.   Valeri, Mark. "The New Divinity and the American Revolution."
        William and Mary Quarterly 46 (October 1989): 741-69.

947.   Webber, Robert E. The Moral Majority: Right or Wrong? West-
        chester: Cornerstone, 1981. 190 p.

        With the Moral Majority on the right and the WCC on the left,
        evangelical Webber carves out a centrist (also called prophetic
        center) position which emphasizes that the church as a divine
        institution "should seek no earthly power," and as the people
        of God "is in constant confrontation and engagement with the
        fallen powers which control all levels of the social order."
        Bibliography. Documents.

948.   Wells, Ronald A. "Recovering the Mind of the Constitution."
         Fides et Historia 19 (June-July 1987): 7-19.

         After surveying constitutional changes over 200 years, Wells,
         following Robert Bellah and Richard John Neuhaus, advocates
         recovering the mind behind the biblical and republican language
         of the founders, but not in the mode of the moral majoritar-
         ians.

949.   Wilson, John F., and Donald L. Drakeman, eds. Church and State in
         American History: The Burden of Religious Pluralism. 2d ed.
         Boston: Beacon Press, 1987. 313 p.

         A fine collection of primary and secondary documents, chrono-
         logically arranged, on the issues that impinged on church-state
         relations from the 17th century to the present. Bibliography.

950.   Wood, James E., Jr. "Religion and Politics--1984." Journal of
         Church and State 26 (Autumn 1984): 401-11.

         The nature of religious (especially the Religious Right)
         political involvement in presidential politics has reached
         "unparallelled" and "unprecedented" proportions, and threatens
         the balance of church and state in political life.

951.   Wuthnow, Robert. "The Political Rebirth of American Evangeli-
         cals." In The New Christian Right: Mobilization and Legitimation,
         eds. Robert C. Liebman and Robert Wuthnow, 167-85. New York:
         Aldine, 1983.

         Evidence of the rebirth, the importance of religious symbols in
         the evangelical ideology, "well served by the blending together
         of politics and morality in the 70s," the whole providing
         "evidence of the capacity of religion to adapt to social
         conditions in ways yet little understood."

See also items 59, 77, 119, 192, 193, 197, 201, 206, 214, 221, 227, 233,
     276, 312, 323, 341, 360, 379, 699, 762, 778, 862, 963, 964, 971, 1050,
     1056, 1145, 1254, 1483, 1619, 1632, 1640, 1649, 1666, 1673, 1904, 1905,
     1907, 1909, 1912, 1913, 1914, 1925, 1926, 1937, 1939, 2550.

                         F.   Society and Religion

952.   Apel, William D. "The Social Gospel in Evangelical Garb." Explor
         2 (Fall 1976): 55-58.

A review of The Young Evangelicals (1974), by Richard
Quebedeaux, The Chicago Declaration (1974), edited by Ronald J.
Sider, and Sojourners (1976-) (was The Post American, 1971-
1975); The Chicago Declaration, for example, "bears witness to
a new kind of evangelical Christian whose basic characteristic
is a commitment to both the personal and public dimensions of
the Gospel."

953.   Armerding, Hudson T. "The Evangelical and Today's World."
        Bibliotheca Sacra 122 (January 1965): 54-62.

        Calls for evangelical social and political involvement, but
        without either "accommodation or secession."

954.   Barlow, Jack. "Response to 'Evangelicals and the Age of Reform,
        1870-1930: An Assessment.'" Fides et Historia 16 (Spring-Summer
        1984): 86-89.

        Responding to Robert R. Mathisen's article in the same issue
        (pp. 74-85), Barlow points up the difficulty of defining
        evangelicalism, social gospel and other terms, and how this in
        turn complicates answering the initial question.

955.   Bockmühl, Klaus. Evangelicals and Social Ethics: A Commentary on
        Article 5 of the Lausanne Covenant. Translated by David T.
        Priestley. Downers Grove: InterVarsity; Exeter, England:
        Paternoster, 1979. 47 p.

        Exposition of the nine verbs of action in Article 5 of the
        Lausanne Covenant (1975), on the social responsibility of
        Christians, pointing "to a truly theological social ethic which
        the whole church needs today." Bibliographical references.

956.   Bosch, David J. "In Search of a New Evangelical Understanding."
        In In Word and Deed: Evangelism and Social Responsibility, ed.
        Bruce J. Nicholls, 63-83. Grand Rapids: Eerdmans, 1985.

        Recent ecumenical developments; the roots of contemporary
        evangelism; some negative influences on evangelical social
        involvement; suggestions on overcoming the evangelism-social
        responsibility dualism inherent in much mission theorizing.

957.   Bridger, Francis. "Review-Article: Ronald Preston's 'The Future
        of Christian Ethics.'" Modern Churchman 30, no. 3 (1988): 40-45.

        Denies Preston's "primary thesis . . . that British
        Evangelicalism has been forced to resort to Dooyerwaardianism

[sic] for its theological basis"; concludes that "the growth of
Evangelical social theology . . . is likely to continue . . .
and that it will make a significant contribution to the
ecumenical context."

958.   Cerillo, Augustus, Jr. "Survey of Recent Evangelical Social
Thought." Christian Scholar's Review 5, no. 3 (1976): 272-80.

Categorizes evangelicals as conservative, liberal, and radical,
by their positions on social issues; a very helpful look at the
literature.

959.   "The Chicago Call: An Appeal to Evangelicals." Christianity Today
21 (17 June 1977): 28-29.

A reprinting of the text of the Chicago Call, issued 1-3 May
1977, urging evangelicals to have greater concern for
traditional "churchmanship."

960.   "The Chicago Call: An Appeal to Evangelicals." In The Orthodox
Evangelicals: Who They Are and What They Are Saying, eds. Robert
E. Webber and Donald Bloesch, 11-18. Nashville: Thomas Nelson,
1978.

In a caution to resurgent evangelicalism, a group of forty-five
diverse evangelical leaders identify and explore eight themes,
historically and theologically, in a call for evangelicalism to
return to historic orthodoxy.

961.   Christenson, Laurence. "What One Charismatic Would Like to Say to
Some Evangelical Social Activists." Transformation 5 (October-
December 1988): 19-20.

962.   Clouse, Robert G. "The Evangelical Christian, Social Concern, and
a Theology of Hope." Evangelical Quarterly 44 (April-June 1972):
68-75.

Premillennialism, especially its dispensational form, mitigates
against social action; Clouse appeals for a change in attitude
that will foster social, political and economic involvement.

963.   Clouse, Robert G., Robert D. Linder, and Richard V. Pierard, eds.
The Cross and the Flag. Carol Stream, IL: Creation House, 1972.
261 p.

Eleven evangelicals write on significant issues in essays
"designed to help Christians bring their faith to bear on the

issues of the day." Good examples of evangelical social
concern early in the evangelical upsurge of the 1970s.
Bibliographical references. Index.

964.   _____, eds. Protest and Politics: Christianity and
Contemporary Affairs. Greenwood, SC: Attic Press, 1968. 271 p.

Eleven essays, early on in the rise of evangelical social
interest, address a number of issues on the relation between
Christianity and participation in the public order.
Bibliographical references. Index.

965.   Crum, Gary. "Fundamentalists and Abortion." New Oxford Review 55
(July-August 1988): 16-21.

Provides the biblical basis--with texts cited--for the
fundamentalist anti-abortion position.

966.   Curry, Dean C., ed. Evangelicals and the Bishops' Pastoral
Letter. Grand Rapids: Eerdmans, 1984. 254 p.

Evangelical response to the significant and controversial
statement, critical of government policy, by American Catholic
Bishops regarding nuclear deterrence and war. Bibliographical
references.

967.   Dayton, Donald W. Discovering an Evangelical Heritage. New York:
Harper & Row, 1976. 147 p.

A significant volume, which contends that nineteenth century
American evangelicalism had a strong social concern and
practice. Bibliography.

968.   _____. "Piety and Radicalism: Ante-bellum Social Evangelicalism in the United States." Radical Religion 3 (1976): 36-40.

Centers on the abolition movement and the role in it played by
Charles Finney, Jonathan Blanchard (founding president of
Wheaton College), and the Wesleyan Methodist Church.

969.   _____. "Social and Political Conservatism of Modern American
Evangelicalism: A Preliminary Search for the Reasons." Union
Seminary Quarterly Review 32 (Winter 1977): 71-80.

Using a three-type understanding of "evangelical." Dayton
explains the "great reversal" (loss of social involvement by
post-fundamentalist evangelicalism) by the rise of

fundamentalism, with its Princeton theology and its emphasis on premillennialism.

970. Edge, Findley B. "The Evangelical Concern for Social Justice." Religious Education 74 (September-October 1979): 471-89.

Contends that the turn-of-the-century social gospel forced conservatives away from social involvement, but now a "new breed" of evangelicals--like Jim Wallis of Sojourners--is picking up the concern.

971. Eells, Robert J. Forgotten Saint: The Life of Theodore Freling-huysen--A Case Study of Christian Leadership. Lanham, MD: University Press of America, 1987. 140 p.

Study of an ante-bellum New Jersey evangelical who held several political posts and supported various parts of the "benevolent empire," as an example of evangelical involvement in social and political issues. Bibliography. Index.

972. Ellison, Craig W. "Understanding Current Urban Realities." United Evangelical Action 48 (May-June 1989): 4-6.

Professor of Counseling and Urban Studies and Director of the Urban Studies Program at Alliance Theological Seminary, he suggests "five key principles for evangelical presence and witness in the city."

973. Essig, James D. The Bonds of Wickedness: American Evangelicals Against Slavery, 1770-1808. Philadelphia: Temple University Press, 1982. 208 p.

Holds that opposition to slavery resulted from the nature of evangelicalism, although the latter was divided in its stance, particularly as it gained in numerical and economic strength. Bibliographical references. Index.

974. Fairfield, James, ed. Probe: For an Evangelism that Cares. Scottdale, PA: Herald Press, 1972. 159 p.

From the Mennonite perspective. Bibliographical references.

975. Ferngren, Gary B. "Caring and Curing: The Evangelical-Fundamen-talist Tradition." In Vol. II of The Best in Theology. gen. ed., J. I. Packer, 141-62. Carol Stream, IL: Christianity Today, 1987.

Chapter 18 of Ronald L. Numbers and Darrel W. Amundsen, eds.,
Caring and Curing: Health and Medicine in the Western Religious
Traditions (1986); Ferngren argues that evangelicalism "has
traditionally shown its primary concern to be with salvation
and the Christian life in a personal, individualistic manner";
still, some interest in health and healing, suffering, mental
health, humanitarianism, and biomedical issues has surfaced,
especially recently.

976.   Forster, Roger. "What Can Charismatics and Evangelical Social
          Activists Learn From Each Other?" Transformation 5 (October-
          December 1988): 3-7.

          Both have a base in biblical Christianity (word) and each needs
          the other: the social activists need spiritual power (wonder),
          and the charismatics need activism (work).

977.   Foster, Charles I. An Errand of Mercy: The Evangelical United
          Front, 1790-1837. Chapel Hill: University of North Carolina
          Press, 1960. 320 p.

          The U.S. received "an intensive, systematic indoctrination in
          the theology of Evangelical Protestantism" in the formative
          years carried out not by denominations but through societies
          (i.e. the united front,) first created in Britain (which Foster
          describes), then in America; the front collapsed in the 1830s,
          due to denominational and societal divisions. Thirty-three-page
          bibliography. Index.

978.   Friedman, Lawrence J. "Confidence and Pertinacity in Evangelical
          Abolitionism: Lewis Tappan's Circle." American Quarterly 31
          (Spring 1979): 81-106.

          Eight evangelicals in the Tappan circle who advocated a variety
          of reforms, including church-centered abolitionism, remained
          close to each other, and exhibited both "insensitivity and
          rigidity" and "pertinacity and innovation."

979.   Furness, Charles Y. The Christian and the Social Order. Old
          Tappan: Fleming Revell, 1974. 254 p.

          Baptist Furness focuses "on human need and on evangelical
          action to meet that need" by discussing past evangelical social
          action, emphasizing the need to address current problems
          (particularly poverty among black Americans), and giving
          biblical and theological reasons for social action.
          Bibliography. Index.

980. Gaebelein, Frank E. "Evangelicals and Social Concern." Journal of the Evangelical Theological Society 25 (March 1982): 17-22.

Applauds the "renaissance of social concern among evangelicals" and lays out some biblical principles that must underlie the concern.

981. Giesbrecht, Herbert. "The Evangelical Church and Social Change: Toward a Broader Perspective." Direction 16 (Fall 1987): 62-70.

Explores "the dynamic relationship between enduring ideals and changing situations," proposing six "dimensions" which an adequate perspective will contain.

982. Goetzman, Martha M. "The Social Gospel and Evangelicalism in America: An Historical Study of the Doctrinal Confrontation." M.A. thesis, Florida Atlantic University, 1974. 190 p.

983. Graffam, Lillian H. "Evangelical Social Concern Expressed Overseas." Evangelical Missions Quarterly 8 (Fall 1971): 17-22.

By the editor of The World Relief Reporter; The World Relief Commission, begun in 1944 as an arm of the National Association of Evangelicals, in 1970 distributed aid worth more than $2,500,000; discusses aspects of the program.

984. Grounds, Vernon C. "Evangelical Views of Today's Moral Crisis." In Evangelicals and Jews in Conversation on Scripture, Theology, and History, eds. Marc H. Tanenbaum, Marvin R. Wilson, and A. James Rudin, 248-65. Grand Rapids: Baker, 1978.

In the face of moral decay and social disruption some evangelicals choose not to act, while others (Grounds included) urge action.

985. _____. Evangelicalism and Social Responsibility. Scottdale, PA: Herald Press, 1969. 39 p.

The biblical data supporting social responsibility, and ten affirmations regarding evangelical social involvement.

986. Hageman, Howard. "Will Evangelicals Penetrate the Inner City?" Eternity 21 (January 1970): 23-25.

After contending in an earlier article (December 1969) that evangelical efforts are ineffective and paralyzed, he argues that we cannot sidestep the inner city, given the biblical mandate for social action.

987.   Halteman, Jim. <u>Market Capitalism and Christianity</u>. Grand Rapids:
        Baker, 1988. 176 p.

        Representing "the Anabaptist approach to Christian practice,"
        economist Halteman discusses the essentials of economic
        systems, offers a model of economic practice for a community of
        believers, describes the Western economic world, and "suggests
        ways for the community of faith to interact effectively with
        market capitalism without selling out to its spirit."
        Glossary. Bibliography. Index.

988.   Hancock, Robert Lincoln, ed. <u>The Ministry of Development in
        Evangelical Perspective: A Symposium on the Social and Spiritual
        Mandate</u>. Convenor Carl F. H. Henry. Pasadena: William Carey
        Library, 1979. 110 p.

        Articles presented by a "diverse group of scholars, missionary
        agency executives and community development specialists," at a
        Symposium sponsored by Development Assistance Services, Inc.,
        and held in November 1978 in Colorado Springs. Henry's contri-
        butions include the concluding chapter: "Evangelicals and the
        Social Scene: God's Plan for Salvation and Justice."
        Bibliographical references.

989.   Heasman, Kathleen J. <u>Evangelicals in Action: An Appraisal of
        Their Social Work in the Victorian Era</u>. London: Bles, 1962.
        310 p.

        Excellent study of English evangelicals and the extensive
        social work in which they engaged. Bibliography. Index.

990.   Helm, Paul. "The British National Evangelical Conference on
        Social Ethics." <u>International Reformed Bulletin</u> no. 73 (1978):
        25-27.

        The Conference (September 11-15, 1978) convened "to work at the
        biblical and methodological foundations of a renewed social
        concern" (UK and USA); 120 invited members met under the
        leadership of John Stott in sessions covering a wide variety of
        subjects in lectures and discussions.

991.   Hendel, Kurt K. "The Care of the Poor: An Evangelical Perspec-
        tive." <u>Currents in Theology and Mission</u> 15 (December 1988):
        526-32.

        Johannes Bugenhagen (1485-1558), friend of Luther, provides a
        carefully constructed model for poor relief, with the creation
        of a "poor chest" as the central means of dispersing help.

992.   Henry, Carl F. H. "Carl Henry on Evangelical Identity."
        Sojourners 5 (April 1976): 27-32.

        A debating-style interview with Jim Wallis and Wes Michaelson
        in which Henry responds to a number of questions and state-
        ments, mostly on social ethics issues.

993.   _____. Christian Countermoves in a Decadent Culture.
        Portland, OR: Multnomah, 1986. 149 p.

        Papers and addresses, all but one from the 1980s, on the
        problem of, the prescription for, and the physicians needed in
        the decadent culture. Bibliographical references. Indexes.

994.   _____. "Evangelical Social Concern." Christianity Today 18
        (1 March 1974): 99-100.

        Supports the "Declaration of Evangelical Social Concern"
        (Thanksgiving 1973) as a statement that avoided both right and
        left ideologies and concentrated "on the social righteousness
        that God demands."

995.   _____. "Evangelicals in the Social Struggle." Christianity
        Today 10 (8 October 1965): 3-11.

        Evangelicalism's history of social concern; evangelical vs.
        liberal social ethics; distinctives and governing principles in
        social ethics.

996.   _____. "Evangelism and Social Action." Crux 16 (September
        1980): 24-29.

        The keynote speech at the 1979 Congress of the Evangelical
        Fellowship of India "on a subject of continuing controversy in
        evangelical circles." Summarizes conflicting views on the
        interrelationship, focuses on the issues involved, and presents
        alternative positions.

997.   Holladay, J. Douglas. "19th Century Evangelical Activism; From
        Private Charity to State Intervention, 1830-50." Historical
        Magazine of the Protestant Episcopal Church 51 (March 1982):
        53-79.

        Develops "the important yet frequently overlooked contribution
        of evangelical reformers in the harnessing of the State to
        supplement and, at times, even replace private initiatives to
        improve England's social condition."

998.   Hollinger, Dennis P. "American Individualism and Evangelical
        Social Ethics: Study of 'Christianity Today,' 1956-1976." Ph.D.
        diss., Drew University, 1981. 371 p.

        By his study of Christianity Today over a 20-year span,
        Hollinger argues an "inexorable link" between American individ-
        ualism and evangelical social ethics. He rejects as inadequate
        the "individualistic world view" of this American-evangelical
        alliance and contends that the community, not the individual,
        should be the basis for social ethics. The basis for
        Hollinger's book, Individualism and Social Ethics: An Evan-
        gelical Syncretism. Lanham, MD: University Press of America,
        1983. 277 p.

999.   Johnson, D. A. "Between Evangelicalism and a Social Gospel; The
        Case of Joseph Rayner Stephens." Church History 42 (June 1973):
        229-42.

        Englishman Stephens, sometime Methodist clergyman, combined
        social concern with individual regeneration in ways that
        foreshadowed the later social gospel but with the political
        resolution of issues left out.

1000.   Jorstad, Erling. "The Born Again Resurgence." Religion in Life
        48 (Summer 1979): 153-61.

        Media emphasis on resurgence has clouded the division over two
        main issues: the what and how of biblical teaching on the
        essentials of discipleship; what the social dimension of that
        discipleship should be.

1001.   Kantzer, Kenneth S. "A Farewell to Harms." Christianity Today 31
        (11 December 1987): 14-15.

        Warns of two dangers: staying out of the culture through
        separation from it; blunting the moral thrust of the gospel by
        accepting the value system of the culture.

1002.   Knott, James P. "Evangelicalism and Its Influence on English
        Social Reform During Part of the Eighteenth and Nineteenth
        Centuries." Ph.D. diss., University of Southern California. 1939.

1003.   Lesick, Lawrence Thomas. The Lane Rebels: Evangelicalism and
        Antislavery in Antebellum America. Metuchen. NJ: Scarecrow Press.
        1980. 278 p.

A 1979 Vanderbilt University dissertation by the same title
that treats the theological underpinnings of the evangelical
contribution to the antislavery movement; instructive as to the
implications of theology for how people act in society; a fine
contribution. Bibliography.

1004.   Lewis, Donald M. "The Evangelical Mission to the Poor in
Nineteenth Century England." Crux 21 (September 1985): 9-16.

Purposes "to demonstrate that English evangelicals were greatly
concerned with evangelizing the city in the nineteenth century,
and that they made enormous efforts to accomplish this goal";
also, that "evangelicals were among those who took the lead in
attempting to make people aware of the appalling conditions of
the urban slums."

1005.   _____. Lighten Their Darkness: The Evangelical Mission to
Working-Class London, 1828-1860. Westport, CT: Greenwood Press,
1986. 369 p.

Describes the development during these decades, of an interdenominational thrust that united the Anglican and dissenting
churches in efforts that were especially highlighted in the
London City Mission and its evangelistic and social work.
Twenty-five-page bibliography. Index.

1006.   Linder, Robert D. "Modern Evangelical Christianity, Social
Concern and Hope: An Historical Perspective." Evangelical
Quarterly 44 (April-June 1972): 76-83.

Cites examples of evangelical social concern from the time of
the Reformation, contends that the fundamentalist-modernist
controversy blunted evangelical social conscience, and appeals
for renewed thinking and action on social issues.

1007.   _____. "The Resurgence of Evangelical Social Concern (1925-
75)." In The Evangelicals: What They Believe, Who They Are, Where
They Are Changing, eds. David F. Wells and John D. Woodbridge,
189-210. Nashville: Abingdon, 1975.

Examines the historical background of this resurgence and
analyzes "the factors which have helped to bring it about."

1008.   Loveland, Anne C. "Evangelicalism and 'Immediate Emancipation' in
American Anti-Slavery Thought." Journal of Southern History 32
(May 1966): 172-88.

Nurturing "a utopian. reformist disposition." evangelicalism
influenced the emergence of immediatism through those radicals
who were converts to evangelicalism and, more importantly,
through its system of beliefs.

1009.   Lutzer, Erwin W. The Morality Gap: An Evangelical Response to
Situation Ethics. Chicago: Moody, 1972. 125 p.

Addresses the defects in the situation ethics espoused by
Joseph Fletcher and others, and offers a biblical alternative.
Bibliography.

1010.   Maclear, J. F. "The Evangelical Alliance and the Antislavery
Crusade." Huntington Library Quarterly 42 (Spring 1979): 141-64.

1011.   Magnuson, Norris A. "The Church in Practical Responsibility: An
Investigation of the Evangelical Church and Social Concern."
Bethel Seminary Journal 14 (Spring 1966): 12-27.

The "necessity and relevance" of social concern, given the
teaching of Scripture and the nature of the new birth/life; the
church's record, both of failure and of frequent remarkable
response to human need; focuses on the late 19th and early 20th
centuries; suggestions for contemporary evangelicals.

1012.   _____. Salvation in the Slums: Evangelical Social Work,
1865-1920. Metuchen, NJ: Scarecrow Press, 1977. 299 p.

Relates the story of the extensive social concern and action of
a number of evangelical groups and organizations between the
Civil War and the end of WWI, showing the interplay of evangelism and "holiness" emphases with social concern and action.
103 pages of "notes" and bibliographical essay. Revision of
his Ph.D. dissertation (University of Minnesota, 1968).

1013.   Marsden, George M. "Demythologizing Evangelicalism: A Review of
Donald W. Dayton's Discovering an Evangelical Heritage."
Christian Scholar's Review 7, no. 2-3 (1977): 203-11.

With a number of qualifications, he thinks this book to be "a
worthwhile contribution to our understanding of the evangelical
past." Includes a reply by Donald Dayton and a "Postscript" by
Marsden.

1014.   _____. "Evangelical Social Concern: Dusting Off the Heritage."
Christianity Today 16 (12 May 1972): 8-11.

Cites several persons (some of whom are later called fundamentalists) and organizations as examples of evangelical social concern in post-Civil War America.

1015.   _____. "Evangelicalism in the Sociological Laboratory: A Review Article." Reformed Journal 34 (June 1984): 20-24.

Review of James Hunter, American Evangelicalism: Conservative Religion and the Quandry of Modernity (1983): a strangely uneven work because it combines the (suspect) use of statistical accounts with the (better) textual analysis of evangelical publications; withal, though, "a valuable, balanced, and informative volume on contemporary evangelicalism."

1016.   _____. "The Gospel of Wealth, the Social Gospel, and the Salvation of Souls in Nineteenth Century America." Fides et Historia 5 (Fall 1972/Spring 1973): 10-21.

Until 1890 orthodox Protestants had as much social gospel as the liberals; further, both espoused the gospel of wealth to some degree; after 1890 the intellectual and theological challenges of modernism froze evangelicals' social and political views in a Gilded Age pattern.

1017.   Mathisen, Gerald S. "Evangelical Social Concern: A Case Study in the Rhetoric of Legitimization." Ph.D. diss., Purdue University, 1982. 171 p.

Mathison traces the increased evangelical involvement in social issues since the 1940s and seeks to analyze "how these socially concerned evangelicals argue their cause and, more specifi-cally, how they have sought to legitimate their involvement in social concern, given evangelicalism's rhetorical tradition of non-involvement."

1018.   Mathisen, Robert R. "Evangelicals and the Age of Reform, 1870-1930: An Assessment." Fides et Historia 16 (Spring-Summer 1984): 74-85.

Mathisen describes the historiographical issue of when the evangelicals' "Great Reversal" (the decline in social concern some time around 1900) occurred: pre-1900, by World War I, after the 1920s; and lays out further research to be conducted. Jack Barlow writes a response in this same issue (pp. 86-89).

184   **American Evangelicalism**

1019.   McGavran, Donald. "Is Social Action Evangelism?" Eternity 17
        (November 1966): 23-24, 44.

        A prominent missiologist presents the two areas, emphasizes the
        danger of confusing them, and while stressing the priority of
        evangelism, also stresses that there has been and is a place
        for social action.

1020.   McKivigan, John R. The War Against Proslavery Religion: Aboli-
        tionism and the Northern Churches, 1830-1865. Ithaca: Cornell
        University Press, 1984. 327 p.

        The northern churches had serious deficiencies in their
        antislavery testimony and, contrary to the usual historical
        judgment, at the same time were positively influenced by the
        abolitionist movement of the 1840s and 1850s. A useful guide
        through the maze of literature on the subject. Thirty-one-page
        bibliography. Index.

1021.   McLoughlin, William G. "Evangelical Childrearing in the Age of
        Jackson: Francis Wayland's Views on When and How to Subdue the
        Willfulness of Children." Journal of Social History 9 (Fall
        1975): 21-34.

        An anonymous letter from Wayland (1790-1865), president of
        Brown University, illustrates childrearing practices in the
        mid-19th century, especially that aspect dealing with
        overcoming the child's will.

1022.   _____. "Indian Slaveholders and Presbyterian Missionaries,
        1837-1861." Church History 42 (December 1973): 535-51.

        Operating in the Indian Territory, the Presbyterian Board of
        Foreign Missions (Old School) was officially neutral regarding
        slaveholding; but missionary correspondence reveals the
        complexity of the issue and demonstrates that neutrality was
        impossible; like some other denominations, the Presbyterians
        could have barred slaveholders from membership, but did not.

1023.   Meadors, Gary T. "John R. W. Stott on Social Action." Grace
        Theological Journal 1 (Fall 1980): 129-47.

        In "a selective review of some of John R.W. Stott's teaching on
        social action," particularly his articles in Christianity
        Today, Meadors concludes that Stott (and possibly the larger
        evangelical movement), has shifted emphasis, and, quoting

Arthur Johnston. "'has dethroned evangelism as the only historical aim for mission.'"

1024.   Meckel, Richard A. "Educating a Ministry of Mothers: Evangelical Maternal Associations, 1815-1860." Journal of the Early Republic 2 (Winter 1982): 403-23.

Description of the maternal organizations, their magazines and their childrearing theories, and the unique role they played in reaching women "below the upper reaches of American society."

1025.   Moberg, David O. The Great Reversal: Evangelism versus Social Concern. Philadelphia: Lippincott, 1972. 194 p.

The "major role in both social reconstruction and social welfare" played by 19th century evangelicals was 'reversed' between 1910 and 1930 to the point where social concern has been lacking among 20th century evangelicals, a condition Moberg wishes to see changed. Influential book whose thesis has since been modified by other studies. Bibliography. Index.

1026.   _____. "Some Practical Steps Toward Evangelical Social Involvement." Gordon Review 11 (Fall 1968): 131-43.

Based upon his assumptions as to the Bible's teachings and implications; presents the Biblical basis, "levels of Christian social concern," "fallacies to avoid," and some areas for implementing concern. including volunteer services, service to groups, education, and research, concluding with a section on "The Renewal of Evangelical Social Concern."

1027.   Moorhead, James H. "Social Reform and the Divided Conscience of Antebellum Protestantism." Church History 48 (December 1979): 416-30.

Analysis of the thought of Charles Finney, "a major symbol of Protestantism's ambiguous relationship to reform." who both "commended useful service and endorsed many reforms, yet was unwilling to proceed as far or as fast as many reformers wished."

1028.   Mouw, Richard J. "Biblical Justice and Peace: Toward an Evangelical--Roman Catholic Rapprochement." Reformed Journal 34 (March 1984): 12-19.

Taken from Dean C. Curry, ed., Evangelicals and the Bishops'
Pastoral Letter (1983), this is a positive response to the
letter because it shows in the Catholic Church a "new, more
explicitly biblical emphasis" and has lessons for evangelicals
about social justice and theology.

1029.   Mullin, Robert Bruce. "Biblical Critics and the Battle Over
Slavery." Journal of Presbyterian History 61 (Summer 1983):
210-26.

The biblical scholars at Andover and Princeton, led by Moses
Stuart and Charles Hodge, held to an exegetical theory which
was "unable to deal successfully with the question of the Bible
and slavery."

1030.   Nix, William. "The Evangelical and War." Journal of the
Evangelical Theological Society 13 (Summer 1970): 133-46.

Looks into "the scriptural teachings on the subject of
believers and war," presenting and critiquing the pacifist,
activist (the position of most evangelicals), and mediativist
positions, the latter presented as having the least problems.

1031.   Oliver, John W., Jr. "A Failure of Evangelical Conscience." Post
American 4 (May 1975): 26-30.

On two major social issues--the civil rights movement and the
Vietnam War--Christianity Today failed to be a prophetic voice,
though to its credit it later abandoned earlier stances; thus,
"Evangelicalism did dare to change and grow."

1032.   Padilla, C. Rene. "Evangelism and Social Responsibility: From
Wheaton '66 to Wheaton '83." Transformation 2 (July-September
1985): 27-32.

More than a dozen documents issued between 1966 and 1983, in
which Two-Thirds World people played a decisive role, went into
shaping an evangelical social conscience that combines
evangelism with meaningful involvement with people.

1033.   Padilla, C. Rene, and Chris Sugden, eds. How Evangelicals
Endorsed Social Responsibility. Bramcote, England: Grove, 1986.

1034.   _____, eds. Texts on Evangelical Social Ethics 1974-1983.
Bramcote, England: Grove, 1986.

1035.   Pannell, William E. "Evangelicals and the Social Crisis." Post
         American 3 (October 1974): 9-12.

         Points out the lack of social conscience among evangelicals
         past and present, but senses a new mood that needs to be tapped
         and encouraged.

1036.   Pendleton, Othniel Alsop. "The Influence of the Evangelical
         Churches Upon Humanitarian Reform: A Case Study Giving Particular
         Attention to Philadelphia, 1790-1840." Ph.D. diss., University of
         Pennsylvania, 1945. 544 p.

1037.   Pierard, Richard V. "Needed: An Evangelical Social Ethic."
         Evangelical Quarterly 44 (April-June 1972): 84-90.

         Premillennialism, individualism and middle-class "success
         culture" have precluded the creation of an adequate social
         ethic.

1038.   Reeves, Earl J. "An Evangelical Position on Birth Control."
         Journal of the American Scientific Affiliation 22 (June 1970):
         50-51.

         Reprinted from Birth Control and the Christian, edited by W. O.
         Spitzer and C. L. Saylor (1969), 192-94. Groups the various
         methods into three categories--abstention, contraception, and
         abortion--and analyses them relative to evangelicals.   o

1039.   Richard, John. "Evangelicals and Human Rights." In Serving Our
         Generation: Evangelical Strategies for the Eighties, ed. Waldron
         Scott, 227-47. Colorado Springs: World Evangelical Fellowship,
         1980.

         A leading evangelical in India treats a variety of human
         issues, the failure of evangelicals to act effectively, reasons
         to act, and some practical measures that can be taken.

1040.   Rosenberg, Carroll Smith. Religion and the Rise of the American
         City: The New York City Mission Movement, 1812-1870. Ithaca:
         Cornell University Press, 1971. 300 p.

         Initially inspired by the Second Awakening. the city missions
         began with very general aims but by the 1840s and 1850s "worked
         almost exclusively among the urban poor": Rosenberg recounts
         their history and aims. disputes the idea that the missions
         were seeking only social control, and shows the relationship

between the missions and the rise of the social work
profession. Appendix. Bibliography. Index.

1041.   Runia, Klaas. "Evangelical Responsibility in a Secularized
World." Christianity Today 14 (19 June 1970): 851-54.

There are signs that evangelicals are no longer neglecting
social problems and the issues of attitudes toward culture;
further, we need a comprehensive world and life view, a correct
picture of the Great Commission, and willingness to cooperate
with others in bringing about social reform.

1042.   Scheunemann, Volkhard. "Some Theses for the Spiritual Renewal and
Revival of Theology: The Church and World-Responsibility."
Evangelical Review of Theology 7 (October 1983): 207-18.

Ninety-three theses gathered around such topics as authority,
theological education, and world responsibility.

1043.   Sider, Ronald J., ed. The Chicago Declaration. Carol Stream, IL:
Creation House, 1974. 144 p.

The Declaration resulting from the 1973 Thanksgiving Workshop
on Evangelicals and Social Concern is explained by participants
through five essays and a number of brief reflections.

1044.   _____, ed. Evangelicals and Development: Toward a Theology of
Social Change. Philadelphia: Westminster, 1981. 132 p.

Papers from the Consultation on the Theology of Development,
held March 10-14, 1980. High Leigh Conference Centre,
Hoddesdon, England, sponsored by the Unit on Ethics and Society
of the Theological Commission of the World Evangelical
Fellowship. Index.

1045.   _____. "Resurrection and Liberation: An Evangelical Approach
to Social Justice." In The Recovery of Spirit in Higher
Education: Christian and Jewish Ministries in Campus Life, ed.
Robert Rankin, 154-77. New York: Seabury, 1980.

Sider lays out the biblical foundations needed for evangelicals
to "correct their heretical neglect of the biblical summons to
do justice."

1046.   _____. with the staff of Evangelicals for Social Action.
Completely Pro-Life: Building a Consistent Stance. Downers Grove:
InterVarsity, 1987. 239 p.

Attempts "to articulate a consistent pro-life stance on public
policy issues that flows from a biblical definition of life."
Chapters on abortion, economics, sexuality, feminism and the
family, and nuclear weapons show the need for "fullness of life
in every area." Bibliography. Index.

1047.   Smedes, Lewis B. "The Evangelicals and the Social Question."
        Reformed Journal 16 (February 1966): 9-13.

1048.   _____. "Evangelicals, What Next?" Reformed Journal 19
        (November 1969): 4-5.

        At a meeting in Minneapolis the evangelical leadership
        publically committed itself to social concern. The next step
        should be an evangelical sweat-session on social ethics!

1049.   Smith, Gary Scott. "The Cross and the Social Order: Calvinist
        Strategies for Social Improvement, 1870-1920." Fides et Historia
        17 (Fall-Winter 1984): 39-54.

        Critiques the view that Reformed Christians gradually abandoned
        social action to proponents of the social gospel. Rather,
        Calvinists made significant efforts to eradicate social ills,
        though they felt that converting individuals was the key to
        solving social problems and therefore rarely challenged
        structural defects in American society. Enlarged on in Smith's
        book, The Seeds of Secularization (1985).

1050.   _____. "The Men and Religion Forward Movement of 1911-12: New
        Perspectives on Evangelical Social Concern and the Relationship
        Between Christianity and Progressivism." Westminster Theological
        Journal 49 (Spring 1987): 91-118.

        This Movement illustrates that evangelicals did not neglect
        social action before 1920 (the break came in the 1920s) and
        "that religious ideologies and groups helped inspire the
        Progessive Movement."

1051.   Smith, H. Shelton. In His Image, but . . .: Racism in Southern
        Religion, 1780-1910. Durham: Duke University Press. 1972. 318 p.

        Highly regarded study of the colonial beginnings of racism in
        the churches, their capitulation to the slavocracy in
        antebellum days, and their continuation of the color line in
        the decades following the Civil War. Bibliographical
        references. Index.

1052.   Smith, Linda Diane. "An Awakening of Conscience: The Changing
         Response of American Evangelicals Toward World Poverty." Ph.D.
         diss., The American University, 1986. 489 p.

1053.   Stewart, James Brewer. "Evangelicalism and the Radical Strain in
         Southern Antislavery Thought During the 1820s." Journal of
         Southern History 39 (August 1973): 379-96.

         A number of upper South writers, a minority group unable to
         bring about concerted action, decried slavery's adverse effects
         on personal morality, interpretation of the Bible, organized
         religion, and white families.

1054.   Stott, John R. W. Christ the Controversialist: A Study in Some
         Essentials of Evangelical Religion. Downers Grove: InterVarsity
         Press, 1970. 214 p.

         A study of the controversies Christ engaged in, gathered around
         eight topics, "to demonstrate that they are live issues still,
         and to argue that the position which Christ adopted in each
         debate is the very position which 'evangelical' Christians have
         always sought to maintain." Bibliographical references.

1055.   . Involvement. Vol. 1, Being a Responsible Christian in
         Non-Christian Society. Old Tappan: Revell, 1984, 1985. 221 p.
         Vol. 2, Social and Sexual Relationships in the Modern World. Old
         Tappan: Revell, 1984, 1985. 286 p.

         Volume one prescribes Christian involvement in the world and
         treats the issues of nuclear war, ecology, north-south economic
         inequality, and human rights. Volume two handles work, labor-
         management issues, racial questions, poverty and wealth, and
         the sexual issues of male-female equality, abortion, and
         homosexuality. Bibliographical references. Indexes.

1056.   Thomas, John L. "Romantic Reform in America, 1815-1865."
         American Quarterly 17 (Winter 1965): 656-81.

         Romantic reform in America originated in "a religious impulse
         [perfectionism] which was both politically and socially
         conservative." The impulse stemmed from Unitarian,
         transcendentalist, and even atheistic (e.g.. Robert Owen)
         religious forms, as well as from the New Divinity.

1057.   Tidball, Derek J. "Evangelicals Rethinking Evangelism." Baptist
         Quarterly 32 (January 1987): 39-42.

Reviews four books--B. Nicholls, In Word and Deed (1985), R. Padilla, Mission Between Times: Essays on the Kingdom (1985), C. Marchant, Signs in the City (1985), and R. Dowley, Towards the Recovery of a Lost Bequest (n.d.)--which reflect the mounting evangelical concern "for a rejection of cultural Christianity . . . in favor of a radical discipleship in which the social implications of the gospel were given full weight."

1058. _____. "Some Contemporary Evangelicals and Social Thinking." Vox Evangelica 8 (1973): 60-80.

Some early 20th century background, followed by discussion of five books of recent years in terms of their nature and context, biblical basis, recurring themes, and two specific issues: race and evolution.

1059. Toms, Paul E. "Evangelical Christians and Social Responsibility." In Evangelicals and Jews in Conversation on Scripture, Theology, and History, eds. Marc H. Tanenbaum, Marvin R. Wilson, and A. James Rudin, 233-47. Grand Rapids: Baker, 1978.

Biblical principles upon which social action is based, and the recent awakening of evangelical social concern.

1060. Vermaat, J. A. E. "Evangelicals and Social Ethics." Reformation Review 25 (October 1980): 236-44.

Comments on "An Evangelical Commitment to Simple Lifestyle" that issued from the International Consultation on Simple Lifestyle, Hoddesdon, England (March 1980); Vermaat takes issue with some of the unclear phrases in the document and their implied condemnation of the state, while he agrees generally on simple lifestyle.

1061. Webster, Douglas. "Evangelicals: Growing Social Awareness." Ecumenist 16 (March-April 1978): 33-38.

Discovery of evangelical social involvement in the 19th century, the Bible's teaching on both evangelism and social action, and social-consciousness statements made recently at conferences and in publications, all point to the growing awareness.

1062. Wirt, Sherwood Eliot. The Social Conscience of the Evangelical. New York: Harper & Row, 1968. 177 p.

A call for social action early in the period when evangelicals
were beginning to show a renewed interest in social concern, by
the then-editor of Decision magazine. Bibliography. Index.

1063.   Woolverton, John F. "Evangelical Protestantism and Alcoholism
1933-1962: Episcopalian Samuel Shoemaker, The Oxford Groups and
Alcoholics Anonymous." Historical Magazine of the Protestant
Episcopal Church 52 (March 1983): 53-65.

The three components, allied only temporarily in the 1930s,
"all had roots in an older American revivalism and in the
progressive era at the turn of the century with its 'anything
can be done' spirit."

1064.   Wright, David F., ed. Essays in Evangelical Social Ethics.
Greenwood, SC: Attic Press, 1978. 192 p.

Papers delivered at the National Evangelical Conference on
Social Ethics (1978: Hoddesdon, Hertfordshire, England).
Bibliographical references. Index.

1065.   Wyatt-Brown, Bertram. "Conscience and Career: Young Abolitionists
and Missionaries." In Anti-Slavery, Religion and Reform, Essays
in Honor of Roger Anstey, eds. Bolt and Drescher, 183-203.
Hamden: Archon Books, 1980.

Concentrates on "the evangelical and chiefly New England
environments" to elucidate child-rearing practices and
conversion and career-choice crises that were common to future
missionaries and abolitionists, leaving as the sole distinction
between them "a parting of the ways in the matter of politics."

1066.   Yoder, John H. "The Contemporary Evangelical Revival and the
Peace Churches." In Mission and the Peace Witness, ed. Robert L.
Ramseyer, 68-103. Scottsdale, PA: Herald Press, 1979.

Rather than assuming that "evangelical revival" and "peace
churches" are two separate entities, Yoder says, the "Peace
church vision is itself the logically consistent form of
evangelical revival"; he illustrates this in the area of social
ethics, and notes five elements in discussion about essentials
and nonessentials.

1067.   _____. "A Critique of North American Evangelical Ethics."
Transformation 2 (January-March 1985): 28-31.

Tied too much to North American culture, evangelical ethics
needs to rethink (biblically) its positions, both in that
culture and in the cultures where North American presumptions
simply do not operate.

See also items 30, 166, 186, 191, 208, 210, 212, 213, 233, 250, 312, 360,
399, 407, 419, 490, 502, 508, 513, 515, 516, 522, 523, 524, 555, 557,
595, 599, 686, 692, 698, 759, 761, 762, 798, 805, 818, 852, 862, 869,
880, 883, 884, 892, 898, 932, 934, 937, 1133, 1239, 1240, 1257, 1433,
1435, 1466, 1470, 1479, 1483, 1527, 1602, 1659, 1779, 1780, 1825, 2525,
2527, 2532, 2579.

G.   Science

1068.   Anderson, V. Elving. "Evangelicals and Science: Fifty Years After
the Scopes Trial (1925-75)." In The Evangelicals: What They
Believe, Who They Are, Where They Are Changing, eds. David F.
Wells and John D. Woodbridge, 249-68. Nashville: Abingdon, 1975.

After reviewing changes during the five decades beginning in
1925, examines "the role of evangelicals in scientific
endeavors and the ways in which some of them deal with . . .
evolution." Divergent views are still prevalent and new
questions have arisen.

1069.   Baldwin, Stanley. "Science and the Evangelical." Eternity 18
(November 1967): 19, 32, 34.

A group of scientists respond to questions such as whether
there is a conflict and whether an evangelical can be a
scientist.

1070.   Bube, Richard H. "Comments on an Article: 'Evangelicals and
Evolution.'" Journal of the American Scientific Affiliation 27
(March 1975): 39-40.

A critique of W. L. Craig's article in the summmer 1974 issue
of the Journal of the Evangelical Theological Society,
entitled, "Creation and Evolution: An Analysis of the Debate
Between the Creation Research Society and the American
Scientific Affiliation."

1071.   Craig, William Lane. "Evangelicals and Evolution: An Analysis of
the Debate Between the Creation Research Society and the American
Scientific Affiliation." Journal of the Evangelical Theological
Society 17 (Summer 1974): 131-48.

Seeks "to explain. compare, and contrast the respective positions . . . as found within their journals"; concludes that the
"two organizations are healthy counterparts. The CRS calls
Christians to examine their Bible more closely, while the ASA
prevents a fundamentalist obscurantism by its persistent demand
for scientific respectability."

1072.   Davis, Dennis Royal. "Presbyterian Attitudes Toward Science and
the Coming of Darwinism in America, 1859 to 1929." Ph.D. diss.,
University of Illinois at Urbana-Champaign, 1980. 444 p.

Using the Presbyterian Church in the USA as a "weathervane,"
Davis traces the Protestant response to post-Darwin science
between the Origin of Species in 1859 and the modernist-
fundamentalist debate of the 1920s. In light of the variety
and complexity of the Protestant response, neither a science
and religion "warfare" approach nor a single issue analysis
(such as biblical literalism) is sufficient.

1073.   Grine, Joanne Del Greco. "A Study of Creationist Pressure:
Strategies Against Evolution Instruction in the Public Schools."
Ph.D. diss., University of Pittsburgh, 1985. 270 p.

1074.   Larson, Edward J. Trial and Error: The American Controversy Over
Creation and Evolution. Rev. ed. New York: Oxford University
Press, 1985. 256 p.

A well done legal-historical study covering the period from
before the 1925 Scopes' trial to cases in the mid-1980s,
concluding "that the creation-evolution legal actions primarily
represented efforts to reconcile public science--that is,
publicly supported science teaching and related activities--
with popular opinion." Bibliography. Index.

1075.   Lindberg, David C., and Ronald L. Numbers. "Beyond War and Peace:
A Reappraisal of the Encounter Between Christianity and Science."
Church History 55 (September 1986): 338-54.

Drawing on recent scholarly studies that critique Andrew
Dickson White's History of the Warfare of Science with Theology
in Christendom (1896), the authors convincingly show "the
warfare metaphor to be neither useful nor tenable in describing
the relationship between science and religion."

1076.   _____. God and Nature: Historical Essays on the Encounter
Between Christianity and Science. Berkeley: University of
California Press, 1986. 516 p.

Eighteen essays, about half on American subjects, countering the older view that posited a "warfare" between science and Christianity. Bibliographical references for each essay; an excellent "Guide to Further Reading."

1077.   Livingstone, David N. "B. B. Warfield, the Theory of Evolution and Early Fundamentalism." Evangelical Quarterly 58 (January 1986): 69-83.

Differing points of view in regard to evolution were presented by four evangelicals in volumes 7 and 8 of The Fundamentals; three articles by Warfield, 1911-1915, show his pro-evolutionary stance.

1078.   _____. Darwin's Forgotten Defenders: The Encounter Between Evangelical Theology and Evolutionary Thought. Grand Rapids: Eerdmans; Edinburgh: Scottish Academic Press, 1987. 210 p.

An important study, mostly of Americans, in revising the ideas that evangelicals were by and large anti-Darwinian from the beginning and that science and religion were at war in the 19th century; shows that "a substantial number of the most distinguished representatives of evangelical orthodoxy [scientists and theologians] found the theological resources to absorb the latest scientific findings." Thirteen-page bibliography. Index.

1079.   _____. "Evangelicals and the Darwinian Controversies: A Bibliographical Introduction." Evangelical Studies Bulletin 4 (November 1987): 1-6.

A bibliographical essay about the relationship of theologically conservative Christians with science, within the context of the larger interaction of religion and science.

1080.   Meeter, Merle. "Theology in the Dark or in Bible Light." International Reformed Bulletin 38 (July 1969): 27-29.

In rebuttal of J. R. van de Fliert's earlier very negative treatment of Morris and Whitcomb's The Genesis Flood (1961) in IRB (nos. 32-33. January-April. 1968: 5-27). Van de Fliert responds later in this issue (34-39).

1081.   Moore, James R. "Evangelicals and Evolution: Henry Drummond. Herbert Spencer, and the Naturalisation of the Spiritual World." Scottish Journal of Theology 38. no. 3 (1985): 383-417.

Extended analysis of Drummond and his Natural Law in the
Spiritual World and his Ascent of Man as indicative of
evangelical life (Drummond was an erstwhile evangelist and
friend of D. L. Moody). tied to the principles of naturalism
which, in the end, led away from evangelicalism.

1082.   Moreland, J. P. Christianity and the Nature of Science: A
Philosophical Investigation. Grand Rapids: Baker, 1989. 263 p.

A professor at Liberty University contends that the complementarity of religion and science is an inadequate view of their
relations, and defends instead three theses: science does not
exclude philosophy or theology from entering its domain, "and
there is nothing unscientific about creation science; the
limits of science preclude scientism and weaken science's
epistemic authority; the integration of science and theology is
best done not by scientific realism but by an eclectic
approach." Bibliography.

1083.   Morison, William James. "George Frederick Wright: In Defense of
Darwinism and Fundamentalism, 1838-1921." Ph.D. diss., Vanderbilt
University, 1971. 462 p.

1084.   Numbers, Ronald L. "The Dilemma of Evangelical Scientists." In
Evangelicalism and Modern America, ed. George Marsden, 150-60.
Grand Rapids: Eerdmans, 1984.

Based in part on his "Creationism in 20th Century America,"
Science 218 (1982): 538-44, Numbers "explores the efforts of
evangelical scientists to come to terms with the issue
origins," from the united opposition to evolution in the 1920s
to the loss of unity by the 1980s.

1085.   Numbers, Ronald L., and Darrel W. Amundsen. eds. Caring and
Curing: Health and Medicine in the Western Religious Traditions.
New York: Macmillan, 1986. 601 p.

Issued from The Park Ridge Center [Illinois]. an Institute for
the Study of Health. Faith. and Ethics; each of the twenty
chapters covers one of the traditions. about half of which are
related to evangelicalism. A helpful reference volume.
Bibliographical references.

1086.   Pinnock, Clark H. "Climbing Out of a Swamp: The Evangelical
Struggle to Understand the Creation Texts." Interpretation 43
(April 1989): 156-69.

Holds that evangelicals are mired in a swamp in their efforts to understand these texts, and affirms that "the way out of the swamp is to begin reading early Genesis appropriately in its own context, in the setting of the life of ancient Israel, and to stop forcing modern agendas upon it."

1087. Ramm, Bernard. The Christian View of Science and Scripture. Grand Rapids: Eerdmans, 1954. 368 p.

A work that became the classic text among those post-WWII evangelicals moving away from their fundamentalist background. Bibliography. Index.

1088. _____. "Evangelical Theology and Technological Shock." Journal of the American Scientific Affiliation 23 (June 1971): 52-56.

Rather than, as in the past, responding to the latest scientific theory, evangelicals need to anticipate scientific discoveries and adjust theology as needed; genetic engineering used as an example.

1089. Remelts, Glenn A. "The Christian Reformed Church and Science, 1900-1930: An Evangelical Alternative to the Fundamentalist and Modernist Responses to Science." Fides et Historia 21 (January 1989): 61-80.

Affected by German philosophy and Kuyper's Neo-Calvinism, the CRC used an "engagement" model to describe the place of science in theological thought; illustrated by the principal thinking and antithetical thinking used in the model's epistemology.

1090. Sider, Ronald J. "Science and Technology: Response." In Evangelicals Face the Future. Scenarios, Addresses, and Responses from the 'Consultation on Future Evangelical Concerns' held in Atlanta, Georgia, December 14-17, 1977, ed. Donald E. Hoke, 55-60. Pasadena: William Carey Library, 1978.

Sounds a note of caution about the negative effects resident in even the positive developments in science and technology.

1091. van de Fliert, J. R. "Bible, Man and Science: A Reply." International Reformed Bulletin no. 38 (July 1969): 34-39.

Responds to two responses (Professors White and Meeter) in this issue to van de Fliert's earlier critique (IRB no. 32-33

(January-April 1968): 5-27) of The Genesis Flood (1961), by
Morris and Whitcomb.

1092.   . "Fundamentalism and the Fundamentals of Geology."
International Reformed Bulletin nos. 32-33 (January-April 1968):
5-27.

A geologist responds with "amazement" in an extended refutation
of the volume The Genesis Flood, the Biblical Record and its
Scientific Implications (1961), by Henry M. Morris and John C.
Whitcomb, Jr. See IRB issue no. 38 (July 1969): 34-39, for
responses to his response. Reprinted in Journal of the
American Scientific Affiliation 21 (September 1969): 69-81.
"The text presented here is the product of editorial revision
by Professor Roger J. Cuffey . . . which has been approved by
the author."

1093.   Wells, Jonathan. Charles Hodge's Critique of Darwinism: An
Historical-critical Analysis of Concepts Basic to the 19th Century
Debate. Lewiston, NY: Edwin Mellen, 1988. 244 p.

Concludes that, contrary to received opinion, Hodge's argument
against Darwin was not from design but to design, an argument
"central to mainstream Christian theology," and one that makes
conflict between Christianity and Darwinism "broader and deeper
than the received view implies." Seventeen-page bibliography.
Index.

1094.   White, William, Jr. "The Fundamentals of Fundamentalism and
Geology." International Reformed Bulletin 38 (July 1969): 30-33.

In response to Professor van de Fliert's article in the IRB
(January-April 1968: 5-27) which had severely criticized Morris
and Whitcomb's volume The Genesis Flood (1961); concludes with
a call for Christian geologists "to produce a geological
science activated by Christian consciences and oriented towards
one and only one goal, pro rege."

See also items 627, 847, 886, 1223, 1650, 1651, 1657, 1670, 1671, 1762,
1962, 2120.

H.   Education

√ 1095.   Bechtel, Paul. Wheaton College: A Heritage Remembered, 1860-1984.
Wheaton: Shaw Publishers, 1984. 384 p.

A balanced account of one of the most prominent evangelical colleges. Bibliography. Index.

1096. Bowers, Lanny Ross. "Religion and Education: A Study of the Interrelationship Between Fundamentalism and Education in Contemporary America." Ed.D. diss., East Tennessee State University, 1985. 312 p.

1097. Boylan, Anne M. Sunday School: The Formation of an American Institution, 1790-1880. New Haven: Yale University Press, 1988. 225 p.

Good survey of the first century of the Sunday School, compared with its British counterpart, and related to the general American culture. A needed corrective to a lack of scholarly study of a one-time pervasive institution. Bibliography. Index.

1098. _____. "Sunday Schools and Changing Evangelical Views of Children in the 1820s." Church History 48 (September 1979): 320-33.

The discovery of childhood as a separate category of human development, along with new childhood experiences, led to the creation of child-oriented institutions such as the Sunday School. Boylan analyzes organization and curriculum in the urban Northeast, showing the emphasis on conversion and religious training through the Bible class.

1099. Bradbury, M. L. "British Apologetics in Evangelical Garb: Samuel Stanhope Smith's Lectures on the Evidences of the Christian Religion." Journal of the Early Republic 5 (Summer 1985): 177-96.

Smith was President of Princeton for 29 years; his Evidences was an early example of a text on that subject, was influential on college education for decades, and indicated the transfer of British anti-deist polemics to the American scene.

1100. Carpenter, Joel A., and Kenneth W. Shipps. eds. Making Higher Education Christian: The History and Mission of Evangelical Colleges in America. Grand Rapids: Christian University Press. 1987. 304 p.

Nineteen essays divided into three topics: assessing the heritage of evangelical higher education. refining the vision of that education. and advancing its mission: most of the essays were given at the conference on The Task of Evangelical

Higher Education. at Wheaton College in May 1985.
Bibliographical references.

1101.   Clutter, Ronald T. "A Background History of Grace Theological
Seminary." Grace Theological Journal 9, no. 2 (1988): 205-32.

Relates the story of its background and beginnings in the 1920s
and 1930s within the context of the fundamentalist-modernist
controversy at large and particularly within the Brethren
Church and its efforts in theological education.

√ 1102.   Findlay, James F., Jr. "Agency, Denominations and the Western
Colleges, 1830-1860: Some Connections Between Evangelicalism and
American Higher Education." Church History 50 (March 1981):
64-80.

Questioning the new educational historians' downplaying the
role of religion in antebellum colleges, Findlay examines the
work of fund-raising agents in seven colleges in Indiana and
Illinois to show the close ties between the schools and
evangelical culture.

1103.   Flood, Robert. "How Evangelicals Launched the Ivy League." Moody
Monthly 76 (March 1976): 32-35.

Condensed from his book, America (1975); the story of
evangelical beginnings, as well as of subsequent drift.

1104.   Fraser, James W. Schooling the Preachers: The Development of
Protestant Theological Education in the U.S. 1740-1875. Lanham,
MD: University Press of America, 1988. 159 p.

The study "focuses on six major changes or crises" in
theological institutions that brought change in theological
education: the Great Awakening, the rise of Unitarianism,
perfectionist abolitionism, the scarcity of ministers, the
demand for denominational colleges, the demand for professional
ministers. Bibliographical references. Index.

1105.   Gangel, Kenneth O. "Thinking Like a Christian: An Evangelical
Analysis of Rationality." Christian Education Journal 8 (Autumn
1987): 61-72.

Asserts that "the Christian leader is our best hope for
rationality in an irrational age. and that the Christian leader
must have a highly developed and thoroughly consecrated mind in
order to meet the challenge of leadership in such an age."

Deals with the importance of the latter, and with how to
develop a healthy Christian mind.

1106.   _____, ed. Toward a Harmony of Faith and Learning: Essays on
Bible College Curriculum. Farmington Hills, MI: William Tyndale
College Press, 1983. 247 p.

1107.   Grounds, Vernon C. "Evangelicalism and Education." Seminary
Study Series. Denver: Conservative Baptist Theological Seminary,
n.d.

1108.   Hafemann, Scott J. "Seminary, Subjectivity, and the Centrality of
Scripture: Reflections on the Current Crisis in Evangelical
Seminary Education." Journal of the Evangelical Theological
Society 31 (June 1988): 129-43.

The evangelical unwillingness to take up the task of biblical
studies stems from the cultural and theological forces that
must be countered to avoid further erosion of biblical
authority.

1109.   Hakes, J. Edward, ed. An Introduction to Evangelical Christian
Education. Chicago: Moody, 1964. 423 p.

Thirty-two authors each write a chapter on some phase of
Christian education, from backgrounds to teaching,
organization, and agencies. Bibliographies. Index.

1110.   Hammond, Phillip E., and James Davison Hunter. "On Maintaining
Plausibility: The World View of Evangelical College Students."
Journal for the Scientific Study of Religion 23 (September 1984):
221-38.

Studying more than 2000 students from ten campuses (nine
evangelical, one public university) the authors conclude that
"education, even evangelical education, weakens the tenacity
with which evangelicals hold on to their world view," though
"on the secular campus the evangelical world view of
evangelical students seems to gain solidity."

1111.   Hatch, Nathan O. "Evangelical Colleges and the Challenge of
Christian Thinking." Reformed Journal 35 (September 1985): 10-18.

Analysis of the institutional obstacles--like constituencies
and competition between schools--to evangelical scholarship,
and a strong call for scholarship based on classic evangelical
orthodoxy.

1112.   Hayes, Edward L. "Evangelicalism and Christian Education." In
         Foundations for Christian Education in an Era of Change, ed.
         Marvin J. Taylor, 198-207. Nashville: Abingdon, 1976.

         The theological stance of evangelicalism, its basic educational
         outlook, the "greening" (lay renewal) of evangelicalism, some
         evangelical organizations, and the future.

1113.   Heaton, C. Adrian. "The Bible in Evangelical Christian
         Education." Bethel Seminary Quarterly 9 (May 1961): 63-70.

         A two-fold place: "it is the primary source of the philosophy
         of Christian education and it is the essential content in the
         curriculum of Christian education."

1114.   Henry, Carl F. H. "The Christian Scholar's Task in a Stricken
         World." Christian Scholar's Review 17 (June 1988): 474-88.

         The post-Christian world suffers from a wide array of
         naturalistic philosophies, none of which offer hope. Christian
         scholarship needs to point to this modernity as transitory,
         "exhibit its weaknesses and, more importantly, exhibit the
         superiority of the theistic view."

1115.   _____. "A Proposal for Evangelical Advance." Christianity
         Today 10 (13 May 1966): 28-29.

         Urges the founding of an Institute for Advanced Christian
         Studies and outlines the advantages.

✓ 1116. Holmes, Arthur F. The Idea of a Christian College. Rev. ed.
         Grand Rapids: Eerdmans, 1987. 106 p.

         A Wheaton College philosophy professor gives an apologetic for
         evangelical higher education in what has become the standard
         text on the subject. Bibliography. Index.

1117.   "How Active is National ETS in Asia? Growing Evangelical Cooper-
         ation in Theological Education." Asia Theological News 15
         (January-March 1989): 4-9, 13, 15.

         Seven leaders in theological education in Asia respond to
         questions, including "the background of Evangelical Theological
         Society (ETS) in your country." and the "main activities of
         your ETS," among others.

1118. International Council of Accrediting Agencies for Evangelical
       Theological Education. "Manifesto on the Renewal of Evangelical
       Theological Education." Asia Theological News 13 (October-
       December 1987): 11-14.

       "A Joint Declaration in Cyprus, 1984," the emphases of which
       include "contextualization," "churchward orientation,"
       "strategic flexibility," and "theological grounding."

1119. Kuhn, Harold B. "The Crisis in Theological Education Today."
       Asbury Seminarian 1 (Spring 1946): 3-13, 21.

       A "sweeping indictment of our theological education today,"
       calling for attention to "the church's one task, the
       proclamation of the message of personal redemption through the
       self-giving of Christ on the cross."

1120. Lewis, Kathryn. "The State of the Art in Evangelical Curriculum
       Publishing." Christian Education Journal 8 (Autumn 1987): 9-24.

       Discusses trends, based on interviews with seven curriculum
       publishers; the movement seems to be away from the transmission
       of content to a more developmental philosophy; "The Evangelical
       community needs to critically examine current trends and to
       purposefully choose those which are consistent with a biblical
       view of the learner and of the process of spiritual
       development."

✓ 1121. Marsden, George M. "The Collapse of Evangelical Academia." In
       Faith and Rationality: Reason and Belief in God, ed. Alvin
       Plantinga and Nicholas Wolterstorff, 219-64. West Bend, IN: Notre
       Dame University Press, 1983.

       Social and cultural factors are inadequate as explanations for
       what caused the collapse; intellectual factors were more
       important, and of these it was Common Sense philosophy and its
       accompanying evidential apologetic that were the crucial
       factors.

1122. _____. "The State of Evangelical Christian Scholarship."
       Reformed Journal 37 (September 1987): 12-16.

       He sees "moderately encouraging signs," cautions that evangel-
       ical scholars are still a "tiny minority," and suggests several
       emphases under which "truly evangelical scholarship can
       flourish."

1123.   Mayers, Marvin K., Lawrence O. Richards, and Robert E. Webber.
         Reshaping Evangelical Higher Education. Grand Rapids: Zondervan,
         1972. 215 p.

         Three Wheaton College professors find a crisis in evangelical
         higher education and argue for "a distinctive world view as the
         source for our educational thought," a more culturally-aware
         system of learning, and the use of new educational options.
         Appendix. Bibliography. Index.

1124.   McLeish, John. Evangelical Religion and Popular Education: A
         Modern Interpretation. London: Methuen, 1969. 206 p.

         Part I gives the historical background of the evangelicals in
         late 18th century Wales and early 19th century England
         (featuring Griffith Jones and Hannah More), who founded charity
         schools for the illiterate peasantry. Part II takes up
         economic, anthropological, psychological, and sociological
         interpretations of the evangelical work, with the last named
         presenting "the most adequate and comprehensive model."
         Glossary. Bibliography. Index.

1125.   Meyer, Kenneth M. "The Purpose of a Seminary Which is Part of the
         Evangelical Movement." Theological Education 14 (Spring 1978):
         100-08.

         The president of Trinity Evangelical Divinity School says the
         "primary distinction of such an institution is its staunch
         commitment to the authority of biblical revelation." Beyond
         that, among other things, it integrates the cognitive and the
         practical, promotes spirituality and missions, and serves a
         broad constituency.

1126.   Moncher, Gary Richard. "The Bible College and American Moral
         Culture." Ph.D. diss., University of California, Berkeley, 1987.
         332 p.

1127.   Mounce, Robert. "The Evangelical Church and Higher Education."
         Eternity 16 (June 1965): 19-21, 48.

         True knowledge does not destroy true spirituality; God wants us
         to love Him with our whole being, including mind: three
         qualities of an educated man: "A mind honed razor sharp by
         excellence in education, coupled with a heart aglow with the
         love of God is the finest contribution we can make to society."

1128.   Noll, Mark A. "Christian Thinking and the Rise of the American University." Christian Scholar's Review 9 (1979): 3-16.

         The revolution in education between the Civil War and WWI, creating "persistently secular" universities, can be traced to the way in which "developmental science and economic Darwinism combined with Christian inflexibility to secularize higher education in America."

1129.   _____. "The Founding of Princeton Seminary." Westminster Theological Journal 42 (Fall 1979): 72-110.

         Describes the motives behind and the roles played by Ashbel Green (1762-1848), Samuel Miller (1769-1850) and Archibald Alexander (1772-1851) in Princeton's founding in 1812, as illuminating American Presbyterianism and "the enduring issues faced by all who are concerned about the education of the church's leaders, or about the relationship between the Christian faith and its cultural setting."

1130.   Pazmino, Robert W. Foundational Issues in Christian Education: An Introduction in Evangelical Perspective. Grand Rapids: Baker, 1988. 232 p.

1131.   Riesman, David. "The Evangelical Colleges: Untouched by the Academic Revolution." Change 13 (January-February 1981): 13-20.

         The academic revolution--faculty "hegemony over a large and growing portion of the academic enterprise," accompanied by increased student freedom--has, in regard to student freedom, made least headway in the evangelical colleges.

1132.   Ringenberg, William C. The Christian College: A History of Protestant Higher Education in America. Grand Rapids: Eerdmans, Christian University Press, 1984. 257 p.

         Using the theme of "the changing influence of the Christian worldview in the intellectual life of the colleges," this fine study traces the history of evangelical higher education from the 17th to the 20th centuries. Bibliographical references. Index.

1133.   Smith, Timothy L. Uncommon Schools: Christian Colleges and Social Idealism in Midwestern America, 1820-1920. Indianapolis: Indiana Historical Society, 1978. 72 p.

A history of church colleges in Illinois and Indiana, which
illustrates the significant role played by Christianity in
higher education "in the cultural and social development of the
Upper Mississippi Valley." Bibliographical references. Index.

1134.   Stephens, Raphael Weller, III. "A History of Governance at Lee
College: A Study in Pentecostal Higher Education." Ed.D. diss.,
The College of William and Mary in Virginia, 1981. 161 p.

✓ 1135.   Stevenson, Louise L. Scholarly Means to Evangelical Ends: The New
Haven Scholars and the Transformation of Higher Learning in
America, 1830-1890. Baltimore: Johns Hopkins University Press,
1986. 221 p.

Argues that a group of evangelical professors at Yale during
this period were pivotal in the movement of American higher
education into a distinctive stage that was marked by
specialist scholars on the German model. Eighteen-page
bibliography. Index.

1136.   Stiles, Gerald Johnston. "Evangelicals and Public Education."
Ed.D. diss., Virginia Polytechnic Institute and State University,
1980. 327 p.

1137.   Trollinger, William Vance, Jr. "Riley's Empire: Northwestern
Bible School and Fundamentalism in the Upper Midwest." Church
History 57 (June 1988): 197-212.

Study supporting the interpretation of "the central role played
by Bible institutes in the survival and growth" of the fundamentalist movement between the world wars; Riley's Northwestern
served "as a denominational surrogate for a regional network of
fundamentalist churches."

1138.   White, John Wesley. "The Case for a Conservative-Evangelical
College in Canada." Evangelical Christian (February 1966): 10-12.

"The substance of an address" given by a prominent evangelist
in October 1965 to twenty leading evangelicals. Answers
affirmatively the questions "does Canada really need such a
college?" and is the formation of such a school possible and
opportune at this time?

1139.   White, John Wesley, et al. "Does Canada Need a Conservative
Evangelical Liberal Arts College? A Study by Some Members of the
Graduate Christian Fellowship, University of Toronto." Crux 4,
no. 1 (1967): 3-29.

Presents the affirmative position of John Wesley White and Elmer McVety, contending for such a college, with the response of other participants a qualified "no" that is "more a preliminary exploration than a final pronouncement."

1140.   Wise, F. Franklyn. "Concerns for the 1970s: A Conservative, Evangelical Assessment." Religious Education 65 (September-October 1970): 402-08.

Five areas of concern for evangelical Christian educators: civil rights, behavioral psychology, social mobility, sex education, and Christian education operations.

1141.   Witmer, John A. "'What Hath God Wrought'--Fifty Years of Dallas Theological Seminary." Bibliotheca Sacra 130 (October-December 1973) [Part 1: "God's Man and His Dream"]; 131 (January-March 1974) [Part 2: "Building Upon the Foundation"]

Dallas Seminary from its founding under Lewis Sperry Chafer (1871-1952) to its growth and expansion under John Walvoord.

See also items 32, 84, 139, 313, 314, 373, 450, 563, 571, 610, 612, 625, 630, 685, 699, 752, 786, 818, 824, 927, 1003, 1254, 1384, 1554, 1567, 1603, 1609, 1610, 1611, 1633, 1636, 1648, 1668, 1746, 1775, 1842, 1865, 1950, 1953, 1960, 1976, 1982, 2041, 2231, 2263, 2515.

I.   Communications

1142.   Dunn, James D. G. "Wise as Serpents, at Least: The Political and Social Perspectives of the Electronic Church." Review and Exposition 81 (Winter 1984): 77-92.

Who the media ministers are, what they want, what they preach, what they have done, and what is their legacy: trivialization, commercialization, politicization, polarization, secularization.

1143.   Durden, Susan. "A Study of the First Evangelical Magazines, 1740-1748." Journal of Ecclesiastical History 27 (July 1976): 255-75.

Important in the history of the periodical press, the three British magazines studied here also show the institutionalization of revivalism, "the development of revival techniques," and "a clear indication of the ways in which information was purveyed" about the awakening.

1144.   Frankl, Razelle. <u>Televangelism: The Marketing of Popular</u>
         <u>Religion</u>. Carbondale: Southern Illinois University Press, 1987.
         204 p.

         This sociological study roots contemporary televangelism in the
         urban revivalism of Finney, Moody and Sunday, and then des-
         cribes the modifications made by the electric church to create
         "a new social-religious institution--a hybrid of revivalism and
         television--which is quantitatively and qualitatively different
         from the social institution of revivalism." Methodology
         appendixes. Thirteen-page bibliography. Index.

1145.   Hadden, Jeffrey K. "Religious Broadcasting and the Mobilization
         of the New Christian Right." <u>Journal for the Scientific Study of</u>
         <u>Religion</u> 26 (March 1987): 1-24.

         Questions the validity of secularization theory that sees a
         decline of religion in secular states; offers instead a
         "resource mobilization" theory that says religious social
         movements (like the NCR) confer legitimacy on both the movement
         and its specific activities. Further, Hadden sees social
         movements as recurring phenomena, and ties the NCR back to
         urban revivalism.

1146.   Hadden, Jeffrey K., and Anson Shupe, eds. <u>Televangelism: Power</u>
         <u>and Politics on God's Frontier</u>. New York: Henry Holt, 1988.
         325 p.

         Using resource mobilization theory, and centering on Jerry
         Falwell and Pat Robertson, the authors contend that a cultural
         revolution "pulling America back to religion and traditional
         values" is taking place, and the New Christian Right will
         continue to play a leading role in it. Bibliographical
         references. Index.

1147.   Hadden, Jeffrey K., and Charles E. Swann. "The New Denomination-
         alism: Franchising the Electronic Church." <u>Foundations</u> 25 (April-
         June 1982): 198-203.

         Prediction that televangelists will franchise their operations,
         creating their own denominations with a steady pool of funds to
         maintain the electronic center.

1148.   Harding, Susan. "The World of the Born-Again Telescandals."
         <u>Michigan Quarterly Review</u> 27 (May 1988): 525-40.

1149. Hicks, Darryl E. "Media-Electronic Evangelism: The Pentecostal Path." Logos Journal 11 (March-April 1981): 46, 48-51.

Brief history of the use of radio and TV media by evangelicals, the rather slow start by pentecostals (until the 1940s), and their surge into the media since WWII.

1150. Hindson, Edward E. "The Mainline Is Becoming the Sideline." Religious Broadcasting 20 (February 1988): 22-23.

Cites studies/articles, in noting losses in the mainline denominations and in liberal seminaries, and the strength in evangelicalism, with special focus on religious broadcasting.

1151. Leonard, Bill J. "The Electric Church: An Interpretive Essay." Review and Expositor 81 (Winter 1984): 43-57.

A history of the electric church, largely in evangelical hands from the radio days of the 1920s to the televangelists of the 1980s.

1152. Lippy, Charles H., ed. Twentieth-Century Shapers of American Popular Religion. Westport, CT: Greenwood Press, 1989. 494 p.

Scholarly examination of more than sixty "shapers" (a number of them evangelicals) who through various media--radio, television, print, music--influenced popular-level religion. Bibliographies. Index.

1153. Litman, Barry R., and Elizabeth Bain. "The Viewership of Religious Television Programming: A Multidisciplinary Analysis of Televangelism." Review of Religious Research 30 (June 1989): 329-43.

Sample in two midwestern cities shows that, contrary to the usual view that church participation is the major stimulus in religious program watching, "religiosity, existing apart from church participation, is a key determinant of such viewing."

1154. Mullins, Mark. "Prime Time Preachers and Popular Religion in America." Crux 18 (September 1982): 14-17.

Reviews the Hadden and Swan study, Prime Time Preachers (1981); concludes that much is wrong in advertising techniques and in the content of the programs, and that if changes are not made, Christian support ought to go to ministries "that do not necessitate capitulation to the materialism of our age."

1155.   Noll, Mark A. "Learning the Language of Heaven? Mainliners and
         Evangelicals Meet in Indianapolis." Reformed Journal 38 (June
         1988): 14-19.

         Some history of the religious press in America, and two reasons
         for the Evangelical Press Association (founded 1949) and the
         Associated Church Press (founded 1916) drawing close together:
         the passage of time has produced a more complicated theological
         landscape, and the awakening of Christian fellowship in the
         world.

1156.   Ostling, Richard N. "Evangelical Publishing and Broadcasting."
         In Evangelicalism and Modern America, ed. George Marsden, 46-55.
         Grand Rapids: Eerdmans, 1984.

         Survey of the various media at the core of the effort by
         evangelicals to create the "remarkable network of denomina-
         tional and parachurch agencies to promote their beliefs and
         programs."

1157.   Pullum, Stephen Jackson. "A Rhetorical Profile of Pentecostal
         Televangelists: Accounting for the Mass Appeal of Oral Roberts,
         Jimmy Swaggart, Kenneth Copeland, and Ernest Angley." Ph.D.
         diss., Indiana University, 1988. 310 p.

1158.   Schultze, Quentin J. "The Wireless Gospel." Christianity Today
         32 (15 January 1988): 18-23.

         Demonstrates through the history of evangelical radio that the
         "combination of evangelical fervor and media sophistication has
         always been explosive." Centers around seven current myths
         about religious broadcasting.

1159.   Steinmetz, Marvin Duane. "The Lost Voice of Mainline Protestant-
         ism or Why Mainline Protestantism Has Been Unable to Establish and
         Maintain a Ministry or Presence on Broadcast Television." D.Min.
         diss., School of Theology at Claremont, 1987. 124 p.

1160.   Taylor, James A. "Progeny of Programmers: Evangelical Religion
         and the Television Age." Christian Century 94 (20 April 1977):
         379-82.

         Draws several parallels between evangelicalism and the patterns
         of behavior on television (not religious programs) "strikingly
         similar to that I see among my evangelical friends."

See also items 2, 154, 831, 1905, 2003, 2247.

J. Literature and the Arts

1161.   Booth, John David. "A Comparative Study of Four Major Non-
        Denominational Evangelical American Hymnals in Current Use."
        D.M.A. diss., New Orleans Baptist Theological Seminary, 1986.
        219 p.

1162.   Child, Philip Albert. "Evangelicalism and English Literature,
        1798-1830: A Study in Literary, Religious, and Social
        Interrelations." Ph.D. diss., Harvard University, 1928.

1163.   Gaebelein, Frank E., ed. A Christianity Today Reader. Edited and
        with an introduction by Frank E. Gaebelein. New York: Meredith
        Press, 1966. 271 p.

        Selections from the first decade of the leading evangelical
        periodical of the era, including articles, editorials, news
        items, poetry, and cartoons. Brief notes on contributors.

1164.   Gambone, Robert L. Art and Popular Religion in Evangelical
        America, 1915-1940. Knoxville: The University of Tennessee Press,
        1989. 304 p.

1165.   Garlock, Donald A. "Fundamentalism and the Fine Arts." Funda-
        mentalist Journal 1 (December 1982): 36-37.

        The arts can play a positive role in the Christian community
        and the world when they are based on the biblical concepts of
        guilt and grace and when they point to a reality in God beyond
        the art form.

1166.   Gill, Frederick Cyril. The Romantic Movement and Methodism: A
        Study of English Romanticism and the Evangelical Revival. London:
        Epworth, 1937. 189 p.

        Defining Methodism rather broadly, Gill believes it "lent an
        indirect hand in the rise of the English novel," helped in the
        "emergence of English biographical and psychological litera-
        ture," and "played a part in the development of the clear style
        and emotional climate of the Romantic period." Bibliography.
        Index.

1167.   Gipson, Betty Jean. "Revolution in the Rectory: A Study of the
        Clergymen in the Novels of Jane Austen and Charlotte Bronte."
        Ph.D. diss., University of Missouri, Columbia, 1984. 243 p.

1168.   Hunter, Lloyd A. "Mark Twain and the Southern Evangelical Mind."
         Missouri Historical Society Bulletin 33 (July 1977): 246-64.

1169.   Kilby, Clyde S. "The Aesthetic Poverty of Evangelicalism."
         Covenant Quarterly 29 (November 1971): 36-43.

         Finds in contemporary evangelicals "a great oddity," namely
         that many of them are the foes of art and imagination, with
         "astonishing indifference to the created world." Concludes
         that orthodoxy is "better retained when regarded as the
         byproduct of a far higher aim, the love of God and the
         expectant search for his truth."

1170.   _____. "The Artistic Poverty of Evangelicalism." Eternity 16
         (December 1965): 16-18.

         Describes the situation, discusses the question Why? and notes
         "the sublime artistic excellence of the Scriptures."

1171.   Kowaleski, Elizabeth Anne. "The Dark Night of Her Soul: The
         Effects of Anglican Evangelicalism on the Careers of Charlotte
         Elizabeth Tonna and George Eliot." Ph.D. diss., Columbia
         University, 1981. 312 p.

1172.   Lundin, Roger. "Offspring of an Odd Union: Evangelical Attitudes
         Toward the Arts." In Evangelicalism and Modern America, ed.
         George Marsden, 135-49. Grand Rapids: Eerdmans, 1984.

         Survey of 19th and 20th century attitudes toward the arts,
         "influenced until very recent years" by "an American disdain
         for tradition, romantic aesthetic assumptions, and
         fundamentalist ideas about culture."

1173.   Moore, R. Laurence. "Religion, Secularization, and the Shaping of
         the Culture Industry in Antebellum America." American Quarterly
         41 (July 1989): 216-42.

         The "virtual revolution in print and oral communication during
         the first half of the nineteenth century" could have meant a
         secularizing of American culture, but religion remained "a
         dominant force in shaping the activities of commercial popular
         culture."

1174.   Nelson, Harland Stanley. "Evangelicalism in the Novels of Charles
         Dickens." Ph.D. diss., University of Minnesota. 1959. 355 p.

1175.   Nelson, Rudolph L. "The Cultural Barrenness of Today's Evangeli-
         calism." Eternity 10 (November 1959): 18-20.

         Evangelicalism is marked "by low-brow cultural level," by
         "aesthetic bankruptcy," partly due to a Puritan tradition that
         has valued conduct above "beauty and intelligence"; gives
         reasons why the Christian ought to value the arts.

1176.   Newell, A. G. "Early Evangelical Fiction." Evangelical Quarterly
         38 (January-March 1966): 3-21; (April-June 1966): 81-98.

         Analysis of the major book of each of four early 19th century
         British novelists--Hannah More, Leigh Richmond, Rowland Hill,
         Mrs. Sherwood--from whom evangelical fiction developed and
         spread.

1177.   Rosman, Doreen M. Evangelicals and Culture. London: Croom Helm,
         1984. 262 p.

         Disputes the received opinion that early 19th century
         evangelicalism was anti-intellectual, ascetic, and philistine,
         and argues that "its adherents shared the cultural and
         intellectual attitudes of their contemporaries to a far greater
         degree than Arnold and many other writers have been prepared to
         admit." Historiographical prologue. Bibliography. Index.

1178.   Rosman, Doreen M. "'What has Christ to do with Apollo?': Evangel-
         icalism and the Novel, 1800-30." In Renaissance and Renewal in
         Christian History [vol. 14 of Studies in Church History], ed.
         Derek Baker, 301-12. Oxford: Basil Blackwell, 1977.

         In the context of general English evangelical disapproval of
         the novel, appeared the religious novel, somewhat grudgingly
         approved by reviewers and generally accepted by the evangelical
         public.

1179.   Smucker, David Joseph. "Philip Paul Bliss and the Musical,
         Cultural and Religious Sources of the Gospel Music Tradition in
         the United States, 1850-1876." Ph.D. diss., Boston University
         Graduate School, 1981. 435 p.

1180.   Spurr, Thurlow, and Darryl E. Hicks. "Gospel Music: Fruit of
         Pentecost." Logos Journal 11 (March-April 1981): 54, 56-61.

         The sources and contemporary nature of pentecostal gospel
         music.

1181.   Tremaine, John S. "Music and Evangelical Christianity." Asbury
         Seminarian 24 (October 1970): 16-19.

         "A few premises to serve as guidelines" for further research
         and thi.king on "the place of music in the evangelical church."

1182.   Tucker, Stephen R. "Pentecostalism and Popular Culture in the
         South: A Study of Four Musicians." Journal of Popular Culture 16
         (Winter 1982): 68-80.

         "A brief examination of the influence of pentecostalism on the
         lives and careers of four key figures in southern music--James
         Blackwood, Johnny Cash, Tammy Wynette and Jerry Lee Lewis--will
         serve to illustrate its importance." From these four, "and
         beyond, the pentecostal experience has been a vivid link in the
         living chain of southern musicians."

1183.   Warren, James I., Jr. O for a Thousand Tongues: The History,
         Nature, and Influence of Music in the Methodist Tradition. Grand
         Rapids: Zondervan 1988. 304 p.

         Contending that "hymn books provide a valuable source for the
         study of church history," Warren follows Methodist hymnody from
         the Wesleys to the 1980s in this well done volume. Biblio-
         graphical references. Indexes.

1184.   Weiss, Ellen. City in the Woods: The Life and Design of an
         American Camp Meeting on Martha's Vineyard. New York: Oxford,
         1987. 167 p.

         An architectural historian describes a 19th century Methodist
         campground with good eye and a sense of the communal nature of
         the institution, "a permanent summer community which was still
         a religious space." Bibliography. Index.

1185.   Wolterstorff, Nicholas. "Evangelicalism and the Arts." Christian
         Scholar's Review 17 (June 1988): 449-73.

         No community opposes all forms of art; every community opposes
         some forms; two streams of thought about the arts prevail in
         the evangelical community: the sacramental (artist as creator)
         and the reformed (artist as worker and steward)--the latter of
         which is Wolterstorff's view.

See also items 94, 127, 217, 222, 229, 230. 558. 756. 845. 1691. 1975.
    2499, 2549.

K. Theology

1186.   Armerding, Carl Edwin, ed. Evangelicals and Liberation. Philadelphia: Presbyterian and Reformed Publishing, 1977. 136 p.

An early look at liberation theology by five evangelical
theologians. Bibliographical references.

1187.   Barr, James. Beyond Fundamentalism. Philadelphia: Westminster,
1983. 195 p.

In a follow-up to the author's earlier Fundamentalism (1977),
Barr concentrates on the issue of biblical authority as central
to understanding (and leaving) fundamentalism. Bibliography.

1188.   _____. Fundamentalism. Philadelphia: Westminster, 1977.
379 p.

A British view of what Barr calls fundamentalism, but what in
the United States is probably evangelicalism. Hostile to the
movement, this book has value in focusing on some of the
difficulties in the traditional evangelical theology.
Bibliography.

1189.   _____. "The Problem of Fundamentalism Today." In Studies in
Isaiah, ed. W. C. Van Wyk, 1-25. Hercules, Pretoria: NHW Press,
1979-80.

The "basic character of fundamentalism," criticisms Barr has
leveled against it, "and in particular the role of conservative
scholarship in relation to the religious core of fundamentalism; a paper read at a congress of the South African Society
for the Study of the Old Testament (OTWSA).

1190.   _____. "Religious Fundamentalism." St. Mark's Review no. 133
(March 1988): 3-10.

1191.   Barth, Karl. Evangelical Theology: An Introduction. Translated
by Grover Foley. Grand Rapids: Eerdmans, 1963. 206 p.

Five lectures delivered in the United States in 1962, with
twelve additional chapters, which together form an "introductory presentation" of the theological stance of the dominant
theologian of the 20th century. Chapters on, for example, "The
Word," "The Spirit," "Commitment," "Faith," "Doubt," "Prayer,"
"Study," "Service," and "Love."

1192.   _____. The Humanity of God. Richmond: John Knox, 1960. 96 p.

Three essays on: 19th century evangelical theology; the revolt
against liberal theology and a call for new and radical
changes; and "The Gift of Freedom" as the "Foundation of
Evangelical Ethics."

1193.   Benn, Wallace, and Mark Burkill. "A Theological and Pastoral
Critique of the Teachings of John Wimber." Churchman 101, no. 2
(1987): 101-13.

Sees "tendencies that are far from helpful and which we believe
are in fact dangerous," in Wimber's theology, practice, and
sprituality.

1194.   Biggar, Nigel. "Attesting the Evangel Evangelically: Toward a
Christian Theology of Religious Pluralism." Evangelical Review of
Theology 13 (October 1989): 314-24. Reprinted from Spectrum 21
(Spring 1989).

With a "tacit assumption of great significance," namely, "that
silence itself may be a most cogent form of Christian
confession," answers the questions: What is a Christian? What
does it mean to bear witness to the gospel evangelically? And
discusses "Religious Pluralism in the Public Place."

1195.   Blaiklock, E. M. "Conservatism, Liberalism, and Neo-Orthodoxy: A
Present Day Survey." Eternity 11 (August 1960): 21-23, 26-27, 33.

A "convinced," and, he hopes, "informed" conservative,
critiques liberalism and neo-orthodoxy, the latter "sympathetically but firmly," cautioning the conservative to cherish no
pride, and to "express . . . cherished truths in the language
and thought forms of the day."

1196.   Bloesch, Donald G. Essentials of Evangelical Theology. Vol. 1,
God, Authority, and Salvation (1978). Vol. 2, Life, Ministry, and
Hope (1979). San Francisco: Harper & Row, 1978-1979. 265, 315 p.

In a theology "hopefully radical as well as conservative," such
that some persons "would not acknowledge me as evangelical in
the traditional sense" because of his views on historical
criticism and the nature of the Bible, Bloesch lays out his
theology in somewhat unconventional format. Bibliographical
references. Indexes.

1197.   . Freedom for Obedience: Evangelical Ethics in
Contemporary Times. San Francisco: Harper & Row, 1987. 342 p.

> Endeavors "to present a viable alternative to legalistic ethics
> . . . and situational and relativistic ethics," and to persuade
> "the evangelical community in particular to explore anew the
> theological foundations for both personal holiness and social
> justice." Bibliography. Indexes.

1198.   . "Toward the Recovery of our Evangelical Heritage."
Reformed Review 39 (Spring 1986): 192-98.

> Call for a return to the solas of the Protestant Reformation
> and the awakening movements of the seventeenth and eighteenth
> centuries as effective means to oppose contemporary distortions
> of the Gospel: liberation theology, existential theology,
> feminist theology.

1199.   . "Whatever Became of Neo-Orthodoxy?" Christianity Today
19 (6 December 1974): 7-12.

> Neo-orthodoxy had certain strengths, such as emphases on
> Scripture, grace and God's transcendence, that overbalanced its
> weaknesses; now we must go beyond it to a full recovery of
> orthodoxy.

1200.   Bloesch, Donald G., and Vernard Eller. "'Evangelical': Integral
to Christian Identity?" TSF Bulletin 7 (November-December 1983):
5-10.

> An exchange between Donald Bloesch and Vernard Eller. Part of
> chapter four of Bloesch's The Future of Evangelical Chris-
> tianity (1983), comments by Eller protesting the term
> "evangelical" as too narrow, and a rejoinder by Bloesch who
> sees Eller as a "closet evangelical."

1201.   Bolich, Gregory G. Karl Barth & Evangelicalism. Downers Grove:
InterVarsity, 1980. 238 p.

> Study of "the relation of Karl Barth to American evangelicalism
> in the light of the need for reform and renewal [italics his]"
> that begins with the present crisis in evangelicalism--the need
> for a "constructive, dynamic, and dogmatic theology"--and
> proceeds to look at evangelicals and Barth. Barth's theology,
> and how evangelicals might learn from Barth. Bibliography.
> Index.

1202.   Bowers, Paul. "Why are Evangelicals Overlooking Mission
         Theology?" Christianity Today 9 (10 September 1965): 5-7.

         Plea for evangelicals to engage in mission theology, with some
         biblical passages cited as the basis for such.

1203.   Braun, Jon. "A Call to Church Authority." In The Orthodox
         Evangelicals: Who They Are and What They Are Saying, eds. Robert
         E. Webber and Donald Bloesch, 166-89. Nashville: Thomas Nelson,
         1978.

         Surveys the biblical, historical, and contemporary evidence
         (including the resistance to leadership in modern times), and
         the characteristics of proper leadership and authority, and
         calls for submissiveness and for authentically Christian
         leadership.

1204.   Brown, Colin. "The Concept of Evangelical." Churchman 95, no. 2
         (1981): 104-09.

         In the current confusion over definitions, Brown argues that
         the word "evangelical" should not have a narrowly defined
         single meaning because it is, to use W. B. Gaillie's term, a
         "contested concept."

1205.   Brown, Paul E. "A New Evangelical Arminianism?" Banner of Truth
         nos. 70-71 (July-August 1969): 28-34.

         An extended review of I. Howard Marshall's book, Kept by the
         Power of God (1969), "an extremely thorough examination of 'The
         Future of Evangelical New Testament' teaching on the persever-
         ence of the saints," but one which, "in the reviewer's opinion,
         bears evidence of an approach to Scripture which departs from
         the full Evangelical position."

1206.   Bruce, Frederick Fyvie. "F. F. Bruce--A Mind that Matters: A
         Conversation with a Pioneer of Evangelical Biblical Scholarship."
         Part one. Christianity Today 33 (7 April 1989): 22-25. Part two,
         "F. F. Bruce--The Apostle Paul and the Evangelical Heritage."
         Harvester 68 (July 1989): 10-12.

         Two part interview with W. Ward Gasque and Laurel Gasque. In
         part one, Bruce responds to questions about biblical authority
         and interpretation. Part two discusses evangelicalism. Paul's
         legacy, interpreters, and attitude toward women.

1207. Bussell. Harold L. "Why Evangelicals are Vulnerable to Cults."
Christian Medical Society Journal 14, no. 2 (1983): 4-6.

Five similarities between cults and evangelical churches,
including a subjectivistic and legalistic spirituality, and
unreasonable expectations for pastors; concludes with brief
suggestions to counteract vulnerability to cults.

1208. Cameron, Nigel M. de S., ed. The Challenge of Evangelical
Theology: Essays in Approach and Method. Edinburgh: Rutherford
House Books. 1987. 153 p.

All but one of these papers were delivered at the first
Edinburgh Conference in Christian Dogmatics (1985).
Contributors from the United States, Britain and Europe.
Bibliographical references. Index.

1209. Carnell, Edward John. The Case for Biblical Christianity, ed.
Ronald H. Nash. Grand Rapids: Eerdmans, 1969. 186 p.

A collection of Carnell's essays, published posthumously,
several of which deal with fundamentalism and evangelicalism
("Conservatives and Liberals," "Orthodoxy: Cultic vs.
Classical," "The Case for Orthodox Theology"). Bibliography
and bibliographical notes.

1210. _____. The Case for Orthodox Theology. Philadelphia:
Westminster, 1959. 162 p.

Classic statement of the neo-evangelical position by an
advocate of irenic evangelicalism. Bibliography.

1211. Chafer, Lewis Sperry. "Dispensational Distinctives Challenged."
Bibliotheca Sacra 100 (July-September 1943): 337-45.

Responds in a lengthy editorial to the "investigation of
so-called Dispensationalism" by the Presbyterian Church, U.S.,
at its recent General Assembly, "as to whether the type of
Bible interpretation known as 'Dispensationalism' is in harmony
with the 'Confession of Faith.'"

1212. Chapman, Colin G. "Going Soft on Islam? Reflections on Some
Evangelical Responses to Islam." Vox Evangelica 19 (1989): 7-31.

In the Laing Lecture for 1988. he shares his evangelical
pilgrimage relative to Islam: Outlines "some of the different
emphases in evangelical responses to Islam in recent years";

attempts to pinpoint what he sees as "the crucial questions";
and suggests "some of the implications of all this for
theological education."

1213.   Coleman, Richard J. Issues of Theological Warfare: Evangelicals
and Liberals. Rev. ed. Grand Rapids: Eerdmans, 1980. 282 p.

Wishing to stimulate dialogue, Coleman compares evangelical and
liberal views of Jesus, the nature of revelation, the
inspiration and authority of Scripture, prayer and providence,
and social involvement. Appendixes. Annotated bibliography.

1214.   Cottrell, Jack W. "Values in Evangelical Theology." Seminary
Review 19 (Summer 1973): 112-28.

Defines evangelical theology, then lays out three of its
values--for doctrine, apologetics, ethics--in the context of
the Christian Church.

1215.   Dahlin, John E. "The Church in Relation to the Cults." Discerner
6 (April-June 1970): 2-4.

Discusses current options, including the National Council of
Churches (accepts the cults), the "non-separatists" (dialog
with the cults), the "do-nothing group," "the ignorant and the
indifferent," and "no compromise with error" ("the unmistakably
clear" position biblically).

1216.   _____. "The Cultic Approach Versus That of Evangelical
Christians." Discerner 11 (July-September 1984): 2-3.

In connection with an exposition of Luke 16:8, contends that
"the cultists . . . reveal a single-hearted earnestness in
going straight for their goal," including "bringing an enormous
amount of literature to the public." Evangelicals "need to
plan wisely."

1217.   _____. "Where Cults Differ With True Believers." Discerner 9
(January-March 1977): 2-5.

Denies that "the cults may have the same goals as genuine
believers, and that they differ mainly on certain details
regarding the Scriptures." Rather, they are marked by "gross
inconsistencies and errors."

1218.   Davis, John Jefferson. Foundations of Evangelical Theology.
Grand Rapids: Baker, 1984. 282 p.

"Evangelical theology is a task-oriented reflection upon
scripture in light of the practical needs of ministry and
mission." Related to the American experience, the book handles
"theological method; revelation; reason; religious experience;
scripture; ecclesiastical tradition; principles of biblical
interpretation." Bibliography.

1219.   Davis, Stephen T. "Evangelicals and the Religions of the World."
TSF Bulletin 5 (September-October 1981): 8-11.

Christianity is an exclusivist, not inclusivist, religion; most
religions make true/false claims; Christianity should not
engage in triumphalism or imperialism in presenting the faith.

1220.   Dayton, Donald W. "Karl Barth and Evangelicalism: The Varieties
of a Sibling Rivalry." TSF Bulletin 8 (May-June 1985): 18-22.

Using "evangelical" as a word of three modes--Reformation,
pietist traditions, defense of orthodoxy--Dayton traces Barth's
ambiguous relationship to each mode, and warns against a too-
quick dismissal of this "sibling" of evangelicals.

1221.   Dean, Lloyd F. "The Withering of Unitarianism." Gordon Review 5
(Spring 1950): 13-29.

Studies the decline of Unitarianism, concluding that its plight
is that "of all denominations under the influence of liberalism," and that American Protestantism needs to keep that
danger continually in mind, along with the solution of establishing itself securely "on God's infallibly revealed Word."

1222.   Dennis, Lane T. "A Call to Holistic Salvation." In The Orthodox
Evangelicals: Who They Are and What They Are Saying, eds. Robert
E. Webber, and Donald Bloesch, 94-117. Nashville: Thomas Nelson,
1978.

Calls for an understanding of salvation as "corporate, physical
and this-worldly" as well as "individual, spiritual and other-
worldly."

1223.   Diehl, David W. "Evangelicalism and General Revelation: An
Unfinished Agenda." Journal of the Evangelical Theological
Society 30 (December 1987): 441-55.

Contends that "an adequate method for relating theology and
science can be found in the evangelical view of general and
special revelation but that the weakness" in that area "stems

especially from an underdevelopment in their doctrine of
general revelation. "

1224.   Dixon, Larry Edward. "The Pneumatology of John Nelson Darby
         (1800-1882)." Ph.D. diss., Drew University, 1985. 396 p.

1225.   Dobson, Edward, and Edward E. Hindson. "Evangelical Tolerance or
         All Things to All Men." Fundamentalist Journal 3 (January 1984):
         10-11.

         Questions and a parable pose the compromise issues facing
         today's evangelicals.

1226.   Dyrness, W. A. "Is Rome Changing? An Evangelical Assessment of
         Recent Catholic Theology." Evangelical Review of Theology 5
         (April 1981): 48-62.

         Issues like infallibility, Scripture and tradition, sacraments
         as mediators of grace and the charismatic renewal are under
         discussion by contemporary Catholics. Evangelicals need to be
         aware of the discussions and to make accurate assessments of
         changes in Rome's thinking.

1227.   Edwards, David L. Evangelical Essentials: A Liberal-Evangelical
         Dialogue. With a response from John Stott. Downers Grove:
         InterVarsity, 1988. 354 p.

         Published in England as Essentials (1988); a self-declared
         "liberal." Anglican Edwards here raises a series of issues
         about the Bible, Jesus, Christian behavior, and missionary
         activity--each of them responded to by Stott. Bibliography.

1228.   Elmore, Floyd S. "An Evangelical Analysis of Process Pneuma-
         tology." Bibliotheca Sacra 145 (January-March 1988): 15-29.

         A review of process theology, with special focus on the Holy
         Spirit, which concludes that "the pneumatology of process
         theology bears scarcely any similarity to a truly biblical
         pneumatology."

1229.   Emmerson, W. L. "Unity in Truth: The Growing Split Among
         Evangelicals." Christian Heritage 33 (January 1972): 10-12. 32.

         From the formation of the Church of South India (1947) through
         the meeting of Anglican evangelicals at Keele (1967).
         evangelical ecumenists have moved away from the historic
         Protestant idea of "unity in truth" toward an "ecumenical
         movement of truth."

1230.   Erickson, Millard J. Christian Theology. Grand Rapids: Baker, 1983-85. 3 volumes.

   One of the most widely used systematic theologies, by a leading evangelical educator and theologian; covers the theological categories and treats theological issues with both contemporary and historical materials.

1231.   _____. "Is Universalist Thinking Now Appearing Among Evangelicals?" United Evangelical Action 48 (September-October 1989): 4-6.

   The teaching "that everyone will be saved," which "has usually been rejected by Bible believing Christians," "has had a significant resurgence in recent years."

1232.   Escobar, Samuel. "The Church: Help or Hindrance to Evangelism." The Evangelical Round Table. Eastern College and Eastern Baptist Theological Seminary (St. Davids, PA: 1986). In Evangelicalism: Surviving Its Success, moderator Kenneth Kantzer, ed. David A. Fraser, 68-76. Princeton: Princeton University Press, 1987.

   A third world evangelical tells his story, defines evangelicalism, discusses tensions within it, and, in the context of those tensions, how evangelical churches can face their mission in the future, in such areas as theology, piety, missions, ethics, and social concern.

1233.   "Evangelical and Liberal Theology." Themelios 14 (October-November 1988): 3-5.

   An editorial responding to David Edwards and John Stott, Essentials: A Liberal-Evangelical Dialogue (1986), concluding that neither position is satisfactory, and urging humility and openness.

1234.   Evangelical Round Table. Eastern College and Eastern Baptist Theological Seminary (St. Davids, PA, 1986). Evangelicalism: Surviving Its Success. Moderator: Kenneth Kantzer. Editor: David A. Fraser. Princeton: Princeton University Press, 1987. 236 p.

   Twenty-two chapters issuing from a conference of leading evangelicals, covering a wide-ranging variety of subjects. historical. biblical. theological. Bibliographical references.

1235.   Evangelical Theological Society. Papers read at National and Regional Meetings, 1980-.

Collected by and available through TREN (Theological Research
Exchange Network). Many of the papers otherwise unpublished.
Bibliographical references. Indexes.

1236.   Fensham, Charles J. "An Evaluation of the Nature of Mission and
the Gospel of Salvation in the 'Evangelical-Roman Catholic
Dialogue on Mission.'" Missionalia 16 (April 1988): 25-39.

Argues that evangelicals and Roman Catholics have "two
different visions of salvation, but that there is an overlap
. . . sufficiently large to allow for further development in
dialogue"; there is also "agreement on scripture and the method
of the interpretation," but the "practical situation on both
sides" is often "far more complicated."

1237.   Finger, Thomas. "Evangelical Theology: Where Do We Begin?" TSF
Bulletin 8 (November-December 1984): 10-14.

After briefly surveying the present situation, and giving
definitions of "Evangelical," he discusses systematic theology,
suggesting that it begin with eschatology, and that "Narrative
Theology" provides the key by which "the Biblical message . . .
can concretely inform, critique and guide the Church today."

1238.   Foss, Michael W. "Rethinking the Mystical: Thoughts From the
Spiritual Closet. An Evangelical Perspective." Word and World 7
(Spring 1987): 148-52.

Roots of the evangelical skepticism about mysticism; and a
reappraisal in which Foss encourages "a new openness toward our
heritage of mystical writings."

1239.   Fowler, Paul B. Abortion: Toward an Evangelical Consensus.
Portland, OR: Multnomah Press, 1987. 225 p.

A biblical and theological study of abortion set in the context
of the church's (and evangelicals') lack of consensus on the
issue, accompanied by a call for an evangelical consensus
against abortion. Bibliographical references. Index.

1240.   Frame, Randy. "Leading Evangelical Scholars Trade Their Latest
Insights." Christianity Today 29 (19 April 1985): 56-57.

Report on "Christian Theology in a Post-Christian World"
Consultation, Wheaton, IL. Features a debate on poverty and a
view of second-chance theology.

1241.   Frei, Hans. "Response to 'Narrative Theology: An Evangelical
         Appraisal.'" Trinity Journal 8 (Spring 1987): 21-24.

         General comments on Carl Henry's article in the same issue of
         Trinity Journal.

1242.   The Fundamentals: A Testimony to the Truth. Los Angeles: Bible
         Institute of Los Angeles, 1917. Four volumes.

         Originally published as twelve volumes, 1910-1915, this set
         (with a few omissions) reproduces the 90-plus articles that
         presented an evangelical approach to a wide range of biblical,
         theological, scientific and other matters; widely received as
         the classic exposition of fundamentalist thought, some of the
         articles would not be accepted by all fundamentalists in the
         1920s and following. Sixty-five of the articles were
         republished as The Fundamentals for Today, ed. Charles L.
         Feinberg. Grand Rapids: Kregel Publications, 1958. 2 volumes
         (657 p.).

1243.   Gager, LeRoy. "The Place of Evangelical Literature in the Battle
         Against the Cults." Discerner 3 (January-March 1959): 7-9.

         Presents three uses: converting non-believers, "identifying
         cults" ("exposing errors"), and "fortifying Christians."

1244.   George, Timothy, and David S. Dockery. Baptist Theologians.
         Nashville: Broadman, forthcoming.

         Several chapters covering Baptist theologians including "Clark
         H. Pinnock: A Theological Odyssey," by Robert V. Rakestraw, a
         version of which will appear in the Christian Scholar's Review
         (June, 1990).

1245.   Gier, Nicholas F. God, Reason, and the Evangelicals: The Case
         Against Evangelical Rationalism. Lanham, MD: University Press of
         America, 1987. 371 p.

         A critique of rightist evangelicalism from the process theology
         perspective of the author; makes much use of contemporary
         evangelical scholarship. Twenty-four-page bibliography.
         Index.

1246.   Goldingay, John. "James Barr on Fundamentalism." Churchman 91
         (October 1977): 295-308.

Barr's analysis is "frequently compelling, though sometimes
misled and often overstated, and over one particular
theological issue (the doctrine of inspiration/infallibility
itself) unsatisfactory."

1247.   Gritsch, Eric Walter. Born Againism: Perspectives on a Movement.
         Philadelphia: Fortress Press, 1982. 111 p.

         The born-again movement, made up of fundamentalism and the
         charismatic renewal, and fueled by millennialism, represents
         "the classic restitutionist ideal," not highly favored by
         Lutheran Gritsch. Annotated bibliography. Index.

1248.   Grounds, Vernon C. "Finis to Fratricide." In The Evangelical
         Round Table. Eastern College and Eastern Baptist Theological
         Seminary (St. Davids, PA: 1986). Evangelicalism: Surviving Its
         Success, moderator Kenneth Kantzer, ed. David A. Fraser, 1-11.
         Princeton: Princeton University Press, 1987.

         Lists charges levelled against the evangelical church--
         mythology, apathy, hypocrisy, bigotry, disunity--and then (pp.
         3-11) explores the charge of disunity, discussing eight "peace-
         producing principles" suggested by Paul to the church at Rome.

1249.   _____. "The Nature of Evangelicalism." Eternity 7 (February
         1956): 12-13, 42-43.

         Not an "ism," evangelicalism is mainstream Christianity,
         characterized by belief in substitutionary atonement,
         justification by faith, human sinfulness, an infallible Bible,
         and a rational apologetic, while avoiding the excesses of
         fundamentalism.

1250.   Gundry, Stanley N. "Evangelical Theology: Where Should We Be
         Going?" Journal of the Evangelical Theological Society 22 (March
         1979): 3-13.

         In his presidential address to ETS, December 1978, Gundry
         argues that "the challenge . . . is to make new advances in the
         definition and implications of inerrancy, the nature of the
         Church and its ministry, and missiological issues." One theme,
         hermeneutics, is common to all three areas.

1251.   Harman, Gordon. "Evangelical Principles and Practices."
         Christianity Today. Part 1 in vol. 11 (6 January 1967): 12-14.
         Part 2 in vol. 11 (20 January 1967): 11-13.

Anglican Harman says that from its root principle of God the
sovereign redeemer flow the four main emphases of evangelical
Christianity: salvation, good works, the priesthood of
believers, and the authority of the Bible.

1252.   Heim, Stephen Mark. "True Relations: D. C. MacIntosh and the
Evangelical Roots of Liberal Theology." Ph.D. diss., Boston
College, 1982. 530 p.

1253.   Hein, Steven Arthur. "The Nature and Existence of Man in the
Apologetic Mission of Edward John Carnell." Ph.D. diss., Saint
Louis University, 1987. 369 p.

1254.   Henry, Carl F. H. The Christian Mindset in a Secular Society:
Promoting Evangelical Renewal & National Righteousness. Portland,
OR: Multnomah, 1984. 156 p.

Eight of Henry's addresses and essays, 1977-1983, "as a
confrontation of the secular contemporary mood" through
formulating biblical principles "that will arrest the drift of
modernity" on political and educational issues. Index.

1255.   _____, ed. "Frontier Issues in Contemporary Theology in
Evangelical Perspective: The Old Testament . . . Arnold C.
Schultz, The New Testament . . . A. Berkeley Mickelsen, Church
History . . . John W. Montgomery, Theology . . . Roger Nicole."
Bulletin of the Evangelical Theological Society 9 (Spring 1966):
63-80.

Papers presented at the seventeenth annual meeting of ETS,
December 1965, with Henry moderating the discussion.

1256.   _____. "Narrative Theology: An Evangelical Appraisal."
Trinity Journal 8 (Spring 1987): 3-19.

Using the work of Hans Frei and Gabriel Fackre, a thorough
analysis of what Henry sees as the problems in narrative
theology: reducing biblical historicity and inerrancy to
second-order questions.

1257.   _____. A Plea For Evangelical Demonstration. Grand Rapids:
Baker, 1971. 124 p.

Gathers several of Henry's addresses and essays, 1967-1971,
which "voice an agonizing concern over the unsure fortunes of
our evangelical witness in the closing decades of this century,
and bear on the need of effective evangelical engagement."

1258.   _____. "Plight of the Evangelicals." Christianity Today 12
         (5 July 1968): 25-27.

         Evangelicals need engagement with four matters: the evangelical
         presence in conciliar denominations; providing alternatives
         rather than just attacking other views; involvement in the
         academic arena; inter-racial liaison between believers.

1259.   _____. "Those Incomprehensible British Fundamentalists."
         Christianity Today. Part 1 in vol. 22 (2 June 1978): 22-26. Part
         2 in vol. 22 (23 June 1978): 22-26. Part 3 in vol. 22 (21 July
         1978): 29-32.

         Barr, Fundamentalism (1977), upset by the success of a theology
         which he utterly dislikes, overstates the simplism and
         triviality of fundamentalism and ignores the distinction
         between it and conservative evangelism. As an alternative,
         Barr offers new views of God, Christ and the Bible which Henry
         sees as another example of "the obscure and ever-shifting
         caprices of liberal criticism."

1260.   _____. "Where is Modern Theology Going?" Bulletin of the
         Evangelical Theological Sciety 11 (Winter 1968): 3-12.

         Noting the "'shrinking' survival span of recent modern
         alternatives to evangelical Christianity," and reviewing those
         developments, he concludes that "'The resurrection of theism'
         after the death of God can be a live option if the evangelical
         vanguard becomes theologically engaged at the frontiers of
         modern doubt."

1261.   _____. "Where Will Evangelicals Cast Their Lot?" This World
         (Summer 1987): 3-11.

         Henry feels that, except for some left-wing evangelicals, the
         evangelical-ecumenical dialogue proposed by Mark Ellingsen in
         The Evangelical Movement (1987) will not lead to constructive
         results because of central disagreement over the meaning of
         Scripture. Along the way, Henry laments the weakened condition
         of evangelical theology.

1262.   Hodge, Archibald Alexander. Evangelical Theology: A Course of
         Popular Lectures. Carlisle, PA: The Banner of Truth Trust. 1976.
         402 p.

         Reprint of original (1890) edition; includes a biographical
         sketch by Francis Patton, a faculty colleague at Princeton

Theological Seminary; nineteen chapters, taken from shorthand
reports, on various theological themes, by one of the leading
American theologians of the 19th century.

1263.   Hoffecker, W. Andrew, and Gary Scott Smith, eds. Building a
Christian World View. Vol. 1, God, Man, and Knowledge.
Phillipsburg, NJ: Presbyterian and Reformed Publ., 1986. 340 p.
Vol. 2, The Universe, Society, and Ethics. Phillipsburg, NJ:
Presbyterian and Reformed Publ., 1988. 478 p.

The authors write "a Reformed and evangelical exposition of the
biblical world view and compare and contrast it with other
Christian and prominent non-Christian perspectives in the
history of Western thought." Using a historical method, the
topics covered are theology, anthropology, and epistemology in
volume one (fifteen essays), and cosmology, the nature of
society, and ethics in volume two (fourteen essays).
Bibliography. Index.

1264.   Holmer, Paul L. "Contemporary Evangelical Faith: An Assessment
and Critique." In The Evangelicals: What They Believe, Who They
Are, Where They Are Changing, eds. David F. Wells and John D.
Woodbridge, 68-95. Nashville: Abingdon, 1975.

Acknowledges his debt to the evangelicals, who "have made it
very clear that God is not to be taken lightly or as one
chooses," and then discusses, within the context of "the formal
notion of epistemological considerations and evangelical
faith," "some rough edges [in evangelicalism] not made by God."

1265.   Holmes, Arthur F. Contours of a World View. Grand Rapids:
Eerdmans, 1983. 240 p.

The initiator of evangelical "world view" studies lays out the
basics: alternative world views; major themes in a Christian
world view; putting the themes into practice. First in a
series of volumes sponsored by the Institute for Advanced
Christian Studies. Bibliographical references. Index.

1266.   House, H. Wayne, and Thomas Ice. Dominion Theology: Blessing or
Curse? Portland, OR: Multnomah, 1988. 460 p.

In the first book-length critique of the Christian
Reconstruction movement, the authors recount the origin and
basis of Reconstructionism, and then analyze the two beliefs
that most separate it from other contemporary evangelicals:
theonomy (the application of Mosaic legislation in the present

era), and post-millennialism. Appendixes. Glossary.
Annotated bibliography. Indexes.

1267.   Housholder, David. "An Evangelical Doctrine of the Ministry."
Currents in Theology and Mission 16 (April 1989): 108-13.

Draws heavily on the work of Arthur Carl Peipkorn, longtime
professor at Concordia Seminary, St. Louis, proposing "an
office of ordained pastors which . . . is dominically-
instituted and functional."

1268.   Howard, Thomas. "Born Again? Who's Born Again?" His 41 (October
1980): 16-18.

Born-Againism has become "The Great New American Thing";
discusses the current situation and the meaning of the "Real
Thing," of "Old-Fashioned Faith."

1269.   _____. "A Call to Sacramental Integrity." In The Orthodox
Evangelicals: Who They Are and What They Are Saying, ed. by Robert
E. Webber and Donald Bloesch, 118-45. Nashville: Thomas Nelson,
1978.

Decries the absence of understanding and emphasis in this area,
and calls for an "authentically gospel sacramentalism."

1270.   Hubbard, David Allan. What We Evangelicals Believe: Expositions
of Christian Doctrine based on "The Statement of Faith" of Fuller
Theological Seminary. Pasadena: Fuller Theological Seminary,
1979. 168 p.

Ten articles of faith expounded in ten chapters that originated
as messages in "The Joyful Sound" radio broadcasts and in the
chapel services of Fuller Seminary. Includes a helpful ten-
page introduction to evangelicalism.

1271.   Hughes, Philip Edgecumbe. "What Does It Mean to be Evangelical?"
New Oxford Review. Part 1 in vol. 47 (June 1980): 13-16. Part 2
in vol. 47 (July-August 1980): 14-16.

Six evangelical distinctives: "the centrality of the Cross, the
sovereignty of God, the authority of Scripture. and priority of
preaching. ministry to the whole man. and the Christian hope."

1272.   Hughes. Richard T., ed. The American Quest for the Primitive
Church. Champaign: University of Illinois Press. 1988. 248 p.

1273.   Hundley, Raymond C. Radical Liberation Theology: An Evangelical
        Response. Wilmore, KY: Bristol Books, 1987. 141 p.

        An introduction to and critique of Liberation Theology from a
        conservative evangelical perspective, by a missionary
        (Colombia) academician. Twenty-three-page bibliography.

1274.   Inch, Morris A. "A Call to Creedal Identity." In The Orthodox
        Evangelicals: Who They Are and What They Are Saying, ed. Robert E.
        Webber and Donald Bloesch, 77-93. Nashville: Thomas Nelson, 1978.

        A warning against the dangers of empty creedalism and
        creedlessness, and a call to articulate the evangelical witness
        against the idolatries of this day.

1275.   Jacobsen, Douglas. "Re-visioning Evangelical Theology." Reformed
        Journal 35 (October 1985): 18-22.

        Whereas a generation ago evangelicalism was a creedal movement,
        it is now becoming a complex theological tradition; in light of
        this Jacobsen proposes five methodological commitments for
        doing theology in the evangelical mode.

1276.   Johnston, Robert K. "The Vocation of the Theologian." TSF
        Bulletin 10 (March-April 1987): 4-8.

        Compares the agendas and results of ecumenical and evangelical
        theologians; the latter may lack a critical spirit and be
        marked by anti-intellectualism, social conservatism, other-
        worldliness and separatism.

1277.   Jordahl, Leigh. "The American Evangelical Tradition and Culture-
        Religion." Dialog 4 (Summer 1965): 188-93.

        19th century evangelicalism, with its strong emphases on
        religious liberty and voluntarism, was basically culture
        religion, as defined by H. R. Niebuhr in his Social Sources of
        Denominationalism (1929); 20th century evangelicalism is also a
        culture religion, but what makes it appear out of step is the
        19th century culture it supports.

1278.   Kaiser, Walter C., Jr. "The Place of Law and Good Works in
        Evangelical Christianity." In A Time to Speak: The Evangel-
        ical-Jewish Encounter. eds. A. James Rudin and Marvin R. Wilson.
        120-33. Grand Rapids: Eerdmans: and Austin, TX: Center for
        Judaic-Christian Studies, 1987.

Based on support from the Bible and the Reformers, Kaiser
concludes that "evangelical Christians can and ought to use the
Mosaic Law."

1279.   Kantzer, Kenneth S. "Evangelical Theology and Paul Tillich."
         Asbury Seminarian 13 (Spring-Summer 1959): 3-9.

         A guest editorial, in an issue devoted to Tillich, critiquing
         Tillich, concluding that "he has fallen off balance far to the
         side of philosophy, and that this fall has rendered him
         nonsensitive to the crucial uniqueness of the Christian
         revelation of God in the person of Jesus Christ."

1280.   Kantzer, Kenneth S., and Stanley N. Gundry, eds. Perspectives on
         Evangelical Theology: Papers from the Thirteenth Annual Meeting of
         the Evangelical Theological Society. Grand Rapids: Baker, 1979.
         289 p.

1281.   King, John Charles. The Evangelicals. London: Hodder &
         Stoughton, 1969. 159 p.

1282.   Kleiner, John W., ed. "Perspectives on Evangelicalism/Fundamen-
         talism/Neo-Conservatism." Consensus: A Canadian Lutheran Journal
         of Theology 13, no. 1 (1987).

         Most of this issue is devoted to six articles on various
         aspects of this subject.

1283.   Krass, Alfred C. "Conversion in the United States Today."
         International Review of Mission 68 (April 1979): 148-55.

         Jesus' teaching about conversion; a comparison of mainline
         Protestant, mainline evangelical and radical evangelical
         concepts of conversion.

1284.   Kurtaneck, Nickolas. "Excellencies of Dispensationalism." Grace
         Journal 3 (Spring 1962): 3-11.

         Holds that, properly understood, much maligned dispensation-
         alism has the following "excellencies": "Harmonizes Scripture."
         "Explains History Adequately," is conducive, in its biblical
         basis, "To a Constructive Influence in the Christian Life," and
         "Provides an Adequate Defense Against the Errors of Liberal
         Theology."

1285.   Larsen, David L. "Aberrations Evangelicals Face: 1. The Teaching
         of R. B. Thieme." Discerner 8 (January-March 1975): 2-4.

The first of a series of articles with the purpose "to pinpoint
certain . . . dangerous delusions," and stressing, for Thieme,
for example, "substantive errors on crucial doctrines,"
including teachings about "the Blood of Christ," and "Twisted
Teachings on Grace." Other articles in the series published
1975-77.

1286.   Lawson, John. An Evangelical Faith for Today. Nashville:
Abingdon, 1972. 95 p.

Briefly presents the distinguishing elements of evangelical
faith. Annotated bibliography.

1287.   Lightner, Robert P. Evangelical Theology: A Survey and Review.
Grand Rapids: Baker, 1986. 303 p.

A college level survey with a practical emphasis, from the pen
of a dispensationalist evangelical. Bibliographies. Indexes.

1288.   Lindsey, F. Duane. "An Evangelical Overview of Process Theology."
Bibliotheca Sacra 134 (January-March 1977): 15-32.

Whiteheadian origins of Protestant process theology, some
current process theologians, exposition of the process doctrine
of God, and some difficulties from the evangelical point of
view.

1289.   Lovelace, Richard F. "Baptism in the Holy Spirit and the
Evangelical Tradition." Pneuma 7 (Fall 1985): 101-23.

1290.   Machen, J. Gresham. Christianity and Liberalism. New York:
Macmillan, 1923. 189 p.

The classic evangelical case against liberalism presented in
clearcut form: "modern liberalism [is] not only a different
religion from Christianity but belongs in a totally different
class of religions." Index.

1291.   Marsden, George M., and Frank Roberts, eds. A Christian View of
History? Grand Rapids: Eerdmans. 1975. 201 p.

Five essays on various aspects of historical study. three on
noteworthy theoreticians--Butterfield. Latourette. Dooyewerd--
and a fine bibliographical essay on Christianity and history.
The purpose of the book is that of "stimulating and broadening
discussion of the relationship between Christianity and
history."

1292.   Mayers, Ronald B. Evangelical Perspectives: Toward a Biblical
         Balance. Lanham, MD: University Press of America, 1987. 193 p.

         A discussion of the major areas of doctrine that tend to divide
         evangelicalism, in an attempt to achieve the balanced position
         he perceives in the Bible and in Christian history.
         Bibliography.

1293.   McClendon, James, Jr. "Evangelical Ethics: A Review-Article."
         Modern Churchman 29, no. 4 (1987): 42-48.

         A generally favorable review, with suggestions for further
         refinement, of Oliver O'Donovan, Resurrection and Moral Order:
         An Outline for Evangelical Ethics (1986), a book that begins
         with moral facts (rather than "meta-ethics") and then moves to
         moral judgments.

1294.   "A Meeting of Minds: Dunn, du Plessis and Hubbard Discuss
         Charismata." Theology, News and Notes 30 (March 1983): 3-7.

         Discussion of the biblical and theological issues, and the
         hopes for renewal in the churches.

1295.   Mouw, Richard J. "Evangelicalism and Philosophy." Theology Today
         44 (October 1987): 329-37.

         Seminary philosophy teaching and scholarship should in its
         approach be "world-viewish" (the forming and evaluating of
         worldviews) as it addresses the pastoral, evangelistic,
         praxical and ecumenical aspects of the Christian community's
         life and witness.

1296.   Murray, Iain. "What is Evangelicalism?" Banner of Truth no. 57
         (June 1968): 33-40.

         The substance of an address which concentrates on three major
         doctrinal features of the movement.

1297.   Nash, Ronald H. Faith and Reason: Searching for a Rational Faith.
         Grand Rapids: Zondervan, 1988. 295 p.

         An evangelical exposition of the current issues in philosophy
         of religion set in the context of several recent and
         contemporary evangelical philosophers. Bibliography. Index.

1298.   _____, ed. Process Theology. Grand Rapids: Baker, 1987.
         389 p.

Though they do not agree on all points, these thirteen
theologians (twelve of them evangelicals), address theological
and philosophical considerations in and give personal reactions
to process theology, providing thereby "a comprehensive
critical assessment." Bibliography. Index.

1299.   "A New Agenda for Evangelical Thought: Issue on the IFACS-ISAE
Conference." Christian Scholar's Review 17 (June 1988): 339-488.

Articles by leading evangelical scholars such as George
Marsden, Nicholas Wolterstorff, and Carl F. H. Henry, which had
been presented as addresses at the Conference.

1300.   New, Benny Lynn. "Religious Orientation and Ethical Thought: A
Profile of Moderate/Fundamentalist Differences Within the Southern
Baptist Convention." Ph.D. diss., University of Texas at Austin,
1987. 241 p.

1301.   Nichols, David R. "The Search for a Pentecostal Structure in
Systematic Theology." Pneuma 6 (Fall 1984): 57-76.

Comes to grips with the need for pentecostal systematics by
rejecting Schleiermacher and Hodge and using some of Barth and
Kierkegaard to arrive at a "spiritual" ontology and at the
analogy of love as the focus for epistemology and hermeneutics.

1302.   Noll, Mark A., ed. The Princeton Theology: 1812-1921: Scripture,
Science, and Theological Method from Archibald Alexander to B. B.
Warfield. Grand Rapids: Baker, 1983. 334 p.

Thirty-one selections from the Princetonians--Alexander, Hodge,
Warfield--preceded by a helpful forty-page introduction.
Fourteen-page bibliography. Index.

1303.   _____. "Revival, Enlightenment. Civic Humanism, and the
Development of Dogma: Scotland and America, 1735-1843." Tyndale
Bulletin 40 (May 1989): 49-76.

With the intent "to interpret comparatively the course of
theological development in Scotland and America over this
period," Noll argues "that study of the relationship between
formal religious thought and its social, political, and
intellectual contexts shows why theology developed differently
in the two regions during this period."

1304.   Noll, Mark A., and David F. Wells, eds. Christian Faith and
Practice in the Modern World: Theology from an Evangelical Point
of View. Grand Rapids: Eerdmans, 1988. 347 p.

Thirteen papers from a conference on theology in a post-
Christian world, held at Wheaton in 1985. The papers come from
center and left-of-center evangelicals in the Reformed,
Anglican, and Baptist communions. Bibliographical references.

1305.   Nunez, Emilio Antonio. Liberation Theology. Trans. Paul E.
         Sywulka. Chicago: Moody, 1985. 304 p.

         A Latin American evangelical assesses liberation theology, both
         Catholic and Protestant, from the standpoint of being faithful
         to the Bible and of listening "to the cry for freedom that
         comes from his [God's] people." Bibliography. Indexes.

1306.   Nyquist, John Paul. "An Evaluation of the Inroads of Process
         Theology Into Contemporary Evangelicalism." Th.D. diss., Dallas
         Theological Seminary, 1984. 298 p.

1307.   O'Byrne, William Lionel, Jr. "A Comparative Study of the Her-
         meneutics of Sun Myung Moon and Contemporary Evangelicalism as
         Represented by James Oliver Buswell, Jr." Ph.D. diss., New York
         University, 1978. 302 p.

         This computer-aided comparison of Sun Myung Moon's "Divine
         Principle" and Buswell's "A Systematic Theology of the
         Christian Religion" focuses on the hermeneutical presup-
         positions and principles of each work and concludes that
         "Moon's hermeneutics and evangelical hermeneutics, as
         represented by Buswell, are 'mutually exclusive.'"

1308.   O'Donovan, Oliver. Resurrection and Moral Order: An Outline for
         Evangelical Ethics. Grand Rapids: Eerdmans, 1986. 284 p.

         Grounds Christian ethics in the Good News of the resurrection
         of Jesus Christ. Christian ethics is, therefore, necessarily
         evangelical in character. An excellent study. Bibliography.
         Index.

1309.   Parker, David D. "Original Sin: A Study in Evangelical Theory."
         Evangelical Quarterly 61 (January 1989): 51-69.

         Concludes that "the biblical data . . . speak of the univer-
         sality of sin and man's needy moral condition." and "the inter-
         vention of divine grace," and that "to discard the terminology
         would be no loss, for it is not biblical in any case."

1310.   Pinnock, Clark H. "Evangelical Theology: Conservative and Con-
         temporary." Christianity Today (5 January 1979): 23-29.

Originally published in McMaster Divinity College's Theological Bulletin (May 1978).

1311. _____. Tracking the Maze: Finding Our Way Through Modern Theology From an Evangelical Perspective.   Grand Rapids: Zondervan, 1990. 224 p.

1312. _____. "Traditions Can Keep Theologians on Track." Christianity Today 22 (22 October 1982): 24-27.

To safeguard against Catholicism, evangelicals need to stress the crucial importance of the Bible; to safeguard against liberalism, they need to stress the importance of tradition.

1313. Popma, J. K. "Evangelical World and Life View." International Reformed Bulletin 41 (Spring 1970): 6-15.

"A view of human life that is governed by the message of the Gospel." Discusses, among other facets, the context of "sin and grace" for the Christian's task, guidance which involves "the usefulness and necessity of Bible study"; the task, which is "an act of world-interpretation," calls for daily and thorough-going correction.

1314. Poythress, Vern S. Understanding Dispensationalists. Grand Rapids: Zondervan, 1987. 137 p.

States the case for dispensationalism and for covenant theology, shows how the classic positions of each have modified toward the other, and gives point-by-point discussion of dispensationalism's major tenets from his non-dispensational stance. Bibliography with brief annotations.

1315. Ramm, Bernard. After Fundamentalism: The Future of Evangelical Theology. San Francisco: Harper & Row, 1983. 225 p.

Leading themes in this "essay in theological methodology" include: the devastating impact of the Enlightenment on orthodox theology; the fact that Barth's theology, the most thorough attempt to come to terms with it, offers the best paradigm for evangelical theologians to follow in seeking to interact with the Enlightenment. Ramm reviews the impact of the Enlightenment upon numerous doctrines and then shows how Barth's approach to each doctrine serves as a model. Bibliography.

1316.   Rightmire. R. David. "The Sacramental Theology of Jonathan
         Edwards in the Context of Controversy." Fides et Historia 21
         (January 1989): 50-60.

         The Northampton controversy in 1749-1750 is the scene for
         Edwards' mature articulation on the sacraments which he sees as
         "primarily subjective, focusing more on what the sacrament
         provides the occasion for in the believer, than on what it is
         or does in an objective sense."

1317.   Runia, Klaas. "Evangelicals and the Doctrine of the Church in
         European Church History." Evangelical Review of Theology 8 (April
         1984): 40-57.

         Overview of various concepts of the church, Reformation to the
         present, and some rather negative comments on "the fact that as
         Evangelicals we are often woefully weak in our ecclesiology."

1318.   Sarles, Ken L. "An Appraisal of the Signs and Wonders Movement."
         Bibliotheca Sacra 145 (January-March 1988): 57-82.

         Emergence of the movement at the hands of C. Peter Wagner and
         John Wimber; and careful evaluation of its assets and
         liabilities in terms of worldview, kingdom theology, and power
         evangelism.

1319.   Schmiechen, Peter M. "The Challenge of Conservative Theology."
         Christian Century 97 (9 April 1980): 402-06.

         Laments the fact that evangelicals have imperialistically (and
         inappropriately) laid claim to the Reformation heritage even
         though they have substituted doctrine for Christ, an inerrant
         Bible for the living Word, and made faith itself a saving work.

1320.   Schrotenboer, Paul G. Roman Catholicism: A Contemporary Evangel-
         ical Perspective. Grand Rapids: Baker, 1988. 99 p.

         A volume by an international group of twelve evangelicals,
         intended "to clarify the relationship of evangelical Christians
         to Roman Catholic faith and practice." Drawing upon official
         documents, presenting and evaluating the Catholic position in
         nine chapters (e.g., "Religious Liberty," "Authority in the
         Church," and "Justification by Faith Alone"), concludes that
         while there is much reason for encouragement, there is also
         much to give evangelicals pause. Bibliography. Index.

1321.   Scott, Waldron. "Evangelical Theology: Rock or Reef?" In The
         Evangelical Round Table. Eastern College and Eastern Baptist
         Theological Seminary (St. Davids, PA, 1986). Evangelicalism:
         Surviving Its Success, moderator Kenneth Kantzer, ed. David A.
         Fraser, 113-19. Princeton: Princeton University Press, 1987.

         Scott asks whether a systematic evangelical theology can be
         constructed that will anchor and unite rather than divide. He
         uses the Evangelical Alliance as a historical case in point,
         considers "centers of current conflict," and then deals with
         future possibilities.

1322.   Sell, Alan P. F. "Conservatives, Liberals and the Gospel." Faith
         and Thought 105 (1978): 62-118.

         Discusses conservative and liberal tendencies in theology, how
         each has measured up to the Gospel, and what our age can learn
         from each camp and from past conflicts.

1323.   Smith, Wilbur M. "The Need for a Vigorous Apologetic in the
         Present Battle for the Christian Faith." Bibliotheca Sacra 100
         (July-September 1943): 407-21; and 100 (October-December 1943):
         532-45.

         From the thought of the day, Smith lists six tendencies that
         oppose Christianity, the results of such tendencies and, using
         Paul's address to the Athenian elders, states that Christians
         should use the truths of creation, resurrection, and judgment
         to answer the opposers.

1324.   Springer, Kevin, ed. Power Encounters Among Christians in the
         Western World. San Francisco: Harper & Row, 1988. 218 p.

         Testimonies of prominent Christians about signs and wonders in
         their ministries; particular emphasis on the Vineyard Christian
         Fellowship (John Wimber). Bibliography.

1325.   Stafford, Tim. "Testing the Wine from John Wimber's Vineyard."
         Christianity Today 30 (8 August 1986): 17-22.

         "The key word in John Wimber's vocabulary is not healing, but
         power." Description of Wimber's success and his teaching, and
         the questions raised by critics.

1326.   Stegner, W. Richard. "Euaggelion: The History of a Word, in the
         New Testament." Explor 2 (Fall 1976): 11-12.

Discusses usage in the Pauline letters and in the Gospels,
concluding that "from a New Testament perspective whoever
preaches the 'good news' of the saving death and resurrection
of Jesus Christ is truly an 'evangelist.'"

1327.   Stoll, John H. "Contemporary Theology and the Bible." Grace
Journal 3 (Winter 1962): 27-32.

Briefly outlines and critiques a few of "the more prominent
contemporary theological philosophies"; liberalism,
existentialism, including the theologies of Karl Barth and
Rudolph Bultmann, and orthodoxy (including evangelicalism and
fundamentalism), concluding with a critique of liberalism and
existentialism.

1328.   Synan, Vinson. "Theological Boundaries: The Arminian Tradition."
Pneuma 3 (Fall 1981): 38-53.

A chapter in Wells and Woodbridge, The Evangelicals (1977); the
Arminian tradition in its Wesleyan, holiness, pentecostal, and
charismatic expressions.

1329.   Toon, Peter. Evangelical Theology, 1833-1856: A Response to
Tractarianism. Atlanta: John Knox, 1979. 242 p.

This excellent study establishes "that there was a large and
powerful Evangelical response to Tractarianism," describes the
history of the response, and evaluates the response along three
theological lines: the rule of faith; justification; and the
church, ministry, and sacraments. Bibliography. Index.

1330.   Trembath, Kern R. "Evangelical Subjectivism: Edward John Carnell
and the Logic of God." Evangelical Quarterly 60 (October 1988):
317-42.

Deals with an aspect ("how Carnell analyzes the God-human
relationship") of the thought of one of the central leaders in
the surge of evangelicalism during the mid-twentieth century.

1331.   Van Til, Cornelius. Defense of the Faith. Philadelphia: Presbyterian and Reformed, 1955. 436 p.

A Reformed theology defense of Christianity. of widespread
influence among evangelicals in the post WWII generation.
Bibliographical references. Index.

1332.   . The New Modernism: An Appraisal of the Theology of
Barth and Brunner. Philadelphia: Presbyterian and Reformed, 1947.
390 p.

1333.   Van Til, Henry R. "In Defense of Orthodoxy." Christianity Today
5 (27 March 1961): 10-12.

A three-fold defense: the argument from history, the scriptural
presupposition about God, and ethical-moral considerations.

1334.   Von Rohr, John. The Covenant of Grace in Puritan Thought.
Atlanta: Scholars Press, 1986. 226 p.

Thorough exploration of English and American Puritan covenant
thought to 1660, against the backdrop of twentieth century
interpretations of covenant theology. Seventeen-page
bibliography. Indexes.

1335.   Ware, Bruce. "An Evangelical Reexamination of the Doctrine of the
Immutability of God." Ph.D. diss., Fuller Theological Seminary
School of Theology, 1984. 477 p.

After reviewing the doctrine's interpretation across the
history of theology, and modern interpretations with special
focus on process theology, Ware briefly examines recent
evangelical contributions and then gives his own "reconstruction of the doctrine," arguing that "the God of the Bible is
both transcendent and immanent and this involves, then, proper
senses both of the divine immutability and mutability."
Bibliography.

1336.   Warfield, Benjamin B. "In Behalf of Evangelical Religion." In
Selected Shorter Writings of Benjamin B. Warfield - I, ed. John E.
Meeter, 385-88. Nutley: Presbyterian and Reformed, 1970.

1337.   Webber, Robert E. "Are Evangelicals Becoming Sacramental?"
Ecumenical Trends 14 (March 1985): 36-38.

Sources of sacramentalism and evidence of the practice among
evangelicals; "evangelicalism as a movement remains non-
sacramental."

1338.   . "Behind the Scenes: A Personal Account." In The
Orthodox Evangelicals: Who They Are and What They Are Saying. eds.
Robert E. Webber and Donald Bloesch. 19-39. Nashville: Thomas
Nelson, 1978.

An account of the organizing of the "Chicago Call." reaction to
it, and an introduction to its emphases and to the hopes the
editor and participants have for it, by a convenor-editor.

1339.   . The Majestic Tapestry. Nashville: Thomas Nelson, 1986.
238 p.

Rewrite and update of his Common Roots (1978), describing how
the early Christian tradition can enrich contemporary faith.
Part of the recent emphasis on worship among evangelicals.
Bibliography.

1340.   . "Worship: A Methodology for Evangelical Renewal." TSF
Bulletin 7 (September-October 1983): 8-10.

How evangelicals got to the present lack of interest in
worship; the rediscovery of the model of scriptural and early
church worship; using the model in contemporary congregations.

1341.   Webber, Robert E., and Donald G. Bloesch, eds. The Orthodox Evangelicals: Who They Are and What They Are Saying. Nashville:
Thomas Nelson, 1978. 239 p.

Thirteen essays based on the Chicago Call of 1977, summoning
evangelicals back to historic Christianity and setting out an
agenda for the late 20th century. The last essay is an
annotated bibliography for further reading. Bibliographical
references.

1342.   Webster, Douglas D. A Passion for Christ: An Evangelical
Christology. Grand Rapids: Zondervan, 1987. 221 p.

1343.   Wells, David F. "An American Evangelical Theology: The Painful
Transition from Theoria to Praxis." In Evangelicalism and Modern
America, ed. George Marsden, 83-93. Grand Rapids: Eerdmans, 1984.

Wells writes about contextualization--unwelcome task,
inescapable responsibility, and necessity--as a primary need if
evangelicalism is to escape "cultural Protestantism."

1344.   , ed. The Princeton Theology. Grand Rapids: Baker, 1989.
127 p.

Four articles, one each on Charles Hodge, B. B. Warfield, and
J. Gresham Machen, and one on the Princeton theology.
Bibliography. Index.

1345.   _____. "Reservations About Catholic Renewal in Evangelical-
ism." In The Orthodox Evangelicals: Who They Are and What They
Are Saying, eds. Robert E. Webber and Donald Bloesch, 213-24.
Nashville: Thomas Nelson, 1978.

A response to the "Chicago Call" that affirms its clarification
of weaknesses in evangelicalism, but critiques positions "that
are essentially incompatible with evangelical belief."

1346.   Wells, Ronald A. History Through the Eyes of Faith: Western
Civilization and the Kingdom of God. New York: Harper & Row,
1989. 262 p.

Careful laying out of a Christian interpretation of western
history, with the idea of "crisis" (of behavior and belief) as
"a guiding principle of the argument in this book."

1347.   Yandell, Keith E. "Evangelical Thought, 1987." Christian
Scholar's Review 17, no. 4 (1988): 341-46.

Report on the June 1987 conference co-sponsored by the
Institute for Advanced Christian Studies (IFACS), and the
Institute for the Study of American Evangelicals (ISAE), with
the theme "A New Agenda for Evangelical Thought." Participants
(whose papers constitute this issue of CSR), represented a wide
range of disciplines and of Christian and secular institutions.

1348.   Zens, Jon. "Moses and the Millennium: An Appraisal of Christian
Reconstructionism." Searching Together 17, nos. 2,3,4 (1988):
1-50, 52.

A historical, theological, and biblical analysis (and rejection
of) reconstruction ideas. A helpful twelve-page topical
bibliography is appended.

See also items 44, 64, 86, 96, 98, 120, 137, 138, 160, 162, 168, 173, 190,
194, 203, 204, 209, 245, 279, 280, 281, 282, 286, 298, 307, 308, 337,
345, 357, 359, 375, 376, 443, 462, 512, 521, 558, 574, 575, 619, 627,
647, 652, 736, 774, 783, 808, 809, 815, 816, 823, 826, 829, 841, 864,
865, 872, 877, 932, 943, 946, 969, 1009, 1042, 1057, 1099, 1352, 1372,
1378, 1384, 1385, 1404, 1413, 1424, 1435, 1442, 1453, 1502, 1514, 1522,
1526, 1532, 1535, 1545, 1546, 1552, 1564, 1582, 1583, 1599, 1621, 1665,
1675, 1676, 1678, 1723, 1724, 1747, 1830, 2398, 2473, 2512, 2610.

L. The Bible

√ 1349. Armerding, Carl Edwin. The Old Testament and Criticism. Grand
         Rapids: Eerdmans, 1983. 134 p.

         After laying out the characteristics of an evangelical Old
         Testament criticism, Armerding treats literary, form, and text
         criticism, and structural analysis, from an evangelical
         perspective. Bibliographical references. Index.

1350.   Barr, James. "The Fundamentalist Understanding of Scripture." In
         Conflicting Ways of Interpreting the Bible, eds. Hans Küng, and
         Jurgen Moltmann, 70-74. Edinburgh: T&T Clark; New York: Seabury,
         1980.

         The dogmatic position, the principles, and the typical
         consequences of fundamentalist understanding, showing it to be
         too devoted not to Scripture but "to a traditional dogmatic
         position about the nature of Scripture in general."

1351.   Bauman, Michael. "Why the Noninerrantists are not Listening: Six
         Tactical Errors Evangelicals Commit." Journal of the Evangelical
         Theological Society 29 (September 1986): 317-24.

         Inerrantist Bauman lays out arguments he believes have not
         worked well for his position--like the slippery-slope and
         definition-of-error arguments--and advises emphasis on the
         biblical data rather than theological deductions from the data.

1352.   Bebbington, David W. "The Advent Hope in British Evangelicalism
         since 1800." Scottish Journal of Religious Studies 9 (Autumn
         1988): 103-14.

1353.   Boer, Harry R. Above the Battle? The Bible and Its Critics.
         Grand Rapids: Eerdmans, 1975. 109 p.

         Distinguishing two views of infallibility, Boer rejects literal
         infallibility [inerrantism], and develops the other view--one
         whose "concern is with the certitude . . . of the gospel which
         only faith can recognize"--by means of discussion of lower and
         higher criticism.

1354.   Bratcher, Robert G. "New International Version--The Bible of
         Evangelicals." Evangelical Review of Theology 4 (October 1980):
         189-96.

Discusses background of the NIV, the "standard textual
principles" followed, the "conservative approach to exegesis,"
and the treatment of "cultural distinctives."

✓ 1355.   Cameron, Nigel M. de S. Biblical Higher Criticism and the Defense
of Infallibilism in 19th Century Britain. Lewiston, NY: Edwin
Mellen, 1987. 419 p.

Careful analysis of the orthodox defense of the Bible against
the inroads of higher criticism, including a survey of
commentaries, and a lengthy description of the work of William
Robertson Smith. Appendixes. Twenty-three-page bibliography.
Index.

1356.   Clearwaters, Richard V. "Causes of the Present Conservative
Baptist Conflict Demanding a New Mission Society." Central C. B.
Quarterly 5 (Summer 1962): 1-8.

The inroads of the new evangelicalism are eroding the historic
"Evangelical-Separatist" position of the Conservative Baptist
movement. Emphasizes the dangers of the ecumenical movement,
and the truth of the dispensational position.

1357.   Coleman, Robert J. "Another View: The Battle for the Bible."
Journal of the American Scientific Affiliation 31 (June 1979):
74-79.

Part of a Symposium on Inerrancy, Coleman uses Lindsell's The
Battle for the Bible (1976), arguing that "almost all defenders
of inerrancy have relied upon some kind of qualification."
Lindsell's volume is one consequence of a qualified doctrine;
Coleman's is another approach, which asks "what is the
essential character of Scripture: dogmatic or kerygmatic?"

1358.   _____. "Biblical Inerrancy: Are We Going Anywhere?" Theology
Today 31 (January 1975): 295-303.

We have not learned from the past: the five issues that divided
persons in the 1890s are still with us; we need to prevent the
issue "from becoming once again the principal barrier between
Christians."

1359.   Conference on Biblical Inerrancy. The Proceedings of the
Conference on Biblical Inerrancy. 1987. Nashville: Broadman.
1987. 554 p.

Collection of papers presented at the Conference held in Ridgecrest, NC in May of 1987, sponsored and coordinated by the six Southern Baptist seminaries, and including scholars, pastors, and laity. Includes (Part 1) major addresses and responses at the plenary sessions, and (Part 2) papers presented at the seminar sessions. Some papers include bibliographical notes, in addition to twelve pages of bibliographies at end of volume.

1360.   Conference on Biblical Interpretation. The Proceedings of the Conference on Biblical Interpretation, 1988. Nashville: Broadman, 1988. 221 p.

Papers presented April 25-27, 1988 at the Ridgecrest Conference Center, NC, at the Conference sponsored by the six Southern Baptist seminaries. Bibliographical notes included with some papers.

1361.   Conn, Harvie M. "Normativity, Relevance and Relativism." TSF Bulletin 10 (January-February 1987): 24-33.

Extended discussion of the two (or more) horizons involved in arriving at the meaning and application of biblical texts, with a laying out of the "Godward" and "manward" elements in hermeneutics. Good example of a contemporary evangelical grappling with the issues in scriptural interpretation.

1362.   Crutsinger, Gene Charles. "The Bible as a Moral Authority: Its Use by Contemporary American Evangelical Theologians." Ph.D. diss., Fuller Theological Seminary, School of Theology, 1988. 308 p.

1363.   Dayton, Donald W. "'The Battle for the Bible': Renewing the Inerrancy Debate." Christian Century 93 (10 November 1976): 976-80.

The variety of reactions to Lindsell's Battle for the Bible (1976), which Dayton here analyzes, indicate the factions appearing in evangelicalism that may lead to new alignments in Protestantism.

1364.   _____. "The Church in the World: 'The Battle for the Bible' Rages On." Theology Today 37 (April 1980): 79-84.

A series of late 1970s books and articles show the ferment over biblical authority producing a crisis point in American evangelicalism which Dayton feels could lead to an easing of "older polarizations."

1365. Fackre, Gabriel. "Evangelical Hermeneutics: Commonality and Diversity." Interpretation 43 (April 1989): 117-29.

Identifies six varieties of evangelicalism, explores the range of views in the interpretation of Scripture, ranging from "oracularity" through "inerrancy" and "infallibity" to "catholicity," while concluding that, "for all its diversity, evangelicalism represents a distinct and important perspective."

1366. Farrow, Douglas. The Word of Truth and Disputes About Words. Winona Lake, IN: Carpenter, 1987. 234 p.

Gathers and analyzes a number of positions in the polarization of the inerrancy debate and offers "functional inerrancy" as the resolution to the problems. Extensive bibliographical references. Indexes.

1367. Feinberg, John S. "Truth, Meaning and Inerrancy in Contemporary Evangelical Thought." Journal of the Evangelical Theological Society 26 (March 1983): 17-30.

Hermeneutical diversity in evangelicalism along three lines: the literal hermeneutic, dispensational versus non-dispensational approaches, and inerrancy.

✓ 1368. France, R. T. "Evangelical Disagreements About the Bible." Churchman 96, no. 3 (1982): 226-40.

The basic evangelical position on the Bible; issues on which evangelicals are divided: biblical criticism, reliability of the Scripture, "plain meaning" of the text; the need for intra-evangelical dialogue so the movement will not split up into "traditionalist" and "modernist" camps.

1369. Grigsby, Bruce. "Compositional Hypotheses for the Lukan 'Magnificat' - Tensions for the Evangelical." Evangelical Quarterly 56 (July 1984): 159-72.

Good example of an evangelical grappling with the hypotheses of redaction criticism while affirming the infallibility of the Bible.

1370. Hagner, Donald A. "The Battle for Inerrancy." Reformed Journal 34 (April 1984): 19-22.

The new, stringent "closed" inerrancy, noted in recent
evangelical battles, is harmful to the cause of evangelical
scholarship and may dishonor the gospel.

1371.   Hatch, Nathan O., and Mark A. Noll, eds. The Bible in America:
Essays in Cultural History. New York: Oxford University Press,
1982. 191 p.

Eight papers from a 1979 conference, dealing chronologically
with the influence of the Bible in American Protestant culture
(save one paper on Catholicism); written from an evangelical
standpoint. Bibliographical references.

1372.   Henry, Carl F. H. "American Evangelicals and Theological
Dialogue." Christianity Today 9 (15 January 1965): 27-31.

Asserts that "the doctrine of the Bible controls all other
doctrines of the Christian faith", and argues that recent works
by evangelicals on biblical authority offer the opportunity to
dialogue with those who hold weak views.

1373.   _____. "'The Chicago Statement on Biblical Inerrancy': Theologian Carl F.H. Henry's Evaluation." Eternity 30 (February 1979):
44-46.

Critiques the eleven-page document produced by almost 300
evangelicals in the fall of 1978, concluding that it "should be
considered an introduction to and not a full elucidation or
even complete outline of an evangelical theology of the Bible."

1374.   _____. Revelation and the Bible: Contemporary Evangelical
Thought. Grand Rapids: Baker, 1958. 413 p.

1375.   Hindson, Edward E. "The Inerrancy Debate and the Use of Scripture
in Counseling." Grace Theological Journal 3 (Fall 1982): 207-19.

Notes the drift away from inerrancy on the part of many
evangelicals, and discusses the significance for counseling of
one's view of Scripture and of "cultural contextualization,"
concluding that "it is time the pastor equipped with the
inerrant Word of God began using it with confidence to the
glory of God and the benefit of his congregation."

√ 1376.   Jacobsen, Douglas. "The Rise of Evangelical Hermeneutical
Pluralism." Christian Scholar's Review 16 (July 1987): 325-35.

A shift from the traditional monist stance, illustrated by
writings of J. Ramsey Michaels and Robert Gundry. Evangelical
hermeneutical pluralism often is more biblical in language and
methodology than its predecessor.

1377.   Johnston, Robert K. Evangelicals at an Impasse: Biblical Authority in Practice. Atlanta: John Knox, 1979. 178 p.

"Evangelicals, all claiming a common Biblical norm, are
reaching contradictory theological formulations" on issues
(which Johnston explores) like women's roles, social ethics,
and homosexuality. Johnson aims for an irenic spirit among
evangelicals and for "consensus-building in theological
formulation." Bibliographical references.

✓ 1378.   , ed. The Use of the Bible in Theology / Evangelical
Options. Atlanta: John Knox, 1985. 257 p.

1379.   Kaiser, Walter C., Jr. Classical Evangelical Essays in Old
Testament Interpretation. Grand Rapids: Baker, 1972. 265 p.

Ranging in date from Ezekiel Hopkins' essay on the Ten
Commandments (published in 1701), to J. Stafford Wright's
article on Ezekiel (1946), and organized by sections of the Old
Testament, these 14 essays share a common evangelical stance.
Bibliographies.

1380.   . "The Eschatological Hermeneutics of 'Evangelicalism':
Promise Theology." Journal of the Evangelical Theological Society
13 (Spring 1970): 91-99.

While covenant theology and dispensationalism have dominated,
"this study . . . offers a third theological and hermeneutical
system with its dual emphasis on the single truth-intention of
the author and the 'corporate solidarity' expressed in many of
the terms found in that one eternal promise."

1381.   Kantzer, Kenneth S., ed. Applying the Scriptures: Papers from the
ICBI Summit III. Grand Rapids: Zondervan, 1987. 514 p.

Seventeen papers, with responses, presented at the
International Council on Biblical Inerrancy meetings in
Chicago, 1986; cover a wide variety of theological and social
issues. Bibliographical references.

1382.   . "Evangelicals and the Inerrancy Question."
Christianity Today 22 (21 April 1978): 16-21.

Adapted from Kantzer's Evangelical Roots (1978); states that while "inerrancy should not be made a test of fellowship in the body of Christ," it is essential for "consistent evangelicalism and for a full Protestant orthodoxy"; suggestions on how to persuade belief in the doctrine.

1383.   Keegan, Terence J. "The Birth of Jesus in Matthew: Two Perspectives." New Catholic World 228 (January-February 1985): 30-33.

Comparison of the differences between fundamentalist (read evangelical) and higher critical approaches to the biblical text, and an attempt to resolve the issue by appeal to churchly faith.

1384.   LaSor, William Sanford. "Life Under Tension - Fuller Theological Seminary and The Battle for the Bible." Theology, News and Notes (Special Issue 1976): 5-10, 23-28.

Faculty member LaSor recounts the history of Fuller Seminary, with special reference to Harold Lindsell and his Battle for the Bible (1976), which, in some regards, misrepresents Fuller faculty and places the issue of the Bible at the point of inerrancy rather than at the point of authority.

1385.   Leahy, Frederick S. "The Place of the Bible in Modern Theology." Banner of Truth no. 86 (November 1970): 1-10.

Opening lecture in the Theological Hall of the Reformed Church in Ireland by the Professor of Systematic Theology and Ethics, on October 17, 1968. Concludes affirming the authority of Scripture and repudiating "the theological liberalism which has proved to be subversive of the very foundations of Christianity."

1386.   Lewis, Gordon R., and Bruce Demarest, eds. Challenges to Inerrancy: A Theological Response. Chicago: Moody, 1984. 414 p.

One of a series of books sponsored by the International Conference on Biblical Inerrancy; these essays look at eleven theologies since the Enlightenment, in order to see their "presuppositions leading to belief in an errant Bible and to assess them in their contexts by standard criteria of truth." Bibliographical references. Indexes.

1387.   Liefeld, David R. "Inerrancy is Not Just 'Fundamentalist.'" Dialog 27 (Spring 1988: 144-47.

A Lutheran pastor, while admitting that fundamentalism had some influence among Lutherans, contends that the concept of inerrancy goes back to Luther and the Lutheran confessions.

1388. Lindsell, Harold. The Battle for the Bible. Grand Rapids: Zondervan, 1976. 218 p.

This controversial book on biblical inerrancy includes Lindsell's view that there has been erosion in certain quarters of evangelicalism which prompted him to argue that loss of inerrancy leads to other deviations from the evangelical faith. Bibliographical references. Index.

1389. _____. The Bible in the Balance. Grand Rapids: Zondervan, 1979. 384 p.

In light of responses to The Battle for the Bible (1976) the author addresses himself "to the objections raised by those who disagree with me" and wishes "to add to the case I presented in the first book" in order that the problems in holding to non-inerrancy be made clear. Index.

1390. _____. "A Historian Looks at Inerrancy." Bulletin of the Evangelical Theological Society 8 (Winter 1965): 3-12.

Concludes that the normative, dominant position until the 18th century was belief in an "infallible and inerrant" Scripture. His account of the subsequent struggle and defections focuses on the slippage within the new evangelicalism (post WWII) and within ETS: "It has been infected itself and its own foundations need to be examined."

1391. Lovelace, Richard F. "Inerrancy: Some Historical Perspectives." In Inerrancy and Common Sense, ed. Roger R. Nicole and J. Ramsey Michaels, 15-47. Grand Rapids: Baker, 1980.

Points out that "entire confidence in biblical inerrancy" was normative in the church down to the 19th century, that loss of full inerrancy is not necessarily a slippery slope to loss of all confidence in the Bible, and urges continuing dialogue between total inerrantists and limited inerrantists.

1392. Marshall, I. Howard. "An Evangelical Approach to 'Theological Criticism.'" Themelios 13 (April-May 1988): 79-85.

Analysis of sachkritik (content criticism, material criticism), which argues for theological contradictions in the Bible;

weaknesses in the method; and its possible limited uses by evangelicals.

1393.   Montgomery, John Warwick. "The Approach of New Shape Roman Catholicism to Scriptural Inerrancy: A Case Study for Evangelicals." Bulletin of the Evangelical Theological Society 10 (Fall 1967): 209-25.

An affirmation of the historic commitment of evangelicals to "the supreme authority of the Bible," with emphasis on the importance of establishing the precise text, achieving accurate translations, and avoiding the perils of undue attachment to tradition or of individual arbitrariness in interpretation.
"[R]ecent developments in Roman Catholic thinking on the revelational issue can provide an invaluable case study for evangelicals facing similar problems." Positive and negative responses to those developments.

1394.   Mott, Stephen. "The Contribution of the Bible to Economic Thought." Transformation 4 (December 1987): 25-40.

Mott centers on the Exodus and the jubilee year as paradigms for economic justice; responses by two commenters.

1395.   Mueller, David L. "The Contributions and Weaknesses of Karl Barth's View of the Bible." In The Proceedings of the Conference on Biblical Inerrancy 1987, 423-47. Nashville: Broadman, 1987.

Sections include, for example, "The Doctrine of the Word of God: The Norm of Evangelical Theology," "The Doctrine of Holy Scripture," "Evangelical Criticisms of Barth's View of Scripture," "Barth's Major Theses on Scripture as the Word of God," and an Appendix: "The History of the Doctrine of the Authority and Inspiration of the Bible."

1396.   Nash, Ronald H. "Truth by Any Other Name." Christianity Today 22 (7 October 1977): 17-23.

Counters the neo-orthodox idea that revelation is non-cognitive by the evangelical belief in propositional revelation, and answers some of the objections to the latter.

1397.   Nichol, John Thomas. "A Call to Biblical Fidelity." In The Orthodox Evangelicals: Who They Are and What They Are Saying, eds. Robert E. Webber and Donald Bloesch, 68-76. Nashville: Thomas Nelson, 1978.

An affirmation of the historic commitment of evangelicals to "the supreme authority of the Bible," with emphasis on the importance of establishing the precise text, achieving accurate translations, and avoiding the perils of undue attachment to tradition or of individual arbitrariness in interpretation.

1398. Noll, Mark A. Between Faith and Criticism: Evangelicals, Scholarship, and the Bible in America. San Francisco: Harper & Row, 1986. 255 p.

Good survey of evangelical interaction with critical scholarship, 1880 to the present; evangelical biblical scholarship remained alive and reemerged during recent decades. Bibliography. Index.

1399. _____. "A Brief History of Inerrancy, Mostly in America." In Proceedings of the Conference on Biblical Inerrancy, 1987, 9-25. Nashville: Broadman, 1987.

The emergence of the question; four late nineteenth century defences: Princeton Presbyterian, dispensational/fundamentalist, "Baptist," and British evangelical; and several conclusions.

1400. _____. "Evangelicals and the Study of the Bible." In Evangelicalism and Modern America, ed. by George Marsden, 103-21. Grand Rapids: Eerdmans, 1984.

1401. Oss, Douglas A. "Canon as Context: The Function of Sensus Plenior in Evangelical Hermeneutics." Grace Theological Journal 9 (Spring 1988): 105-27.

Sensus plenior, distinguished from allegory and eisegesis, is "recognition of the canon of Scripture as a single and unified literary work," whose "circumspect and judicious use . . . should be part of a proper hermeneutical method for evangelicals."

1402. Packer, James I., ed. Beyond the Battle For the Bible. Westchester: Cornerstone Books, 1980. 159 p.

A collection of Packer's writings (one piece is new) and reviews addressed "to the task of restoring the Bible to its rightful place in the lives of present-day Christians and churches." Bibliographical references.

1403. Phillips, Timothy R. "The Argument for Inerrancy: An Analysis." Journal of the American Scientific Affiliation 31 (June 1979): 80-87.

Concludes that "foundationalism" ("an epistemological argument which claims that one is able to obtain genuine knowledge only from a foundation of apodictic certitudes"), "is not a proper model for biblical authority."

1404.   Pinnock, Clark H. Biblical Revelation--The Foundation of
         Christian Theology. Chicago: Moody, 1971. 256 p.

         A study of revelation, inspiration, and theology around the
         thesis "that our understanding of revelation radically affects
         our view of Scripture (its medium and witness) and, in turn,
         our conception of the character and role of theology"; from the
         evangelical point of view, including inerrancy "as an essential
         concomitant of the doctrine of inspiration." Bibliography.
         Indexes.

1405.   _____. "Evangelicals and Inerrancy: The Current Debate."
         Theology Today 35 (April 1978): 65-69.

         Draws the battle lines in the debate (noting the "crisis of the
         Scripture principle" beyond evangelicalism)--militants,
         moderates, opponents--and sees a new theology of inspiration on
         the horizon, one stressing the "spiritual power and authority
         of Scripture."

1406.   _____. "The Inerrancy Debate Among Evangelicals." Theology,
         News and Notes (Special Issue 1976): 11-13.

         Three theses: the category "inerrancy" should not create
         controversy; Scripture is inerrant in all it affirms; the
         urgent need of the moment is the relation between inspiration
         and interpretation.

1407.   _____. "The Ongoing Struggle Over Biblical Inerrancy."
         Journal of the American Scientific Affiliation 31 (June 1979):
         69-74.

         With a view to reducing hostilities, discusses the positions of
         "the militant advocates of biblical inerrancy," "advocates of
         modified biblical inerrancy," and "evangelical opponents of
         biblical inerrancy," arguing that the latter position needs to
         be more fully developed; concludes by setting the debate in the
         larger context of contemporary theology.

√ 1408. _____. The Scripture Principle. San Francisco: Harper & Row,
         1984. 251 p.

         While believing that the old (orthodox) view of the Bible "is
         not biblical and serviceable in every detail today," Pinnock
         calls for maintaining the normative authority of the Bible as
         he presents an understanding of biblical authority "in a
         positive, systematic and relevant way"; defends "the full

authority and trustworthiness of the Bible," and assists
evangelicals "to move ahead in the understanding of their
convictions." Bibliography. Indexes.

1409.   Price, Robert M. "The Crisis of Biblical Authority: The Setting
and Range of the Current Evangelical Crisis." Ph.D. diss., Drew
University, 1981. 290 p.

1410.   _____. "Inerrant the Wind: The Troubled House of North
American Evangelicals." Evangelical Quarterly 55 (July 1983):
129-44.

The current crisis of biblical authority; five non-inerrantist
positions (some of them opposed to each other) which will
probably lead their advocates slowly out of the evangelical
orbit.

1411.   Reid, Stephen. "An Evangelical Approach to Scripture." TSF
Bulletin 8 (March-April 1985): 2-5.

Argues for the use of canon/canonical criticism and the
materialist reading of Scripture as the hermeneutical methods
to replace form critical and tradition history methods.

1412.   Riggs. Jack R. "The 'Fuller Meaning' of Scripture: A
Hermeneutical Question for Evangelicals." Grace Theological
Journal 7 (Fall 1986): 213-27.

Reviews the "sensus plenior" ("fuller meaning") debate within
Roman Catholicism, as a foundation for examining the fuller
meaning and single meaning views as held by evangelicals,
concluding with difficult questions evangelicals need to
address in order to further accurate interpretation of the
Bible.

1413.   Rogers. Jack B., and Donald L. McKim, eds. The Authority and
Interpretation of the Bible: An Historical Approach. San
Francisco: Harper & Row, 1979. 484 p.

A controversial book central in the inerrancy debate among
evangelicals; the authors argue for a return to "the central
Christian tradition. especially as it came to expression at the
time of the Reformation." rather than continuing the scholastic
(inerrancy) tradition aided as it was by Scottish common sense
philosophy and 19th century Princeton theology. Extensive
bibliographical references. Indexes.

1414.   Roth, Wolfgang. "The Bible Among Evangelicals: Recent Pronounce-
         ments and Study Aids for the Bible." Explor 2 (Fall 1976): 23-34.

         Reviews "The Wheaton Declaration," "The Lausanne Covenant," and
         "The Junaluska Affirmation." The Living Bible and The New
         Scofield Reference Bible, The Wycliffe Bible Encyclopedia, and
         The Zondervan Pictorial Encyclopedia of the Bible.

1415.   Shepherd, William H., Jr. "Revelation and the Hermeneutics of
         Dispensationalism." Anglican Theological Review 71 (Summer 1989):
         281-99.

         Traces "the historical background and main tenets of dispensa-
         tionalism," then its "hermeneutical and exegetical principles,"
         showing that, "in order to affirm the primacy of literal
         interpretation and the unity of the biblical message, [it]
         embraces figurative interpretation and biblical diversity; what
         is ultimately at stake is biblical inerrancy."

1416.   Sheppard, Gerald T. "Biblical Hermeneutics: The Academic Language
         of Evangelical Identity." Union Seminary Quarterly Review 32
         (Winter 1977): 81-94.

         "Certain formulations of biblical hermeneutics have a unique
         rhetorical function" as they help to define the boundaries of
         the term evangelical.

1417.   _____. "An Overview of the Hermeneutical Situation of Biblical
         and Theological Studies in the United States." In Conflict and
         Context: Hermeneutics in the Americas, eds. Mark Lau Branson and
         C. Rene Padilla, 11-21. Grand Rapids: Eerdmans, 1986.

         Some negative comments about evangelical hermeneutics,
         especially in connection with inerrancy, and a survey of
         hermeneutics among non-evangelicals.

1418.   Stonehouse, Ned B. "The Infallibility of Scripture and
         Evangelical Progress." Bulletin of the Evangelical Theological
         Society 1 (Winter 1958): 9-13.

         Annual presidential address (1957); "there is a very intimate
         connection between the maintenance of the infallibility of
         Scripture and the attainment of any significant progress" for
         the evangelical cause; involves observing "A qualitative
         distinction between Scripture and tradition"; and diligently
         searching out Scripture regarding issues "on which evangelicals
         are seriously divided."

1419. Trembath. Kern R. Evangelical Theories of Biblical Inspiration: A Review and Proposal. New York: Oxford University Press, 1987. 154 p.

> Examines seven major theories and proposes a new definition that he holds to be most compatible with a Thomistic doctrine of God. Bibliography. Indexes.

1420. _____. "Evangelicals and Biblical Inspiration." Evangelical Review of Theology 12 (January 1988): 29-40.

> Reprinted from the Evangelical Quarterly, July 1986. A summary of his recent doctoral dissertation (University of Notre Dame): "Evangelical Theories on Biblical Inspiration." Stresses the three categories of inspiration: the initiating agent, the receiving agent, and the means.

1421. Turner, David L. "Evangelicals, Redaction Criticism, and Inerrancy: The Debate Continues." Grace Theological Journal 5 (Spring 1984): 37-45.

> A brief updating on "recent developments in evangelicalism, many of which center in the Evangelical Theological Society and the commentary of R. H. Gundry on Matthew," concluding that there remains a "crucial need of clarifying what evangelicals mean by inerrancy, without which there is a danger both of heresy and of a vigilante approach to these issues."

1422. _____. "Evangelicals, Redaction Criticism, and the Current Inerrancy Crisis." Grace Theological Journal 4 (Fall 1983): 263-88.

> Introduces the current situation, summarizes and then evaluates three important approaches, notes the situation within the Evangelical Theological Society, and offers a summary and conclusions, with an "Addendum: The Case of J. Ramsey Michaels" of Gordon-Conwell Theological Seminary.

1423. _____. "The Structure and Sequence of Matthew 24:1-41: Interaction with Evangelical Treatments." Grace Theological Journal 10 (Spring 1989): 3-27.

> Evaluates evangelical interpretations (four basic views). concluding "that a substantial portion of the chapter describes the present age." with the destruction of Jerusalem acting as an "earnest" anticipating the "eschatological tribulation."

1424.   Turner, George A. "Biblical Theology Revived." Asbury Seminarian
         35 (October 1980): 26-30.

         Presents and compares the evangelical and other viewpoints in
         what he sees as a welcome change for the evangelical, "the end
         of an era in Biblical scholarship--an era in which the
         historical critic was too often critical of the theologian."

1425.   Walters, Stanley D. "The World Will End in 1919: Daniel Among the
         Victorians." Asbury Theological Journal 44 (Spring 1989): 29-50.

         Description of the historical understanding of the book of
         Daniel as seen in the work of Henry G. Guinness, Irish-born
         evangelist and missionary. Exemplifies the last of that group
         of interpreters who are overtaken in the late 19th century by
         the futurists; part of the fascination with prophecy so common
         at the end of the 19th century.

1426.   Waltke, Bruce K. "An Evangelical Christian View of the Hebrew
         Scriptures." In Evangelicals and Jews in an Age of Pluralism,
         eds. Marc H. Tanenbaum, Marvin R. Wilson, and A. James Rudin,
         105-39. Grand Rapids: Baker, 1984.

         Definition of evangelical; Reformation hermeneutics; principles
         of exegesis; New Testament rules for interpreting the Old
         Testament; applying the Hebrew Scriptures today.

1427.   Woodbridge, John D. Biblical Authority: A Critique of the
         Rogers/McKim Proposal. Grand Rapids: Zondervan, 1982. 237 p.

         Woodbridge effectively answers the Rogers/McKim contention that
         inerrancy was a recent (19th century) development as he
         demonstrates the "deeply-rooted deficiences" in the
         Rogers/McKim book, The Authority and Interpretation of the
         Bible (1979). Bibliographical references. Indexes.

1428.   _____. "Is Biblical Inerrancy a Fundamentalist Doctrine?"
         Bibliotheca Sacra 142 (October-December 1985): 292-305.

         Over against a number of authors, who seem to classify
         inerrancy with fundamentalism but not with evangelicalism.
         Woodbridge argues (especially against George Marsden) that
         inerrancy is "the central tradition of the Christian churches."

1429.   Youngblood, Ronald, ed. Evangelicals and Inerrancy. Nashville:
         Thomas Nelson, 1984. 265 p.

Twenty-three papers on biblical inerrancy, most of them
published in the Journal of the Evangelical Theological
Society, covering the years from 1954 to 1979. Bibliographical
references.

See also items 50, 119, 190, 203, 238, 340, 402, 442, 456, 462, 468, 589,
594, 774, 965, 985, 1029, 1108, 1113, 1187, 1239, 1250, 1256, 1327,
1549, 1557, 1582, 1613, 1711, 1742, 1771, 1801, 2180.

M.   Wesleyanism

1430.   Abraham, William J. The Coming Great Revival: Recovering the Full
          Evangelical Tradition. San Francisco: Harper & Row, 1984. 125 p.

          Current evangelicalism "is falling apart theologically,"
          primarily because it is attempting to "rescue the doctrinal
          content of early twentieth-century fundamentalism." John
          Wesley is offered as "a viable model" to reinvigorate the
          evangelical tradition. Bibliographical references. Index.

1431.   _____. "Redeeming the Evangelical Experiment." TSF Bulletin 8
          (January-February 1985): 11-13.

          Abraham calls for a return to the use of John Wesley's thought
          as the way to keep evangelicalism alive and well. More fully
          developed in Abraham's book, The Coming Great Revival (1984).

1432.   Alderfer, Owen H. "British Evangelical Response to the American
          Revolution: The Wesleyans." Fides et Historia 8 (Fall 1976):
          7-34.

          Explores how Wesleyans, as an expression of British evangel-
          icalism, responded to the crisis of the Revolution, and the
          steps they took in working out and expressing their position,
          with special focus on John Wesley and Francis Asbury; concludes
          that Wesleyans responded in contrasting ways, with some, as in
          the case of Wesley after 1775, "thoroughly Tory," and others
          like Asbury responding differently.

1433.   Bready, John Wesley. England: Before and After Wesley; The
          Evangelical Revival and Social Reform. New York: Harper. 1938.
          463 p.

          Bready describes "an epochal movement" by looking at its
          "social and moral backgrounds, then proceed[s] to the origin
          and evolution of the movement itself, and finally examine[s]

the fruitage of its maturity in different spheres of cultural
attainment on different continents." Bibliographical
references. Index.

1434.   Burkett, Charles E. "The Common Fire: An Examination of the
Theological/Spiritual Kinship Between the Wesleyan Holiness
Movement and the Catholic Charismatic Renewal." Thesis, Ashland
Theological Seminary, 1983. 88 p.

"Differences obviously exist," but "the hard facts of
experience are the same and the conclusions of theology are
essentially similar."

1435.   Carter, Charles W. [gen. ed.], R. Duane Thompson, and Charles R.
Wilson [assoc. eds.]. A Contemporary Wesleyan Theology: Biblical,
Systematic, and Practical. Grand Rapids: Zondervan/Francis Asbury
Press, 1983. 2 volumes (1,178 p.).

Twenty-four chapters by a score of evangelical Wesleyans cover
the historical significance of Wesleyan theology, treat each
component of the systematic theology corpus, and address social
issues. Glossaries. Bibliographies. Indexes.

1436.   Coppedge, Allan. "Entire Sanctification in Early American
Methodism: 1812-1835." Wesleyan Theological Journal 13 (Spring
1978): 34-50.

Counters the accepted interpretation that there was a lull of
interest in entire sanctification in the first third of the
19th century by showing that interest in the doctrine remained
steady in the period.

1437.   Goen, C. C. "The 'Methodist Age' in American Church History."
Religion in Life 34 (Autumn 1965): 562-72.

The century following the Great Awakening was the age, not so
much because of the Methodist denomination, but because
American religion shifted "from the theocratic ideal of God's
rule in society to an introspective pietism concerned with
little beyond individual conversion," a legacy whose price we
are still paying.

1438.   Hamilton, James E. "Academic Orthodoxy and the Arminianizing of
American Theology." Wesleyan Theological Journal 9 (Spring 1974):
52-59.

Focusing on Asa Mahan (1800-1899). "perhaps the most complete single representative of this movement," Hamilton describes the change, notes its mingling with Methodism, and how with Methodism "it gave rise to the holiness movement of the latter half of the century."

1439.   Harrison, Archibald W. The Evangelical Revival and Christian Reunion. London: Epworth, 1942. 207 p.

1440.   Mickey, Paul A. Essentials of Wesleyan Theology: A Contemporary Affirmation. Grand Rapids: Zondervan, 1980. 185 p.

In the series, "Contemporary Evangelical Perspectives"; based on the Junaluska Affirmation (1975). an evangelical statement issued by the Good News movement in the United Methodist Church; Mickey explicates the preamble and the nine points in the affirmation, each of which begins, "Spiritual Christianity affirms." Bibliographical references. Index.

1441.   Rattenbury, John Ernest. Wesley's Legacy to the World: Six Studies in the Permanent Values of the Evangelical Revival. London: Epworth, 1928. 309 p.

The Quillian Lectures given at Emory University in 1928 recount Wesley's life and theology, and describe Wesleyan influence on religion, the secular world, and in hymnody.

1442.   Snyder, Howard A. "Wesley's Concept of the Church." Asbury Seminarian 33 (January 1978): 34-59.

Continues the Ryan Lectures with "a largely systematic treatment of Wesley and his understanding of the Church."

1443.   Snyder, Howard A., with Daniel V. Runyon. The Divided Flame: Wesleyans and the Charismatic Renewal. Grand Rapids: Francis Asbury, 1986. 120 p.

The central question raised by charismatic Christianity is. "In what sense is Christian experience. or the church. charismatic?" The author answers that dependence on grace. the action of the Holy Spirit. the church as community. and tension with the church as institution. are elements shared by Wesleyans and charismatics. Bibliographical references. Index.

1444.   Turner. George A. "Were the First Methodists Like the Early Christians?" Asbury Seminarian 38 (Winter 1982-1983): 26-34.

Concludes affirmatively. "despite the retention of the
hierarchical elements." "It was in the area of holy living
that the Wesleys were most distinctive and nearest to the
genius of the New Covenant."

1445.   Tuttle, Robert G. Mysticism in the Wesleyan Tradition. Grand
         Rapids: Zondervan, 1989. 192 p.

1446.   Van Die, Margaret. Evangelical Mind: Nathaniel Burwash and the
         Methodist Tradition in Canada, 1839-1918. Toronto: University of
         Toronto Press, 1989. 290 p.

1447.   Wood, A. Skevington. "The Eighteenth Century Methodist Revival
         Reconsidered." Evangelical Quarterly 53 (July-September 1981):
         130-48.

         Conditions in 18th century England; origins of the revival;
         effects of the revival, most noteworthy of which was personal
         transformation.

See also items 127, 184, 247, 386, 529, 546, 551, 602, 788, 870, 1166,
    1183, 1328, 1448, 1479, 1485, 1541, 1542, 1543, 1544, 2005, 2025, 2109,
    2539, 2551.

N.   The Holiness Movement

1448.   Bassett, Paul Merritt. "A Study in the Theology of the Early
         Holiness Movement." Methodist History 13 (April 1975): 61-84.

         Stressing theology rather than sociology, uses the Church of
         the Nazarene to exemplify the holiness movement: finds two
         kinds of Nazarenes, those consistently Wesleyan (H. Orton
         Wiley), and those at odds with classical Wesleyanism (A. M.
         Hills).

1449.   Dayton, Donald W. "The Doctrine of the Baptism of the Holy
         Spirit: Its Emergence and Significance." Wesleyan Theological
         Journal 13 (Spring 1978): 114-26.

         Well-nuanced description of the two ways of articulating entire
         sanctification, a Christocentric one (John Wesley) and a
         "pneumatocentric" one (Oberlin and Phoebe Palmer): the latter
         became background for the pentecostal movement by way of the
         late 19th century holiness movement. Expanded in Dayton's
         Theological Roots of Pentecostalism (1987).

1450.   . "From 'Christian Perfection' to the 'Baptism of the
Holy Ghost.'" In Aspects of Pentecostal-Charismatic Origins, ed.
Vinson Synan, 41-54. Plainfield: Logos, 1975.

   Traces the pentecostal baptism-of-the-Spirit terminology and
   theology to the works of the Oberlin perfectionist Asa Mahan,
   influential in the mid-19th century holiness movement.

1451.   , ed. "The Higher Christian Life": Sources for the Study
of the Holiness, Pentecostal, and Keswick Movements. New York:
Garland, 1984-.

   Forty-eight volumes in a facsimile reprint series of significant documents for the study of 19th century religious and
   social history.

1452.   . "The Holiness and Pentecostal Churches: Emerging from
Cultural Isolation." Christian Century 96 (15-22 August 1979):
786-92.

   Now fundamentalism, the charismatic movement, ecumenism, and
   social witness are adding to the ferment in these maturing
   church bodies, a diverse group to begin with.

1453.   . "Pneumatological Issues in the Holiness Movement."
Greek Orthodox Theological Review 31 (Fall-Winter 1986): 361-87.

   After a description of the beginnings and course of the
   holiness churches, Dayton treats their views of the filioque
   controversy, pneumatology, pentecostalism, and political
   concern.

1454.   . "The Rise of the Evangelical Healing Movement in 19th
Century America." Pneuma 4 (Spring 1982): 1-18.

   Traces the healing movement prior to the rise of pentecostalism
   to a number of sources, including Wesley and Finney, and
   centers on Charles Cullis, A. B. Simpson, A. J. Gordon and
   R. Kelso Carter as representative of the movement and its
   leaders; close tie with some holiness teaching.   Expanded in
   Dayton's dissertation.

1455.   . "Yet Another Layer of the Onion: Or Opening the
Ecumenical Door to Let the Riffraff In." Ecumenical Review 40
(Janary 1988): 87-110.

This fine article traces the emergence of the holiness,
pentecostal, and Keswick movements, plots the reorientations in
historiography and theology required by knowledge of these
movements, and suggests both a methodological and content level
as the significances of the holiness tradition.

1456.   Dayton, Donald W., David W. Faupel, and David D. Bundy. The
Higher Christian Life: A Bibliographical Overview. New York:
Garland, 1985. 201 p.

Brings together three earlier bibliographies, each published by
the Fisher Library of Asbury Seminary: Dayton's "The American
Holiness Movement: A Bibliographic Introduction" (1971);
Faupel's "The American Pentecostal Movement: A Bibliographical
Essay" (1972); and Bundy's "Keswick: A Bibliographic Introduction to the Higher Live Movements" (1975). Though exceeded
in volume by Jones' A Guide to the Study of the Holiness
Movement (1974), these annotated essays provide good access
into the subjects. Index.

1457.   Dieter, Melvin E. "The Development of Nineteenth Century Holiness
Theology." Wesleyan Theological Journal 20 (Spring 1985): 61-77.

Historical milieu of Wesleyan holiness; Phoebe Palmer's
theology; post Civil War developments; pentecost and holiness;
the age of the Spirit.

1458.   _____. "From Vineland to Manheim to Brighton and Berlin: The
Holiness Revival in Nineteenth-Century Europe." Wesleyan Journal
of Theology 9 (Spring 1974): 15-27.

Description of how from the 1830s on the holiness movement in
America was carried to Europe, first to England and then in the
1870s to the Continent; with implications for further study.

1459.   _____. The Holiness Revival of the Nineteenth Century.
Metuchen, NJ: Scarecrow Press, 1980. 356 p.

Good description of the Holiness movement that was so influential on nineteenth and twentieth century evangelicalism; some
reference to the rise of pentecostalism. Fifty-page
bibliography. Index.

1460.   Moule, Handley Carr Glyn, et al. Holiness by Faith: A Manual of
Keswick Teaching. London: Religious Tract Society. 1906. 156 p.

Bishop of Durham, New Testament scholar, holiness advocate, leading evangelical; chapters also by Hubert Brooke, J. Elder Cumming, and F. B. Meyer; aim "to give very plain instruction in the doctrine of Holiness by Faith, its Scriptural basis, and its application in daily life."

1461.   Raser, Harold E. "The Way of Holiness: Phoebe Palmer and Perfectionistic Revivalism in Nineteenth-Century American Religion." Ph.D. diss., The Pennsylvania State University, 1987. 373 p.

1462.   Shelley, Bruce L. "Sources of Pietistic Fundamentalism." Fides et Historia 5 (Fall 1972/Spring 1973): 68-78.

Identifies "pietistic fundamentalism," presenting its 19th century holiness background in several key leaders (W. E. Boardman, Hannah Whitall Smith, D. L. Moody, and A. B. Simpson) and the conferences and Bible schools through which their influence spread.

1463.   Snyder, Howard A. "The Church as Holy and Charismatic." Wesleyan Theological Journal 15 (Fall 1980): 7-32.

Reprinted in Evangelical Review of Theology 6 (October 1982): 172-201. The church is charismatic in nature, Wesleyanism was a charismatic movement (though not fully biblical), the holiness movement of the 19th century was not fully Wesleyan, and this holiness feature characterizes pentecostal and charismatic groups; then, an agenda for holiness-charismatic dialogue.

1464.   Stevenson, Herbert F., ed. Life More Abundant: Spirit-filled Messages from the Keswick Convention. Grand Rapids: Francis Asbury, 1987. 120 p.

Ten messages typify the Keswick approach to Christian Living, selected from Stevenson's much fuller books of Keswick messages: Keswick's Authentic Voice (1959), and Keswick's Triumphant Voice (1963).

See also items 8, 38, 334, 694, 712, 758, 785, 848, 854, 881, 1328, 1434, 1474, 1475, 1524, 1597, 1674, 1742, 1834, 2005, 2007, 2008, 2010, 2016, 2025, 2026, 2038, 2110, 2142, 2650.

O.   Millennialism

1465.   Barkun, Michael. Crucible of the Millennium: The Burned-Over District of New York in the 1840s. Syracuse: Syracuse University Press, 1986. 194 p.

Examination of the leading millennial movements, from
Millerites to the utopian societies, through the lens of
disaster theory, leading to the conclusion that these movements
may be seen "as the end stage of a process through which human
groups seek to accommodate collective stress. Twelve-page
bibliography. Index.

1466.   Buss, Dietrich G. "The Millennial Vision as Motive for Religious
        Benevolence and Reform: Timothy Dwight and the New England
        Evangelicals Reconsidered." Fides et Historia 16 (Fall-Winter
        1983): 18-34.

        Critique of the "social control" interpretation of the early
        19th century benevolent empire, centering on Berk's study of
        Dwight. Suggests that Dwight continued the view of his
        grandfather, Jonathan Edwards, seeing the approaching millen-
        nium as the strongest motive for reform through religious
        societies.

1467.   Butler, Jonathan M. "From Millerism to Seventh-day Adventism:
        'Boundlessness to Consolidation.'" Church History 55 (March
        1986): 50-64.

        Description of how the boundlessness and spontaneity of
        Millerism changed to the "consolidation, control, stability,
        uniformity, and order" of Seventh-day Adventism, providing
        thereby "access to the inner core of a profound transition in
        mid-nineteenth century American culture."

1468.   Hatch, Nathan O. "Millennialism and Popular Religion in the Early
        Republic." In The Evangelical Tradition in America, ed. Leonard
        I. Sweet, 113-30. Macon, GA: Mercer University Press, 1984.

        Emphasizes the importance of the Bible and of millennialism in
        popular religious history.

1469.   Hempton, David. "Evangelicalism and Eschatology." Journal of
        Ecclesiastical History 31 (April 1980): 179-94.

        Among 19th century British evangelicals are the sources and
        developments of a pre-millennialism pessimistic about society
        and the church, that left "evangelicalism wide open to the
        mid-century attacks from biblical criticism and science."

1470.   Maddex, Jack P., Jr. "Proslavery Millennialism: Social
        Eschatology in Antebellum Southern Calvinism." American Quarterly
        31 (Spring 1979): 46-62.

Southern Presbyterians gradually formulated a view of slavery
made more humane, but continuing in the coming millennial age,
only to have the eschatology dashed by the Civil War.

1471.   Moorhead, James H. American Apocalypse: Yankee Protestants and
the Civil War, 1860-1869. New Haven: Yale University Press, 1978.
278 p.

1976 Brewer Prize. Baptists, Methodists, Presbyterians and
Congregationalists in the North who were convinced that the
Civil War was the climactic test of the redeemer nation and its
millennial role, only to be unprepared for the perplexities and
problems that beset the nation after the war. Twenty-five-page
bibliography. Index.

1472.   ____. "The Erosion of Postmillennialism in American Religious
Thought, 1865-1925." Church History 53 (March 1984): 61-77.

Charts the loss of postmillennial thought not only among
premillennial conservatives but among liberals as well, so that
it became "a relic of a lost world."

1473.   Numbers, Ronald L., and Jonathan M. Butler, eds. The Disap-
pointed: Millerism and Millenarianism in the Nineteenth Century.
Bloomington: Indiana University Press, 1987. 235 p.

A collection of eleven essays from a 1984 conference on
Millerism and Millenarianism; current historiography on a
variety of nineteenth century adventist topics. Most recent
book reflecting the renewed interest in adventism.
Bibliographical references.

1474.   Smith, Timothy L. "Christian Perfectionism and American Idealism,
1820-1900." Asbury Seminarian 31 (October 1976): 7-34.

Argues that the two concepts worked together in the nineteenth
century, millennialism and the American dream uniting as a
catalyst to promote the perfectionism urged by the Oberlin
theologians and the Methodist holiness advocates.

1475.   ____. "Righteousness and Hope: Christian Holiness and the
Millennial Vision in America, 1800-1900." American Quarterly 31
(Spring 1979): 21-45.

Perfectionist religion and political ideology from Andrew
Jackson to the end of the century; the Bible's authority "was a
principal factor in shaping that ideology"; religious

millennialism combined with the American dream "was a prime
catalyst . . . of the quest for personal and social holiness."
Reprinted as "Holiness and Radicalism in Nineteenth Century
America," in Sanctification and Liberation: Liberation
Theologies in Light of the Wesleyan Tradition, ed. Theodore
Runyon, 116-41. Nashville: Abingdon, 1981.

1476.   Tuveson, Ernest Lee. Redeemer Nation: The Idea of America's
        Millennial Role. Chicago: University of Chicago Press, 1968.
        238 p.

        The book that established the U.S. as playing "a starring role
        as world redeemer," present "from the beginning of the
        republic; it is present even yet"; includes the identification
        of that role with evangelical destiny; carries the concept
        through WWI. Appendix. Bibliography. Index.

1477.   Weber, Timothy P. Living in the Shadow of the Second Coming:
        American Pre-millennialism, 1875-1982. Enl. edition. Grand
        Rapids: Zondervan, 1983. 305 p.

        A fine study of dispensational premillennialism: its emergence
        late in the 19th century; the behavioral consequences of its
        belief; its effects on evangelical social reform and world
        evangelization; its response to several 20th century issues.
        Twenty-three-page bibliography. Index. Previous edition
        (1979) entitled Living in the Shadow of the Second Coming:
        American Pre-millennialism, 1875-1925. 232 p.

See also items 10, 181, 819, 837, 906, 1831, 2462, 2500.

P.   Pietism

1478.   Brown, Dale W. Understanding Pietism. Grand Rapids: Eerdmans,
        1978. 182 p.

1479.   Kincheloe, Joe L., Jr. "European Roots of Evangelical Revivalism:
        Methodist Transmission of the Pietistic Socio-Religious Tradi-
        tion." Methodist History 18 (July 1980): 262-71.

        Ignores the Reformed tradition in arguing for the Methodist
        role in transmitting 17th century pietism to the American
        scene.

1480.   Kuenning, Paul P. "Pietism: A Lutheran Resource for Dialogue with
        Evangelicalism." Dialog 24 (Fall 1985): 285-92.

What evangelicalism is, the 19th century Lutheran pietist
tradition and its relation to evangelicalism, and the pietist
heritage as source for dialogue with contemporary evangelicals.

1481.   . The Rise and Fall of American Lutheran Pietism: The
        Rejection of an Activist Heritage. Macon, GA: Mercer University
        Press, 1988. 271 p.

Relates the dominance (for nearly 150 years), and the demise
(in the pre-Civil War years), of the pietist tradition within
American Lutheranism. Sympathetic to that tradition, but a
careful and well-written study. Thirty-page bibliography.
Index.

1482.   McLoughlin, William G. "Pietism and the American Character."
        American Quarterly 17 (Summer 1965): 163-86.

McLoughlin ranges through politics, literature and art to
illustrate his belief that pietism (actually "pietistic-
perfectionism") in its Christian and post-Christian version
"lies at the basis of American civilization."

1483.   Meiring, P. G. J. "Pietists, Evangelicals and Liberation."
        Missionalia 5 (August 1977): 196-99.

Though pietists gave precedence to individual conversion, they
also were socially and politically involved; evangelicals,
their heirs, are just now making social and political
statements.

1484.   Olson, Virgil A. "The Baptist General Conference and Its Pietis-
        tic Heritage." Bethel Seminary Quarterly 4 (May 1956): 54-66.

In the context of a rapid transition into an Americanized
Christianity, a church historian reviews the pietistic heritage
within evangelicalism and then discusses some "Pietistic
characteristics" of "Conference Baptists": "the centrality of
the Bible," "a born-again experience," "holy living," "a
layman's movement," and "revival."

1485.   Snyder, Howard A. "Pietism, Moravianism, and Methodism as Renewal
        Movements: A Comparative and Thematic Study." Ph.D. diss.,
        University of Notre Dame, 1983. 326 p.

Study by a prominent participant in the church renewal movement
of the late 20th century, of three significant and vital
strands within historic evangelicalism. Sixteen-page
bibliography.

1486.   Stoeffler, F. Ernest. Continental Pietism and Early American
         Christianity. Grand Rapids: Eerdmans, 1976. 276 p.

         Seven studies on the influence of Pietism on 18th century
         denominations, aimed at pointing out that besides Puritanism
         there were other influences "which rightly share in the glory
         and the shame of what happened in our history." Biblio-
         graphies. Index.

1487.   _____. German Pietism During the Eighteenth Century. Leiden:
         Brill, 1973. 281 p.

         Thorough exposition of German Pietism from its founding at
         Halle to its various 18th century expressions: Moravianism,
         Wurttemberg Pietism, radical Pietism, Reformed Pietism, and
         neo-Pietism; a movement which was in time "transplanted to
         North America by a substantial number of immigrants." Biblio-
         graphical references. Bibliography of secondary sources.
         Index.

1488.   _____. The Rise of Evangelical Pietism. Lieden: Brill, 1971.
         252 p.

         Development of the Pietistic movement, 1590 to 1690, concen-
         trating on Pietism among English Puritans, the origin of
         Reformed Pietism in Europe, and the beginning of Lutheran
         Pietism. Bibliography. Index.

1489.   Thompson, Clark Alva. "Motifs in Eighteenth Century Evangelical-
         Pietism." Ph.D. diss., Brown University, 1974. 264 p.

         A double focus: argues that the evangelicals constituted "an
         evangelical community and an evangelical reformation"; and
         discusses a number of motifs that are common to the literature
         of evangelical pietism. Bibliography.

See also items 421, 1462, 2380.

Q. Spiritual Life

1490.   Adams, Doug. Meeting House to Camp Meeting: Toward a History of
         American Free Church Worship From 1620-1835. Saratoga. NY: Modern
         Liturgy-Resource Publ.. 1981. 158 p.

         A study of a significant aspect of the evangelical experience.
         stressing the Puritan origins of worship patterns. when worship

forms were more free than they became later. Bibliography.
Index.

1491. Allen, Maurice. "Reflections on My Former Evangelicalism." Crux
5 (1 February 1968): 16-31.

Discusses why he is no longer an evangelical; lists reasons for
his "disaffection," and outlines an alternative position,
inviting dialog.

1492. Ballard, Paul H. "Evangelical Experience: Notes on the History of
a Tradition." Journal of Ecumenical Studies 13 (Winter 1976):
51-68.

Survey of Anglo-Saxon evangelicalism from Luther and Calvin to
post-World War II, stressing experience rather than doctrinal
formulations, leading the author to see a strong potential for
support of ecumenism among evangelicals.

1493. Barrett, Roger. "Can an Evangelical Not Be a Christian?"
Eternity 21 (February 1970): 17-19.

A professor of psychology at an evangelical college attempts to
show "how one can be raised to do all the right evangelical
sort of things--praying, testifying, etc.--and still not be a
Christian," trusting in "sound religious behavior" rather than
"in the grace of God in Christ."

1494. _____. "How an Evangelical Can Be a Christian." Eternity 21
(July 1970): 15-16.

Affirms that neither religious experience nor correct beliefs
constitute saving faith; the locus of faith is rather in the
person of Jesus Christ; an awareness of lostness is pivotal,
with the focus on our sinful nature rather than on sinful acts.

1495. Benson, John E. "Two Types of Evangelicalism: The Inner Life as
Mirror and as Lamp." Dialog 24 (Summer 1985): 193-96.

Brief description of spirituality as imitation (the mirror) and
as activity (the lamp), with evangelicals falling mostly into
the first camp. Benson tends to equate fundamentalism with
evangelicalism.

1496. Bradley, James. "Varieties of Spirituality in the Evangelical
Tradition." A lecture presented at Fuller Theological Seminary.
September 18, 1980.

Covers evangelical spirituality from the Reformation to the
20th century, as well as the central strands in medieval
Catholic spirituality.

1497.   Dockery, David S. "An Outline of Paul's View of the Spiritual
Life: Foundation for an Evangelical Spirituality." Criswell
Theological Review 3 (Spring 1989): 327-40.

"[T]here is hardly any aspect of the Christian experience that
is not influenced by the Spirit's activities. . . . We observed
that the ethical teaching concerning life in the Spirit is
shaped by the list of vices and virtues, by the indicative/
imperative statements carried out in time in the already/not
yet tension. Life in the Spirit brings freedom to the
believers in the community."

1498.   Hefley, James C. Unique Evangelical Churches. Waco: Word, 1977.
164 p.

Characterizes eight churches, varying in size, location, style,
and ministries, to provide a cross-section of how conservative
churches are growing.

1499.   Hoffecker, W. Andrew. "The Devotional Life of Archibald
Alexander, Charles Hodge, and Benjamin B. Warfield." Westminster
Theological Journal 42 (Fall 1979): 111-29.

Argues that this trio of prominent professors, whose lives span
the 19th century, shared not only a common Princeton (Reformed)
theology, with which they are generally associated, but a
common piety or devotional life that also marked Princeton, and
that was of profound importance for them. See also his book,
Piety and the Princeton Theologians (1981).

1500.   Howard, Thomas. Evangelical Is Not Enough. Nashville: Thomas
Nelson, 1984.

Continues the autobiographical sketches begun in Christ the
Tiger (1967) and An Antique Drum (1979), depicting Howard's
pilgrimage from his fundamentalist upbringing to his avowed
episcopalianism.

1501.   Inch, Morris A. Paced by God. Waco: Word Books, 1973. 129 p.

Out of his work with evangelical college students, Inch
presents a lay-oriented study of the evangelical movement and
"the cardinal issues concerning God, man, and their
relationship." Bibliography.

1502.　　Johnston, Robert K. "Of Tidy Doctrine and Truncated Experience."
Christianity Today 21 (18 February 1977): 10-14.

Recognizes the danger of emphasis on the Word to the neglect of
the Spirit, but warns of the dangers of relational theology and
the emphasis on experience.

1503.　　Jones, Bob, Sr. "After 58 Years of Evangelism." Sword of the
Lord 13 (7 December 1956): 1, 8-10.

1504.　　Lovelace, Richard F. Dynamics of Spiritual Life: An Evangelical
Theology of Renewal. Downers Grove: InterVarsity, 1979. 455 p.

A manual for both individual spiritual growth and renewal in
the church; Part I describes and analyzes the key elements in
the history of awakenings since the Reformation, and Part II
"re-examines some of these elements in greater depth and
enlarges on their significance for reformation and renewal in
the church of the future." Bibliographical references. Index.

1505.　　　　　　. "Evangelical Spirituality: A Church Historian's
Perspective." Journal of the Evangelical Theological Society 31
(March 1988): 25-35.

Against the backdrop of Reformation spirituality, and the
spirituality of Puritanism, pietism and the evangelical
awakenings, Lovelace assesses the need for a reinvigorated
spirituality for contemporary evangelicals.

1506.　　Lundin, Roger, and Mark A. Noll, eds. Voices from the Heart:
Four Centuries of American Piety. Grand Rapids: Eerdmans, 1987.
396 p.

While not confined to evangelicals, this collection of
fifty-five readings includes many evangelicals. Helpful
headnotes accompany each selection. Bibliographical
references.

1507.　　Marshall, I. Howard. "Personal View: Evangelical Foundations."
TSF Bulletin (Spring 1971): 1-2.

A plea for evangelical scholarly attention to four matters:
pentecostalism, revival, holiness, and Sunday observance.

1508.　　Palmer, Bernard, and Marjory Palmer. The Winds of God are
Blowing. Wheaton: Tyndale House, 1973. 186 p.

Stories of spiritual awakening--some charismatic, some not--
recounted from first-hand interviews made by the authors in a
several-months tour of the United States and Canada.

1509.   Pike, Kenneth Lee. With Heart and Mind: A Personal Synthesis of
Scholarship and Devotion. Grand Rapids: Eerdmans, 1962. 140 p.

A "new evangelical" of the 1950s and 1960s, professor of
linguistics at Michigan and a linguist with Wycliffe
Translators, presents twenty-five essays which carefully work
out his understanding of intellect, viewpoint, commitment, and
outreach.

1510.   Rogers, Jack B. Confessions of a Conservative Evangelical.
Philadelphia: Westminster, 1974. 144 p.

Autobiographical account (through theological essays) of
Rogers' move away from the false dilemma of conservatism vs.
liberalism to the evangelical center, much influenced by G. C.
Berkouwer.

1511.   Rolland, Ross W. "The Continuity of Evangelical Life and
Thought." Religion in Life 13 (Spring 1944): 245-53.

Four twice-born men--Paul, Augustine, Luther, Wesley--illus-
trate "the most penetrating point of power in the Christian
religion": evangelical experience.

1512.   Stevenson, Herbert F., comp. Light Upon the Word: An Anthology of
Evangelical Spiritual Writings. Selected and introduced by
Herbert F. Stevenson. Old Tappan: Revell, 1979. 182 p.

Selections ranging in time from Doddridge, Wesley, Whitefield,
Newton and others in the 18th century, to A. W. Tozer, D.
Martyn Lloyd-Jones, and John Stott in the 20th. Includes a
brief subject index and an introductory essay as well as a
biographical sketch of each author.

1513.   Waltke, Bruce K. "Evangelical Spirituality: A Biblical Scholar's
Perspective." Journal of the Evangelical Theological Society 31
(March 1988): 9-24.

A God-centered life, a kingdom-centered life (love for others),
and the dynamics of spiritual life: defensively, against the
kingdom of Satan; offensively, within the kingdom of Christ
("the law, the Spirit, and the sacraments").

1514.   Webber, Robert E. Evangelicals on the Canterbury Trail: Why
         Evangelicals Are Attracted to the Liturgical Church. Waco: Word,
         1985. 174 p.

         A leading evangelical advocate of the liturgical tradition with
         six others explain their move into the Episcopal Church.

1515.   Yancey, Philip. "Evangelicals and Spiritual Schizophrenia."
         Eternity 27 (June 1976): 22-23, 32, 37-38.

         "A plea for wholeness in the Christian life," in the context of
         his assertion that "the tendency to split off and compartmen-
         talize doctrine (. . . or just about anything) is one of the
         main trademarks of evangelicalism." Gives suggestions for
         bringing wholeness.

1516.   _____. "Growing Up Fundamentalist." Christianity Today 61 (17
         February 1989): 56.

         Tells of some "handicaps" associated with "growing up Funda-
         mentalist," yet concludes that the positive has outweighed the
         negative.

See also items 17, 235, 561, 938, 1445, 1622, 1641, 2048, 2097, 2201, 2232.

                              R.   Denominations

1517.   Ascol, Tom. "1984 Founders' Conference." Banner of Truth no. 255
         (December 1984): 19-20.

         Report on the second annual "Southern Baptist Conference on the
         Faith of the Founders." Twelve presentations to 159 conferees,
         in which the speakers "expounded the doctrines of grace from
         expositional, devotional, doctrinal, and historical
         perspectives."

1518.   Bartholomew, Alfred Clinton. "An Interpretation of the Evangeli-
         cal and Reformed Church in a Changing American Society." Ph.D.
         diss., Drew University. Madison, NJ. 1950. 246 p.

1519.   Bass, Dorothy C. "The Reformation Heritage of the UCC and Its
         Meaning for Twentieth-Century Christians." Chicago Theological
         Seminary Register 75 (Spring 1985): 3-13.

         Relates how central Reformation themes (the priesthood of all
         believers, "radical trust in God," and emphasis on the Bible)

influenced personal piety, congregational life, and social
transformation across the generations.

1520.   Blumhofer, Edith Waldvogel. Pentecost in My Soul: Explorations in
the Meaning of Pentecostal Experience in the Early Assemblies of
God. Springfield, MO: Gospel Publishing House, 1989. 265 p.

1521.   Boice, James Montgomery. "United Presbyterians: Evangelical
Victory?" Eternity 29 (August 1978): 10-11.

Regarding the "lopsided triumph in homosexual vote" at the
188th General Assembly of the United Presbyterian Church on the
issue of "the ordination of avowed, practicing homosexuals,"
discusses sobering considerations relative to the process and
vote, and "troubling" elements in the final policy statement.

1522.   Bratt, James D. Dutch Calvinism in Modern America: A History of a
Conservative Subculture. Grand Rapids: Eerdmans, 1984. 329 p.

Originally a Yale doctoral dissertation, this excellent study
"explores the intellectual history of those communities
established by the Dutch who immigrated to the U.S. between the
1840s and World War I," concentrating on the 20th century
communities; a work in religious history because religion
supplied both the terms and the forum of intellectual
discourse. Eighteen-page bibliography. Index.

1523.   Burkhart, John E. "Evangelical, Biblical, and Reformed."
McCormick Quarterly 19 (January 1966): 74-82.

Occasioned by "The Proposal to Revise the Confessional Position
of the United Presbyterian Church in the United States of
America"; "this paper explores the thesis . . . that the
proposed formula is Evangelical, Biblical, and Reformed."

1524.   Burkiser, W. T. Called Unto Holiness (Vol. 2): The Second Twenty-
Five Years, 1933-58. Kansas City: Nazarene Publishing House,
1983. 356 p.

Sequel to T. L. Smith's 1962 volume on the formative years of
the holiness denomination (also entitled Called Unto Holiness),
this volume sees the Nazarenes through their move to a second
generation of leadership, the global crises surrounding World
War II and the maintaining of their founding principles; from
the perspective of one of the participants. Bibliography;
extensive lists of Nazarene leaders.

1525.   Cooper, John C. "Ultra-Conservatives and Lutherans Today."
         Lutheran Quarterly 18 (August 1966): 214-26.

         Lutherans are predominantly progressive in their outlook,
         stressing the fruits as much as the roots of their faith, but a
         threat is posed by a small group of fundamentalism-influenced
         Lutherans who are right-wing both in their theology and in
         their political and social views.

1526.   Davis, D. Clair. "Evangelicals and the Presbyterian Tradition: An
         Alternative Perspective." Westminster Theological Journal 42
         (Fall 1979): 152-56.

         Contra Lovelace, "Evangelical Revivals . . . ," in this issue,
         Davis argues that evangelicals will probably not persuade
         moderate Presbyterians that the moderates need the evangel-
         icals.

1527.   Davis, Lawrence B. Immigrants, Baptists, and the Protestant Mind
         in America. Urbana: University of Illinois Press, 1973. 230 p.

         Northern Baptist responses to immigrants, 1880-1925, as typical
         of Protestant responses. Seventeen-page bibliography. Index.

1528.   Dennison, Charles G., and Richard C. Gamble, eds. Pressing Toward
         the Mark: Essays Commemorating Fifty Years of the Orthodox
         Presbyterian Church. Philadelphia: Orthodox Presbyterian Church,
         1986. 489 p.

         Thirty essays, historical and theological, on the denomination
         that emerged after the modernist controversy of the 1920s.
         Bibliographical references; bibliography of the writings of J.
         G. Machen.

1529.   Dunkerly, Donald A. "Conservatives in the U.S.A. Form National
         Presbyterian Church." Banner of Truth no. 125 (February 1974):
         13-15, 18.

         Reports the proceedings of the first General Assembly held in
         Birmingham, AL, in December 1973.

1530.   Evangelicals: American and European. Stockholm: International
         Federation of Free Evangelical Churches. 1966. 86 p.

         Survey of the Free Church in fourteen nations, and the text of
         the Federation's constitution.

1531.   Fackre, Gabriel. "Theological Soul-Searching in the United Church
         of Christ." TSF Bulletin 8 (November-December 1984): 5-9.

         Survey of the theological diversity in the UCC from the
         evangelical subgroups to the left-wing elements, stressing the
         Craigville Letter of 1984 as an attempt to found a centrist
         position in the denomination.

1532.   Friesen, Duane K. "Biblical Authority: The Contemporary Theologi-
         cal Debate." Response by Donald Longbottom. Mennonite Life 44
         (September 1989): 26-33.

         The issue of biblical authority from conservative and liberal
         perspectives within the Mennonite community.

1533.   Garrett, James Leo, Jr. "Southern Baptists as Evangelicals."
         Baptist History and Heritage 18 (April 1983): 10-20.

         Varieties of meaning of the term evangelical; commonalities in
         doctrine, ethics, and evangelism and missions; differences of
         Southern Baptists from other evangelicals; conclusion: Southern
         Baptists are "denominational evangelicals," that is, subscri-
         bers to the central doctrines of the Protestant Reformation.

1534.   _____. "W. T. Conner: Contemporary Theologian." Southwestern
         Journal of Theology 25 (Spring 1983): 43-60.

         Description of Southern Baptist Conner (1877-1952), whose
         "theology was characterized by fixity and flexibility," and the
         relevance of his writings for four contemporary SBC issues:
         dispensationalism, charismaticism, biblical inerrancy, and
         resurgent Calvinism.

1535.   Garrett, James Leo, Jr., E. Glenn Hinson, and James E. Tull. Are
         Southern Baptists "Evangelicals"? Macon, GA: Mercer University
         Press, 1983. 239 p.

         Historical and theological study leads to contrasting answers;
         with responses. Annotated bibliography.

1536.   Goen, C. C. Broken Churches, Broken Nation: Denominational
         Schisms and the Coming of the American Civil War. Macon, GA:
         Mercer University Press, 1985. 198 p.

         Attaches significant importance to the denominations in
         antebellum America, because the divisions of the Presbyterian,
         Methodist and Baptist churches severed "an important bond of

national union." and were "both portent and catalyst of the
imminent national tragedy." Bibliographical references.
Index.

1537.   Hamm, Thomas D. The Transformation of American Quakerism:
         Orthodox Friends, 1800-1907. Bloomington: Indiana University
         Press, 1988. 261 p.

         Filling a gap in the history of American evangelicalism, Hamm
         chronicles the loss of most of the marks of Quaker distinc-
         tiveness through "a combination of internal tensions, socio-
         economic change, and the influence of non-Quaker religious
         thought, especially evangelicals"; by 1900 created one more
         evangelical denomination. Twenty-four-page bibliography.
         Index.

1538.   Harwell, Jack U. "Can Baptists Survive the Evangelicals."
         Southern Baptist Journal 6 (April 1978): 1.

         A reprint of an editorial in the Christian Index of Georgia,
         extensively quoting the president of Golden Gate Baptist
         Theological Seminary.

1539.   Hedlund, Roger Eugene. "Conservative Baptists in Mid-Passage: The
         Study of a Movement; Its Growth and Self-Understanding, Its
         Present Crisis of Uncertainty." D.Miss. diss., Fuller Theological
         Seminary, School of World Mission, 1974. 418 p.

1540.   Hefley, James C. "The Historic Shift in America's Largest
         Protestant Denomination." Christianity Today 27 (5 August 1983):
         38-41.

         Conservatives are moving the Southern Baptist Convention away
         from its leftward drift, a move to the right unprecedented in
         American denominational history.

1541.   Heidinger, James V., II, ed. Basic United Methodist Beliefs: An
         Evangelical View. Wilmore, KY: Good News Books. 1986. 124 p.

         Thirteen evangelical Methodists write thirteen chapters (all
         but one originally appeared in Good News magazine) on Wesleyan
         doctrinal distinctives. Two appendixes.

1542.   _____. ed. United Methodist Renewal: What Will it Take?
         Wilmore, KY: Bristol Books. 1988. 115 p.

The Executive Secretary of Good News, and editor of Good News
magazine, discusses the prospects for renewal, the historical
background, including the evangelical/liberal controversy of
the 1930s, for what he thinks to be the present deplorable
condition, and suggestions for regaining vitality.
Bibliography.

1543.   Heidinger, James V., II, and Steve Long. "Our Theological
Confusion: Its Roots . . . & . . . Its Fruits." Good News 22
(May/June 1989): 27-31.

Good News editor Heidinger discusses the defection of Methodism
from evangelical theology during the "Social Gospel era" and
Long treats the "unfortunate results" of that defection.

1544.   Heisey, Terry M. "Immigration as a Factor in the Division of the
Evangelical Association." Methodist History 19 (October 1980):
41-57.

A Methodist Episcopal branch called the Evangelical Association, aimed at converting 19th century German immigrants,
divided over doctrine, polity and especially immigration
factors in the 1880s and 1890s.

1545.   Hinson, E. Glenn. "Baptists and Evangelicals: What is the
Difference?" Baptist History and Heritage 16 (April 1981): 20-32.

Hinson sees critical distinctions between evangelicals and
Baptists: Baptists emphasize reception of the Word
(experience) over the Word itself; Baptists cry for religious
liberty (soul competence).

1546.   _____. "Southern Baptists and the Liberal Tradition in
Biblical Interpretation, 1845-1945." Baptist History and Heritage
19 (July 1984): 16-20.

Ideas and influence of C. H. Toy and W. L. Poteat, the only two
SBC seminary teachers who openly advocated the liberal
tradition.

1547.   Hood, Fred J. Reformed America: The Middle and Southern States,
1783-1837. University City: University of Alabama Press. 1980.
254 p.

Important study of a neglected body of thought--the Reformed
tradition, especially its Presbyterian manifestation--in a
neglected region--the middle and southern states in the early

national period. Hood shows how the Reformed faced and dealt
with disestablishment, and developed a revivalism that was
"both rational and community-oriented"; in both cases, with
national implications. Bibliographical essay. Index.

1548.   Howe, Claude L., Jr. "British Evangelical Response to the
American Revolution: The Baptists." Fides et Historia 8 (Fall
1976): 35-49.

Identifies "some of the principal spokesmen as well as "persistent themes," so as to better understand Baptist involvement;
"does not challenge the conclusion that English Baptists
sympathized with and supported the Americans."

1549.   _____. "Southern Baptists and the Moderate Tradition in
Biblical Interpretation, 1845-1945." Baptist History and Heritage
19 (July 1984): 21-28.

After some discussion, Howe concludes that the moderate
position is "more moralistic and pietistic than doctrinal and
cultural"; among Southern Baptists, E. Y. Mullins and W. T.
Conner embodied the position.

1550.   Ingle, H. Larry. Quakers in Conflict: The Hicksite Reformation.
Knoxville: University of Tennessee Press, 1986. 310 p.

Definitive study of the break in the 1820s and 1830s that led
to the 125-year division between evangelical Friends who
sympathized with mainstream 19th century Protestantism and the
more traditional Hicksites who stressed reliance on the spirit
of truth. Bibliographical essay. Index.

1551.   International Federation of Free Evangelical Churches. Evangelicals, American and European. Stockholm, Sweden: n.p., 1966.
Various pagings.

Papers (in English and German) by contributors who include Karl
A. Olson, Clark H. Pinnock, F. Burton Nelson, Kenneth Kantzer,
and others, on similarities and differences between the
Evangelical Free Church of America, and the Evangelical Mission
Covenant Church, covering a wide range of theological topics.

1552.   Klassen, A. J. "The Bible in the Mennonite Brethren Church."
Direction 2 (April 1973): 34-55.

Surveys the role of the Bible in Anabaptist-Mennonite history,
and in the development and life of the Mennonite Brethren
Church.

1553.   Leonard, Bill J. "Fragmentation Grows for Southern Baptists."
         Christian Century 106 (5-12 July 1989): 644-46.

         An account of the annual convention (1989) of Southern
         Baptists, held in Las Vegas, with special focus on the ongoing
         theological controversy.

1554.   _____. "The Future of Theological Education in the Southern
         Baptist Convention." Faith and Mission 6 (Fall 1988): 36-46.

         Set amidst the fundamentalist-moderate controversy in the SBC,
         moderate Leonard says that "in the short term the travail will
         surely continue," but the long term "may not seem so uncertain
         after all."

1555.   Lewis, Donald M. "Anglican Evangelicals and 'No Popery': The
         Formation of the Reformed Episcopal Church in Canada." Crux 22
         (December 1986): 26-36.

         Deals with one facet of the broad anti-Catholicism in Canada
         during the 19th century, namely the secession from the Anglican
         Church of persons who formed the Reformed Episcopal Church "in
         their reaction to the ritualist phase of the Oxford Movement."

1556.   Lovelace, Richard F. "Evangelical Revivals and the Presbyterian
         Tradition." Westminster Theological Journal 42 (Fall 1979):
         130-51.

         A survey of spiritual awakenings, including an extended section
         covering the period from the modernist/fundamentalist
         controversy to the current evangelical resurgence. Set in the
         context of recent controversy within Presbyterianism
         surrounding that resurgence.

1557.   Maring, Norman H. "Baptists and Changing Views of the Bible,
         1865-1918." Part 1, Foundations 1 (July 1958): 52-75; Part 2,
         Foundations 1 (October 1958): 30-61.

         Beginning with a belief in inerrancy, in this period a
         significant number of northern Baptists (many seminary
         professors, some pastors and laymen) "came to acknowledge the
         presence of a fallible human element in the Scriptures: they
         adopted critical conclusions about the authorship and date of
         various books, and reformulated conceptions of biblical
         authority," thereby helping foster the conflicts of the 1920s.

1558.   Marshall, Herbert J. "Evangelical Catholicity: The Lutheran
        Tradition." Word and World 9 (Summer 1989): 262, 264.

        Lutherans have lost the catholicity concept, which is a part of
        their roots, of "pietistic individualism and enlightenment
        liberalism."

1559.   Marty, Martin E. "Denominations: Surviving the '70s." Christian
        Century 94 (21 December 1977): 1186-88.

        Although America "has been undergoing some sort of religious
        revival," it "has not led to prosperity for most of the
        denominations."

1560.   Menzies, William W. Anointed to Serve: The Story of the Assem-
        blies of God. Springfield, MO: Gospel Publishing House, 1971.
        436 p.

        Best history of the Assemblies of God, by a teacher at the
        Assemblies seminary. Nineteen-page bibliography.

1561.   _____. "The Assemblies of God, 1941-1967: The Consolidation of
        a Revival Movement." Ph.D. diss., The University of Iowa, 1968.
        341 p.

1562.   Miller, Glenn T. "God's Light and Man's Enlightenment:
        Evangelical Theology of Colonial Presbyterianism." Journal of
        Presbyterian History 51 (Summer 1973): 97-115.

        "Transitional figures between the Federal theologians of the
        seventeenth century and the Evangelicals of the nineteenth,"
        the 18th century evangelical Calvinists centered their theology
        and preaching on the conversion experience in the context of
        certain aspects of Enlightenment thought.

1563.   Mouw, Richard J. "Evangelicalism and the CRC." Banner 121 (16
        June 1986): 14-17.

        Contending that relations with the Dutch churches "will never
        again be what it once was" and that "we are evangelicals." Mouw
        urges the CRC to join the National Association of Evangelicals.

1564.   Naumann, William Henry. "Theology and German-American Evangeli-
        calism: The Role of Theology in the Church of the United Brethren
        in Christ and the Evangelical Association." Ph.D. diss., Yale
        University, 1966. 506 p.

1565.   Neil, William. "The Good News Movement (1960s and '70s)." Explor
         2 (Fall 1976): 68-72.

         Relates the story of Charles Keysor and the Good News Movement,
         an influential movement of conservative evangelicals within
         Methodism.

1566.   Noll, Mark A. "Children of the Reformation in a Brave New World."
         Dialog 24 (Summer 1985): 176-80.

         Argues that what divides American evangelicals from Lutheran
         evangelicals in America is primarily the events of American
         history, not sixteenth century doctrinal differences between
         Lutheran and Reformed theologies.

1567.   _____. "The Irony of the Enlightenment for Presbyterians in
         the Early Republic." Journal of the Early Republic 5 (Summer
         1985): 149-75.

         Turning their backs on Jonathan Edwards, Presbyterians made
         compromises with the moderate enlightenment which turned out
         not to buttress the faith, yet "[t]he Enlightenment and
         Presbyterian orthodoxy continued to travel side by side through
         the nineteenth century."

1568.   _____. "Rethinking Restorationism--A Review Article."
         Reformed Journal 39 (November 1989): 15-21.

         Four volumes by present or former professors at Abilene
         Christian University (Churches of Christ), whose work consti-
         tutes "nothing less than a full-scale, rigorous, and critically
         informed investigation of the notion of 'restoration.'"

1569.   _____. "The Spirit of Old Princeton and the Spirit of the
         OPC." In Pressing Toward the Mark, eds. Charles G. Dennison and
         Richard C. Gamble, 235-46. Philadelphia: Orthodox Presbyterian
         Church, 1986.

         Four comparisons between the Princeton of Hodge and Warfield
         and the Orthodox Presbyterian Church (OPC), some showing a
         continuation between the two bodies, others showing how the OPC
         has improved on Princeton.

1570.   Olson, Adolf. "The Theology of Conference Baptists." Bethel
         Seminary Quarterly 1 (May 1953): 18-32.

A study of the theology of the mid-19th century Swedish Baptist founders and pioneers, which concludes that their mid-20th century heirs, although "still walking in the faith of the pioneers," do not "believe as profoundly and intensely in the great fundamentals of Christianity."

1571.   Olson, Arnold T. Believers Only. Minneapolis: Free Church Publications, 1964. 367 p.

"An outline of the history and principles of the Free Evangelical movement in Europe and North America affiliated with the International Federation of Free Evangelical Churches," by the president of the Evangelical Free Church of America. Bibliography. Index.

1572.   Plowman, Edward E. "The Assemblies of God: 75 Years of Faith, Outreach and Growth." Charisma 15 (August 1989): 37-44.

"Assemblies of God . . . a worldwide family of diverse congregations testifying to the Pentecostal reality and seeking to touch every area of human need."

1573.   Poloma, Margaret M. The Assemblies of God at the Crossroads: Charisma and Institutional Dilemmas. Knoxville: University of Tennessee Press, 1989. 368 p.

1574.   Redekop, Calvin. "The Embarrassment of a Religious Tradition." Mennonite Life 36 (September 1981): 17-21.

Focuses on the Evangelical Mennonite Brethren Church, a group in process of severing its relationship with the Mennonite family of churches and moving into the fundamentalist evangelical community, tracing its story, and then looking from a sociological perspective at religious heritage and religious community.

1575.   Regehr, William, and Calvin Redekop. "Research Notes: Evangelical Mennonite Brethren." Mennonite Life 37 (March 1982): 29-31.

A response by Regehr to Redekop's earlier article [Mennonite Life 36 (September 1981): 17-21]. and a rejoinder by Redekop.

1576.   "The Revival in Southern Presbyterian Literature." Banner of Truth no. 142 (July 1975): 7-8.

Brief comments on the reissuing of several 19th century Presbyterian works, theological and biblical.

1577.   Roberts, Arthur O. The Association of Evangelical Friends: A
         Story of Quaker Renewal in the Twentieth Century. Newberg:
         Barclay Press, 1975. 58 p.

         History of the Association (1947 to 1970), an evangelical
         renewal movement that influenced a number of Yearly Meetings
         and several Quaker colleges. Appendix.

1578.   Rudnick, Milton L. "Fundamentalism and the Missouri Synod: A
         Historical Study of Their Interaction and Mutual Influence."
         Concordia Theological Monthly 43 (April 1972): 252-57.

         Five years after publication of his Fundamentalism and the
         Missouri Synod (1966), the author comments on books about
         fundamentalism recently published, gives the outline, argument
         and conclusion of his work, and asserts that his conclusions
         are still valid.

1579.   Russell, Charles Allyn. "The Northern (American) Baptist
         Experience with Fundamentalism." Review and Expositor 79 (Winter
         1982): 45-61.

         The experience in the 1920s and 1940s; the issues of contro-
         versy were theological, organizational and ecclesiastical in
         nature; the denomination lost many churches and members, but
         fundamentalists did not stop splintering after leaving the NBC.

1580.   Schlabach, Theron F. Peace, Faith, Nation: Mennonites and Amish
         in Nineteenth-Century America. Scottdale, PA: Herald Press, 1988.
         415 p.

1581.   Shelley, Bruce L. A History of Conservative Baptists. Wheaton:
         Conservative Baptist Press, 1971. 140 p.

         An extensively rewritten and expanded version of Conservative
         Baptists (1960), dropping the dissent motif that had marked
         that earlier volume; "Today I prefer to see Conservative
         Baptist history as the story of one group of conservatives
         making their way through the jungle of theological debate from
         1920 to 1970." Bibliographical references. Index.

1582.   Shurden, Walter B. "The Inerrancy Debate: A Comparative Study of
         Southern Baptist Controversies." Baptist History and Heritage 16
         (April 1981): 12-19.

         Compares the inerrancy debate of the 1970s and 1980s with three
         other SBC debates in the 20th century, noting the contrasts and
         similarities.

1583.   Sider, Ronald J. "Evangelicalism and the Mennonite Tradition."
         In Evangelicalism and Anabaptism, ed. C. Norman Kraus, 149-68.
         Scottdale, PA: Herald Press, 1979.

         Two theses: If evangelicals were consistent they would be
         Anabaptists; and, Mennonites and evangelicals need each other.
         Emphasis on the need for both orthodoxy and orthopraxis.

1584.   Sine, Tom. "Calling Anabaptists Back to Their Roots: An Interview
         With Tom Sine." Gordon Houser, interviewer. Mennonite 104 (11
         July 1989): 317.

         Negative on the evangelicalism he sees some Mennonites
         embracing.

1585.   Steely, John E. "Current Issues in the Southern Baptist Conven-
         tion in Historical Perspective." Faith and Mission 1 (Spring
         1984): 5-14.

         Identifies issues involved, and interprets them in the light of
         their historical background, and of their broader context
         currently, concluding by identifying some ongoing questions.

1586.   Sundberg, Walter. "Evangelical Catholicity: A Lutheran
         Tradition." Word and World 9 (Summer 1989): 263, 265.

         Contrary to Herbert J. Marshall, Sundberg says that "Evan-
         gelical Catholicity" is not a term symbolic of wholeness in
         Lutheranism but the label of a faction.

1587.   Synan, Vinson. "From the Hills of Tennessee." Charisma 12
         (January 1987): 58-62.

         Brief historical overview of one of the earliest and largest
         Pentecostal denominations, the Church of God.

1588.   _____. "That Old-Time Pentecostal Religion." Charisma 12
         (August 1986): 53-57.

         The founding and spread of the largest Pentecostal
         denomination, the Assemblies of God.

1589.   Taggart, Morris. "Ecumenical Attitudes in the Evangelical
         Covenant Church of America." Covenant Quarterly 26 (August 1968):
         30-41.

The results of a referendum conducted among adult members of the ECC in 1965; focuses on non-theological factors in attempting "to indicate in a tentative way the possible role of some of the more widely used sociological variables." The most significant variations were in attitudes toward affiliation with the WCC and the NCC.

1590.   Toews, J. B. "The Influence of Fundamentalism on Mennonite Brethren Theology." Direction 10 (July 1981): 20-29.

Discusses five areas that in his view have been negatively affected by "fundamentalism and some forms of American Evangelicalism"; concluding that "Fundamentalism has exalted the 'work of the Cross' but has been strangely silent about the 'way of the cross' and the demand of Christian discipleship."

1591.   Toews, John E. "Theological Reflections." Direction 14 (Fall 1985): 60-68.

The "Mennonite Brethren Church Membership Profile 1972-1982," reveals that they are "theologically orthodox and conservative," that their "piety shows signs of erosion," and that their "commitment to Anabaptist faith and ethics is weakening," the latter revealed by "major indices in the Profile."

1592.   Waller, Wilson Loran. "Cumberland Presbyterian Evangelicalism Before and After Default in Ecumenical Union in 1906." D.Div. diss., Vanderbilt University Divinity School, 1971. 291 p.

1593.   Weborg, John. "Lutherans in Their Theology: Luther and the Evangelical Covenant Church." Explor 8 (Spring 1986): 23-30.

Identifies similarities ("the fathers and mothers were Lutherans, most certainly in their consciousness and, . . . in a certain conceptual framework") and differences (e.g., Covenant concern for the purity of the church as against Lutheran emphasis on purity of doctrine).

1594.   Weniger, G. Archer. "Questions and Answers About Conservative Baptists." Central C. B. Quarterly 1 (Winter 1958): 17-22.

A helpful compilation of facts from a fundamentalist perspective in the areas of general information, doctrine, missionary program, interchurch relationships, and educational facilities, with concluding comments.

1595.   West, Earl Irvin. "1827 Annus Mirabilis and Alexander Campbell."
         Restoration Quarterly 16, nos. 3 and 4 (1973): 250-59.

         An important year in the movement (Alexander Campbell, et al.);
         this article points up the difference between Restoration
         revivalism and that of other revivalists of the era.

1596.   Whiteman, Curtis Wayne. "The General Association of Regular
         Baptist Churches, 1932-1970." Ph.D. diss., Saint Louis
         University, 1982. 388 p.

1597.   Wilson, Ernest Gerald. "The Christian and Missionary Alliance:
         Developments and Modifications of Its Original Objectives." Ph.D.
         diss., New York University, 1984. 602 p.

1598.   Wood, Richard E. "Evangelical Quaker Acculturation in the Upper
         Mississippi Valley, 1850-1875." Quaker History 76 (Fall 1987):
         128-44.

         Joining forces with evangelicals after 1850, the majority of
         Quakers "came to share much more than before the economic,
         educational, and political attitudes of other revivalistic
         Protestants," while preserving their pacifist ideal.

1599.   Zabriskie, Alexander Clinton. Anglican Evangelicalism. With
         foreword by the Presiding Bishop. Philadelphia: The Church
         Historical Society, 1943. 283 p.

         Essays written and published as a testimonial to Wallace E.
         Rollins by members of the faculty of Virginia Theological
         Seminary (Episcopal), on historical, theological, and practical
         application subjects. Eleven-page bibliography. Index.

See also items 31, 124, 128, 163, 180, 192, 199, 209, 213, 232, 237, 241,
    245, 250, 253, 254, 255, 290, 291, 322, 388, 392, 403, 426, 427, 526,
    598, 631, 650, 663, 682, 823, 835, 843, 855, 856, 857, 858, 860, 923,
    927, 974, 1022, 1029, 1066, 1072, 1089, 1101, 1244, 1282, 1300, 1359,
    1360, 1387, 1470, 1471, 1480, 1481, 1484, 1656, 1689, 1741, 1744, 1750,
    1753, 1755, 1764, 1769, 1772, 1775, 1783, 1785, 1787, 1788, 1793, 1810,
    1812, 1826, 1841, 1878, 1879, 1948, 1958, 2034, 2036, 2042, 2043, 2073,
    2084, 2087, 2092, 2103, 2109, 2110, 2195, 2231, 2235, 2251, 2290, 2304,
    2333, 2336, 2339, 2342, 2358, 2435, 2438, 2453, 2485, 2489, 2504, 2544,
    2546, 2551, 2552, 2648.

S.   Parachurch Organizations

1600.   Balmer, Randall H.   "Adirondack Fundamentalism."   Reformed Journal
        39 (June 1989): 14-21.

        A chapter in Balmer's book, Mine Eyes Have Seen the Glory: A
        Journey into the Evangelical Subculture in America (1989);
        about one aspect of the multi-faceted work of Jack Wyrtzen, the
        Word of Life youth camp at Schroon Lake in the Adirondack
        mountains of upstate New York.

1601.   Board, Stephen.   "The Great Evangelical Power Shift."   Eternity 30
        (June 1979): 16-21.

        The executive editor of Eternity on the growth of parachurch
        organizations, and their impact upon the evangelical churches.
        Discusses qualities in evangelicalism that have contributed to
        the flourishing of the parachurch groups, asks "a few hard
        questions" about both and suggests practical steps to reduce
        the tensions.

1602.   Brown, Nate.   "Introducing Prison Fellowship."   Evangelism 3
        (August 1989): 162-70.

        A brief account of the development and program of PF, founded
        in 1976 by Charles Colson: in-prison ministry, family ministry,
        "aftercare" ministry, and "justice fellowship"; organized
        internationally, with ministry in forty countries.

1603.   Campus Crusade for Christ International.   "The Campus Crusade for
        Christ Story Part II."   Evangelical Christian (December 1966):
        10-12.

        Briefly relates, for Canadian readers, the history of one of
        the prominent evangelical organizations of the latter 20th
        century.   One of a number of articles on evangelical
        organizations, history, and revival.

1604.   Carpenter, Joel A.   "Youth for Christ and the New Evangelicals'
        Place in the Life of the Nation."   In Rowland, Sherrill, ed..
        American Recoveries: Religion in the Life of the Nation.
        Champaign, IL: University of Illinois Press, 1989.

1605.   Hills, James W. L.   "How It All Began: The Birth & Growth of
        Inter-Varsity."   His 40 (April 1980): 29-31.

Presents the "heritage. some essential truths, and organizational characteristics," concluding with his vision of "Inter-Varsity continuing the finest in the evangelical tradition."

1606. MacLeod. A. Donald. "Inter-Varsity in Canada: The First Fifty Years." His 39 (January 1979): 24-26.

Discusses its beginnings in 1928 under the leadership of Howard Guinness, some "observable trends," the problems posed by geography, and the kinds of ministries.

1607. Murray, John. "Child Evangelism Fellowship of Canada." Evangelical Christian (September 1966): 5-6.

Operating in Canada since 1943. CEFC became "truly Canadian" in March 1966 with its incorporation in Canada. Presents CEF approach and emphasis.

1608. Olyott, Stuart. "Campus Crusade for Christ International Inc." Banner of Truth no. 64 (January 1969): 27-30.

A description of the movement which, while commending certain features, comes to a basically negative evaluation.

1609. Pippert, Rebecca Manley. "Evangelical Spirituality on College Campuses." In The Recovery of Spirit in Higher Education: Christian and Jewish Ministries in Campus Life, ed. Robert Rankin, 68-83. New York: Seabury, 1980.

False and true approaches to evangelical spirituality, and "evidences of the Spirit's work" on campus.

1610. Rambo, Lewis R. "TSF: A Quest To Be Conservative and Contemporary." Christian Century 97 (6-13 February 1980): 161-63.

Programs, aims and brief history of the Theological Students Fellowship. devoted to serving the needs of evangelical students in non-evangelical educational settings.

1611. Rossen, Betsy. "The International Fellowship of Evangelical Students: (Say That Ten Times. Fast)." His 41 (November 1980): 25-27.

After reviewing diversity within IFES. lists some of the many common characteristics. and describes the organization's origins and programs.

1612.   Shelley, Bruce L. "The Rise of Evangelical Youth Movements."
         Fides et Historia 18 (January 1986): 47-63.

         The origins in the 1930s and the 1940s and the course, down to
         1957, of Youth for Christ, Young Life, and Inter-Varsity
         Christian Fellowship as exemplars of para-church youth
         ministries.

1613.   Swamidoss, A. W. "The Biblical Basis of the Para-Church Move-
         ments." Evangelical Review of Theology 7 (October 1983): 192-206.

         Exegetical study of the structure of the church and the
         theology of the church and para-church, in which Indian
         evangelical Swamidoss finds prototypes of para-church
         organizations as an arm of the universal church.

1614.   Waters, Kenny. "Full Gospel Business Men: Fulfilling a Vision."
         Logos Journal (January-February 1978): 15-17.

         "Miracles . . . are common occurrences . . . in meetings hosted
         by the Full Gospel Business Men's Fellowship International
         (FGBMFI)." Relates the story of the beginnings in the early
         1950s and subsequent "escalating growth."

See also item 1646.

T. Social Science Studies

1615.   Bibby, Reginald W., and Merlin B. Brinkerhoff. "Circulation of
         the Saints Revisited: A Longitudinal Look at Conservative Church
         Growth." Journal for the Scientific Study of Religion 22
         (September 1983): 253-63.

         Ten years later, "the number and proportion of new members who
         entered these conservative churches changed very little,"
         consisting as before primarily of "geographically mobile
         evangelicals and members' children."

1616.   _____. "Circulation of the Saints: A Study of People Who Join
         Conservative Churches." Journal for the Scientific Study of
         Religion 12 (September 1973): 273-83.

         A study of twenty evangelical congregations in a western Canada
         city shows that of those added as church members "[l]ess than
         10 percent were proselytes or converts from outside the
         evangelical community."

1617.   Bruce, Steve. "A House Divided: Protestant Schisms and the Rise of Religious Tolerance." Sociological Analysis 47 (Spring 1986): 21-28.

    Delineates the main divisions of modern Christianity by citing four basic sources for authoritative religious knowledge: culture/reason, Bible, church, Spirit; unfortunately the term evangelical is difficult to pin down because it is used "with wild abandon."

1618.   Burkholder, J. Lawrence. "Popular Evangelicalism: An Appraisal." In Evangelicalism and Anabaptism, ed. C. Norman Kraus, 23-37. Scottdale, PA: Herald Press, 1979.

    Analyzes evangelicalism as a socio-religious phenomenon, including its historical precedents and spiritual integrity.

1619.   Campolo, Anthony. "A Sociologist Looks at the Church." His 39 (June 1979): 1, 4-6.

    An interview with His magazine, exploring the content of an address delivered in May 1978 at the Urban Congress sponsored by the Seminary Consortium for Urban Pastoral Education in Chicago, an address printed in its entirety in his book Metro-Ministry (1979).

1620.   Clelland, Donald A., et al. "In the Company of the Converted: Characteristics of a Billy Graham Crusade Audience." Sociological Analysis 35 (Spring 1974): 45-56.

1621.   Dennis, Lane T. "Conversion in an Evangelical Context: A Study in the Micro-Sociology of Religion." Ph.D. diss., Northwestern University, 1980. 382 p.

    Dennis studies the nature of evangelical conversion in the context of L'Abri Fellowship founded by Francis Schaeffer. An analysis of the theology, the community life, and the influence of L'Abri is followed by a discussion of the importance and nature of conversion in that setting.

1622.   Doland, Virginia M. "Totalitarian Evangelicalism." Christian Century 100 (4 May 1983): 429-31.

    Evangelicals "seem to have a built-in weakness for some aspects of totalitarianism." A warning against such, based in part on the author's experience in a rigid evangelical college.

1623.   Dolby, James R., et al. "Cultural Evangelicalism: The Background
         for Personal Despair." Journal of the American Scientific
         Affiliation 24 (September 1972): 91-101.

         Reprint of Dolby's "Help for the Disillusioned Evangelical"
         (Christian Herald, 1969). Evangelicalism is "an almost
         inseparable combination of a cultural style and a theological
         belief system," and to attempt to leave it produces inner
         conflicts because of fear of separation, guilt, need for
         answers or loss of meaning. Seven responses to Dolby's
         article.

1624.   Ellison, Craig W., and William S. Mattila. "The Needs of
         Evangelical Christian Leaders in the United States." Journal of
         Psychology and Theology 11 (Spring 1983): 28-35.

         One thousand subscribers to Leadership magazine give "incon-
         clusive, but instructive" data on time demands, unrealistic
         expectations, and other factors affecting evangelical leaders.

1625.   Ellwood, Robert S. One Way: The Jesus Movement and Its Meaning.
         Englewood Cliffs: Prentice-Hall, 1973. 150 p.

         Places the Jesus movement in the context of American culture,
         draws parallels from other religions, and shows how the
         movement affected its adherents (and American culture), all of
         which illustrates "the nature of evangelicalism, popular
         culture, and the present religious situation in America"--
         though the movement "will probably end up as a cultural drift."
         Bibliography. Index.

1626.   Epperson, Cheryl Lynn. "The Relationship of General Tolerance
         with Education, Ultimate Religious Motivation, Theological
         Position, and Denominational Affiliation." M.A. thesis,
         University of Richmond, 1988.

1627.   Finke, Roger, and Rodney Stark. "How the Upstart Sects Won
         America: 1776-1850." Journal for the Scientific Study of Religion
         28 (March 1989): 27-44.

         The upstart sects (Baptists and Methodists) flourished in the
         "unregulated religious economy" of the new nation, while the
         "mainline" denominations (Prebyterians, Episcopalians,
         Congregationalists) slumped, an indication that the mainline
         declined long before WWII.

1628.   Frank, Douglas W. "The Evangelical and Modernity." Reformed
         Journal 37 (June 1987): 27-29.

         A positive review article of sociologist James Davison Hunter's
         Evangelicalism: The Coming Generation (1987), which contends
         that the evangelical academic subculture is succumbing to the
         forces of modernity.

1629.   _____. "Reply." Reformed Journal 37 (September 1987): 9-10.

         A response to James Mathison's negative response (same issue,
         pp. 8-9) to Frank's earlier favorable review of Hunter's
         volume.

1630.   Gibson, Dennis L. "The Obsessive Personality and the Evangel-
         ical." Journal of Psychology and Christianity 2 (Fall 1983):
         30-35.

         Discusses obsessions of perfectionism, ritualism, and
         indecision, and offers some curative techniques.

1631.   Gordon-McCutchan, R. C. "Great Awakenings?" Sociological
         Analysis 44 (Summer 1983): 83-96.

         Helpful presentation of the historiographic controversy on
         whether there are such things as awakenings (Gordon-McCutchan
         believes there are) and what are the social causes and effects
         of revivalism.

1632.   Harper, Charles L., and Kevin Leicht. "Religious Awakenings and
         Status Politics: Sources of Support for the New Religious Right."
         Sociological Analysis 45 (Winter 1984): 339-53.

         This Nebraska study concludes that "It is unjustifiable to
         explain the social origins of the contemporary NRR by status
         politics explanations which emphasize structural factors and
         de-emphasize cultural and religious factors themselves." On
         the larger issue of awakenings, the authors choose the linear
         view over the episodic view.

1633.   Hubbard, David Allan, and Cinton W. McLemore. "Evangelical
         Churches." In Ministry in America, eds. David S. Schuller, Merton
         P. Strommen, and Milo L. Brekke, 351-94. San Francisco: Harper &
         Row, 1980.

         A study-summary of 800 evangelicals in twelve denominations
         whose seminaries are in the Association of Theological Schools

(part of a larger study by the ATS and the Search Institute,
summed up in this volume); very detailed analysis of eleven
factors of evaluation, comparison with other denominational
families, and forecasts of future trends in evangelicalism.

1634.   Hunter, James Davison. American Evangelicalism: Conservative
Religion and the Quandary of Modernity. New Brunswick, NJ:
Rutgers University Press, 1983. 171 p.

The interplay of American evangelicals, modernity, and the
modernization process and its impact, by a University of
Virginia sociologist. Extensive bibliography. Index.
Originally Hunter's 1981 Rutgers University Ph.D. dissertation,
"Contemporary American Evangelicalism: Conservative Religion
and the Quandary of Modernity."

1635.   _____. "Christianity Today Talks to James Davison Hunter." By
David Neff and Beth Spring. Christianity Today 31 (20 November
1987): 64-65.

Questions and answers based on Hunter's controversial book,
Evangelicalism: The Coming Generation (1987).

1636.   _____. Evangelicalism: The Coming Generation. Chicago:
University of Chicago Press, 1987. 302 p.

Based upon a wide range of sources and literature, but especially upon a survey taken between 1982 and 1985 of faculty and
students at nine liberal arts colleges and seven seminaries;
contends that evangelicalism is succumbing to the forces of
modernity. Bibliography.

1637.   _____. "The New Class and the Young Evangelicals." Review of
Religious Research 22 (December 1980): 155-69.

Based on analysis of Sojourners and The Other Side. Hunter
asserts that "there is a relationship structurally, politically, and ideologically" between the new class (left-liberal
class members in the knowledge industry) and the young
evangelicals (the left-wing of the evangelical movement).

1638.   _____. "Operationalizing Evangelicalism: A Review. Critique
and Proposal." Sociological Analysis 42 (Winter 1981): 363-72.

Review of the literature (and its shortcomings) on American
evangelicalism; guidelines for future study that include
Protestantism, core beliefs, and various traditions.

1639.   . "The Perils of Idealism: A Reply." Review of Religious Research 24 (March 1983): 267-76.

Hunter replies to Boyd Reese, contending that the new class construct is validly applied to young evangelicals.

1640.   . "Religion and Political Civility: The Coming Generation of American Evangelicals." Journal for the Scientific Study of Religion 23 (December 1984): 364-80.

A national sample of students attending evangelical colleges (9) and seminaries (7) to test "the ethic of civility" (being tolerant of others and tolerable to others), discloses that evangelical "religious exclusivism . . . has not been translated into a political exclusivism."

1641.   . "Subjectivization and the New Evangelical Theodicy." Journal for the Scientific Study of Religion 21 (March 1982): 39-47.

In light of modern culture's subjectivism--preoccupation with the "undiscovered" complexities of the self--mainstream evangelicalism, shown in this study of mass market and trade monographs, has expanded its theodicy beyond suffering and death to "intrasubjective exploration."

1642. Johnson, Benton. "Taking Stock: Reflections on the End of Another Era." Journal for the Scientific Study of Religion 21 (September 1982): 189-200.

One reason for the recent rise of evangelicalism, Johnson affirms, is that it adopted much of the liberal program, but placed it within a different authority system.

1643. Joy, Donald M. "Kohlberg Revisited: An Evangelical Speaks His Mind." Asbury Seminarian 35 (January 1980): 6-17.

Moves beyond his "basic position--that there is abundant common ground . . . to focus upon specific objections--. . . to Lawrence Kohlberg's presuppositions. his methodology. and his theory about moral development."

1644. Kahoe, Richard D. "Religious Conservatism: A Quasi-Longitudinal Perspective." Journal of Psychology and Theology 5 (Winter 1977): 40-47.

142 former students of a midwestern religious college were questioned six years after their freshman year to sort out personality and institutional factors that explain the increase in liberal attitudes among members of the group.

1645.   Kelley, Dean M. Why Conservative Churches Are Growing: A Study in Sociology of Religion. New and updated edition. New York: Harper & Row, 1977. 184 p.

A widely cited study published in 1972, just before the full resurgence of the evangelical movement, arguing that the ecumenical, mainline Protestant churches are not doing well in explaining the ultimate meaning of life, while the conservative churches are explaining that meaning with a strictness and costliness that only enhances their success. Bibliographical references. Index.

1646.   Kesler, Jay. "Jesus, Rambo and the Gates of Hell." Transformation 4 (January-March 1987): 7-11.

Using his experience in Youth for Christ as a model, Kesler points out the need of reaching youth across racial, ethnic, and socioeconomic barriers and of rejecting North American nationalism (which is often inextricably bound up with the gospel message).

1647.   Kraft, Charles H. "Conservative Christians and Anthropologists: A Clash of Worldviews." Journal of the American Scientific Affiliation 32 (September 1980): 140-45.

Suggests ten areas of polarized viewpoints, although he maintains that "the opposition is not necessary," and makes suggestions toward a synthesis in each of the areas.

1648.   Lindskoog, Donald, and Roger E. Kirk. "Some Life-History and Attitudinal Correlates of Self-Actualization Among Evangelical College Students." Journal for the Scientific Study of Religion 14 (March 1975): 51-55.

Study of forty-five students from a southwestern U.S. school, divided into high, moderate, and low levels of self-actualization, shows certain social-background characteristics that seem to explain the high self-actualizers.

1649.   Lorentzen, Louise J. "Evangelical Life Style Concerns Expressed in Political Action." Sociological Analysis 41 (Summer 1980): 144-54.

Applies the theory of status politics to explain "the onset of
political activism among previously uninvolved, conservative
evangelical Christians" in the 1978 race for U.S. Senator from
Virginia.

1650. Lyon, David. Sociology and the Human Image. Downers Grove, IL:
InterVarsity Press, 1983. 224 p.

A British evangelical surveys sociological theory and
contemporary social issues from the standpoint of "critical
Christian social thinking in constant dialogue and interaction
with contemporary sociology." Bibliography. Index.

1651. _____. The Steeple's Shadow: On the Myths and Realities of
Secularization. Grand Rapids: Eerdmans, 1985. 165 p.

A "state-of-the-art survey of secularization studies"; Lyon
takes secularization seriously, and also takes seriously
"criticisms of it for distorting and obscuring social and
religious reality." Bibliography. Index.

1652. Marsden, George M. "Does Evangelicalism Have a Future." Reformed
Journal 39 (April 1989): 2-3.

Report in part from a "gathering" with participants primarily
from the Reformed wing of American evangelicalism, and focused
on evangelical sociologist James D. Hunter's Evangelicalism:
The Coming Generation (1987). Marsden concludes that "the
situation looks grim indeed," but that "things are no worse
than they ever have been."

1653. Maynard, Kent Arthur. "Christianity and Religion: Evangelical
Identity and Sociocultural Organization in Urban Ecuador." Ph.D.
diss., Indiana University, 1981. 294 p.

1654. McKenzie, John Grant. Psychology, Psychotherapy and Evangelicalism. London: Allen and Unwin, 1940. 238 p.

An early attempt to integrate evangelicalism and psychology,
with the heavier emphasis on psychology. Index.

1655. Minor, John E. "Understanding as the First Step in an Evangelical
Approach to World Religions: Some Methodological Considerations."
Journal of the Evangelical Theological Society 19 (Spring 1976):
121-28.

An appeal to avoid mistakes in describing other religions
through erroneous definitions or reductionism. and to begin
with a thorough knowledge of the religion under consideration.

1656.   Muelder, W. A. "From Sect to Church." Christendom 10 (Autumn
        1945): 450-62.

        Standard approach of the migration from sect to church in this
        look at some Assemblies of God and Nazarene congregations in
        California.

1657.   Noll, Mark A. "'And the Lion Shall Lie Down with the Lamb': The
        Social Sciences and Religious History." Fides et Historia 20
        (October 1988): 5-30.

        Noll sees a happier relationship developing between social
        science and religious history, especially in the social science
        granting of religion as a domain in its own right and therefore
        not to be explained away in social terms, and in historians'
        proper use of social science in understanding religious history
        at the empirical, "lower-order" level. A far-ranging and
        insightful survey of the literature.

1658.   O'Neal, Glenn. "The Evangelical Looks At Pastoral Counseling."
        Grace Journal 2 (Fall 1961): 30-36.

        Shortcomings and contributions of psychoanalysis, concluding
        with a section on the advantages of the evangelical approach to
        counseling.

1659.   Ostrom, Richard M., Robert E. Lazerlere, and Stephen K. Reed.
        "The Views of Selected Evangelical Christians on Sex Education."
        Journal of Psychology and Christianity 1 (Winter 1982): 17-22.

        Evangelicals in a large metropolitan area were "less favorable
        toward sex education in the public schools than the general
        population. Those favoring sex education were found to be less
        conservative politically than evangelicals generally."

1660.   Ownby, Ted. "Evangelicalism and Male Culture: Recreation and
        Religion in the Rural South, 1865-1920." Ph.D. diss.. The Johns
        Hopkins University, 1986. 387 p.

1661.   Perkins, Richard B. "The Orthodox Bigot: A Sociological
        Analysis." Journal of the American Scientific Affiliation 28
        (September 1976): 116-22.

Investigates two areas of recent research related to the
correlation between orthodoxy and ethnocentrism: the
"commitment dimension," and the approach from a worldview
perspective; attempts "to establish a theoretical synthesis" to
resolve "logical inconsistencies" that develop between the two
approaches; examines implications for Christian faith.

1662.   Quebedeaux, Richard, and Rodney Sawatsky, eds. Evangelical-
Unification Dialogue. Barrytown, NY: Unification Theological
Seminary; New York: Distributed by the Rose of Sharon Press, 1979.
374 p.

Transcription of a dialogue held in June and October, 1978, at
Unification Theological Seminary, Barrytown, NY.

1663.   Reese, Boyd. "'The New Class and the Young Evangelicals': Second
Thoughts." Review of Religious Research 24 (March 1983): 261-67.

James D. Hunter's attempt to employ the New Class construct
fails because the construct is "internally inconsistent as
applied to religious movements."

1664.   Robertson, Darrel M. The Chicago Revival, 1876: Society and
Revivalism in a Nineteenth-Century City. Metuchen, NJ: Scarecrow,
1989. 225 p.

The Moody-Sankey meetings are narrated from the standpoint of
the city itself and the techniques used by the evangelists; the
meetings "strengthened and contributed to a sense of evangelical and middle-class solidarity based on common sentiments and
attitudes," but had little impact on the working classes, and
did not lessen the "existing religious and ethnic tensions in
Chicago." Appendix. Bibliography. Index.

1665.   Shriver, George. "When Conservatism Is Liberalism." Christian
Century 86 (6 August 1969): 1040-41.

The liberalism of these southern evangelicals-fundamentalists
is culture-accommodation to racism.

1666.   Smidt, Corwin. "'Praise the Lord' Politics: A Comparative
Analysis of the Social Characteristics and Political Views of
American Evangelical and Charismatic Christians." Sociological
Analysis 50 (Spring 1989): 53-72.

Addresses the issue of "the nature of the relationship between
the two movements and whether . . . [they] might be united

politically under one banner." by "comparing and contrasting
the social bases and political perceptions" of each; if the
differences persist, it is "highly unlikely" that the two
movements will merge into a unified political movement.

1667.   Smith, Gary Scott. The Seeds of Secularization: Calvinism,
           Culture, and Pluralism in America, 1870-1915. Grand Rapids:
           Christian University Press and Eerdmans, 1985. 239 p.

           The Calvinists (more numerous than members of the Reformed
           denominations) tried to contain the growth of secular humanism
           by (mistakenly) advocating a Christian world view to dominate
           American institutions and practices; that approach helped form
           20th century American culture. Bibliographical references.
           Index.

1668.   Stone, Howard W. "Liberals and Conservatives: Differences in
           Demographic Characteristics, Interests and Service Orientation
           Among Those Entering Ministry." Journal of Psychology and
           Christianity 8, no. 3 (1989): 24-37.

           A study of 692 first year students at a mainline Protestant
           seminary suggests differences.

1669.   Tyson, Ruel W., Jr., James L. Peacock, and Daniel W. Patterson,
           eds. Diversity of Gifts: Field Studies in Southern Religion.
           Champaign: University of Illinois Press, 1988. 224 p.

           A useful volume of eleven anthropological essays derived from
           field studies of North Carolina "independent Protestants."
           churches with "no national bureaucracies [or] . . . uptown
           churches"; stresses the concept of "gesture" in the religious
           communities and organizations and in the experience and forms
           of the congregations. Bibliographical references. Index.

1670.   Van Leeuwen, Mary Stewart. "North American Evangelicalism and the
           Social Sciences: A Forty-Year Appraisal." Theology, News and
           Notes 34 (December 1987): 15-20.

           The perspectival view of Bernard Ramm and Donald MacKay.
           problems in perspectivalism, and modifications made by the
           post-empiricist response to "value-free" science that have
           importance for evangelicals.

1671.   _____. "North American Evangelicalism and the Social Sciences:
           A Historical and Critical Appraisal." Journal of the American
           Scientific Affiliation 40 (December 1988): 194-203.

"[T]races the nineteenth and twentieth century relationship of
evangelicalism to the social sciences, particularly via the
question of how the natural and social sciences should relate
to each other and how both should relate to world view
considerations." Contends for "a more 'hermeneutic' and
'value-critical' approach to the social sciences." Reprinted
as "Evangelicals and the Social Sciences" in Evangelical Review
of Theology 13 (July 1989).

1672.   . The Person in Psychology: A Contemporary Christian
Appraisal. Leicester, England: Inter-Varsity Press; Grand Rapids:
Eerdmans, 1985. 264 p.

Well-done appraisal of both theoretical and methodological
approaches to the person, offering a Christian worldview as
alternative to the other views prevalent in psychological
studies. Bibliographical references. Index.

1673.   Wald, Kenneth D., Dennis E. Owen, and Samuel S. Hill, Jr. "Evangelical Politics and Status Issues." Journal for the Scientific
Study of Religion 28 (March 1989): 1-16.

Offers an empirical assessment of the "status politics"
interpretation of the "New Christian Right," concluding, with
cautions, that that model continues to be a viable one.

1674.   Warburton, T. Rennie. "Holiness Religion: An Anomaly of Sectarian
Typologies." Journal for the Scientific Study of Religion 8
(Spring 1969): 130-39.

Differentiated from pentecostalism (with which it shares some
characteristics), the holiness movement has not produced
widespread and large sects, making it "anomalous when examined
within the usual framework of sect typologies."

1675.   Warner, R. Stephen. "Theological Barriers to the Understanding of
Evangelical Christianity." Sociological Analysis 40 (Spring
1979): 1-9.

Warner argues against the barriers--"the identification of
evangelicalism with social class [disinherited], political
[conservative], and historical [atavistic] correlates"--
especially in trying to understand evangelicalism in mainline
and middle class churches.

1676.   Weddle, David L. "The Image of the Self in Jonathan Edwards: A
Study of Autobiography and Theology." Journal of the American
Academy of Religion 43 (March 1975): 70-83.

Using categories from Erik Erikson, Weddle explores the
relationship between Edwards' understanding of his "self" and
the "'ideology' in his sermons and theological treatises."

1677.   . "The Law and the Revival: A 'New Divinity' for the
Settlements." Church History 47 (June 1978): 196-214.

Charles Finney's "new divinity" resolved "the conflict between
autonomy and order in the religious life of the [Western]
settlements" in that his revival theology, like the lawyers'
legal codes, "directed, rather than suppressed, human energies
and encouraged human initiative," providing the vision of a
just social order common to both law and revival.

1678.   Wells, David F. "No Offense, I am an Evangelical: A Search for
Self-Definition." In A Time to Speak, eds. A. James Rudin and
Marvin R. Wilson, 20-40. Grand Rapids: Eerdmans, 1987.

Doctrinal belief is only part of the reality, so Wells looks at
evangelicalism sociologically: the changes experienced as it
outgrew fundamentalism, and "the changes wrought upon it by its
function within the modern world."

1679.   Williams, Peter W. Popular Religion in America: Symbolic Change
and the Modernization Process in Historical Perspective.
Champaign: University of Illinois Press, 1989. 288 p.

Wide-ranging study of popular religion, from behavioral science
and historical perspectives; some treatment of evangelicalism,
fundamentalism, pentecostalism. Glossary. Bibliographical
references. Index.

1680.   Wilson, Sandra D. "Evangelical Christian Adult Children of
Alcoholics: A Preliminary Study." Journal of Psychology &
Theology 17 (Fall 1989): 263-73.

"Using the Sixteen Personality Factor Test evangelical
Christian adult children of alcoholics and nonalcoholics from
17 Protestant churches . . . were compared on five personality
characteristics." Discusses the findings and gives suggestions
for further research.

1681.   Windemiller, Duane Arlo. "The Psychodynamics of Change in
Religious Conversion and Communist Brainwashing, with Particular
Reference to the 18th Century Evangelical Revival and the Chinese
Thought Control Movement." Ph.D. diss., Boston University, 1960.
186 p.

1682. Wuthnow, Robert. "Religious Commitment and Conservatism: In
Search of an Elusive Relationship." In Religion in Sociological
Perspective, ed. Charles Y. Glock, 117-32. Belmont: Wadsworth,
1973.

1683. _____. The Restructuring of American Religion: Society and
Faith Since World War II. Princeton: Princeton University Press,
1988. 374 p.

A volume in the Project on Church and State at Princeton, this
sociological analysis of society and faith stresses the
polarization between religious liberals and religious
conservatives, and the growth of special purpose religious
groups since World War II. Bibliography. Index.

1684. _____. The Struggle for America's Soul: Evangelicals,
Liberals, and Secularism. Grand Rapids: Eerdmans, 1989. 208 p.

Sociological analysis of the main elements in American society,
the social and political battles waged by the churches, and
areas of special concern to American religion. Bibliography.
Index.

1685. Young, Frank W. "Adaption and Pattern Integration of a California
Sect." Review of Religious Research 1 (Summer 1959): 137-50.

Supports the theory that "anomic social conditions are
associated with sect activity"; when the anomic conditions were
relieved the congregation moved to a "church" type.

1686. Zimbelman, Ernie. Human Sexuality and Evangelical Christians.
Lanham, MD: University Press of America, 1985. 374 p.

Thorough discussion of all aspects of sexuality from the
standpoint of evangelical commitment. More a book of information than of advice. Twenty-four page bibliography.

See also items 10, 154, 189, 195, 210, 230, 259, 276, 291, 353, 413, 481,
519, 597, 642, 770, 781, 786, 891, 904, 912, 923, 1015, 1036, 1065,
1110, 1145, 1146, 1153, 1277, 1394, 1466, 1842, 1918, 1962, 1977, 1988,
2499, 2523, 2549, 2550, 2570, 2580.

IV

FUNDAMENTALISM

A. General Studies

1687.   Ashcraft, Morris. "The Strengths and Weaknesses of Fundamentalism." In Proceedings of the Conference on Biblical Inerrancy,
1987, 531-41. Nashville: Broadman, 1987.

> Definition, brief historical summary, and theology of fundamen-
> talism; seven strengths and seven weaknesses; "Fundamentalism
> has made numerous contributions to the Christian movement, but
> its exclusive claim to the whole truth" has been injurious.

1688.   _____. "The Theology of Fundamentalism." Review and Expositor
79 (Winter 1982): 31-44.

> Fundamentalism holds to the doctrines typical of Protestant
> conservatives but its delineating characteristic is a basic
> theology of one major feature: the inerrancy of the biblical
> autographs, present in the fundamentalists of the 1920s and in
> the evangelicals (which he more or less lumps with
> fundamentalists) of the 1980s.

1689.   Bartlett, Billy Vick. A History of Baptist Separatism. Springfield, MO: Roark, 1972. 79 p.

1690.   Beale, David O. "Fundamentalism: Past and Present." Faith for
the Family 10 (October 1982): 12-13.

> Very brief recounting of the basics of fundamentalism, written
> from the Bob Jones University perspective.

1691.   Boone, Kathleen C. The Bible Tells Them So: The Discourse of
Protestant Fundamentalism. Albany: State University of New York
Press, 1989. 139 p.

Originally a SUNY at Buffalo Ph.D. dissertation (1987), Boone's
approach is via literary theory as she seeks to describe the
fundamentalist in discourse rather than fundamentalism. Fundamentalist discourse centers on the Bible as final authority,
and Boone treats the discourse as literary text. Empathetic
and provocative. Bibliography. Index.

1692.   Brown, Harold O. J. "Fundamentalism, Intolerance, and the 'Threat
to Liberty.'" Fundamentalist Journal 5 (November 1986): 14, 16.

Fundamentalism, not a threat to liberty, needs honestly to ad-
mit its mistakes, but also to reject false charges against it.

1693.   _____. "What's in a Name?" Fundamentalist Journal 3 (December
1984): 21-22.

Proposes that value still remains in the term fundamentalist.

1694.   Childerston, James Kent. "Understanding Religious 'Fundamentalists': A Study of Typology and Moral Judgment." Ph.D. diss.,
Fuller Theological Seminary, School of Psychology, 1985. 155 p.

1695.   Chilson, Richard. "Two Visions." New Catholic World 228
(January-February 1985): 42-44.

Points up the differences between Catholics and fundamentalists, noting that the differences are rooted in opposing
understanding of grace.

1696.   Christopherson, Kenneth E. "Fundamentalism: What Led Up To It,
How It Got Among Us, and What We In Academe Do About It." Dialog
19 (Summer 1980): 209-14.

The church has seen many literalists and many inerrantists in
regard to the biblical text, but few who combine the two like
the fundamentalists do, who raise literal inerrantism to be
"the first and most basic Christian doctrine, keystone of all
the other doctrines."

1697.   Clearwaters, Richard V. "Fundamentalism and Ecumenicity."
Central C. B. Quarterly 2 (Spring 1959): 17-26.

In an extended response to an article with that same title in
the Christian Century (1 October 1958), occasioned by the
defection of a Denver Seminary professor from fundamentalist
ranks, he contrasts "historic fundamentalism" with the

ecumenical movement, finding disturbing "incompatibilities" of structure, goal and gospel.

1698.   Conway, Flo, and Jim Siegelman. Holy Terror: The Fundamentalist War on America's Freedoms in Religion, Politics and Our Private Lives. Garden City, NY: Doubleday, 1982. [Updated edition. New York: Dell, 1984.] 402 p.

The Holy Terror "is the exploitation of religion as the vehicle for a larger social and political movement, a drive for power . . . in every domain," public and private, engaged in by the fundamentalists; written from a communication research perspective, in rather inflated language. Bibliography. Index.

1699.   Cordis, Robert. "The Revival of Religion and the Decay of Ethics." Christian Century 101 (28 November 1984): 1122-26.

Draws lines of similarity (and some differences) between Jewish and Christian fundamentalists, "more alike than they are different," emphasizing their anti-intellectualism, indifference to human needs, and materialism.

1700.   Curley, Brian E. "Fundamentalism and Its Challenge to Catholic Religious Education." New Catholic World 228 (January-February 1985): 34-37.

Fundamentalism, "an attitude of defensive retrenchment and militant evangelization," is transcendent, confrontational, and escapist.

1701.   De Oliveira, Silas. "The Victory of Fundamentalism." Reformation Review 29 (July 1984): 148-59.

The various isms that threaten but will not vanquish fundamentalism, followed by five reasons for separation from ecumenical groups.

1702.   Dobson. Edward. "Fundamentalism and Evangelicalism: A Comparison and Contrast." Fundamentalist Journal 5 (March 1986): 12.

Five strengths of each, "two distinct groups among conservative Protestants."

1703.   _____. "Fundamentalist Fanaticism: Private Religion and Public Policy." Fundamentalist Journal 4 (March 1985): 14-15.

It is incorrect to see fundamentalists as waging a holy war and
to judge the whole movement by extremists on the fringe.

1704.   . "I am Proud to be a Fundamentalist." Fundamentalist
Journal 4 (June 1985): 12.

Dobson is a fundamentalist both by convictions and by choice.

1705.   . "In Search of Unity." Fundamentalist Journal 4
(January 1985): 12-13.

A fourfold appeal to fundamentalists: recommit to the truth;
reshape the image of fundamentalism; revive personal holiness;
reclaim the world for Christ.

1706.   . "Learning From Our Weaknesses." Fundamentalist Journal
5 (April 1986): 12.

Five weaknesses each of fundamentalists and evangelicals; and a
warning against the fringes of each movement.

1707.   . "The Lunatic Fringe." Fundamentalist Journal 3 (April
1984): 10-11.

Lists fringe elements in fundamentalism and evangelicalism;
neither far right nor far left represents biblical
Christianity.

1708.   Dollar, George W. "Facts for Fundamentalists to Face." Bibliotheca Sacra 124 (April-June 1967): 144-49.

The facts are the new evangelicalism, Romanism, worldliness,
secularism and paganism.

1709.   Dollar, Truman. "What is a Fundamentalist?" Fundamentalist
Journal 1 (September 1982): 6-8.

A plea for "right spirit" to characterize fundamentalists,
along with their already-in-place emphases on right doctrine
and right behavior. Fundamentalists have carried the military
analogy too far and warred among themselves to the detriment of
the gospel.

1710.   Edwards, Paul R. "Some Thoughts on Fundamentalist Infallibility."
Eternity 8 (September 1957): 6-7, 48.

A "'chastened fundamentalist,' who is shocked and appalled not only by his movement's contentiousness but also by its total unwillingness to acknowledge its glaring weaknesses and to repent of them," critiques fundamentalist theology.

1711.   Eenigenburg, Elton M. "Critical Distinctions Between the Reformed Tradition and Fundamentalism in Eschatology." Reformed Review 18 (December 1964): 3-17.

Compares the premillennialism of fundamentalists with the amillennialism of the Reformed, emphasizing the variety in each and the differing hermeneutical approaches they take.

1712.   Enslin, Morton S. "Gamaliel and the Fundamentalist." Crozer Quarterly 25 (October 1948): 332-36.

Asks why, if the fundamentalist is so confident of having divine truth, he is "so bitter and venomous to his misguided brothers and sisters," rather than taking a calm and reasoned position like that of Gamaliel? Urges liberals to contend more aggressively for their positions.

1713.   Evans, Rod L., and Irwin M. Berent. Fundamentalism: Hazards and Heartbreaks. La Salle, IL: Open Court, 1988. 175 p.

Centering on understanding the Bible, the authors propose "to point out some potential hazards associated with viewing the Bible in the ways in which many fundamentalists typically view it," and offer alternative views. Bibliography. Index.

1714.   Fromow, George H. "Fundamentalist Doctrine Defined and Defended." Reformation Review 4 (July 1957): 206-12.

Debates the comments against fundamentalism made by a British liberal, and appends a nine-point statement of fundamentalist beliefs.

1715.   Gillespie, Paul F., ed. Foxfire 7. Garden City: Anchor/Doubleday, 1982. 510 p.

Some references to Appalachian religion. Bibliographical references. Index.

1716.   Hamann, Henry P. The Bible Between Fundamentalism and Philosophy. Minneapolis: Augsburg, 1980. 76 p.

Lectures delivered by Australian Lutheran Hamann at Valparaiso University, April 1979, in which he defends "the safe, middle ground" between the deviation by fundamentalism and the threat by philosophy (philosophy is the more destructive) to true biblical understanding. Bibliographical references.

1717.   Hebert, Gabriel. "The Bible and Modern Religions: VI. Fundamentalism." Interpretation 11 (April 1957): 186-203.

While commending their enthusiasm, Australian Catholic Hebert points out the differences between fundamentalists and other Christians in regard to the nature of the church and the nature and meaning of the Bible, leading to their retreat from "the menacing difficulties of the world."

1718.   Helgeland, John. "The Pain and Itch of Fundamentalism." Dialog 21 (Spring 1982): 133-37.

Driven by the desire to limit subjectivity, fundamentalism has rapport with Cartesian thinking, relates to papal infallibility (the Catholic parallel to Scriptural infallibility), and fits the mechanistic culture of contemporary technology, in all making it "mostly detrimental to religious sensitivity."

1719.   Keyser, Leander S. "The Position of the Fundamentalists." Discerner 7 (January-March 1971): 13-14.

"The fundamentalists have stood firmly and unalterable [sic] for the doctrines of the Scriptures," accepting "without compromise the great doctrines of the Bible"; they "hold it to be a Christian duty to defend the faith," and, "as a rule" "use less invective and vituperation than the liberals."

1720.   Lapierre, Emmanuel. "Understanding Fundamentalism." Ecumenism no. 91 (September 1988): 3-22.

1721.   LaVerdiere, Eugene. "Fundamentalism: A Pastoral Concern." Bible Today 21 (January 1983): 5-11.

A Roman Catholic outlines fundamentalist beliefs and contends that fundamentalism is "a symptom of broad socio-religious and personal problems" that requires pastoral faith and love to overcome.

1722.   Lightner, Robert P. "A Plea to Fellow Fundamentalists." Fundamentalist Journal 5 (June 1986): 14-15.

Suggests five other fundamentals--more behavioral than
doctrinal--as a means to contend "earnestly for the faith, but
to do so in a way that is pleasing to God."

1723.   McCune, Rolland D. "Eschatology of 'Historic' Premillennialism."
Central Bible Quarterly 18 (Winter 1975): 2-49.

"In its fundamental underpinnings and leading motifs it is
Biblically unacceptable to a dispensationalist."

1724.   _____. "Hermeneutics and Church Among 'Historic' Premillen-
nialists." Central Bible Quarterly 18 (Fall 1975): 2-34.

Examines the hermeneutical grounds with special focus on the
doctrine of the church, concluding that the position of
"historic" premillennialism is untenable.

1725.   Michalsky, Walt. "The Masquerade of Fundamentalism." Humanist 41
(July-August 1981): 15-18, 52.

Fundamentalism is a "misanthropic cult" that asks its followers
to capitulate to the movement, pushes creationism, and has
blueprints to follow when making moral decisions.

1726.   Pickering, Ernest. Should Fundamentalists Support the Billy
Graham Crusades? Minneapolis: Central Conservative Baptist
Seminary, n.d.

1727.   Pratt, Raymond. "Prejudice Against Fundamentalists Seen On Rise
In Latest Survey." Emerging Trends 11 (March 1989): 1-2.

"A new Gallup Poll reveals a broad pattern of prejudice
against diverse religious and ethnic minorities and persons
with unconventional life styles."

1728.   Ramm, Bernard. "Fundamentalism: Doctrine is Theology." Eternity
33 (April 1982): 43-44.

The strategies, theses, and affirmations of fundamentalism.

1729.   Rausch, David A. "Paranoia About Fundamentalism." Judaism 28
(Summer 1979): 304-08.

Evangelicals/fundamentalists are strong supporters of the
nation of Israel and are philo-semites, not the anti-semites
they are often portrayed to be.

1730.   "Resolutions of the 10th Assembly, Far Eastern Council of
          Christian Churches." Reformation Review 26 (July 1981): 146-61.

          Includes resolutions opposing the ecumenical movement, the Holy
          Spirit renewal movement, and neo-evangelicalism.

1731.   Rice, John R. Earnestly Contending for the Faith. Murfreesboro,
          TN: Sword of the Lord, 1965. 361 p.

          Sixteen articles from Rice's Sword of the Lord demonstrate his
          militant fundamentalist stance.

1732.   _____. "Modernism-Religious Liberalism." Sword of the Lord 43
          (24 June 1977): 1-2, 14-15.

          Describing religious liberals as "infidels who claim to be
          Christians," Rice cites the biblical warnings, reviews the
          "absolute essentials" of the faith, contends that those who
          deny the essentials are not Christian, and seeks to answer the
          question as to how to identify the modernist/religious liberal,
          providing "some marks" of such persons.

1733.   Sandeen, Ernest R. "Fundamentalism and American Identity."
          Annals of the American Academy of Political and Social Science 56
          (January 1970): 387.

          Fundamentalism (evangelicalism) is "classically American" and
          represents "one of the few authentic conservative traditions in
          American history."

1734.   Sanders, James A. "Fundamentalism and the Church: Theological
          Crisis for Mainline Protestants." Biblical Theology Bulletin 18
          (April 1988): 43-49.

1735.   Stevick, Daniel. Beyond Fundamentalism. Richmond: John Knox,
          1964. 239 p.

          "[A]n essay in friendly polemic" that grew out of letters to
          friends and that argues "that there is nothing of value in
          Fundamentalism which could not be retained--and in fact
          heightened and fulfilled--by its moving" into the broader
          church fellowship. Focus on biblical inerrancy, other
          subjects. Bibliography.

1736.   Stransky, Thomas F. "A Catholic Looks at American Fundamen-
          talists." New Catholic World 228 (January-February 1985): 10-13.

Careful and sympathetic summary of the fundamentalist position.

1737. Summerhill, William Roy, Jr. "Holy War Within the Mythic Horizon of American Christian Biblical Fundamentalism." Ph.D. diss., The Catholic University of America, 1985. 336 p.

1738. Sweet, Leonard I. "The Four Fundamentals of Oldline Protestants." Christian Century 102 (13 March 1985): 266-70.

The fundamentalisms are distortions of the "fundamentals" of oldline [mainline] Protestants: a heartfelt faith that is too pietistic; a Christbody community caught up in procedures; a transforming mission that is too activist; the lack of magic, mystery, miracle.

1739. Tulga, Chester E. The Doctrine of Separation in These Times. Chicago: Conservative Baptist Fellowship, 1952. 64 p.

A Baptist militant expounds the fundamentalist view of separation at a time when the new evangelicalism was beginning.

1740. Valbracht, Louis H. The Follies of Fundamentalism. Lima, OH: C.S.S. Pub., 1974. 53 p.

Four sermons by an Iowa Lutheran pastor refuting what he sees as the follies of which fundamentalists are guilty--about the Bible.

See also items 58, 89, 92, 93, 131, 455, 518, 794, 878, 886, 975, 1092, 1165, 1187, 1188, 1189, 1259, 1284, 1314, 1350, 1428, 1525, 1574, 1778, 1787, 1790, 1795, 1846, 1917, 1953, 2635.

B. History

1741. Ashworth, Robert A. "The Fundamentalist Movement Among the Baptists." Journal of Religion 4 (November 1924): 611-31.

Detailed narrative, including persons and publications, of fundamentalist attempts from 1919 to 1924 to secure control of the Northern Baptist Convention.

1742. Bassett, Paul Merritt. "The Fundamentalist Leavening of the Holiness Movement, 1914-1940: The Church of the Nazarene: A Case Study." Wesleyan Theological Journal 13 (Spring 1978): 65-91.

The gradual acceptance among Nazarenes of the Princeton position on biblical inerrancy, foreign to the traditional Nazarene stress on the testimony of the Holy Spirit rather than the words of the Bible, which traditional teaching was upheld by its chief theologian, H. Orton Wiley.

1743.   Beale, David O. In Pursuit of Purity: American Fundamentalism Since 1850. Greenville, SC: Unusual Publications, 1986. 457 p.

The best of the histories of fundamentalism from an insider point of view. Some overstating of issues, but also a recognition of failings in the movement. Thirty-page bibliography. Index.

1744.   Becklund, David E. "A History of the Minnesota Baptist Convention." Central Bible Quarterly 10 (Summer 1967): 2-72.

Includes the background of the Convention in the 19th and early 20th centuries, "The Rise of the Fundamentalist Forces in Minnesota (1933-1946)," and "The Struggle for Separatism in the Minnesota Baptist Convention." A case study of the national struggle.

1745.   Blakemore, Peter James. "Toward an Honest Portrait of Fundamentalism, 1930-1980: A Historical Study of Progressive Development in the Working Definition of Fundamentalism." Ph.D. diss., Bob Jones University, 1982. 314 p.

1746.   Brereton, Virginia Lieson. "Protestant Fundamentalist Bible Schools, 1882-1940." Ph.D. diss., Columbia University, 1981. 470 p.

1747.   Bridges, Horace James. The God of Fundamentalism and Other Studies. Chicago: P. Covici, 1925. 319 p.

The title refers to chapter one, 3-58, wherein Bridges, a member of Ethical Culture, makes an extended critique of the Calvinism in J. G. Machen's Christianity and Liberalism (1923).

1748.   Carpenter, Joel A. "Fundamentalist Institutions and the Rise of Evangelical Protestantism, 1929-1942." Church History 49 (March 1980): 62-75.

The 1925 Scopes Trial did not defeat fundamentalism. Carpenter sees vitality in missions, education, media, and Bible conferences--even though some loss of political and social visibility

--as indicators of the strength of a popular religious movement
that continued to grow in the 1930s and 1940s.

1749.   , ed. The Fundamentalist-Modernist Conflict: Opposing
Views on Three Major Issues. New York: Garland, 1988. Various
pagings.

Reprints tracts that "illustrate three important friction
points that sparked and sustained" the conflict: attacks on
premillennialism, the debate about the Interchurch World
Movement during 1919-1920, and the preaching and writing of
Harry Emerson Fosdick. Helpful introduction with notes.

1750.   Coggins, Jim. "A Lesson From History." Mennonite Brethren Herald
28 (23 June 1989): 2-3.

Reviews the history of Baptist conflict in Canada during the
fundamentalist era, as a warning to present-day Mennonite
Brethren.

1751.   Cole, Stewart G. A History of Fundamentalism. New York: R. R.
Smith, 1931. 319 p.

Earliest book-length analysis of fundamentalism; sees the
movement as the result of a psychological attachment to certain
doctrines, coupled with the loss of social status. Bibliography. Index.

1752.   . "The Psychology of the Fundamentalist Movements."
Ph.D. diss., University of Chicago, 1929. 193 p.

1753.   Compton, Bobby D. "J. Frank Norris and the Southern Baptists."
Review and Expositor 79 (Winter 1982): 63-84.

Well-documented survey of the life of a major controversialist
in the fundamentalist movement until his death in 1952.

1754.   Dahlin, John E. "Liberalism and Fundamentalism (A Review of the
Conflict in the United States)." Discerner 6 (October-December
1969): 12-13.

Attempts "to place the development in its right historical
context." Discusses the social gospel, the organization and
position of the fundamentalist groups, and the on-going
struggle.

1755.   Delnay, Robert. "The Crucial Buffalo Debate in the Northern
         Baptist Convention." Central C. B. Quarterly 6 (Winter 1963):
         15-20.

         A church historian at Central Conservative Baptist Seminary
         reviews the pre-Convention and Convention meetings of 1920,
         with the three large issues of modernist control of the
         denomination, its press and its schools; with concluding
         observations.

1756.   Dobson, Edward. "Fundamentalism--Its Roots." Fundamentalist
         Journal 1 (September 1982): 24, 26-27.

         Origins of the movement; the five fundamentals. Reprinted in
         New Catholic World 228 (January-February 1985): 4-9.

1757.   _____. In Search of Unity: An Appeal to Fundamentalists and
         Evangelicals. Nashville: Thomas Nelson, 1985. 168 p.

         At the time attached to Liberty University and the senior
         editor of Fundamentalist Journal, Dobson describes the history
         of fundamentalism and its divisions, examines the issue of
         unity (with the doctrine of separation as a key factor), and
         calls for unity and revival. Annotated bibliography. Index.

1758.   Dollar, George W. "Early Days of American Fundamentalism."
         Bibliotheca Sacra 123 (April-June 1966): 115-23.

         The fundamentalist fathers of 1875-1900, some of their central
         beliefs (biblical literalism, fulfillment of prophecy), and the
         institutions they founded.

1759.   _____. A History of Fundamentalism in America. Greenville,
         SC: Bob Jones University Press, 1973. 415 p.

         A survey of the separatist branch of fundamentalism, for the
         years 1875-1970; an insider's look at the course of funda-
         mentalism. A number of factual mistakes, and a rather militant
         tone. Overshadowed by the Beale book (q.v.). Bibliography.
         Index.

1760.   Edmondson, William Douglas. "Fundamentalist Sects of Los Angeles.
         1900-1930." Ph.D. diss.. Claremont Graduate School. 1969. 465 p.

1761.   Findlay. Alice M. "The Fundamentalist Controversy (1920-1927).
         and Its Effect on the American Baptist Foreign Mission Society."
         M.A. thesis, Andover-Newton Theological School, 1969. 156 p.

An account of the origins and the controversy within the
American Baptist Convention, with special focus on the ABFMS,
told by an ABFMS missionary. Appendixes. Bibliographical
references.

1762. Foster, Allyn K. "Where the Evangelical Faith Lives With the New
Learning." Crozer Quarterly 1 (October 1924): 416-21.

Attempts to demonstrate that evolution can live nicely with the
Christian faith, albeit some of the doctrines get restated;
good example of what disturbed the 1920s fundamentalists.

1763. Foster, John W. Four Northwest Fundamentalist Portland, OR:
n.p., 1975. 128 p.

Rather adulatory sketches of early 20th century pastors John J.
Staub, Mark A. Matthews, Walter B. Hinson, and Albert G.
Johnson.

1764. Freitag, Walter. "Fundamentalism and Canadian Lutheranism."
Consensus 13 (1987): 23-39.

Historical and theological survey of fundamentalism, a movement
that has influenced Lutheranism but "is not the same thing as
Lutheranism."

1765. Furnlss, Norman. The Fundamentalist-Modernist Controversy, 1918-
1938. New Haven: Yale University Press, 1954. 199 p.

Classic, and dated, exposition of fundamentalists as bigoted,
illiterate, egocentric searchers for certainty in a climate of
fear. Bibliographical references. Index. Revision of his
Ph.D. dissertation entitled "The Fundamentalist Controversy,
1918-1931," Yale University, 1950. 256 p.

1766. Gasper, Louis. The Fundamentalist Movement. The Hague, Netherlands: Mouton, 1963. 181 p.

Fine study of the American Council of Christian Churches and
the National Association of Evangelicals from 1930 to the
1950s. Originally Gasper's 1958 Ph.D. dissertation at Case
Western Reserve University entitled "Fundamentalist Movement in
American Protestant Christianity Since 1930." Bibliographical
references. Index.

1767. Gatewood, Willard B., Jr. Controversy in the Twenties: Fundamentalism, Modernism, and Evolution. Nashville: Vanderbilt
University Press, 1969. 459 p.

Handy volume of documents and commentary on modernists and
fundamentalists related to their cultural and psychological
milieu. Notes on secondary sources.

1768.   Gaustad, Edwin Scott. "Did the Fundamentalists Win?" In Religion
and America: Spirituality in a Secular Age. eds. Mary Douglas and
Steven M. Tipton, 169-78. Boston: Beacon, 1983.

Using as his point of departure Fosdick's famous sermon, "Shall
the Fundamentalists Win," Gaustad surveys the two generations
since, and writes, "Did liberal protestantism lose? Yes. This
round."

1769.   Glass, William R. "The Ministry of Leonard G. Broughton at Tabernacle Baptist Church, 1898-1912: A Source of Southern Fundamentalism." American Baptist Quarterly 4 (March 1985): 35-60.

Contrary to the usual belief that fundamentalism did not arrive
in the South until the 1920s, this study of an Atlanta pastor
whose church held Bible conferences in the Northfield pattern
shows that contact with Northern fundamentalists and Northern
issues and debates were present in the pre-WWI South.

1770.   Goen. C. C. "Fundamentalism in America." Southwestern Journal of
Theology 2 (October 1959): 52-62.

Views fundamentalism rather positively, "in terms of the
developments which provoked it, the course of the controversy,
and the issues involved."

1771.   Grabbe, Lester L. "Fundamentalism and Scholarship: The Case of
Daniel." In Scripture: Meaning and Method, ed. Barry P. Thompson.
Hull, England: University of Hull Press, 1987.

1772.   Hall, Joseph Hill. "The Controversy Over Fundamentalism in the
Christian Reformed Church, 1915-1966." Ph.D. diss., Concordia
Seminary, 1974. 229 p.

1773.   Handy, Robert T. "Fundamentalism and Modernism in Perspective."
Religion in Life 24 (Summer 1955): 381-94.

Puritans "sought to keep faith and reason in creative tension"
but in the course of time faith and reason became separated.
one example of which was the fundamentalist-modernist
controversy of the 1920s. Handy sees hope for reconciliation
in the theological renaissance of the 1950s.

1774. _____. "The New Fundamentalism in America: Theological
Foundations and Political Temptations." In Faith and Freedom, ed.
Richard Libowitz. New York: Pergamon, 1987. 268 p.

1775. Harper, James Clyde. "A Study of Alabama Baptist Higher Education
and Fundamentalism, 1890-1930." Ph.D. diss., The University of
Alabama, 1977. 148 p.

1776. Harrington, Carroll Edwin. "The Fundamentalist Movement in
America." Ph.D. diss., University of California, 1959.

1777. Hart, Nelson Hodges. "The True and the False: The Worlds of an
Emerging Evangelical Protestant Fundamentalism in America,
1890-1920." Ph.D. diss., Michigan State University, 1976. 248 p.

1778. Hebert, Gabriel. Fundamentalism and the Church. Philadelphia:
Westminster, 1957. 156 p.

An Anglican priest and theological educator in Australia
concludes that the fundamentalists have rightly emphasized "the
fundamentals of the faith," that "the doctrine of the Inerrancy
of Scripture" is an inadequate one, and that the Church is
composed of sinners, a fact which is the ground of Christian
unity. A careful assessment by one who feels "that
Fundamentalism (in the evil sense) is a grave menace to the
Church of God." Bibliographical references.

1779. Henry, Carl F. H. The Uneasy Conscience of Modern Fundamentalism.
Grand Rapids: Eerdmans, 1947. 89 p.

Called for, and signalled, the reawakening of fundamentalism to
the social dimensions of the Gospel. To a generation increas-
ingly troubled about the "frequent failure" to apply great
Biblical truths effectively to "crucial problems," he called
for "a progressive fundamentalism with a social message."

1780. _____. "The Uneasy Conscience Revisited: Current Theological,
Ethical and Social Concerns." Theology, News and Notes 34
(December 1987): 3-9.

Forty years after the publication of his Uneasy Conscience of
Modern Fundamentalism (1947), Henry reflects on the book and on
the questions that remain for evangelicals to discuss: unity,
academic engagement, political influence, materialism,
naturalism.

1781. Herman, Douglas Edward. "Flooding the Kingdom: The Intellectual
Development of Fundamentalism, 1930-1941." Ph.D. diss., Ohio
University, 1980. 265 p.

1782.   Howard, Philip E., Jr. "Unashamed Fundamentalists." Reformation
         Review 7 (July 1960): 200-06.

         Reprinted from the Sunday School Times (26 May 1945); lists
         early 20th century leaders, a statement of faith, and comments
         on The Fundamentals.

1783.   Johnson, Dell G. "The Victory of Fundamentalism in the Minnesota
         Baptist Convention." Central Bible Quarterly 20 (Spring 1977):
         26-59.

         History, from the inside, of the several decades battle between
         the Minnesota Baptist Convention and the Northern (American)
         Baptist Convention, culminating in the early 1960s.

1784.   _____. "W. B. Riley and the Developing New Evangelicalism."
         Central Bible Quarterly 21 (Fall 1978): 2-28.

         Documents some of the initial questions and controversies from
         a fundamentalist standpoint; cites Riley's ambiguous attitudes
         about the National Association of Evangelicals in the 1940s.

1785.   Kim, Ki Hong. "Presbyterian Conflict in the Early Twentieth
         Century: Ecclesiology in the Princeton Tradition and the Emergence
         of Presbyterian Fundamentalism." Ph.D. diss., Drew University,
         1983. 235 p.

1786.   King, Larry L. "Bob Jones University: The Buckle on the Bible
         Belt." Harper's 232 (June 1966): 51-58.

         Character sketches of the Jones family; description of campus
         life and ethos.

1787.   Land, Richard D. "Southern Baptists and the Fundamentalist
         Tradition in Biblical Interpretation, 1845-1945." Baptist History
         and Heritage 19 (July 1984): 25-32.

         Sees two fundamentalisms, both strong on the central matter
         of Scripture, but one without the isolationism and anti-
         intellectualism of the other.

1788.   Leonard, Bill J. "Independent Baptists: From Sectarian Minority
         to 'Moral Majority.'" Church History 56 (December 1987): 504-17.

         A fairly recent phenomenon (post-WWI). independent Baptists are
         autonomous (though losely bound in groups like the Baptist
         Bible Fellowship), fundamentalist, and separatist, but have

modified their separatism "in an effort to promote their
particular moral and spiritual agendas" in what they see as a
humanistic culture.

1789.   . "The Origin and Character of Fundamentalism." Review
and Expositor 79 (Winter 1982): 5-17.

Discussion of the historiography of fundamentalism with special
attention to Sandeen, Marsden and Russell. While each has
contributed to an understanding of the diversity and complexity
of fundamentalism, Leonard feels we need further study on the
grass roots: how laity and local churches responded to the
movement.

1790.   Marsden, George M. "Defining Fundamentalism." Christian
Scholar's Review 1 (Winter 1971): 141-51.

Hails Sandeen's work, The Roots of Fundamentalism (1970), as
the best to date on fundamentalism; recognizes the clear
exposition of millennialism in the book, but doubts Sandeen's
interpretation that millennialism is the root of fundamentalism. Reply by Sandeen in "Defining Fundamentalism: A
Reply to Professor Marsden." CSR 1 (Spring 1971).

1791.   . Fundamentalism and American Culture: The Shaping of
Twentieth-Century Evangelicalism, 1870-1925. New York: Oxford
University Press, 1980. 306 p.

Best study to date of the rise and course of fundamentalism to
the Scopes trial. Marsden is balanced and judicious in his
interpretation, sympathetic to fundamentalism without losing
the ability to give a critical analysis. The book to start
with in any study of the subject. Seventy-six pages of notes.
Index.

1792.   . "Fundamentalism as an American Phenomenon, A Comparison
With English Evangelicalism." Church History 46 (June 1977):
215-32.

English evangelicalism lacked widespread militancy and lacked
impact on both churches and culture. while in America social
factors, religious factors (especially revivalism) and intellectual factors aided the fundamentalist cause.

1793.   . "The New School Heritage and Presbyterian Fundamentalism." Westminster Theological Journal 32 (May 1970): 129-47.

As "an integral part of the evangelical revival of the first
half of the nineteenth century," New School Presbyterianism
"had at least as much affinity to twentieth-century fundamentalism" as to liberalism. Based on Marsden's The Evangelical
Mind and the New School Presbyterian Experience (1970).

1794.   Mattison, Elvin Keith. "A Movement Study of Fundamentalism
Between 1900 and 1960." Ph.D. diss., Wayne State University,
1977. 178 p.

1795.   Mattson, Vernon Eugene. "The Fundamentalist Mind: An Intellectual
History of Religious Fundamentalism in the United States." Ph.D.
diss., University of Kansas, 1971. 298 p.

1796.   Mayer, F. E. The Religious Bodies of America. St. Louis:
Concordia, 1954. 591 p.

Includes critical articles on premillennialism and
fundamentalism. Bibliography.

1797.   McArthur, Harvey. "Liberal Concessions to Fundamentalism."
Religion in Life 14 (Autumn 1945): 535-44.

Three concessions should be made to fundamentalism: its
numerical and spiritual power; its being in line with historic
Christianity; its exclusivism as consistent with its basic
pattern.

1798.   McBirnie, Robert Sheldon. "Basic Issues in the Fundamentalism of
W. B. Riley." Ph.D. diss., The University of Iowa, 1952. 169 p.

1799.   McCahon, Thomas J. "Protestant Fundamentalism: Public Education
and the Politics of Regression." Ph.D. diss., Kansas State
University, 1987. 268 p.

1800.   McCowan, Kenneth. "Historic Contemporary Fundamentalism."
Christianity Today 7 (5 July 1963): 12.

Distinguishes this group (author's position; most fall here, he
says) from the new fundamentalism (ultra-separatist) and the
new evangelicalism (too interested in quarreling with
fundamentalism).

1801.   McCrossan, T. J. The Bible: Its Christ and Modernism. Seattle:
The Author, 1929. 213 p.

Considers "Reasons why we know the Bible is inspired of God,"
reasons Jesus "ought to be our highest and final authority,"
teachings of Jesus "which modernists deny," reasons "Modernists
dare to criticize the Bible," "How the Bible estimates
Modernists" and "How Christians should treat Modernists."

1802. McGlone, Lee Roy. "The Preaching of J. Frank Norris: An
'Apologia' for Fundamentalism." Ph.D. diss., The Southern Baptist
Theological Seminary, 1983. 268 p.

1803. McIntire, Carl T. "The Renewed Attack Upon the Fundamentalists."
Reformation Review 15 (July 1968): 201-16.

Review of fundamentalist history and the anti-fundamentalist
attacks in a journal called Diaspora and from the WCC.

1804. _____. Twentieth Century Reformation. Second and revised
edition. Collingswood, NJ: Christian Beacon, 1945. 226 p.

Seeing the "Ecumenical Movement" and "the New Reformation, or
Twentieth Century Reformation," as the two dominant movements
of the mid-twentieth century, he calls for Christians "to stand
together" in the latter movement "on the platform of the
historic Christian church against the widespread apostasy in
the church today."

1805. McKinney, Larry J. "The Fundamentalist Bible School as an
Outgrowth of the Changing Patterns of Protestant Revivalism,
1882-1920." Religious Education 84 (Fall 1989): 589-605.

Examines "many of the early fundamentalist Bible schools and
their relationship to Protestant revivalism that took place in
America in the late nineteenth and early twentieth centuries."

1806. Meadows, Milo Martin, Jr. "Fundamentalist Thought and Its Impact
in Kentucky, 1900-1928." Ph.D. diss., Syracuse University, 1972.
272 p.

1807. Meehan, Brenda M. "A. C. Dixon: An Early Fundamentalist."
Foundations 10 (January-March 1967): 50-63.

Dixon (1854-1925), editor of six volumes of The Fundamentals,
is seen here as a symbol of "early" fundamentalism (1890s and
1900s), "a conservative, Northern urban reaction to modernism
and the social Gospel," and a precursor of post-WWI
fundamentalism.

1808.   Moore. Leroy. Jr. "Another Look at Fundamentalism: A Response to
        Ernest R. Sandeen." Church History 37 (June 1968): 195-202.

        Praises Sandeen's work for seeing fundamentalism as a religious
        phenomenon; however, "Sandeen's genetic approach--his concern
        for origins--is, in its way, liable to the same sort of failing
        as the socio-political approach of Cole and Furniss."

1809.   Nash, Lee. "Unbowed to Baal: The Fundamentalist Remnant in
        America." Fides et Historia 7 (Fall 1974): 37-40.

        A negative review essay of George Dollar's A History of
        Fundamentalism in America (1974); judges that Dollar's "most
        notable contribution" is in his numerous biographical sketches
        of fundamentalist preachers.

1810.   Nelson, Roland Tenus. "Fundamentalism and the Northern Baptist
        Convention." Ph.D. diss., The University of Chicago, 1965.

1811.   Nelson, Rudolph L. "Fundamentalism at Harvard: The Case of Edward
        John Carnell." Quarterly Review (Methodist) 2 (Summer 1982):
        79-98.

        Among a dozen fundamentalist doctoral graduates at Harvard in
        the 1940s and 1950s Carnell typifies fundamentalism come of
        intellectual age as he retains his conservative faith while
        grappling with the ideas presented in his graduate studies.

1812.   Nichols, Robert Hastings. "Fundamentalism in the Presbyterian
        Church." Journal of Religion 5 (January 1925): 14-36.

        The rise and development of fundamentalism--the heart of which
        is scriptural literalism and millennialism--from the agitations
        of the 1890s to the Fosdick issue in the 1920s, and the
        enduring issue in the controversy: "The freedom of the
        Christian man against ecclesiastical authority."

1813.   Nix, William. "The Fundamentals: A Blend of 'Common-Sense'
        Doctrine and Personal Application." Fundamentalist Journal 8 (May
        1989): 28-30.

        Discussing the historical context and the contents of The
        Fundamentals, he concludes that they "blend a 'common-sense'
        doctrinal approach with personal application built upon the
        foundation of the inspired and inerrant scriptures." an
        approach that remains relevant today.

1814.   North American Pre-Convention Conference. Buffalo, New York, 1920.
        <u>Baptist Fundamentals: Being Addresses Delivered at the Pre-Conven-
        tion Conference at Buffalo, June 21 and 22, 1920</u>. Philadelphia:
        Judson, 1920. 202 p.

        Papers by prominent Baptist conservative evangelicals, in
        response to a call issued "To all Baptists within the Bounds of
        the Northern Convention"; doctrinal drift, particularly in
        Baptist educational institutions, and growing worldliness in
        the churches. Bibliography.

1815.   Ockenga, Harold John. "Can Fundamentalism Win America?"
        <u>Christian Life and Times</u> 2 (June 1947): 13-15.

1816.   Opie, John. "The Modernity of Fundamentalism." <u>Christian Century</u>
        82 (12 May 1965): 608-11.

        Fundamentalism "could not have emerged without the Enlighten-
        ment and the scientific revolution," and it approaches
        religious questions "through a special use of rational inquiry,
        scientific method and ideological theory," and freezes them in
        an authoritarianism.

1817.   Parker, David D. "The Bible Union: A Case Study in Australian
        Fundamentalism." <u>Journal of Religious History</u> 14 (June 1986):
        71-99.

        While escaping some of the controversies faced in the U.S.,
        Australian "moderate fundamentalism," here seen through a case
        study of the Bible Union (founded 1923), had its own battles
        with modernism, using lectures, publications, and comments in
        the press to foster a program which produced little impact.

1818.   _____. "Fundamentalism and Conservative Protestantism in
        Australia, 1920-1980." Ph.D. diss., University of Queensland
        (Australia), 1982. Two volumes (865 p.).

1819.   Peterson, Walter Ross. "John Roach Straton: Portrait of a
        Fundamentalist Preacher." Ph.D. diss., Boston University, 1965.
        488 p.

1820.   Pettegrew, Larry D. "The Historical and Theological Contributions
        of the Niagara Bible Conference to American Fundamentalism."
        Th.D. diss., Dallas Theological Seminary, 1976.

1821.   _____. "The Niagara Bible Conference and American Fundamental-
        ism." <u>Central Bible Quarterly</u> 20 (Winter 1977): 3-30.

Last of a five-part series. from his 1976 Th.D. dissertation at
Dallas Theological Seminary.

1822.   Pettingill, William Leroy. The Christian Fundamentals: A Brief
Review of "Those Things Which are Surely Believed Among Us."
Findlay, OH: Fundamental Truth Publishers, 1941. 64 p.

Brief studies on the Bible, the virgin birth, atonement,
resurrection, the new birth, and the second coming. Reprinted
from The Sunday School Times.

1823.   Poorter, John. "The Road to Modernism." Central C. B. Quarterly
3 (Fall 1960): 19-22.

Contends that among the marks of the subtle road were: "utter
confusion concerning the nature of tolerance"; a "speculative
vagueness"; a tendency to "disparage doctrine"; "a feigned
horror of what is called Pharisaism."

1824.   Price, Oliver. "The Historical Background of the Five
Fundamentals." Bibliotheca Sacra 118 (January-March 1961): 35-40.

Mostly looks at liberalism's tenets--evolution, higher
criticism. inclusive church unity--as provoking the move to
stating the fundamentals.

1825.   Rhim, Soon Man. "The Responses of American Protestantism to
Selected Social Problems in the 1930s with Particular Reference to
the Liberals, the Fundamentalists and the Sectarians." Ph.D.
diss., Drew University, 1972. 261 p.

1826.   Rudnick, Milton L. Fundamentalism and the Missouri Synod: A
Historical Study of Their Interaction and Mutual Influence. St.
Louis: Concordia, 1966. 152 p.

A study of a major conservative denomination that includes
critiquing of the larger fundamentalist movement. Based on his
Ph.D. dissertation (Concordia Seminary, 1963). Bibliography.

1827.   Russell, Alfred U. "In Defence of Fundamentalism." Central C. B.
Quarterly 2 (Spring 1959): 43-44.

Relates the history of the terms "evangelical" and "fundamental," defending and urging the use of the latter. in part
because of the wide range of persons identifying themselves
with the former.

1828.   Russell, Charles Allyn. Voices of American Fundamentalism: Seven
         Biographical Studies. Philadelphia: Westminster, 1976. 304 p.

         Good study of seven leading fundamentalists of the 1920s,
         showing the movement's variety of personality and belief.
         Twenty-five-page annotated bibliography. Index.

1829.   Sandeen, Ernest R. "Defining Fundamentalism: A Reply to Prof.
         Marsden." Christian Scholar's Review 1 (Spring 1971): 227-33.

         Suggests that Marsden misunderstood and misinterpreted parts of
         Sandeen's book, The Roots of Fundmentalism (1970).

1830.   _____. "The Problem of Authority in American Fundamentalism."
         Review and Expositor 75 (Spring 1978): 211-17.

         Authority questions revolve around two poles, the mythic and
         the factual; these options presented themselves when the Bible
         came under attack in the late 19th century, and the funda-
         mentalists were among those who chose the factual--in their
         case, biblical literalism.

1831.   _____. The Roots of Fundamentalism: British and American
         Millenarianism, 1800-1930. Chicago: University of Chicago Press,
         1970; Grand Rapids: Baker, reprinted 1978. 328 p.

         In the first of the more judicious looks at fundamentalism,
         Sandeen sees the movement as one phase of the larger
         millenarian movement. Though Sandeen overstated his case, he
         provided a needed corrective to earlier interpretations of
         fundamentalism. Thirty-page bibliography. Index.

1832.   _____. "Toward a Historical Interpretation of the Origins of
         Fundamentalism." Church History 36 (March 1967): 66-83.

         Anticipating his book The Roots of Fundamentalism (1970),
         Sandeen asserts that, until about 1918, fundamentalism "was
         comprised of an alliance between two newly-formulated
         nineteenth-century theologies, dispensationalism and the
         Princeton Theology."

1833.   Sawatsky, Ronald George. "'Looking for That Blessed Hope': The
         Roots of Fundamentalism in Canada, 1878-1914." Ph.D. diss.,
         University of Toronto (Canada). 1985. 366p.

1834.   Shipley, Maynard. The War on Modern Science: A Short History of
         the Fundamentalist Attacks on Evolution and Modernism. New York &
         London: Knopf, 1927. 415 p.

Classic statement in the old warfare style that sees
fundamentalists as encroachers on science and the American
system of government, and tied to the KKK, creating "a grave
peril to our modern civilization"; also, a state-by-state
analysis of the fundamentalist threat regarding the teaching of
evolution in the public schools.

1835.   Smith, Timothy L. "Historical Fundamentalism." Fides et Historia
         14 (Fall-Winter 1981): 68-72.

         Review of George M. Marsden's Fundamentalism and American
         Culture: The Shaping of Twentieth Century Evangelicalism:
         1870-1925 (1980); commends what Marsden did in the book, but
         calls in question what he did not do, viz., sharply draw the
         divergences of fundamentalism from other expressions of
         evangelicalism.

1836.   Sodergren, Carl Johannes. Fundamentalists and Modernists. Rock
         Island: Augustana Book Concern, 1925. 80 p.

         Finds right and left wing (pseudo) fundamentalists and right
         and left wing (naturalistic) modernists, and espouses an
         alliance between right wing fundamentalism and right wing
         modernism as the way out of the controversy.

1837.   Stott, John R. W. Fundamentalism and Evangelism. Grand Rapids:
         Eerdmans, 1959. 80 p.

         An early attempt, from the standpoint of a sympathetic English
         observer, to see the values and the dangers in fundamentalism.

1838.   Straton, John Roach. The Famous New York Fundamentalist Modernist
         Debates: The Orthodox Side. New York: Geo. H. Doran, 1925.
         256 p.

         The main addresses and rebuttals on the orthodox side given in
         Straton's four debates with the Unitarian pastor, Charles
         Francis Potter.

1839.   Streiker, Lowell D. The Gospel Time Bomb: Ultrafundamentalism and
         the Future of America. Buffalo, NY: Prometheus Books, 1984.
         200 p.

         Basically a book about cults, with which Streiker groups
         revivalism, fundamentalism, and pentecostalism, producing an
         unsophisticated melange of religious categories and skewing his
         analysis. Scattered references.

1840.   Szasz, Ference Morton. "Three Fundamentalist Leaders: The Roles
         of William Bell Riley, John Roach Straton, and William Jennings
         Bryan in the Fundamentalist-Modernist Controversy." Ph.D. diss.,
         The University of Rochester, 1969. 408 p.

1841.   Tinder, Donald. "Fundamentalist Baptists in the Northern and
         Western United States." Ph.D. diss., Yale University, 1972.
         475 p.

1842.   Trollinger, William Vance, Jr. "One Response to Modernity:
         Northwestern Bible School and the Fundamentalist Empire of William
         Bell Riley." Ph.D. diss., The University of Wisconsin, Madison,
         1984. 321 p.

1843.   Unger, Walter. "'Earnestly Contending for the Faith': The Role of
         the Niagara Bible Conference in the Emergence of American
         Fundamentalism, 1875-1900." Ph.D. diss., Simon Fraser University
         (Canada), 1982.

1844.   Vanderlaan, Eldred C. "Modernism and Historic Christianity."
         Journal of Religion 5 (May 1925): 225-38.

         The fundamentalist charges, the liberal defense (with its
         ambiguities), and the "real" modernism: a "rediscovery of the
         historical Jesus, and an attempt to organize devotion to him
         rather than in relation to the standardized doctrines about
         him."

1845.   Walvoord, John F. "What's Right About Fundamentalism?" Eternity
         8 (June 1957): 6-7, 34-35.

         "A conservative scholar traces the history of Fundamentalism
         and pleads for retention of the descriptive term."

1846.   Wenger, Robert Elwood. "Social Thought in American Fundamen-
         talism, 1918-1933." Ph.D. diss., The University of Nebraska,
         Lincoln, 1973. 354 p.

See also items 13, 19, 147, 169, 244, 246, 271, 272, 289, 302, 450, 470,
    474, 728, 730, 731, 735, 765, 799, 803, 825, 826, 831, 854, 855, 856,
    857, 858, 859, 860, 861, 862, 873, 874, 875, 878, 969, 1091, 1094,
    1101, 1137, 1247, 1290, 1387, 1415, 1462, 1503, 1578, 1579, 1590,
    1596, 1731, 1732, 1861, 1930, 1940, 1961, 1990, 1993.

C. Post-World War Two

1847.   Academy of Humanism. Neo-Fundamentalism: The Humanist Response.
         Presented by the Academy of Humanism. Buffalo, NY: Prometheus
         Press, 1988. 186 p.

         Papers presented in Oslo, Norway, in 1986, by a group of
         distinguished international scholars, sponsored by the Academy
         of Humanism (established in 1983) and the International
         Humanist and Ethical Union, in response to what they perceive
         to be the threat to reason and freedom posed by the resurgence
         of fundamentalism as a world-wide phenomenon. Bibliographical
         references. Cf. item 1882.

1848.   Allen. Robert. "Must a Fundamentalist Fight?" Fundamentalist
         Journal 1 (November 1982): 28-29, 64.

         Not all the early fundamentalists were fighters. and current
         fundamentalists need to learn to get along, not how to fight
         one another; four points on how to handle disagreements.

1849.   Arnold, Patrick M. "The Rise of Catholic Fundamentalism."
         America 156 (11 April 1987): 297-302.

         Sees fundamentalism in its worldwide context (not just the
         twentieth century Protestant version) as a reaction to cultural
         change; lists five "unhealthy characteristics"; offers an
         analysis of Roman Catholic fundamentalism (which Arnold calls
         "neo-orthodoxy").

1850.   Balmer, Randall H. "Fundamentalism Redux." Reformed Journal 33
         (June 1983): 26-28.

         A review of Eric Gritsch's Born Againism: Perspectives on a
         Movement (1982), "a competent, if uninspiring" addition to the
         growing body of literature about resurgent fundamentalism.

1851.   Barber. Raymond W. "Fundamentalism: A Coming Together."
         Fundamentalist Journal 1 (October 1982): 6-7. 37.

         Fundamentalism has "come of age"; division. dissension and
         isolationism are too high a price to pay for the task of
         preserving the truth of the gospel.

1852.   Brown, Bruce. "Report on the 1980 World Congress of Funda-
         mentalists." Faith for the Family 9 (February 1981): 6-8.

> Meetings held in Manila by the Bob Jones University sort of militant fundamentalism; a list of speakers, meetings and resolutions.

1853. Coskren, Thomas M. "Fundamentalists on Campus." New Catholic World 228 (January-February 1985): 38-41.

> Fundamentalism is a religious novelty that appeals to some Catholic youth; offers help to Catholic leaders to avert the appeal.

1854. Davis, Jimmy Thomas. "Organizational Ideographs: A Case Study of the Recent Rise of Southern Baptist Fundamentalism." Ph.D. diss., Indiana University, 1987. 200 p.

1855. Dobson, Edward, and Edward E. Hindson. "A Critical Self-Evaluation of Fundamentalism." Fundamentalist Journal 2 (March 1983): 12-13, 43.

> Describes ten "characteristic weaknesses of fundamentalism."

1856. Dowell, Bill, Jr. "The New Fundamentalism." Fundamentalist Journal 1 (November 1982): 8-10.

> The soul of fundamentalism is not opposing education or name-calling against liberals. It is the belief in the Bible as the absolute, universal truth.

1857. Fackre, Gabriel. "Ministry in the Emerging Religious Context: The Neo-Fundamentalist Phenomenon." Word and World 5 (Winter 1985): 12-23.

> Neo-fundamentalism (Jerry Falwell, et al.) is presented in terms of the threefold office of the ministry: prophetic, priestly, royal; followed by Fackre's responses from "the classical Christian tradition."

1858. Falwell, Jerry, with Edward Dobson and Edward E. Hindson. The Fundamentalist Phenomenon: The Resurgence of Conservative Christianity. Garden City, NY: Doubleday, 1981. 269 p.

> An insider's optimistic evaluation of late 20th century conservative evangelicalism, concluding with "An Agenda for the Eighties" written by Falwell. Sixteen-page bibliography.

1859. Flake, Carol. Redemptorama: Culture, Politics and the New Evangelicalism. Garden City, NY: Doubleday, 1984. 300 p.

Well-written depiction of the variety of approaches that
evangelicalism (mostly fundamentalism) makes toward American
culture; reflects the ambivalence of one who was raised in and
later left fundamentalism. Bibliographical references. Index.

1860.   Grindal, Bruce T. "Creationism, Sexual Purity, and the Religious
Right." Humanist 43 (March-April 1983): 19-23, 32.

Using anti-rock music, anti-long hair and anti-Jewish events as
examples, the author recognizes the sincerity of fundamentalists and the malaise in American society, but fears that
fundamentalist thinking could "form the basis of an atavistic
fascism."

1861.   Grounds, Vernon C. "Fundamentalism Needs a Reformation."
Eternity 12 (December 1961): 21-24, 29.

Uses examples of "Jewish traditionalism and Lutheran Protestantism" (for the former, bibical phariseeism and for the
latter, Soren Kierkegaard's critique of 19th century Protestantism), "to help us understand the course of American
Fundamentalism."

1862.   Haiven, Judith. Faith, Hope, No Charity: An Inside Look at the
Born Again Movement in Canada and the United States. Vancouver,
Canada: New Star Books, 1984. 221 p.

1863.   Hearn, Arnold. "Fundamentalist Renascence." Christian Century 75
(30 April 1958): 528-30.

In light of the renascence in intellectual activity of
fundamentalist (conservative evangelical) scholars, the author
pleads for mainline seminaries to give serious attention to
fundamentalist thought.

1864.   Henry, Carl F. H. "The Fundamentalist Phenomenon: The Ricochet of
Silver Bullets." Christianity Today 25 (4 September 1981): 30-31.

A rather positive appraisal of Jerry Falwell, ed., The
Fundamentalist Phenomenon (1981), "a bid for larger evangelical
perspective and cooperation" that "dare not be neglected."

1865.   Hindson, Edward E. "Fundamentalist Education Comes of Age."
Fundamentalist Journal 4 (September 1985): 15.

The future is bright for fundamentalist schools of higher
learning.

1866. Hinson, E. Glenn. "Neo-Fundamentalism: An Interpretation and Critique." Baptist History and Heritage 16 (April 1981): 33-42, 49.

In contrast to some of its earlier manifestations, contemporary fundamentalism shows a decline in the quality of its spokesmen, its theology is truncated and unbalanced, and its social and political involvement tends toward self-righteousness.

1867. Inbody, Tyron. "The Common Ground of Liberals and Fundamentalists." Perspectives in Religious Studies 13 (Fall 1986): 197-206.

"For all their momentous differences, then, liberals and fundamentalists inhabit the same universe of the liberal Western Enlightenment and its heirs: romanticism, modernism, and even post-modernism"; but that universe is being challenged, especially for liberals.

1868. Jaberg, Russell L. "Is There Room for Fundamentalists?" Christianity Today 4 (18 July 1960): 6-7.

Analysis of the pejorative use of the term fundamentalism.

1869. Jenkins, John W. "Toward the Anti-Humanist New Christian Nation." Humanist 41 (July-August 1981): 20-23.

Pat Robertson, James Robison and Jerry Falwell as advocates of a new right-wing religious and cultural America.

1870. Jorstad, Erling. "Two on the Right: A Comparative Look at Fundamentalism and New Evangelicalism." Lutheran Quarterly 23 (May 1971): 107-17.

The "origins, membership, doctrines, and social involvement" of fundamentalism and evangelicalism, whose "many differences must be weighted against the several commitments they share in common."

1871. Keating, Karl. Catholicism and Fundamentalism: The Attack on "Romanism" by "Bible Christians." San Francisco: Ignatius Press. 1988. 360 p.

From the standpoint of traditional Catholic beliefs, the editor of Catholic Answers handles issues raised by the anti-Catholic wing of fundamentalism. Bibliography. Index.

1872.   Lazear, Robert W., Jr. "Fundamentalism's Facades." Eternity 7
          (December 1956): 16-17, 43-44.

          Discusses the facades of legalism, traditionalism, separatism,
          and evangelism.

1873.   Lee, Earl. "Christian Cults: How Fundamentalists React to
          Unitarians and Minority Religious Groups." Religious Humanism 23
          (Summer 1989): 139-44.

          A consideration of the changing meaning of cults, with special
          attention to Walter Martin's The Kingdom of the Cults (new
          edition, 1985); charges Martin with ignoring the changes in
          understanding that have occurred during the past two decades.

1874.   Marsden, George M. "The New Fundamentalism." Reformed Journal 32
          (February 1982): 7-11.

          Analysis of Tim LaHaye, The Battle for the Mind (1980) and
          Falwell, Dobson and Hindson, The Fundamentalist Phenomenon
          (1981), reveals in addition to the traditional "doctrinal
          fundamentalism" of the separatist the existence of the "new"
          fundamentalism, the leading feature of which is its political
          character.

1875.   Marty, Martin E. "Insiders Look at Fundamentalism." Christian
          Century 98 (18 November 1981): 1195-97.

          Review of Falwell, Dobson and Hindson, The Fundamentalist
          Phenomenon (1981) which Marty sees as staking a claim to the
          left of hyper-fundamentalists and to the right of non-
          separatist evangelicals.

1876.   _____. "Modern Fundamentalism." America 155 (27 September
          1986): 133-35.

          Modern as in "modernity": origins are recent; centers on
          choice; inventive, eclectic; and now, "post-modern."

1877.   Marty, Martin E., Joseph Cardinal Bernardin, Rabbi Yechiel
          Eckstein, and Carl F. H. Henry, commentators. "What Others Say
          About Fundamentalism." Fundamentalist Journal 3 (December 1984):
          14-19.

          A series of pro and con statements, analytic Marty and
          sympathetic Bernardin are quite irenic, Epstein and Henry quite
          negative in tone.

1878. McBeth, Leon. "Baptist Fundamentalism: A Cultural Interpretation." Baptist History and Heritage 13 (July 1978): 12-19.

Traces the fundamentalist-moderate controversy in the current Southern Baptist Convention to the debate that began in the 1960s over SBC-published materials, and the hardening of lines since then.

1879. _____. "Fundamentalism in the Southern Baptist Convention in Recent Years." Review and Expositor 79 (Winter 1982): 85-103.

Traces fundamentalism from the Elliott controversy (1960s) to the Broadman commentary series (1970s), the Baptist Faith and Message Fellowship group (formed in 1973), the inerrancy controversies (1970s), to the attempts to capture control of SBC agencies by 1980.

1880. McCune, Rolland D. "The Battle Updated." Central Bible Quarterly 21 (Spring 1978): 31-41.

A presentation at the 21st annual Bible Workshop at Central Baptist Seminary (March 1977), reviewing Harold Lindsell's The Battle for the Bible (1976). Summarizes Lindsell's book and analyzes evangelical reactions to it.

1881. Muesse, Mark William. "The Significance of Contemporary Fundamentalism for Academic Liberal Theology." Ph.D. diss., Harvard University, 1987. 384 p.

1882. Neo-Fundamentalism: The Humanist Response. Buffalo: Prometheus Books, 1988. 186 p.

1883. Olds, Mason. "The Humanist and Fundamentalism." Religious Humanism 23 (Summer 1989): 126-38.

With "the resurgence of fundamentalism, especially its support of the political right," Olds considers its "basic tenets," to determine whether "it can survive the tests of critical reflection required by the humanist"; concludes that "the political philosophy of fundamentalism is as questionable as its theology, and we would do well to repudiate it."

1884. Parker, Monroe. "Wolves in Sheep's Clothing." Central C. B. Quarterly 1 (Summer 1958): 13-16.

Contends that while the old modernism had "utterly failed" and was dead, a "New Modernism," neo-orthodoxy, equally dangerous, had arisen in its place.

1885.   Pickering, Ernest. "What's Wrong With the National Council of
         Churches?" Discerner 6 (January-March 1969): 8-16.

         Presented as rooted in the social gospel of the late 19th
         century, and characterized by "theological liberalism,"
         "political radicalism," and "economic socialism."

1886.   "The Resurgence of Fundamentalism: A Symposium." Humanist
         (January-February 1977): 36-43.

         Essays by leading scholars in response to the resurgence of
         conservative evangelicalism.

1887.   Selvidge, Marla J. Fundamentalism Today: What Makes It So
         Attractive? Elgin: Brethren Press, 1984. 134 p.

         Twelve essays on a variety of subjects from the standpoint of
         those outside the movement.

1888.   Smith, Charles R. "Review Article: The Fundamentalist
         Phenomenon." Grace Theological Journal 3 (Spring 1982): 33-37.

         Sympathetic chapter-by-chapter summary of Jerry Falwell, ed.,
         The Fundamentalist Phenomenon (1981).

1889.   Szasz, Ference Morton. "Religious Fundamentalism and the
         Ecumenical Movement." Ecumenical Trends 12 (May 1983): 70-72.

         Fears of the conservative evangelicals about the ecumenical
         movement, though some possibilities for dialogue on subjects
         like abortion, race, and social programs.

1890.   Tarr, Leslie K. "The Hermetically Sealed World of Neo-Funda-
         mentalism." Eternity 27 (August 1976): 24-27, 46.

         Noting the regularity of attacks by fundamentalists on new
         evangelicals. he presents ten "recurring basic tenets and life
         outlooks that are all completely unrelated to the fundamentals
         of the faith." and which, he contends, reveal "a frightening
         similarity between fundamentalism and the cults."

1891.   Towns, Elmer L. "Trends Among Fundamentalists." Christianity
         Today 17 (6 July 1973): 12-19.

         Fundamentalists, different "in life style and methodology" from
         evangelicals. are building larger campus-style churches.
         emphasizing education, and moving into the media.

1892.   Van Impe, Jack. "I Am a Fundamentalist." Sword of the Lord 43
         (30 December 1977): 1, 10.

         "Includes letters and statements" written in late 1977 by
         numerous prominent fundamentalists, including Jerry Falwell,
         Jack Hyles, and Lee Roberson, among others.

1893.   Wheaton, John F. "Challenging Fundamentalism." America 155 (27
         September 1986): 136-38.

         Facing many defections to "Bible churches" the Catholic Church
         needs to stress identity, evangelicalization, and above all
         else, Bible study.

1894.   Whelan, Timothy D. "Falwell and Fundamentalism." Christianity
         and Crisis 47 (12 October 1987): 328-31.

         Falwell's takeover of the PTL ministry illustrates further that
         he is "no longer a [quintessential] fundamentalist," even
         though he is still so perceived by most non-fundamentalists.

See also items 344, 384, 397, 424, 447, 453, 456, 466, 476, 527, 614, 830,
    1073, 1096, 1282, 1356, 1375, 1516, 1600, 1645, 1698, 1717, 1718,
    1719, 1722, 1725, 1734, 1739, 1800, 1803, 1917, 1919, 1920, 1921,
    1922, 1951, 1965, 1966.

D.   Fundamentalism and Politics

1895.   Averill, Lloyd J. Religious Right, Religious Wrong: A Critique of
         the Fundamentalist Phenomenon. New York: Pilgrim Press, 1989.
         196 p.

         Averill sees fundamentalism in many of its features as "a faith
         turned in upon itself and consequently ungenerous and unlovely
         in its religion, flawed in its understanding of history, and
         dangerous in its politics"; his last chapter, however,
         describes "some important redeeming characteristics in the
         movement." Glossary. Bibliography. Index.

1896.   Blackwelder, Julia Kirk. "Fundamentalist Reactions to the Civil
         Rights Movement Since 1964." Ph.D. diss., Emory University. 1972.
         256 p.

1897.   Bledsoe, W. Craig. "The Fundamentalist Foundations of the Moral
         Majority." Ph.D. diss., Vanderbilt University. 1985. 352 p.

1898.   Bonham, Jerry Lee. "Fundamentalism and the Radical Right: A
         Theoretical Exploration and Analysis." Ph.D. diss., University of
         Illinois at Urbana-Champaign, 1975. 496 p.

1899.   Brinkerhoff, Merlin B., Jeffrey R. Jacob, and Marlene M. Mackie.
         "Mormonism and Moral Majority Make Strange Bedfellows? An
         Exploratory Critique." Review of Religious Research 28 (March
         1987): 236-51.

         The authors conclude that while the two have a "high degree of
         value consensus," traditional hostility against Mormonism by
         conservative Christians makes "ongoing coalitions problematic"
         and alliances will likely occur only on the periphery of both
         movements.

1900.   Brown, L. Duane. Confronting Today's World: A Fundamentalist
         Looks at Social Issues. Schaumburg, IL: Regular Baptist Press,
         1986. 205 p.

         Speaking for the anti-Falwell wing of fundamentalism, Brown
         explores the biblical and theological bases for social action,
         and reviews fourteen social issues; his conclusion is that
         though Christians individually should help others and be good
         citizens, "any social ministry should be limited to believers
         in their needs" and the church must avoid "drifting into purely
         benevolent social activity." Thirty-one-page bibliography.

1901.   Brown, Robert McAfee. "Listen, Jerry Falwell!" Christianity and
         Crisis 40 (22 December 1980): 360-64.

         Scores Falwell's book Listen, America! (1980), for its poor
         sources, selective use of evidence, presuppositions, and for
         using the Bible as the norm for (conservative) economic and
         politial action.

1902.   Bruce, Steve. "The Moral Majority: The Politics of Fundamentalism
         in Secular Society." In Lionel Caplan, ed., Studies in Religious
         Fundamentalism, 177-94. Albany: SUNY Press, 1987. 216 p.

         Analysis of the New Christian Right: rejects status-defense
         theory and inconsistencies-of-status theory, in favor of a
         cultural defense approach: shows the difficulty for a group
         like MM both to enlarge its base and sustain its core
         consistency.

1903.   Buckelew, Roy Edward. "The Political Preaching of Jerry Falwell:
         A Rhetorical Analysis of the Political Preaching of Rev. Jerry

Falwell in Behalf of the Moral Majority During the 1980 Political
Campaign." Ph.D. diss., University of Southern California, 1983.
Two volumes (456 p.).

1904.   Cain, Michael Scott. "Crazies at the Gate: The Religious Right
and the Schools." Humanist 43 (July/August 1983): 16-21, 38.

Presents examples of censorship, describes secular humanism as
presented by the religious right, which he sees as marked by
"paranoid delusion," and concludes that to protect the
schools, non-crazies must "refuse to remain complacent," must
insist that parents "have no right to prescribe education for
all children," and must "demand that our schools be all that
they can be."

1905.   Chandler, Ralph C. "The Wicked Shall Not Bear Rule: The
Fundamentalist Heritage of the New Religious Right." Quarterly
Review (Methodist) 4 (Summer 1984): 8-27.

A critic, Chandler says that parts of the doctrines of the
Second Coming and biblical inerrancy have been re-interpreted
"toward political interest group activity" and placed in the
hands of the electronic church, producing the myth of a pax
Americana.

1906.   Clabaugh, Gary K. Thunder on the Right: The Protestant
Fundamentalists. Chicago: Nelson-Hall, 1974. 261 p.

Description of "fundradists"--like Carl McIntire, Billy James
Hargis, and Edgar Bundy--including their "historical background, ideology, leaders, organizations, resources, methods,
and impact on our contemporary culture." Bibliographical
references. Index.

1907.   Dobson, Edward, and Edward E. Hindson. The Seduction of Power.
Old Tappan, NJ: Revell, 1988. 192 p.

Formerly associated with the Moral Majority and Liberty
University, the authors, through several analyses, question the
effectiveness and direction of the 1980s religious right, but
argue the need for evangelical political involvement.
Bibliography. Index.

1908.   Fackre, Gabriel. The Religous Right and the Christian Faith.
Grand Rapids: Eerdmans, 1982. 126 p.

Tests the "long-standing norms of Scripture and Christian
tradition" against "the substructure of theological belief"
held by the religious right, a movement that "has made its
witness in one area [personal ethics] and remained silent in
major portions of another [social ethics]." Bibliographical
references. Index.

1909.   Falwell, Jerry. "Can We Restore Morality by Political Means?"
         Logos Journal 11 (May-June 1981): 13-15.

         The attempt to do so is well in keeping with American
         principles, and needs to be fostered.

1910.   _____. Listen, America! Garden City, NY: Doubleday, 1980.
         269 p.

         The book that described the reasons for the Moral Majority's
         political involvement, summed up in the statement: "our very
         moral existence is at stake." Bibliography.

1911.   "'Fundamentalists' an Issue in '88 Elections." Christian Beacon
         53 (11 February 1988): 1, 5-6.

         In support of Robertson and a defence of fundamentalism in the
         face of attacks following Robertson's strong showing in the
         Iowa caucuses.

1912.   Gilbert, Timothy Dwain. "Critical Analysis of the Development of
         the New Right in America with Particular Emphasis from 1964 to
         1985." Ph.D. diss., Southwestern Baptist Theological Seminary,
         Fort Worth, TX, 1987. 377 p.

         Sees the New Right "as an attempt at a cultural re-synthesis in
         terms of civil religion"; sections on the rise and decline of
         the Old Right, the recrudescence of evangelical social
         conscience, the rise of the New Right, and an alternate
         synthesis for American churches. Forty-page bibliography.

1913.   Hastey, Stan. "The New Christian Right: Retrospect and Prospect."
         American Baptist Quarterly 6 (December 1987): 264-72.

         Argues that the NCR peaked in the 1980 presidential election
         and slowly lost power through the 1980s. but that it is too
         early to say that the NCR has "died."

1914.   Hill, Samuel S., Jr., and Dennis E. Owen. The New Religious
         Political Right in America. Nashville: Abingdon. 1982. 160 p.

The makeup, operation, and appeal of the New Religious
Political Right in America seen here as a totalitarian movement
to be taken seriously, but one unlikely "to alter the basic
course of American life" because it "is neither biblical nor
Constitutional enough to recommend itself as a constructive
element." Bibliography.

1915.   Hindson, Edward E. "Thunder in the Pulpit: The Social-Political
Involvement of the New Right." Foundations 25 (April-June 1982):
144-52.

A member of the new right answers three questions about its
members: Where did they come from? Why are they getting
involved? Should they get involved? "A new era has dawned for
conservative religion."

1916.   Hofstadter, Richard. "Fundamentalism and Status, Politics on the
Right." Columbia University Forum (Fall 1965): 18-24.

Status politics--the interest in certain moral values; not the
same as interest-group politics--plays a role among the
fundamentalists who give support to right-wing politics,
especially anti-communism.

1917.   Ide, Arthur Frederick. Evangelical Terrorism: Censorship,
Falwell, Robertson, & the Seamy Side of Christian Fundamentalism.
Irving, TX: Scholars Books, 1986. 193 p.

1918.   Johnson, Stephen D., and Joseph B. Tamney. "Support for the Moral
Majority: A Test of a Model." Journal For the Scientific Study of
Religion 23 (June 1984): 183-96.

Study of 284 Muncie, Indiana, residents indicates that "a
Christian Right orientation, cultural ethnocentrism, and
authoritarianism had a major impact on Moral Majority support";
age, education, and religious television had secondary
influence.

1919.   Jorstad, Erling. "The Church in the World: The New Christian
Right." Theology Today 38 (July 1981): 193-200.

The rise of the NCR, its influence mediated especially by means
of the electronic church and direct mail, and an open question
as to whether its influence will increase or diminish.

1920.   _____. "How New is the New Right?" Ecumenist 19 (January-
February 1981): 25-27.

Shares several components with the old right (Hargis, McIntire) but the differences make it a potentially more powerful force: uses full power of the federal government for its morality agenda, and sophisticated technology to get the message across.

1921.   . The New Christian Right, 1981-1988: Prospects for the Post-Reagan Decade. Lewiston, NY: Edwin Mellon, 1987. 286 p.

An update of Jorstad's Evangelicals in the White House (1981), this work describes the NCR's theology, the details of its political ideology, and the mode of its operations, to show how the NCR "has altered the traditional ground rules of blending religion and politics." Bibliographical references. Index.

1922.   . The Politics of Doomsday: Fundamentalists of the Far Right. Nashville: Abingdon, 1970. 190 p.

Uses Carl McIntire, Billy James Hargis, Edgar Bundy and Verne Kaub to describe the creation of the ultrafundamentalist wing, and as exemplars of the theology, ideology, and programs of action espoused by the movement. Bibliographical references. Index.

1923.   Kater, John L., Jr. Christians on the Right: The Moral Majority in Perspective. New York: Seabury, 1982. 157 p.

Thoughtful mainline critique of the Christian right, which Kater faults for its populist cultural perspective and particularly for its failure to truly mirror traditional Christian belief; followed by an appeal to mainstream Protestants to meet the challenge of the Moral Majority. Notes.

1924.   Kauffmann, Donna R. "The New Christian Right: The Network Structure and Support for the Movement." Ph.D. diss., Bowling Green State University, OH, 1987. 175 p.

1925.   Kossel, Clifford G. "The Moral Majority and Christian Politics." Communio: International Catholic Review 9 (Winter 1982): 339-54.

In a generally sympathetic portrayal, Kossel gives the historical origins of the Moral Majority, describes agreements and disagreements--on ecclesial unity and relationship to culture--between evangelicals and Catholics, and notes the lessons Catholics can learn from evangelicals.

1926.   Liebman, Robert C. "Mobilizing the Moral Majority." In The New Christian Right: Mobilization and Legitimation, eds. Robert C. Liebman and Robert Wuthrow, 49-73. New York: Aldine, 1983.

1927.   Linder, Robert D. "Religion and the American Dream: A Study in Confusion and Tension." TSF Bulletin 8 (January-February 1985): 13-17.

The new religious right shares with 17th century Puritans the determination to change the moral and religious climate, but to impose such changes will (as for the Puritans) only lead to frustration and, in the end, the possible destruction of the American dream.

1928.   Maguire, Daniel C. The New Subversives: Anti-Americanism of the Religious Right. New York: Continuum, 1982. 153 p.

Hostile approach to the "fascist" new right, replete with warnings about the "mean purposes" of their programs, designed to "offend both religion and the cause of political peace and justice." Bibliography. Index.

1929.   Marsden, George M. "The New Paganism." Reformed Journal 38 (January 1988): 2-4.

Reflections on the support that the religious right gives to unabashed patriotism.

1930.   _____. "Preacher of Paradox: The New Religious Right in Historical Perspective." In Religion and America: Spirituality in a Secular Age, ed. Mary Douglas and Steven M. Tipton, 150-68. Boston: Beacon, 1983.

A movement "fraught with paradoxes" (Marsden describes at least eight), due to its complex history, fundamentalism offers a "combination of traditions and beliefs that is filled with more ambiguity" than many of its supporters or opposers realize.

1931.   Marty, Martin E. "Fundamentalism as a Social Phenomenon." In Evangelicalism and Modern America, ed. George Marsden, 56-68. Grand Rapids: Eerdmans, 1984.

A revision of an article with the same title In Review and Expositor 79 (Winter 1982): 19-29. While fundamentalism begins with individual religiosity, it then moves into voluntary associations of various kinds and also engages in political expression, the major element described in this finely-nuanced discussion.

1932.   Measures, Royce. "J. Frank Norris: A Forerunner of the New Right." Fides et Historia 15 (Fall-Winter 1982): 61-70.

Overview of Norris's life and description of his political
involvement (especially the 1928 presidential campaign); a
tenuous link from Norris to G. Beauchamp Vick to Jerry Falwell
via Baptist Bible College in Springfield, MO.

1933.   Mouw, Richard J. "Assessing the Moral Majority." Reformed
Journal 31 (June 1981): 13-15.

Five positive and five negative comments.

1934.   _____. "Understanding the Fundamentalists' Retreat." New
Oxford Review 54 (September 1987): 11-15.

1935.   Negri, Maxine. "Humanism Under Fire: The Moral Majority Vs.
Humanism." Humanist 41 (March/April 1981): 4-7, 50.

Briefly surveys the record of attacks on humanism across recent
decades, including several pages of examples of "recent attacks
. . . in newspapers and magazines"; appeal to "stand up and be
counted" as anti-humanism attacks increase.

1936.   Neuhaus, Richard John. "Can the New Right Turn America Around?"
Fundamentalist Journal 4 (July-August 1985): 36-38.

An excerpt from Neuhaus's The Naked Public Square (1984); the
majority of Americans just might agree with the Moral Majority,
in which case the country can be turned around.

1937.   _____. "Richard John Neuhaus on Religion in the Public
Square." Fundamentalist Journal 4 (July-August 1985): 39-40.

In this interview, Neuhaus answers questions about the role of
religion in public life and the role of the New Right in the
present situation.

1938.   _____. "What the Fundamentalists Want." Commentary 79 (May
1985): 41-46.

The American people have always been "determinedly, some would
say incorrigibly, religious"; fundamentalists continue in that
vein, wanting "a few rules changed right away," but they are
not a threat to liberal democracy.

1939.   Pierard, Richard V. "Religion and the New Right in the 1980s."
In Religion and the State, ed. James E. Wood, Jr., 393-417. Waco:
Baylor University Press, 1985.

The New Christian Right in its historical context; its relation
to President Reagan; the Christian schools issue; five
organizations/ movements pursuing the NCR agenda.

1940.   Ribbufo, Leo. The Old Christian Right: The Protestant Far Right
from the Great Depression to the Cold War. Philadelphia: Temple
University Press, 1983. 369 p.

Nuanced study of the careers and complexities of character of
William Dudley Pelley, Gerald B. Winrod, and Gerald L. K.
Smith, whose extremism in the 1930s and 1940s produced both
followers and opponents. Eighty pages of bibliographical
references. Index.

1941.   Roof, Wade Clark. "The New Fundamentalism: Rebirth of Political
Religion in America." In Prophetic Religions and Politics:
Religion and the Social Order, eds. Jeffrey K. Hadden and Anson
Shupe, 18-34. New York: Paragon, 1986.

Roof says that the recovery of some of its own heritage of
political activity, combined with new themes, new demographics,
and a sense of moral crisis, has led to the reemergence of
fundamentalism.

1942.   Simpson, John H. "Some Elementary Forms of Authority and
Fundamentalist Politics." In Prophetic Religions and Politics:
Religion and the Public Order, eds. Jeffrey K. Hadden and Anson
Shupe, 391-409. New York: Paragon, 1986.

Since "societal authority patterns are fundamentally independent of so-called modernization phenomena," fundamentalist
politics in the U.S. "are not a simple function of modernization"; further, fundamentalist politics are more likely in ex
parte (U.S.) than in ex toto (Canada) authority systems.

1943.   Southern, James Richard. "Fundamentalism and Political Activism:
A Study of the New Christian Right." Ph.D. diss., Claremont
Graduate School, 1987. 196 p.

1944.   Stob, Henry. "Fundamentalism and Political Rightism." Reformed
Journal 15 (January 1965): 12-14.

Stob lays out the features of fundamentalist individualism (an
unwitting ally to the spirit of modernity), which "discloses an
inner connection between it [fundamentalism] and political
rightism."

1945.   Sturm, Douglas. "Reagan's New Fundamentalism." Christianity and
         Crisis 45 (26 August 1985): 318-20.

         Reagan's opposition to Nicaragua and support of school prayer
         are examples of the dichotomous nature of the new
         fundamentalism.

1946.   Vinz, Warren L. "The Politics of Protestant Fundamentalism in the
         1950s and 1960s." Journal of Church and State 14 (Spring 1972):
         235-60.

         Represents "the results of some limited empirical studies of
         rank and file Fundamentalists, and it represents the politics
         of key Fundamentalist leaders"; its purpose is to convey what
         the politics of Protestant fundamentalists were "and to
         demonstrate that these political convictions were compatible
         with and justified by their theological convictions."

1947.   Willoughby, William. Does America Need the Moral Majority?
         Plainfield: Haven Books, 1981. 186 p.

         "Yes," says the author in this journalistic account of the
         Moral Majority and the positive role it can play in American
         life. Notes.

1948.   Wood, James E., Jr. "The New Religious Right and Its Implications
         for Southern Baptists." Foundations 25 (April-June 1985): 153-66.

         The NRR differs from earlier fundamentalism in its call to "a
         political theology, a political agenda, and to partisan
         political action." Coupled with the resurgence of
         fundamentalism in the SBC, Wood sees beliefs in the NRR that
         threaten a number of historic SBC stances on political and
         social issues.

1949.   _____. "Religious Fundamentalism and the New Right." Journal
         of Church and State 22 (Autumn 1980): 409-21.

         No one denies the right of fundamentalists to be involved in
         politics; it is "the nature of that involvement which is at
         issue," and of which editor Wood disapproves.

1950.   _____. "Religious Fundamentalism and the Public Schools."
         Journal of Church and State 29 (Winter 1987): 7-17.

         Analyzes the public pressure and the court cases used by
         fundamentalists in the 1980s in their drive against "secular
         humanism."

See also items 59, 379, 704, 725, 726, 778, 888, 890, 894, 897, 920, 925,
936, 942, 944, 945, 947, 1145, 1632, 1649, 1673, 1774, 1788, 1799,
1959, 1964, 1966, 1968, 1971, 1973, 1998, 1999, 2000, 2001, 2002,
2003.

E. Social Science Studies

1951.   Ammerman, Nancy Tatom. Bible Believers: Fundamentalism in the
Modern World. New Brunswick: Rutgers University Press, 1987.
247 p.

An examination of fundamentalist faith and life, based on a
sociologist's research through participant observation of a
fundamentalist congregation in Connecticut. Some history
included. Good analysis. Fourteen-page bibliography.

1952.   Berg, Philip L. "Self-Identified Fundamentalism Among Protestant
Seminaries: A Study of Persistence and Change in Value-Orienta-
tions." Review of Religious Research 12 (Winter 1977): 88-94.

1953.   Burton, Ronald, Stephen D. Johnson, and Joseph B. Tamney.
"Education and Fundamentalism." Review of Religious Research 30
(June 1989): 344-59.

Although there was "a weak, negative relationship between
education and Fundamentalism," "converts to Fundamentalism were
not less educated people" (contrary to the authors' expectations). Finally, "the Fundamentalist perspective differs by
educational group."

1954.   Caplan, Lionel, ed. Studies in Religious Fundamentalism. Albany:
State University of New York Press, 1987. 216 p.

Ten specialists with a "predominantly anthropological emphasis"
discuss movements and organizations within five major world religions from the standpoint of religious fundamentalism. Index.

1955.   Cecil, Kedric Hugh. "Attitudes Toward the Etiology of Psycho-
pathology in Members of a Fundamentalist Christian Church Compared
to Members of a Non-Fundamentalist Church." Ph.D. diss.. United
States International University. 1986. 136 p.

1956.   DeJong. Gordon J.. and Thomas R. Ford. "Religious Fundamentalism
and Denominational Preference in the Southern Appalachian Region."
Journal for the Scientific Study of Religion 5 (October 1965):
24-33.

1957.   Dudley, Robert Louis. "Alienation From Religion in Adolescents
         from Fundamentalist Religious Homes." Journal for the Scientific
         Study of Religion 17 (December 1978): 389-98.

         Study of four hundred Seventh Day Adventist students in
         Adventist secondary schools indicates that alienation
         correlates "with the quality of their relationships with
         parents and other religious authority figures, especially as
         those relationships concern religious values."

1958.   Feagin, Joe R. "Prejudice and Religious Types: A Focused Study of
         Southern Fundamentalists." Journal for the Scientific Study of
         Religion 4 (October 1964): 3-13.

         1963 study of five Southern Baptist congregations in Texas and
         Oklahoma, supporting the idea that, contrary to the view that
         church members are more prejudiced than non-members, there are
         different types of church members displaying a variety of
         prejudice attitudes (though some tie emerged between
         fundamentalism and prejudice).

1959.   Georgianna, Sharon Linzey. "The Moral Majority and Fundamen-
         talism: Plausibility and Dissonance." Ph.D. diss., Indiana
         University, 1984. 178 p.

1960.   Gilbert, Earl Jean. "Some Personality Correlates of Certain
         Religious Beliefs, Attitudes, Practices, and Experiences in
         Students Attending a Fundamentalist Pentecostal Church College."
         Ed.D. diss., The University of Tennessee, 1972. 127 p.

1961.   Gorman, Benjamin Lee. "Fundamentalism and the Frontier: Value
         Clusters in the Texas Panhandle." Ph.D. diss., Tulane University,
         1965. 212 p.

1962.   Gray, Virginia. "Anti-Evolution Sentiment and Behaviour: The Case
         of Arkansas." Journal of American History 57 (September 1970):
         352-66.

         Gray uses Arkansas' 1928 anti-evolution law, the only one to be
         enacted through the initiative, to test the conventional theory
         about the social characteristics of fundamentalism, and finds
         support for only some features of the theory.

1963.   Gustafson, Cloyd V. "The Sociology of Fundamentalism: A Topo-
         logical Analysis Based on Selected Groups in Portland, Oregon, and
         Vicinity." Ph.D. diss., The University of Chicago. 1956. 479 p.

1964.   Hadden, Jeffrey K., and Anson Shupe, eds. Religion and the
         Political Order. Vol. 3: Secularization and Fundamentalism
         Reconsidered. New York: Paragon House, 1989.

1965.   Hartz, Gary W., and Henry C. Everett. "Fundamentalist Religion
         and Its Effect on Mental Health." Journal of Religion and Health
         28 (Fall 1989): 207-17.

             "[W]e outline assertions about the mental problems caused by
             membership in fundamentalist religion, illustrate these with
             two case histories, briefly discuss intervention strategies and
             describe conceptual and empirical issues"; "a causal link
             between . . . symptoms and . . . religious membership has not
             yet been established."

1966.   Hendricks, John Stephen. "Religious and Political Fundamentalism:
         The Links Between Alienation and Ideology." Ph.D. diss., The
         University of Michigan, 1977. Two volumes (489 p.).

             Hendricks demonstrates that fundamentalism, far from being a
             shrinking segment of the church, has expanded in the 1960s and
             has come to include not only working class but middle class
             congregations.

1967.   Hittle, Gary Dean. "The Relationship Between Extreme Religious
         Fundamentalism and Non-Actualizing Modes of Intrapersonal and
         Marital Adjustment." Ph.D. diss., United States International
         University, 1977. 175 p.

1968.   Hood, Ralph W., Jr., and Ronald J. Morris. "Boundary Maintenance,
         Social-Political Views, and Presidential Preference Among High and
         Low Fundamentalists." Review of Religious Research 27 (December
         1985): 134-45.

             Tests the assumption that to be conservative in religious
             matters is to be conservative in extra-religious matters;
             concludes that while fundamentalists share certain religious
             beliefs, "on broader social and political issues [they] are as
             divergent as other groups."

1969.   Hood, Ralph W., Jr., Ronald J. Morris, and P. J. Watson.
         "Maintenance of Religious Fundamentalism." Psychological Reports
         59 (October 1986): 547-59.

1970.   Hudson, Charles. "The Structure of a Fundamentalist Christian
         Belief System." In Religion and the Solid South, ed. Samuel S.
         Hill Jr., 122-42. Nashville: Abingdon, 1972.

Anthropologist Hudson argues that, like some nonwestern
religions, southern fundamentalism holds to the (apparently)
contradictory beliefs of both supernatural justice and fate,
which does not weaken the system but "is largely responsible
for the generality of the system."

1971.   Jelen, Ted G. "The Effects of Religious Separatism on Partisan
Identification, Voting Behaviour, and Issue Positions Among
Evangelicals and Fundamentalists in 1984." Sociological Analysis
48 (Spring 1987): 30-45.

Based on the General Social Survey of 1985, this study suggests
that "fundamentalists are significantly more likely to trans-
late personal values into demands for the legal enforcement of
those values than are evangelicals, though both groups are
personally conservative on moral issues."

1972.   Lechner, Frank J. "Fundamentalism and Socio-Cultural Revitaliza-
tion in America: A Sociological Interpretation." Sociological
Analysis 46 (Fall 1985): 243-60.

Uses action-theory to understand Puritanism and the first,
second and third awakenings, and asserts that "fundamentalism
can no longer be seen as merely reactive, and fundamentalism
and modernity can no longer be treated simply as polar
opposites."

1973.   Liebman, Robert C., and Robert Wuthnow, eds. The New Christian
Right: Mobilization and Legitimation. New York: Aldine, 1983.
256 p.

Twelve chapters, drawing on original research and all
previously unpublished, by eleven authors from sociology,
political science, and religious studies, on the general shape
of the movement, "the forms of its mobilization, the character
of its constituency, and the major tenets of its ideology," and
a section on the cultural environment of the NCR. Twelve-page
bibliography. Index.

1974.   Lupfer, Michael B., Patricia L. Hopkinson, and Patricia Kelley.
"An Exploration of the Attributional Styles of Christian
Fundamentalists and of Authoritarians." Journal for the
Scientific Study of Religion 27 (September 1988): 389-98.

Contrary to the usual view, the authors find "no evidence of a
distinctive attributional style among Christian fundamentalists," while authoritarians "committed more normative attribu-

tional errors" but "were less inclined than nonauthoritarians to use dispositional explanations when such explanations were expected."

1975. Mathisen, Gerald S., and James A. Mathisen. "The New Fundamentalism: A Sociohistorical Approach to Understanding Theological Change." Review of Religious Research 30 (September 1988): 18-32.

Rhetorical-critical analysis of 100 articles from Fundamentalist Journal, 1982-1984, indicates "conservative religious cognitive bargaining with the more secular culture, especially by its renegotiation of symbolic boundaries."

1976. McCall, Clarence Victor, Jr. "An Investigation of the Differences in Religious Conflict and Anxiety Among Religiously Fundamentalist Students Enrolled in Hiwassee College, Johnson Bible College, and The University of Tennessee, Knoxville." Ed.D. diss., The University of Tennessee, 1981. 229 p.

1977. Miller, Wesley Edward, Jr. "A Sociological Analysis of the New Christian Right." Ph.D. diss., Loyola University of Chicago, 1984. 206 p.

1978. Monaghan, Robert R. "Three Faces of the True Believer: Motivations for Attending a Fundamentalist Church." Journal for the Scientific Study of Religion 6 (Fall 1967): 236-45.

Members of a midwestern church fall into one of three categories: authority-seekers, comfort-seekers, social participators.

1979. O'Donohue, John. "Fundamentalism: A Psychological Problem." AFER: African Ecclesial Review 29 (December 1987): 344-50.

1980. Penner, David Robert. "The MMPI Religious Fundamentalism Content Scale Related to Personality Characteristics of Psychiatric Inpatients." Ph.D. diss., Western Conservative Baptist Seminary, 1983.

1981. Perry, Everett L. "Socio-Economic Factors in American Fundamentalism." Review of Religious Research 1 (Summer 1959): 57-61.

Summary of Perry's 1959 University of Chicago Ph.D. dissertation entitled "The Role of Socio-Economic Factors in the Rise and Development of American Fundamentalism," which explains fundamentalism, "a reactionary tendency in religion," in terms of five factors.

1982.   Peshkin, Alan. <u>God's Choice: The Total World of a Fundamentalist</u>
         <u>Christian School</u>. Chicago: University of Chicago Press, 1986.
         349 p.

         The result of an eighteen-month study, this work presents with
         sympathy and understanding the picture of the special world of
         a fundamentalist school; an unusual inside view of the workings
         and dynamics of this fast-growing segment of education.
         Appendixes. Bibliography. Index.

1983.   Photiadis, John D., and John F. Schnabel. "Religion: A Persistent
         Institution in a Changing Appalachia." <u>Review of Religious</u>
         <u>Research</u> 19 (Fall 1977): 32-42.

         Study of 1,051 adult male heads of households in West Virginia
         "suggests that fundamentalism persists because it acts as a
         buffer for the large number of rural and low income
         Appalachians who feel alienated because of dislocations that
         took place in the region in the last few decades."

1984.   Ray, Vernon Oliver. "A Rhetorical Analysis of the Political
         Preaching of The Reverend Jerry Falwell: The Moral Majority
         Sermons, 1979." Ph.D. diss., The Louisiana State University and
         Agricultural and Mechanical College, 1985. 276 p.

1985.   Rhodes, Albert Lewis. "The Effects of Status, Social Participa-
         tion, Religious Fundamentalism, and Alienation on a Measure of
         Authoritarianism." Ph.D. diss., Vanderbilt University, 1956.
         272 p.

1986.   Richardson, James T. "New Forms of Deviancy in a Fundamentalist
         Church: A Case Study." <u>Review of Religious Research</u> 16 (Winter
         1975): 134-41.

         Study of the dismissal of a church member over a financial (not
         doctrinal) matter to illustrate the concepts of boundary main-
         tenance, moral entrepreneurship, and degradation ceremonies.

1987.   Richardson, James T., Mary White Stewart, and Robert B. Simmonds.
         "Conversion to Fundamentalism." In <u>In Gods We Trust: New Patterns</u>
         <u>of Religious Pluralism in America</u>, eds. Tony Robbins and Dick
         Anthony, 127-39. New Brunswick: Transaction, 1981.

         Investigation of the Christ Communal Organization by means of a
         five-element conversion model (mostly social factors):
         supported by the data, but further investigation is needed.

1988. _____. "Researching a Fundamentalist Commune." In Understanding t. New Religions, eds. Jacob Needleman and George Baker, 235-51. New York: Seabury, 1978.

> Comparison of research methods between the Richardson group and the Robbins, Anthony, Curtis research team, the former being the more successful; with implications for the conduct of research on evangelical groups.

1989. Rogers, Martha L. "A Fundamentalist Church as an Autonomous Community and Its Relationship to the Larger Community." Journal of Psychology and Theology 3 (Summer 1975): 210-15.

> A partially-flawed study of a small congregation (twenty families) supports the hypotheses of autonomy and separation.

1990. Scanzoni, John. "Resurgent Fundamentalism: Marching Backward into the '80s?" Christian Century 97 (10-17 September 1980): 847-49.

> Using Troeltsch's model, Scanzoni sees earlier fundamentalism (sect) moving to evangelicalism (church) and now back to fundamentalism (reverting to sect).

1991. Shriver, Peggy L. "Guardians of Fundamentalism's Fortress." New Catholic World 288 (January-February 1985): 15-19.

> Sociological and psychological dimensions of fundamentalism.

1992. Simmonds, Robert B., James T. Richardson, and Mary W. Harder. "A Jesus Movement Group: An Adjective Check List Assessment." Journal for the Scientific Study of Religion 15 (December 1976): 323-37.

> "Reports results of a personality assessment of members of a fundamentalist Jesus movement commune"; compared with a normative group, "the results generally indicate a 'maladaptive' pattern of self-conceptions" (with qualifications due to "substantial cultural differences" in the two groups).

1993. Smith, William Henry. "A Psychological Study of Three Non-Roman Religious Attitudes: Modernism. Fundamentalism. Catholicism." Ph.D. diss., The Hartford Seminary. 1925.

1994. Stones, Christopher R. "The Jesus People: Fundamentalism and Changes in Factors Associated With Conservatism." Journal for the Scientific Study of Religion 17 (June 1978): 155-58.

Caucasian members of the Jesus movement in South Africa, says
Stones, are "more Biblically fundamentalistic, and less
conservative, less militaristic, less antihedonistic, and less
ecclesiastically fundamentalistic" than their mainline peers.

1995.   Tamney, Joseph B., and Stephen D. Johnson. "Fundamentalism and
Self-Actualization." Review of Religious Research 30 (March
1989): 276-86.

1981 study of 281 Muncie, IN, residents found no direct
relation, positive or negative, between fundamentalism and
self-actualization, leading the authors to conclude that
self-actualization ideology has affected fundamentalist
thinking more than the authors anticipated.

1996.   ____. "The Moral Majority in Middletown." Journal for the
Scientific Study of Religion 22 (June 1983): 145-57.

Support for the Moral Majority has three independent sources:
"persuasion via religious television;" an attitude "that
desires continuation of the status quo"; appeal "to those who
have a Christian Right perspective."

1997.   Tekippe, Charles John. "Religious Fundamentalism, Paranoia and
Homicide: A Further Exploration of the Gastil-Hackney Southern
Subculture of Violence Thesis." Ph.D. diss., The University of
Texas at Austin, 1984. 264 p.

1998.   Vinz, Warren L. "A Comparison Between Elements of Protestant
Fundamentalism and McCarthyism." Ph.D. diss., The University of
Utah, 1968. 280 p.

1999.   Wilcox, Clyde. "America's Radical Right Revisited: A Comparison
of the Activists in Christian Right Organizations From the 1960s
and the 1980s." Sociological Analysis 48 (Spring 1987): 46-57.

Members of the Ohio Moral Majority in 1982 and the Christian
Anti-Communism Crusade in 1962 display some differences but
resemble each other in significant ways: education, occupation,
and conservative political thought.

2000.   ____. "Evangelicals and Fundamentalists in the New Christian
Right: Religious Differences in the Ohio Moral Majority." Journal
for the Scientific Study of Religion 25 (September 1986): 355-63.

Suggests "the utility of differentiating between fundamentalists and evangelicals in future research," because

fundamentalists "are more likely than evangelicals to perceive a strong connection between their political and religious beliefs," and evangelicals "are more politically active and sophisticated."

2001. _____. "The Fundamentalist Voter: Politicized Religious Identity and Political Attitudes and Behavior." Review of Religious Research 31 (September 1989): 54-67.

Explores "one of the main fault lines in the evangelical community: the difference between fundamentalists and other evangelicals," concluding that only given the influence of elites, seeking a "politicized group consciousness," are fundamentalists more conservative, more Republican, than other evangelicals.

2002. _____. "Political Action Committees of the New Christian Right: A Longitudinal Analysis." Journal For the Scientific Study of Religion 27 (March 1988): 60-71.

Uses data from the Federal Election Commission and the resource mobilization theory to disclose the strategy and tactics of the NCR PACs to back nonincumbents (usually) in close races.

2003. Will, Jeffry, and Rhys Williams. "Research Note: Political Ideology and Political Action in the New Christian Right." Sociological Analysis 47 (Summer 1986): 160-68.

Uses the Tamney and Johnson Muncie, Indiana, data to search for differential effects from politicized televangelists vs. salvation-oriented televanglists, but no significant differences emerge; suggestions for further study.

See also items 912, 1145, 1146, 1153, 1632, 1649, 1673, 1679, 1685, 1694, 1727, 1751, 1846, 1859, 1902, 1917, 1918, 1931, 1942.

V

PENTECOSTALISM

A. Origins

2004. Bartleman, Frank. Azusa Street. With a foreword by Vinson Synan. Plainfield: Logos, 1980. 184 p.

Reprint of Bartleman's 1925 book, How Pentecost Came to Los Angeles--How It Was in the Beginning, his eyewitness account of the Azusa Street revival in 1906 and the effects in the years following. to 1910. Helpful introduction by Vinson Synan.

2005. Brandt-Bessire, Daniel. Aux Sources de la Spiritualite Pente-cotiste. Paris: Labor et Fides, 1986. 222 p.

Discusses theological and ethical influences on the pentecostal movement, examining such antecedents as the Wesleyan and Keswick movements and the Welsh Revival. An important book. Extensive bibliography.

2006. Davison, Leslie. Pathway to Power: The Charismatic Movement in Historical Perspective. Watchung, NJ: Charisma Books, 1971. 93 p.

Popular study of charismatic matters--the Bible, Wesley, the holiness movement--down to 1900.

2007. Dayton, Donald W. The Theological Roots of Pentecostalism. Metuchen, NJ: Scarecrow Press, 1987. 199 p.

Uses the four-fold view of Christ--Savior. Sanctifier. Leader. Christ King--to show that penteoostalism derives from the Wesleyan tradition In the nineteenth century Holiness Movement. Helpful bibliographical essay. Index.

2008. _____. "Theological Roots of Pentecostalism." Pneuma 2 (Spring 1980): 3-21.

With the foursquare gospel as a paradigm. Dayton points up both the Methodist and Reformed roots of pentecostalism by way of the 19th century holiness movement. A condensed version of Dayton's University of Chicago dissertation and his book of the same title (1987). A similar article is his "Toward a Theological Analysis of Pentecostalism." In The Distinctiveness of Pentecostal-Charismatic Theology. D1-D26. Fifteenth Annual Meeting, Society for Pentecostal Studies, Mother of God Community, Gaithersburg, MD: 1985.

2009.   Del Monte Sol, Teresa. "Pentecostalism and the Doctrine of Saint Teresa and Saint John of the Cross." Spiritual Life 17 (Spring 1971): 21-33.

Fourteen characteristics of pentecostalism that are evident to some degree in the writings of these two mystics.

2010.   Dieter, Melvin E. "Wesleyan-Holiness Aspects of Pentecostal Origins: As Mediated Through the 19th Century Holiness Revival." In Aspects of Pentecostal-Charismatic Origins, ed. Vinson Synan, 55-80. Plainfield: Logos, 1975.

2011.   Goff, James Rudolph, Jr. Fields White Unto Harvest: Charles F. Parham and the Missionary Origins of Pentecostalism. Fayetteville: The University of Arkansas Press, 1988. 255 p.

2012.   Hunter, Harold D. "Spirit-Baptism and the 1896 Revival in Cherokee County, North Carolina." Pneuma 5 (Fall 1983): 1-17.

Extensive research leads Hunter to conclude that leaders of the Church of God (Cleveland) and the Church of God of Prophecy likely got their formulations from the Azusa Street revival of 1906, not the 1896 revival.

2013.   McGee, Gary B. "The Azusa Street Revival and Twentieth Century Missions." International Bulletin of Missionary Research 12 (April 1988): 58-61.

The missionary thrust that resulted from the Azusa Street revival produced characteristics unique to pentecostal missions: signs and wonders. indigenous churches. democratic leveling in the churches. missionary education. and a pragmatic view of organizational development.

2014.   _____. "A Brief History of the Modern Pentecostal Outpouring." Paraclete 18 (Spring 1984): 18-23.

From the 19th century to Azusa Street, and the organizations
that developed.

2015.   . "This Gospel Shall Be Preached": A History and Theology
of Assemblies of God Foreign Missions to 1959. Springfield, MO:
Gospel Publishing House, 1986. 288 p.

Based on a dissertation (St. Louis University), this volume
explores the history and missiology of the largest of the
Pentecostal denominations and one of the most important strands
in the twentieth century world missions movement.
Fifty-seven-page bibliography.

2016.   Menzies, William W. "The Non-Wesleyan Origins of the Pentecostal
Movement." In Aspects of Pentecostal-Charismatic Origins, ed.
Vinson Synan, 81-98. Plainfield: Logos, 1975.

Influences from (non-Wesleyan) fundamentalism and from Keswick
teaching, in the context of the "finished work" and "oneness"
controversies, 1910-1916.

2017.   Minor, John E. "The Mantle of Elijah: Nineteenth Century Primitive Methodism and Twentieth Century Pentecostalism." Proceedings
of the Wesley Historical Society 43 (December 1982): 141-49.

The 19th century Primitive Methodists in this British study
were democratic, lay-oriented, socially based among the poor,
and had church activities and spirituality that have to a large
extent become part of pentecostal experience.

2018.   Myland, D. Wesley, G. F. Taylor, and B. F. Lawrence. Three Early
Pentecostal Tracts, with a preface by Donald Dayton. New York:
Garland, 1985. 215, 138, 119 p.

Contents: The Latter Rain Covenant and Pentecostal Power
(1910), by D. Wesley Myland; The Spirit and the Bride (1907),
by G. F. Taylor; The Apostolic Faith Restored (1916), by B. F.
Lawrence.

2019.   Reed, David Arthur. "Aspects of the Origins of Oneness
Pentecostalism." In Aspects of Pentecostal-Charismatic Origins.
ed. Vinson Synan, 143-68. Plainfield: Logos, 1975.

Synopsis of Reed's Boston University dissertation which sees
oneness doctrine originating in the 19th century, forming in
1913-1916, and operating as "a non-ethnic, sectarian expression
of Jewish Christianity."

2020.   _____. "Origins and Development of the Theology of Oneness
Pentecostalism in the United States." Pneuma 1 (Spring 1979):
31-37.

Summary of his 1978 Ph.D. dissertation of the same title at
Boston University.

2021.   Robeck, Cecil M., Jr. "The International Significance of Azusa
Street." Pneuma 8 (Spring 1986): 1-4.

Some comments about the bibliography of the Azusa Street
revival.

2022.   Strachan, Gordon. "Theological and Cultural Origins of the 19th
Century Pentecostal Movement." In Essays on Apostolic Themes, ed.
Paul Elbert, 144-57. Peabody, MA: Hendrickson, 1985.

Three Scottish ministers--John McLeod Campbell, Alexander J.
Scott, Edward Irving--together "produced the first clearly
understood and theologically based Pentecost since the early
days of the church."

2023.   Synan, Vinson, ed. Aspects of Pentecostal-Charismatic Origins.
Plainfield: Logos, 1975. 252 p.

Eleven papers from the third annual meeting of the Society for
Pentecostal Studies, 1973, covering a variety of historical and
theological subjects. Bibliographical references. Index.

2024.   _____. "Beginnings: Azusa Street--The Roots of Revival."
Logos Journal 11 (March-April 1981): 10-13.

Survey of the Azusa Street revival and its worldwide results,
and five reflections on the meaning and continuation of the
revival in the present.

2025.   _____. The Holiness-Pentecostal Movement in the United States.
Grand Rapids: Eerdmans, 1971. 248 p.

Based on Synan's 1974 University of Georgia Ph.D. dissertation;
sets the pentecostal-holiness tradition in the context of U.S.
social and intellectual history, and argues that "the
historical and doctrinal lineage of American pentecostalism is
to be found in the Wesleyan tradition"; covers from the 1860s
to the 1960s. Bibliography. Index.

2026.   _____. "The Holiness-Pentecostal Movement." Paraclete 23
(Fall 1989): 1-8.

Describes historically the response to "The Biblical Call to Holiness," discusses "Responses to Pentecostalism," and "The Unfinished Theological Task," emphasizing again the call to holiness, a call that, "for many Pentecostals . . . has ceased to be part of the personal spiritual agenda."

2027.   ____. "A New Third Force in Christendom: Part 1." Charisma 10 (November 1984): 92-96, 103-105. "The Latter Rain Falls in America." Charisma 10 (December 1984): 71-72, 77-78, 80, 83, 85-86. "Pentecost Scorned, Pentecost Reconsidered." Charisma 10 (January 1985): 54-56, 76, 78-80. "The Renewal Intensified." Charisma 10 (February 1985): 73-74, 76, 79, 81-82, 84.

Four excerpts from Synan's book In the Latter Days (1984), tracing the Holy Spirit awakening from the early church to the 19th and 20th centuries, its initial rejection by many and its ultimate approval and continued extension by the 1960s and 1970s.

2028.   ____. "The Role of the Holy Spirit and the Gifts of the Spirit in the Mystical Tradition." One in Christ 10, no. 2 (1974): 193-202.

The reality if not the name of the baptism in the Holy Spirit can be found in the mystical tradition; there are both similarities and differences In the phenomena in pentecostalism and the mystical tradition.

2029.   Valdez, A. C., Sr., with James F. Scheer. Fire on Azusa Street. Costa Mesa, CA: Gift, 1980. 139 p.

Eyewitness account by a man present during the Azusa Street revival of 1906 and who went on to a long career as a pentecostal evangelist.

2030.   Warner, Wayne E., ed. Touched by the Fire: Eyewitness Accounts of the Early Twentieth-Century Pentecostal Revival. Plainfield: Logos, 1978. 163 p.

Popular, brief accounts by thirty-five of the early 20th century participants in the pentecostal revival.

See also items 38, 39, 693, 694, 695, 790, 876, 1449, 1450, 1457, 1459, 1463, 2032, 2077, 2110, 2152, 2171, 2335, 2555.

B. History

2031.   Alexander, David A. "Bishop J. H. King and the Emergence of
Holiness Pentecostalism." Pneuma 8 (Fall 1986): 159-83.

Life and teachings of an early leader in the Pentecostal Holiness denomination, a group advocating a three-stage work of the
Spirit: justification, entire sanctification, Spirit-baptism
accompanied by glossolalia.

2032.   Anderson, Robert Mapes. Vision of the Disinherited: The Making of
American Pentecostalism. New York: Oxford University Press, 1979.
334 p.

Excellent study of the development of pentecostalism to the
1930s, from the standpoint of social and psychological origins.
Study of forty-five pentecostal leaders. Thirty-six-page
bibliography. Index.

2033.   Barfoot, Charles H., and Gerald T. Sheppard. "Prophetic vs.
Priestly Religion: The Changing Role of Women Clergy in Classical
Pentecostal Churches." Review of Religious Research 22 (September
1980): 2-17.

Documents "the shift in Pentecostalism from 'prophetic'
religion (1901 to 1920s), in which women played key roles in
the founding and functioning of churches, to 'priestly'
religion (since the 1920s), in which women's roles have
declined."

2034.   Bicket, Zenas J. "Fashioned by the Spirit." Pentecostal Evangel
no. 3908 (2 April 1989): 4-9.

One of several articles in this issue relating to the 75th
anniversary of the Assemblies of God; by the president of the
denomination's Berean College.

2035.   Blumhofer, Edith Waldvogel. "American Pentecostalism in
Historical Perspective." Paraclete 19 (Winter 1985): 10-14.

Late 19th century evangelicalism emphasized Spirit baptism and
divine healing; "[b]y the first decades of the 20th century
this concept was the province of the Pentecostals."

2036.   _____. The Assemblies of God: A Chapter in the Story of
American Pentecostalism. Volume 1: to 1941. Springfield, MO:
Gospel Publishing House, 1989.

2037.   _____. "Divided Pentecostals: Bakker vs. Swaggart." <u>Christian Century</u> 104 (6 May 1987): 430-31.

The feud between Swaggart and Bakker "helps illumine internal tensions that some think threaten to polarize this fast-growing Pentecostal community. At issue is the basic definition of Pentecostalism, especially in its relationship to culture."

2038.   _____. "The 'Overcoming' Life: A Study in the Reformed Evangelical Contribution to Pentecostalism." <u>Pneuma</u> 1 (Spring 1979): 7-19.

In a summary of her Harvard 1977 Ph.D. dissertation entitled "The 'Overcoming Life': A Study in the Reformed Evangelical Origins of Pentecostalism," she contends for a Reformed influence on pentecostalism (especially the Assemblies of God) in three areas: premillennialism, an "overcoming" life rather than the Wesleyan "second blessing," and a practical emphasis on divine healing.

2039.   _____. "A Woman Used by the Spirit." <u>Paraclete</u> 21 (Summer 1987): 5-9.

Account of Marie Burgess and the beginnings of Glad Tidings Tabernacle, established in 1907 as New York City's first pentecostal mission.

2040.   Bromiley, Geoffrey W. "The Charismata in Christian History." <u>Theology, News and Notes</u> 20 (March 1974): 3-5, 24.

Traces charismata in the church from the post-apostolic age to the modern era, calling for "a comprehensive reassessment of charismata."

2041.   Brooks, M. Paul. "Bible Colleges and the Expansion of the Pentecostal Movement." <u>Paraclete</u> 23 (Spring 1989): 9-17.

Brief survey of the role of the Bible college as an educational force among pentecostals, especially in the Assemblies of God.

2042.   Brumback, Carl. <u>Like a River</u>. Springfield, MO: Gospel Publishing House, 1977. 169 p.

Narrative, heavy with the persons involved, of the Assemblies of God from its founding in 1914 to the late 1920s. Appendix. Bibliography. Index. Originally published as Part Two of the author's <u>Suddenly . . . From Heaven</u> (1961).

2043.   . A Sound From Heaven. Springfield, MO: Gospel
           Publishing House, 1977. 153 p.

           Detailed narrative of the early years of pentecostalism, 1900
           to 1910. Originally published as Part One of the author's
           Suddenly . . . From Heaven (1961). Bibliography. Index.

2044.   Bundy, David D. "Louis Dalliere: Apologist for Pentecostalism in
           France and Belgium, 1932-1939." Pneuma 10 (Fall 1988): 85-115.

           Study of one who "has long been ignored in the historiography
           of Pentecostalism and of the French and Belgian Protestant
           churches." Includes appendix (pp. 111-15): "Bibliography of
           Louis Dalliere, 1932-1939."

2045.   Chappell, Paul Gale. "The Divine Healing Movement in America."
           Ph.D. diss., Drew University, 1983. 410 p.

2046.   Damboriena, Prudencio. Tongues as of Fire: Pentecostalism in
           Contemporary Christianity. Washington: Corpus Books, 1969.
           256 p.

2047.   Davies, Horton. "Threat or Promise?" Expository Times 76 (March
           1965): 197-99.

           Review of Nils Bloch-Hoehl, The Pentecostal Movement (1964),
           "the best study of Pentecostalism yet to have appeared," but in
           need of updating.

2048.   Davis, Arnor S. "The Pentecostal Movement in Black Christianity."
           Black Church 2 (1972): 65-88.

           Memories of the author's experiences in a small Georgia town in
           the 1930s and 1940s, and in a community program in Washington,
           DC, in the 1950s and 1960s.

2049.   Dayton, Donald W. "The Evolution of Pentecostalism." Covenant
           Quarterly 32 (August 1974): 28-40.

           Seeing Pentecostalism as "a complex or gestalt of theological
           ideas." he discusses roots. traces origins and early
           development. and concludes with a brief consideration of
           "Neo-Pentecostalism" or the "Charismatic Movement."

2050.   Dollar, George W. "Who's Who in the New Pentecostalism." Central
           Bible Quarterly 19 (Fall 1976): 2-5.

Lists twenty-seven pentecostals and charismatics, with annotations on denomination, education, and publications.

2051. Du Plessis, David J. "Golden Jubilees of Twentieth Century Pentecostal Movements." International Review of Missions 47 (1958): 193-201.

Beginnings of the 20th century pentecostal movement, and its global extension through fifty years.

2052. _____. The Spirit Bade Me Go: The Astounding Move of God in the Denominational Churches. Dallas: David J. du Plessis, 1961. Rev. ed. Plainfield: Logos, 1970. 122 p.

A potpourri of talks and lectures by "Mr. Pentecost" on some of the distinctives in pentecostalism and its place in the ecumenical movement.

2053. Durasoff, Steve. Bright Wind of the Spirit: Pentecostalism Today. Englewood Cliffs: Prentice-Hall, 1972. 277 p.

Pentecostalism in the 20th century, Oral Roberts (two chapters), the charismatic renewal, and pentecostals in Russia, done appreciatively by a professor at Oral Roberts University. Bibliography. Index.

2054. Forster, Greg S. "The Third Arm: Pentecostal Christianity." TSF Bulletin. Part 1, 63 (Summer 72): 5-9; Part 2, 64 (Autumn 72): 16-21.

Definition of pentecostalism (including the charismatics), antecedents and growth of the movement, its general beliefs, and a detailed, sympathetic study of the pentecostal experience, followed by reasons why pentecostalism arouses opposition.

2055. Fry, C. George. "Pentecostalism in Historical Perspective." Springfielder 39 (March 1976): 183-93.

A Missouri Synod Lutheran contends that despite some differences, pentecostalism and liberalism "have much more in common than in opposition"; based on his reading of sociological data, historical distortions, and repudiation of theology and a rejection of biblical authority.

2056. Garlock, Ruthanne. "Women: Pentecost and the Release of Women in Ministry." Logos Journal 11 (March-April 1981): 42, 44-45.

Biblical examples of women in ministry, the presence of many
women leaders, especially early in the pentecostal movement,
and women in the charismatic movement.

2057.   Gilbert, Arthur. "Pentecost Among the Pentecostals." Christian
Century 78 (28 June 1961): 794-96.

An American Jewish rabbi reports on a pentecostal conference in
Jerusalem, coming away with both apprehension about pentecostal
zeal and a feeling of common ground that might lead to
conversations with Catholics, Protestants and Jews.

2058.   Gott, Lois. "Donald Gee: The Apostle of Balance." In Essays on
Apostolic Themes: Studies in Honour of Howard M. Ervin, ed. Paul
Elbert, 173-83. Peabody, MA: Hendrickson, 1985.

British pentecostal Gee (1891-1966) balanced his pentecostalism
with ecumenism, and had a balanced view of divine healing.

2059.   Harrell, David Edwin, Jr. All Things are Possible: The Healing
and Charismatic Revivals in Modern America. Bloomington: Indiana
University Press, 1975. 622 p.

Study of the major figures in healing revival history,
1947-1975; doctrines, claims, successes, and failures, and the
principal themes of the revival; 1958 was the transition year
to a new phase, successfully transited by some, but not all;
places "the charismatic movement in a historical perspective."
Fifteen-page bibliographical essay. Index.

2060.   Hart, Larry D. "Problems of Authority in Pentecostalism." Review
and Expositor 75 (Spring 1978): 249-66.

Historical/sociological description of pentecostalism's
charismatic personalities, bureaucracies, and developing and
hardening traditions, together with the contemporary problem of
authoritarian leadership that affects both pentecostal and
charismatic groups.

2061.   Hocken, Peter. "The Pentecostal-Charismatic Movement as Revival
and Renewal." Pneuma 3 (Spring 1981): 31-47.

Terminology differences--revival and renewal--between
pentecostals and charismatics; the differences "symbolize the
way in which division between Christians limits the work of
God"; the resolution of the differences is to see continuity
and complementarity in the terminology.

2062.   _____. "Wiser Than Human Wisdom." Theology, News and Notes 30
         (March 1983): 8-12, 34.

         Description of the general pentecostal movement in the 20th
         century, and a theology of the work of the Holy Spirit in
         conversion and in baptism in the Spirit.

2063.   Hollenweger, Walter J. "Charisma and Oikoumene: The Pentecostal
         Contribution to the Church Universal." One in Christ 7, no. 4
         (1971): 324-43.

         Challenges the following misconceptions about pentecostalism:
         it caters solely to the underprivileged; it exists for the poor
         and the Third World; it contributes nothing to serious
         theology.

2064.   _____. Pentecost Between Black and White: Five Case Studies on
         Pentecost and Politics. Belfast, Ireland: Christian Journals
         Ltd., 1974. 143 p.

2065.   _____. "The Pentecostal Movement and the World Council of
         Churches." Ecumenical Review 18 (July 1966): 310-20.

         Discusses "The Rise and Significance of Pentecostalism" (in six
         groups), considers it as "an ecumenical revival movement,"
         discusses "The Criticism of the WCC by the Pentecostals" (with
         appropriate WCC responses), and reviews "New Attempts at a
         Dialogue," particularly those of the British Pentecostal,
         Donald Gee.

2066.   _____. The Pentecostals: The Charismatic Movement in the
         Churches. Minneapolis: Augsburg, 1972. 572 p.

         Translation by R. A. Wilson of Hollenweger's large history of
         pentecostalism in the U.S. and elsewhere: Brazil, South Africa,
         Europe. Section on belief and practice. Most notable European
         pentecostal historian. Forty-five-page bibliography. Index.

2067.   Howell, Joseph H. "The People of the Name: Oneness Pentecostalism
         in the United States." Ph.D. diss., The Florida State University.
         1985. 320 p.

2068.   Hummel, Charles E. Fire in the Fireplace: Contemporary
         Charismatic Renewal. Downers Grove: InterVarsity. 1978. 275 p.

         Sympathetic biblical and theological study of the fire (the
         action of the Holy Spirit) in the fireplace (the church), in

four parts: the rise of pentecostalism and the charismatic
renewal, studies in Acts, studies in Paul, and contemporary
issues. Bibliographical references. Index.

2069.   Hunter, Harold D. "Tongues-Speech: A Patristic Analysis."
Journal of the Evangelical Theological Society 23 (June 1980):
125-37.

With some careful qualifications, Hunter cites evidence for
tongues-speech (most of which was xenolalia) through the second
century, and its gradual demise by the fifth century.

2070.   Kantzer, Kenneth S. "The Charismatics Among Us." Christianity
Today 24 (22 February 1980): 25-29.

Christianity Today-Gallup Poll on the extent and variety of
beliefs of pentecostals and charismatics; less than 20% had the
tongues experience.

2071.   Kendrick, Klaude. "The History of the Modern Pentecostal
Movement." Ph.D. diss., The University of Texas at Austin, 1959.
388 p.

2072.   _____. "The Pentecostal Movement: Hopes and Hazards."
Christian Century 80 (8 May 1963): 608-10.

As pentecostals move from sect to church they need to engage in
such institutionalizing matters as better training and improved
facilities.

2073.   Kenyon, Howard Nelson. "An Analysis of Ethical Issues in the
History of the Assemblies of God." Ph.D. diss., Baylor
University, 1988. 486 p.

2074.   _____. "An Analysis of Racial Separation Within the Early
Pentecostal Movement." M.A. thesis, Baylor University, 1978.
173 p.

2075.   Mackey, Lloyd. "Pentecostals Proliferate and Bridge Barriers."
Christianity Today 23 (2 November 1979): 61-63.

News report on the twelfth Pentecostal World Conference.
Vancouver (1979).

2076.   Marty, Martin E. "Pentecostalism in the Context of American Piety
and Practice." In Aspects of Pentecostal-Charismatic Origins. ed.
Vinson Synan, 193-233. Plainfield: Logos, 1975.

History and characteristics of pentecostal beliefs and
practices, their social and psychological dimensions, and their
part in America as a "nation of behavers."

2077.   McClung, L. Grant, Jr., ed. "Azusa Street and Beyond": Pentecostal Missions and Church Growth in the Twentieth Century. South
Plainfield, NJ: Bridge, 1986. 245 p.

Sixteen articles and documents on theological and missiological
developments, as well as articles with a special focus on the
relationship of pentecostal missiology to the church growth
movement and the future of pentecostal missions. Sixty-page
annotated bibliography. Index.

2078.   _____. "Explosion, Motivation, and Consolidation: The
Historical Anatomy of the Pentecostal Missionary Movement."
Missiology 14 (April 1986): 159-72.

Contending that pentecostalism was missionary-minded from its
birth, though affected by doctrinal naivete and financial
immaturity, McClendon shows the consolidation that occurred by
1920.

2079.   _____. "From Bridges (McGavran 1955) to Waves (Wagner 1983):
Pentecostals and the Church Growth Movement." Pneuma 7 (Spring
1985): 5-18.

Documents the interfacing of pentecostalism with the church
growth movement from the 1940s to the 1980s, such that the two
have mutually reinforced each other.

2080.   _____. "Truth on Fire: Pentecostals and an Urgent Missiology."
In The Distinctiveness of Pentecostal-Charismatic Theology,
K1-K73. Fifteenth Annual Meeting, Society for Pentecostal
Studies, Mother of God Community, Gaithersburg, MD: 1985.

The underlying assumptions of pentecostal missions; missionary
practices; the next 100 years. Very helpful appended annotated
bibliography on missions.

2081.   McDonnell, Kilian. "Catholic Charismatic Renewal and Classical
Pentecostalism: Growth and the Critique of a Systematic
Suspicion." One In Christ 23. nos. 1-2 (1987): 36-61.

Statistical evidence of the growth of classical pentecostals
and Roman Catholic charismatics. reasons for the growth.
theologies of the baptism in the Holy Spirit. and analysis of

the exodus of Catholic charismatics to pentecostal churches,
written by a leading authority on the Catholic charismatic
movement.

2082.   . "The Pentecostals and Drug Addiction." America 118 (30
March 1968): 402-06.

Analysis of the work among male addicts at David Wilkerson's
Brooklyn center of Teen Challenge, concluding that the staff,
strong biblical message, and dependence on God are the reasons
for its effectiveness.

2083.   McGavran, Donald. "What Makes Pentecostal Churches Grow?"
Pastoral Renewal 2 (October 1977): 25-27.

Pentecostal churches emphasize the work of the Holy Spirit, the
importance of ordinary Christians, they engage in exorcisms and
healing, and they are innovative.

2084.   McGee, Gary B. "Assemblies of God Missions History." Mountain
Movers 31 (August 1989): 4-11.

The origins and development of the missionary enterprise of the
Assemblies of God, 1914-1989.

2085.   . "Pentecostal Awakenings at Nyack." Paraclete 18
(Summer 1984): 22-28.

Influence from the Azusa Street revival, and some later
influence from Nyack on the Assemblies of God.

2086.   Millard, A. D. "The Classical Pentecostal Movement: A Profile."
Paraclete 11 (Winter 1977): 24-27.

Twelve characteristics of the 20th century movement.

2087.   Mitchell, Robert Bryant. Heritage and Horizons: The History of
Open Bible Standard Churches. Des Moines: Open Bible Publishers,
1982. 414 p.

Thorough survey, written from the inside. Bibliography.

2088.   Money, Ann-Janine. "Empowerment, Control, and Consolation:
Pentecostal Women Talk About the Spirit." Cross Currents 37
(Winter 1987-1988): 427-31.

Brief accounts of the spiritual experience of three pentecostal
women who "share a commitment to affective, experiential
religion"; similar in tone to heroines in 19th century novels.

2089.   Nichol, John Thomas. Pentecostalism. Rev. ed. New York: Harper
& Row, 1971. 264 p.

First published in 1966, the earliest of the critical studies
of the beginnings and course of pentecostalism; based on his
Boston University Ph.D. dissertation (1965) entitled
"Pentecostalism: A Descriptive History of the Origin, Growth,
and Message of a Twentieth Century Religious Movement"
(526 p.). Bibliography. Index.

2090.   _____. "The Role of the Pentecostal Movement in American
Church History." Gordon Review 2 (December 1956): 127-38.

A paper originally read before the eastern division of the
Evangelical Theological Society; deals with the origins,
definition and appraisal of pentecostalism a half century after
its origins.

2091.   Parkes, William. "Pentecostalism: Its Historical Background and
Recent Trends." London Quarterly and Holborn Review 35 (April
1966): 147-53.

On the occasion of some of the pentecostal bodies joining the
WCC (New Delhi, 1961) Parkes outlines pentecostal history
worldwide through the 1940s.

2092.   Pierce, Talmadge Burton. "Integrating a Charismatic Group With An
Assemblies of God District." D.Min. diss., Drew University, 1982.
251 p.

2093.   Pollock, Algernon J. Modern Pentecostalism, Foursquare Gospel,
"Healings" & "Tongues": Are They of God? 6th ed. London: Central
Bible Depot. 64 p.

2094.   Pomerville, Paul A. The Third Force in Missions: A Pentecostal
Contribution to Contemporary Mission Theology. Peabody, MA:
Hendrickson, 1985, 208 p.

2095.   Ranaghan, Kevin M. "Rites of Initiation In Representative
Pentecostal Churches in the United States, 1901-1972." Ph.D.
diss., University of Notre Dame, 1974. 802 p.

2096.   Riss. Richard M. "The Latter Rain Movement of 1948." Pneuma 4
         (Spring 1982): 32-45.

         The movement. part of the healing revival of 1947-1952, began
         in Saskatchewan and spread to other parts of North America,
         producing persons of influence in charismatic and pentecostal
         groups in the 1960s and 1970s.

2097.   Robeck, Cecil M., Jr. "Growing Up Pentecostal." Theology, News
         and Notes 35 (March 1988): 4-7, 26.

         A pentecostal boyhood in the 1940s and 1950s, with some of its
         stereotypes and mythologies about Roman Catholicism now
         shattered.

2098.   _____. "Pentecostalism and Ecumenical Dialogue: A Potential
         Agenda." Ecumenical Trends 16 (December 1987): 185-88.

         Fears separate the two groups, but fair treatment and respect,
         support and encouragement, and a review of priorities and
         practices can be helpful in overcoming the fears.

2099.   _____. "Pentecostals and the Apostolic Faith: Implications for
         Ecumenism." Pneuma 9 (Fall 1986): 61-84.

         Description of pentecostalism's difficulties (until the 1940s
         and 1950s) in getting involved with ecumenical movements of
         various kinds, followed by a list of issues between
         pentecostals and conciliarists and a plan for furthering
         ecumenical dialogue.

2100.   _____. "The Society for Pentecostal Studies." Ecumenical
         Trends 14 (February 1985): 28-30.

         The origins. meetings and publications of the society as
         indicative of the recent pentecostal emphasis on scholarship.

2101.   Sahlberg, Carl E. "From Ecstacy to Enthusiasm: Some Trends in the
         Scientific Attitude to the Pentecostal Movement." Evangelical
         Review of Theology 9 (January 1985): 70-77.

         Terms of the 1920s like ecstasy. lack of conscience. and
         fanatic were replaced by the 1970s with words like healthy.
         therapeutic and spontaneity; the change was due to pentecostal
         expansion. awareness of its own history. loss of exclusivity.
         and the charismatic renewal.

2102.   Saunders, Monroe R. "Some Historical Pentecostal Perspectives For a Contemporary Developmental Pentecost." D.Min. diss., Howard University, 1974.

2103.   Sheppard, Gerald T. "Pentecostals and the Hermeneutics of Dispensationalism: The Anatomy of an Uneasy Relationship." Pneuma 6 (Fall 1984): 5-33.

With six Assemblies of God publications 1930 to 1955 as examples, Sheppard shows how the dispensational eschatology (pre-tribulation rapture) accepted by many pentecostals conflicts with dispensational ecclesiology (with its implications for Acts 2).

2104.   Sims, Patsy. Can Somebody Shout Amen! (Inside the Tents and Tabernacles of American Revivalists). New York: St. Martin's Press, 1988. 234 p.

First-hand report, in journalistic style, of southern pentecostal revival meetings in the 1980s, centering on half a dozen evangelists, aiming to offer "an unbiased rendering, to show the good and the bad, the strengths and the weaknesses" of the revivalists and their audiences. Bibliography.

2105.   Smith, Harold B. "America's Pentecostals: Where They are Going." Christianity Today 31 (16 October 1987): 27-30.

Four pentecostal leaders discuss three challenges facing their denominations: maintaining distinctives; being cordial with the charismatics; keeping doctrines firmly planted in the Bible.

2106.   Smith, Timothy L. "The Disinheritance of the Saints." Religious Studies Review 8 (January 1982): 22-28.

Detailed analysis of Robert M. Anderson's Vision of the Disinherited (1979), a volume Smith finds sympathetic and judicious toward pentecostals, but flawed by Anderson's thesis: "ecstatic religion reflects the need for dislocated and disinherited persons to find a compensatory sense of identification with the divine."

2107.   Society for Pentecostal Studies. Papers of the Sixteenth Annual Meeting; Azusa Street Revisited: Facets of the American Pentecostal Experience. Costa Mesa: Society for Pentecostal Studies, 1986. Various pagings.

Thirteen papers read at the conference, most of them on topics in pentecostal history; valuable indication of the range of current studies. Bibliographical references.

2108.   Spittler, Russell P. "Bar Mitzvah for Azusa Street: Features, Fractures, and Futures of a Renewal Movement Come of Age." Theology, News and Notes 30 (March 1983): 13-17, 35.

Fine survey by an Assembly of God teacher of the characteristics, the threat to division in, and the future of, the movement.

2109.   Synan, Vinson. "Christian Initiation in the Pentecostal Holiness Church." Studia Liturgica 10, no. 1 (1974): 56-64.

The PHC "has distilled and preserved the three great spiritual reforms of historic Christianity--the Lutheran, the Wesleyan, and the Pentecostal"; taken together they constitute initiation: spiritual rebirth, entire sanctification, baptism in the Spirit.

2110.   _____. The Old-time Power. Franklin Springs, GA: Advocate Press, 1973. 296 p.

An official history of the Pentecostal-Holiness Church, from its roots in the late-19th century holiness movement through the beginnings of pentecostalism at the turn of the century, and down to the 1960s. Bibliography. Index.

2111.   _____. "The Pentecostal Tide is Coming in." Christianity Today 21 (5 November 1976): 78-80.

News report of the eleventh triennial meeting of the World Pentecostal Conference, held in London, September 1976.

2112.   _____. "Pentecostalism: Varieties and Contributions." One in Christ 23, nos. 1-2 (1987): 97-109.

Helpful classification of the variety of Pentecostal movements, their theologies, and their contributions to the church at large.

2113.   _____. The Twentieth-Century Pentecostal Explosion: The Exciting Growth of Pentecostal Churches and Charismatic Renewal Movements. Altamonte Springs, FL: Creation House, 1987. 235 p.

A brief, popular narrative history of the major pentecostal
churches and charismatic renewal. Primary sources and
interviews of pioneer figures provide new data for some of the
movement. Bibliography. Index.

2114.   Tinney, James S. "Pentecostals Refurbish the Upper Room."
Christianity Today 10 (1 April 1966): 47-48.

Changes in theology and practice in pentecostal churches make
them appear less sect-like than previously.

2115.   Trigg, Joseph William, and William Lewis Sachs. Of One Body:
Renewal Movements in the Church. Atlanta: John Knox, 1986. 164
p.

From their mainline Protestant perspective, the authors describe the renewal movements (pentecostalism and the charismatics), respond to it in terms of tradition, worship and order,
and the personal and social dimensions of Christian living, and
suggest ways of rapproachement. Bibliography. Index.

2116.   Tugwell, Simon. New Heaven? New Earth?: An Encounter with
Pentecostalism, by Simon Tugwell, et al. Preface by Walter
Hollenweger. Springfield, IL: Templegate, 1977. 206 p.

2117.   Wacker, Grant. "America's Pentecostals: Who They Are."
Christianity Today 31 (16 October 1987): 16-21.

Pentecostalism: what it is, roots, denominations, the
charismatic movement, recent trends, prospects.

2118.   _____. "Are the Golden Oldies Still Worth Playing?
Reflections on History Writing Among Early Pentecostals." Pneuma
8 (Fall 1986): 81-100.

Interpretation of histories by first-generation pentecostals
from the standpoint of their views of the nature of history,
origins and significance of the movement: the books are marred
by defensiveness, lack of critical standards, and
ritualization, yet have value.

2119.   _____. "The Functions of Faith in Primitive Pentecostalism."
Harvard Theological Review 77 (July-October 1984): 353-75.

2120.   _____. "Marching to Zion: Religion in a Modern Utopian
Community." Church History 54 (December 1985): 496-511.

The story of John Alexander Dowie (1847-1907) and his Zion, IL, community, best understood not through the concepts of social disorganization, cultural deprivation, or personal maladjustment (though these are present), but through "the central and irreducible role of religious motivations."

2121. _____. "The Pentecostal Tradition." In Caring and Curing: Health and Medicine in the Western Religious Traditions, eds. Ronald L. Numbers and Darrel W. Amundsen, 514-38. New York: Macmillan, 1986.

The Pentecostal views of health and medicine, from the 19th century background to the present; along with speaking in tongues, "the doctrine and practice of divine healing . . . has been the enduring backbone of the Pentecostal tradition."

2122. _____. "Taking Another Look at the Vision of the Disinherited." Religious Studies Review 8 (January 1982): 15-22.

Commends Robert M. Anderson's vision of the disinherited as a landmark in the historiography of American pentecostalism, but doubts the validity of Anderson's "strain thesis" (certain social strains lead to certain religious expressions) along four social lines: position, anxiety, change, behavior.

2123. Ward, Horace S. "The Anti-Pentecostal Movement." In Aspects of Pentecostal-Charismatic Origins, ed. Vinson Synan, 99-122. Plainfield: Logos, 1975.

Handles the shifting nature of criticisms from the "early charges of demon possession to the present-day serious exegetical and theological evaluations."

2124. Whittaker, Colin C. Seven Pentecostal Pioneers. Springfield, MO: Gospel Publishing House, 1983. 224 p.

Descriptions of the ministries of seven British pentecostal leaders: Smith Wigglesworth, Stephen Jeffreys, Donald Gee, Howard Carter, Harold Horton, William F. P. Burton, and Terry Hodson. Endnotes. Index.

2125. Williams, J. Rodman. The Pentecostal Reality. Plainfield: Logos, 1972. 109 p.

Collection of six articles previously published by Williams, on historical, biblical, and theological themes in the charismatic renewal. Bibliographical references.

2126. _____. "The Upsurge of Pentecostalism: Some Presbyterian/ Reformed Comment." Reformed World 31 (December 1971): 339-48.

Summary of twenty years of statements, comments and appraisals that see in pentecostalism "a vital renewal of Christianity at its original sources."

2127. Williams, Jerry D. "The Modern Pentecostal Movement in America: A Brief Sketch of its History and Thought." Lexington Theological Quarterly 9 (April 1974): 50-60.

Survey by a student at Lexington Theological Seminary.

2128. Zimmerman, Thomas F. "The Reason for the Rise of the Pentecostal Movement." In Aspects of Pentecostal-Charismatic Origins, ed. Vinson Synan, 5-13. Plainfield: Logos, 1975.

"The pentecostal revival is a fulfillment of prophecy--a sign of the last days."

See also items 9, 24, 39, 46, 52, 62, 65, 69, 73, 244, 309, 648, 692, 695, 703, 712, 716, 753, 780, 790, 800, 801, 814, 879, 1134, 1149, 1180, 1182, 1247, 1451, 1452, 1456, 1560, 1561, 1572, 1573, 1587, 1588, 1839, 2011, 2023, 2025, 2026, 2030, 2137, 2147, 2157, 2164, 2168, 2185, 2196, 2197, 2218, 2220, 2235, 2247, 2253, 2261, 2264, 2276, 2286, 2287, 2441, 2493, 2582, 2624.

C. Biblical and Theological Studies

2129. Aldrich, Roy L. "Is the Pentecostal Movement Pentecostal?" Bibliotheca Sacra 108 (January-March 1951): 44-52; and (April-June 1951): 172-85.

Concludes that the movement is not "Pentecostal" in the biblical sense in scope, power, or doctrine (discusses "the promise of the father," "miraculous gifts," "evidence of the baptism," "entire sanctification," and "divine healing").

2130. Barnett, Donald Lee, and Jeffrey P. McGregor. Speaking in Other Tongues: A Scholarly Defence. Seattle: Community Chapel Publications, 1987. 840 p.

Announced as "the most comprehensive work ever produced on the baptism in the Holy Spirit and speaking in tongues," this work answers allegations against and provides evidence for the tongues experience. Appendixes. Index.

2131.   Beverly, Jim. "Truly Pentecostal? A Critique of the United
          Pentecostal Church." Journal of Pastoral Practice 4, no. 3
          (1980): 109-12.

          The major "oneness" pentecostal group is not pentecostal, he
          argues, "in the biblical or historical sense of the word," but
          is rather "an extreme deviation from classical Pentecostalism"
          with views that are in error "in three major dimensions" (God,
          Salvation, and Holiness).

2132.   Bruner, Frederick Dale. A Theology of the Holy Spirit: The
          Pentecostal Experience and the New Testament Witness. Grand
          Rapids: Eerdmans, 1970. 390 p.

          Among the best works on the subject, this carefully done "essay
          in case-study theology" on "the doctrine and experience of the
          Holy Spirit," through "the missionary movement known as
          pentecostalism," analyzes the teachings of pentecostalism, then
          proceeds to biblical exegesis, particularly of the relevant
          passages in Acts and I Corinthians. Thirty-five-page
          bibliography. Documents. Index.

2133.   Burgess, Stanley M. The Spirit and the Church: Antiquity.
          Peabody, MA: Hendrickson Publishers, 1984. 216 p.

          An analysis of the "minor tradition" (emphasis on the Spirit),
          from Clement of Rome to Augustine, with selected passages from
          the Fathers. Bibliographical references.

2134.   Canty, George. In My Father's House: Pentecostal Expositions of
          the Major Christian Truths. London: Marshall, Morgan & Scott,
          1969. 128 p.

          An English pentecostal evangelist describes the major doctrines
          from the pentecostal viewpoint.

2135.   Chantry, Walter J. Signs of the Apostles: Observations on
          Pentecostalism Old and New. Second rev. ed. Edinburgh, Scotland/
          Carlisle, PA: Banner of Truth Trust, 1976. 147 p.

          Primarily a biblical study, concluding that we "must deny that
          miracles are being performed today by men who are filled with
          God's Spirit." Appendix. Bibliography.

2136.   Chinn, Jack J. "May We Pentecostals Speak?" Christianity Today 5
          (17 July 1961): 8-9.

An appeal to evangelicals to see in pentecostalism the work of
the Spirit.

2137.   Clement, Arthur J. Pentecost or Pretense? An Examination of the
Pentecostal and Charismatic Movements. Milwaukee: Northwestern
Publishing House, 1981. 256 p.

Historical, theological, and biblical analysis of the
movements, which Clement concludes are not "the answer to the
crying need for spiritual renewal in the churches."
Bibliographical references. Index.

2138.   Craig, Robert. "Pentecostalism." Theology 68 (December 1965):
563-69.

Extended review of Nils Bloch-Hoehl, The Pentecostal Movement
(1964), laying out the main tenets of pentecostal theology.

2139.   Dahlin, John E. "Resurgence of the Tongues Movement." Discerner
4 (October-December 1962): 2-3.

A very negative evaluation introduces an issue devoted to the
"Tongues Movement": "The current over-emphasis on speaking in
tongues and physical healing reveal a gross misunderstanding of
New Testament teachings."

2140.   Dalton, Robert Chandler. Tongues Like as of Fire: A Critical
Study of Modern Tongue Movements in the Light of Apostolic and
Patristic Times. Springfield, MO: Gospel Publishing House, 1945.
127 p.

Attempts to compile evidence, especially historical,
"concerning the genuineness" of the modern tongues phenomenon,
and then to draw the conclusions demanded by that evidence;
conclusions include the "tremendous error that the main body of
the evangelical Christian churches are making" in neglecting
the phenomenon.

2141.   Damboriena, Prudencio. "The Pentecostal Fury." Catholic World
202 (January 1966): 217-23.

Appreciation for pentecostalism's zeal and emphasis on
community, dismay over its proselytizing, especially in Roman
Catholic countries, hope that pentecostals will be drawn into
ecumenical dialog.

2142.   Davies, Horton. "Centrifugal Christian Sects." Religion in Life
         25 (Summer 1956): 323-35.

         These sects--holiness, adventist, perfectionist, pentecostal--
         are "imitations, yet distortions, of the historic churches"
         whose challenge must "be met constructively by appreciation as
         well as negatively by criticism."

2143.   The Distinctiveness of Pentecostal-Charismatic Theology.
         Fifteenth Annual Meeting, Society for Pentecostal Studies.
         Gaithersburg, MD: Mother of God Community, 1985. Various pagings.

         Twelve papers on a variety of theological issues illustrate the
         diversity in contemporary pentecostal thinking.
         Bibliographies.

2144.   Doane, James. "Pentecostalism and Reformation Faith." Reformed
         Journal 24 (April 1974): 17-20.

2145.   Du Plessis, Justus T. "The Pentecostal Viewpoint." One in Christ
         12, no. 4 (1976): 347-50.

         The sacraments section of a paper (by a pentecostal) from the
         pentecostal-Roman Catholic dialogues, 1974-1976. "Obedience
         and faith is required from both the dispenser and recipient of
         the sacraments."

2146.   Dunn, James D. G. "Spirit-Baptism and Pentecostalism." Scottish
         Journal of Theology 23 (November 1970): 397-407.

         Wide-ranging survey of Spirit-baptism from the Puritans to the
         charismatic movement, followed by analysis of the doctrine;
         Dunn sees Spirit-baptism occurring at conversion-initiation;
         all subsequent experiences with the Spirit as fillings.

2147.   Elbert, Paul, ed. Essays on Apostolic Themes: Studies in Honor of
         Howard M. Ervin Presented to Him by Colleagues and Friends on His
         Sixty-Fifth Birthday. Peabody, MA: Hendrickson, 1985. 239 p.

         Valuable sixteen-article festschrift on a variety of
         pentecostal subjects: biblical, theological, historical.
         Extensive bibliographical references. Indexes.

2148.   Farah, Charles. "America's Pentecostals: What They Believe."
         Christianity Today 31 (16 October 1987): 22-26.

Outlines pentecostal beliefs, points up shortcomings, asks
questions of evangelicals, and distinguishes among
pentecostals, charismatics and neo-pentecostals.

2149.   Faupel, D. William. "The Function of 'Models' in the Interpretation of Pentecostal Thought." Pneuma 2 (Spring 1980): 51-71.

2150.   Forbes, James A. "A Pentecostal Approach to Empowerment for Black
Liberation." Ph.D. diss., Colgate Rochester Divinity School/
Crozer Theological Seminary, 1975. 135 p.

2151.   Fullam, Everett L. Riding the Wind: Your Life in the Holy Spirit.
Altamonte Springs, FL: Creation House, 1986. 179 p.

An Episcopal rector, prominent in the charismatic movement,
gives pastoral talks on the Spirit-led life. Index.

2152.   Gaede, Charles S. "Glossolalia at Azusa Street: A Hidden
Presupposition?" Westminster Theological Journal 51 (Spring
1989): 77-92.

Purposes "to examine the place of biblical authority in the
glossolalia beliefs and practices in the Azusa Street revival,"
suggesting that "a comparative study of modern Pentecostal
glossolalia beliefs and practice would demonstrate the survival
of the early doctrines"; with the claim of scriptural support,
glossolalia became the focal point for a number of beliefs and
practices; Gaede attempts to reconstruct their hermeneutical
system from the historical record of other activities.

2153.   Gee, Donald. "The Adventure of Pentecostal Meetings." Paraclete
17 (Spring 1983): 27-30.

British pentecostal Gee notes that the "Pentecostal testimony
was born of God to be extraordinary," and this is what
justifies its separate existence.

2154.   _____. Concerning Spiritual Gifts. Springfield, MO: Gospel
Publishing House, 1972. 119 p.

Influential British pentecostal Gee (d. 1966) provides an
exposition of the classic biblical doctrines of pentecostalism
in this reprint of studies originally done in the 1920s.

2155.   Gelpi, Donald L. Pentecostalism, a Theological Viewpoint. New
York: Paulist Press, 1971. 234 p.

2156.   Hart. Larry D. "A Critique of American Pentecostal Theology."
         Ph.D. diss., Southern Baptist Theological Seminary, 1978.

2157.   Hellstern, Mark. "The 'Me Gospel': An Examination of the Histori-
         cal Roots of the Prosperity Emphasis Within Current Charismatic
         Theology." Fides et Historia 21 (October 1989): 78-90.

         Concludes that the message of men like Copeland, Capps,
         Savelle, and Tilton is "merely the most recent edition of an
         American theology with abundant precedent"; such a message in
         the 1980s "should come as no surprise," given the tendency of
         the church "to absorb and to mirror the values of secular
         society."

2158.   Hickman, James T. "Let's Find Pentecostal Balance." Eternity 25
         (April 1974): 16-17.

         A pentecostal answers the question, "How can we have meaningful
         fellowship between Pentecostal and non-Pentecostal?"; grants
         "that tongues is a legitimate though not universal gift of the
         Spirit"; concludes that "the potential for fellowship in the
         Spirit is great."

2159.   Hoekema, Anthony A. "The Holy Spirit in Christian Experience."
         Reformed Review 28 (Spring 1975): 183-91.

         Excerpted from Hoekema's Holy Spirit Baptism (1972), an
         exegetical and historical study: "the New Testament does not
         support Neo-Pentecostal teaching on Spirit-baptism."

2160.   Holdcroft, L. Thomas. The Holy Spirit: A Pentecostal
         Interpretation. Springfield, MO: Gospel Publishing House, 1979.
         252 p.

         An Assemblies of God college president gives a thorough
         biblical and theological exposition of the doctrine and work of
         the Holy Spirit in the classic pentecostal tradition.
         Appendixes. Bibliography. Index.

2161.   Hollenweger, Walter J. "Creator Spiritus: The Challenge of
         Pentecostal Experience to Pentecostal Theology." Theology 81
         (January 1978): 32-40.

         Summarizes briefly "the understanding of charismata in Paul,"
         exemplifies that "understanding in relation to speaking in
         tongues and a charismatic theology of the world." and draws
         "some conclusions for the modern debate on development and

underdevelopment and for ecumenical relationships between western and Third World churches."

2162. _____. "Pentecostalism and Black Power." Theology Today 30 (October 1973): 228-38.

Based on his own observations and on Gerlach and Hine, People, Power, Change (1970), Hollenweger argues that both Black Power and pentecostalism are oral religions and revolutionary movements posing a threat to the "literary" theology of white religion and culture.

2163. Howe, Leroy T. "Pentecostalism Today: Theological Reflections." South East Asia Journal of Theology 18 (1977): 32-37.

Theological reflection on three areas: baptism and grace, the identity and gifts of the Spirit, and the moral dimensions of sanctification.

2164. Hunter, Harold D. Spirit-Baptism: A Pentecostal Alternative. Lanham, MD: University Press of America, 1983. 310 p.

A revised edition of the author's Fuller Seminary Ph.D. dissertation, this careful study of biblical material, patristic literature, and selected literature down to 1900, followed by an evaluation of the doctrines of salvation and sanctification, was made "to see if there is any basis for the essence of Classical Pentecostal doctrine of Spirit-baptism"; the author concludes there is such a basis. Bibliography. Addendum on tongues-speech.

2165. "The Initial Physical Evidence of the Baptism in the Holy Spirit." Paraclete 16 (Spring 1982): 1-7.

Adopted by the Assemblies of God, August 1981, the paper explains terms and gives the biblical and theological basis for tongues-speaking.

2166. Johnson, S. Lewis, Jr., et al. "A Symposium on the Tongues Movement." Bibliotheca Sacra 120 (July-September 1963): 224-33, and 120 (October-December 1963): 309-21.

Contributions from Dallas Seminary faculty, reflecting "recent discussion" there and focusing on relevant biblical passages (e.g., 1 Corinthians 13 and Acts), concluding with an historical survey.

2167.   Johnston, Robert K. "Pentecostalism and Theological Hermeneutics:
         Evangelical Options." Pneuma 6 (Spring 1984): 51-66.

         Centers on the options available for pentecostals, given
         continuing questions in evangelicalism: contextualization, role
         of tradition, sensus plenior, critical study of the Bible, and
         the work of the Spirit.

2168.   Kelsey, Morton. Tongue Speaking: The History and Meaning of
         Charismatic Experience. New York: Crossroad, 1981. 252 p.

         Glossolalia from Bible times to the present; explanations and
         evaluation of tongues-speaking, which Episcopalian Kelsey sees
         as a valid expression of a lesser gift that should be kept in
         the bounds of the Christian community. Appendixes.
         Bibliography.

2169.   Klaus, Byron. "A Theology of Ministry: Pentecostal Perspectives."
         Paraclete 23 (Summer 1989): 1-10.

         Attempts, "not to develop a definitive Pentecostal theology of
         ministry, but to chart some major focal points in a theology of
         ministry from a Pentecostal perspective."

2170.   Klempa, William. "Ecstasy and the Experience of the Holy Spirit."
         Reformed World 32 (September-December 1972): 110-21.

         The concept of ecstasy; pentecostalism and neo-pentecostalism;
         the biblical critique of ecstatic phenomena; theological issues
         and dangers in regard to ecstasy.

2171.   Kydd, Ronald. Charismatic Gifts in the Early Church. Peabody, MA:
         Hendrickson, 1984. 100 p.

2172.   MacDonald, William G. "Glossolalia in the New Testament."
         Bulletin of the Evangelical Theological Society 7 (Spring 1964):
         59-68.

         A careful, sympathetic treatment: "The 'command of the Lord'--
         do not forbid glossolalia, but do all things properly and in
         order--has never been revoked!"

2173.   Maxwell, James. "Jesus Only" Doctrines and Pentecostalism:
         Debates by Maxwell-Johnson Debate and the Maxwell-Liner Debate.
         Co-sponsored by Maxwell Publications and Family Ideas. Terrell,
         TX: Maxwell, 1983. 247 p.

A Church of Christ minister and college administrator debates with those who espouse the "Jesus Only" doctrine. Scattered references.

2174.   McDonnell, Kilian. "The Ecumenical Significance of the Pentecostal Movement." Worship 40 (December 1966): 608-29.

Pentecostal views on speaking in tongues, experience of the Holy Spirit, conversion and sanctification, worship, ecclesiology. Important for the ecumenical movement is its emphasis on a Spirit-led life, which poses for the established churches "the question of holiness."

2175.   _____. "Holy Spirit and Pentecostalism." Commonweal 89 (8 November 1968): 198-204.

Empathetic description of pentecostalism and the charismatic movement, analysis of the teachings about tongues-speaking and healing, and a list of the difficulties in assessing pentecostalism.

2176.   _____. "Ideology of Pentecostal Conversion." Journal of Ecumenical Studies 5 (Winter 1968): 105-26.

Evaluates the growth process of pentecostalism in terms of its ideology: emphasis on experience, closing the gap between the real and the ideal, the push to witness, missionary endeavor, eschatology, healing, and the rising economic standard among converts.

2177.   _____. "Pentecostal Culture: Protestant and Catholic." One in Christ 7, no. 4 (1971): 310-18.

Pentecostalism is often misjudged; this article suggests that some of the misjudgment is based on "the rather consistent neglect to comprehend Pentecostalism within its own cultural framework," which McDonnell sees as pre-literary and oral.

2178.   McLean, Mark D. "Toward a Pentecostal Hermeneutic." Pneuma 6 (Fall 1984): 35-56.

Since both liberal and non-pentecostal evangelical hermeneutics pose a threat, pentecostalism needs to chart out its own hermeneutic.

2179.   Meeks, Fred E. "The Pastor and the Tongues Movement." Southwestern Journal of Theology 19 (Spring 1977): 73-85.

Baptist Meeks surveys the heritage of glossolalia and its
contemporary context, analyzes the experience, and counsels
pastors to have "[a]cceptance, patience, and loving tolerance"
of glossolalists.

2180.   Millard, A. D. "The Pentecostal Movement and Inerrancy."
Paraclete 20 (Spring 1986): 4-7.

Contends that pentecostalism began with belief in an inerrant
Bible and continues to hold that position.

2181.   Mills, Watson E. A Theological/Exegetical Approach to
Glossolalia. Landam, MD: University Press, 1985. 179 p.

Aims to set forth "the theological relevance of glossolalia, if
any, and to relate the experience of tongues to the larger
context of biblical theology"; studies in the Judeo-Christian
tradition, Acts, and I Corinthians. Forty-three-page
bibliography. Indexes.

2182.   _____. "Ecstaticism as a Background for Glossolalia." Journal
of the American Scientific Affiliation 24 (December 1975): 167-71.

Examines ecstaticism in the ancient world, both within and
outside of the Hebrew tradition, to assist in answering
questions about the origins and interpretation of glossolalia.

2183.   Muller, Jac. "Neo-Pentecostalism: A Theological Evaluation of
Glossolalia, with Special Reference to the Reformed Churches."
Journal of Theology for Southern Africa no. 7 (June 1974): 41-49.

2184.   Packer, James I. "Piety on Fire." Christianity Today 33 (12 May
1989): 18-23.

From a Christianity Today book entitled Tough Questions
Christians Ask (1989), Packer lists twenty-three
characteristics of "a recognizably Charismatic approach to
Christian and church life"; discusses the movement "from all
angles," sociologically, spiritually, doctrinally, culturally,
and theologically, and treats at length the "impossible"
contention of some that the movement is "not from God." A
balanced, critical, and positive treatment.

2185.   Parnell, Chris W. "What About Speaking in Tongues?" Eternity 24
(March 1973): 20-22, 78-79.

Concludes that "the contemporary emphasis on tongues-speaking seems out of perspective and proportion"; while a valid gift, tongues is a minor one, not to be sought.

2186. Pitcher, Leonard S. "Pentecostalism." Reformation Review 2 (April 1955): 158-63.

2187. Quebedeaux, Richard. "The Old Pentecostalism and the New Pentecostalism." Theology, News and Notes 20 (March 1974): 6-8, 23.

Differences center around theology, worship, ecclesiology, intellectuality, socio-political awareness, culture attitudes, and members' social status.

2188. Ramm, Bernard. "Varieties of Belief: Acts, Chapter 2." Eternity 33 (May 1982): 45-46.

Some preliminary statements, and ten characteristics of pentecostalism.

2189. Ranaghan, Kevin M. "Conversion and Baptism: Personal Experience and Ritual Celebration in Pentecostal Churches." Studia Liturgica 10, no. 1 (1974): 65-76.

"The normal denominational Pentecostal public worship is itself the basic Pentecostal rite or event of initiation," with a crisis conversion experience the most fundamental event of initiation and water baptism a dependent rite of initiation.

2190. Reddin, Opal Laurene. "The Application of Biblical Principles for Church Growth, From a Pentecostal Perspective." D.Min. diss., Fuller Theological Seminary, School of Theology, 1985. 323 p.

2191. Reitzel, Charles F. The Errors of Pentecostalism. 3d ed. Altoona, PA: n.p., n.d. 32 p.

2192. Righter, James D. "A Critical Study of the Charismatic Experience of Speaking in Tongues." D.Min. diss., Wesley Theological Seminary, 1974.

2193. Sala, Harold James. "Investigation of the Baptizing and Filling Work of the Holy Spirit in the New Testament Related to the Pentecostal Doctrine of Initial Evidence." Ph.D. diss., Bob Jones University, 1966. 196 p.

2194. Samarin, William J. "Sacred and Profane." Crux 9 (May 1972): 4-11.

Contends that glossolalia is "normal, not supernatural" and not
abnormal; it is part of a "world-wide inventory of varieties of
religious language," a "linguistic symbol of the sacred."
Other articles in the same issue interact with his position.

2195.   Selness, David Bruce. "A Baptist Understanding of the
         Charismatic's Baptism in the Holy Spirit." D.Min. diss., Bethel
         Theological Seminary, 1987. 132 p.

2196.   Sheppard, Gerald T. "The Nicean Creed, Filioque, and Pentecostal
         Movements in the United States." Greek Orthodox Theological
         Review 31 (Fall-Winter 1986): 401-16.

         For most of their history pentecostals have not shown much
         interest in creeds (though the "Jesus Only" movement of the
         1910s prompted some interest), but their concern with the Holy
         Spirit gives them a natural entry into discussions of the
         filioque clause.

2197.   _____. "The Seduction of Pentecostals Within the Politics of
         Exegesis: The Nicene Creed, Filioque, and Pentecostal Ambivalence
         Regarding an Ecumenical Challenge of a Common Confession of
         Apostolic Faith." In The Distinctiveness of Pentecostal Charis-
         matic Theology, G1-G15. Fifteenth Annual Meeting, Society for
         Pentecostal Studies, Mother of God Community, Gaithersburg, MD:
         1985.

         Discussion of the ambivalence of pentecostals in regard to
         church history in general and the Nicene Creed in particular,
         especially in light of pentecostals' desire for church unity.

2198.   Stibbs, Alan Marshall, and James I. Packer. The Spirit Within
         You: The Church's Neglected Possession. Grand Rapids: Baker,
         1979. 93 p.

         Reprint of a 1967 study by two Anglican evangelicals,
         emphasizing the need for a renewed emphasis on the Spirit;
         written from a nonpentecostal point of view.

2199.   Stronstad, Roger. "The Hermeneutics of Lucan Historiography."
         Paraclete 22 (Fall 1988): 5-17.

         Luke-Acts as historical books: two approaches to historical
         narrative that Stransky rejects: Stransky's proposal:
         narratives have exemplary, typological, programmatic, or
         paradigmatic functions, not just informational functions. Part
         two of a two part series.

2200.   _____. "Trends in Pentecostal Hermeneutics." Paraclete 22
            (Summer 1988): 1-12.

            Beginning with a pragmatic hermeneutic, pentecostalism has now
            moved to other possibilities: genre (Gordon Fee); pneumatic
            (Howard Ervin); holistic [which includes genre] (William
            Menzies). Part one of a two part series.

2201.   Tugwell, Simon. "Reflections on the Pentecostal Doctrine of
            'Baptism in the Holy Spirit.'" Heythrop Journal 13 (July 1972):
            268-81, (October 1972): 402-14.

            Stating that "Pentecostal-inspired renewal movements represent
            one of the major religious stirrings of our time," he argues
            "that the New Testament does not bear out the Pentecostal
            doctrine that there is a 'baptism in the Holy Spirit' distinct
            from sacramental baptism." The concluding article series
            includes "various testimonia from very different sources
            describing experiences of spiritual breakthrough."

2202.   Van Elderen, Marlin J. "Glossolalia in the New Testament."
            Bulletin of the Evangelical Theological Society 7 (Spring 1964):
            53-58.

            Discusses "the material to be included in glossolalia," and the
            "significance and relevance of the phenomenon," concluding that
            "'tongues' are certainly llmited in usefulness and virtually
            undesirable as a communal activity."

2203.   Villafane, Eldin. "Toward an Hispanic American Pentecostal Social
            Ethic, With Special Reference to North Eastern United States."
            Ph.D. diss., Boston University, 1989. 493 p. Two volumes.

2204.   Ward, Julian. "Pentecostal Theology and the Charismatic
            Movement." In Strange Gifts? A Guide to Charismatic Renewal,
            eds. David Martin and Peter Mullen, 192-207. New York: Basil
            Blackwell, 1984.

            Raises and answers five questions about the attitudes and
            relationships between pentecostals and charismatics, who "have
            an important prophetic function in the years that lie ahead."

2205.   Weaver, Gilbert B. "Tongues Shall Cease." Grace Journal 14
            (Winter 1973): 12-24.

            Explores several questions: What is meant by the term
            "tongues"? What is meant by shall cease? Under what

conditions will tongues cease? And, "when is the condition
fulfilled?" Concludes that tongues are not a continuation of
the New Testament practice of the gift.

2206.   Whalley, W. E. "Pentecostal Theology." Baptist Quarterly 27
(July 1978): 282-89.

2207.   Wiebe, Phillip H. "The Pentecostal Initial Evidence Doctrine."
Journal of the Evangelical Theological Society 27 (December 1984):
465-72.

Exegetical study that concludes that when glossolalia occurs it
is "probably caused by the Spirit," but "[t]he view that
glossolalia is the first effect of Spirit baptism receives no
conclusive textual support."

2208.   Williams, Cyril Glyndwr. Tongues of the Spirit: A Study of
Pentecostal Glossolalia and Related Phenomena. Cardiff:
University of Wales Press, 1981. 276 p.

2209.   Williams, J. Rodman. "Pentecostal Spirituality." One in Christ
10, no. 2 (1974): 180-92.

Eight elements in the (non-Catholic) pentecostal understanding
of baptism in the Holy Spirit.

2210.   Zimmerman, Thomas F. "Plea for the Pentecostals." Christianity
Today 7 (4 January 1963): 11-12.

Apologetic for pentecostal belief in baptism in the Holy Spirit
and speaking in tongues.

2211.   _____. "Priorities and Beliefs of Pentecostals." Christianity
Today 24 (4 September 1981): 36-7.

Six priorities and beliefs place pentecostalism "in the
mainstream of theological orthodoxy."

See also items 39, 46, 53, 54, 69, 73, 710, 1289, 1301, 1328, 1614, 2006,
2019, 2020, 2023, 2046, 2054, 2059, 2062, 2068, 2073, 2095, 2100, 2103,
2109, 2116, 2123, 2125, 2212, 2222, 2226, 2248, 2291, 2373, 2376.

D.   Pentecostalism Outside the United States

2212.   Bond, John. "Pentecostalism in the Pentecostal Churches."
Journal of Theology for Southern Africa no. 7 (June 1974): 10-22.

Glossolalia. the beginnings of pentecostalism, pentecostalism
in South Africa. its doctrines and distinctives, and relation
to the charismatic movement; a list is appended with brief
descriptions of the twelve pentecostal denominations in South
Africa. This issue of JTSA is devoted to pentecostalism in the
region.

2213.   Castro, Emilio. "Pentecostalism and Ecumenism in Latin America."
Christian Century 89 (27 September 1972): 955-57.

Latin American pentecostals are not dependent on North America
and Europe; are not fundamentalists; center their worship and
practice on the Bible; now face the issue of what to do about
political and social problems; and can play a role in the
ecumenical movement.

2214.   Endruveit, Wilson Harle. "Pentecostalism in Brazil: A Historical
and Theological Study of Its Characteristics." Ph.D. diss.,
Northwestern University, 1975. 222 p.

2215.   Gaxiola, Manuel J. "The Pentecostal Ministry." International
Review of Mission 66 (January 1977): 57-63.

A Mexican pentecostal describes success in Latin America, warns
of tensions and dilemmas to be faced by pentecostal ministers,
and regards liberation theology as of little import to pentecostals since they take a more individualistic approach to
poverty.

2216.   Glazier, Stephen D., ed. Perspectives on Pentecostalism: Case
Studies From the Caribbean and Latin America. Washington, DC:
University Press of America, 1980. 197 p.

Eleven papers chart the growth and the social and political
effects of pentecostalism in selected Caribbean and Latin
American locations. Bibliography. Index.

2217.   Handspicker. M. B.. and Lukas Vischer. "The Pentecostal Movement
in Europe." Ecumenical Review 19 (January 1967): 37-47.

Considers the historical roots, doctrine. and "illustrations of
some ways various Christian doctrines are worked out in the
lives of persons who are members of Pentecostal churches."
concluding that there is "immense variety in the Bible." and
that "there is both the possibility and necessity for
continuing conversation" with pentecostals.

2218.   Hedlund, Roger C. "Why Pentecostal Churches Are Growing Faster in
          Italy." Evangelical Missions Quarterly 8 (Spring 1972): 129-36.

          Recounts the spread from the Azusa Street origins in 1906, to
          Chicago and then to Italy, noting their remarkable success in
          Italy, and suggesting a number of reasons for that success
          (e.g., they are Italian, aggressive, emphasize the Holy Spirit,
          grow along family lines).

2219.   Hodges, Melvin L. "A Pentecostal's View of Mission Strategy."
          International Review of Missions 57 (July 1968): 304-10.

          With the Holy Spirit and the local church at the forefront,
          pentecostal strategy creates church growth and social concern.

2220.   Hollenweger, Walter J. "After Twenty Years' Research on
          Pentecostalism." Theology 87 (November 1984): 403-12.

          Survey of the status of Third World pentecostal denominations,
          charismatic movements, and non-white indigenous churches;
          emphasis on the effects on white, Western Christianity.

2221.   _____. "Pentecostalism and the Third World." Dialog 9 (Spring
          1970): 122-29.

2222.   _____. "Social and Ecumenical Significance of Pentecostal
          Liturgy." Studia Liturgica 8 (1971-1972): 207-15.

          Based primarily on the author's experience among Chilean
          pentecostals; a plea for the validity of an oral liturgy.

2223.   _____. "Theology of the New World: III. The Religion of the
          Poor is not a Poor Religion: The Example of Latin American
          Pentecostal and African Independent Spirituality." Expository
          Times 87 (May 1976): 228-32.

          Convinced that "there is theology hidden in this spirituality,"
          Hollenweger analyzes four features of this "religion of
          travail": song and story, prayer for the sick, exorcism, and
          glossolalia.

2224.   Johnson, Norbert E. "The History, Dynamic, and Problems of the
          Pentecostal Movement in Chile." Th.M. thesis. Union Theological
          Seminary, Richmond, VA, 1970. 132 p.

2225.   _____. "Pentecostalism in Chile." Covenant Quarterly 29
          (February 1971): 21-29.

Discusses the background of 19th century Protestant missions in
Chile, particularly the Methodist Mission and the Willis
Hoovers, treats the early development of the pentecostal church
in Chile, concluding with a positive assessment of its success.

2226.   Lartey, Emmanuel Y. "Healing: Tradition and Pentecostalism in
Africa Today." International Review of Mission 75 (January 1986):
75-81.

Fictionalized account, though true in details, of how the
independent indigenous pentecostal churches in Ghana and
Nigeria are combining Christian faith with traditional healing.

2227.   Lee, Jae Bum. "Pentecostal Type Distinctives and Korean
Protestant Church Growth." Ph.D. diss., Fuller Theological
Seminary, School of World Mission, 1986. 377 p.

2228.   Matre, Frank Martin. "A Theological Foundation to Design a
Strategy for the Renewal and Growth of the Norwegian Pentecostal
Movement." D.Min. diss., Fuller Theological Seminary, 1985.
277 p.

2229.   Medcraft, John P. "The Roots and Fruits of Brazilian Pentecostalism." Vox Evangelica 17 (1987): 67-94.

History of pentecostalism in Brazil, external social and
religious factors in its growth, and the internal factors:
doctrines, communication, ecclesiology.

2230.   Pederson, W. Dennis. "Pentecost South of the Border."
Christianity Today 7 (19 July 1963): 32.

Facts of and reasons for pentecostal growth in Latin America
gathered from a number of observers.

2231.   Perez, Torres Ruben. "The Pastor's Role in Educational Ministry
in the Pentecostal Church of God in Puerto Rico." D.Min. diss.,
School of Theology at Claremont, 1979. 122 p.

2232.   Pethrus, Lewi. Lewi Pethrus: A Spiritual Memoir. Plainfield:
Logos, 1973, 164 p.

The author, important in the beginnings of pentecostalism in
Scandinavia, recounts his own long experience and reflects on
some of the important needs of the churches.

2233.   Pillay, Gerald J. "The Antithetical Structure of Pentecostal
         Theology." Journal of Theology for Southern Africa no. 50 (March
         1985): 27-36.

                 Pentecostal charismatics are plagued by antithetical beliefs in
                 four areas: authority, freedom, history, and certainty; the
                 antitheses are resolved by "experience of the spirit."

2234.   Poloma, Margaret M. "Pentecostals and Politics in North and
         Central America." In Prophetic Religions and Politics: Religion
         and the Social Order, eds. Jeffrey K. Hadden and Anson Shupe,
         329-52. New York: Paragon, 1986.

                 Well-drawn comments about the pentecostals in both regions lead
                 Poloma to conclude that "the charismatic movement worldwide is
                 characterized by political passivity," particularly on public
                 issues, but it has the potential to become a "revolutionary
                 political force."

2235.   Pothen, Abraham Thottumkal. "The India Pentecostal Church of God
         and Its Contribution to Church Growth." M.A. thesis, Fuller
         Theological Seminary, School of World Mission, 1988. 184 p.

2236.   Raj, P. Solomon. "The Influence of Pentecostal Teaching on Some
         Folk Christian Religions in India." International Review of
         Mission 75 (January 1986): 39-46.

2237.   Rowe, Michael. "Pentecostal Documents From The USSR." Religion
         in Communist Lands 3 (January-June 1975): 16-18.

                 Analysis of the documents, and the hope they suggest for better
                 treatment of pentecostals; two of the documents are reproduced
                 (25-30).

2238.   Saracco, J. Norberto. "The Type of Ministry Adopted by the
         Pentecostal Churches in Latin America." International Review of
         Mission 66 (January 1977): 64-70.

2239.   Sepulveda, Ivan. "Pentecostalism as Popular Religiosity." Inter-
         national Review of Mission 78 (January 1989): 80-88.

                 A Chilean pentecostal discusses pentecostalism's idea of
                 salvation ("individuals recover from a total lack of meaning").
                 its effects on peasants. on urban workers. and its success at
                 the popular levels.

2240.   Van der Laan. Paul N. "Dynamics in Pentecostal Mission: A Dutch
          Perspective." International Review of Mission 75 (January 1986):
          47-50.

          Ten factors in Dutch pentecostalism. all of which "contain the
          dangers of extremism and exclusivism"; still, "in which way can
          the church benefit from the positive elements?"

2241.   Westmeier. Karl-Wilhelm. "The Enthusiastic Protestants of Bogota,
          Colombia: Reflections on the Growth of a Movement." International
          Review of Mission 75 (January 1986): 13-24.

          Demonstrates the "fit" between pentecostalism and the
          spiritual, psychological, and community needs of Bogotanos.

2242.   Willens, Emillio. "Validation of Authority in Pentecostal Sects
          of Chile and Brazil." Journal for the Scientific Study of
          Religion 6 (Fall 1967): 253-58.

          Despite the egalitarian tendency of these groups (two in Chile,
          one in Brazil) there is a strong leadership, whose authority is
          legitimated by supernatural sanctions (appeals to the Holy
          Spirit).

2243.   Wilson, Everett A. "Latin American Pentecostals: Their Potential
          for Ecumenical Dialogue." Pneuma 9 (Fall 1986): 85-90.

2244.   _____. "Sanguine Saints: Pentecostalism in El Salvador."
          Church History 52 (June 1983): 186-98.

          Origins. growth. and especially the organizational development
          of the El Salvador pentecostal churches.

See also items 580, 599, 621, 2044, 2066, 2134. 2183. 2253, 2263, 2650.

E.   Social Science Studies

2245.   Barker, Montagu G. "Psychological Aspects of the Charismatic
          Movement." Journal of the Christian Brethren Research Fellowship
          no. 29 (1977); 27-37.

          Proposes to treat not the reality or validity. but "to comment
          upon the expectation of experience and the differing status
          given to it in the lives of Christians": draws several
          conclusions about tongue speakers and charismatic groups.

2246.   Beckmann, David M. "Trance: From Africa to Pentecostalism."
         Concordia Theological Monthly 45 (January 1974): 11-26.

         Speaking in tongues is a trance experience brought by
         Afro-Americans into Christianity, with the speaking entirely
         unlike ordinary language; based on six points, some of which,
         like the debate on Herskovits, need further exploration.

2247.   Bourgault, Louise. "The Electric Church: The 'PTL Club.'"
         Journal of Religious Studies 12, no. 1 (1984): 76-95.

         Derived from her Ohio University 1980 Ph.D. dissertation, "An
         Ethnographic Study of the 'Praise the Lord Club,'" this 1979
         survey of churches in an Ohio town reveals entertainment users
         and inspiration seekers among the viewers.

2248.   Clark, Donald L. "An Implicit Theory of Personality, Illness, and
         Cure Found in the Writings of Neo-Pentecostal Faith Teachers."
         Journal of Psychology and Theology 12 (Winter 1984): 279-85.

         Faith confessionalists like E. W. Kenyon, Kenneth Hagin, et
         al., produce "a cohesive theory of personality, illness and
         cure."

2249.   Connelly, James Thomas. "The Pentecostal Movement and Speaking in
         Tongues." In Does Jesus Make a Difference? (Proceedings of the
         College Theology Society), ed. Thomas M. McFadden, 167-85. New
         York: Seabury, 1974.

         Helpful critical survey of some of the social science
         literature on glossolalia.

2250.   Davies, Douglas. "The Charismatic Ethic and the Spirit of
         Post-Industrialism." In Strange Gifts? A Guide to Charismatic
         Renewal, eds. David Martin and Peter Mullen, 137-50. New York:
         Basil Blackwell, 1984.

         The "psychological aspects of speaking in tongues," the
         "sociological factors touching" the "tongues-speakers," and
         "some theological issues which inevitably arise from these
         reflections."

2251.   Dearman, Marion. "Christ and Conformity: A Study of Pentecostal
         Values." Journal for the Scientific Study of Religion 13
         (December 1974): 437-53.

Study of the United Pentecostal Church. a "oneness" group;
subjects (a group of males. aged twenty to forty, from several
UPC churches in Oregon) share many of the dominant values of
American society, values taught in the local congregations;
hostility to society, commonly seen as a characteristic of
sects, does not apply here.

2252.   Dominian, J. "Psychological Evaluation of the Pentecostal
         Movement." Expository Times 87 (July 1976): 292-97.

         Recognizes the values to the church produced by pentecostalism
         (including charismatics). but its emphasis on emotions, visible
         demonstration of the gifts of the Spirit. and its dynamic
         characteristics make it especially attractive to the mentally
         disturbed.

2253.   Gerlach, Luther P. "Pentecostalism: Revolution or Counter-
         Revolution?" In Religious Movements in Contemporary America, eds.
         Irving I. Zaretsky and Mark P. Leone, 669-99. Princeton:
         Princeton University Press, 1974.

         Rather than "examining religion as the consequence of or
         reaction to change," this essay uses two detailed case studies
         --pentecostalism in the U.S., and in Haiti--to see "how
         religion generates individual and social change."

2254.   Gerlach. Luther P., and Virginia H. Hine. "Five Factors Crucial
         to the Growth and Spread of a Modern Religious Movement." Journal
         for the Scientific Study of Religion 7 (Spring 1968): 23-40.

         Based on pentecostal groups in Minnesota and in four Latin
         American countries. the authors conclude that organization,
         recruitment, a commitment act, ideology, and real or imagined
         opposition are the five factors.

2255.   Gilmore, Susan K. "Personality Differences Between High and Low
         Dogmatism Groups of Pentecostal Believers." Journal for the
         Scientific Study of Religion 8 (Spring 1969): 161-66.

         The low dogmatism pentecostals "score significantly higher on
         measures of personal adjustment and interpersonal skill (i.e..
         the CPI) than do closed or dogmatic Pentecostals."

2256.   Gritzmacher. Steven A.. Brian Bolton. and Richard H. Dana.
         "Psychological Characteristics of Pentecostals: A Literature
         Review and Psychodynamic Synthesis." Journal of Psychology and
         Theology 16 (Fall 1988): 233-45.

Extends previous literature reviews by including studies from
1976 through 1985 as well as earlier studies. Conclusions
include that "the psychological and sociological literature has
progressed from viewing Pentecostalism from a perspective of
psycho-pathology, trance, and social disorganization/
deprivation to an assessment of personality characteristics,
social learning variables, and competing social commitments
associated with Pentecostalism."

2257.   Hine, Virginia H. "Pentecostal Glossolalia: Toward a Functional
         Interpretation." Journal for the Scientific Study of Religion 8
         (Fall 1969): 211-26.

         Citing the inadequacy of psychological and sociological
         explanations, Hine's study of 289 subjects offers a functional
         explanation of glossolalia as "one component in the generation
         of commitment," operating in both social and personal change.

2258.   Jennings, George J. "An Ethnological Study of Glossalalia [sic]."
         Journal of the American Scientific Affiliation 20 (March 1968):
         5-16.

         Applies "ethnological analysis to glossolalia by reference to
         its occurrence among non-Christian cultures."

2259.   Lankford, John. "David Edwin Harrell, Jr., All Things Are
         Possible: The Healing and Charismatic Revivals in Modern America;
         A Review Essay." Historical Magazine of the Protestant Episcopal
         Church 46 (June 1977): 251-65.

         Positive evaluation of Harrell's book, followed by Lankford's
         own sociological description of pentecostalism's move into the
         mainline denominations: "the charismatic message stands in
         stark contrast to the public/bureaucratic world."

2260.   Lovekin, Adams, and H. Newton Malony. "Religious Glossolalia: A
         Longitudinal Study of Personality Changes." Journal for the
         Scientific Study of Religion 16 (December 1977): 383-93.

         A pioneering study, measuring persons in the "Life in the
         Spirit" seminar "on personality and attitudinal variables pre,
         post, and three months after the seminar." While "all persons
         changed in the direction of personality integration" the
         changes were interpreted "primarily as a function of attending
         the seminar rather than of the glossolalic experience."

2261. Shopshire, James Maynard. "A Socio-Historical Characterization of the Black Pentecostal Movement in America." Ph.D. diss., Northwestern University, 1975. 246 p.

2262. Tappeiner, Daniel A. "The Function of Tongue-Speaking for the Individual: A Psycho-Theological Model." Journal of the American Scientific Affiliation 26 (March 1974): 29-32.

> Assuming the identity of present day tongues with that of the New Testament, he examines the biblical, psychological and theological descriptions of tongues; concludes that "to make too much of tongues as a means is an understandable error--to ignore tongues is an unfortunate one."

2263. Verge, Carl. "A Comparison of the Beliefs and Practices of Two Groups of Pentecostal Assemblies of Canada Ministers: Those With a Master's Degree and Those With Only Three Years of Bible College Training." Ph.D. diss., New York University, 1987. 232 p.

2264. Wilson, John, and Harvey K. Clow. "Themes of Power and Control in a Pentecostal Assembly." Journal for the Scientific Study of Religion 20 (September 1981): 241-50.

> Two-year study of a southern "Jesus Only" congregation questions the deprivation thesis, and offers the idea that pentecostal worship symbols replicate reality rather than simply compensate for it.

2265. Wood, William Woodhull. "Culture and Personality Aspects of the Pentecostal Holiness Religion." Ph.D. diss., The University of North Carolina at Chapel Hill, 1961. 184 p.

See also items 53, 69, 146, 642, 1679, 2032, 2060, 2064, 2101, 2242.

VI

THE CHARISMATIC MOVEMENT

A. History

2266.　Audemard, Philip. "Bardon: A Puzzle for the Protestant
Evangelical." Fraternal no. 168 (September 1973): 40-44.

Reports on a charismatic Roman Catholic congregation in Bardon,
a suburb of Brisbane, Australia, the center of pentecostalism
in Brisbane and the "parent body" of a growing movement in
Australia, that began in 1970.

2267.　Bennett, Dennis. "Dennis Bennett: Mainline Charismatic."
Interview by Miriam Murphy. Christian Century 89 (27 September
1972): 952-55.

One of the first mainline clergymen in the charismatic
movement, Episcopalian Bennett here outlines the basic beliefs
and then-current status of its operation.

2268.　Bishop, Richard W. "An Investigation of the Relationship of the
Baptism in the Spirit to the Devotional Life of Charismatic
Christians as Reflected by Charismatic Literature From 1959 to
1980." D.Min. diss., North American Baptist Seminary, 1982.

2269.　Bord, Richard J., and Joseph E. Faulkner. "Religiosity and
Secular Attitudes: The Case of Catholic Pentecostals." Journal
for the Scientific Study of Religion 14 (March 1975): 257-70.

Study of nearly one thousand members of Catholic charismatic
prayer groups reveals that "religiosity indices are associated
only with those social attitudes having direct implications for
ongoing doctrinal or church-related consideration."

2270.　Bourassa, Louise. "A Man of the Spirit." New Covenant 12 (June
1983): 4-8.

403

Sketch of the life and work of Belgian Cardinal Leo Joseph
Suenens, foremost European leader in the Catholic renewal
movement.

2271.　"Charismatic Unity in Kansas City." Christianity Today 27 (12
August 1977): 36-37.

Reports "The 1977 Conference on Charismatic Renewal in the
Christian Churches," with 40,000 registrants, almost half of
them Roman Catholics. Ten "denominational or fellowship
groups" co-sponsored the event, with independents, Lutherans,
and Methodists next largest.

2272.　Colledge, Edward. "Enthusiasm in 1976." The Way 17 (April 1977):
95-103.

An ambiguous description of the Catholic charismatic movement
as one in a series of renewals in the church's history.

2273.　Connelly, James Thomas. "Neo-Pentecostalism: The Charismatic
Revival in the Mainline Protestant and Roman Catholic Churches in
the United States, 1960-1971." Ph.D. diss., The University of
Chicago, 1977. 417 p.

2274.　Danielson, Dan. "Charismatic Renewal and Social Concern." Post
American 4 (February 1975): 24-25.

Previously printed in New Convenant (June 1974) and Link (29
October 1973); the renewal is still in its "novitiate" but has
the potential for "solid, long-term radical commitment to
social justice."

2275.　Davison, Leslie. "Conscious Awareness: A New Phase in the
Pentecostal Movement." Frontier 14 (November 1971): 235-38.

Bibliographical article charting the rise of the charismatic
movement as the "new phase."

2276.　Dayton, Donald W. "Pentecostal/Charismatic Renewal and Social
Change: A Western Perspective." Transformation 5 (October-
December 1988): 7-13.

2277.　Ensley, Eddie. Sounds of Wonder: Speaking in Tongues in the
Catholic Tradition. New York: Paulist Press, 1977. 140 p.

Glimpses of the "jubilation tradition" (glossolalic prayer)
from the church fathers to the present. Bibliographical
references. Index.

2278.   Ewin, Wilson. "Key '73 and Roman Catholic Pentecostal
         (Charismatic) Power." Reformation Review 20 (July 1973): 227-43.

         The Catholic charismatic movement and its ecumenical approaches
         to classical pentecostals and to new evangelicals are
         indicators of no change in traditional Catholic doctrine nor in
         the desire to unite all Christians with the Pope.

2279.   Fargher, Brian. "The Charismatic Movement in Ethiopia 1960-1980."
         Evangelical Review of Theology 12 (October 1988): 344-58.

         A movement initiated by young people in the 1960s, reactions to
         it, excesses in it, and its gradual toning down and acceptance
         in the 1970s as it made contributions in music, enthusiasm,
         participation and gifts of the Holy Spirit.

2280.   Forrest, Tom. "The Renewal Reaches the World." New Covenant 12
         (July-August 1982): 22-28.

         Interview of Forrest, chairman of the International Catholic
         Charismatic Renewal Office (Rome), who describes the worldwide
         extent of the movement.

2281.   Gross, Don H., and Donald Hands. "A Charismatic Dictionary for
         Psychotherapists." Journal of Pastoral Counseling 16 (Fall/Winter
         1981): 32-34.

         Fourteen popular charismatic phrases are given "partial
         translation."

2282.   Hamilton, Michael Pollock, ed. The Charismatic Movement. Grand
         Rapids: Eerdmans, 1975. 196 p.

2283.   Harper, Michael. "Charismatic Renewal-A New Ecumenism?" One in
         Christ 9, no. 1 (1973): 59-65.

         In spite of weaknesses--illuminism, pietism, elitism--Anglican
         Harper sees great hopes for the renewal "in all areas of
         Christian life and concern."

2284.   _____. "The Holy Spirit Acts in the Church, Its Structure, Its
         Sacramentality, Its Worship and Sacraments." One In Christ 12,
         no. 4 (1976): 319-28.

         Components in the renewal movement: eschatology, ecclesiology,
         house churches, music.

2285.   Heino, Harri. "The Charismatic Movement in Finland and North
         America." Pneuma 10 (Spring 1988): 50-61.

         Explores the (1) "Charismatic Movement as a Research Problem,"
         (2) "The Charismatic Movement in the Lutheran Church of
         Finland," (3) "Differences in the Charismatic movements in
         North America and Finland," and (4) "Factors influencing the
         formation of the Finnish Charismatic Movement."

2286.   Heron, B. M. "Roman Catholics and Pentecostals." One in Christ
         10, no. 1 (1974): 2-4.

         "The Charismatic Renewal or Pentecostal Movement can powerfully
         forward the movement towards true Christian unity," but there
         are "special difficulties in this direction."

2287.   Hills, James W. L. "The New Charismatics, 1973." Eternity 24
         (1973): 23-25, 33.

         American pentecostalism has entered phase three, phase one
         being from the turn of the century (Asuza Street), phase two
         from 1960 (neo-pentecostalism in main line Protestant
         churches), and phase three with beginnings of Roman Catholic
         pentecostalism and the Jesus People, both of which Hills deals
         with here.

2288.   _____. "The New Pentecostalism: Its Pioneers and Promoters."
         Eternity 14 (July 1963): 17-18.

         Sympathetic approach to the charismatic movement in its early
         stages, focusing on Dennis Bennett, David DuPlessis, Harold
         Bredesen and James Brown as representative.

2289.   Hollenweger, Walter J. "Roots and Fruits of the Charismatic
         Renewal in the Third World." In Strange Gifts? A Guide to
         Charismatic Renewal, ed. David Martin and Peter Mullen, 172-91.
         New York: Basil Blackwell, 1984.

         Transcribed tape of an address on the origin and scope of the
         movement and its relation to the WCC, followed by responses to
         audience questions.

2290.   Howe, Claude L., Jr. "Charismatic Movement in Southern Baptist
         Life." Baptist History and Heritage 13 (July 1978): 20-27, 65.

         Survey of SBC seminary professors, Convention presidents and
         association leaders, concludes that while Southern Baptists are

a diverse group, most of them see the charismatic movement as divisive, "stressing a minor gift [tongues] out of proportion to the biblical evidence."

2291.   Hughes, R. H. "A Traditional Pentecostal Looks at the New Pentecostals." Christianity Today 18 (7 June 1974): 6-10.

Raises and discusses several questions--the role of doctrine; relation between tongues-speaking and baptism in the Spirit; the issue of unity; life style; relation to the church--and sees some dangers in the new pentecostalism.

2292.   Hummel, Charles E. "The Renewal's Effect on Churches Today." Logos Journal 11 (March-April 1981): 18-24.

Lists the variety of forms the charismatic renewal takes in Roman Catholic and in Protestant mainline denominations.

2293.   Jensen, Peter F. "Calvin, Charismatics and Miracles." Evangelical Quarterly 51 (July-September 1979): 131-44.

Calvin believed that miracles adorned the Scriptures when given, but faith is in the Word which we now have, therefore miracles are no longer needed; Calvin would no doubt reject decisively the contemporary charismatic movement.

2294.   John Paul II, Pope. "Authentic Renewal." New Covenant 10 (June 1981): 4-6.

Positive comments about the renewal, and apostolic blessing on the 16,000 Italian Catholics addressed by the Pope, October 1980.

2295.   Jones, James William. Filled With New Wine: The Charismatic Renewal of the Church. New York: Harper & Row, 1974. 141 p.

Episcopalian Jones describes the pentecostal experience and offers "a practical theology of church renewal based on the charismatic movement."

2296.   Jorstad, Erling. "Agenda for Charismatic Renewal." Ecumenist 14 (January/February 1976): 27-31.

Four sources of division among charismatics need to be placed on the agenda: evangelicals vs. mainline Protestants, the theology of the Spirit, charismatics and their parent churches, controversy over "discipleship" [authority].

2297.   _____. Bold in the Spirit: Lutheran Charismatic Renewal in
America Today. Minneapolis: Augsburg, 1974. 128 p.

The origins of Lutheran charismatic renewal, case studies of
individuals and congregations who experienced renewal, the
present conditions of the Lutheran renewal, and "some of the
issues to be faced by both charismatics and non-charismatics in
the future of the church." Bibliography.

2298.   _____. The Holy Spirit in Today's Church: A Handbook of the
New Pentecostalism. Nashville: Abingdon, 1973. 160 p.

2299.   Kerkhofs, J., ed. Catholic Pentecostals Now. Canfield, OH: Alba
Books, 1977. 118 p.

Material from Pro Mundi Vita Bulletin, no. 60.

2300.   Koenig, John. "Documenting the Charismatics." Word and World 1
(Summer 1981): 287-89.

Review of some of the current literature produced by Episcopal,
Lutheran and Roman Catholic charismatics.

2301.   Laurentin, Rene. Catholic Pentecostalism. Translated by Matthew
J. O'Connell. Garden City: Doubleday, 1977. 239 p.

A French charismatic describes the rise, course, meaning, and
dangers of the renewal movement, writing "historically and
doctrinally, while also being open to the interdisciplinary
contributions of the human sciences." Helpful multilingual
bibliography.

2302.   Lilly, Fred. "A Charismatico Explosion." New Covenant 13 (May
1984): 8-12.

The work of two Roman Catholic charismatic organizations among
Hispanics in the U.S.: Hispanic Missions and Charisma in
Missions.

2303.   _____. "Spiritual Powerhouses." New Covenant 15 (October
1985): 16-18.

The account of two Catholic parishes (Langdon. ND. and Grand
Rapids. MI) that have been touched by the Charismatic renewal
movement.

2304.   Lindberg, Carter. The Third Reformation? Charismatic Movements
         and the Lutheran Tradition. Macon, GA: Mercer University Press,
         1983. 345 p.

            A look at Lutheran charismatics, set against the backdrop of
            Lutheran history since the sixteenth century. Sixteen-page
            bibliography. Index.

2305.   Magno, Joseph A. "An Interview with Fr. Richard Rohr, O.F.M. on
         the Key Issues of the Charismatic Renewal." Listening 12 (Winter
         1977): 3-15.

            A principal leader in the renewal, Rohr answers questions about
            and objections to the Catholic charismatic movement. This
            issue of Listening has essays on various aspects of the renewal
            in the Catholic Church.

2306.   Maier, Walter A. "Charismatic Renewal in the Lutheran Church:
         'Renewal in Missouri.'" Concordia Theological Quarterly 53
         (January-April 1989): 21-38.

            Gives a historical sketch, including the founding in the spring
            of 1988 of an organization named "Renewal in Missouri"
            (abbreviated "RIM"), with a newsletter with the same name, then
            devotes the balance of the article to "Comments on Certain of
            RIM's Distinctive Theological Affirmations."

2307.   Martin, David, and Peter Mullen, eds. Strange Gifts? A Guide to
         Charismatic Renewal. New York: Blackwell, 1984. 254 p.

            Contributions from supporters and critics of the charismatic
            movements in Britain, intended to "illuminate as many aspects
            of the movement as possible - theological, historical,
            philosophical, sociological and aesthetic." Bibliographies.

2308.   Martin, Ralph. Unless the Lord Build the House: The Church and
         the New Pentecost. Notre Dame, IN: Ave Maria Press, 1971. 63 p.

            A leader in the Catholic charismatic movement states that the
            theological confusion in his Church can only be overcome by
            preaching the gospel in the power of the Spirit and by building
            community.

2309.   McDonnell, Kilian. "The Catholic Charismatic Renewal: Reassess-
         ment and Critique." Religion in Life 44 (Summer 1975): 138-54.

Careful discussion of terms; social and theological elements in
the movement; and the patterns in which the Catholic renewal is
expressed, the chief of which is summed up in the word
presence.

2310.   . "Catholic Pentecostalism: Problems in Evaluation."
Dialog 9 (Winter 1970): 35-54.

Based on four years of extensive print and field research in
various parts of the world, McDonnell lays out the difficulties
in making an objective evaluation, the Scriptural basis for
baptism in the Spirit, origins of the movement in Catholicism;
even though it has dangers and abuses, concludes that "the
Pentecostal spirituality . . . is of an assailable validity."
Shorter version in Theology Digest 19 (Spring 1971): 46-53.

2311.   . Charismatic Renewal and Ecumenism. New York: Paulist
Press, 1978. 125 p.

Neither academic nor exhaustive, this document (based on
comments by an international team of theologians) aims "to
indicate what norms should guide ecumenism at the local level"
of the Catholic Church in relating to the Orthodox, Anglicans,
and Protestants. Bibliographical references.

2312.   . Charismatic Renewal and the Churches. New York:
Seabury Press, 1976. 202 p.

McDonnell is the chief among historians and analyzers of the
Catholic charismatic movement. Bibliography. Index.

2313.   . "The Relationship of the Charismatic Renewal to the
Established Denominations." Dialog 13 (Summer 1974): 223-29.

Explores the Lutheran "theological ecclesial culture" to argue
that Lutheran charismatics (like those in other denominations)
ought to work in their own theological culture for mutual
enrichment.

2314.   . "Towards a Critique of the Churches and the Charismatic
Renewal." One in Christ 16, no. 4 (1980): 329-37.

A two-part list: criticism of the documents about the renewal
issued by a number of churches: criticisms leveled by McDonnell
at the movement: isolation from the world, the church and
theology.

2315.   McGuire, Meredith B. Pentecostal Catholics: Power, Charisma, and
         Order in a Religious Movement. Philadelphia: Temple University
         Press, 1982. 270 p.

2316.   McKinney. Joseph, Bill Beatty, et al. "Perspectives on the
         Charismatic Renewal." New Covenant 16 (February 1987): 19-23.

         Seven leaders share their evaluations of the renewal's past and
         present, and they look forward to a bright future."

2317.   Moonie, Peter Meredith. "The Significance of Neo-Pentecostalism
         for the Renewal and Unity of the Church in the United States."
         Th.D. diss., Boston University School of Theology, 1974. 499 p.

2318.   Mouw, Richard J. "Catholic Pentecostalism Today." Reformed   <
         Journal 22 (July-August 1972): 8-15.

         Mouw sees Catholic pentecostalism as "a powerful work of the
         Holy Spirit in the Roman Catholic Church"; occasioned by his
         attendance at the International Conference on the Charismatic
         Renewal In the Catholic Church, held at Notre Dame (1973).

2319,   O'Connor, Edward D. "The Hidden Roots of the Charismatic Renewal   <
         in the Catholic Church." In Aspects of Pentecostal-Charismatic
         Origins, ed. Vinson Synan, 169-91. Plainfield: Logos, 1975.

         The variety of persons, movements, and theologies from the 19th
         century to Vatican II that formed the backdrop for the
         charismatic renewal that began in the late 1960s.

2320.   _____. The Pentecostal Movement in the Catholic Church. Notre   <
         Dame, IN: Ave Maria Press, 1971. 301 p.

2321.   _____, ed. Perspectives on Charismatic Renewal. Notre Dame: <
         University of Notre Dame Press, 1975. 216 p.

         Series of articles on charismatic movements from ancient Israel
         to the modern movement; extremely helpful forty-page
         bibliography on the Roman Catholic renewal, covering the years
         1967-1975. Index.

2322.   O'Mara, Philip F. "Ecumenism in the Catholic Charismatic Renewal   <
         Movement." Journal of Ecumenical Studies 17 (Fall 1980): 647-60.

         Looks at worship and at spiritual formation in renewal groups,
         and discusses the ecumenical tensions produced thereby.

2323.   "Official and Private Views on the Orthodox Charismatic Renewal."
         Logos (November-December 1977): 13-16.

         Noting the absence of official statements, and that "almost
         every assessment of the Charismatic Renewal, whether private or
         semi-official, has been negative." cites, often quoting at
         length, many of those assessments, and reprints the full text
         of the portion of a Spring 1976 Encyclical dealing with the
         charismatic renewal.

2324.   Opsahl, Paul D., ed. The Holy Spirit in the Life of the Church:
         From Biblical Times to the Present. Minneapolis: Augsburg, 1978.
         287 p.

         "Essays representing first phase of a study project conducted
         by the Division of Theological Studies of the Lutheran Council
         in the U.S.A. and presented at four national conferences,
         1974-1976." Historical and theological. Bibliographies.

2325.   Otterland, Anders, and Lennart Sunnergren. Upwinds: A Short
         Report on Spiritual Upwinds in Our Time. Nashville: Thomas
         Nelson, 1975. 162 p.

         Two sympathetic investigators look at the components, changed
         lives, and other factors in the charismatic renewal in Sweden.

2326.   Painter, John. "Background to 'Charismatic Christianity.'"
         Journal of Theology For Southern Africa no. 8 (June 1974): 4-9.

         Report on a course on "Charismatic Christianity" given for more
         than 100 selected individuals at the University of Cape Town
         (February 1974).

2327.   Pederson, W. Dennis. "A Time to Mend." Christian Life 45 (April
         1984): 40-42.

         Charismatics can "bridge the gap between evangelical and more
         liberal denominations" and "provide a linkage between historic
         churches and . . . Third World bodies."

2328.   Quebedeaux, Richard. The New Charismatics II. Rev. ed. San
         Francisco: Harper & Row, 1983. 272 p.

         Revision of his The New Charismatics (1976), with a helpful
         annotated bibliography.

2329.   ___. The New Charismatics: The Origins, Development, and
             Significance of Neo-Pentecostalism. Garden City: Doubleday, 1976.
             252 p.

             A revised version of the author's Oxford D.Phil. dissertation
             (1975), this fine work looks at the background and beginnings
             of pentecostalism, then describes the post-WWII rise of the
             charismatic movement, its leadership, faith and practice,
             relation to classical pentecostalism, and reasons for its
             success. Appendix. Bibliography. Index.

2330.   Ranaghan, Kevin M. "The Catholic Charismatic Renewal." Logos
             Journal 11 (March-April 1981): 25-29.

             An early leader in the movement gives a positive appraisal of
             its effects in the Roman Catholic Church.

2331.   Ranaghan, Kevin M., and Dorothy Ranaghan, eds. Catholic
             Pentecostals. Paramus: Paulist Press, 1969. 266 p.

             First of the books giving a historical and theological
             introduction to the Catholic renewal, by two persons prominent
             in the movement. Bibliography with some annotations.

2332.   Reid, W. S. "Some Questions About the New Pentecostalism."
             Christianity Today 18 (7 June 1974): 6-10.

             Use of the term charismatic; paucity of historical evidence of
             tongues-speaking; fruit of the present charismatic movement.

2333.   Reinertsen, Lawrence Gustav. "The Charismatic Renewal and The
             Presbyterian Church (U.S.A.): A Survey of the Attitudes and
             Perceptions of the Presbytery Executives (United States)." D.Min.
             diss., Eastern Baptist Theological Seminary, 1984. 267 p.

2334.   Religious Reawakening in America. Books by U.S. News and World
             Report. Joseph Newman - Directing Editor. Washington, DC: U.S.
             News and World Report, 1972. 191 p.

             Surveys the national scene of the late 1960s and early 1970s.
             Considerable attention to the charismatic movement, but little
             or no explicit attention to evangelicalism or fundamentalism.
             Index.

2335.   Robeck, Cecil M., Jr., ed. Charismatic Experiences in History.
             Peabody, MA: Hendrickson, 1985. 180 p.

Articles on charismatic matters, both historical and
theological. Bibliographies.

2336.   Stephanou, Eusebius A. Pathway to Orthodox Renewal. Fort Wayne:
Logos Ministry for Orthodox Renewal, 1978. 159 p.

An Orthodox priest issues to his Church a prophetic call for
"repentance and reconversion to the living Christ" in a day
when the outpouring of the Holy Spirit is occurring;
continuation of the themes in his Desolation and Restoration in
the Orthodox Church (1977).

2337.   Stockwell, Eugene. "Charismatics." International Review of
Missions 75 (April 1986): 113-16.

Four areas where the charismatic movement poses danger to
Christian unity.

2338.   Suenens, Leon Joseph Cardinal. "We Need a Spiritual Renewal."
New Covenant 11 (July 1981): 5-7.

The interview (1973) in which Belgian Cardinal Suenens "became
the foremost Catholic bishop to identify himself with the
charismatic renewal."

2339.   Synan, Vinson. "Baptists Ride the Third Wave." Charisma 12
(December 1986): 52-57.

Overview of the influence of the charismatic renewal among
Baptist churches.

2340.   _____. "Bringing the Charismatic Renewal to Maturity." New
Covenant 16 (October 1986): 14-16.

Anticipating the 1986 and 1987 Holy Spirit conferences in New
Orleans, Synan sees the 1990s as the most important decade for
Holy Spirit evangelization.

2341.   _____. "Discerning the Charismatic Renewal." Theology Today
39 (July 1982): 187-93.

Appreciative review of Kilian McDonnell. Presence. Power.
Praise: Documents on the Charismatic Renewal (1980).

2342.   _____. "A Long Road to Renewal." Charisma 12 (October 1986):
61-65.

Reaction to the Pentecostal experience within Wesleyan-Holiness
and Orthodox churches.

2343.   _____. "A Surprise of the Spirit." Charisma 12 (March 1978):   <
26-29.

Survey of the twenty years of the Catholic charismatic renewal
movement.

2344.   Thielemann, Bruce W. "Annotated Bibliography (Neo-Pentecostalism)." Theology, News and Notes 20 (March 1974): 20-21.

List of sixteen books "designed to benefit the busy pastor
. . . [who] does not have time to undertake an extended study"
of neo-pentecostalism.

2345.   Williams, J. Rodman. "Profile of the Charismatic Movement."
Christianity Today 19 (28 February 1975): 9-13.

Seven characteristics of the movement, by the then-president of
Melodyland School of Theology.

See also items 9, 36, 47, 51, 52, 65, 73, 497, 621, 667, 1463, 1520, 2023,
2049, 2050, 2061, 2068, 2081, 2092, 2113, 2115, 2220, 2359, 2364,
2365, 2366, 2388, 2397, 2444, 2449, 2493, 2597, 2598, 2608.

B. Biblical and Theological Studies

2346.   Agrimson, J. Elmo, ed. Gifts of the Spirit and the Body of
Christ: Perspectives on the Charismatic Movement. Minneapolis:
Augsburg, 1974. 112 p.

Six Lutherans, only one a charismatic, write about the
movement--biblical, historical, psychological, practical--
hoping to create guidance for congregations facing
charismatics. Bibliography.

2347.   Antekeier, Charles, Janet K. Vandagriff, and Van Vandagriff.   <
Confirmation: The Power of the Spirit; a Charismatic Preparation
Program for Youth, Their Parents, and Sponsors. Notre Dame, IN:
Ave Maria Press, 1972. 128 p.

Seven lessons given to groups of seventh- and eighth-graders
being instructed for confirmation in a Grand Rapids, Michigan,
parish, based on The Life in the Spirit Seminars "developed to
teach adults who are seeking the 'baptism in the Holy Spirit.'"

> 2348.   Bagiackas, Joseph. The Future Glory: Charismatic Renewal and the
          Implementation of Vatican II. South Bend, IN: Charismatic Renewal
          Services, 1983. 130 p.

          A Catholic charismatic considers different aspects of the
          Catholic mentality and how charismatic life enriches them, and
          attempts "to show how life in the Spirit is in harmony with the
          spirit of Vatican II."

2349.   Beeg, John Frederich. "Beliefs and Values of Charismatics: A
          Survey." Ph.D. diss., Colgate Rochester Divinity School/Crozer
          Theological Seminary, 1977.

> 2350.   Bishops' Liaison Committee With the Catholic Charismatic Renewal.
          A Pastoral Statement on the Catholic Charismatic Renewal: A
          Statement of the Bishops' Liaison Committee With the Catholic
          Charismatic Renewal. Washington, DC: United States Catholic
          Conference, 1984. 19 p.

2351.   Bittlinger, Arnold. "Charismatic Renewal: An Opportunity for the
          Church?" Ecumenical Review 31 (July 1979): 247-51.

          Upbeat description of a renewal that offers half a dozen
          opportunities for the church and the individual.

2352.   _____, ed. The Church is Charismatic. Geneva, Switzerland:
          Renewal and Congregational Life, World Council of Churches, 1981.
          241 p.

2353.   _____. "Presence, Power, Praise: An Evaluation of Documents on
          the Charismatic Renewal." Ecumenical Review 35 (January 1983):
          75-80.

          Review essay of Kilian McDonnell's Presence, Power, Praise:
          Documents on the Charismatic Renewal (1980). Bittlinger gives
          high marks to McDonnell for his objective approach in including
          both pro and con statements, but regrets the lack of documents
          from Africa and Latin America.

2354.   Bloesch, Donald G. "The Charismatic Revival: A Theological
          Critique." Religion in Life 35 (Summer 1966): 364-80.

          Biblical, psychological and theological appraisal of the
          revival, which Bloesch approves of as a "fragment of the
          Christian truth"; the Christian faith is fuller and more
          catholic than charismatic experiences.

2355.   Board, Stephen. "Are the Catholic Charismatics 'Evangelicals.'"
        Eternity 29 (July 1978): 12-16.

        Label them "evangelicals," because they are Christ-centered,
        grace-centered, emphasize "personal faith response to Christ
        and passionate love for Him," and "increasingly minimize" what
        have been objectionable features for Protestants.

2356.   Breckenridge, James F. The Theological Self-Understanding of the
        Catholic Charismatic Movement. Washington, DC: University Press
        of America, 1980. 144 p.

2357.   Bredesen, Harold. "Momentum: The Second Wave of Pentecost."
        Logos Journal 11 (March-April 1981): 14-16.

        The fifteen years from Bredesen's experience of tongues-
        speaking to the birth of the charismatic renewal in 1960.

2358.   Brown, Dale W. Flamed by the Spirit: Biblical Definitions of the
        Holy Spirit: A Brethren Perspective. Elgin, IL: Brethren Press,
        1978. 80 p.

        Four Bible studies on the work and role of the Holy Spirit in
        the community of believers. Bibliographical references.

2359.   Buskey, Jack Ronald. "The Charismatic Movement in Relationship to
        the Church." D.Min. diss., Drew University, 1978. 267 p.

        Buskey posits that the charismatic renewal is "not inherently
        divisive" and that it has an "important contribution" to make
        to the established church, such as a renewed interest in the
        Holy Spirit. At the same time, he cautions, the charismatic
        renewal needs the "perspective and balance" of the church at
        large.

2360.   Butler, C. S. "Is the Charismatic Movement a Revival?"
        Reformation Today 80 (July-August 1984): 28-31.

        Compares the charismatic renewal with past revivals and states
        that revival "has not come through the charismatic movement."

2361.   Byrne, James E. Living in the Spirit: A Handbook on Catholic
        Charismatic Christianity. New York: Paulist Press. 1975. 184 p.

        Writing to charismatics, Byrne sees the baptism in the Holy
        Spirit as a work of grace, not a panacea, therefore stresses
        developing a spiritual life, the gifts and their functions.

guidance by the Spirit, and the charismatic's relation to the church. Bibliography.

2362.   "The Charismatics and Their Churches: Report on Two Conferences." Dialog 15 (Spring 1976): 142-44.

Lutheran charismatics in Minneapolis and Catholic charismatics in Detroit (both meeting in August 1975), though similar "in approach, content and style," are "marked by significant differences."

2363.   Christenson, Laurence. A Charismatic Approach to Social Action. Minneapolis: Bethany Fellowship, 1974. 122 p.

2364.   _____. The Charismatic Renewal Among Lutherans: A Pastoral and Theological Perspective. Minneapolis: Lutheran Charismatic Renewal Services, distributed by Bethany Fellowship, 1976. 160 p.

Outlines "the contribution which Lutherans and Lutheranism have to make to the charismatic renewal, and which the renewal offers to the Lutheran Church." Ten-page annotated bibliography.

2365.   _____. A Message to the Charismatic Movement. Minneapolis: Bethany Fellowship, 1972. 119 p.

Study of the teachings and church life of the 19th century Catholic Apostolic church (founded by Edward Irving) and their application to the 20th century renewal movement. Bibliographical references.

2366.   _____, ed. Welcome, Holy Spirit: A Study of Charismatic Renewal in the Church. Minneapolis: Augsburg, 1987. 432 p.

Based on papers presented at the International Lutheran Charismatic Theological Consultation held outside Helsinki, Finland, in the Summer of 1981. Forty-page bibliography. Index.

2367.   Cole. G. A. "Renewal: Catholic. Charismatic and Calvinist." Evangelical Review of Theology 9 (October 1985): 323-33.

Reprinted from Reformed Theology Review (January-April 1985): Cole uses Cardinal Suenens. Michael Harper. and James I. Packer to represent the three positions. and draws some theological conclusions.

2368.   Culpepper, Robert H. Evaluating the Charismatic Movement: A
         Theological and Biblical Appraisal. Valley Forge: Judson, 1977.
         192 p.

              Profile, historical background, and theological appraisal of
              baptism in the Holy Spirit, gifts of the Spirit, and other
              components in the movement, done in an irenic fashion by
              Baptist Culpepper. Annotated bibliographies. Index.

2369.   _____. "Survey of Some Tensions Emerging in the Charismatic
         Movement." Scottish Journal of Theology 30, no. 5 (1977): 439-52.

              Tensions include "The Gifts . . . Versus the Fruit of the
              Spirit," "Experience Versus Doctrine," "Crisis Experience
              Versus Growth Experience," "Emotionalism Versus Intellec-
              tualism," "Spiritual Elitism Versus Spiritual Complacency,"
              "Pietism Versus Social Activism," and "Ecumenism Versus
              Divisiveness."

2370.   Fahey, Sheila Macmanus. Charismatic Social Action: Reflection/
         Resource Manual. New York: Paulist Press, 1977. 174 p.

              Many specific suggestions on how prayer groups can address
              themselves to social problems. Bibliographies.

2371.   Fichter, Joseph Henry. The Catholic Cult of the Paraclete. New
         York: Sheed and Ward, 1975. 183 p.

2372.   Fiddes, Paul S. "The Theology of the Charismatic Movement." In
         Strange Gifts? A Guide to Charismatic Renewal, eds. David Martin
         and Peter Mullen, 19-40. New York: Basil Blackwell, 1984.

              The theology of renewal--particularly the concept of "break-
              through"-- and theological discussion of charisms and
              submission, are the main areas of charismatic theological
              contribution.

2373.   Ford, J. Massyngberde. Baptism of the Spirit: Three Essays on the
         Pentecostal Experience. Techny, IL: Divine Word Publications,
         1971. 133 p,

              Discusses "Charismatic Renewal," the "Pentecostal Blueprint,"
              and "Speaking in Tongues." Bibliographical references.

2374.   _____. "Fly United--But Not In Too Close Formation:
         Reflections on the Catholic Pentecostal Movement." Spiritual Life
         17 (Spring 1971): 12-20.

A convinced charismatic, Ford addresses two issues that cause
her concern: misunderstanding about baptism in the Holy Spirit,
and the creation of exclusive pentecostal communities in the
church.

> 2375.   . "Neo-Pentecostalism Within the Churches." Ecumenist 13
(March-April 1975): 33-36.

Shorter version of Ford's book Which Way for Catholic
Pentecostals? (1976), in which she characterizes two different
models in the Catholic charismatic movement.

> 2376.   . The Pentecostal Experience. Paramus, NJ: Paulist
Press, 1970. 60 p.

Brief description of the Holy Spirit in history, and a relating
of pentecostal experience to Catholic teaching.

> 2377.   . "Pentecostal Poise or Docetic Charismatics?" Spiritual
Life 19 (Spring 1973): 32-47.

Raises several issues about the nature of the Catholic charismatic movement; notes two threats to poise: illuminism and
paraclericalism; suggests a recipe for "pentecostal delight."

2378.   . "Tongues-Leadership-Women: Further Reflections on the
Neo-Pentecostal Movement." Spiritual Life 17 (Fall 1971): 186-97.

The New Testament, while reverencing glossolalia "as a divine
gift and ministry," teaches Christians to seek the higher
gifts; leadership in charismatic groups needs to be controlled;
women "should not hesitate to take leadership in the . . .
movement."

> 2379.   . Which Way For Catholic Pentecostals? New York: Harper
& Row, 1976. 143 p.

Careful analysis of two types of Catholic charismatics: the
structured, convenanted kind embodied in the South Bend and Ann
Arbor communities, which follow "a theology not dissimilar to
that of the Radical Reformation"; and a more open, more pro-
women, more Catholic type--the author's preference. Bibliography. Index.

2380.   Gelpi, Donald L. "Conversion: The Challenge of Contemporary
Charismatic Piety." Theological Studies 43 (December 1982):
606-28.

Defines conversion as affective, speculative, moral and
religious; shows how both evangelical and Catholic piety is
inadequate in some regards; holds out a broader definition of
"charismatic" than pentecostals espouse, as a means of
combining thought, feeling and action.

2381.   . Experiencing God: A Theology of Human Experience. New
York: Paulist Press, 1978. 406 p.

A Jesuit charismatic relates his experience and the ideas of a
number of American philosophers to the charismatic renewal in
this work on fundamental theology. Bibliographical references.
Glossary. Index.

2382.   Ghezzi, Bert. Build With the Lord: Pastoral Advice for Prayer
Groups in the Charismatic Renewal. Ann Arbor: Word of Life, 1976.
129 p.

2383.   Gilling, Bryan. "Charismatics, Grace and Works." Evangelical
Review of Theology 13 (April 1989): 125-36.

"The central thesis of this exegetical study is that man
basically relates himself to his fellow human beings, and the
world around, by work."

2384.   Granfield, Patrick. "The Ecumenical Significance of the Charismatic Movement." Ecumenical Trends 9 (July/August 1980): 97-99.

"Primarily involved with spiritual ecumenism" (rather than
theological or social ecumenism), the charismatic renewal may
make two principal contributions, and faces two possible
problems.

2385.   Harper, George W. "Renewal and Causality: Some Thoughts on a
Conceptual Framework for a Charismatic Theology." Journal of
Ecumenical Studies 24 (Winter 1987): 93-103.

Rather than seeing God's extraordinary activities--tongues,
healing, and the like--as abrogations in a view of natural law
no longer tenable, we should see them panentheistically, as the
different modalities of God's presence.

2386.   Harris, Jackson Lee, II. "A Pastoral Approach to the Charismatic
Renewal." D.Min. diss., School of Theology at Claremont, 1976.
108 p.

2387.   Haughey, John C., ed. Theological Reflections on the Charismatic
          Renewal: Proceedings of the Chicago Conference, October 1-2, 1976.
          Ann Arbor: Servant Books, 1978. 129 p.

          Four papers, with responses, given at the conference sponsored
          by the National Service Committee of the Catholic Charismatic
          Renewal, on biblical hermeneutics, spiritual direction,
          tradition, and authority and church office. Bibliographical
          references.

2388.   Hendrix, Scott H. "Charismatic Renewal: Old Wine in New Skins."
          Currents in Theology and Mission 4 (June 1977): 158-66.

          The charismatic renewal stands in the tradition of "renewal as
          the restoration of the New Testament Church"; a prescriptive
          use of the Bible, a theology of power, and speaking in tongues,
          are signs of restoration. The danger is that charismatics may
          not settle for the Reformation ideal of revitalization, but
          insist on repristination.

2389.   Hesselink, I. John. "The Charismatic Movement and the Reformed
          Tradition." Reformed Review 28 (Spring 1975): 147-56.

          Though he has some reservations about the charismatic movement,
          Hesselink contends that the Reformed tradition's strong
          biblical understanding of the work of the Spirit can complement
          the pentecostal emphasis on the experience of the Spirit.

2390.   Hinnebusch, Paul, ed. Contemplation and the Charismatic Renewal.
          New York: Paulist Press, 1986. 138 p.

          Papers from the 1982 Tampa meeting of the (Catholic) National
          Association of Diocesan Liaisons provide "guidelines for
          directing and promoting contemplative prayer" among charis-
          matics. Bibliographical references.

2391.   Hitt, Russell T. "The New Pentecostalism: An Appraisal."
          Eternity 14 (July 1963): 10-16.

          Judicious analysis of the burgeoning charismatic movement,
          centering on tongues, which the author, though sympathetic,
          holds is not biblical.

2392.   Hocken, Peter. "Catholic Pentecostalism: Some Key Questions. I."
          Heythrop Journal 15 (April 1974): 131-43. "Catholic Pente-
          costalism: Some Key Questions. II." 15 (July 1974): 271-84.

Part I explores "the relationship and distinction between 'Classical' and Catholic Pentecostalism," and "the experience and doctrine of 'baptism in/of the Spirit.'" Part II considers "the Laying-on of Hands, Gifts of the Spirit, Glossolalia, the Place of Reason, and Conclusions, concerning the nature of renewal movements, the central insights and values in Catholic neo-Pentecostalism, and the reactions provoked by it."

2393.   _____. "Charismatic Renewal, The Churches and Unity." One in Christ 15, no. 4 (1979): 310-21.

Though ecumenical from its origin, the renewal has produced a church-ecumenism dilemma, which the author resolves through a three-fold fidelity: to one's denomination, and to the familiar and the unfamiliar in the renewal experiences.

2394.   Johnston, Raymond. "Creation, Culture and Charismatics." Scottish Bulletin of Evangelical Theology 2 (1984): 23-31.

An Anglican sympathetic to the charismatic movement admits some excesses in its adherents, but stresses the positive notes, particularly those tied to the doctrine of creation.

2395.   Judisch, Douglas. An Evaluation of Claims to the Charismatic Gifts. Grand Rapids: Baker, 1978. 96 p.

An evangelical Lutheran's exegetical study of the New Testament, Daniel, and Zechariah, leads him to conclude "that it is contrary to the Word of God to claim prophetic gifts in the postapostolic era." Appendix. Bibliography. Indexes.

2396.   Lederle, Henry I. "The Charismatic Movement: The Ambiguous Challenge." Missionalia 14 (August 1986): 61-75.

The charismatic renewal movement lacks "in challenging the world on the level of structural and systematic evil, but does, in fact, present a significant and praiseworthy challenge on the level of contemporary idolatries such as individualism and materialism."

2397.   _____. Treasures Old and New: Interpretations of "Spirit-Baptism" in the Charismatic Renewal Movement. Peabody, MA: Hendrickson, 1988. 264 p.

A theological rather than exegetical or historical study: after a chapter on the pre-charismatic era (pre-1960), the book centers on interpretations of Spirit-baptism by analyzing forty

writers in three categories: neo-pentecostal, sacramentarian,
and integrative; the author offers his own "ecumenical" view.
The introduction has a helpful "demography" of charismatic
groups. Twenty-page bibliography. Index.

2398.   Lindsell, Harold. The Holy Spirit in the Latter Days. Nashville:
         Thomas Nelson, 1983. 205 p.

         Biblical and theological study of the Holy Spirit and the
         Spirit-filled believer, against the background of the charis-
         matic movement, a movement Lindsell sees as in part Spirit-
         directed, but with tendencies that need to be curtailed.
         Bibliography.

2399.   MacArthur, John F., Jr. The Charismatics: A Doctrinal Perspec-
         tive. Grand Rapids: Zondervan, 1978. 224 p.

         Examines the charismatic movement on ten issues in light of the
         Bible, and while noting strengths sees a fatal flaw at the
         center of the movement: a tendency to place experience above
         the Bible. Bibliography.

2400.   MacKenzie, John S. "Charismatic Confusion." Reformation Review
         25 (July 1980): 171-84.

         Because of its ties to Roman Catholicism, women in authority,
         subjectivism, sensitivity training, and doctrinal errors, the
         charismatic movement is condemned as "the logical end of
         liberalism."

2401.   _____. "The Charismatic Movement and the Word of God."
         Reformation Review 24 (January 1979): 12-20.

         Bible study from which the author concludes that pentecostal
         teaching about tongues and healing is not biblical; the Roman
         Catholic presence further indicates problems in the movement.

2402.   Martin, George, ed. Scripture and the Charismatic Renewal:
         Proceedings of the Milwaukee Symposium, December 1-3, 1978. Ann
         Arbor: Servant Books, 1978. 127 p.

2403.   Mather, Anne. "Talking Points: The Charismatic Movement."
         Themelios 9 (April 1984): 17-21.

         Presentation of the biblical and theological bases of the
         movement; questions about its theology; the increasing
         rapprochement between charismatics and non-charismatics.

2404.   McDonnell, Kilian. "The Distinguishing Characteristics of the
         Charismatic-Pentecostal Spirituality." One in Christ 10, no. 2
         (1974): 117-28.

         One among a number of spiritualities, charismatic spirituality
         is marked by the expansion of awareness, expectation of
         openness and by a theological focus on the Spirit; shorter
         version: "Charismatic Spirituality: One Among Many?" in
         Theology Digest 22 (Autumn 1974): 211-16.

2405.   _____. "The Experience of the Holy Spirit in the Catholic   <
         Charismatic Renewal." In Conflicts About the Holy Spirit, ed.
         Hans Küng and Jürgen Moltmann, 95-102. New York: Seabury, 1979.

         Description of "the actual historical shape of that experience,
         its modalities and accents," rather than critical analysis
         thereof.

2406.   _____. ed. The Holy Spirit and Power: The Catholic Charismatic   <
         Renewal. Garden City: Doubleday, 1975. 186 p.

         Eight essays by seven Catholics on substantive theological
         issues: the work of the Spirit, Christian experience, liturgy,
         ecclesiology, and ecumenism. Bibliographical references.

2407.   _____. "Statement of the Theological Basis of the Catholic   <
         Charismatic Renewal." Worship 47 (December 1973): 610-20.

         Prepared by McDonnell and signed by others at an international
         conference near Rome, October 1973. places the renewal in the
         context of initiation (baptism) and the Spirit-given charisms;
         points up questions, strengths and problems.

2408.   Mühlen, Heribert. "Charismatic and Sacramental Understanding of   <
         the Church: Dogmatic Aspects of Charismatic Renewal." One in
         Christ 12, no. 4 (1976): 333-47.

         Technical description of the work of the Spirit, seen through a
         Roman Catholic understanding of the nature of the church and
         the operation of the sacraments: asks non-Catholic pentecostals
         to accept the charisms of government and unity via the RC
         Church.

2409.   _____. A Charismatic Theology: Initiation in the Spirit.   <
         Translated by Edward Quinn and Thomas Linton. New York: Paulist
         Press, 1978. 360 p.

2410.   Morris, John Warren. "The Charismatic Movement: An Orthodox
         Evaluation." Greek Orthodox Theological Review 28 (Summer 1983):
         103-34.

         Historical background of the movement, and a series of
         doctrinal considerations: ecclesiology, gifts of the Spirit,
         glossolalia, prayer, baptism of the Spirit and spiritual
         renewal. Morris concludes that the charismatic movement
         ultimately derives from American Protestantism and "embodies a
         spirituality that is foreign to Orthodoxy."

2411.   Oudersluys, Richard C. "Charismatic Theology and the New
         Testament." Reformed Review 28 (Autumn 1974): 48-59.

         A non-tongues-speaker sympathetically addresses the charismatic
         movement in the Reformed churches, "clearing away some current
         exegetical misconceptions with regard to spiritual gifts."

2412.   Packer, James I. "Charismatic Renewal: Pointing to a Person and a
         Power." Christianity Today 24 (7 March 1980): 16-20.

         Raises and evaluates the concerns commonly voiced by those who
         question the movement, then suggests the positive contributions
         charismatics make to other Christians in worship, ministry,
         communication and community.

2413.   Pannell, William E. "What Do I Want to Say to Charismatics?"
         Transformation 5 (October-December 1988): 20-23.

         Pannell has several concerns: seeing the work of the Spirit
         only in individual terms; being seduced into nationalism; an
         interest in affluence; overemphasis on experience.

2414.   Plowman, Edward E. "The Deepening Rift in the Charismatic
         Movement." Christianity Today 20 (10 October 1975): 52-54.

         The most serious question is the issue of "shepherd-leaders"
         with their heavy control over the flock, supported by people
         like Bob Mumford of Christian Growth Ministries and opposed by
         older charismatics.

2415.   Ranaghan, Kevin M. "The Church, the Spirit, and the Charismatic
         Renewal." New Covenant 11 (August 1981): 10-13.

2416.   Richards, John. "The Church's Healing Ministry and Charismatic
         Renewal." In Strange Gifts? A Guide to Charismatic Renewal, eds.
         David Martin and Peter Mullen, 151-58. New York: Basil Blackwell,
         1984.

Discusses two streams of healing, "sacramental" and
"charismatic", which belong together, in order that the church
can be "mature and aflame at the same time."

2417. Saracco, J. Norberto. "Charismatic Renewal and Social Change: A
Historical Analysis From a Third World Perspective."
Transformation 5 (October-December 1988): 14-18.

Argentinian Saracco places the renewal in its social, political
and religious context, depicts its characteristics and
teachings, and describes its generally conservative social
outlook (with potential for use in social liberation).

2418. Scaer, David P. "The Charismatic Movement as Ecumenical
Phenomenon." Concordia Theological Quarterly 45 (January-April
1981): 81-83.

Warns that the ecumenical enthusiasm of charismatics reflects
"a deeper problem--an aberrant understanding that detaches the
Spirit from the Word and Sacrament, and proclaims His freedom
from the Scripture."

2419. Schonebaum, William J. The Holy Spirit in the Life of the
Believing Community: A Study in Pneumatology, Ecclesiology and
Neo-Pentecostalism. St. Paul, MN: n.p., 1979. 268 p.

2420. Schreck, Alan Edward. "Ronald Knox's Theory of Enthusiasm and Its   <
Application to the Catholic Charismatic Renewal." Ph.D. diss.,
St. Michael's College, University of Toronto (Canada), 1979.
344 p.

2421. Suenens, Leon Joseph Cardinal. Ecumenism and Charismatic Renewal: <
Theological and Pastoral Orientations. Ann Arbor: Servant Books,
1978. 109 p.

The second document in the Malines series, this one stressing
the ecumenical potential of the charismatic renewal; by the
leading European Catholic churchman in the renewal movement.
Bibliographical references.

2422. _____. Theological and Pastoral Orientations on the Catholic   <
Charismatic Renewal. Notre Dame, IN: Word of Life, 1974. 71 p.

The first "Malines Document." from the conference Cardinal
Suenens called in 1974 in Belgium: gives "a tentative answer to
the main problems raised by the charismatic renewal and its
integration into the normal life of the Church." Bibliography.

⟩ 2423.   Suenens, Leon Joseph Cardinal, and Dom Helder Camara. Charismatic
           Renewal and Social Action: A Dialogue. Ann Arbor: Servant Books,
           1979. 98 p.

           Malines Document 3; shows "that prayer and the sociopolitical
           work of evangelization" are the characteristics that "define
           the complete Christian." Notes. Index.

⟩ 2424.   Sullivan, Francis Aloysius. Charisms and Charismatic Renewal: A
           Biblical and Theological Study. Ann Arbor: Servant Books, 1982.
           184 p.

           A Jesuit at the Gregorian University in Rome carefully and
           irenically treats the chief emphases in the renewal movement,
           with the purpose of clearing up the confusion and controversy
           among Catholics about the movement. Bibliographical
           references. Index.

⟩ 2425.   Walsh, Vincent M. A Key to Charismatic Renewal in the Catholic
           Church. St. Meinrad, IN: Abbey Press, 1974. 286 p.

           Set up as a study guide for interested Catholics, the book
           answers scores of questions about the gifts of the Spirit,
           charismatic prayer groups, and issues raised by the movement.
           Bibliography.

    2426.   Watson, David. "David Watson on Spiritual Gifts." Interview by
           Cecil Robeck. Theology, News and Notes 30 (March 1983): 18-23,
           34.

           Anglican charismatic Watson answers a variety of questions on
           the nature and use of spiritual gifts.

    2427.   Williams, J. Rodman. Renewal Theology: God, the World, &
           Redemption: Systematic Theology From a Charismatic Perspective.
           Grand Rapids: Academie Books, Zondervan, 1988. 443 p.

    2428.   Zens, Jon. "An Appraisal of the Charismatic Movment." Baptist
           Reformation Review 11 (1982): 43-47.

           The "movement's attributes are suspect" because of "[c]ertain
           clear deviations from the Word of God," which Zens lists.

See also items 961, 976, 1434, 1443, 2061, 2070, 2081, 2151, 2175, 2187,
    2204, 2295, 2296, 2297, 2305, 2307, 2309, 2310, 2332, 2458.

C. Personal Accounts

2429.   Battley, D. H. "Charismatic Renewal: A View From Inside."
Ecumenical Review 38 (January 1986): 48-56.

A charismatic Anglican from England describes his own
experience, and points out the dangers facing the movement:
discerning true from false; hostility toward non-charismatics;
social conservatism; adventism.

2430.   Bittlinger, Arnold. "The Significance of Charismatic Experiences
for the Vision of the Church." International Review of Mission 75
(April 1986): 117-22.

Distinguishes the charismatic movement (which tends to get
"confessionalized") from charismatic experiences (both inside
and outside the church); the latter offers greater hope for the
church.

2431.   Chervin, Ronda. Why I am a Charismatic: A Catholic Explains.   <
Liguori, MO: Liguori Publications, 1978. 123 p.

"Reflections on charismatic prayer and the longings of the
human heart."

2432.   Ellison, R. W. "Charismatic Renewal and Practical Usage." Dialog
13 (Winter 1974): 33-39.

A Lutheran pastor from Omaha recounts his experience and that
of his congregation, from which are derived principles for
understanding charismatic renewal.

2433.   Ghezzi, Bert. "The Big Switch: A Memoir on Catholic Charismatic   <
Renewal." New Covenant 16 (February 1987): 8-11.

Autobiographical account of his switch from self-reliance to
reliance on the Holy Spirit.

2434.   Gunstone, John Thomas Arthur. Greater Things Than These: A
Personal Account of the Charismatic Movement. Leighton Buzzard,
Meds, England: The Faith Press; New York: Morehouse-Barlow, 1974,
111 p.

A personal account by a priest of the Church of England,
concluding with "the lessons to be learned from pentecostalism
and how these can be applied to the worship and life-style of
the institutional churches today." Bibliographical references.

2435.   Hall, Robert B. "The Charismatic Movement in the Episcopal
         Church." St. Luke's Journal of Theology 15 (January 1972): 12-17.

         A description, definition and evaluation of the movement.

2436.   Hocken, Peter. "The Charismatic Experience." The Way 18 (January
         1978): 44-55.

         Elements in the charismatic experience, developments in the
         charismatic renewal, and charismatic experience as Christian
         experience--"basic Christianity will more and more include what
         is now seen as distinctively charismatic."

2437.   Irish, Charles. "Parishes Can Be Renewed." New Covenant 15
         (October 1985): 13-15.

         The Rector of an Episcopal parish and the national coordinator
         of Episcopal Renewal Ministries recounts the charismatic
         renewal of his Bath, Ohio, parish.

2438.   Koch, Roy S., and Martha Koch, eds. My Personal Pentecost.
         Foreword by Kevin Ranaghan. Scottdale, PA: Herald Press, 1977.
         275 p.

         Twenty-four accounts by Menonnites who have experienced the
         charismatic renewal.

2439.   Martin, Ralph. "A Catholic Assesses Charismatic Renewal in His
         Church." Christianity Today 24 (7 March 1980): 18-19.

         Though it has dangers in spirituality and theology, the
         movement "is part of a broader evangelical renewal in the
         catholic church."

2440.   McDonnell, Kilian. "Charismatic Renewal and Ecumenism." One in
         Christ 14, no. 3 (1978): 247-58.

         An extract from the final chapter of McDonnell, Charismatic
         Renewal and Ecumenism (1978), giving twenty-eight suggestions
         to help priests to handle pastorally the renewal, and a reprint
         of the book's epilogue.

2441.   Phillipson, John S. "Two Pentecostal Experiences." America 120
         (29 March 1969): 360-63.

         The author gives positive reports of his attendance at a
         pentecostal meeting in Youngstown, OH, and a Catholic
         charismatic meeting near Lansing, MI.

2442. Ranaghan, Kevin M., and Dorothy Ranaghan, eds. As the Spirit <
Leads Us. Paramus: Paulist Press, 1971. 250 p.

Eleven Catholics, "firmly rooted in Scripture, the liturgy,
spirituality and teaching of the [Catholic] Church," reflect on
"worship, witness, ecumenism, and the present condition and
future development of the Church." Bibliography.

2443. Snyder, Dean J. "Confessions of a Closet Charismatic." Christian
Century 100 (5 October 1983): 878-81.

Charismatics are coping with the disillusion of science "and
the faltering technological culture it legitimizes," and, if
they can avoid their privatistic tendencies, will challenge the
church's bondage to culture.

2444. Watson, David. You Are My God: A Pioneer of Renewal Recounts His
Pilgrimage in Faith. Wheaton: Harold Shaw, 1984. 192 p.

A noted charismatic Anglican shares his spiritual journey in
church and family.

See also items 1508, 2267, 2295, 2303, 2374, 2458.

D. Social Science Studies

2445. Bergquist, Susan L. "The Revival of Glossolalic Practices in the <
Catholic Church: Its Sociological Implications." Perkins Journal
26 (Summer 1973): 32-37.

Personal observation and thirteen in-depth interviews lead the
author to say that the revival is partly a reaction to the "God
is Dead" movement and partly an attempt to reconstruct the
spiritual aspect of Catholic church life.

2446. Bord, Richard J., and Joseph E. Faulkner. The Catholic Charis- <
matics: The Anatomy of a Modern Religious Movement. University
Park: Pennsylvania State University Press, 1983. 162 p.

2447. Bradfield, Cecil David. "He's Not One of Us - Yet! Research in a
Neo-Pentecostal Group." Pneuma 1 (Spring 1979): 49-57.

A neo-pentecostal group in western Virginia is analyzed via
three data-gathering techniques.

2448.   . Neo-Pentecostalism: A Sociological Assessment.
Washington, DC: University Press of America, 1979. 75 p.

Studying neo-pentecostals in western Virginia, Bradfield used
Glock's deprivation theory, which was helpful in demonstrating
the role of "non-objective forms of deprivation such as ethical
or psychic" in the emergence of sectarian groups, but which was
too static in nature to account for the social change factors.
Bibliographical references.

2449.   Harrison, Michael I., and John K. Maniha. "Dynamics of Dissenting
Movements Within Established Organizations: Two Cases and a
Theoretical Interpretation." Journal for the Scientific Study of
Religion 17 (September 1978): 207-24.

Tests the Turner and Killian theory on the relationship between
parent organizations and internal movements of dissent by
looking to Episcopal and Catholic charismatics, suggesting that
Turner and Killian, good to a point, needs to be extended into
a fuller theory of movement dynamics.

2450.   McDonnell, Kilian. "A Sociologist Looks at the Catholic
Charismatic Renewal." Worship 49 (August-September 1975): 378-92.

Extended review of Fr. Joseph Fichter, The Catholic Cult of the
Paraclete (1975), especially where McDonnell disagrees with
Fichter's findings: "about social engagement, clergy-laity
relations, the influence of fundamentalist exegesis, the role
of women, deliverance ministries."

2451.   McGaw, Douglas B. "Commitment and Religious Community: A
Comparison of a Charismatic and a Mainline Congregation." Journal
for the Scientific Study of Religion 18 (January 1979): 146-63.

Two Connecticut Presbyterian congregations are compared, with
the charismatic one displaying stronger commitment (i.e. "is
more effective at providing meaning and belonging to its
members")--with belonging more important to members than
meaning.

2452.   . "Meaning and Belonging in a Charismatic Congregation:
An Investigation into Sources of Neo-Pentecostal Success." Review
of Religious Research 21 (Summer 1980): 284-301.

Further elaboration of the above study: meaning (beliefs) "is
most effective when the belonging mechanisms are strong."

2453.   _____. A Tale of Two Congregations: Commitment and Social
Structure in a Charismatic and Mainline Congregation. Foreword by
Jackson Carroll. Hartford: Hartford Seminary Foundation, 1979.
110 p.

> Tests Dean Kelley's thesis in Why Conservative Churches are
> Growing (1972, 1977) that "high demand" religion is more
> successful than pluralism, and finds support for the thesis in
> this sociological study of two suburban Hartford Presbyterian
> congregations in that when looking at religion as the provider
> of meaning in life "[t]he key factor is commitment--the degree
> of tenacity." Appendix.

2454.   McGuire, Meredith B. "The Social Context of Prophecy: 'Word-
Gifts' of the Spirit Among Catholic Pentecostals." Review of
Religious Research 18 (Winter 1977): 134-47.

> Study of seven Catholic pentecostal groups, 1971-1975, shows
> that communication from God to group members fosters an
> atmosphere of expectancy and mystery, promotes group unity,
> provides control by the leaders and serves as a teaching
> authority.

2455.   _____. "Testimony as a Commitment Mechanism in Catholic
Pentecostal Prayer Groups." Journal for the Scientific Study of
Religion 16 (June 1977): 165-68.

> The data from seven Catholic charismatic prayer groups "show
> that testimony (or 'witnessing') is the central commitment
> mechanism," more so even then glossolalia.

2456.   _____. "Toward a Sociological Interpretation of the 'Catholic
Pentecostal' Movement." Review of Religious Research 16 (Winter
1975): 94-104.

> Earlier analysis of same groups as above; here the emphasis is
> on the needs for security and the plausibility of the religious
> worldview that the groups provide for their members.

2457.   Northcott, John E. "The Congregation in Crisis: A Contextual
Approach to Managing the Unresolved Conflict Between a Controlled
or An Enabled Concept of Christianity as Precipitated by the
Encounter Between Negative Pseudo Neo-Pentecostal Authoritarianism
and Traditional Lutheran Patterns of Ministry and Church Life."
D.Min. diss., United Theological Seminary, 1980.

> 2458.   Poloma, Margaret M. The Charismatic Movement: Is There a New
          Pentecost? Boston: Twayne, 1982. 284 p.

          Poloma analyzes the movement both from within and without as a
          sociologist involved in charismatic Catholicism. Her research
          is a balanced view between scientific analysis of the movement
          and its prophetic nature, covering a wide range of topics.
          Thirty-one-page bibliography. Index.

  2459.   Prieguez, Raquel Maria. "The Power of Demeanor: Charismatic
          Leadership in a Spiritual Organization." Ph.D. diss., University
          of California, San Diego, 1987. 342 p.

> 2460.   Sneck, William Joseph. Charismatic Spiritual Gifts: A
          Phenomenological Analysis. Washington, DC: University Press of
          America, 1981. 298 p.

          Concentrates on the gifts of prophecy and healing as evidenced
          in the Word of God community, a Catholic renewal group in Ann
          Arbor, aimed at understanding (rather than prediction or
          control), and producing a tightly-drawn picture of the group.
          Sixteen-page bibliography.

  2461.   Syreck, William J. "Neo-Pentecostals and Healing: A
          Phenomenological Approach to the Spiritual Gifts." The Way 18
          (October 1978): 263-71.

          Five years of participant observation in a Catholic charismatic
          community leads Syreck to draw conclusions via Object Relation
          Theorists.

See also items 1666, 2252, 2269, 2281, 2307.

VII

REVIVALISM

A. General Studies

2462.   Barkun. Michael. "The Awakening-Cycle Controversy." Sociological Analysis 46 (Winter 1985): 425-43.

In light of the cyclical models of Whitney Cross, E. P. Thompson, Anthony F. C. Wallace and Thomas Kuhn, "the awakening-cycle theory remains promising but requires modification, principally by assigning greater significance to outbursts of millennialism as a key indicator."

2463.   Bast, Henry. "What is Revival?" Reformed Review 13 (March 1960): 3-8.

Applies Charles Hodge's three tests (doctrines preached, nature of the religious experience, abiding results) to conclude that "we are far from a real revival in our day."

2464.   Cairns, Earle E. An Endless Line of Splendor: Revivals and Their Leaders from the Great Awakening to the Present. Wheaton: Tyndale House, 1986. 373 p.

Survey of revivalism in the U.S., concentrating on biography; a bit laudatory. Twenty-one-page bibliography. Index.

2465.   Crawford. Michael J. "The Invention of the American Revival." Ph.D. diss., Boston University. 1978. 401 p.

2466.   Donovan, John J. "Religious Revivals as a Counter-Culture." Spiritual Life 18 (Spring 1972): 47-57.

Compares radicalism inside the church with that outside the church; believes the inside ("trad") version will last longer.

2467.   Evans, Eifion. "Preaching and Revival." Banner of Truth no. 87
         (December 1970): 11-20.

         A biblical and historical treatment, emphasizing the signifi-
         cant role of preaching in revival.

2468.   Evans, W. Glyn. "A Survey of Evangelism in America." Journal of
         the Evangelical Theological Society 14 (Summer 1971): 165-72.

         Contrasts the mass evangelist (promoter, mechanical means) and
         the revivalist (endued with power), concluding from the
         ministries of Edwards, Finney, Moody, Sunday, and Graham, that
         "early American evangelism was of the revivalistic type, while
         later American evangelism (specifically after 1830) has
         followed the evangelistic type."

2469.   Frantz, John B. "Revivalism: A Thesis Concerning its Effect on
         Protestant Denominations." Theology and Life 8 (Summer 1965):
         127-40.

         With the German Reformed Church as a case study, Frantz
         suggests that rather than contributing to uniformity,
         revivalism encouraged "renewed devotion to doctrines and
         practices consistent with" each denomination.

2470.   Hammond, John L. "The Reality of Revivals." Sociological
         Analysis 44 (Summer 1983): 111-16.

         Agrees with William McLoughlin that revivals really occurred,
         but disagrees on why they occurred. how many people
         participated, the nature of the beliefs propagated, and the
         effects (if any) on society at large.

2471.   Hardman, Keith J. The Spiritual Awakeners: American Revivalists
         from Solomon Stoddard to D. L. Moody. Chicago: Moody, 1983.
         228 p.

         Survey of revivalism in the great sweep of awakenings down to
         1900. Bibliography. Index.

2472.   Lane, Belden C. "The Spirituality of the Evangelical Revival."
         Theology Today 43 (July 1986): 169-77.

         Liminality as an explainer of a revivalist spirituality: God
         cannot be contained in one place: being in transit forms a
         primary metaphor of the encounter with God: identification with
         the marginal peoples of the world.

2473. Leonard. Bill J. "Evangelism and Contemporary American Life."
       Review and Expositor 77 (Fall 1980): 493-506.

       Influenced by pluralism, revivalism, nationalism and funda-
       mentalism, present-day evangelism is diverse because of the
       variety of evangelicals and the variety of styles among
       evangelists.

2474. Mathews, Donald G. "The Second Great Awakening as an Organizing
       Process: 1780-1830: An Hypothesis." American Quarterly 21
       (Spring 1969): 23-43.

       More than just theological or ecclesiastical change, the
       awakening gave "meaning to people suffering in various degrees
       from the social strains of a nation on the move into new
       political, economic, and geographic areas."

2475. McLoughlin, William G. Modern Revivalism: Charles Grandison
       Finney to Billy Graham. New York: Ronald, 1959. 551 p.

       Still the standard text on American revivalism from 1825 on,
       explaining "the part revivalism has played, and is playing
       today, in the social, intellectual, and religious life of
       America," from the sympathetic stance of seeing revivalism as a
       significant factor in American history. Bibliography. Index.

2476. _____. Revivals, Awakenings, and Reform: An Essay on Religion
       and Social Change in America, 1607-1977. Chicago: University of
       Chicago Press, 1978. 239 p.

       Provocative look at "great awakenings" in American history
       through the lens of social science; religious revivals
       accompany, with supports or opposition, the awakenings (which
       are social revitalizations). Bibliography. Index.

2477. Menzies, William W. "Lessons From Great Revivals." Paraclete 8
       (Winter 1974): 7-16.

2478. Murray, Iain. "Necessary Ingredients of a Biblical Revival."
       Banner of Truth no. 184 (January 1979): 19-27.

       "The substance of an address . . . at the annual meeting of the
       Reformed Fellowship at Grand Rapids. Michigan. on October 12.
       1978"; seeks to explain the increasing doubt about revivals.
       followed by a listing of the marks of authentic revivals.

2479.   _____. "Prayer and Revival." Banner of Truth no. 133
           (October 1974): 1-5.

           An appeal for prayer, and a treatment of the means of being
           "brought to increasing prayerfulness."

2480.   _____. "The Puritans and Revival Christianity." Banner of
           Truth no. 72 (September 1969): 9-19.

           The "main features" of the Reformation and of Puritanism, "as,
           for instance, the extensiveness of their influence, the
           singular position given to Scripture and the transformation in
           character of the morally careless, are all effects of revival."

2481.   _____. "Reflections on Revivals." Banner of Truth no. 12
           (September 1958): 3-10.

           Discusses "Some General Characteristics of Revival" (rapidity
           and suddenness, power, multiple conversions), "Some Dangers
           . . .," and "The Case of John Wesley (1703-1791)"; with
           conclusions that include the importance of "the degree of
           Scriptural purity held by . . . participants," and the "Immense
           good which a revival can bring."

2482.   Opie, John. "Conversion and Revivalism: An Internal History from
           Jonathan Edwards through Charles Grandison Finney." Ph.D. diss.,
           University of Chicago, 1964.

2483.   Orr, J. Edwin. Campus Aflame: Dynamic of Student Religious
           Revolution: Evangelical Awakenings in Collegiate Communities.
           Glendale: Regal Books, 1972. 277 p.

           An account of "Evangelical awakenings in collegiate commun-
           ities" during the 19th and 20th centuries, set in the context
           of the larger evangelical movement and its awakenings.
           Thirteen-page bibliography.

2484.   Packer, James I. "Puritanism as a Movement of Revival."
           Evangelical Quarterly 52 (January-March 1980): 2-16.

           The case is made because "spiritual revival was central to what
           Puritans professed to be seeking," "personal revival was the
           central theme of Puritan devotional literature," and "God-
           brought revival" occurred under the ministry of Puritan
           pastors.

2485.   Quere, Ralph Walter. Evangelical Witness: The Message, Medium, Mission, and Method of Evangelism. Minneapolis: Augsburg, 1975. 160 p.

Study guide prepared by Harold H. Zietlow. Bibliographical references.

2486.   Rambo, David. "Revival Begins With Leaders." United Evangelical Action 48 (March-April 1989): 4-7.

The President of the Christian and Missionary Alliance "calls evangelicals to renew their commitment to 'inner disciplines.'"

2487.   Rawlyk, George A. "Writing About Canadian Religious Revivals." Paper read at the Conference on Modern Christian Revivalism: A Comparative Perspective, at Wheaton College. March 30-April 1, 1989. Photocopied.

Influenced by A.F.C. Wallace, Victor Turner and George Marsden, Rawlyk interprets maritime Canada revivalism in the 18th and 19th centuries and the decline of Canadian revivalism and evangelicalism in the 20th century.

2488.   Rood, Paul W. Can We Expect a World-Wide Revival? Grand Rapids: Zondervan, 1940. 154 p.

"Evangelical addresses of intense spiritual fervor" by a prominent fundamentalist pastor and author and President of the World's Christian Fundamentals Association. Messages preached in many of the large conservative churches and Bible conferences across the United States.

2489.   Schlabach, Theron F. "Mennonites, Revivalism, Modernity--1683-1850." Church History 48 (December 1979): 398-415.

In some ways already accommodating to modernity, the Mennonites who were revival converts and joined the United Brethren made further accommodations, as did the Mennonite bodies which after 1880 accepted revivalism, "a potent agent of modernization."

2490.   Schmidt, Leigh Eric. "Scottish Communions and American Revivals: Evangelical Ritual, Sacramental Piety, and Popular Festivity From the Reformation Through the Mid-Nineteenth Century." Ph.D. diss., Princeton University. 1987. 355 p.

"[E]xplores a sacramental festival that developed and flourished in post-Reformation Scotland and that in turn was

prominent among Presbyterian immigrants in early America."
Patterned "some of the largest revivals in American history."
In book form: Holy Fairs: Scottish Communions and American
Revivals in the Early Modern Period (1990).

2491.   Smith, Paul B. "Revival in Canada." Evangelical Christian
(October 1966): 8-9.

Discusses "unprecedented national prosperity" and "an uncertain
view on the inspiration of the Bible" as "the roadblocks that
are holding back revival in Canada today."

2492.   Smith, Timothy L. "My Rejection of a Cyclical View of 'Great
Awakenings.'" Sociological Analysis 44 (Summer 1983): 97-102.

Recites his own interest in the complexities of American
religious history to show his preference for "determined
efforts to apprehend and understand the complex facts" rather
than beginning with "flashy theories."

2493.   Smylie, James H. "Testing the Spirits in the American Context:
Great Awakenings, Pentecostalism, and the Charismatic Movement."
Interpretation 33 (January 1979): 32-46.

The First and Second Awakenings as Spirit movements, and now in
the 20th century a third Spirit awakening, the effects of which
need to be tested by the Scripture.

2494.   Sonnack, Paul G. "A Perspective on Evangelism and American
Revivalism." Word and World 1 (Winter 1981): 52-58.

"Basically, revivalism is a technique" that has adversely
affected American Protestantism (anti-intellectual and
culture-defending), and ultimately narrows and constricts "the
multifaceted richness of evangelism."

2495.   Spurgeon, Charles H. "The Kind of Revival Wanted by the Church."
Banner of Truth no. 73 (October 1969): 4-10.

A widely influential 19th century preacher discusses authentic
religion in terms of "old-fashioned doctrine." "personal
godliness," "domestic religion." and the "vigorous consecrated
strength" of "saints."

2496.   Sweet, William Warren. Revivalism in America: Its Origin. Growth
and Decline. New York: Scribner's, 1944. 192 p.

An early text on the history of revivalism that sees it in the
context of a nation whose people were in motion and which,
through most of its history, was marked by individualism.
Bibliography. Index.

2497.   Weisberger, Bernard A. They Gathered at the River: The Story of
the Great Revivalists and Their Impact on Religion in America.
Chicago: Quadrangle Books, 1966. 345 p.

The story of American revivalism from the camp meeting to the
1920s, concentrating on Finney, Moody, and Sunday.
Twenty-eight pages of bibliographical references. Index.

See also items 66, 123, 205, 611, 817, 1303, 1556, 1595, 1677, 2502, 2531,
2533, 2537, 2539, 2564, 2575, 2576.

B.   Eighteenth Century

2498.   Balmer, Randall H.   "Eschewing the 'Routine of Religion':
Eighteenth-Century Middle Class Pietism and the Revival Tradition
in America." Paper read at the Conference on Modern Christian
Revivalism: A Comparative Perspective, at Wheaton College,
March 30-April 1, 1989. Photocopied.

This study of German and especially Dutch pietism sees it as
"the earliest harbinger of eighteenth-century revival" and as
providing "a new paradigm for understanding both ecclesiastical
and political activism" of the time.

2499.   Belden, Albert David. George Whitefield, the Awakener: A Modern
Study of the Evangelical Revival. New York: Macmillan, 1953.
302 p.

British Congregationalist Belden chronicles "the romantic and
thrilling story of Whitefield" in a rather laudatory fashion,
and from the story derives theological, ethical, psychological,
and sociological implications for the 20th century. Bibliographical references. Index.

2500.   Bergman, Marvin L. "Millennialism Among Virginia Revivalists,
1740-1800." Fides et Historia 18 (October 1986): 56-72.

Bergman concludes that millennialism did not play a decisive
role for the six Virginia revivalists he uses to test the
interpretations of Nathan Hatch, The Sacred Cause of Liberty
(1977), and James West Davidson, The Logic of Millennial

Thought (1977). both of whom centered on New England for their
contention that millennial thinking played an important role in
the revolutionary generation.

2501.   Blauvelt, Martha Tomhave, and Rosemary Skinner Keller. "Women and
Revivalism: The Puritan and Wesleyan Traditions." Women and
Religion, vol. 2. The Colonial and Revolutionary Periods, 316-67.
San Francisco: Harper & Row, 1983.

Women who played a role in the Great Awakening in America and
the Evangelical Revival in Britain; accompanied by twelve
documents.

2502.   Butler, Jonathan M. "Enthusiasm Described and Decried: The Great
Awakening as Interpretative Fiction." Journal of American History
69 (September 1982): 305-25.

Persuasive argument that historians "should abandon the term
'the Great Awakening' because it distorts the character of
eighteenth-century American religious life and misinterprets
its relationship to prerevolutionary American society and
politics."

2503.   Foster, Mary C. "Theological Debate in a Revival Setting:
Hampshire County in the Great Awakening." Fides et Historia 6
(Spring 1974): 31-47.

The debate. begun in Hampshire County, MA, in November 1734,
was about "the character of true Christianity: a reasonable
faith of a supernatural spiritual experience"; and, while the
Great Awakening contributed to the debate it "was not the
primary cause of the division of theological thought in the
late eighteenth century."

2504.   Goodwin, Gerald J. "The Anglican Reaction to the Great
Awakening." Historical Magazine of the Protestant Episcopal
Church 35 (December 1966): 343-72.

Using the terms awakening. revivalism. and evangelicalism to
refer to the Great Awakening. Goodwin reviews the story of "the
one major church hostile to the Great Awakening." noting its
success in "staving off evangelicalism." but concluding that it
was a "hollow victory." that sealed its own fate as "a minority
church in America."

2505.   Heimert, Alan, and Perry Miller, eds. The Great Awakening:
Documents Illustrating the Crisis and its Consequences.
Indianapolis/New York: Bobbs-Merrill, 1967. 663 p.

2506. McLoughlin, William G. "Timepieces and Butterflies: A Note on the Great Awakening Construct and Its Critics." Sociological Analysis 44 (Summer 1983): 103-10.

McLoughlin's point-by-point responses to the attacks on the Great-Awakening-construct.

2507. Moran, Gerald F. "Christian Revivalism and Culture in Early America: Puritan New England as a Case Study." Paper read at the Conference on Modern Christian Revivalism: A Comparative Perspective, at Wheaton College, March 30-April 1, 1989. Photocopied.

Contrary to the view that the cultural meaning of revivalism in Puritan America is found in the theme of religious declension, Moran says "the Great Awakening represented not a dramatic break from the Puritan past but rather a popular reaffirmation of it."

2508. Murray, Iain. "Jonathan Edwards 16: The First Revival at Princeton." Banner of Truth no. 261 (June 1985): 22-29.

Part of an extended series drawing upon The Journal of Esther Edwards Burr, ed. Carol F. Karlsen and Laurie Crumpacker (1984).

2509. _____. "Whitefield and the Evangelical Revival in Scotland." Banner of Truth no. 79 (April 1970): 8-24.

Describes the course of the Revival, including a section on the effects on Scotland, in an address given at the "Evangelical Library Meeting" in Glasgow in January 1970.

2510. O'Brien, Susan. "A Transatlantic Community of Saints: The Great Awakening and the First Evangelical Network, 1735-1755." American Historical Review 91 (October 1986): 811-32.

Extensive writing and circulation of letters, the founding of newspapers and magazines, and coordinated prayer days, demonstrate that while revivals took place locally, a whole network of information "about works elsewhere shaped individual behavior and individual understanding" of the international nature of the awakening.

2511. Overton, John Henry. The Evangelical Revival in the Eighteenth Century. 4th ed. London: Longmans, Green, 1898. 208 p.

Narrative of the people and events of the movement in England, with chapters on the literature, results, opposition to and doctrines of the revival. Index.

2512.   Reeve, Ronald. "John Wesley, Charles Simeon, and the Evangelical Revival." Canadian Journal of Theology 2 (October 1956): 203-14.

The Evangelical Revival "represents another phase in the development of the doctrine of the Holy Spirit," notable in the work of Wesley and Simeon.

2513.   Reid, Roddey, Jr. "The Eighteenth Century Evangelical Revival Especially in Regard to the Ministry of the Laity." St. Luke's Journal of Theology 7 (Spring 1964): 3-21.

Somewhat rambling account of the beginnings, the spread and method, and the accomplishments of the revival, with conclusions and application for the 20th century.

2514.   Rutter, Robert Sherman. "The New Birth: Evangelicalism in the Transatlantic Community During the Great Awakening, 1739-1745." Ph.D. diss., Rutgers University, 1982. 449 p.

2515.   Sangster, Paul E. Pity My Simplicity: The Evangelical Revival and the Religious Education of Children, 1738-1800. London: Epworth, 1963. 200 p.

2516.   Shaw, Ian. "Young People in the Great Awakening." Banner of Truth no. 169 (October 1977): 21-28.

"One of the most remarkable aspects . . . was the profound effect upon . . . children and young people." Describes that effect, with special attention to Edwards and Northampton.

2517.   Smyth, Charles Hugh Egerton. Simeon and Church Order: A Study of the Origins of the Evangelical Revival in Cambridge in the Eighteenth Century. Cambridge: University Press, 1940. 316 p.

Four lectures on "the historic background of Simeon's ministry in the Church of England," two lectures on "the two major problems by which Simeon found himself confronted: the problem of Continuity, and the problem of Church Order." Appendixes. Bibliography. Index.

2518.   Thomas, Geoffrey. "The Westminster Conference: Geoffrey Thomas Reflects on the Conference Held in Westminster Chapel 17-18 December 1985." Banner of Truth no. 270 (March 1986): 10-15.

Papers include one on the awakening in Northampton, MA, in 1735.

2519. Westerkamp, Marilyn J. Triumph of the Laity: Scots-Irish Piety and the Great Awakening, 1625-1760. New York: Oxford University Press, 1987. 266 p.

Sees the Great Awakening as deriving from Scots-Irish revivalism, promoted by the laity, centrally defined by ritual, primarily religious in nature, and occurring in a time of growth. Bibliography. Index.

See also items 66, 188, 199, 200, 512, 545, 832, 866, 1143, 1447, 2490.

C. Nineteenth Century

2520. Altschuler, Glenn C., and Jan M. Saltzgaber. Revivalism, Social Conscience, and Community in the Burned-Over District: The Trial of Rhoda Bement. Ithaca: Cornell University, 1983. 177 p.

With the transcript of the trial (in 1843) as the centerpiece, the authors "set the stage by examining the religious and social ramifications of the Second Great Awakening" and "reassess the divisive tendencies of revivalism"; they conclude that "organized religion was central to the stability and cohesiveness of village life in antebellum America." Bibliographical references. Index.

2521. Anderson, Douglas Firth. "San Francisco Evangelicalism, Regional Religious Identity, and the Revivalism of D. L. Moody." Fides et Historia 15 (Spring-Summer 1983): 44-66.

Uses the two Moody campaigns in the 1880s, in a largely overlooked region in religious studies, to point out the ambivalent nature of religious identity with the rest of the nation for West Coast evangelicals both then and now.

2522. Autrey, C. E. "The Revival of 1858." Southwestern Journal of Theology 1 (October 1958): 9-20.

Factors contributing to. characteristics. methods, spread and effects of the revival.

2523. Bilhartz, Terry D. Urban Religion and the Second Great Awakening: Church and State in Early National Baltimore. Rutherford, NJ: Farleigh Dickenson University Press, 1986. 236 p.

Sociological analysis of Baltimore as a case study of how the
voluntary systems affected American church life, with important
implications for interpreting the Second Awakening. Thirty-
page bibliography. Index.

2524.   Bocock, John H. "The Beginning of a Revival." Banner of Truth
no. 104 (May 1972): 1-6.

An extract from the Selections From the Writings of John H.
Bocock (Richmond, 1871), describing the 1858 revival in his
parish in Virginia.

2525.   Boles, John B. "Revivalism, Renewal, and Social Mediation in the
Old South." Paper read at the Conference on Modern Christian
Revivalism: A Comparative Perspective, Wheaton College, March
30-April 1, 1989. Photocopied.

The predominant denominations (Presbyterian, Methodist,
Baptist) accepted revivalism as normative, "domesticated"
relations between the races, and also "mediated between
different social classes of whites."

2526.   Bowden, Henry Warner. "Oberlin and Ojibwas: An Evangelical
Mission to Native Americans." In The Evangelical Tradition in
America, ed. Leonard I. Sweet, 149-79. Macon, GA: Mercer
University Press, 1984.

Discusses what he views as the relatively unsuccessful
missionary efforts out of Finney's Oberlin College to reach the
Ojibwa Indians during the 1840s and 1850s.

2527.   Brinks, Herbert. "Revivalism and Reform in America." Reformed
Journal 18 (November 1968): 16-21.

Contends, with examples, that in the period 1800-1860 the
revivalistic churches, with their revolutionary potential,
"became models for reformers both in and out of the church."

2528.   Bruce, Dickson D., Jr. And They All Sang Hallelujah: Plainfolk
Camp-Meeting Religion, 1800-1845. Knoxville: University of
Tennessee Press, 1974. 155 p.

Important study of the religion of the Methodist and Baptist
camp-meeting (rather than its social or intellectual elements),
seen through the symbols and songs used at the meetings by and
for the plain folk: the mass of farmers and townspeople in the
antebellum South, outside the plantation system, "Who were

neither rich nor starving." Fourteen-page bibliography. Indexes.

2529.   Carwardine, Richard. "The Second Great Awakening in Comparative Perspective: Revivals and Culture in the United States and Britain." Paper read at the Conference on Modern Christian Revivalism: A Comparative Perspective, at Wheaton College, March 30-April 1, 1989. Photocopied.

Less well-known but equally important, the British "second awakening" of the early 19th century shows several similarities to its American counterpart, and some "starkly conflicting" qualities as well.

2530.   _____. Transatlantic Revivalism: Popular Evangelicalism in Britain and America, 1790-1865. Westport, CT: Greenwood Press, 1978. 249 p.

Description of the ties between British and American revivalism in the antebellum era; emphasis on the personnel from both sides who made the Atlantic a British-American lake. Bibliography. Index.

2531.   _____. "The Welsh Evangelical Community and Finney's Revival." Journal of Ecclesiastical History 29 (October 1978): 463-80.

Rather than arguing that Finney's Lectures (1835) "caused" the awakenings in Wales, 1839-1843, Carwardine says that the character of Welsh evangelical religion, the transatlantic nature of revivalism, and the modification of High Calvinism made the reading of Finney's book "unsurprising, especially as the publication appeared at a time when the revival pendulum was on the upswing."

2532.   Cross, Whitney R. The Burned-Over District: The Social and Intellectual History of Enthusiastic Religion in Western New York, 1800-1850. Ithaca: Cornell University Press, 1950; New York: Harper & Row, 1965; Reissued, 1982. 383 p.

Pathbreaking book on the revivals and other religious movements that swept through the region. Its implications go beyond the time, subject and area confines suggested by a microcosmic study of this sort. Bibliographical references. Index.

2533.   Doan, Ruth Alden. "Order, Space, and Time: Rhetoric and Retreat in Mid-Nineteenth Century American Revivalism." Paper read at the Conference on Modern Christian Revivalism: A Comparative Perspective, at Wheaton College, March 30-April 1, 1989. Photocopied.

The place of revivalism in American culture, 1830s to 1870s, seen in the relation between revival time and (insane) asylum space, and in camp meetings and camp meeting resorts.

2534.   Elias, John. "Revival." Banner of Truth no. 125 (February 1974): 1-4.

An 1840 letter describing the various components in true revival.

2535.   England, Daniel. "Baptist Boanerges: Jacob Knapp and Revivalism." American Baptist Quarterly 4 (June 1985): 184-99.

New measures evangelist Knapp (1799-1874), confrontational and accused of being money-hungry, symbolizes the mid-century issues about revivalism that, in Knapp's case, "had less to do, perhaps, with theology than it did with temperament, intelligence, and the heat of the moment."

2536.   Faust, Drew Gilpin. "Christian Soldiers: The Meaning of Revivalism in the Confederate Army." Journal of Southern History 53 (February 1987): 63-68.

A neglected area of study; extensive revivals among Confederate soldiers had both personal and social implications, as religion became "the vehicle and symbol of broader cultural innovation and change."

2537.   Finney, Charles G. Memoirs of Charles Finney: The Complete Restored Text, eds. Richard DuPuis and Garth Rosell. Grand Rapids: Zondervan, 1989. 736 p.

New, critical edition of Finney's memoirs contains the complete text of the original manuscript (as contrasted to Fairchild's somewhat expurgated version), with extensive footnotes, providing a valuable source for revivalism studies.

2538.   Johnson, James E. "Charles G. Finney and the Great 'Western' Revivals." Fides et Historia 6 (Spring 1974): 13-30.

Town-by-town narrative of Finney's revival meetings in western New York in 1825-1826, at the beginning of Finney's long career, wherein he "fashioned a popular Christianity" and in several ways "set the pattern for later evangelists."

2539.   Luker, David. "Revivalism in Theory and Practice: The Case of Cornish Methodism." Journal of Ecclesiastical History 37 (October 1986): 603-19.

2540.   Macphail, S. R. "Reminiscences of the 1859 Revival." Banner of
         Truth no. 174 (March 1978): 25-30.

         An address given in 1909 and reported in the book by the same
         title (Aberdeen: 1910).

2541.   Morrison, Howard Alexander. "The Finney Takeover of the Second
         Great Awakening During the Oneida Revivals of 1825-1827." New
         York History 59 (January 1978): 17-53.

2542.   Murray, Iain. "Archibald Alexander and Revival in Virginia."
         Banner of Truth no. 186 (March 1979): 16-26.

         The early life of Alexander (1772-1851), who was a long time
         professor of Church History at Princeton Seminary, and who was
         at once a participant in and a historian of revival.

2543.   Nicholls, John. "The Revival of 1859 in Scotland." Banner of
         Truth no. 259 (April 1985): 1-7.

         Account of the revival that had begun in the United States and
         reached Scotland via Ireland. Special focus on lay preaching.

2544.   Olson, Virgil A. "Revivalism in Early Conference History."
         Bethel Seminary Quarterly 8 (August 1960): 79-88.

         Review of Swedish Baptist General Conference history, begun in
         a "spirit of revival" which continued in the "church centered
         revivalism" of the early twentieth century, and in mid-century
         continued to mark the heirs of the Swedish Baptists.

2545.   Orr, J. Edwin. The Light of the Nations: Evangelical Renewal and
         Advance in the Nineteenth Century. Grand Rapids: Eerdmans, 1965.
         302 p.

         A leading historian of the evangelical revivals describes the
         waves of renewal and advance during the great evangelical
         century. Bibliography. Index.

2546.   Owens, Raymond Eugene. "Preaching in a Revivalist Tradition: The
         Influence of Revivalism on Southern Baptist Preaching, 1845-1877."
         Th.D. diss.. Union Theological Seminary in the City of New York,
         1967. 348 p.

2547.   Prim, C. Clinton, Jr. "Colporteurs: Propagandists and Revivalists
         in the Confederate Army." American Baptist Quarterly 2 (September
         1983): 228-35.

Summary of Prim's Florida State Ph.D. dissertation; traces a large part of the extensive religious revivals in the Confederate armies to the work of colporteurs' distribution efforts.

2548.   Shiels, Richard D. "The Scope of the Second Great Awakening: Andover, Massachusetts, as a Case Study." Journal of the Early Republic 5 (Summer 1985): 223-46.

Describes the two phases of the awakening in Andover, with their accompanying changes in age, gender, kinship, and economic status, "impressive for its universality."

2549.   Sizer, Sandra S. Gospel Hymns and Social Religion: The Rhetoric of Nineteenth-Century Revivalism. Philadelphia: Temple University Press, 1978. 222 p.

Using the theoretical perspectives of anthropologists Geertz and Levi-Strauss and literary critic Kenneth Burke, Sizer's influential book offers "a historical sociology of religious language" of the hymnody of Moody and Sankey (set in the context of 19th century revivalism), which hymnody "represent[s] an interpretive strategy and a technique of transcendence." Appendix. Extensive bibliographical references. Index.

2550.   _____. "Politics and Apolitical Religion: The Great Urban Revivals of the Late 19th Century." Church History 48 (March 1979): 81-98.

Coupling concepts from Charles Finney with the revivals of 1857-1858 and 1873-1875, Sizer pursues the hypothesis that revivals occurred when "the evangelical community was under threat and the wrong sort of people [the slave Power, or the Pope] seemed to be gaining control, the necessity of purification was pressing, to strengthen from within and protect from the dangers without."

2551.   Thacker, Joseph A. "Methodism and the Second Great Awakening." Asbury Seminarian 39 (Summer 1984): 46-61.

Describes numerous revivals of the early 19th century, illustrating the "infinite variety that the Holy Spirit uses," concluding with an emphasis on prayer, the "one thread" that runs through all the revivals studied.

2552.   Walzer, William C. "Charles Grandison Finney and the Presbyterian Revivals of Central and Western New York." Ph.D. diss., University of Chicago, 1945. 254 p.

See also items 66, 68, 264, 758, 770, 792, 797, 798, 817, 828, 838, 839, 852, 881, 1027, 1040, 1144, 1184, 1461, 1547, 1595, 1664, 1677, 2474, 2483, 2490, 2572, 2573, 2574, 2575, 2578.

D. Twentieth Century

2553.   Barnhart, Joe E. The Billy Graham Religion. Philadelphia: United Church Press, 1972. 255 p.

Concentrates on Graham's theology, from a "thoughtful critique" point of view, to elaborate Graham's role as advocate of evangelicalism and sponsor of "Christian Americanism." Bibliographical references.

2554.   Blair, William, and Bruce Hunt. "The Korean Pentecost and the Sufferings Which Followed." Banner of Truth no. 164 (May 1977): 1-4.

An extract, describing the revival of 1907, from a volume by Blair (a contemporary of the events), and Hunt, of the latter twentieth century.

2555.   Blumhofer, Edith Waldvogel. "The Welsh Revival 1904-1905." Paraclete 20 (Summer 1986): 1-5.

Course of the revival and its influence elsewhere. "In several important ways it contributed to the specific context in which Pentecostalism emerged."

2556.   Briggs, Kenneth A. "The Church in the World: The Post-War Revival. Where is it Going?" Theology Today 31 (January 1975): 324-30.

Religion "was not the prime cause of the revival, but a response to it"; in any case, "the revival has peaked and is already in rapid decline, at least in most measurable respects."

2557.   Fuller, Daniel P, Give the Winds a Mighty Voice: The Story of Charles E. Fuller, Waco: Word, 1972, 247 p.

History of the famed revivalist, a figure important in the transition from fundamentalism to new evangelicalism.

2558.   Harrell, David Edwin, Jr. "American Revivalism from Graham to Robertson." Paper read at the Conference on Modern Christian

Revivalism: A Comparative Perspective, at Wheaton College,
March 30-April 1, 1989. Photocopied.

Deft portrayals of the raft of southerners--especially Graham,
Falwell, Swaggart, Roberts and Robertson--in whose hands
current revivalism is held.

2559.   Hunter, Jim Ernest, Jr. "A Gathering of Sects: Revivalistic
Pluralism in Tulsa, Oklahoma, 1945-1985." Ph.D. diss., The
Southern Baptist Theological Seminary, 1986. 328 p.

2560.   Kuyvenhoven, Andrew. "U.S. Evangelicals Talk Revival." Banner
124 (10 April 1989): 6-7.

Forty-seventh annual meeting of the NAE, in Columbus, Ohio,
March 1989; notes the strength of NAE; reports the varied
participants and emphases, including revival.

2561.   Marty, Martin E. "Ubiquitous Evangelists." Christian Century 95
(19 April 1978): 431.

The second in a series "illustrating our thesis that America is
so full of evangelism organizations that no one can escape
being targeted." Focuses in part on organizations aiming at
Jewish people.

2562.   McLeod, William L. Demonism Among Evangelicals and the Way to
Victory. Saskatoon, Saskatchewan, Canada: Western Tract Mission,
1975. 183 p.

Written by one of the central persons in the revival in Canada
during the early 1970s. Bibliography.

2563.   Orr, J. Edwin. "A Decade of Revival, 1900-1910." Evangelical
Review of Theology 9 (October 1985): 296-303.

The "most extensive evangelical awakening of all time," winning
more than five million persons in the two years of greatest
impact. Notes its beginnings in prayer, its worldwide scope,
and its social impact.

2564.   Rhee, Yoon-Ho. "Towards a Theory of Revival: A Case Study of the
Biblical and Korean Revivals." Th.M. thesis. Fuller Theological
Seminary, Pasadena, 1988. 228 p.

2565.   Riss, Richard M. A Survey of 20th Century Revival Movements in
North America. Peabody, MA: Hendrickson, 1988. 302 p.

Riss sees three awakenings in 20th century North America: the 1900-1910 rise of pentecostalism; the post-WWII era of Graham and Roberts; the 1960s and 1970s charismatic renewal, Jesus movement, and evangelicalism in the mainstream of American life. Includes a study of lesser-known revivalists and revival movements. Bibliography.

2566.   Shepherd, Richard Lawson. "The Awakening of 1904-08 and its Effects on Baptists in the United States." Ph.D. diss., Southwestern Baptist Theological Seminary, 1982. 519 p.

2567.   Stanley, Brian. "East African Revival - African Initiative Within a European Tradition." Evangelical Review of Theology 2 (October 1978): 188-207.

Description of the revival in the 1930s; analysis of how the European sources--Keswick teaching, the Scofield Reference Bible, and Oxford Group teaching--were coupled with African leadership and direction. Positive effects of the revival well past WWII.

2568.   Thomas, Geoffrey. "The Welsh Revival of 1904." Banner of Truth no. 74 (November 1969): 16-21.

A review of the book by that title by Eifion Evans, concluding that "while the book is the best on the 1904 revival to have appeared, we still await a more definitive work on what the reviewer regards as a sad episode in Welsh church history."

See also items 66, 298, 431, 800, 1144, 1503, 1839, 2024, 2029, 2473, 2483, 2488, 2544, 2569.

E.   Social Effects of Revivalism

2569.   Goldsmith, Peter. "Revivalism and the Advent of Cash Economy on the Georgia Coast." Review of Religious Research 29 (June 1988): 385-97.

Revivals and changes in the economy on St. Simon's Island, Georgia, in 1928 show (at variance with some expressions of deprivation theory) that one cannot assume "that religious innovation is in the service of either ideological hegemony or political protest": there is no "universal relationship between religious movements and a given political ideology."

2570. Gordon-McCutchan, R. C. "The Irony of Evangelical History."
       Journal for the Scientific Study of Religion 20 (December 1981):
       309-26.

       Religious awakenings--such as the Reformation and the first and
       second great awakenings--are essentially calming and stabiliz-
       ing forces in times of social dislocation, but ironically "have
       become, in a few short steps, themselves agencies for vastly
       accelerating the pace of social change," due to freedom from
       institutional restraint, the activist nature of evangelicalism,
       and its millennial tendencies.

2571. Guelzo, Allen C. "Revivalism and Social History: Some Observa-
       tions on a Reprint." Fides et Historia 14 (Spring-Summer 1982):
       61-69.

       Comments prompted by the 1980 reprint of Timothy L. Smith's
       Revivalism and Social Reform (1955); Guelzo sees it as an
       evangelical classic, but "doubt[s] its effectiveness as a piece
       of history."

2572. Hammond, John L. "Revival Religion and Antislavery Politics."
       American Sociological Review (April 1974): 175-86.

       Several counties in antebellum Ohio serve to demonstrate that
       "religious belief had a direct effect on political behavior,
       because doctrine prescribed that a particular political choice
       was required by the believers' religious obligations."

2573. _____. "Revivals, Consensus, and American Political Culture."
       Journal of the American Academy of Religion 46 (September 1978):
       293-314.

       Rejects the interpretation of early 19th century revivalism
       which sees it as one part of the era's political consensus;
       rather, revivalism "provided moral conviction more than group
       loyalties," "did not reinforce Jacksonian political culture,"
       and inspired political movements that "divided the nation far
       more than unified it."

2574. Johnson, Paul E. A Shopkeeper's Millennium: Society and Revivals
       in Rochester, New York, 1815-1837. New York: Hill and Wang. 1978.
       293 p.

       Reconstructing the biographies of hundreds of converts, Johnson
       explores the relationships between revivalism and the social
       and political order; focuses on "domestic relations, work,

community relationships, and the means of institutionalizing
political conflict and of arriving at political decisions"; and
sees revivals as solutions to massive spiritual crises.
Twenty-page bibliography. Index.

2575. Luker, Ralph E. "Revivalism and Revisionism Revisited." Fides et
Historia 14 (Spring-Summer 1982): 70-74.

Rejoinder to Guelzo's "Revivalism and Social History: Some
Observations on a Reprint." Fides et Historia 14 (Spring-
Summer 1982): 61-69, in part defending T. L. Smith's Revivalism
and Social Reform (1955; reprint 1980).

2576. McLoughlin, William G. "Professional Evangelism: The Social
Significance of Religious Revivals Since 1865." Ph.D. diss.,
Harvard University, 1953. 239 p.

2577. Orr, J. Edwin. "Revival and Social Change." Fides et Historia 6
(Spring 1974): 1-12.

Surveying the five "great awakenings" of modern times, he
contends that they revived the church and mobilized "believers
for evangelism, teaching, and social action," and that it is a
"popular fallacy that Evangelical Christians have lacked a
social conscience."

2578. Smith, Timothy L. Revivalism and Social Reform: American
Protestantism on the Eve of the Civil War. Baltimore: Johns
Hopkins University Press, 1980. 269 p.

Reprint of Revivalism and Social Reform in Mid-Nineteenth
Century America (New York: Abingdon, 1957, 253 p.) with
"Afterword" and "Selected Bibliography, 1960-1980" added. An
epochal book that reestablished the fact of evangelical social
Christianity, finding in pre-Civil War evangelicalism the roots
of the Social Christianity of the late 19th and early 20th
centuries. Eleven-page bibliographical essay. Index.

2579. Van Deburg, William L. "William Lloyd Garrison and the 'Pro-
Slavery Priesthood': The Changing Beliefs of an Evangelical
Reformer, 1830-1840." Journal of the American Academy of Religion
43 (June 1975): 224-37.

Demonstrates that Garrison entered the 1830s an apparently
convinced evangelical, was rebuffed by many orthodox clergy
over his immediatism, was influenced by non-orthodox thinkers,
and gave up orthodoxy in the 1840s and 1850s.

2580.   Whitam. Frederick L. "Revivalism as Institutionalized Behavior:
          An Analysis of the Social Base of a Billy Graham Crusade." Social
          Science Quarterly (June 1968): 115-27.

          Persons who made decisions at the 1957 crusade came not at
          random from the general population, but "from the ranks of
          white. middle class, 'old' Americans who were already
          identified with major Protestant denominations."

See also items 68, 1598, 1631, 2466, 2470, 2474, 2476, 2523, 2525, 2527,
     2532, 2548.

VIII

ECUMENISM

2581.   Baker, Tony. "Evangelical Approaches to Theological Dialogue."
Churchman 102, no. 1 (1988): 44-53.

Addressing Anglican evangelicals in Britain, Baker lists six
dangers in dialogue, six principles to guide dialogue, and
reports on the mixed results of twenty years of dialogue.

2582.   Barnhouse, Donald Grey. "Finding Fellowship With Pentecostals."
Eternity 9 (April 1958): 8-10.

Reports a meeting in 1957 at the headquarters of the Assemblies
of God, that revealed substantial agreement, and a willingness
to fellowship despite some frank disagreement; notes the rapid
growth of the Assemblies.

2583.   _____. "One Church." Eternity 9 (July 1958): 17-23.

Address to an InterVarsity Missions Conference in December 1957
by a new evangelical arguing for unity among all those (whatever their denominational affiliation) who are true believers.

2584.   Berkhof, Hendrikus. "Berlin Versus Geneva: Our Relationship with
the 'Evangelicals.'" Ecumenical Review 28 (January 1976): 80-86.

In the context of what he terms no longer a "problem" but a
"war" for the WCC, a leading Dutch Reformed theologian
interacts with the book Reich Gottes oder Weltgemeinschaft?
("Kingdom of God or World Community?: The Berlin Ecumenical
Manifesto on the Utopian Vision of the World Council of
Churches"), eds. Walter Kunneth and Peter Beyerhaus (1975),
Seeks to be open to "the Berlin book," arguing that dialogue is
the best approach, that there ought to be some shift in WCC
emphases, and noting changes that might occur.

2585.   Berkouwer, G. C. "What Conservative Evangelicals Can Learn From
         the Ecumenical Movement." Christianity Today 10 (27 May 1966):
         17-20.

         Evangelicals can learn about "the unity of the church and the
         dangers of an unbiblical eschatology."

2586.   Beyerhaus, Peter, Arthur Johnston, and Myung Yuk Kim. "An Evan-
         gelical Evaluation of the WCC's Sixth Assembly in Vancouver." TSF
         Bulletin 7 (September-October 1983): 19-20.

         After noting some positives, these three evangelicals list ten
         matters of concern, leading to the assessment that the WCC
         still has "shortcomings and distortions" that need to be
         addressed.

2587.   Bloesch, Donald G. The Future of Evangelical Christianity: A Call
         for Unity Amid Diversity. Garden City: Doubleday, 1983. 202 p.

         An ecumenical evangelical warns of the dangers (to the right
         and the left) that could disrupt the evangelical movement.
         Extensive bibliographical references.

2588.   Bromiley, Geoffrey W. "Fundamentalism-Modernism: First Step in
         the Controversy." Christianity Today 2 (11 November 1957): 3-5.

         Calls for a renewal of discussion, if modernists will be
         "genuinely historical and scientific," and fundamentalists will
         be "radically and consistently biblical."

2589.   Cairns, Earle E. "An Evangelical Approach to Ecumenicity."
         Asbury Seminarian 21 (January 1967): 31-36.

         "[A]ny 'dialogue' must come to terms with the message, mission,
         motivation and machinery to express spiritual unity in
         organizational union." If true to those basic principles,
         evangelicals "can have a strategic role in Christendom."

2590.   Chapman, G. Clark. "Ecumenism Under the Cross: Toward a New
         Coalition of Liberals and Evangelicals." Sojourners 6 (November
         1977): 28-30.

2591.   "The Charismatics and Ecumenism." Discerner 9 (January-March
         1978): 5-10.

2592.   Colquhon, Frank. The Fellowship of the Gospel: A New Testament
         Study in the Principles of New Testament Co-operation. Grand
         Rapids: Zondervan, 1957. 60 p.

Discusses the "limits of cooperation" evangelicals should make with other professing Christians, stressing fellowship over separatism.

2593. "The Consultation on Confessing the Apostolic Faith: From the Perspective of the Pentecostal Churches (October 22-24, 1986)." Ecumenical Trends 16 (February 1987): 29-30.

Brief news report of the fourth in a series of conciliar-pentecostal meetings.

2594. Cubie, David L. "An Evangelical Response." Ecumenical Trends 15 (July/August 1986): 116-18.

A response to Emmanuel Sullivan's article in the same issue; defines evangelical as "those churches which continue the revivalistic tradition of the eighteenth and nineteenth centuries," he discusses their resistance to ecumenism and concludes that "what is needed is a new sense of urgency" about Christian unity.

2595. Curtis, C. J. "Evangelical Catholicity." Ecumenical Review 17 (October 1965): 374-81.

Holding that "our contemporary situation has been virtually revolutionized by the ecumenical thinking . . . in our day," he sees "the ecumenical movement as dynamic process," as being, "in a sense, . . . another manifestation of progressive revelation."

2596. Dahlin, John E. "Problems Facing Evangelical Protestantism." Discerner 4 (October-December 1964): 2-5.

In the context of the great pressure for "external church unity," problems include: being in a "minority status," "being considered un-cooperative," and "spiritual discernment" (evangelicals must stand on "a solid doctrinal base").

2597. Darby, George. "'The Charismatics and Ecumenicism.'" Discerner 9 (January-March 1978): 5-10.

Contends that the two movements are closely interrelated, and that with the emphasis on ecumenism comes a de-emphasis on doctrine; due to lack of interest in doctrinal basics, the charismatic movement is in danger of being ensnared by the ecumenists, who are clearly apostate.

2598.   Davis, Rex. Locusts and Wild Honey: The Charismatic Renewal and the Ecumenical Movement. Geneva, Switzerland: World Council of Churches, 1978. 123 p.

2599.   Dayton, Donald W. "Evangelicals and the World Council of Churches: A (Very!) Personal Analysis." TSF Bulletin 7 (September-October 1983): 14-17.

Sees three kinds of Evangelicals--defender of the faith, pietist, sectarian--each with differing views of the WCC; hope in the latter two categories for some kind of rapprochement between evangelicals and the WCC.

2600.   Douglas, James D., ed. Evangelicals and Unity: Six Essays. Appleford, England: Marcham Manor Press, 1964. 96 p.

Six British evangelicals look at the ecumenical scene, "evaluate it in light of Evangelical principles, and express some of their hopes and fears in such a situation."

2601.   "An Evangelical Perspective on Roman Catholicism." Evangelical Review of Theology 10 (October 1986): 342-64.

The first of two articles issuing from the task force established by the World Evangelical Fellowship in 1980.

2602.   "The Evangelical-Roman Catholic Dialogue on Mission, 1977-1984: A Report." International Bulletin of Missionary Research 10 (January 1986): 2-21.

"[T]he full report of the Evangelical-Roman Catholic Dialogue on Mission (ERCDOM) . . . a product of three international meetings that took place . . . from 1977 to 1984." An important first step in a search for common ground.

2603.   "Evangelicals and Church Unity." Churchman 101, no. 3 (1987).

Papers given at the Church Society Spring Conference at Swanwick.

2604.   "Evangelicals at Vancouver: An Open Letter." TSF Bulletin 7 (September-October 1983): 18-19.

Signed by more than 200 persons. reflecting their "growing conviction that evangelicals should question biblically the easy acceptance of withdrawal. fragmentation and parochial isolation."

2605.   "Evangelicals in the Church of Rome." Christianity Today 10 (18
         March 1966): 22-23.

         Contends that large changes are occurring, and that evangeli-
         cals "should reach out . . . to those who . . . are our
         spiritual brothers and sisters in Christ," and should engage in
         dialogue with the Church within the principle of complete
         fidelity to the Scriptures.

2606.   Ewin, Wilson. "Is there an Evangelical Movement in the Catholic
         Church?" Discerner 7 (April-June 1972): 4-10.

         Concludes that "Reports of born-again people and evangelical
         trends within the Church of Rome were absolutely untrue and
         without foundation."

2607.   Frame, Randy. "Evangelical Voice Heard at World Council Meeting."
         Christianity Today 33 (14 July 1989): 45-46.

         A meeting of the WCC's Commission of World Mission and
         Evangelism at San Antonio, TX, May 22-31, 1989.

2608.   Garver, Stuart P. "Charismatic Renewal: Is It the Key to the
         Reunion of Protestants and Catholics." Christian Heritage 33 (May
         1972): 8-9, 28-9.

         In the author's view, the establishment in Illinois of a
         Catholic non-territorial congregation, "The Community of the
         Holy Spirit," means that "reunion" is "under the restraint and
         control of the Church of Rome."

2609.   Glasser, Arthur F. "Can This Gulf Be Bridged? Reflections on the
         Ecumenical/Evangelical Mission Debate." Missiology 6 (July 1978):
         275-82.

         Some doubts about whether the gulf can be bridged, given
         sharply different views on "the role of the Church and the
         authority of the Bible."

2610.   _____, "Evangelicals and the WCC." Ecumenical Trends 7 (June
         1978): 90-92.

         Discusses points of disagreement with the WCC, centering on the
         nature of the Church and the authority of the Scriptures,
         concluding that until there is "a measure of agreement on them
         . . . there is little hope of significant Evangelical
         involvement in the WCC."

2611.   _____. "What Evangelicals Can Learn From Bangkok." Eternity
          24 (April 1973): 27-29, 75-76, 78.

          Glasser is interviewed about the WCC-sponsored Bangkok con-
          ference on "Salvation Today"; notes earlier world missions
          conferences and discusses three differences: a shift from the
          evangelistic mandate to the "cultural mandate," the centrality
          of the church rather than of the missionary enterprise; the
          almost complete absence of the Person and Work of the Holy
          Spirit.

2612.   _____. "What Has Been the Evangelical Stance, New Delhi to
          Uppsala?" Evangelical Missions Quarterly 5 (Spring 1969): 129-50.

          Presents trends and attitudes during the period between the two
          congresses (1961 and 1968), concluding with the "significant
          role" played by evangelicals at Uppsala, though with
          unsatisfactory impact.

2613.   _____. "A Paradigm Shift? Evangelicals and Inter-Religious
          Dialogue." Missiology 9 (1981): 393-408.

          There are two paradigms, the evangelical one centering on the
          unity and authority of the Bible, and the conciliarists' on the
          view that authority rests in the encounter with Christ.
          Glasser questions whether meaningful dialogue is possible
          "across the gulf of these two paradigms."

2614.   Goodall, Norman. "Evangelicalism and the Ecumenical Movement."
          Ecumenical Review 15 (July 1963): 399-409.

          Role of the Evangelical Alliance in the beginnings of the
          modern ecumenical movement; the opposition to the ecumenical
          movement within evangelicalism; the nature of the opposition as
          related to doctrine, to the realm of faith; a reviewal of the
          doctrinal basis of evangelicalism and the ecumenical movement;
          the question of social Christianity.

2615.   _____. "'Evangelicals' and WCC-IMC." International Review of
          Missions 47 (April 1958): 210-15.

          Summarizes basic evangelical beliefs, notes the reluctance of
          evangelicals to cooperate with the WCC, and suggests some ways
          to improve the possibility of encounter between the two.

2616.   Hastings, C. Brownlow. "Reborn Christians: Their Significance for
          the Ecumenical Movement." Ecumenical Trends 8 (January 1979):
          13-16.

Defines evangelicalism (in terms of being born again) and
ecumenicalism, and proposes that: "There is an ad-hoc kind of
ecumenism within evangelicalism." "There are signs that
ecumenicalism and evangelicalism are at least beginning to
recognize one another's worth today."

2617. Henry, Carl F. H. "A Door Swings Open." Christianity Today 9 (18
June 1964): 24-26.

The ecumenical movement shows "a dilution of evangelical
theology and a diminution of evangelistic mission," opening the
door for an evangelical alliance to offer a dynamic faith and
authoritative voice to America.

2618. _____. "Evangelicals and Ecumenism." Christianity Today 10
(27 May 1966): 10-13.

Cites an increase in transdenominational cooperation as
indicative of the evangelical brand of ecumenism; points to the
large segment of evangelicals in the conciliar denominations;
offers suggestions by which conciliarists can show respect for
evangelicals.

2619. _____. "Looking Back at Key 73." Reformed Journal 24
(November 1974): 6-12.

Key 73 "aimed at a cooperative evangelistic witness by
evangelical believers" across America, and, despite criticisms
from right and left, made some strides toward evangelical
transdenominational cooperation.

2620. _____. "The New Coalitions." Christianity Today 33 (17
November 1989): 26-29.

"Evangelicals can count on having to join forces with non-
evangelicals before significant social change can come";
evangelicals ought to "take the initiative in setting the
agenda."

2621. _____. "Will the Gap Narrow or Widen?" Christianity Today 10
(4 February 1966): 27-30.

The gap between ecumenists and evangelicals will widen unless
ecumenism shows "a lively indignation over its non-evangelical
and anti-evangelical ingredients."

2622.   Hills, James W. L. "Evangelicals and Roman Catholics."
          Christianity Today 5 (3 July 1961): 3-5.

          Warns against a too-easy comradeship with Roman Catholicism, in
          light of the differences between it and evangelicalism,
          particularly in the matter of the role of the Bible in church
          and personal life.

2623.   Hitt, Russell T. "The World Council at 25 Years: An Evangelical
          Appraisal." Eternity 24 (October 1973): 18-20.

          Describes conservative evangelicalism, including its doctrine
          and praxis, and its relationship to the WCC; in Hitt's judgment
          the two movements have "never been further apart."

2624.   Hollenweger, Walter J. "Pentecostalism's Contribution to the
          World Church." Theology Digest 19 (Spring 1971): 54-57.

          Has ecumenical possibilities and is a good model of a theology
          of doing, but questions need to be raised about some
          pentecostal practices.

2625.   Justinian, Patriarch of Rumania. "Evangelical Humanism and
          Christian Responsibility." Ecumenical Review 19 (April 1967):
          157-60.

          "The struggle for Christian unity . . . cannot achieve its aim
          without carrying out a common service for the world." Emphases
          include peace, justice, equality. The WCC, "in every branch of
          its activities . . . should express its resolution to
          strengthen the service of Christianity in its pan-human and
          dynamic perspective."

2626.   Kelley, Dean M. "The NCC Shares What is on Its Mind."
          Christianity Today 26 (17 September 1982): 24-26.

          Provides a conciliatory attitude toward evangelicals and
          answers several questions posed by CT.

2627.   Kik, J. Marcellus. Ecumenism and the Evangelical. Philadelphia:
          Presbyterian and Reformed, 1957. 152 p.

          "The evangelical"--defined as one who "holds firmly to the sola
          scriptura and sola gratia of the Reformation"--"cannot afford
          to remain aloof," but must evaluate ecumenism in the light of
          Scripture and must set forth the scriptural concept of unity

and of the church. a task in which the evangelical "has been sadly remiss," and in which the author engages.

2628.   Kromminga, John H. "Evangelical Influence on the Ecumenical Movement." Calvin Theological Journal 11 (November 1976): 149-80.

Focusing on the Fifth Assembly of the WCC at Nairobi (1975), treats the "issues of central importance to the evangelical group [evangelism, syncreticism, social/political issues], the evidences of moderation in dealing with these issues. the sources from which the moderation may have sprung, and the limitations to be noted in the effect [on WCC] of the evangelical impact."

2629.   Lane, Tony. "Evangelicalism and Roman Catholicism." Evangelical Quarterly 61 (October 1989): 351-64.

Revision of a paper given at the conference of the Fellowship of European Evangelical Theologians at Altenkirchen, W. Germany (August 1988); how should evangelicals respond to recent changes in Roman Catholicism? Discusses those changes; concludes with an appeal to evangelicals for "warm hearts and a cool head"; despite changes, "fundamental differences" remain.

2630.   Lehmann. Daniel J. "Evangelizing the Evangelicals." Christian Century 105 (19 October 1988): 916-17.

Discusses the conversion of a number of evangelical clergy to Eastern Orthodoxy and their acceptance into the Antiochan Orthodox Church.

2631.   Lorenzen, Thorwald. "'Evangelical' and 'Ecumenical': Alternative Approaches to a Theology of Mission?" Foundations 25 (January-March 1982): 45-66.

Better to speak of different distinctions or emphases than to polarize evangelicalism and ecumenism. but there are areas of theological conflict (such as the Bible and its interpretation. the person and work of Christ. the understanding of reality. and the relation between faith and doctrine). and there are areas of consensus.

2632.   Lovelace. Richard F. "Evangelicals and the COCU Covenanting Process." Ecumenical Trends 15 (October 1986): 144-46.

Sets the new round of negotiations for COCU in the historical context of renewal and ecumenism under Count Zinzendorf; sees evangelicals as a crucial factor.

2633.   MacKay, John A. "What the Ecumenical Movement Can Learn From
        Conservative Evangelicals." Christianity Today 10 (27 May 1966):
        17, 20-23.

        Major difference is that ecumenists seek visible, structured
        unity of the church, while evangelicals seek the expression of
        biblical revelation in the thought and life of persons.
        Ecumenists can learn the importance of conversion and the role
        of the Bible in personal and corporate life.

2634.   Marcoux, Jacques. "Evangelical Catholics and the Ignored
        Paradox." Discerner 8 (April/June 1974): 6-11.

        In the context of changes in the Church, the increasing number
        of Roman Catholics who claim to have had a new birth
        experience, and the resultant optimism among Protestant
        evangelicals, emphasizes the paradox that "the fundamental
        position of the Church has not been modified." Accordingly,
        "the Evangelical Protestants' attitude should be reservation
        and moderation."

2635.   Maris, J. C. "The Ecumenical Movement: A Historical Perspective."
        Reformation Review 26 (July 1981): 138-45.

        Distinguishes true from false unity, the latter embodied in the
        WCC ecumenical movement.

2636.   Martin, Ralph. "Catholics, Evangelicals and Catholic Evangeli-
        cals." In Serving Our Generation: Evangelical Strategies for the
        Eighties, ed. Waldron Scott, 249-65. Colorado Springs: World
        Evangelical Fellowship, 1980.

        A leading Catholic charismatic presents the case for the
        possibility of being both Catholic and evangelical.

2637.   Martin, Roger H. Evangelicals United: Ecumenical Stirrings in
        Pre-Victorian Britain, 1795-1830. Metuchen, NJ: Scarecrow Press,
        1983. 230 p.

        Early experiments in ecumenism seen through the effect on
        churches in Britain by four pan-evangelical organizations: the
        London Missionary Society, the Religious Tract Society, the
        British and Foreign Bible Society, and the London Society for
        Promoting Christianity Amongst the Jews. Bibliographical
        references. Index.

2638. McDonnell, Kilian. "The Experiential and the Social: New Models From Pentecostal/Roman Catholic Dialogue." One in Christ 9, no. 1 (1973): 43-58.

> Lists the contributions classical pentecostalism could make in the Roman Catholic-pentecostal dialogue in the areas of witness, experience, and arriving at a new social and political consciousness.

2639. _____. "The International Roman Catholic Pentecostal Dialogue: The Meeting of a Structural Church and a Movement." One in Christ 10, no. 1 (1974): 4-6.

> "There is much that the historic Churches can learn from the classical Pentecostals in the area of evangelization."

2640. Meeking, Basil. "The Roman Catholic/Pentecostal Dialogue." One in Christ 10, no. 2 (1974): 117-28.

> Brief description of the five-year long series of meetings between the Roman Catholic Church and representatives of some of the pentecostal churches.

2641. Meeking, Basil, and John R. W. Stott, eds. The Evangelical-Roman Catholic Dialogue on Mission, 1977-1984: A Report. Grand Rapids: Eerdmans, 1986. 96 p.

> A report on the meetings at Venice (1977), Cambridge (1982), and Landevennec, France (1984). Concludes that "every possible opportunity for common witness should be taken, except where conscience forbids." Bibliography.

2642. Montgomery, John Warwick. "Evangelical Unity and Contemporary Ecumenicity." Gordon Review 9 (Winter 1966): 69-90.

> Discusses questions related to evangelical stance toward current ecumenical interaction; the need for "depth analysis" in various areas: "The Cruciality of Theological Motif-Research," "The 'Geist' of Eastern Orthodoxy," and a "new Western Theological Zeitgeist," concluding with a section on "The Potential Crisis and the Evangelical Responsibility."

2643. Mouw, Richard J. "An Evangelical Response." Ecumenical Trends 15 (July/August 1986): 113-15.

> A cautiously positive response to Emmanuel Sullivan's article, in the same issue, on "Reception . . .." with acknowledgement of evangelical shortcomings.

2644.   Nelson, F. Burton. "A Call to Church Unity." In The Orthodox
         Evangelicals: Who They Are and What They Are Saying, eds. Robert
         E. Webber and Donald Bloesch, 190-210. Nashville: Thomas Nelson,
         1978.

         Presents the biblical and historical case, concluding with a
         strong challenge for evangelicals to join energetically in the
         contemporary quest for church unity.

2645.   One in Christ (Magazine). Roman Catholic-Pentecostal Dialogue:
         Zurich-Horgen, June, 1972; Rome, 1973; Schloss Craheim, 1974;
         Venice, 1975; Rome, 1976. London: One in Christ, 1974-1977.
         Three volumes in one.

2646.   "The Perils of Ecumenicity." Christianity Today 1 (26 November
         1956): 20-22.

         The ecumenical movement in general elevates the doctrine of the
         unity of the [church] body above every other doctrine," leaving
         theological vagueness and ecclesiasticalism in its wake.

2647.   Petersen, Rodney L. "Evangelical Ecumenism: The Frustration and
         the Hope." Ecumenical Trends 15 (June 1986): 89-91.

         With "cautious optimism" reviews developments in WCC and COCU,
         and relates those trends to evangelical renewal. For
         evangelicals who do participate in ecumenical dialogue he
         offers guidelines for ecumenists to recognize.

2648.   Prenter, Regin. "Catholic and Evangelical: A Lutheran View."
         Ecumenical Review 1 (Summer 1949): 382-88.

         Argues that there is, "beneath our apparently irreparable
         divisions, a deeper concord than we usually imagine to exist,"
         and concludes that the question to ask is not whether there is
         hope for some result from ecumenical efforts, but whether it is
         "permissible for us to refrain from making the attempt?"

2649.   Quebedeaux, Richard. "Evangelicals: Ecumenical Allies."
         Christianity and Crisis 31 (27 December 1971): 286-88.

         Ecumenists should welcome evangelicals into dialogue because
         the latter are present in large numbers in mainline
         denominations, are increasingly social in outlook, and are
         taking new tacks in understanding the Bible.

2650. Randall, Claire. "The Importance of the Pentecostal and Holiness Churches in the Ecumenical Movement." One in Christ 23, no. 1-2 (1987): 83-92.

> Shows that the NCC and WCC are open to dialogue with pentecostal and holiness churches, points up areas of differences between conciliarists and these groups, and notes the contributions the latter can make.

2651. Read, Francis W. "Evangelicals and Anglo-Catholics." Christianity Today 6 (5 January 1962): 9-10.

> In spite of unresolvable differences at this time, Episcopalian Read says that evangelicals and Anglo-Catholics have many things in common that could lead to mutual understanding and respect.

2652. Rees, Paul S. "Attitudes of Conservative Evangelicals Toward the World Council of Churches." Covenant Quarterly 27 (February 1969): 34-36.

> Remarks made at a plenary session of the WCC Commission on Faith and Order, August 2, 1967, by a prominent evangelical pastor and editor of World Vision magazine, about perceived low view of Scripture, superchurch orientation, sacramentarian and liturgical tendency, universalism and syncretism, among others.

2653. Samuel, David. "Ecumenism: A Dilemma for Evangelicals." Churchman 101, no. 3 (1987): 198-212.

> Background and history of the ecumenical movement; an analysis of the Anglican-Roman Catholic dialogue and the threat it makes to evangelical Anglicans, for whom separation from the Anglican Church is not yet but could become the right response.

2654. Schrotenboer, Paul G. "An Evangelical Response to Baptism, Eucharist and Ministry." Evangelical Review of Theology 13 (October 1989): 291-313.

> A constructive, critical response, prepared by the World Evangelical Fellowship in June 1989, in response to the WCC's Lima Document on Baptism, Eucharist and Ministry (BEM) (Faith and Order Paper No. 111): general background for the Document, followed by a point-by-point treatment, a four-point conclusion, and two appendixes.

2655.   Shelley. Marshall. "What Catholics and Evangelicals Have in
         Common." Christianity Today 26 (26 November 1982): 66.

         Report on "Christianity Confronts Modernity" Conference in Ann
         Arbor, Michigan, 20-23 October 1982.

2656.   Sider, Ronald J. "Evangelicals and the WCC." Engage/Social
         Action 4 (February-March 1976): 41-45.

         After attending the WCC Fifth Assembly (Nairobi 1975), Sider
         still has reservations about the WCC, but the new emphasis on
         evangelism can mean hope for "dialogue and interchange with
         non-conciliar evangelicals."

2657.   Smith, Eugene L. "The Conservative Evangelicals and the World
         Council of Churches." Ecumenical Review 15 (January 1963):
         182-91.

         Noting the great importance and rapid growth of conservative
         evangelicals, calls for recognition of the validity of
         evangelical concerns; concludes that the primary concern of
         ecumenists must be with truth rather than unity.

2658.   Smith, Timothy L. "The Evangelical Kaleidoscope and the Call to
         Christian Unity." Christian Scholars' Review 15 (1986): 125-40.

         In broad strokes Smith pictures a multiform evangelicalism that
         has concerns similar to ecumenism, and notes the irony (even
         tragedy) in the failure of evangelicals to foster conversation
         with ecumenists.

2659.   Stewart, James Alexander. "The Evangelicals and the World Council
         of Churches." Reformation Review 11 (July 1964): 216-27.

         Evangelicals wrongly compromise with the WCC in ecumenical
         evangelism, the end result of which will be loyalty to the
         Church at Rome.

2660.   Stott. John R. W. "Evangelicals and Roman Catholics."
         Christianity Today 21 (12 August 1977): 30-31.

         How to relate to Roman Catholics in the context of Vatican II.
         Concludes that "the right way forward seems to be that of
         personal friendship. joint Bible study. and candid dialogue"
         and cites his experience as a part of "the Evangelical-Roman
         Catholic Dialogue on Mission" in April 1977; hopes for
         additional evangelical initiatives.

2661.   Stransky, Thomas F. "Catholics and Evangelicals: A Roman Priest
         Looks Across the Divide." Christianity Today 26 (22 October
         1982): 28-30.

         Historical reasons for estrangement, convergences taking place,
         and fundamental issues: "the Bible of the church, and the
         church of the Bible."

2662.   Winter, Harry E. "Evangelical and Catholic?" America 127 (5
         August 1972): 63-66.

         Outline of the evangelical past, contemporary growth and
         vitality; evangelical-Catholic relationships; hope for closer
         cooperation.

2663.   Witte, Paul W. "Can Catholics Learn Anything From Evangelical
         Protestants?" Christianity Today 15 (18 December 1970): 268-70.

         Six lessons on discovering a "purity and freshness" of the
         faith.

2664.   _____. On Common Ground: Protestant and Catholic Evangelicals.
         Waco: Word, 1975. 135 p.

See also items 48, 82, 107, 135, 149, 239, 241, 243, 244, 292, 303, 336,
    360, 364, 366, 577, 578, 663, 674, 676, 678, 679, 680, 823, 842, 1028,
    1226, 1227, 1236, 1238, 1261, 1320, 1372, 1463, 1492, 1589, 1592,
    1697, 1889, 2052, 2058, 2063, 2065, 2098, 2099, 2136, 2158, 2174,
    2213, 2217, 2222, 2243, 2283, 2286, 2311, 2322, 2351, 2367, 2384,
    2418, 2421.

SELECTED PERIODICALS

The following list of quarterly journals is a source for the variety of scholarly endeavors in which contemporary evangelicals engage:

Asbury Theological Journal (formerly Asbury Seminarian)
Bibliotheca Sacra
Calvin Theological Journal
Christian Education Journal
Christian Legal Society Quarterly
Christian Medical and Dental Society Journal
Christian Scholar's Review
Christianity and Literature
Churchman
Creation Research Quarterly
Criswell Theological Review
Evangel
Evangelical Journal
Evangelical Missions Quarterly
Evangelical Review of Theology
Evangelical Studies Bulletin
Faith and Philosophy
Fides et Historia
Grace Theological Journal
Journal of Psychology and Christianity
Journal of Psychology and Theology
Journal of the Academy for Evangelism in Theological Education
Journal of the Evangelical Theological Society
Paraclete
Perspectives on Science and Christian Faith: Journal of the American Scientific Affiliation
Pneuma
Presbyterion
Reformation Review
Review and Expositor
Science and Christian Belief
Scottish Bulletin of Evangelical Theology
Studia et Biblica Theologica
Southwestern Journal of Theology

Themlios
Transformation
Trinity Journal
Tyndale Bulletin
Wesleyan Theological Journal
Westminster Theological Journal

For a more popular understanding of the nature of evangelicalism consult the scores of denominational and other organizational publications, and general magazines like:

Charisma
Christian Herald
Christianity Today
Eternity
Moody Monthly

INDEX OF AUTHORS/EDITORS

(Numbers refer to entries, not pages)

Abell, Aaron Ignatius, 210
Abraham, William J., 1430, 1431
Academy of Humanism, 1847
Adams, Charles, 211
Adams, Doug, 1490
Adeyemo, Tokunboh, 579
Agrimson, J. Elmo, 2346
Ahlstrom, Sydney E., 1, 78, 267
Ahonen, Lauri, 648
Alderfer, Owen H., 1432
Aldrich, Roy L., 2129
Alexander, David A., 2031
Alexander, John W., 649
Alexander, Patrick H., 9
Allan, J. D., 79
Allen, David Grayson, 196
Allen, Maurice, 1491
Allen, Robert, 1848
Alley, Cletus E., 80
Alline, Henry, 179
Altschuler, Glenn C., 2520
Alvarez, Carmelo E., 580
Ammerman, Nancy Tatom, 1951
Amundsen, Darrel W., 1085
Anderson, Clifford V., 313
Anderson, Douglas Firth, 2521
Anderson, Marvin W., 81
Anderson, Robert Mapes, 2032
Anderson, V. Elving, 1068
Antekeier, Charles, 2347
Apel, William D., 952
Aren, Gustav, 581
Armerding, Carl Edwin, 718, 1186, 1349
Armerding, Hudson T., 953

Arnold, Patrick M., 1849
Ascol, Tom, 1517
Ashbrook, William A., 417
Ashbrook, William E., 418
Ashcraft, Morris, 1687, 1688
Ashworth, Robert A., 1741
Askew, Thomas A., 83, 174, 314
Audemard, Philip, 2266
Autrey, C. E., 2522
Averill, Lloyd J., 84, 1895

Bagiackas, Joseph, 2348
Bain, Elizabeth, 1153
Baker, Thomas Eugene, 316
Baker, Tony, 2581
Balda, Wesley D., 529, 530
Baldwin, Stanley, 1069
Ballard, Paul H., 1492
Balleine, George Reginald, 531
Balmer, Randall H., 180, 317, 1600, 1850, 2498
Bandow, Doug, 885
Banki, Judith H., 719
Banks, William L., 682
Banner, Lois W., 212
Banner, Ray, 318
Barabas, Steven, 532
Barber, Raymond W., 1851
Barfoot, Charles H., 2033
Baring-Gould, Sabine, 533
Barker, Montagu G., 2245
Barker, William S., 213
Barkley, Gary, 2
Barkun, Michael, 1465, 2462
Barlow, Jack, 954

Barnard, John, 214
Barnett, Donald Lee, 2130
Barnhardt, III, Luther (Lee) E.,
    650
Barnhardt, Joy A., 650
Barnhart, Joe E., 2553
Barnhouse, Donald Grey, 319, 2582,
    2583
Barr, James, 1187, 1188, 1189,
    1190, 1350
Barrett, Roger, 1493, 1494
Barth, Karl, 1191, 1192
Bartholomew, Alfred Clinton, 1518
Bartleman, Frank, 2004
Bartlett, Billy Vick, 1689
Bass, Clarence B., 3
Bass, Dorothy C., 1519
Bassett, Paul Merritt, 1448, 1742
Bast, Henry, 2463
Bates, Vernon Lee, 886
Battley, D. H., 2429
Bauman, Michael, 1351
Baumann, Fred E., 887
Baumann, J. Daniel, 320
Baxter, James Sidlow, 85
Bayly, Joseph, 321
Beale, David O., 1690, 1743
Beatty, Bill, 2316
Bebbington, David W., 86, 534, 535,
    1352
Bechtel, Paul, 1095
Becklund, David E., 1744
Beckmann, David M., 2246
Beckwith, Burnham P., 268
Bedell, Kenneth B., 481
Beeg, John Frederich, 2349
Belden, Albert David, 2499
Bendroth, Margaret L., 751
Benjamin, Paul, 322
Benn, Wallace, 1193
Bennett, Arthur, 536, 537
Bennett, Dennis, 2267
Benson, John E., 1495
Benware, Paul, 419
Berent, Irwin M., 1713
Berg, John Leland, 888
Berg, Philip L., 1952

Berger, Peter L., 323
Bergman, Marvin L., 651, 2500
Bergquist, James A., 4
Bergquist, Susan L., 2445
Berk, Stephen E., 215
Berkhof, Hendrikus, 2584
Berkouwer, G. C., 2585
Bernardin, Joseph Cardinal, 1877
Best, G. F. A., 538
Beverly, Jim, 2131
Beyerhaus, Peter, 652, 2586
Bibby, Reginald W., 1615, 1616
Bicket, Zenas J., 2034
Biggar, Nigel, 1194
Bilhartz, Terry D., 2523
Billington, Louis, 5, 209
Bishop, Richard W., 2268
Bishops' Liaison Committee With the
    Catholic Charismatic Renewal,
    2350
Bittlinger, Arnold, 2351, 2352,
    2353, 2430
Blackwelder, Julia Kirk, 1896
Blackwood, Andrew W., 324, 325
Blaiklock, E. M., 1195
Blair, William, 2554
Blakemore, Peter James, 1745
Blauvelt, Martha Tomhave, 2501
Bledsoe, W. Craig, 1897
Bloch, Ruth H., 181
Blocker, Jacques, 583
Bloesch, Donald G., 421, 422, 720,
    1196, 1197, 1198, 1199, 1200,
    1341, 2354, 2587
Blumhofer, Edith Waldvogel, 14,
    1520, 2035, 2036, 2037, 2038,
    2039, 2555
Board, Stephen, 1601, 2355
Bockmühl, Klaus, 87, 955
Bocock, John H., 2524
Boer, Harry R., 1353
Boice, James Montgomery, 1521
Boles, John B., 512, 513, 2525
Bolich, Gregory G., 1201
Bolton, Brian, 2256
Bond, John, 2212
Bong, Rin Ro, 584, 585, 586

Bonham, Jerry Lee, 1898
Bonomi, Patricia U., 182
Boone, Kathleen C., 1691
Booth, John David, 1161
Bord, Richard J., 2269, 2446
Bosch, David J., 956
Bourassa, Louise, 2270
Bourgault, Louise, 2247
Bowden, Henry Warner, 88, 216, 2526
Bowers, Lanny Ross, 1096
Bowers, Paul, 587, 1202
Boyd, Forrest J., 588
Boyd, Nancy, 269
Boylan, Anne M., 752, 1097, 1098
Bozeman, Theodore Dwight, 183
Bradbury, M. L., 1099
Bradfield, Cecil David, 2447, 2448
Bradley, Ian C., 539
Bradley, James, 1496
Brandt-Bessire, Daniel, 2005
Branson, Mark Lau, 6, 89, 589
Bratcher, Robert G., 1354
Bratt, James D., 1522
Braun, Jon, 1203
Bready, John Wesley, 1433
Breckenridge, James F., 2356
Bredesen, Harold, 2357
Breisch, Francis, 889
Brereton, Virginia Lieson, 1746
Bridger, Francis, 957
Bridges, Horace James, 1747
Brien, Robert C., 423
Briggs, J. H. Y., 217
Briggs, Kenneth A., 2556
Brinkerhoff, Merlin B., 1615, 1616,
    1899
Brinks, Herbert, 2527
Bromiley, Geoffrey W., 2040, 2588
Bromley, David G., 890
Brooks, M. Paul, 2041
Brown, Bruce, 1852
Brown, C. G., 184, 540
Brown, Clifton L., 76
Brown, Colin, 1204
Brown, Dale W., 1478, 2358
Brown, Ford K., 218
Brown, Harold O. J., 90, 1692, 1693

Brown, John Bossert, Jr., 91
Brown, Joseph, 683
Brown, L. Duane., 1900
Brown, Nate, 1602
Brown, Paul E., 1205
Brown, Robert McAfee, 1901
Bruce, Calvin E., 684
Bruce, Dickson D., Jr., 2528
Bruce, Frederick Fyvie, 1206
Bruce, Steve, 891, 1617, 1902
Brumback, Carl, 2042, 2043
Brumberg, Joan Jacobs, 219
Bruner, Frederick Dale, 2132
Brunkow, Robert de V., 7
Brusco, Elizabeth Ellen, 590
Bube, Richard H., 1070
Buckelew, Roy Edward, 1903
Buckley, T. E., 185
Bundy, David D., 8, 1456, 2044
Burgess, Stanley M., 9, 2133
Burkett, Charles E., 1434
Burkhart, John E., 1523
Burkholder, J. Lawrence, 1618
Burkill, Mark, 1193
Burkiser, W. T., 1524
Burton, Ronald, 1953
Buskey, Jack Ronald, 2359
Buss, Dietrich G., 10, 1466
Bussell, Harold L., 1207
Butchart, Ronald E., 685
Butler, C. S., 2360
Butler, Farley P., Jr., 270
Butler, Francis Joseph, 220
Butler, Jonathan M., 186, 1467,
    1473, 2502
Byrne, James E., 2361

Cailliet, Emile, 92
Cain, Michael Scott, 1904
Cairns, Earle E., 2464, 2589
Calhoon, Robert M., 514
Camara, Dom Helder, 2423
Cameron, Nigel M. de S., 1208, 1355
Campbell, Will D., 326
Campolo, Anthony, 1619
Campus Crusade for Christ
    International, 1603

Canty, George, 2134
Caplan, Lionel, 1954
Carden, Allen, 12, 187
Carnell, Edward John, 93, 1209, 1210
Carpenter, Joel A., 13, 14, 271, 272, 1100, 1604, 1748, 1749
Carper, James C., 32
Carroll, R., 591
Carter, Charles W., 1435
Carter, Paul A., 15
Cartwright, Desmond W., 753
Carwardine, Richard, 221, 2529, 2530, 2531
Castlen, James Eudelle, 94
Castro, Emilio, 2213
Catherwood, Christopher, 273
Cattell, Everett L., 327, 592
Cauthen, Kenneth, 16
Cecil, Kedric Hugh, 1955
Cerillo, Augustus, Jr., 892, 958
Chafer, Lewis Sperry, 274, 1211
Chandler, Ralph C., 1905
Chantry, Walter J., 2135
Chao, Jonathan T'ien-en, 593
Chapman, Colin G., 1212
Chapman, G. Clark, 2590
Chappell, Paul Gale, 2045
Chase, Elise, 17
Chervin, Ronda, 2431
Child, Philip Albert, 1162
Childerston, James Kent, 1694
Chilson, Richard, 1695
Chinn, Jack J., 2136
Chow, Wilson W., 594
Christenson, Laurence, 961, 2363, 2364, 2365, 2366
Christopherson, Kenneth E., 1696
Citron, Bernhard, 95
Cizik, Richard, 893
Clabaugh, Gary K., 1906
Clancy, Thomas, 329
Clark, Donald L., 2248
Clark, Gordon H., 330
Clearwaters, Richard V., 424, 425, 426, 427, 428, 1356, 1697
Clegg, Herbert, 542

Clelland, Donald A., 1620
Clement, Arthur J., 2137
Clifford, Alan, 543, 544
Clouse, Robert G., 962, 963, 964, 2264
Clutter, Ronald T., 1101
Clymer, Kenton J., 653
Coalter, Milton J., Jr., 188
Coggins, Jim, 1750
Cohen, Charles L., 189, 190
Cole, G. A., 2367
Cole, Stewart G., 1751, 1752
Coleman, Richard J., 1213
Coleman, Robert J., 1357, 1358
Colledge, Edward, 2272
Collier, William, 222
Collins, Gary, 331
Colquhon, Frank, 2592
Compton, Bobby D., 1753
Conference on Biblical Inerrancy, 1359
Conference on Biblical Interpretation, 1360
Conforti, Joseph, 223, 224
Conn, Harvie M., 654, 754, 1361
Connelly, James Thomas, 2249, 2273
Conser, Walter Hurley, Jr., 225
Conway, Flo, 1698
Cooper, John C., 894, 1525
Coote, Robert T., 655
Coppedge, Allan, 1436
Cordis, Robert, 1699
Corley, Kathleen E., 755
Corrigan, John E., 191
Corwin, Charles, 595
Coskren, Thomas M., 1853
Costas, Orlando E., 596
Cotham, Perry C., 895
Cottrell, Jack W., 1214
Cragg, George G., 545
Craig, Robert, 2138
Craig, William Lane, 96, 1071
Craufurd, A. H., 226
Crawford, Michael J., 2465
Cromartie, Michael, 896, 925
Crooks, George R., 546
Cross, Whitney R., 2532

Crowther. Edward Riley, 515
Crum. Gary, 965
Crunden, Robert M., 227
Crutsinger. Gene Charles, 1362
Cubie, David L., 2594
Culpepper, Robert H., 2368, 2369
Curley, Brian E., 1700
Currey, Cecil B., 192
Curry, Dean C., 966
Curry, Lerond. 97
Curtis, C. J., 2595

d'Epinay, Christian LaLive, 597
Dabney, Robert L., 228
Dahlin. John E., 1215, 1216, 1217,
    1754, 2139, 2596
Dalton, Robert Chandler, 2140
Damboriena, Prudencio, 2046, 2141
Dana, Richard H., 2256
Daniel, M., 591
Danielson. Dan. 2274
Darby, George, 2597
Davies, Douglas, 2250
Davies, George Colliss Boardman,
    547
Davies, Horton, 2047, 2142
Davis, Arnor S., 2048
Davis, Christian R., 229
Davis, D. Clair, 1526
Davis, Dennis Royal, 1072
Davis, Jimmy Thomas, 1854
Davis, John Jefferson, 98, 99, 1218
Davis, Lawrence B., 1527
Davis, Rex, 2598
Davis, Robin Reed, 756
Davis, Stephen T., 1219
Davison, Leslie. 2006, 2275
Dawsey, James, 18
Dayton, Donald W., 334, 483, 484,
    757, 758, 897, 967, 968, 969,
    1220, 1363, 1364, 1449, 1450,
    1451, 1452, 1453, 1454, 1455,
    1456, 2007, 2008, 2049, 2276,
    2599
Dayton. Lucille Sider. 758
De Chalandeau. Alexander. 598
De Gruchy, John W., 485

De Oliveira. Silas, 1701
Dean, Lloyd F., 1221
Dearman, Marion, 2251
Deck, Allan Figueroa, 335
DeHoney, Wayne, 100
Dejong, Gerben, 898
DeJong, Gordon J., 1956
DeJong, Mary A., 230
Del Monte Sol, Teresa, 2009
Delnay, Robert, 1755
Demarest, Bruce, 1386
Dempster, Murray W., 892
Dennis, Lane T., 506, 1222, 1621
Dennison, Charles G., 1528
DePetrella, Lidia Susana Vaccaro,
    599
Derham, A. Morgan, 548, 600
Diehl, David W., 1223
Dieter, Melvin E., 1457, 1458,
    1459, 2010
Dixon, Larry Edward, 1224
Doan, Ruth Alden, 2533
Doane, James, 2144
Dobson, Edward, 101, 486, 1225,
    1702, 1703, 1704, 1705, 1706,
    1707, 1756, 1757, 1855, 1858,
    1907
Dockery, David S., 487, 1244, 1497
Doland, Virginia M., 1622
Dolby, James R., 1623
Dole, C. F., 231
Dollar, George W., 19, 429, 1708,
    1758, 1759, 2050
Dollar. Truman. 1709
Dominian, J., 2252
Donahoo, William D., 656
Donovan, John J., 2466
Douglas. James D., 2600
Douglass, R. Bruce. 336
Dowell. Bill, Jr., 1856
Doyle, Barry. 601
Drakeman. Donald L., 949
Du Plessis. David J., 2051, 2052
Du Plessis. Justus T., 2145
Dudley. Robert Louis. 1957
Dudley-Smith. Timothy. 102
Duffield, Gervase. 549, 550

Dunkerly, Donald A., 1529
Dunn, James D. G., 1142, 2146
Durasoff, Steve, 2053
Durden, Susan, 1143
Dyrness, W. A., 1226

Earle, Ralph M., Jr., 103
Eckstein, Rabbi Yechiel, 1877
Edge, Findley B., 970
Edmondson, William Douglas, 1760
Edwards, David L., 1227
Edwards, Paul R., 1710
Eells, Robert J., 971
Eenigenburg, Elton M., 1711
Eens-Rempel, Kevin, 232
Ehrenstein, Herbert Henry, 791
Elbert, Paul, 2147
Elias, John, 2534
Eller, Vernard, 1200
Ellingsen, Mark, 104, 337
Elliott-Binns, L. E., 551
Ellis, George M., 233
Ellison, Craig W., 972, 1624
Ellison, R. W., 2432
Ellwood, Robert S., 1625
Elmore, Floyd S., 1228
Elwell, Walter A., 20, 21
Emery, George N., 602
Emmerson, W. L., 1229
Endruveit, Wilson Harle, 2214
England, Daniel, 2535
Ensley, Eddie, 2277
Enslin, Morton S., 1712
Epperson, Cheryl Lynn, 1626
Epstein, Barbara Leslie, 759
Erickson, Millard J., 430, 1230,
  1231
Escobar, Samuel, 657, 1232
Essig, James D., 973
Evangelical Archives Conference,
  22, 105
Evangelical Theological Society,
  1235
Evangelicals for Social Action,
  1046
Evans, Eifion, 2467
Evans, James H., Jr., 23

Evans, Rod L., 1713
Evans, W. Glyn, 2468
Evans, William Joseph, 340
Everett, Henry C., 1965
Ewin, Wilson, 2278, 2606
Ezell, Macel D., 341

Fackre, Gabriel, 1365, 1531, 1857,
  1908
Fahey, Sheila Macmanus, 2370
Fairfield, James, 974
Falwell, Jerry, 1858, 1909, 1910
Farah, Charles, 2148
Fargher, Brian, 2279
Farley, Ian David, 552
Farrow, Douglas, 1366
Faught, J. Harry, 605
Faulkner, Barbara L., 686
Faulkner, Joseph E., 2269, 2446
Faupel, D. William, 24, 1456, 2149
Faust, Drew Gilpin, 516, 2536
Feagin, Joe R., 1958
Feinberg, John S., 1367
Fensham, Charles J., 1236
Ferm, Robert O., 431
Ferngren, Gary B., 975
Fichter, Joseph Henry, 2371
Fiddes, Paul S., 2372
Findlay, Alice M., 1761
Findlay, James F., Jr., 792, 1102
Finger, Thomas, 1237
Finke, Roger, 1627
Finlayson, R. A., 553
Finney, Charles G., 2537
Fison, Joseph Edward, 106
Flake, Carol, 1859
Flood, Robert, 1103
Flowers, Ronald B., 899
Foley, Michael W., 900
Forbes, Bruce David, 659
Forbes, James A., 2150
Ford, J. Massyngberde, 2373, 2374,
  2375, 2376, 2377, 2378, 2379
Ford, Leighton, 342
Ford, Thomas R., 1956
Forrest, Tom, 2280
Forster, Greg S., 2054

Forster, Roger, 554, 976
Foss, Michael W., 1238
Foster, Allyn K., 1762
Foster, Charles I., 977
Foster, John W., 1763
Foster, Mary C., 2503
Fowler, Paul B., 1239
Fowler, Robert Booth, 901
Frame, Randy, 793, 1240, 2607
France, R. T., 1368
Frank, Douglas W., 234, 1628, 1629
Frankl, Razelle, 1144
Frantz, John B., 2469
Fraser, Elouise Renich, 760
Fraser, James W., 1104
Frei, Hans, 1241
Freitag, Walter, 1764
Frey, Harald Christian Andreas, 107
Friedman, Lawrence J., 978
Friesen, Duane K., 1532
Fromow, George H., 1714
Fry, C. George, 2055
Fullam, Everett L., 2151
Fuller, Daniel P., 2557
Fuller, David Otis, 108
Furness, Charles Y., 979
Furniss, Norman, 1765

Gabriel, Ralph H., 235
Gaebelein, Frank E., 980, 1163
Gaede, Charles S., 2152
Gager, LeRoy, 1243
Gallagher, Sharon, 488
Gallichan, W. M., 236
Gamble, Richard C., 1528
Gambone, Robert L., 1164
Gangel, Kenneth O., 1105, 1106
Garlock, Donald A., 1165
Garlock, Ruthanne, 2056
Garrett, James Leo, Jr., 1533, 1534, 1535
Garver, Stuart P., 2608
Gasper, Louis, 1766
Gatewood, Willard B., Jr., 1767
Gaustad, Edwin Scott, 25, 1768
Gaxiola, Manuel J., 2215
Gee, Donald, 2153, 2154

Gehman, Richard J., 607
Geisler, Norman, 373
Geissler, Suzanne B., 193
Gelpi, Donald L., 2155, 2380, 2381
Genet, Harry, 608
George, Timothy, 1244
Georgianna, Sharon Linzey, 1959
Gerlach, Luther P., 2253, 2254
Gerstner, John H., 109
Ghezzi, Bert, 2382, 2433
Gibson, Dennis L., 1630
Gier, Nicholas F., 1245
Giesbrecht, Herbert, 981
Gifford, Carolyn De Swarte, 26
Gilbert, Arthur, 2057
Gilbert, Earl Jean, 1960
Gilbert, Timothy Dwain, 1912
Gill, Frederick Cyril, 1166
Gillespie, Paul F., 1715
Gillie, Robert Calder, 275
Gilling, Bryan, 2383
Gilmore, Susan K., 2255
Ginzberg, Lori D., 761, 762
Gipson, Betty Jean, 1167
Glass, William R., 1769
Glasser, Arthur F., 660, 661, 662, 663, 664, 2609, 2610, 2611, 2612, 2613
Glazier, Stephen D., 2216
Glover, Willis B., 237, 238, 432
Goen, C. C., 1437, 1536, 1770
Goetzman, Martha M., 982
Goff, James Rudolph, Jr., 2011
Goldingay, John, 1246
Goldsmith, Peter, 2569
Goodall, Norman, 344, 2614, 2615
Goodwin, Gerald J., 2504
Gordon-McCutchan, R. C., 1631, 2570
Gorman, Benjamin Lee, 1961
Gott, Lois, 2058
Gouldstone, Tim, 345
Grabbe, Lester L., 1771
Graffam, Lillian H., 983
Graham, Billy, 346, 347, 348, 349, 350, 351, 794, 795
Graham, Stephen R., 239
Granfield, Patrick, 2384

Gray, Virginia, 1962
Grenz, Stanley J., 902
Gribbin, William, 903
Grier, W. J., 796
Griffin, Leslie, 27
Grigsby, Bruce, 1369
Grindal, Bruce T., 1860
Grine, Joanne Del Greco, 1073
Gritsch, Eric Walter, 1247
Gritzmacher, Steven A., 2256
Gross, Don H., 2281
Grounds, Vernon C., 352, 353, 433,
    434, 435, 721, 984, 985, 1107,
    1248, 1249, 1861
Grubb, Kenneth, 609
Grubb, Luther L., 354
Guelzo, Allen C., 194, 2571
Guinness, Os, 355
Gundry, Stanley N., 1250, 1280
Gunstone, John Thomas Arthur, 2434
Gustafson, Cloyd V., 1963

Hadden, Jeffrey K., 1145, 1146,
    1147, 1964
Hafemann, Scott J., 1108
Hageman, Howard, 986
Hagner, Donald A., 1370
Haiven, Judith, 1862
Hakes, J. Edward, 1109
Hale, Frederick, 67
Hall, David D., 28, 195, 196
Hall, Joseph Hill, 1772
Hall, Robert B., 2435
Halteman, Jim, 987
Hamann, Henry P., 1716
Hamilton, James E., 797, 1438
Hamilton, Michael Pollock, 2282
Hamm, Thomas D., 1537
Hammond, John L., 2470, 2572, 2573
Hammond, Phillip E., 276, 904, 1110
Hancock, Robert Lincoln, 988
Hands, Donald, 2281
Handspicker, M. B., 2217
Handy, Robert T., 277, 1773, 1774
Hansell, Joy, 763
Harder, Mary W., 1992
Hardesty, Nancy A., 764

Harding, D. N., 356
Harding, Susan, 1148
Hardman, Keith J., 798, 2471
Harkness, Robert A., 799
Harman, Gordon, 1251
Harper, Charles L., 1632
Harper, George W., 2385
Harper, James Clyde, 1775
Harper, Michael, 2283, 2284
Harrell, David Edwin, Jr., 517,
    800, 801, 2059, 2558
Harrington, Carroll Edwin, 1776
Harris, Eleanor K., 802
Harris, Jackson Lee, II, 2386
Harrison, Archibald W., 1439
Harrison, Michael I., 2449
Harrison, Patricia J., 610
Hart, Benjamin, 905
Hart, Darryl Glenn, 803
Hart, Larry D., 2060, 2156
Hart, Nelson Hodges, 1777
Hartz, Gary W., 1965
Harwell, Jack U., 1538
Hassey, Janette, 765
Hastey, Stan, 1913
Hastings, C. Brownlow, 2616
Hatch, Nathan O., 178, 357, 804,
    906, 930, 1111, 1371, 1468
Haughey, John C., 2387
Hayes, Edward L., 1112
Haynes, Michael E., 687
Hearn, Arnold, 1863
Heasman, Kathleen J., 989
Heath, Richard , 240
Heaton, C. Adrian, 1113
Hebert, Gabriel, 1717, 1778
Hedlund, Roger C., 2218
Hedlund, Roger Eugene, 1539
Hedstrom, James A., 29, 278
Hefley, James C., 1498, 1540
Heidebrecht, Paul H., 805
Heidinger, James V., II, 1541,
    1542, 1543
Heim, Stephen Mark, 1252
Heimert, Alan, 197, 2505
Hein, Steven Arthur, 1253
Heino, Harri, 2285

Heisey, Terry M., 1544
Helgeland, John, 1718
Helgerson, Carlton, 436
Hellstern, Mark, 2157
Helm, Paul. 110, 990
Hempton, David, 30, 1469
Hendel, Kurt K., 991
Hendricks, John Stephen, 1966
Hendrix, Scott H., 2388
Hennell, Michael, 555, 556, 844
Henry, Carl F. H., 279, 280, 281,
    282, 358, 359, 360, 361, 362,
    437, 806, 807, 808, 809, 907,
    992, 993, 994, 995, 996, 1114,
    1115, 1254, 1255, 1256, 1257,
    1258, 1259, 1260, 1261, 1372,
    1373, 1374, 1779, 1780, 1864,
    1877, 2617, 2618, 2619, 2620,
    2621
Henry, Paul B., 908
Herman, Douglas Edward, 1781
Heron, B. M., 2286
Hesselgrave, David J., 665
Hesselink, I. John, 2389
Hestenes, Roberta, 363
Hewitt, Nancy A., 766, 767
Hewitt, Thomas, 364
Hickman, James T., 111, 2158
Hicks, Darryl E., 1149, 1180
Hill, Samuel S., Jr., 518, 519,
    520, 1673, 1914
Hills, James W. L., 1605, 2287,
    2288, 2622
Hindson, Edward E., 101, 486, 1150,
    1225, 1375, 1855, 1858, 1865,
    1907, 1915
Hine, Leland D., 283
Hine, Virginia H., 2254, 2257
Hinnebusch, Paul, 2390
Hinson, E. Glenn, 1535, 1545, 1546,
    1866
Hitt, Russell T., 810, 2391, 2623
Hittle, Gary Dean, 1967
Hoch, Carl B., Jr., 768
Hocken, Peter, 2061, 2062, 2392,
    2393, 2436
Hodge, Archibald Alexander, 1262

Hodges, Melvin L., 2219
Hoekema, Anthony A., 2159
Hoeveler, J. David, Jr., 241, 811
Hoffecker, W. Andrew, 1263, 1499
Hoffelt, Robert David, 812
Hofstadter, Richard, 1916
Hogan, William, 909
Hogg, W. Richie, 666
Hoke, Donald E., 365
Holdcroft, L. Thomas, 2160
Holifield, E. Brooks, 198, 521
Holladay, J. Douglas, 557, 997
Hollenweger, Walter J., 667, 2063,
    2064, 2065, 2066, 2161, 2162,
    2220, 2221, 2222, 2223, 2289,
    2624
Hollinger, Dennis P., 998
Holloway, J. Y., 326
Holmer, Paul L., 1264
Holmes, Arthur F., 438, 1116, 1265
Hood, Fred J., 1547
Hood, Ralph W., Jr., 1968, 1969
Hopkins, Jerry Berl, 688
Hopkinson, Bill, 558
Hopkinson, Patricia L., 1974
Houghton, Myron J., 439
House, H. Wayne, 1266
Housholder, David, 1267
Howard, Philip E., Jr., 1782
Howard, Ted, 157, 158
Howard, Thomas, 1268, 1269, 1500
Howden, J. Russell, 284
Howe, Claude L., Jr., 1548, 1549,
    2290
Howe, Leroy T., 2163
Howell, Joseph H., 2067
Hubbard, David Allan, 1270, 1633
Hudson, Charles, 1970
Hudson, Winthrop S., 769
Hughes, Philip Edgecumbe, 1271
Hughes, R. H., 2291
Hughes, Richard T., 31, 1272
Hummel, Charles E., 2068, 2292
Humphreys, Fisher, 242
Hundley, Raymond C., 1273
Hunt, Bruce, 2554
Hunt, Thomas C., 32

Hunter, Harold D., 2012, 2069, 2164
Hunter, James Davison, 1110, 1634,
   1635, 1636, 1637, 1638, 1639,
   1640, 1641
Hunter, Jim Ernest, Jr., 2559
Hunter, Lloyd A., 1168
Hurley, James B., 813
Hutcheson, Richard G., Jr., 366,
   910
Hutchison, William R., 33, 34, 285,
   668
Hylson-Smith, Kenneth, 559
Hywel-Davies, Jack, 814

Ice, Thomas, 1266
Ide, Arthur Frederick, 1917
Inbody, Tyron, 1867
Inch, Morris A., 112, 1274, 1501
Ingle, H. Larry, 1550
Institute for the Study of American
   Evangelicals, 35
International Conference for
   Itinerant Evangelists, 611
International Council of
   Accrediting Agencies for
   Evangelical Theological
   Education, 1118
International Federation of Free
   Evangelical Churches, 1551
Ippel, Henry P., 113
Irish, Charles, 2437
Isaac, Rhys, 199

Jaberg, Russell L., 1868
Jackson, Harvey H., 200
Jacob, Jeffrey R., 1899
Jacobs, Anton K., 114
Jacobs, Sylvia M., 689
Jacobsen, Douglas, 286, 1275, 1376
Jay, Elizabeth, 560
Jeffrey, David Lyle, 561
Jelen, Ted G., 1971
Jenkins, John W., 1869
Jennings, George J., 2258
Jensen, Kenneth M., 887
Jensen, Peter F., 2293
Jenson, Robert W., 815, 816

Johannesen, Stanley, 911
John Paul II, Pope, 2294
Johnson, Benton, 1642
Johnson, D. A., 999
Johnson, Dell G., 1783, 1784
Johnson, James E., 817, 2538
Johnson, Norbert E., 2224, 2225
Johnson, Paul E., 2574
Johnson, S. Lewis, Jr., 2166
Johnson, Stephen D., 912, 1918,
   1953, 1995, 1996
Johnston, Arthur, 652, 2586
Johnston, Jon, 368
Johnston, Raymond, 2394
Johnston, Robert K., 1276, 1377,
   1378, 1502, 2167
Jones, Bob, Sr., 1503
Jones, Charles Edwin, 37, 38, 39
Jones, James William, 2295
Jordahl, Leigh, 1277
Jordan, Philip D., 243
Jorstad, Erling, 369, 913, 1000,
   1870, 1919, 1920, 1921, 1922,
   2296, 2297, 2298
Joy, Donald M., 1643
Judisch, Douglas, 2395
Juster, Susan, 770
Justinian, Patriarch of Rumania,
   2625

Kahoe, Richard D., 1644
Kaiser, Walter C., Jr., 1278, 1379,
   1380
Kane, J. Herbert, 669, 670
Kantzer, Kenneth S., 115, 116, 117,
   118, 370, 371, 372, 373, 442,
   722, 914, 1001, 1279, 1280,
   1381, 1382, 2070
Karmarkovic, Alex, 915
Kater, John L., Jr., 1923
Kato, Byang, 612
Katsh, Abraham I., 119
Kauffmann, Donna R., 1924
Kay, Thomas O., 120
Keating, Karl, 1871
Keck, Herbert A., 287
Keegan, Terence J., 1383

Keller, Rosemary Skinner, 788, 2501
Kelley, Dean M., 1645, 2626
Kelley, Patricia, 1974
Kelsey, Morton, 2168
Kendrick, Klaude, 2071, 2072
Kenyon, Howard Nelson, 2073, 2074
Kerkhofs, J., 2299
Kesler, Jay, 1646
Kevan, E. F., 121
Keyser, Leander S., 1719
Kik, J. Marcellus, 2627
Kilby, Clyde S., 818, 1169, 1170
Killen, R. Allen, 443
Kim, Ki Hong, 1785
Kim, Myung Yuk, 652, 2586
Kincheloe, Joe L., Jr., 1479
Kinder, Ernst, 122
King, John Charles, 1281
King, John Owen, III, 123
King, Larry L., 1786
Kirk, Roger E., 1648
Kirkwood, Wilson D., 444
Klassen, A. J., 1552
Klaus, Byron, 2169
Kleiner, John W., 1282
Klempa, William, 2170
Knapp, Stephen C., 489, 671
Knippers, Diane, 771
Knott, James P., 1002
Koch, Martha, 2438
Koch, Roy S., 2438
Koenig, John, 2300
Koop, Allen V., 672
Kossel, Clifford G., 1925
Kowaleski, Elizabeth Anne, 1171
Kraft, Charles H., 1647
Krass, Alfred C., 1283
Kraus, C. Norman, 124, 125, 126, 244
Kromminga, John H., 2628
Kucharsky, David, 374
Kuenning, Paul P., 1480, 1481
Kuhn, Annie W., 127
Kuhn, Harold B., 1119
Kuklick, Bruce, 40
Kurtaneck, Nickolas, 1284
Kuykendall, John W., 522

Kuyvenhoven, Andrew, 2560
Kuzmic, Peter, 613
Kydd, Ronald, 2171

Land, Gary, 819
Land, Richard D., 1787
Lane, A. N. S., 375
Lane, Belden C., 2472
Lane, Bill, 490
Lane, Tony, 376, 2629
Lankford, John, 2259
Lapierre, Emmanuel, 1720
Larsen, David L., 1285
Larson, Edward J., 1074
Lartey, Emmanuel Y., 2226
LaSor, William Sanford, 723, 1384
Laurentin, Rene, 2301
LaVerdiere, Eugene, 1721
Lawrence, Albert Sumner, 562
Lawrence, B. F., 2018
Lawson, John, 1286
Lazear, Robert W., Jr., 1872
Lazerlere, Robert E., 1659
Leahy, Frederick S., 1385
LeBlanc, Douglas, 690
Lechner, Frank J., 1972
Lederle, Henry I., 2396, 2397
Lee, Earl, 820, 1873
Lee, Jae Bum, 2227
Lehmann, Daniel J., 2630
Leicht, Kevin, 1632
Leonard, Bill J., 128, 1151, 1553, 1554, 1788, 1789, 2473
Lernoux, Penny, 614
Lesick, Lawrence Thomas, 1003
Lesser, M. X., 42, 821
Levine, Hillel, 724
Lewis, Donald M., 822, 1004, 1005, 1555
Lewis, Gordon R., 1386
Lewis, Kathryn, 1120
Liebman, Robert C., 1926, 1973
Liefeld, David R., 823, 1387
Liefeld, Walter L., 789
Lightner, Robert P., 445, 446, 1287, 1722
Lilly, Fred, 2302

Lincoln, C. Eric, 691
Lindberg, Carter, 2304
Lindberg, David C., 1075, 1076
Linder, Robert D., 916, 963, 964,
    1006, 1007, 1927
Lindsell, Harold, 129, 130, 131,
    377, 673, 1388, 1389, 1390,
    2398
Lindsey, F. Duane, 1288
Lindskoog, Donald, 1648
Linton, Thomas H., 447
Lippy, Charles H., 43, 44, 1152
Lipset, Seymour Martin, 917
Litman, Barry R., 1153
Livingstone, David N., 1077, 1078,
    1079
Lloyd-Jones, D. M., 121
Loane, Marcus Lawrence, 563, 564
Loetscher, Lefferts A., 824
Long, Steve, 1543
Lorentzen, Louise J., 1649
Lorenzen, Thorwald, 2631
Lotz, Davis M., 288
Lovekin, Adams, 2260
Lovelace, Richard F., 132, 133,
    373, 1289, 1391, 1504, 1505,
    1556, 2632
Loveland, Anne C., 523, 1008
Lovett, Leonard, 692, 693, 694
Luchies, John E., 448
Luidens, Donald A., 923
Luker, David, 2539
Luker, Ralph E., 2575
Lundin, Roger, 1172, 1506
Lundquist, Carl H., 378
Lupfer, Michael B., 1974
Lutzer, Erwin W., 1009
Lyon, David, 1650, 1651
Lyra, Synesio, Jr., 491

Mabie, Henry Clay, 134
MacArthur, John F., Jr., 2399
MacDonald, William G., 2172
MacEwen, H. F., 449
Machen, J. Gresham, 1290
MacKay, Donald M., 135
MacKay, John A., 492, 2633

MacKenzie, John S., 2400, 2401
Mackey, Lloyd, 2075
Mackie, Marlene M., 1899
Maclear, J. F., 1010
MacLeod, A. Donald, 565, 1606
MacLeod, John, 566
Macphail, S. R., 2540
MacRobert, Iain, 695
Maddex, Jack P., Jr., 1470
Magno, Joseph A., 2305
Magnuson, Norris A., 1011, 1012
Maguire, Daniel C., 1928
Maier, Walter A., 2306
Malony, H. Newton, 2260
Maniha, John K., 2449
Mann, James, 615
Manspeaker, Nancy, 45
Manwaring, Randle, 567
Marcoux, Jacques, 2634
Mariner, Kirk, 136
Maring, Norman H., 1557
Maris, J. C., 2635
Marsden, George M., 137, 138, 245,
    246, 289, 379, 450, 825, 826,
    918, 930, 1013, 1014, 1015,
    1016, 1121, 1122, 1291, 1652,
    1790, 1791, 1792, 1793, 1874,
    1929, 1930
Marshall, Herbert J., 1558
Marshall, I. Howard, 827, 1392,
    1507
Martin, David, 2307
Martin, George, 2402
Martin, Ira Jay, III, 46
Martin, Ralph, 2308, 2439, 2636
Martin, Roger H., 139, 247, 2637
Marty, Martin E., 140, 141, 142,
    248, 380, 381, 451, 452, 493,
    1559, 1875, 1876, 1877, 1931,
    2076, 2561
Mason, Frances, 772
Massey, James Earl, 696
Mather, Anne, 2403
Mathews, Donald G., 524, 525, 2474
Mathisen, Gerald Stephen, 1017,
    1975
Mathisen, James A., 1975

Mathisen. Robert R.. 1018
Matre, Frank Martin, 2228
Mattila, William S.. 1624
Mattison, Elvin Keith, 1794
Mattson, John Stanley, 828
Mattson, Vernon Eugene. 1795
Mattson-Boze, M. Howard, 201
Maxwell, James. 2173
Mayer, F. E., 1796
Mayers, Marvin K., 1123
Mayers, Ronald B., 1292
Maynard, Kent Arthur, 1653
McAllister, Ronald J., 919
McArthur, Harvey. 1797
McBeth, Leon, 1878, 1879
McBirnie, Robert Sheldon. 1798
McCahon, Thomas J., 1799
McCall, Clarence Victor. Jr., 1976
McCants, David A., 773
McClain, Alva J., 453
McClanahan, James Samuel, Jr., 829
McClendon, James, Jr., 1293
McClung, L. Grant, Jr., 2077, 2078,
    2079. 2080
McConnell. Francis John. 568
McCowan, Kenneth. 1800
McCrossan, T. J., 1801
McCune, Rolland D.. 454, 455, 494,
    1723, 1724, 1880
McCutcheon, William, 290
McDonald, Morris, 456
McDonnell. Kilian, 47, 143, 2081.
    2082, 2174, 2175, 2176, 2177,
    2309, 2310, 2311, 2312, 2313,
    2314, 2404, 2405, 2406, 2407,
    2440. 2450, 2638, 2639
McGavran, Donald, 48, 1019, 2083
McGaw, Douglas B.. 2451, 2452. 2453
McGee, Gary B., 9. 2013, 2014.
    2015, 2084, 2085
McGiffert, Michael, 49
McGlone. Lee Roy. 1802
McGoldrick. James E.. 144
McGregor. Jeffrey P.. 2130
McGuire. Meredith B.. 2454. 2455.
    2456, 2315
McIntire. Carl. 145

McIntire. Carl T., 1803, 1804
McKenna, David, 382
McKenzie, John Grant, 1654
McKim, Donald K., 1413
McKim, Donald L., 50
McKinney, Joseph, 2316
McKinney, Larry J., 1806
McKivigan. John R., 1020
McLean, Mark D., 2178
McLeish, John, 1124
McLemore, Cinton W.. 1633
McLeod, William L., 2562
McLoughlin, William G., 146, 249,
    250, 920, 1021, 1022, 1482,
    2475, 2476, 2506, 2576
Mead, Sidney E., 147
Meadors, Gary T., 1023
Measures, Royce, 1932
Meckel, Richard A., 1024
Medcraft, John P., 2229
Meehan, Brenda M., 1807
Meeking, Basil, 2640, 2641
Meeks, Fred E., 2179
Meeter, Merle, 1080
Meiring, P. G. J., 1483
Melton, J. Gordon, 51
Mendez, Guillermo W., 591
Menendez, Albert J., 383
Menzies, William W., 1560, 1561,
    2016, 2477
Meyer, Kenneth M., 1125
Mühlen, Heribert, 2408, 2409
Michalsky, Walt, 1725
Mickelsen, Alvera, 774
Mickey, Paul A., 1440
Miguez-Bonino, Jose, 616
Millard, A. D.. 2086, 2180
Miller. Glenn Thomas. 202, 1562
Miller, Perry. 252, 2505
Miller, Wesley Edward. Jr.. 1977
Mills. Watson E.. 52. 53, 54. 2181,
    2182
Minor. John E.. 1655. 2017
Mitchell. Robert Bryant. 2087
Moberg. David O.. 291. 384. 1025.
    1026
Moellering. Ralph L.. 495

Mollenkott, Virginia Ramey, 775, 776
Monaghan, Robert R., 1978
Moncher, Gary Richard, 1126
Money, Ann-Janine, 2088
Monsma, Stephen V., 921
Montgomery, John Warwick, 148, 1393, 2642
Montgomery, Michael S., 55
Moonie, Peter Meredith, 2317
Moore, James R., 1081
Moore, Leroy, Jr., 1808
Moore, R. Laurence, 1173
Moorhead, James H., 1027, 1471, 1472
Moran, Gerald F., 2507
Moreland, J. P., 1082
Morison, William James, 1083
Morris, John Warren, 2410
Morris, Ronald J., 1968, 1969
Morrison, Howard Alexander, 2541
Mott, Stephen, 1394
Moule, Handley Carr Glyn, 1460
Mouly, Ruth W., 725, 726
Mounce, Robert, 496, 1127
Mouw, Richard J., 149, 385, 922, 1028, 1295, 1563, 1933, 1934, 2318, 2643
Moyles, R. G., 56
Muck, Terry, 830
Muelder, W. A., 1656
Mueller, David L., 1395
Muesse, Mark William, 1881
Muir, Andrew Forest, 253
Mulholland, Robert Joseph, 831
Mullen, Peter, 2307
Muller, Jac, 2183
Mullin, Robert Bruce, 254, 1029
Mullins, Mark, 1154
Murch, James D., 292
Murdoch, Norman H., 255
Murphy, Cullen, 386
Murray, Iain, 293, 294, 832, 833, 1296, 2478, 2479, 2480, 2481, 2508, 2509, 2542
Murray, John, 1607
Myland, D. Wesley, 2018

Nash, Lee, 1809
Nash, Ronald H., 388, 389, 457, 1297, 1298, 1396
National Association of Evangelicals, 295
National Conference of Evangelicals and Jews, 727
Naumann, William Henry, 1564
Negri, Maxine, 1935
Neil, William, 1565
Neill, Stephen, 296
Nelson, F. Burton, 2644
Nelson, Harland Stanley, 1174
Nelson, Roland Tenus, 1810
Nelson, Rudolph L., 834, 1175, 1811
Nelson, Wilton M., 617
Nemeth, Roger J., 923
Nesdoly, Samuel J., 618
Nesmith, Bruce Forrester, 924
Neuhaus, Richard John, 925, 1936, 1937, 1938
New, Benny Lynn, 1300
Newbigin, Lesslie, 674
Newell, A. G., 1176
Newman, Amy L., 777
Newman, Elias, 728
Newport, Frank, 942
Nichol, John Thomas, 1397, 2089, 2090
Nicholls, John, 2543
Nichols, David R., 1301
Nichols, James Hastings, 256
Nichols, John Broadhurst, 150
Nichols, Robert Hastings, 1812
Niebuhr, Gustav, 697
Nix, William, 1030, 1813
Noll, Mark A., 57, 151, 152, 178, 203, 204, 205, 391, 392, 835, 836, 926, 927, 928, 929, 930, 1128, 1129, 1155, 1302, 1303, 1304, 1371, 1398, 1399, 1400, 1506, 1566, 1567, 1568, 1569, 1657
North American Pre-Convention Conference, 1814
Northcott, John E., 2457
Norton, Wilbert, 675

Norton, Will, 698
Numbers, Ronald L., 837, 1075, 1076, 1084, 1085, 1473
Nunez, Emilio Antonio, 619, 620, 1305
Nyquist, John Paul, 1306

O'Brien, Susan, 2510
O'Byrne, William Lionel, Jr., 1307
O'Connor, Edward D., 2319, 2320, 2321
O'Donohue, John, 1979
O'Donovan, Oliver, 1308
O'Mara, Philip F., 2322
O'Neal, Glenn, 1658
Oatley-Willis, B. R., 459
Ockenga, Harold John, 297, 460, 461, 1815
Odunaike, Samuel, 621
Olds, Mason, 1883
Oliver, John W., Jr., 699, 1031
Olson, Adolf, 1570
Olson, Arnold T., 1571
Olson, Virgil A., 1484, 2544
Olyott, Stuart, 1608
One in Christ (Magazine), 2645
Opie, John, 838, 839, 1816, 2482
Opsahl, Paul D., 2324
Orr, J. Edwin, 2483, 2545, 2563, 2577
Oss, Douglas A., 1401
Ostling, Richard N., 395, 1156
Ostrom, Richard M., 1659
Oswalt, John N., 729
Otterland, Anders, 2325
Oudersluys, Richard C., 2411
Overton, John Henry, 2511
Owen, Dennis E., 1673, 1914
Owens, Raymond Eugene, 2546
Ownby, Ted, 1660

Packard, A. Appleton, 840
Packard, William, 298
Packer, James I., 396, 462, 1402, 2184, 2198, 2412, 2484
Padilla, C. Rene, 153, 589, 1032, 1033, 1034

Paine, Stephen W., 397
Painter, John, 2326
Palmer, Bernard, 1508
Palmer, Marjory, 1508
Pannell, William E., 700, 701, 1035, 2413
Parker, David D., 622, 623, 624, 625, 1309, 1817, 1818
Parker, Harold M., Jr., 526
Parker, Monroe, 1884
Parkes, William, 2091
Parnell, Chris W., 2185
Patterson, Bob E., 841
Patterson, Daniel W., 1669
Patterson, James Alan, 931
Paulson, Eric Edwin, 299
Payne, Eric, 702
Pazmino, Robert W., 1130
Peacock, James L., 1669
Peck, George, 676
Pederson, W. Dennis, 2230, 2327
Pendleton, Othniel Alsop, 1036
Penner, David Robert, 1980
Perez, Pablo E., 626
Perez, Torres Ruben, 2231
Perkins, Richard B., 1661
Perry, Edmund F., 307
Perry, Everett L., 1981
Peshkin, Alan, 1982
Petersen, Rodney L., 312, 2647
Peterson, Paul D., 58
Peterson, Walfred H., 932
Peterson, Walter Ross, 1819
Peterson, William J., 398
Pethrus, Lewi, 2232
Pettegrew, Larry D., 1820, 1821
Pettingill, William Leroy, 1822
Phillips, Timothy R., 1403
Phillips, Walter, 627
Phillipson, John S., 2441
Photiadis, John D., 1983
Pickering, Ernest, 464, 465, 466, 1726, 1885
Pierard, Richard V., 59, 60, 399, 842, 916, 933, 934, 935, 936, 937, 963, 964, 1037, 1939
Pierce, Talmadge Burton, 2092

Piggin. Stuart. 628. 677
Pike, Garnet Elmer. 703
Pike, Kenneth Lee, 1509
Pike, Richard, 629
Pillay, Gerald J., 2233
Pinnock, Clark H., 497, 938, 1086,
    1310, 1311, 1312, 1404, 1405,
    1406, 1407, 1408
Pippert, Rebecca Manley, 1609
Pitcher, Leonard S., 2186
Pitzer, Donald E., 939
Plowman, Edward E., 1572, 2414
Pocock, Emil, 257
Pointer, Richard W., 206, 207
Politzer, Jerome, 843
Pollard, Arthur, 844
Pollock, Algernon J., 2093
Poloma, Margaret M., 1573, 2234,
    2458
Pomerville, Paul A., 2094
Poole-Conner, E. J., 569
Poorter, John, 1823
Popma, J. K., 1313
Porter, Thomas Henry, 845
Pothen, Abraham Thottumkal, 2235
Poythress, Vern S., 1314
Pratt, Andrew Leroy, 940
Pratt, Raymond, 467, 1727
Prenter, Regin, 2648
Price, Oliver, 1824
Price, Robert M., 468, 498, 846,
    1409, 1410
Prieguez, Raquel Maria, 2459
Prim, C. Clinton, Jr., 2547
Pritchard, Linda K., 258, 259
Proctor, Samuel D., 704
Proctor, W. C. G., 300
Proctor, William, 61
Pullum, Stephen Jackson, 1157
Pyles, Volie E., 469

Quebedeaux, Richard, 154, 499, 500,
    501, 1662, 2187, 2328, 2329,
    2649
Quere, Ralph Walter, 2485

Raab, Earl, 917

Raboteau, Albert J., 705
Radl, Shirley, 778
Raj, P. Solomon, 2236
Rambo, David, 2486
Rambo, Lewis R., 1610
Ramm, Bernard, 155, 847, 1087,
    1088, 1315, 1728, 2188
Ranaghan, Dorothy, 2331, 2442
Ranaghan, Kevin M., 2095, 2189,
    2330, 2331, 2415, 2442
Randall, Claire, 2650
Raser, Harold E., 848, 1461
Raskopf, Roger W., 62
Rattenbury, John Ernest, 1441
Rausch, David A., 156, 260, 730,
    731, 732, 733, 734, 735, 743,
    1729
Rawlinson, Leslie, 849
Rawlyk, George A., 2487
Ray, Vernon Oliver, 1984
Read, Francis W., 2651
Reasoner, Esther, 779
Reddin, Opal Laurene, 2190
Redekop, Calvin, 1574, 1575
Reed, David Arthur, 2019, 2020
Reed, Stephen K., 1659
Rees, Paul S., 2652
Reese, Boyd, 1663
Reeve, Ronald, 2512
Reeves, Earl J., 1038
Regehr, William, 1575
Reid, Roddey, Jr., 2513
Reid, Stephen, 1411
Reid, W. S., 2332
Reinertsen, Lawrence Gustav, 2333
Reitzel, Charles F., 2191
Remelts, Glenn A., 1089
Rennie, Ian Scott, 570
Renwick, A. M., 301
Reynolds. John Stewart. 571
Rhee, Yoon-Ho. 2564
Rhim. Soon Man. 1825
Rhodes. Albert Lewis. 1985
Ribbufo. Leo. 1940
Ricard. Laura B., 63
Rice, John R., 1731, 1732
Richard, John, 630, 1039

Richards, John, 2416
Richards, Lawrence O., 1123
Richardson, James T., 1986, 1987, 1988, 1992
Rienstra, M. Howard, 64
Riesman, David, 1131
Rifkin, Jeremy, 157, 158
Riggans, Walter, 736
Riggs, Jack R., 1412
Righter, James D., 2192
Rightmire, R. David, 1316
Riley, William Bell, 302
Ringenberg, William C., 1132
Riss, Richard M., 2096, 2565
Robeck, Cecil M., Jr., 65, 2021, 2097, 2098, 2099, 2100, 2335
Robert, Dana Lee, 850
Roberts, Arthur O., 1577
Roberts, Frank, 1291
Roberts, Richard Owen, 66
Roberts, Ronald E., 706
Robertson, Darrel M., 1664
Robertson, Roland, 726
Rochelle, Larry, 941
Roebuck, David G., 780
Rogers, J. Guinness, 261
Rogers, Jack B., 502, 851, 1413, 1510
Rogers, Martha L., 1989
Rolland, Ross W., 1511
Rood, Paul W., 2488
Roof, Wade Clark, 1941
Rooks, Charles Shelby, 707
Rosell, Garth M., 852, 852
Rosenberg, Carroll Smith, 1040
Rosman, Doreen M., 1177, 1178
Rossen, Betsy, 1611
Roth, Wolfgang, 159, 1414
Rothenberg, Stuart, 942
Rowdon, Harold H., 303
Rowe, Michael, 2237
Rubinstein, Murray A., 631
Rudin, A. James, 737, 738, 741, 742
Rudnick, Milton L., 1578, 1826
Ruegsegger, Ronald W., 853
Runia, Klaas, 1041, 1317
Runyon, Daniel V., 1443

Russell, Alfred U., 470, 1827
Russell, Charles Allyn, 854, 855, 856, 857, 858, 859, 860, 861, 862, 1579, 1828
Rutter, Robert Sherman, 2514
Ryan, Mary P., 781

Sachs, William Lewis, 572, 2115
Sahlberg, Carl E., 2101
Sala, Harold James, 2193
Saltzgaber, Jan M., 2520
Samarin, William J., 2194
Samuel, David, 2653
Sanasac, Rupert L., 471
Sandeen, Ernest R., 67, 1733, 1829, 1830, 1831, 1832
Sanders, James A., 1734
Sangster, Paul E., 2515
Saperstein, Marc, 739
Saracco, J. Norberto, 2238, 2417
Sarles, Ken L., 1318
Saunders, Monroe R., 2102
Sawatsky, Rodney, 1662
Sawatsky, Ronald George, 1833
Sawatsky, Walter, 632, 633
Scaer, David P., 2418
Scanzoni, John, 1990
Scanzoni, Letha Dawson, 782
Scarf, Alan, 634
Schaeffer, Francis A., 400, 863
Schaff, Philip, 160
Scheer, James F., 2029
Scheunemann, Volkhard, 1042
Schlabach, Theron F., 1580, 2489
Schmidt, Leigh Eric, 2490
Schmiechen, Peter M., 1319
Schnabel, John F., 1983
Schneider, Lenore, 208
Scholer, David M., 783
Schonebaum, William J., 2419
Schreck, Alan Edward, 2420
Schrotenboer, Paul G., 304, 1320, 2654
Schultze, Quentin J., 1158
Schwarz, Fred, 161
Scorgie, Glen, 864, 865
Scott, Donald Moore, 262

Scott, Waldron, 401, 635, 1321
Scroggs, Robin, 402
Secrett, A. G., 866
Sell, Alan P. F., 162, 1322
Selness, David Bruce, 2195
Selvidge, Marla J., 1887
Sepulveda, Ivan, 2239
Sernett, Milton C., 163, 708
Setta, Susan, 782
Sharp, Larry Dean, 867
Shaw, Ian, 2516
Shaw, James T., 472
Shaw, Mark R., 164
Sheehan, R. J., 573
Shelley, Bruce L., 305, 403, 404,
    1462, 1581, 1612
Shelley, Marshall, 2655
Shepherd, Richard Lawson, 2566
Shepherd, William H., Jr., 1415
Sheppard, Gerald T., 1416, 1417,
    2033, 2103, 2196, 2197
Shiels, Richard D., 2548
Shipley, Maynard, 1834
Shipps, Kenneth W., 1100
Shopshire, James Maynard, 2261
Shriver, Donald W., Jr., 288
Shriver, George, 1665
Shriver, Peggy L., 1991
Shupe, Anson, 890, 943, 1146, 1964
Shurden, Walter B., 1582
Sider, Ronald J., 503, 504, 1043,
    1044, 1045, 1046, 1090, 1583,
    2656
Siegelman, Jim, 1698
Simeon, Charles, 868
Simmonds, Robert B., 1987, 1988,
    1992
Simpson, John H., 1942
Sims, Patsy, 2104
Sine, Tom, 1584
Sizer, Sandra S., 2549, 2550
Skoglund, Herbert, 636
Smedes, Lewis B., 1047, 1048
Smeeton, Donald Dean, 637
Smidt, Corwin, 1666
Smith, Anthony Christopher, 638
Smith, Charles R., 1888

Smith, Eugene L., 2657
Smith, Gary Scott, 1049, 1050,
    1263, 1667
Smith, H. Shelton, 1051
Smith, Harold B., 2105
Smith, Linda Diane, 1052
Smith, Paul B., 2491
Smith, Timothy L., 165, 166, 405,
    473, 740, 1133, 1474, 1475,
    1835, 2106, 2492, 2578, 2658
Smith, Wilbur M., 1323
Smith, Willard H., 869
Smith, William Henry, 1993
Smith-Rosenberg, Carroll, 68
Smucker, David Joseph, 1179
Smylie, James H., 2493
Smyth, Charles Hugh Egerton, 2517
Sneck, William Joseph, 2460
Snyder, Dean J., 2443
Snyder, Howard A., 870, 1442, 1443,
    1463, 1485
Society for Pentecostal Studies,
    2107
Sodergren, Carl Johannes, 1836
Sonnack, Paul G., 2494
Southern, James Richard, 1943
Speck, W. A., 209
Spencer, Ralph Wakefield, 784
Spittler, Russell P., 69, 2108
Springer, Kevin, 1324
Spurgeon, Charles H., 2495
Spurr, Thurlow, 1180
Sroka, Barbara, 871
Stackhouse, John G., Jr., 306, 406,
    872
Stafford, Thomas Albert, 167
Stafford, Tim, 1325
Staggers, Kermit L., 873
Stanley, Brian, 2567
Stark, Rodney, 1627
Steely, John E., 1585
Steeves, Paul D., 639
Stegner, W. Richard, 1326
Stein, K. James, 168
Steinmetz, Marvin Duane, 1159
Stephanou, Eusebius A., 2336
Stephens, Raphael Weller, III, 1134

Stephens, W. Richard, 505
Stevenson, Herbert F., 1464, 1512
Stevenson, Louise L., 1135
Stevick, Daniel, 1735
Stewardson, Jerry L., 307
Stewart, James Alexander, 2659
Stewart, James Brewer, 1053
Stewart, Mary White, 1987, 1988
Stibbs, Alan Marshall, 2198
Stiles, Gerald Johnston, 1136
Stob, Henry, 1944
Stober, Gerald S., 944
Stockwell, Eugene, 2337
Stoeffler, F. Ernest, 1486, 1487,
    1488
Stoll, John H., 1327
Stone, Howard W., 1668
Stonehouse, Ned B., 874, 1418
Stones, Christopher R., 1994
Stott, John R. W., 407, 474, 1054,
    1055, 1837, 2641, 2660
Stout, Harry S., 804
Strachan, Gordon, 2022
Strachey, Barbara, 785
Stransky, Thomas F., 408, 1736,
    2661
Straton, John Roach, 1838
Streiker, Lowell D., 944, 1839
Stronstad, Roger, 2199, 2200
Stuart, Bruce Wayne, 70
Stunt, Timothy C., 640
Sturm, Douglas, 1945
Suenens, Leon Joseph Cardinal,
    2338, 2421, 2422, 2423
Sugden, Chris, 1033, 1034
Sullivan, Francis Aloysius, 2424
Summerhill, William Roy, Jr., 1737
Sundberg, Walter, 1586
Sunnergren, Lennart, 2325
Swamidoss, A. W., 1613
Swann, Charles E., 1147
Swanson, Michael Richard Hans, 263
Sweet, Leonard I., 71, 72, 409,
    410, 786, 787, 1738
Sweet, William Warren, 2496
Swift, Alan, 601
Swift, David E., 709

Synan, Vinson, 1328, 1587, 1588,
    2023, 2024, 2025, 2026, 2027,
    2028, 2109, 2110, 2111, 2112,
    2113, 2339, 2340, 2341, 2342,
    2343
Syreck, William J., 2461
Szasz, Ference Morton, 169, 1840,
    1889

Taggart, Morris, 1589
Tamney, Joseph B., 912, 1918, 1953,
    1995, 1996
Tanenbaum, Marc H., 741, 742
Tappeiner, Daniel A., 2262
Tarr, Leslie K., 411, 412, 875,
    1890
Taylor, G. F., 2018
Taylor, James A., 1160
Taylor, William, 620
Tekippe, Charles John, 1997
Tenney, Merrill C., 308
Thacker, Joseph A., 2551
Thielemann, Bruce W., 2344
Tholin, Richard, 506
Thomas, Cal, 945
Thomas, Geoffrey, 2518, 2568
Thomas, Hilah F., 788
Thomas, John L., 1056
Thompson, Clark Alva, 1489
Thompson, James J., Jr., 527
Thompson, R. Duane, 1435
Tidball, Derek J., 1057, 1058
Tinder, Donald, 73, 1841
Tinney, James S., 710, 876, 2114
Toews, J. B., 1590
Toews, John E., 1591
Toms, Paul E., 1059
Toon, Peter, 574, 575, 576, 1329
Torjesen, Karen J., 755
Tow, Siang Hwa, 475
Towns, Elmer L., 1891
Tremaine, John S., 1181
Trembath, Kern R., 1330, 1419, 1420
Trigg, Joseph William, 2115
Trollinger, William Vance, Jr.,
    1137, 1842
Troutman, Charles H., 642

Trueblood. D. Elton. 877
Tucker, Ruth A., 789
Tucker, Stephen R., 1182
Tugwell. Simon, 2116, 2201
Tulga, Chester E., 1739
Tull, James E., 1535
Turner, David L., 1421, 1422, 1423
Turner, George A., 1424, 1444
Turner, William C., Jr., 711, 712
Tuttle, Robert G., 1445
Tuveson, Ernest Lee, 1476
Tyson, Ruel W., Jr., 1669

Underwood, Brian, 170
Unger, Walter, 1843
Utuk, Efiong S., 678

Valbracht, Louis H., 1740
Valdez, A. C., Sr., 2029
Valeri, Mark, 946
van de Fliert, J. R., 1091, 1092
Van Deburg, William L., 2579
Van der Laan, Paul N., 2240
Van Die, Margaret, 1446
Van Elderen, Marlin J., 507, 2202
Van Impe, Jack, 1892
Van Leeuwen, Mary Stewart, 1670,
    1671, 1672
Van Til. Cornelius, 1331, 1332
Van Til. Henry R., 1333
Vandagriff, Janet K., 2347
Vandagriff, Van, 2347
Vanderlaan, Eldred C., 1844
Vanhetloo, Warren, 476
Verge, Carl, 2263
Vermaat, J. A. E., 1060
Villafane, Eldin, 2203
Vinz. Warren L., 1946, 1998
Vischer, Lukas, 2217
Voll. Dieter, 577
Von Rohr, John, 1334
Voss, Carl Hermann, 156, 260, 743

Wacker, Grant, 74, 413, 2117, 2118,
    2119, 2120, 2121, 2122
Wagner, C. Peter, 643, 644
Wald, Kenneth D., 1673

Walhout. E., 477
Walker, Charles Lynn, 878
Walker, Robert, 309
Waller, Wilson Loran, 1592
Wallis, Jim, 508, 509, 510, 511
Walsh, Vincent M., 2425
Walters, Stanley D., 1425
Waltke, Bruce K., 1426, 1513
Walvoord, John F., 1845
Walzer, William C., 2552
Warburton, T. Rennie, 1674
Ward, Horace S., 2123
Ward, Julian, 2204
Ware, Bruce, 1335
Warfield, Benjamin B., 1336
Warner, R. Stephen, 414, 1675
Warner, Wayne E., 790, 2030
Warren, James I., Jr., 1183
Washington, James Melvin, 713, 714
Washington, Joseph R., Jr., 715
Waters, Kenny, 1614
Watson, David, 2426, 2444
Watson, P. J., 1969
Watt, David Harrington, 310
Wauzzinski, Robert Alan, 171
Weaver, C. Douglas, 879
Weaver, Gilbert B., 2205
Webber, Robert E., 947, 1123, 1337,
    1338, 1339, 1340, 1341, 1514
Weber, Timothy P., 1477
Weborg, John, 880, 1593
Webster, Douglas D., 578, 1061,
    1342
Weddell, John Weaver, 311
Weddle, David L., 1676, 1677
Weimer, Ferne Lauraine, 75
Weisberger, Bernard A., 2497
Weiss, Ellen, 1184
Wells, David F., 172, 173, 1304,
    1343, 1344, 1345, 1678
Wells, Jonathan, 1093
Wells, Ronald A., 145, 174, 948,
    1346
Wells, William W., 175
Wenger, Robert Elwood, 1846
Weniger, G. Archer, 1594
West, Earl Irvin, 1595

Westerkamp. Marilyn J., 2519
Westmeier, Karl-Wilhelm, 2241
Whalley, W. E., 2206
Wheaton, John F., 1893
Whelan, Timothy D., 1894
Whitam, Frederick L., 2580
White, Charles Edward. 881
White, John Wesley. 1138, 1139
White, William, Jr., 1094
Whiteman, Curtis Wayne, 1596
Whittaker, Colin C., 2124
Wiebe, Phillip H., 2207
Wilcox, Clyde, 1999, 2000, 2001,
    2002
Will, Jeffry, 2003
Willens, Emillio, 2242
Williams, Cyril Glyndwr, 2208
Williams, Ethel L., 76
Williams, George H., 312
Williams, J. B., 478
Williams, J. Rodman, 2125, 2126,
    2209, 2345, 2427
Williams, Jerry D., 2127
Williams, Melvin Donald, 716
Williams, Michael Patrick, 717
Williams, Peter W., 44, 1679
Williams, Rhys, 2003
Willoughby, William, 1947
Wilson, Charles Reagan, 528, 1435
Wilson, Ernest Gerald. 1597
Wilson, Everett A., 645, 2243, 2244
Wilson, John F., 77, 288, 949, 2264
Wilson, Major L., 264
Wilson, Marvin R., 738, 741, 742,
    744, 745, 746, 747, 748
Wilson, Sandra D., 1680
Windemiller, Duane Arlo, 1681
Winter, Harry E., 679, 2662
Winter, Ralph D., 680
Winter, Rebecca J., 265
Wirt, Sherwood Eliot. 1062
Wise, F. Franklyn, 1140
Witmer. John A., 1141
Witte. Paul W., 2663, 2664
Wolterstorff. Nicholas. 1185
Wood, A. Skevington. 177, 1447
Wood, Gordon S., 266

Wood, James E., Jr., 950, 1948,
    1949, 1950
Wood, Richard E., 1598
Wood, William Woodhull, 2265
Woodbridge, Charles J., 479
Woodbridge, John D., 172, 173, 178,
    1427, 1428
Woodward, Kenneth L., 416
Woolverton, John F., 1063
Wozniak, Kenneth William
    Mulholland, 882
Wright, David F., 1064
Wuthnow, Robert, 951, 1682, 1683,
    1684, 1973
Wyatt-Brown, Bertram, 883, 884,
    1065
Wyschogrod, Michael, 749

Yamauchi, Edwin M., 750
Yancey, Philip, 1515, 1516
Yandell, Keith E., 1347
Yoder, Bill, 646
Yoder, Derek S., 647
Yoder, John H., 1066, 1067
Young, Frank W., 1685
Young, Warren C., 480
Youngblood, Ronald, 1429

Zabriskie, Alexander Clinton, 1599
Zens, Jon, 1348, 2428
Zimbelman, Ernie, 1686
Zimmerman, Thomas F., 2128, 2210,
    2211